Principles of Service Marketing and Management

Christopher Lovelock
Lovelock Associates

Lauren Wright
California State University, Chico

 Prentice Hall
Upper Saddle River, New Jersey 07458

Acquisitions Editor: Gabrielle Dudnyk/Leah Johnson
Editorial Assistant: Michele Foresta
Editor-in-Chief: Natalie Anderson
Marketing Manager: Shannon Moore
Production Editor: Aileen Mason
Permissions Coordinator: Monica Stipanov
Managing Editor: Dee Josephson
Associate Managing Editor: John Roberts
Manufacturing Buyer: Diane Peirano
Manufacturing Supervisor: Arnold Vila
Manufacturing Manager: Vincent Scelta
Senior Designer/Cover Design: Cheryl Asherman
Design Manager: Pat Smythe
Interior Design: Judy Allan/TopDesk Publisher's Group
Photo Research Supervisor: Melinda Lee Reo
Image Permission Supervisor: Kay Dellosa
Photo Researcher: Melinda Alexander
Illustrator (Interior): Electra Graphics and Preparé
Cover and Chapter Illustration: Mark Jasin
Composition: Preparé

Credits and acknowledgments for materials borrowed from other sources and reproduced, with permission, in this textbook appear on page 404.

Published by Prentice-Hall, Inc.
A Simon & Schuster Company
Upper Saddle River, New Jersey 07458

Library of Congress Cataloging-in-Publication Data

Lovelock, Christopher H.
    Principles of service marketing and management / Christopher
Lovelock, Lauren Wright.
      p.   cm.
    Includes bibliographical references and index.
    ISBN 0-13-676875-X
    1. Service industries—United States—Marketing. 2. Service
industries—United States—Management. I. Wright, Lauren.
II. Title.
HD9981.5\.L68 1998
658.8—dc21   98-49946
                                          CIP

Prentice-Hall International (UK) Limited, London
Prentice-Hall of Australia Pty. Limited, Sydney
Prentice-Hall Canada, Inc., Toronto
Prentice-Hall Hispanoamericana, S.A., Mexico
Prentice-Hall of India Private Limited, New Delhi
Prentice-Hall of Japan, Inc., Tokyo
Simon & Schuster Asia Pte. Ltd., Singapore
Editora Prentice-Hall do Brasil, Ltda., Rio de Janeiro

Printed in the United States of America

10 9 8 7 6 5 4 3 2 1

Brief Contents

iii

Contents

Preface

The study of service businesses first emerged as an academic field during the 1970s. But it took almost 20 years for courses in service marketing and management to reach the status of mainstream course offerings, widely taught in business schools around the world. Many people are surprised that it should have taken so long for service courses to move into the mainstream because service industries, in fact, have dominated the economies of most industrialized nations for more than half a century; even in developing economies, the contribution made by services to both employment and the gross domestic product is growing rapidly. But the fact is that research and teaching in management were historically dominated by a focus on manufacturing industries.

That imbalance is now being corrected. Paralleling growing research efforts in both academia and business is the increased student interest in taking courses that focus on management of service organizations. This makes a lot of sense from a career standpoint because most business school graduates will be working in service industries, and existing managers report that manufacturing-based models of business practice are not always useful to them.

The service sector of the economy can best be characterized by its diversity. No single conceptual model can embrace organizations ranging in size from huge international corporations (in such fields as airlines, banking, insurance, telecommunications, hotel chains, and freight transportation) to locally owned and operated small businesses (such as restaurants, laundries, taxis, optometrists, and many business-to-business services). Thus this book provides a carefully designed toolbox for service managers, teaching students how different frameworks and analytical procedures can best be used to examine the varied challenges faced by managers in different situations. In particular, we stress the importance of understanding the underlying processes of service delivery and the way in which new technologies are affecting them. These processes can be grouped into four categories, each of which has distinctive implications for the role played by customers and, thus, for management practice.

As the title suggests, *Principles of Service Marketing and Management* presents an integrated approach to the study of services that places marketing issues within a broader general management context. Whatever a manager's specific job may be, he or she has to recognize and acknowledge the close ties that link the marketing, operations, and human resource functions. With that perspective in mind, this book has been designed so that instructors can use it for teaching courses in either services marketing or service management.

The theme of this book is that service organizations differ in many important respects from manufacturing businesses, requiring a distinctive approach to planning and implementing marketing strategy. By this, we don't mean to imply that services marketing is uniquely different from goods marketing. If that were true, it would undercut the whole notion of marketing as a coherent management function. Rather, we stress the importance of understanding service organizations on their own terms and then tailoring marketing goals and strategies accordingly. Within this group we include not-for-profit service organizations, as well as the service divisions of manufacturing firms.

The text has 16 chapters and 12 short to medium-length cases. Discussing cases in a classroom (or analyzing them for written projects) gives students a chance to apply what they have learned to real-world settings and to understand the complexities of service management—including the interactions among marketing, operations, and human resources, which are much more closely intertwined in services than in manufacturing.

The service sector presents many exciting work opportunities. We hope that you will also find it an exciting field to study.

Acknowledgments

Over the years, many colleagues in both the academic and business worlds have provided us with valuable insights into the management and marketing of services, through their writings or in conference and seminar discussions. In particular, we want to express our appreciation to John Bateson of Gemini Consulting; Leonard Berry of Texas A&M University; Bernard Booms of the University of Washington; Steven Brown and Mary Jo Bitner of Arizona State University; Pierre Eiglier of Universite d'Aix-Marseille III; Ray Fisk of the University of New Orleans; Liam Glynn of University College, Dublin; Christian Grönroos of the Swedish School of Economics in Finland; Stephen Grove of Clemson University; Eric Langeard, formerly of Universite d'Aix-Marseille III; Jean-Claude Larreché and James Teboul of INSEAD; Theodore Levitt, James Heskett, Earl Sasser, and Len Schlesinger of Harvard Business School; "Parsu" Parasuraman of the University of Miami; Paul Patterson of the University of New South Wales; Fred Reichheld of Bain & Co.; Sandra Vandermerwe of Imperial College, London; Rhett Walker of the University of Tasmania; Charles Weinberg of the University of British Columbia; Jochen Wirtz of the National University of Singapore; and Valarie Zeithaml of the University of North Carolina.

We are grateful to the reviewers, Eileen Bridges of Kent State University, Tom Brown of Oklahoma State University, Douglas Dalrymple of Indiana University, Dawn Iacobucci of Northwestern University, and Surendra N. Singh of Oklahoma State University, whose insightful comments were very helpful to us.

Special thanks also go to the people at Prentice Hall for their valued assistance in helping to bring this book into being. They include Don Hull, our former acquisitions editor, who commissioned the book; Aileen Mason, our production editor; Cheryl Asherman, cover designer; Judy Allan (interior book design); Mark Jasin (cover and chapter opener art—boat shells); and Barbara Conner (copy editing). Finally, we want to express our appreciation to Gabrielle Dudnyk, our editor, for her enthusiasm and support.

Christopher Lovelock
Lauren Wright

About the Authors

Christopher Lovelock, one of the pioneers of service marketing, divides his professional life among writing, teaching, and consulting. Based in New England, he gives seminars and workshops in the United States and around the world. He has also lived and worked in Britain, Canada, France, and Switzerland. His past academic career includes 11 years on the faculty of the Harvard Business School; two years as a visiting professor at the International Institute for Management Development (IMD) in Switzerland, and short-term appointments at Berkeley, Stanford, the Sloan School at MIT, Theseus Institute, and INSEAD. Christopher is author of 60 articles, over 100 teaching cases, and 20 books including *Services Marketing* 3/e (Prentice Hall, 1996) and *Product Plus* (McGraw-Hill, 1994). He is a recipient of the *Journal of Marketing*'s Alpha Kappa Psi Award, the American Marketing Association's Award for Career Contributions to the Services Discipline, and many awards for outstanding cases. He holds MA and BCom degrees from the University of Edinburgh, an MBA from Harvard, and a PhD from Stanford.

Lauren Wright is professor and former marketing department chair at California State University (CSU), Chico. In 1998, she was a visiting faculty fellow at the University of Canterbury in Christchurch, New Zealand. Winner of an award for outstanding undergraduate teaching, Lauren has been recognized as a Master Teacher at CSU-Chico and advises faculty on effective teaching campus-wide. Her name is listed in the 1998 publication *Who's Who among America's Teachers*. She is chair of the American Marketing Association's Special Interest Group for Services Marketing (SERVSIG), founded the annual SERVSIG Doctoral Consortium, and has served as research director for the International Service Quality Association. She has published numerous articles on service quality, new service success, business process redesign, and action learning. Lauren holds a BS from the University of Oregon and MBA and PhD degrees from Pennsylvania State University.

PART One

Understanding Services

CHAPTER One

Why Study Services?

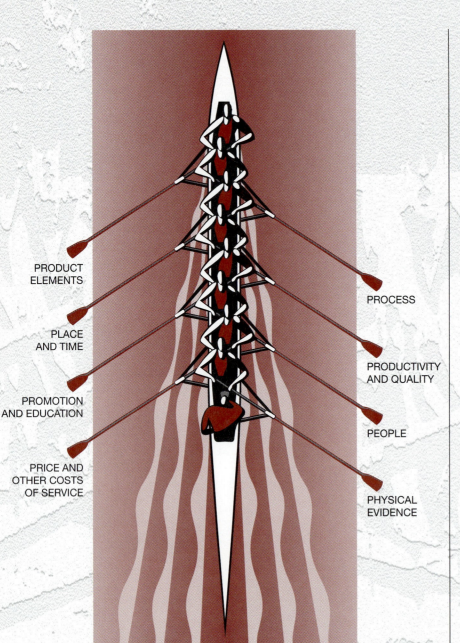

PRODUCT ELEMENTS

PLACE AND TIME

PROMOTION AND EDUCATION

PRICE AND OTHER COSTS OF SERVICE

PROCESS

PRODUCTIVITY AND QUALITY

PEOPLE

PHYSICAL EVIDENCE

Learning Objectives

After reading this chapter, you should be able to

- describe what kinds of businesses are classified as services

- recognize the major changes occurring in the service sector

- identify the characteristics that make services different from goods

- understand the 8Ps of integrated service management

- explain why service businesses need to integrate the marketing, operations, and human resource functions

Service Evolution in an Era of Change

Financial services, freight and passenger transportation, and the wine trade are among the oldest of business activities, dating back to biblical times. At the turn of a new millennium, each is part of the dynamic service sector of the economy. Modern service industries are in an almost constant state of change. Innovators continually launch new ways to satisfy existing needs and to meet needs that people did not even know they had (how many people ever thought they would need electronic mail?). Most of these new ventures fail sooner or later, but a few succeed. Many long-established firms are also failing, but others are making spectacular progress by continually rethinking the way they do business. Consider the following examples.

Federal Express (FedEx) was launched by Frederick W. Smith in 1973. As an undergraduate at Yale in 1965, Fred wrote a term paper on the opportunities for an efficient airfreight service dedicated to the movement of small, high-priority shipments like medicine, electronics, and computer parts. His professor was unimpressed; citing the twin barriers of heavy regulation and intense competition, he gave the paper a C. But Smith later turned the concept into reality. After some difficult early years, Federal Express finally prospered as shippers began to appreciate the value of fast, door-to-door transportation and guaranteed delivery times, backed by exceptional customer service. Central to the firm's success have been its path-breaking applications of information technology, including package tracking. Today, FedEx is a global company, serving 212 countries and carrying more than 3 million packages a day. In its quarter century of existence, it has totally transformed the way in which business people view the logistics function.

Recognized as one of the best companies to work for in America, FedEx's business philosophy is expressed by the motto "People, Service, Profits."

Virtual Vineyards dates from 1995, when Robert Olson, a computer systems specialist, joined forces with his brother-in-law, Peter Granoff, a wine expert, to sell fine California wines. Customers don't need to travel to this wine store, for it has no physical location. Instead, it exists in cyberspace as a Web site, using the address www.virtualvin.com. Although wine itself is a physical product, distributing it is a service. Virtual Vineyards is now one of the most popular wine-buying sites on the Internet and the firm will ship wine wherever it is legal to do so. Attractive but easily

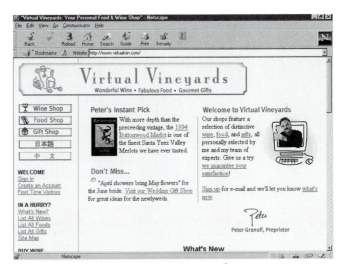

Web sites enable small businesses to reach national and even global markets.

downloadable graphics include wine descriptions, custom-designed tasting charts, and photographs of the specific vineyards whose products the company distributes. Customers can order wines and specialty foods on-line and pay by credit card transactions protected by encryption. They can also request information and advice by e-mail.

British Airways, now one of the world's largest and most profitable airlines, was formed in 1972 by merging two smaller, government-owned carriers. For many years, it had a reputation for inefficiency and incompetence; in fact, people joked that the initials BA stood for "bloody awful." Following major efforts to reduce costs, shares were offered to private investors in 1984. Through a series of transformations, every aspect of the airline's operation and the passenger's experience has been improved, with particular attention being paid to recruitment and training of staff. British Airways offers a variety of service categories, from the supersonic Concorde across the Atlantic to the Shuttle that operates between major British cities. Each class of service is managed as a "subbrand," with distinctive, clearly defined features and standards. The airline's global reach has been extended through investments in Australian, French, and German airlines and alliances with carriers in Canada, Hong Kong, and the United States. It has also pioneered the use of franchising by licensing several smaller airlines to operate certain European routes in its name, featuring aircraft painted in its colors and cabin crews trained to offer British Airways standards of service. Recently, *Fortune* magazine named British Airways the world's most admired airline.

Bank of Montreal, Canada's first bank, was founded in 1817. Today it is more interested in describing itself as one of the largest banks in the North American Free Trade Association (NAFTA). To the 1,100 branches stretching across Canada can be added the 140 branches of its subsidiary, Chicago-based Harris Bank, and the more than 1,000 branches of Mexico's Grupo Financiero Bancomer, in which it holds an equity position. As a result, the bank can deliver retail and commercial banking capabilities in all three countries of NAFTA. It also has offices in key financial centers around the world. With Harris Bank, the Bank of Montreal has created mbanx, the first North American virtual banking enterprise, offering a complete range of banking products and services to millions of customers 24 hours a day, seven days a week, via Internet, toll-free phone or fax, and automated teller machines (ATM)—plus courier and mail service during more conventional hours. The bank's original employees wouldn't recognize the business! Further changes may be in store. Recognizing the challenges of worldwide competition, Bank of Montreal announced plans in January 1998 to merge with Royal Bank of Canada. If approved, this "merger of equals" would create a Canadian financial services institution of global stature.

SERVICES IN THE MODERN ECONOMY

As consumers, we use services every day. Turning on a light, watching television, talking on the telephone, riding a bus, visiting the dentist, mailing a letter, getting a haircut, refueling a car, writing a check, and sending clothes to the cleaners are all examples of service consumption at the individual level. The institution at which you are studying is itself a complex service organization. In addition to educational services, today's college facilities usually include libraries and cafeterias, counseling, a bookstore and placement offices, copy services, telecommunications, and even a bank. It you are enrolled at a residential university, campus services are also likely to include dormitories, health care, indoor and outdoor athletic facilities, a theater, and perhaps a post office.

Unfortunately, customers are not always happy with the quality and value of the services they receive. People complain about late deliveries, rude or incompetent personnel, inconvenient service hours, poor performance, needlessly complicated procedures, and a host of other problems. They grumble about the difficulty of finding salesclerks to help them in retail stores, express frustration about mistakes on their credit card bills or bank statements, shake their heads over the complexity of new self-service equipment, mutter about poor value, and sigh as they are forced to wait in line almost everywhere they go.

Suppliers of services often seem to have a very different set of concerns. Many complain about how difficult it is to make a profit, how hard it is to find skilled and motivated employees, or how difficult to please customers have become. Some firms seem to believe that the surest route to financial success lies in cutting costs and eliminating "unnecessary" frills. A few even give the impression that they could run a much more efficient operation if it weren't for all the stupid customers who keep making unreasonable demands and messing things up!

Happily, in almost every field of endeavor there are service suppliers who know how to please their customers while also running a productive, profitable operation, staffed by pleasant and competent employees. By studying organizations such as FedEx, Virtual Vineyards, British Airways, Bank of Montreal, and the many others featured in this book, we can draw important insights about the most effective ways to manage the different types of services in today's economy.

What Is a Service?

Because of their diversity, services have traditionally been difficult to define. Complicating matters further is the fact that the way in which services are created and delivered to customers is often hard to grasp, because many inputs and outputs are intangible. Most people have little difficulty in defining manufacturing or agriculture, but defining **service** can elude them. Here are two approaches that capture the essence.

service: an act or performance that creates benefits for customers by bringing about a desired change in—or on behalf of—the recipient.

- A service is an act or performance offered by one party to another. Although the process may be tied to a physical product, the performance is essentially intangible and does not normally result in ownership of any of the factors of production.

- Services are economic activities that create value and provide **benefits** for customers at specific times and places, as a result of bringing about a desired change in—or on behalf of—the recipient of the service.

benefit: an advantage or gain that customers obtain from performance of a service or use of a physical good.

More humorously, services have also been described as "something that may be bought and sold but that cannot be dropped on your foot."

Understanding the Service Sector

Services make up the bulk of today's economy, not only in the United States and Canada, where they account for 72 percent and 67 percent of the gross domestic product (GDP), respectively, but also in other developed industrial nations throughout the world.[1] The **service sector** accounts for most of the growth in new jobs in these countries. Unless you are already predestined for a career in a family manufacturing or agricultural business, the probability is high that you will spend most of your working life in companies (or public agencies and nonprofit organizations) that create and deliver services.

service sector: the portion of a nation's economy represented by services of all kinds, including those offered by public and nonprofit organizations.

As a national economy develops, the share of employment among agriculture, industry (including manufacturing and mining), and services changes dramatically. Figure 1.1 (p. 6) shows how the evolution to a service-dominated employment base is likely to take place over time as per capita income rises. Service jobs now account for 76 percent of private sector payrolls in the United States, with wages growing at a faster pace than in manufacturing jobs.[2] In most countries, the service sector of the economy is very diverse, comprising a wide array of different industries, ranging in size from huge enterprises that operate on a global basis to small entrepreneurial firms that serve a single town.

It comes as a surprise to most people to learn that the dominance of the service sector is not limited to highly developed nations. For instance, World Bank statistics show that the service sector accounts for more than half the gross

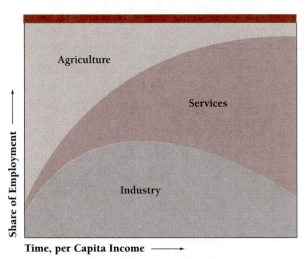

FIGURE 1.1
Changing Structure of Employment as an Economy Develops

Source: International Monetary Fund, *World Economic Outlook*, Washington, D.C.: International Monetary Fund, May 1997.

national product (GNP) and employs more than half the labor force in many Latin American and Caribbean nations, too (see Table 1.1).[3] In many of these countries, there is a large underground economy that is not captured in official statistics. In Mexico, it has been estimated that as much as 40 percent of trade and commerce is "informal."[4] Significant service output is created by undocumented work in domestic jobs (e.g., cook, housekeeper, and gardener) or small, cash-based enterprises such as restaurants, laundries, rooming houses, and taxis.

Service organizations range in size from huge international corporations like airlines, banking, insurance, telecommunications, hotel chains, and freight transportation to a vast array of locally owned and operated small businesses, including restaurants, laundries, taxis, optometrists, and numerous business-to-business services. Franchised service outlets—in fields ranging from fast foods to bookkeeping—combine the marketing characteristics of a large chain that offers a standardized product with local ownership and operation of a specific facility. Some firms that create a time-sensitive physical product, such as printing or photographic processing, are now describing themselves as service businesses because much of the value

TABLE 1.1   Size of the Service Sector in Selected Latin American and Caribbean Countries

Country	Services as Percent of GNP	Labor Force Distribution		
		Agriculture	Industry	Services
Argentina	63	12	32	57
Brazil	52	22	23	53
Costa Rica	59	25	27	48
Dominican Republic	62	24	18	58
Ecuador	50	31	18	51
El Salvador	66	11	29	60
Guatemala	55	50	18	32
Honduras	50	37	21	42
Mexico	63	23	28	50
Panama	72	27	15	67
Puerto Rico	57	4	26	70
Trinidad & Tobago	55	10	33	57
Uruguay	64	15	26	60
Venezuela	53	11	28	61

Source: The World Bank, *El Mundo del Trabajo en una Economia Integrada*, Washington, D.C.: The World Bank, 1995.

added is created by speed, customization, and convenient locations. Regis McKenna wrote, "Companies best equipped for the twenty-first century will consider investment in real time systems as essential to maintaining their competitive edge and keeping their customers."[5]

There is a hidden service sector, too, in many large corporations that are classified by government statisticians as being in manufacturing, agricultural, or natural resources industries. So-called **internal services** cover a wide array of activities, including recruitment, publications, legal and accounting services, payroll administration, office cleaning, landscape maintenance, freight transport, and many other tasks. To a growing extent, organizations are choosing to outsource those internal services that can be performed more efficiently by a specialist subcontractor.[6] As these tasks are outsourced, they become part of the competitive marketplace and therefore are categorized as contributing to the services component of the economy. Even when such services are not outsourced, however, managers of the departments that supply them would do well to think in terms of providing good service to their internal customers.

Governments and nonprofit organizations are also in the business of providing services, although the extent of such involvement may vary widely from one country to another, reflecting both tradition and political values. In many countries, colleges, hospitals, and museums are in public ownership or operate on a not-for-profit basis, but for-profit versions of each type of institution also exist.

internal services: service elements in any type of business that facilitate creation of, or add value to, its final output.

THE EVOLVING ENVIRONMENT OF SERVICES

The service sector of the economy is going through a period of almost revolutionary change. Around the world, innovative newcomers that offer new standards of service have succeeded in markets where established competitors have failed to please today's demanding customers. Many barriers to competition are being swept away, allowing the entry of eager newcomers, ranging from tiny start-up operations like Virtual Vineyards to well-financed multinational firms that import service concepts previously developed and tested in other countries. Established businesses often find it hard to maintain customer loyalty in the face of new product features; improved performance; price cutting; clever promotions; and introduction of more convenient, technology-driven delivery systems.

One example of a service industry caught in the vortex of change is cable television. Cable companies have long been on customers' lists of most-complained about services, but their monopoly in many geographic areas has allowed them to ignore customer's frustrations. Their complacency has allowed new competitors to make significant inroads into the cable TV market by beaming transmissions from multichannel satellites to small dishes mounted on the roofs or walls of customers' homes. However, cable companies have since been exploring some new business opportunities of their own. They are seeking permission to provide local phone service and working on ways to provide easy access to the Internet, using the television sets that exist in virtually every home. However, the competition will be stiff in this area, not only from existing, computer-based Internet service providers, but also from telecommunications companies that wish to enter this rapidly expanding market.

The cable companies are not alone in their struggle to cope with an increasingly challenging environment. Many service industries around the world are currently undergoing dramatic changes. Depending on the industry and the country in which the service firm does business, the underlying causes of such changes may include any of the 12 forces listed in Figure 1.2 (p. 8). Like the factors that underlie

FIGURE 1.2 Forces for Change in Service Management

- changing patterns of government regulation
- relaxation of professional association restrictions on marketing
- privatization of some public and nonprofit services
- technological innovations
- growth of service chains and franchise networks
- internationalization and globalization
- pressures to improve productivity
- the service quality movement
- expansion of leasing and rental businesses
- manufacturers as service providers
- need for public and nonprofit organizations to find new income
- hiring and promotion of innovative managers

any revolution, some of the origins of today's service sector revolution go back a number of years, whereas others reflect a chain of relatively recent events that continues to unfold. Let's look at each of these aspects in more detail.

Changing Patterns of Government Regulation

Traditionally, many service industries were highly regulated. Government agencies mandated price levels, placed geographic constraints on distribution strategies, and, in some instances, even defined the product's attributes. In the late 1970s, the United States began a trend toward complete or partial federal deregulation in several major service industries. Federal Express lobbied for and won deregulation of the domestic airfreight industry. Changes in the regulatory environment took place at the state level, too.

Other nations watched the American experience and began making changes of their own. Relaxation of regulations on trade in services between members of the European Union has already started to reshape the economic landscape of Europe. Meanwhile, in Latin America, democratization and new political initiatives are creating economies that are much less regulated than in the past. In the United States, reduced government regulation has already eliminated or minimized many constraints on competitive activity in such industries as airfreight, airlines, railroads, trucking, banking, securities, insurance, and telecommunications. Americans will soon be able to choose from whom to buy their electricity, following further deregulation of public utilities. Barriers to entry by new firms have been dropped in many instances, geographic restrictions on service delivery have been reduced, there is more freedom to compete on price, and existing firms have been able to expand into new markets or new lines of business.

But reduced regulation is not an unmixed blessing. It is feared that if successful firms become too large—through a combination of internal growth and acquisitions—there may eventually be a decline in the level of competition. Conversely, lifting restrictions on pricing may benefit customers in the short run as competition lowers prices, but it leaves insufficient profits for needed future investments. For instance, fierce price competition among American domestic airlines led to huge financial losses in the industry, bankrupting several airlines. This made it difficult for unprofitable carriers to invest in new aircraft and raised troublesome questions about service quality and safety.[7] Profitable foreign airlines, such as British Airways and Singapore Airlines, gained market share by offering better service than American carriers on international routes. Of course, not all regulatory changes represent a relaxation of government rules. In many countries, steps continue to be taken to strengthen consumer protection laws, to safeguard employees, to improve health and safety, and to protect the environment.

Relaxation of Professional Association Restrictions on Marketing

Another American initiative, also copied elsewhere, has been government or legal pressure to force professional associations to remove or relax bans on advertising and promotional activities. Among professionals affected by such rulings are accountants, architects, doctors, lawyers, and optometrists, who now can engage in much more vigorous competitive activity. On the one hand, the freedom to engage in advertising, promotion, and overt selling is essential in bringing innovative services, price cuts, and new delivery systems to the attention of prospective customers. On the other hand, critics worry that the huge surge in, say, legal advertising in the United States simply encourages people to file more and more lawsuits, many of them frivolous.

Privatization of Some Public and Nonprofit Services

The term **privatization** was coined in Great Britain to describe the policy of transforming government organizations into investor-owned companies. Led by Britain, privatization of public corporations has been moving rapidly ahead in a number of countries, notably in Europe, as well as in Canada, Australia, and New Zealand, and more recently in some Asian and Latin American nations. The transformation of such service operations as national airlines (including British Airways), telecommunications, and natural gas utilities into private enterprises has led to restructuring, cost cutting, and a more market-focused posture. When privatization is combined with a relaxation of regulatory barriers to allow entry of new competitors, as in the British telecommunications industry, the marketing implications can be dramatic.

privatization: transforming government-owned organizations into investor-owned companies.

Privatization can also apply to regional or local public agencies. At the local level, for instance, services such as trash removal have been shifted from the public sector to private firms. A slightly different form of privatization occurs when nonprofit organizations, notably hospitals in the United States, convert to for-profit status. Not everyone is convinced, however, that such changes are beneficial to all segments of the population. When services are provided by public agencies, there are often cross subsidies, designed to achieve broader social goals. With privatization, there are fears that the search for efficiency and profits will lead to cuts in service and price increases. The result may be to deny less affluent segments the services they need at prices they can afford—hence the argument for continued regulation of prices and terms of service in key industries such as health care and telecommunications.

Technological Innovations

New technologies are radically altering the ways in which many service organizations do business with their customers, as well as what goes on behind the scenes. Perhaps the most powerful force for change today comes from the integration of computers and telecommunications. Companies operating information-based services, such as financial service firms, are seeing the nature and scope of their businesses totally transformed by the advent of national (or even global) electronic delivery systems, including the Internet and its best known component, the World Wide Web. Virtual Vineyards and the local wine shop both sell wine, but they are

Automated teller machines have become a symbol of how technology is changing the banking industry.

radically different enterprises in both organization and geographic scope. Similarly, mbanx and an individual branch of the Bank of Montreal offer customers radically different ways to conduct financial transactions.

Technological change affects many other types of services, too, from airfreight to hotels to retail stores. FedEx claims that information about packages is as important as their physical movement to customers. Technology does more than enable the creation of new or improved services. It may also facilitate the reengineering of such activities as delivery of information, order taking, and payment; enhance a firm's ability to maintain more consistent service standards; permit creation of centralized customer service departments; allow replacement of personnel by machines for repetitive tasks; and lead to greater involvement of customers in operations through self-service technology.

Growth of Service Chains and Franchise Networks

franchising: the licensing of independent entrepreneurs to produce and sell a branded service according to tightly specified procedures.

More and more services are being delivered through national or even global chains. Respected brand names like Burger King, Body Shop, Citicorp, Hertz, and Mandarin Oriental Hotels have spread far from their original national roots. In some instances, these chains are entirely company owned; in others, the creator of the original concept has entered into partnership with outside investors. **Franchising** involves the licensing of independent entrepreneurs to produce and sell a branded service according to tightly specified procedures. It is an increasingly popular way to finance the expansion of multisite service chains that deliver a consistent service concept. Large franchise chains are replacing (or absorbing) a wide array of small, independent service businesses in fields as diverse as bookkeeping, car rentals, haircutting, muffler repair, photocopying, plumbing, quick-service restaurants, and real estate brokerage. Among the requirements for success are creation of mass media advertising campaigns to promote brand names nationwide (and even worldwide); standardization of service operations; formalized training programs; an ongoing search for new products; continued emphasis on improving efficiency; and dual marketing programs directed at customers and franchisees, respectively.

Internationalization and Globalization

The internationalization of service companies is readily apparent to any tourist or business executive traveling abroad. Airlines and airfreight companies that were formerly just domestic in scope today have extensive foreign route networks. Numerous financial service firms, advertising agencies, hotel chains, fast-food restaurants, car rental agencies, and accounting firms now operate on several continents. This strategy may reflect a desire to serve existing customers better, to penetrate new markets, or both. The net effect is to increase competition and to encourage the transfer of innovation in both products and processes from country to country. Many well-known service companies in the United States are owned by foreign investors; for instance, Burger King is owned by a British company, and the upscale Four Seasons hotel chain is Canadian owned. But American service businesses, including such industries as banks, quick-service restaurants, and consulting firms, have also been expanding abroad, helping to create a surplus in so-called "invisible" trade. A walk around many of the world's major cities quickly reveals numerous famous service names that originated in other parts of the globe. Franchising allows a service concept developed in one nation to be delivered around the world through distribution systems owned by local investors.

Internationalization of service businesses such as the Bank of Montreal is being facilitated by free-trade agreements such as those among Canada, Mexico, and the United States (NAFTA), among the South American countries that make up Mercosur or Pacto Andino, and among the 15 member nations of the European Union. However, there are fears that barriers will be erected to impede trade in services between free-trade blocs and other nations, as well as between the blocs themselves. Developing a strategy for competing effectively across numerous countries is becoming a major marketing priority for many service firms.

Pressures to Improve Productivity

With increasing competition, often price based, has come greater pressure to improve productivity. Demands by investors for better returns on their investments have also fueled the search for new ways to increase profits by reducing the costs of service delivery. Historically, the service sector has lagged behind the manufacturing sector in productivity improvement, although there are encouraging signs that some services are beginning to catch up, especially when allowance is also made for simultaneous improvements in quality. Using technology to replace labor (or to permit customer self-service) is one cost-cutting route that has been followed in many industries. Reengineering of processes often results in speeding up operations by cutting out unnecessary steps. However, managers need to be aware of the risk that cost-cutting measures, driven by finance and operations personnel without regard for customer needs, may lead to a perceived deterioration in quality and convenience.

The Service Quality Movement

The 1980s were marked by growing customer discontent with the quality of both goods and services. Many of the problems with manufactured products concerned poor service at the point of purchase—the retail store—and with difficulties in solving problems, obtaining refunds, or getting repairs made after the sale. Service industries such as banks, hotels, rental car firms, restaurants, and cable television companies were as much criticized for human failings on the part of their employees as for failures in the technical aspects of service.

With growing realization that improving quality was good for business and necessary for effective competition, a radical change in thinking took place. Traditional notions of quality (based on conformance to standards defined by operations managers) were replaced by the new imperative of letting quality be customer driven, which had enormous implications for the importance of service marketing and the role of customer research.[8] Numerous service organizations have invested in research to determine what their customers want on every dimension of service, in quality improvement programs designed to deliver what customers want, and in ongoing measurement of how satisfied their customers are with the quality of service received. FedEx, the first company to win the Baldrige Quality Award in the service category, is widely recognized for its efforts to link both quality and productivity improvement.

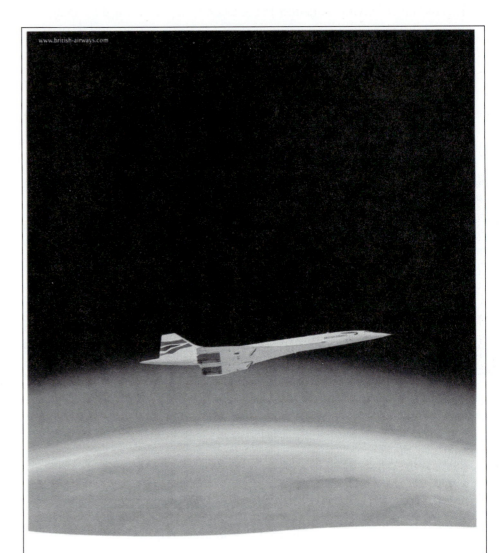

www.british-airways.com

BA : 726,766
NASA : 271

Awesome statistics are what Concorde has always been about. On each mission it flies at 1,336 mph and climbs into the earth's stratosphere to gain an altitude of 10.2 miles. But the most impressive figure of all? The astronomical number of 'astronauts' it's launched into space over the years. Even NASA would look up to that. **The world's favourite airline.**

BRITISH AIRWAYS

One of only two airlines able to fly passengers at supersonic speeds, British Airways has built a reputation for quality in all its services.

Expansion of Leasing and Rental Businesses

Leasing and rental businesses represent a marriage between service and manufacturing. Increasingly, both corporate and individual customers find that they can enjoy the use of a physical product without actually owning it. Long-term leases may involve use of the product alone—such as a truck—or provision of a host of related services at the same time. In trucking, for instance, full-service leasing (also known as "wet leasing") provides almost everything, including painting, washing, maintenance, tires, fuel, license fees, road service, substitute trucks, and even drivers. Personnel, too, can be rented rather than employed full time, as seen by the growth of firms supplying temporary workers, from secretaries to security guards (sometimes jokingly called "rent-a-cops").

Manufacturers as Service Providers

Service profit centers in manufacturing firms are transforming many well-known companies in such fields as computers, automobiles, and electrical and mechanical equipment. Supplementary services once designed to help sell equipment—including consultation, credit, transportation and delivery, installation, training, and maintenance—are now offered as profit-seeking services in their own right, even to customers who have chosen to purchase competing equipment.

Several large manufacturers (including General Electric and Ford) have become important players in the financial services industry as a result of developing credit financing and leasing divisions. Similarly, numerous manufacturing firms now seek to base much of their competitive appeal on the capabilities of their worldwide consultation, maintenance, repair, and problem-solving services. In fact, service profit centers often contribute a substantial proportion of the revenues earned by such well-known manufacturers as IBM, General Electric, DuPont, Hewlett-Packard, and General Motors.

Pressures on Public and Nonprofit Organizations to Find New Income Sources

The financial pressures confronting public and nonprofit organizations are forcing them not only to cut costs and develop more efficient operations but also to pay more attention to customer needs and competitive activities. In their search for new sources of income, many "nonbusiness" organizations are developing a stronger marketing orientation, which often involves rethinking their product lines; adding profit-seeking services such as shops, retail catalogs, restaurants, and consultancy; becoming more selective about the market segments they target; and adopting more realistic pricing policies.[9]

Hiring and Promotion of Innovative Managers

Traditionally, many service industries were very inbred. Managers tended to spend their entire careers working within a single industry, even within a single organization. Each industry was seen as unique, and outsiders were suspect. Relatively few managers had graduate degrees in business, such as an MBA, although they might have held an industry-specific degree in a field such as hotel management or health care administration. In recent years, however, competition and enlightened self-interest have led companies to recruit better qualified managers who are willing to question traditional ways of doing business and are able to bring new ideas from previous work experience in another industry. In many firms, intensive training programs are now exposing employees at all levels to new tools and concepts.

None of the industries in the service sector have been untouched by any of the factors just described. In many industries, notably transportation and financial services, several elements are converging—like a gale, a new moon, and heavy rains—to produce a flood tide that will wreck organizations whose management tries to maintain the status quo. Other managers with more foresight recognize, like Shakespeare's Brutus, that a tide taken at the flood can lead to fortune. But where does this tide lead, and what does it imply for the role of marketing in the service sector? We have described some of the challenges facing service managers, but these changes also bring opportunities. The companies portrayed in the chapter introduction have taken advantage of the changing environment to create new offerings or enhance their competitive positions.

MARKETING SERVICES VERSUS PHYSICAL GOODS

The dynamic environment of services today places a premium on effective marketing. Although it is still very important to run an efficient operation, that no longer suffices for success. The service product must be tailored to customer needs, priced realistically, distributed through convenient channels, and actively promoted to customers. New market entrants are positioning their services to appeal to specific market segments, through their pricing, communication efforts, and service delivery, rather than trying to be all things to all people. But are the marketing skills that have been developed in manufacturing companies directly transferable to service organizations? The answer is often no because marketing management tasks in the service sector tend to differ in several important respects.

Basic Differences between Goods and Services

product: the core output (either a service or a manufactured good) produced by a firm.

goods: physical objects or devices that provide benefits for customers through ownership or use.

Every **product**—a term used in this book to describe the core output of any type of industry—delivers benefits to the customers who purchase and use it. **Goods** can be described as physical objects or devices; services are actions or performances.[10] Early research into services sought to differentiate them from goods, focusing particularly on four generic differences—intangibility, heterogeneity (or variability), perishability of output, and simultaneity of production and consumption.[11] Although these characteristics are still cited, they have been criticized for being too academic and for oversimplifying the real-world environment. More practical insights are provided in Figure 1.3, which lists nine basic differences that can help us to distinguish the tasks associated with services marketing and management from those involved with physical goods.

It's important to note that in identifying these differences we're still dealing with generalizations that do not apply equally to all services. (In chapter 2, we classify services into distinct categories, each of which presents somewhat different challenges for marketers and other managers.) Let's examine each characteristic in more detail.

Customers do not obtain ownership.   Perhaps the key distinction between goods and services lies in the fact that customers usually derive value from services without obtaining permanent ownership of any tangible elements. In many instances, service marketers offer customers the opportunity to rent the use of a physical object, like a car or hotel room, or to hire for a short period of time the labor and expertise of people whose skills range from brain surgery to knowing how to check customers into a hotel. As a purchaser of services yourself, you know that although your main interest is in the final output, the way in which you are treated during service delivery can also have an important impact on your satisfaction.

FIGURE 1.3 **Basic Differences Between Goods and Services**

- customers do not obtain ownership of services
- service products are intangible performances
- there is greater involvement of customers in the production process
- other people may form part of the product
- there is greater variability in operational inputs and outputs
- many services are difficult for customers to evaluate
- there is typically an absence of inventories
- the time factor is relatively more important
- delivery systems may involve both electronic and physical channels

Service products as intangible performances.   Although services often include tangible elements—such as sitting in an airline seat, eating a meal, or getting damaged equipment repaired—the service performance itself is basically **intangible**. The benefits of owning and using a manufactured product come from its physical characteristics (although brand image may convey benefits, too). In services, the benefits come from the nature of the performance. The notion of service as a performance that cannot be touched or wrapped up and taken away leads to a theatrical metaphor for service management—visualizing service delivery as being like staging a play, with service personnel as the actors and customers as the audience. (We discuss the managerial implications of this metaphor in chapter 10.) Some services, such as rentals, include a physical object like a car or a power tool. But marketing a car rental is very different from attempting to market the physical object alone. For instance, in the former, customers usually reserve a particular category of vehicle rather than a specific brand and model. Instead of worrying about colors and upholstery, customers focus on such elements as price, location and appearance of pickup and delivery facilities, extent of insurance coverage, cleanliness and maintenance of vehicles, provision of free shuttle buses at airports, availability of 24-hour reservations service, hours when rental locations are staffed, and quality of service provided by customer-contact personnel. In contrast, the core benefit derived from owning a physical good normally comes specifically from its tangible elements, even though it may also provide intangible benefits, too. An interesting way to distinguish between goods and services is to place them on a scale from tangible dominant to intangible dominant (illustrated in Figure 1.4, p. 16).[12]

intangible: something that is experienced and cannot be touched or preserved.

Customer involvement in the production process.   Performing a service involves assembling and delivering the output of a mix of physical facilities and mental or physical labor. Often customers are actively involved in helping to create the service product—either by serving themselves (as in using a laundromat or withdrawing cash from a bank's ATM) or by cooperating with service personnel in such settings as hair salons, hotels, colleges, or hospitals. Thus, service firms have much to gain from trying to educate their customers to make them more competent.[13] As we see in chapter 2, services can be categorized according to the extent of contact that the customer has with the service organization. Changing the production process often affects the role that customers play.

People as part of the product.   In high-contact services, customers not only come into contact with service personnel but also rub shoulders with other customers (literally so, if they ride a bus or subway during the rush hour). The difference between service businesses often lies in the quality of employees who are serving customers. Similarly, the type of customer who patronizes a particular service business helps to define the nature of the service experience. Thus, people become part of

FIGURE 1.4 Dominance of Tangible versus Intangible Elements in Goods and Services

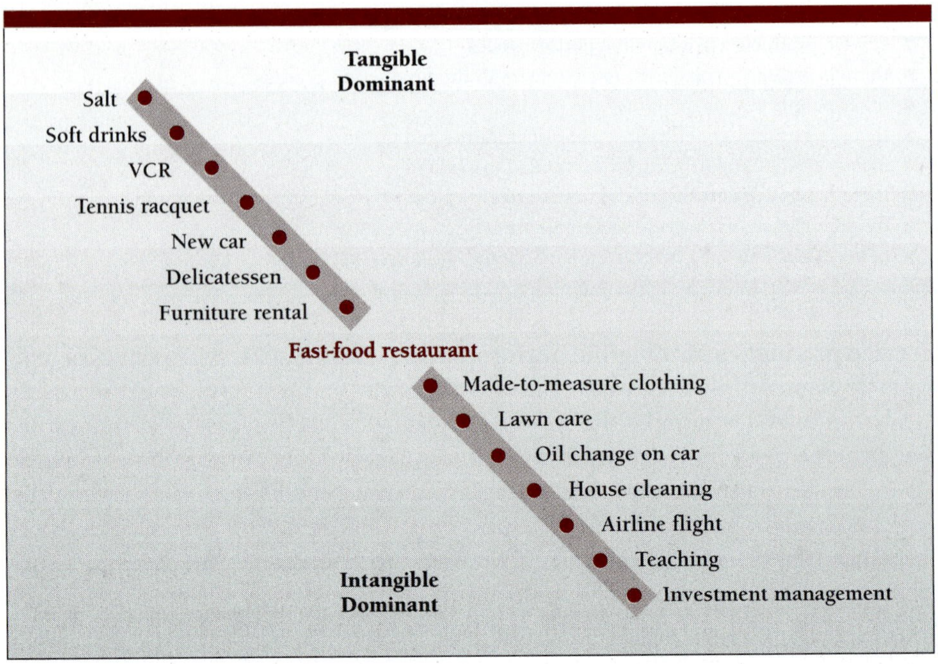

the product in many services. Managing these service encounters—especially those between customers and service providers—with a view to creating a satisfactory experience is a challenging task.

Greater variability in operational inputs and outputs.   The presence of personnel and other customers in the operational system makes it difficult to standardize and control **variability** in both service inputs and outputs. Manufactured goods can be produced under controlled conditions, designed to optimize both productivity and quality, and then checked for conformance with quality standards long before they reach the customer. (Of course, their subsequent use by customers will vary widely, reflecting customers' needs and skills, as well as the nature of the occasion.) But when services are consumed as they are produced, final "assembly" must take place under real-time conditions, which may vary from customer to customer and even from one time of the day to another. As a result, mistakes and shortcomings are both more likely and harder to conceal. These factors make it difficult for service organizations to improve productivity, control quality, and offer a consistent product. As a former packaged goods marketer observed some years ago after moving to a new position at Holiday Inn,

> We can't control the quality of our product as well as a Procter and Gamble control engineer on a production line can. ... When you buy a box of Tide, you can reasonably be 99 and 44/100ths percent sure that this stuff will work to get your clothes clean. When you buy a Holiday Inn room, you're sure at some lesser percentage that it will work to give you a good night's sleep without any hassle, or people banging on the walls and all the bad things that can happen in a hotel.[14]

However, not all variations in service delivery are necessarily negative, and modern service businesses are starting to recognize the value of customizing at least some aspects of the service offering to the needs and expectations of individual customers. In fields such as health care, it's essential.[15]

variability: a lack of consistency in inputs and outputs during the service production process.

Harder for customers to evaluate.   Most physical goods tend to be relatively high in "search attributes"—characteristics a customer can determine before purchasing a product, such as color, style, shape, price, fit, feel, hardness, and smell. Other goods and some services, in contrast, may emphasize "experience attributes," which can only be discerned after purchase or during consumption—as with taste, wearability, ease of handling, quietness, and personal treatment. Finally, there are "credence attributes"—characteristics that customers find hard to evaluate even after consumption. Examples include surgery and technical repairs that are not readily visible.[16]

No inventories for services.   Because a service is a deed or performance, rather than a tangible item that the customer keeps, it is "perishable" and cannot be inventoried. Of course, the necessary facilities, equipment, and labor can be held in readiness to create the service, but these simply represent productive capacity, not the product itself. Having unused capacity in a service business is rather like running water into a sink without a stopper. The flow is wasted unless customers (or possessions that require service) are present to receive it. When demand exceeds capacity, customers may be sent away disappointed because no inventory is available for backup. An important task for service marketers, therefore, is to find ways of smoothing demand levels to match capacity.

Importance of time.   Many services are delivered in real time. Customers have to be physically present to receive services from such organizations as airlines, hospitals, haircutters, and restaurants. There are limits to how long customers are willing to be kept waiting; also, services must be delivered fast so that customers do not waste time receiving them. Even when a service takes place in the back office, customers have expectations about how long a particular task should take to complete—whether it is repairing a machine, completing a research report, cleaning a suit, or preparing a legal document. Today's customers are increasingly time sensitive, and speed is often a key element in good service.

Different distribution channels.   Unlike manufacturers, which require physical distribution channels to move goods from the factory to customers, many service businesses either use electronic channels (as in broadcasting or electronic funds transfer) or combine the service factory, retail outlet, and point of consumption at a single location. In the latter, service firms are responsible for managing customer-contact personnel. They may also have to manage the behavior of customers in the service factory to ensure smoothly running operations and to avoid situations in which one person's behavior irritates other customers who are present at the same time.

AN INTEGRATED APPROACH TO SERVICE MANAGEMENT

This book is not just about services marketing. Throughout the chapters, there are continuing references to two other important functions: service operations and human resource management. Imagine yourself as the manager of a small travel agency. Or think big, if you like, as the chief executive officer (CEO) of a major airline. In both instances, you need to be concerned on a day-to-day basis that your customers are satisfied, that your operational systems are running smoothly and efficiently, and that your employees are not only working productively but are also doing a good job either of serving customers directly or of helping other employees to do so. Even if you see yourself as a middle manager, with specific responsibilities in either marketing or operations or human resources, your success in the job will often involve understanding these other functions and periodic meetings with colleagues in these areas. In short, integration of activities between functions is the goal. If there is a problem in any one of these three areas, it may signal financial problems ahead.

The Eight Components of Integrated Service Management

When discussing strategies to market manufactured goods, marketers usually address four basic strategic elements: product, price, place (or distribution), and promotion (or communication).[17] But the nature of services, which involves such aspects as customer involvement in production and the importance of the time factor, requires that other strategic elements be included. To capture this challenge, we use the 8Ps model of **integrated service management**, which highlights eight decision variables for managers of service organizations.[18]

Our visual metaphor for the 8Ps is the racing eight, a lightweight boat or shell powered by eight rowers, made famous by the Oxford and Cambridge boat race that has taken place annually on the Thames near London for almost 150 years. Today, similar races involving many different teams are a staple of rowing competitions around the world, as well as a featured sport in the Summer Olympics. Speed comes from the rowers' physical strength, but it also reflects their harmony and cohesion. To achieve optimal effectiveness, each of the eight rowers must pull on his or her oar in unison with the others, following the direction of the coxswain, who is seated in the stern. A similar synergy and integration between each of the 8Ps is required for success in any competitive service business (Figure 1.5). The coxswain (cox)—who steers the boat, sets the pace, motivates the crew, and keeps a close eye on competing boats in the race—is a metaphor for management.

Product elements. Managers must select the features of both the core product (either a good or service) and the bundle of supplementary service elements surrounding it, with reference to the benefits desired by customers and how well competing products perform.

Place and time. Delivering product elements to customers involves decisions on both the place and the time of delivery and may involve physical or electronic distribution channels (or both), depending on the nature of the service being provided. Firms may deliver service directly to customers or through intermediary organizations, such as retail outlets owned by other companies, which receive a fee or percentage of the selling price to perform certain tasks associated with sales, service, and customer contact.

Process. Creating and delivering product elements to customers requires the design and implementation of effective processes. A process describes the method and sequence in which service operating systems work. Badly designed processes are likely to annoy customers because of slow, bureaucratic, and ineffective service delivery. Similarly, poor processes make it difficult for front-line staffs to do their jobs well, result in low productivity, and increase the likelihood of service failures.

Productivity and quality. Productivity and quality, often treated separately, should be seen as two sides of the same coin. No service firm can afford to address either element in isolation. Improved **productivity** is essential to keep costs under control, but managers must beware of making inappropriate cuts in service levels that are resented by customers (and perhaps by employees, too). Service **quality**, as defined by customers, is essential for product differentiation and for building customer loyalty. However, investing in quality improvement without understanding the trade-off between incremental costs and incremental revenues may place the profitability of the firm at risk.

---

integrated service management: the coordinated planning and execution of those marketing, operations, and human resources activities that are essential to a service firm's success.

product elements: all components of the service performance that create value for customers.

place and time: management decisions about when, where, and how to deliver services to customers.

process: a particular method of operations or series of actions, typically involving steps that need to occur in a defined sequence.

productivity: how efficiently service inputs are transformed into outputs that add value for customers.

quality: the degree to which a service satisfies customers by meeting their needs, wants, and expectations.

FIGURE 1.5 The Eight Components of Integrated Service Management

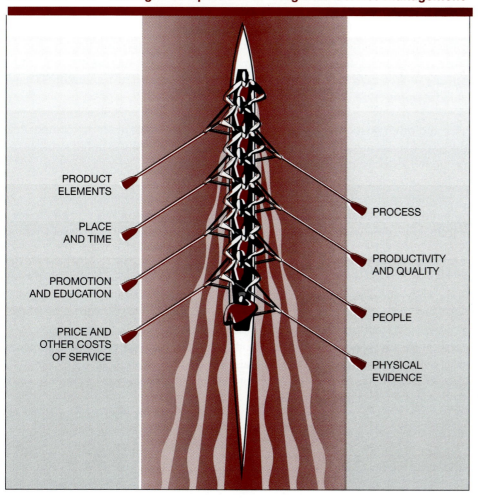

People.   Many services depend on direct, personal interaction between customers and a firm's employees (as in getting a haircut or eating at a restaurant). The nature of these interactions strongly influences the customer's perceptions of service quality.[19] Customers will often judge the quality of the service they receive largely on their assessment of the people who are providing the service. Successful service firms devote significant efforts to recruiting, training, and motivating their personnel, especially—but not exclusively—those who are in direct contact with customers.

> **people:** personnel (and sometimes other customers) who are involved in service production.

Promotion and education.   No marketing program can succeed without an effective communication program that provides promotion and education. This component plays three vital roles: providing needed information and advice, persuading target customers of the merits of a specific product, and encouraging customers to take action at specific times. In service marketing, much communication is educational in nature, especially for new customers. Companies may need to teach them the benefits of the service, where and when to obtain it, and how to participate in service processes. Communications can be delivered by such individuals, as salespeople and trainers or through such media as television, radio, newspapers, magazines, billboards, brochures, and Web sites.

> **promotion and education:** all communication activities and incentives designed to build customer preference for a specific service or service provider.

physical evidence: visual or other tangible clues that provide evidence of service quality.

Physical evidence.   The appearance of buildings, landscaping, vehicles, interior furnishing, equipment, staff members, signs, printed materials, and other visible cues all provide tangible evidence of a firm's service quality. Service firms need to manage physical evidence carefully because it can have a profound impact on customers' impressions. In services with few tangible elements, such as insurance, advertising is often used to create meaningful symbols. For instance, an umbrella may symbolize protection and a fortress, security.

price and other costs of service: expenditures of money, time, and effort that customers incur in purchasing and consuming services.

Price and other costs of service.   The price and other costs of service component addresses management of the various *costs* incurred by customers in obtaining benefits from the service product. Responsibilities are not limited to the traditional pricing tasks of establishing the selling *price* to customers, setting trade margins, and establishing credit terms. Service managers also recognize and, where practical, seek to minimize other costs that customers may bear in purchasing and using a service, including time, mental and physical effort, and negative sensory experiences.

Linking Service Marketing, Operations, and Human Resources

As shown by the component elements of the 8Ps model, marketing cannot operate in isolation from other functional areas in a successful service organization. Three management functions play central and interrelated roles in meeting customer needs: marketing, operations, and human resources. Figure 1.6 illustrates this interdependency. In future chapters, we raise the question of how marketers should relate to and involve their colleagues from other functional areas in planning and implementing marketing strategies.

Service firms must understand the implications of the eight components of integrated service management, as previously described, to develop effective strategies. Firms whose managers succeed in developing integrated strategies will have a better chance of surviving and prospering. Those that fail to grasp these implications, in contrast, are likely to be outmaneuvered by competitors

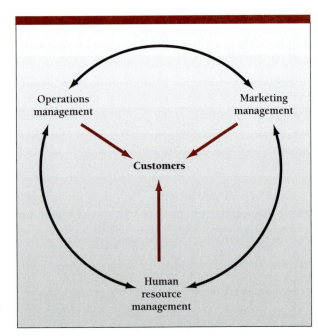

FIGURE 1.6
Interdependence of Marketing, Operations, and Human Resources in Service Management

that are more adept at responding to the dramatic changes affecting the service economy.

You can expect to see the 8Ps framework used throughout this book. Although any given chapter is likely to emphasize just one (or a few) of the eight components, you should always keep in mind the importance of integrating the component(s) under discussion with each of the others when formulating an overall strategy. For a quick clue about the principal focus of each chapter, find the boat diagram on its first page. Each oar represents one of the 8Ps. See which of the eight oars are highlighted. Red highlights indicate which of the 8Ps will be covered extensively in a particular chapter; pink highlights show which components play a more minor role.

Creating Value in a Context of Values

Managers need to be concerned about giving good **value** to customers and treating them fairly in decisions involving all elements of the 8Ps. Firms create value by offering the types of services that customers need, accurately presenting their capabilities, and delivering them in a pleasing and convenient fashion at a fair price. In return, firms receive value from their customers, primarily in the form of the money paid to purchase and use the services in question. Such transfers of value illustrate one of the most fundamental concepts in marketing, that of **exchange**, which takes place when one party obtains value from another in return for something else of value. These exchanges aren't limited to buying and selling. An exchange of value also takes place when employees work for an organization. The employer gets the benefit of the worker's efforts; in turn, the employee receives wages, benefits, and possibly such valued experiences as training, on-the-job experience, and working with friendly colleagues.

As a customer yourself, you regularly make decisions on whether or not to invest time, money, and effort to obtain a service that promises the specific benefits you seek. Perhaps the service in question solves an immediate need, such as getting a haircut, eating a pizza, repairing your bike or car, or passing a couple of hours at a movie theater or another entertainment facility. Alternatively, as with getting an education, you may be prepared to take a long-term perspective before the payoff is realized. But if, after the fact, you find you have had to pay more than you expected or received fewer benefits than anticipated, you are likely to feel cheated. At a minimum, you will be muttering darkly about "poor value" (more likely, your discontent will be loudly and colorfully expressed). If you feel you were badly treated during service delivery, although the service itself provided the desired benefits, you may conclude that this treatment diminished the value received. Perhaps you or people you know have worked for an organization that treated its employees poorly, even to the extent of not computing wages fairly or failing to deliver promised job-related benefits. That's not the best way for management to build employees' commitment to the firm or dedication to serving customers. In fact, customers are quick to pick up on a bad aura from unhappy service workers.

No firm that seeks long-term relationships with either customers or employees can afford to mistreat them or to provide poor value on an ongoing basis. At a minimum, it's bad business; at worst, it's unethical. Sooner or later, shortchanging or mistreating customers and employees is likely to rebound to the firm's disadvantage. Unfortunately, not all firms, employees, or even customers have the other parties' best interests at heart. The potential for abusive behavior is perhaps higher in services than in manufacturing, reflecting the difficulty of evaluating many services in

value: the worth of a specific action or object relative to an individual's needs at a particular time.

exchange: the act of giving or taking one thing of value in return for something else of value.

Checking in: People are part of the product in hotel services, so customer satisfaction depends on both employee performance and the behavior of the other customers.

values: underlying beliefs held by people about the way life should be lived and business conducted, including what constitutes appropriate behavior for both individuals and organizations.

advance (and even after the fact), the need to involve customers in service production and delivery in many instances, and the face-to-face encounters that customers often have with service personnel and other customers.[20] Companies need a set of morally and legally defensible **values** to guide their actions and to shape their dealings with both employees and customers. To the extent possible, managers would be wise to use these values as criteria in recruiting and motivating employers. They should also clarify the firm's values and expectations in dealing with prospective customers, as well as making an effort to attract and retain customers who share and appreciate these same values.

Businesses and business schools are devoting more attention today to discussions of what constitutes ethical behavior. However, there's nothing new in the notion of ethical conduct of business affairs nor in the recognition of the merit of good values. More than 30 years ago, Siegmund Warburg of the investment banking house of S.G. Warburg (now SBC Warburg) remarked that the reputation of a firm for "integrity, generosity, and thorough service is its most important asset, more important than any financial item. However, the reputation of a firm is like a very delicate living organism which can easily be damaged and which has to be taken care of incessantly, being mainly a matter of human behavior and human standards."[21]

business ethics: the principles of moral conduct that should guide behavior in the business world.

What's new today is the greater scrutiny given to a firm's **business ethics** and the presence of tougher legislation designed to protect both customers and employees from abusive treatment. In this book, we try not to be preachy, but we periodically raise ethical issues as they relate to different aspects of service management. Don't be surprised to find occasional questions relating to ethical practice, as well as some examples and case studies. We also look at the responsibility of customers to behave in considerate ways toward suppliers and other customers. In chapter 6, we discuss how managers should deal with customers who behave in unethical or abusive ways.

Conclusion

Why study services? Because modern economies are driven by service businesses, both large and small. Services are responsible for the creation of a substantial majority of new jobs, both skilled and unskilled, around the world. The service sector has a tremendous variety of different industries, including many activities provided by public and nonprofit organizations. It accounts for over half the economy in most developing countries and for over 70 percent in many highly developed economies.

As we've shown in this chapter, services differ from manufacturing organizations in many important respects and require a distinctive approach to marketing and other management functions. As a result, managers cannot continue to rely solely on tools and concepts developed in the manufacturing sector. In the remainder of this book, we discuss in more detail the unique challenges and opportunities faced by service businesses. It's our hope that you'll use the material in this text to enhance your future experiences not only as a service employee or manager but also as a customer of many different types of service businesses.

Study Questions and Exercises

1. Business schools have traditionally placed more emphasis on manufacturing industries than on service industries in their courses. Why do you think this is so? Does it matter?
2. Why is time so important in services?
3. What are the implications of freer competition for managers in service industries that used to be heavily regulated?
4. Give examples of how computer and telecommunications technology has changed the services that you use during the past 10 years.
5. Choose a service company with which you are familiar and show how each of the eight elements (8Ps) of integrated service management applies.
6. Is the risk of unethical business practices greater or lesser in service businesses than in manufacturing firms. Why or why not?
7. Why do marketing, operations, and human resources have to be more closely linked in services than in manufacturing? Give examples.

CHAPTER
Two

Understanding Service Processes

Learning Objectives

After reading this chapter, you should be able to

■ appreciate the value of classification in services marketing

■ understand useful ways of classifying differences between various types of services

■ define a service process

■ describe four different types of service processes and their implications for management strategy

■ recognize that the nature of a customer's contact with a service varies according to the underlying process

Product elements

Place and Time

Promotion and education

Price and other costs of service

PROCESS

Productivity and quality

People

Physical Evidence

Susan Munro, Service Consumer

Susan Munro, a final-year business student, had breakfast and then turned on the television to watch the weather forecast. It predicted rain, so she grabbed an umbrella before leaving the apartment and walking to the bus stop for her daily ride to the university. On the way, she dropped a letter in a mailbox. The bus arrived on schedule. It was the usual driver, who recognized her and gave a cheerful greeting as she showed her commuter pass. The bus was quite full, carrying a mix of students and office workers, so she had to stand.

Arriving at her destination, Susan left the bus and walked to the School of Business. Joining a throng of other students, she took a seat in the large classroom where her finance class was held. The professor lectured in a near monotone for 75 minutes, occasionally projecting charts on a large screen to illustrate certain calculations. Susan reflected that it would be just as effective—and far more convenient—if the course were transmitted by television or recorded on videotapes that students could watch at their leisure. She much preferred the marketing course that followed because this professor was a very dynamic individual who believed in having an active dialog with the students. Susan made several contributions to the discussion and felt that she learned a lot from listening to others' analyses and viewpoints.

She and three friends ate lunch at the recently modernized Student Union. The old cafeteria, a gloomy place that served boring food at high prices, had been replaced by a well-lit and colorfully decorated new food court, featuring a variety of small kiosks. These included both local suppliers and brand-name fast-food chains, which offered choices of sandwiches, as well as health foods and a variety of desserts. Although she had wanted a sandwich, the line of waiting customers at the sandwich shop was rather long, so Susan joined her friends at Burger King and then splurged on a caffe latte from the adjacent Hav-a-Java coffee stand. The food court was unusually crowded today, perhaps because of the rain now pouring down outside. When they finally found a table, however, they had to clear off the dirty trays. "Lazy slobs!" commented her friend Mark, referring to the previous customers.

After lunch, Susan stopped at the cash machine, inserted her bank card, and withdrew some money. Remembering that she had a job interview at the end of the week, she telephoned her hairdresser and counted herself lucky to be able to make an appointment for later in the day because of a cancellation by another client. Leaving the Student Union, she ran across the rain-soaked plaza to the Language Department. In preparation for her next class, Business Spanish, she spent an hour in the language lab, watching an engaging videotape of customers making purchases at different types of stores, then repeating key phrases and listening to her own recorded voice. "My accent's definitely getting better!" she said to herself.

The class over, it was time to visit the hairdresser, whose salon was within walking distance. She liked the store, which had a bright, trendy decor and well-groomed, friendly staff. Unfortunately, the cutter was running late and Susan had to wait 20 minutes, which she used to review a chapter for tomorrow's human relations course. Some of the other waiting customers were reading magazines provided by the store. Eventually, it was time for a shampoo, after which the cutter proposed a slightly different cut, to which

Susan agreed, although she drew the line at the suggestion to lighten her hair color. She sat very still, watching the process in the mirror and turning her head when requested. She was pleased with the result and complimented the cutter on her work. Including the shampoo, the process had lasted about 40 minutes. She tipped the cutter and paid at the reception desk.

The rain had stopped and the sun was shining as Susan left the store, so she walked home, stopping on the way to pick up clothes from the cleaners. This store was rather gloomy, smelled of cleaning solvents, and badly needed repainting. She was annoyed to find that although her silk blouse was ready as promised, the suit she would need for her interview was not. The assistant, who had dirty fingernails, mumbled an apology in an insincere tone without making eye contact. Although the store was convenient and the quality of work quite good, Susan considered the employees unfriendly and not very helpful. Back at the

apartment building, she opened the mailbox in the lobby and collected the mail for herself and her roommates. Her own mail, which was rather dull, included a quarterly bill from her insurance company, which required no action since she had signed an agreement to deduct the funds automatically from her bank account. There was also a postcard from her optometrist, reminding her that it was time to schedule a new eye exam. Susan made a mental note to call for an appointment, anticipating that she might need a revised prescription for her contact lenses. She was about to discard the junk mail when she noticed a flyer promoting a new dry-cleaning store and including a coupon for a discount. She decided to try the new firm and pocketed the coupon.

Since it was her turn to cook dinner, she wandered into the kitchen and started looking in the refrigerator and then the cupboards to see what was available, which was not much. Maybe she would make a salad and call for home delivery of a large pizza.

HOW DO SERVICES DIFFER FROM ONE ANOTHER?

The service sector is amazingly varied, and the array of transactions made by Susan Munro represents only a small sample of all the services directed at individual consumers. As a review of the listings in the Yellow Pages will show, there is also a vast number of business services directed at corporate purchasers. It's surprising how many managers in service businesses consider their industries to be unique—or at least distinctively different. Certainly, there are distinctions to be drawn, but it would be a mistake to assume that any one service used by Susan has nothing in common with any of the others she might use.

In chapter 1, we looked at some of the ways in which services might differ from goods. In this chapter, our focus is on developing useful ways of grouping services into categories that share managerially relevant characteristics, particularly as they relate to marketing strategy. We find that important insights can be gained by looking for similarities between "different" service industries. The more service managers can identify meaningful parallels to their own firms' situations, the better their chances of beating the competition by borrowing good ideas from other businesses. One hallmark of innovative service firms is that their managers have been willing to look outside their own industries for useful ideas that they can try in their own organizations. We start our search for useful categorization schemes by examining how goods have traditionally been classified.

The Value of Classification Schemes

Marketing practitioners have long recognized the value of developing distinctive strategies for different types of goods. One of the most famous classification schemes divides goods into convenience, shopping, and specialty categories, according to how frequently consumers buy them and how much effort they are prepared to put into comparing alternatives and locating the right product to match their needs.[1] This scheme helps managers obtain a better understanding of consumer expectations and behavior and provides insights into the management of retail distribution

Purchasing decisions for business services often involve managers from several different departments.

systems. This same classification can also be applied to retail service institutions, from financial service providers to hair salons.

Another major classification is between durable and nondurable goods. Durability is closely associated with purchase frequency, which has important implications for the development of both distribution and communications strategies. Although service performances are intangible, the durability of benefits is relevant to repurchase frequency. For example, you probably purchase a haircut less often than you buy a cafe latte (at least if you are a typical student or a coffee connoisseur).

Yet another classification is consumer goods (those purchased for personal or household use) versus industrial goods (those purchased by companies and other organizations). This classification relates not only to the types of goods purchased—although there is some overlap—but also to methods for evaluating competing alternatives, purchasing procedures, size of purchase orders, and actual usage. Once again, this classification is transferable to services. For example, you may be the only one involved in a decision about whether to purchase America Online (AOL) or another Internet provider for your own computer, but a corporate decision about what on-line services to select for employees may involve managers and technical specialists from several departments. Business-to-business services, as the name suggests, comprise a large group of services targeted at corporate customers and may range from executive recruiting to security and from payroll management to sandblasting.

Although these goods-based classification schemes are helpful, they don't go far enough in highlighting the key strategic issues. We need to classify services into marketing-relevant groups, looking for points of similarity among different industries. We can use the insights from these classifications to help us focus on marketing strategies that are relevant to specific service situations.

How Might Services Be Classified?[2]

The traditional way of grouping services is by industry. Service managers may say, "We're in the transportation business" (or hospitality, banking, telecommunications, or repair and maintenance). These groupings help us to define the core products

FIGURE 2.1 Selected Ways of Classifying Services

- degree of tangibility or intangibility of service processes
- direct recipient of the service process
- place and time of service delivery
- customization versus standardization
- nature of the relationship with customers
- extent to which demand and supply are in balance
- extent to which facilities, equipment, and people are part of the service experience

offered by the firm and to understand both customer needs and competition. However, they may not capture the true nature of each business the industry because service delivery can differ widely even within a single category. (For example, food can be provided to customers in settings that range from airport Taco Bells to four-star restaurants.) Various proposals have been made for classifying services. Among the meaningful ways in which services can be grouped or classified are those listed in Figure 2.1 and discussed next.

Degree of tangibility or intangibility of service processes.   Does the service do something physical and **tangible** (like food services or dry cleaning), or do its processes involve a greater amount of **intangibility** (like teaching or telephoning)? Different service processes not only shape the nature of the service delivery system but also affect the role of employees and the experience of customers.

Direct recipient of the service process.   Some services, like haircutting or public transportation, are directed at customers themselves. Some customers seek services (like dry cleaning) to restore or improve objects that belong to them, but they remain uninvolved in the process of service delivery and do not consume the benefits until later. The nature of the service encounter between service suppliers and their customers varies widely according to the extent to which customers themselves are integrally involved in the service process. Contrast Susan's extended interactions with the haircutter and her brief encounter with the mailbox on her way to school.

Place and time of service delivery.   When designing delivery systems, service marketers must ask themselves whether customers need to visit the service organization at its own sites (as Susan did with the university, the hair salon, and the cleaners) or whether service should come to the customer (like the pizza delivery to her apartment). Or perhaps the interaction can occur through physical channels like mail (as with her insurance) or electronic channels (as with her banking transaction). These managerial decisions involve consideration of the nature of the service itself, where customers are located (both home and workplace may be relevant), their preferences relating to time of purchase and use, the relative costs of different alternatives, and—in some instances—seasonal factors.

Customization versus standardization.   Services can be classified according to the degree of **customization** or **standardization** involved in service delivery. An important marketing decision is whether all customers should receive the same service or whether service features (and the underlying processes) should be adapted to meet individual requirements. Susan's insurance policy is probably one of several standard options. The bus service is standardized, with a fixed route and schedule (unlike a taxi), but passengers can choose when to ride and where to get on and off. By encouraging student discussion and debate, Susan's marketing professor is offering a more customized course than her finance professor. Her haircut is

tangible *(adjective)*: capable of being touched, held, or preserved in physical form over time.

intangibility: a distinctive characteristic of services that makes it impossible to touch or hold on to them in the same manner as physical goods.

customization: tailoring service characteristics to meet each customer's specific needs and preferences.

standardization: reducing variation in service operations and delivery.

If you want to enjoy whitewater rafting, you will have to go to a rafting company on the right river at the right season of the year.

customized (although other young women may wear the same style), and her future eye exam will have to be totally customized if the prescription for new contacts is to be accurate.

Nature of the relationship with customers.   Some services involve a formal relationship, in which each customer is known to the organization and all transactions are individually recorded and attributed (like Susan's bank or optometrist). But in other services, unidentified customers undertake fleeting transactions and then disappear from the organization's sight (for instance, the phone company has no record of her call from the pay phone, nor the TV station of her watching the weather forecast). As we see in chapter 6, some services lend themselves naturally to a "membership" relationship, in which customers must apply to join the "club" and their subsequent performance is monitored over time (as in insurance or college enrollment). Other services, like buses, hair salons, dry cleaners, and restaurants, need to undertake proactive efforts to create an ongoing relationship. Although the bus company does not record Susan's rides, it could keep records of all monthly pass holders so that it can mail out passes every month, plus a newsletter describing service improvements or route and schedule changes. Sometimes companies create special club memberships or frequent user programs to reward loyal users. For instance, both the hair salon and the dry cleaner could record customers' names and addresses and periodically make them special offers.

Extent to which demand and supply are in balance.   Some service industries face steady demand for their services, whereas others encounter significant fluctuations. In chapter 14, we address the problem faced by marketers when the demand for service fluctuates widely over time. In these situations, either capacity must be adjusted to accommodate the level of demand or marketing strategies must be implemented to predict, manage, and smooth demand levels to bring them into balance with capacity. On a wet day, more students are eating lunch at the Student Union at Susan's university, and so there are lines at the sandwich shop and tables are hard to find.

Extent to which facilities, equipment, and people are part of the service experience.   Customers' service experiences are shaped, in part, by the extent to which they are exposed to tangible elements in the service delivery system (the bus that Susan rides is very tangible; so are her classrooms, the table and chairs in the food court, and the videocassette recorder [VCR] in the language lab). In contrast, the physical evidence of her insurance company may be limited to occasional letters, and she may see little more of her bank than monthly statements and the ATM that she uses at the Student Union.

The cheerful bus driver humanizes Susan's bus ride. She appears to think better of her dynamic marketing professor than of her dull finance professor. She likes her trendy hair salon and the friendly cutter but not the smelly dry-cleaning store and its surly employees, even though the quality of cleaning is good. When the cleaner fails to deliver her suit on time and, coincidentally, she receives a discount coupon in the mail from a competitor, she's ready to switch.

The service classification strategies we've just discussed can help managers better raise the following questions: What does our service operation actually do? What sorts of processes are involved in creating the core product that we offer to customers? And speaking of customers, where do they fit into our operation? The answers will differ, depending on the nature of the underlying service process required to create and deliver a particular service. So now we turn to the most fundamental of the 8Ps of integrated service management: the *processes* by which service products are created and delivered.

SERVICE AS A PROCESS

Marketers don't usually need to know the specifics of how physical goods are manufactured—that is the responsibility of the people who run the factory. However, the situation is different in services. Because customers are often involved in service production, marketers do need to understand the nature of the processes to which

SkyTel makes its paging service more tangible by providing its customers with a pager and putting its name next to the manufacturer's.

SkyTel features advanced messaging pagers by Motorola.

their customers may be exposed. A *process* is a particular method of operation or a series of actions, typically involving multiple steps that often need to take place in a defined sequence. Think about the steps that Susan went through at the hair salon: phoning in advance to make an appointment, arriving at the store, waiting, having a shampoo, discussing options with the cutter, having her hair cut and styled, tipping, paying, and finally leaving the store.

Service processes range from relatively simple procedures involving only a few steps—such as filling a car's tank with fuel—to highly complex activities like transporting passengers on an international flight. In later chapters, we show how these processes can be represented in diagrams known as flowcharts, which help us to understand what is going on (and perhaps how a specific process might be improved).

Categorizing Service Processes

A process involves transforming input into output. But what is each service organization actually processing and how does it perform this task? Two broad categories are processed in services: people and objects. In many cases, ranging from passenger transportation to education, customers themselves are the principal input to the service process (as in Susan's haircut); in other instances, the key input is an object like a malfunctioning computer or a piece of financial data. In some services, as in all manufacturing, the process is physical: Something tangible takes place. But in information-based services, the process can be intangible.

By looking at services from a purely operational perspective, we see that they can be categorized into four broad groups. Table 2.1 shows a four-way classification scheme based on tangible actions to either people's bodies or to customer's physical possessions and intangible actions to people's minds or to their intangible assets.

TABLE 2.1   Understanding the Nature of the Service Act

What Is the Nature of the Service Act?	Who or What Is the Direct Recipient of the Service?	
	People	*Possessions*
Tangible Actions	*(People Processing)* **Services directed at people's bodies:** Passenger transportation Health care Lodging Beauty salons Physical therapy Fitness centers Restaurants/bars Haircutting Funeral services	*(Possession Processing)* **Services directed at physical possessions:** Freight transportation Repair and maintenance Warehousing/storage Janitorial services Retail distribution Laundry and dry cleaning Refueling Landscaping/lawn care Disposal/recycling
Intangible Actions	*(Mental Stimulus Processing)* **Services directed at people's minds:** Advertising/PR Arts and entertainment Broadcasting/cable Management consulting Education Information services Music concerts Psychotherapy Religion Voice telephone	*(Information Processing)* **Services directed at intangible assets:** Accounting Banking Data processing Data transmission Insurance Legal services Programming Research Securities investment Software consulting

Each of these four categories involves fundamentally different forms of processes, with vital implications for marketing, operations, and human resource managers. We refer to the categories as people processing, possession processing, mental stimulus processing, and information processing. Although the industries within each category may appear at first sight to be very different, analysis will show that they do, in fact, share important process-related characteristics. As a result, managers in one industry may be able to obtain useful insights by studying another one and then create valued innovations for their own organization.

people processing: services that involve tangible actions to people's bodies.

1. **People processing** *involves tangible actions to people's bodies.* Examples of people-processing services include passenger transportation, haircutting, and dental work. Customers need to be physically present throughout service delivery to receive its desired benefits.

possession processing: tangible actions to goods and other physical possessions belonging to customers.

2. **Possession processing** *includes tangible actions to goods and other physical possessions belonging to the customer.* Examples of possession processing include airfreight, lawn mowing, and cleaning services. In these instances, the object requiring processing must be present, but the customer need not be.

mental stimulus processing: intangible actions directed at people's minds.

3. **Mental stimulus processing** *refers to intangible actions directed at people's minds.* Services in this category include entertainment, spectator sports, theater performances, and education. In such instances, customers must be present mentally but can be located either in a specific service facility or in a remote location connected by broadcast signals or telecommunication linkages.

information processing: intangible actions directed at customers' assets.

4. **Information processing** *describes intangible actions directed at a customer's assets.* Examples of information-processing services include insurance, banking, and consulting. In this category, little direct involvement with the customer may be needed once the request for service has been initiated.

Let's examine why these four different types of processes often have distinctive implications for marketing, operations, and human resource strategies.

People Processing

From ancient times, people have sought out services directed at themselves (e.g., being transported, fed, lodged, restored to health, or made more beautiful). To receive these types of services, customers must physically enter the service system. Because they are an integral part of the process, they cannot obtain the benefits they desire by dealing at arm's length with service suppliers. They must enter the **service**

service factory: the physical site where service operations take place.

factory, which is a physical location (sometimes mobile like Susan's bus) where people or machines (or both) create and deliver service benefits to customers. Sometimes, of course, service providers are willing to come to customers, bringing the necessary tools of their trade to create the desired benefits in the customers' choice of locations.

If customers want the benefits that a people-processing service has to offer, they must be prepared to cooperate actively with the service operation. The level of involvement required of customers may entail anything from boarding a city bus for a five-minute ride to undergoing a lengthy course of unpleasant treatments at a hospital. In between these extremes are such activities as ordering and eating a meal; having one's hair washed, cut, and styled; and spending some nights in a hotel room. The output from these services (after a period of time that can vary from minutes to months) is a customer who has reached her destination or satisfied his hunger or is now sporting clean and stylishly cut hair or has had a good night's sleep away from home or is now in physically better health. Susan cooperates with her hair stylist by sitting still and turning her head as requested. She will also have to be part of the process when she visits the optometrist for her next eye exam.

It's important for managers to think about process and output in terms of what happens to the customer (or other object being processed) because it helps them to identify what benefits are being created. Reflecting on the service process itself helps to identify some of the nonfinancial costs—such as time, mental and physical effort, and even fear and pain—that customers incur in obtaining these benefits.

Possession Processing

Often, customers ask a service organization to provide treatment to some physical possession—which could be anything from a house to a hedge, a car to a computer, or a dress to a dog. Many such activities are quasi-manufacturing operations and do not always involve simultaneous production and consumption. Examples include cleaning, maintaining, storing, improving, or repairing physical objects—both live and inanimate—that belong to the customer in order to extend their usefulness. Additional possession-processing services include transport and storage of goods; wholesale and retail distribution; and installation, removal, and disposal of equipment—in short, the entire value-adding chain of activities that may take place during the lifetime of the object in question.

Customers are less physically involved with this type of service than with people-processing services. Consider the difference between passenger and parcel transportation. In the former you have to go along for the ride to obtain the benefit of getting from one location to another. But with package service, you drop the package off at a mailbox or post office counter (or request a courier to collect it from your home or office) and wait for it to be delivered to the recipient. In most possession-processing services, the customer's involvement is usually limited to dropping off the item that needs treatment, requesting the service, explaining the problem, and later returning to pick up the item and pay the bill (like Susan's visit to the cleaners to pick up her blouse and suit). If the object to be processed is something that is difficult or impossible to move, like landscaping, installed software, heavy equipment, or part of a building, the service factory must come to the customer,

FedEx couriers visit customers to pick up and deliver packages.

with service personnel bringing the tools and materials necessary to complete the job on-site. If a pipe bursts in Susan's apartment, a plumber will have to go there to fix it (and the sooner the better).

The service process could involve applying insecticide in a house to get rid of ants, trimming a hedge at an office park, repairing a car, installing software in a computer, cleaning a jacket, or giving an injection to the family dog. The output in each instance should be a satisfactory solution to the customer's problem or some tangible enhancement of the item in question. In Susan's case, the cleaners disappointed her because her suit was not ready when promised.

Mental Stimulus Processing

Services that interact with people's minds include education, news and information, professional advice, psychotherapy, entertainment, and certain religious activities. Anything touching people's minds has the power to shape attitudes and influence behavior. So, when customers are in a position of dependency or there is potential for manipulation, strong ethical standards and careful oversight are required.

Receiving these services requires an investment of time on the customer's part. However, recipients don't necessarily have to be physically present in a service factory—just mentally in communication with the information being presented. There's an interesting contrast here with people-processing services. Although passengers can sleep through a flight and still arrive at their desired destination, if Susan falls asleep in class or during an educational TV broadcast, she will not be any wiser at the end than at the beginning!

Services like entertainment and education are often created in one place and transmitted by television or radio to individual customers in distant locations. However, they can also be delivered to groups of customers at the originating location in a facility such as a theater or lecture hall. (Susan would prefer the broadcast approach for her finance class.) We need to recognize that watching a live concert on television in one's home is not the same experience as watching it in a concert hall in the company of hundreds or even thousands of other people. Managers of concert halls face many of the same challenges as their colleagues in people-processing services. Similarly, the experience of participating in a discussion-based class through interactive cable television lacks the intimacy of people debating one another in the same room.

Because the core content of all services in this category is information based (whether music, voice, or visual images), it can easily be converted to digital bits or analog signals; recorded for posterity; and transformed into a manufactured product, such as a compact disk, videotape, or audiocassette, which may then be packaged and marketed much like any other physical good. These services can thus be "inventoried" because they can be consumed at a later date than when they were produced. For instance, Susan's Spanish videotape can be used over and over again by students visiting the language lab.

Information Processing

Information processing, one of the buzzwords of our age, has been revolutionized by computers. But not all information is processed by machines: Professionals in a wide variety of fields use their brains, too. Information is the most intangible form of service output, but it may be transformed into more enduring, tangible forms as letters, reports, books, tapes, or diskettes. Among the services that are highly de-

She could watch the circus on television or videotape—but would it be the same experience or even the same service?

pendent on the effective collection and processing of information are financial services and professional services like accounting, law, marketing research, management consulting, and medical diagnosis.

The extent of customer involvement in both information and mental stimulus processing is often determined more by tradition and a personal desire to meet the supplier face to face than by the needs of the operational process. Strictly speaking, personal contact is quite unnecessary in industries like banking or insurance. Why subject your firm to all the complexities of managing a people-processing service when you could deliver the same core product at arm's length? As a customer, why go to the service factory when there's no compelling need to do so? Susan appears comfortable dealing at arm's length with both her bank and her insurance company, using a self-service ATM for her banking transactions and receiving mail communications from her insurance company.

Habit and tradition often lie at the root of existing service delivery systems and service usage patterns. Professionals and their clients may say they prefer to meet face to face because they feel they thus learn more about each other's needs, capabilities, and personalities. However, experience shows that successful personal relationships, built on trust, can be created and maintained purely through telephone or e-mail contact.

DIFFERENT PROCESSES POSE DISTINCTIVE MANAGEMENT CHALLENGES

The challenges and tasks facing managers who work in each of the four different service categories just described are likely to vary to some extent. The classification scheme displayed earlier is central in understanding these differences and developing effective service strategies. Not only does it offer insights into the nature of service benefits in each instance, but it also provides an understanding of the behavior that is required of the customer. There are also implications for developing channel strategy, designing and locating the service delivery system, and using information technology to best advantage.

Identifying Service Benefits

Managers need to recognize that operational processes, however important, are basically just a means to an end. The key is to understand the specific benefits that a service provides for its users. Many firms bundle together lots of different activities as part of their effort to provide good service. But innovation in service delivery requires a constant spotlight to be maintained on the processes underlying delivery of the core product—a bed for the night in the lodging industry, fast transportation of people in the airline industry, or cleaning and pressing clothes in the laundry industry. New technology often allows service organizations to deliver the same (or improved) benefits to customers through distinctly different processes. Sometimes customers are delighted to receive service through faster, simpler, and more convenient procedures. However, operations managers need to beware of imposing new processes, in the name of efficiency, on customers who prefer the existing approach (particularly when the new approach relies on technology and equipment to replace personal service by employees). By working with marketing personnel, operations specialists will improve their chances of designing new processes that deliver the benefits desired by customers in user-friendly ways.

Designing the Service Factory

Every service has customers (or hopes to find some), but not every service interacts with them in the same way. Customer involvement in the core activity may vary sharply for each of the four categories of service process. Nothing can alter the fact that people-processing services require the customer to be physically present in the service factory. If you're currently in New York and want to be in London tomorrow, you simply can't avoid boarding an international flight and spending time in a jet high above the Atlantic. If you want your hair cut, you can't delegate this activity to somebody else's head—you have to sit in the haircutter's chair yourself. If you have the misfortune to break your leg, you will personally have to submit to the unpleasantness of having the bone X-rayed, reset by an orthopedic surgeon, and then encased in a protective cast for several weeks.

When customers visit a service factory, their satisfaction will be influenced by such factors as

- encounters with service personnel
- appearance and features of service facilities—both exterior and interior
- interactions with self-service equipment
- characteristics and behavior of other customers

When customers are required to be physically present throughout service delivery, the process must be designed around them from the moment they arrive at the service factory. Customers may initially need parking (or other assistance in traveling to and from the service facility). The longer they remain at the site, the more likely they are to need other services, including hospitality basics like food, beverages, and toilets. In many instances, they will have to play active roles in the creation and delivery of the service. Well-managed service firms teach their customers how to participate effectively in service operations.

Air travel requires sitting in an airline seat high above the earth (some seats are more comfortable than others).

Service delivery sites that customers need to visit must be located and designed with their convenience in mind. If the service factory is noisy, smelly, confusingly laid out, and in an inconvenient location, customers are likely to have negative impressions. Marketing managers need to work closely with their counterparts in operations to design facilities that are both pleasing to customers and efficient to operate. At Susan's college, the redesigned food court at the Student Union replaced a cafeteria that provided a less attractive experience (as well as worse food). The exterior of a building creates important first impressions, whereas the interior can be thought of as the "stage" on which the service performance is delivered. The longer customers remain in the factory, and the more they expect to spend, the more important it is to offer facilities that are comfortable and attractive. The interior of Susan's hair salon appeals to her but that of the dry cleaner does not.

Marketers need to work with human resource managers, too. Here the task is to ensure that those employees who are in contact with customers present an acceptable appearance and have both the personal and technical skills needed to perform well. The workers at the dry-cleaning store appear to lack such skills. If service delivery requires customers to interact with employees, both parties may need some basic training or guidance on how to work together cooperatively to achieve the best results. If customers are expected to do some of the work themselves—as in self-service—facilities and equipment must be user-friendly.

Finding Alternative Channels for Service Delivery

Unlike the situation in people-processing services, managers responsible for possession processing, mental stimulus processing, and information processing need not oblige their customers to visit a service factory. Instead, they may be able to offer a choice of several alternative delivery channels: (1) letting customers come to a user-friendly factory, (2) limiting contact to a small retail office that is separate from the factory, (3) coming to the customer's home or office, and (4) conducting business at arm's length.

Let's consider the cleaning and pressing of clothes—a possession-processing service—as an example. One approach is to do your laundry at home. If you lack the necessary machines, you can pay to use a laundromat, which is essentially a self-service cleaning factory. If you prefer to leave the task of laundry and dry cleaning to professionals, as Susan chose to do with her best clothes, you can go to a retail store that serves as a drop-off location for dirty clothes and pickup point for newly cleaned items. Sometimes, cleaning is conducted in a space behind the store; at other times, the clothing is transported to an industrial operation some distance away. Home pickup and delivery is available in some cities, but this service tends to be expensive because of the extra costs involved. Innovation in service delivery sometimes takes the form of changing the conventional approach to location strategy to offer customers greater convenience (see the box, "Entrepreneur Sells Mobile Oil Changes").

Both physical and electronic channels allow customers and suppliers to conduct service transactions at arm's length. For instance, instead of shopping at the mall, you can study a printed catalog and order by telephone for mail delivery; or you can shop on the Internet, entering your orders electronically after reviewing your choices at a Web site. Information-based items, like software, research reports, or real estate listings can be downloaded immediately to your own computer.

ENTREPRENEUR SELLS MOBILE OIL CHANGES
His market is busy delivery fleets and people on the go.

By Mike Karath
Staff Writer

HYANNIS—Andrew Todoroff discovered oil on Cape Cod.

For people who don't have time to take their car in for an oil change, Todoroff brings the auto shop to them.

About two years ago he opened Lube On Location, which services commercial fleets and personal autos across the Cape. It provides oil changes for $26.95; tire rotation for $21.15; wiper blades starting at $15 and air filter changes starting at $12, tax included.

In the next several months he will add a vacuum system to his van and offer complete interior cleanings for about $30.

Todoroff popped up from beneath a red Mazda recently after finishing an oil change in the parking lot of a Main Street Hyannis business. A drop of motor oil ran down his face as he wiped his hands.

"The woman who owns the car, her husband called and said she wasn't really taking care of it." Todoroff said. "I had been doing work on his truck, so he asked if I could do his wife's car while she was at work." He added, "People at the bank saw me doing her car, and I got more business from it."

Lube On Location specializes in fleets like courier companies. Todoroff services them early in the morning while the trucks are being loaded and in the late afternoon while they are being unloaded.

"He saves me a ton of money," said Edward Matz, fleet manager of Cape Allied Transit in West Yarmouth, a courier service. "Just in manpower alone he saves me a lot because I don't have to pay a guy to take the truck to a station, sit and wait for an oil change."

Matz said Todoroff is so "efficient and clean" with the company's 70 trucks that he hired him for the company's New Hampshire and Rhode Island terminals as well.

Todoroff is registered with the state Environmental Protection Agency to carry waste oil, which is burned at a Hyannis car dealership's waste oil furnace. He also has a general insurance policy that covers accidents or spills.

Todoroff, 27, a Poughkeepsie, N.Y., native is married and is the father of a one-year-old son and another on the way. In 1989 he moved to the Cape to be near his brother.

Today's managers need to be creative because the combination of information technology and modern package transportation services like those of FedEx offers many opportunities to rethink the *place and time* of service delivery. Some manufacturers of small pieces of equipment allow customers to bypass retail dealers when a product needs repair. Instead, a courier will pick up the defective item (suitably packaged, of course), ship it to a repair site, and return it a few days later when it has been fixed. Electronic distribution channels offer even more convenience because transportation time can be eliminated. For instance, using telecommunication links, engineers in a central facility (which could even be on the other side of the world) may be able to diagnose problems in defective computers and software at distant customer locations and send signals to correct the defects.

As noted in chapter 1, advances in telecommunications and in the design of user-friendly terminals have played an important role in creating new services and new delivery channels for existing services. Later, we describe in more detail some of the key developments that are changing the traditional face of retail banking.

Rethinking service delivery procedures for all but people processing may allow a firm to get customers out of the factory and transform a high-contact service into a low-contact one. When the nature of the *process* makes it possible to deliver service at arm's length, the design and location of the factory can focus on purely operational priorities. Some industry observers are predicting that by early in the 21st

---

He had been working as a cook and a carpet cleaner when a friend suggested he start an auto maintenance business.

"I've always worked on my own cars," Todoroff said. "He got me thinking about it, and soon after that, I read about a guy in Entrepreneur magazine who manufactures equipment to do oil changes on location."

Todoroff sold his car to buy used equipment he saw in a trade magazine classified ad.

The business has about 600 clients, Todoroff said, but he would not disclose his yearly sales. He plans to hire his first employee in May as sales continue to climb.

Despite Todoroff's success, skeptics like John Paul, a spokesman for the American Automobile Association in Rockland, don't see on-location businesses as a hot new trend.

"I don't know if you're going to see it take off." Paul said. "The idea never really caught on in this part of the country because it is contingent on good weather. I'd also say that if it wasn't for places like Jiffy Lube, it would be a service whose time had come."

But Todoroff may have the edge over those businesses. Jiffy Lube in Hyannis charges $28 including tax for an individual oil change. That is $1.39 more than what Lube On Location charges.

"My target customer during the day is someone who doesn't want to waste a Saturday to get an oil change done," Todoroff said. "They have such busy work weeks that when the weekend comes, they'd rather go for a ride or spend their time doing something fun or interesting."

Service on the go

Lube On Location oil change includes:

■ Change oil and oil filter lube all fittings; check and fill antifreeze, automatic transmission fluid, power steering fluid, brake fluid, windshield washer fluid; check battery, wipers, belts, radiator hoses, air pressure in tires, and headlights.

■ Price: $26.95 (including tax)

Jiffy Lube in Hyannis:

■ Change oil and oil filter, lube the chassis, check and top off all fluids except antifreeze, vaccum interior, check tires, and clean front and rear outside windows.
Price: $28.34 (including tax)

Source: Reprinted with permission from the *Cape Cod Times*, 28 March 1998, C-9.

century the traditional bank branch will cease to exist, and we will be conducting most of our banking and credit union transactions through ATMs, telephones, or personal computers (PCs) and modems (not everybody agrees with this prediction). The chances of success in such an endeavor will be enhanced when the new procedures are user-friendly and offer customers greater convenience.

Balancing Supply and Demand

Sharp fluctuations in demand are a bane in the lives of many managers, although manufacturing firms can inventory supplies of their product as a hedge against fluctuations in demand. This enables them to enjoy the economies derived from operating factories at steady production levels. Few service businesses can do this easily. For example, the potential income from an empty seat on an airliner is lost forever once that flight takes off. Hotel rooms are equally perishable, and the productive capacity of an auto repair shop is wasted if no cars come in for servicing on a day when the shop is open. Conversely, when demand for service exceeds supply, the excess business may be lost. If someone cannot get a seat on one flight, another carrier gets the business or the trip is canceled. In other situations, customers may be forced to wait in line until sufficient productive capacity is available to serve them.

In general, services that process people and physical objects are more likely to face capacity limitations than those that are information based. Radio and television transmissions, for instance, can reach any number of homes within their receiving area or cable distribution network. In recent years, information-processing and transmission capacity has been vastly increased by greater computer power, digital switching, and the replacement of coaxial cables by fiber-optic ones. Yet technology has not found similar ways to increase the capacity of those service operations that process people and their physical possessions without big jumps in cost. Thus managing demand becomes essential in improving productivity in those types of services that involve tangible actions. Either customers must be given incentives to use the service outside peak periods or capacity must be allocated in advance through reservations. For example, a golf course may employ both of these strategies by discounting greens fees during off-peak hours and requiring reservations for the busier tee times.

The problem in people-processing services is that there are limits to how long customers will wait in line. They have other things to do and become bored, resentful, tired, and hungry. Susan was not prepared to wait for a sandwich at the food court, so she chose a burger instead. One strategy for reducing or eliminating the need for waiting is to institute a reservation systems, but the times offered should be realistic (note that Susan's hair salon offered appointments but was not running on schedule the day that she visited it). In contrast, physical possessions rarely suffer if they have to wait (unless they are highly perishable). More relevant to customers is the cost and inconvenience associated with delays. (How will Susan cope if her suit is not returned from the dry cleaner in time for her job interview?) The issue of demand and capacity management is so central to productive use of assets (and thus profitability) that we devote significant coverage to the topic in chapter 14, with further coverage of managing reservations and waiting lines in chapter 15.

Making the Most of Information Technology

information-based services: all services in which the principal value comes from the transmission of data to customers (includes both mental stimulus processing and information processing).

It's clear that **information-based services** (a term that covers both mental stimulus processing and information processing) have the most to gain from advances in information technology, because they allow the operation to be physically sep-

Web sites allow real estate listings in cyberspace that can be accessed from around the world.

arate from customers. Modern telecommunications and computer technologies allow customers to connect their own computers (or other input–output devices) with the service provider's system in another location.[3] For example, customers of a discount brokerage, such as Charles Schwab or e-trade, can manage their own portfolios, buying and selling stocks by keying in orders on their home or office computers.

technology: the application of a scientifically designed system for using procedures, materials, equipment, and facilities to achieve practical purposes.

Many examples of using **technology** to transform the nature of the core product and its delivery system are based on radio and television. From studio symphony performances to electronic churches to call-in gardening advice programs, broadcasting—and now interactive cable—have created new ways to bring advice, entertainment, culture, and spiritual enlightenment to widely scattered audiences. In many countries, education is offered through electronic channels as an alternative to the traditional mode of face-to-face presentations in a physical classroom. One of the largest efforts of this nature is the Open University (OU) in Great Britain. The OU has been offering degree programs to students nationwide through the electronic campus of the British Broadcasting Corporation (BBC) for over 30 years. Anyone can watch or hear the programs, of course, but students also receive printed course material through the mail and communicate with tutors by mail, e-mail, or telephone.

Seeing People as Part of the Product

The more involved customers become in the service delivery process, the more they see service personnel (the *people* element of the 8Ps). In many people-processing services, customers meet lots of employees and often interact with them for extended periods of time. They are also more likely to run into other customers; after all, many service facilities achieve their operating economies by serving large numbers of customers simultaneously. Susan's bus ride, classes, meal, and haircut all involved other customers. When other people become a part of the service experience, they can enhance it or detract from it. Susan enjoyed the comments made by other students in her marketing class. At the food court, lazy customers had failed to clear their table; so even though they had already left, their behavior still detracted in a small way from the experience of Susan and her friends. The poor attitude and appearance of the employee at the dry cleaner compounded the problem of delays in cleaning Susan's suit and may lead to the loss of her custom in the future.

Direct involvement in service production means that customers evaluate the quality of employees' appearance and social skills, as well as their technical skills; and because customers also make judgments about other customers, managers find themselves trying to manage customer behavior, too. Service businesses of this type tend to be harder to manage because of the human element. As a manager, how would you get everyone to clear their table after eating at the food court? How would you make the staff at the dry cleaner more friendly? How would you ensure that all bus drivers give a pleasant greeting to passengers boarding their vehicles?

Conclusion

We've seen in this chapter that although not all services are the same, many do have important characteristics in common. Rather than focusing on broad distinctions between goods and services, it is more useful to identify different categories of services and to study the marketing, operations, and human resource challenges that they raise.

The four-way classification scheme in this chapter focuses on different types of service *processes*. Some services require direct physical contact with customers (hair-cutting and passenger transport); others center on contact with people's minds (education and entertainment). Some involve processing of physical objects (cleaning and freight transport); others process information (accounting and insurance). As you can now appreciate, the processes that underlie the creation and delivery of any service have a major impact on marketing and human resources. Process design (or redesign) is not just a task for the operations department. Both managers and employees must understand underlying processes (particularly those in which customers are actively involved) in order to run a service business that is both efficient and user-friendly.

Study Questions and Exercises

1. Consider each of the services used by Susan Munro.
   a. What needs is she attempting to satisfy in each instance?
   b. What alternative product or self-service could solve her need in each instance?
   c. What similarities and differences are there between the dry-cleaning store and the hair salon? What could each learn from the other?
2. Make a list of all the services that you have used during the past week. Then categorize them by type of process.
3. Note the different types of service factories that you visit in the course of a typical month and how many times you visit each type.
4. Review each of the different ways in which services can be classified. How would you explain the usefulness of these systems to the manager of a health and fitness center?
5. Give examples of durable and nondurable benefits in services and describe the implications.
6. Identify the strategies used by your long-distance phone company or favorite restaurant to manage demand.
7. What do you see as the major ethical issues for those responsible for creating and delivering mental-stimulus-processing services?
8. How have other customers affected your service experiences—either positively or negatively?

CHAPTER
Three

Customer Contact with Service Organizations

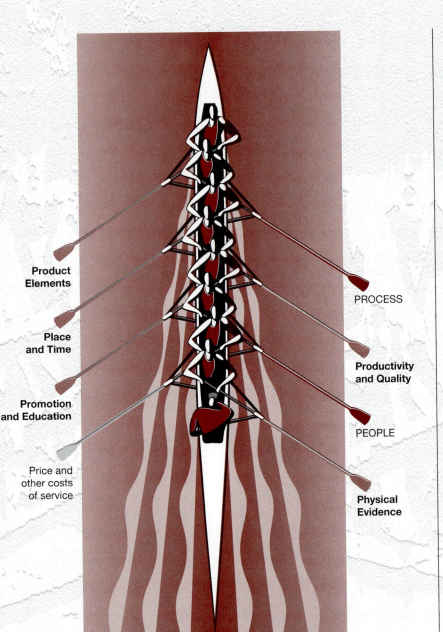

Product Elements

Place and Time

Promotion and Education

Price and other costs of service

PROCESS

Productivity and Quality

PEOPLE

Physical Evidence

Learning Objectives

After reading this chapter, you should be able to

■ recall that the extent of customer contact with a service varies according to the nature of the underlying processes

■ recognize that there are significant differences in managing service businesses according to the level of customer contact

■ distinguish between backstage and front-stage operations

■ understand service encounters, especially in situations where other people are part of the product

■ understand the nature of critical incidents and recognize their significance for customer satisfaction and dissatisfaction

■ appreciate the potential role of customers as "coproducers" of services

The Bank with No Branches

"Hello, First Direct. How may I help you?" says a friendly voice to a customer who has telephoned in the middle of the night to conduct some banking transactions. First Direct, a division of Britain's Midland Bank, has no branches. It serves customers throughout the United Kingdom (and abroad) from several customer service call centers located far from the financial powerhouses of London.[1]

Many banks now offer telephone service, but it's usually just a supplement to traditional branch operations. However, there is a trend in larger banks toward offering person-to-person contact by phone 24 hours a day, every day of the year. Bankers from all over the globe come to study First Direct to see what they can learn from the world's first, all-telephone bank.

The idea for what became First Direct grew out of research undertaken by Midland in 1988. A national survey of British bank customers revealed some surprising findings:

- ❏ 51 percent of account holders said they would rather visit their branch as little as possible
- ❏ 20 percent had not visited their branch in the past month
- ❏ 38 percent said banking hours were inconvenient
- ❏ 27 percent wished they could conduct more business by telephone (but with a real person)

In response, Midland decided to create a brand new bank without branches. To serve customers entirely by telephone required new *processes* that would be user-friendly for both staff and customers. As one operations manager remarked, "We had to be able to respond in seconds, not minutes—normal banking procedures simply did not apply. We had to create a workable system that would be the servant, not the master, of those using it." Planners traveled widely to find existing computer and telecommunication systems that could deliver service with the speed, productivity, and quality needed to attract customers and make the new bank profitable. Access to cash was a simple matter—customers would use a national ATM network.

In hiring what it called "banking representatives," First Direct did not look for traditional bank tellers. Instead, it sought people with strong communication capabilities to create trust and confidence among customers, who would never meet employees face to face and would almost certainly deal with a different staff member every time they called. Another important criterion was excellent listening skills. Intensive training honed these skills and added knowledge of banking products and procedures.

Despite gloomy predictions by traditional bankers and other skeptics that the new venture would soon fail, First Direct has become profitable and successful. Its staffing and transaction costs are sharply below those of conventional banks with branches. A high proportion of its new customers are attracted by recommendations from existing, satisfied customers. The bank anticipates more than a million customers by the year 2000. More significantly, First Direct has stimulated an industry-wide shift from high-contact bank branches to low-contact banking by telephone plus ATMs.

The logical next step is home banking by Web site. Summing up the bank's philosophy, a marketing manager remarked, "People do not see banks as a fundamental part of their lives. We're trying to market First Direct as a background activity. The whole idea … is that it's efficient, easy, and available when you want it. You simply tap into it and then you go away and do something more interesting."

CUSTOMERS AND THE SERVICE OPERATION

Where does the customer fit in a service organization? Clearly, First Direct's customers have a different type of relationship with their bank than do those who continue to visit a traditional retail bank branch. The former benefit from convenience of place and time rather than having to enter a service factory. Their only physical contact is with ATMs, which can be found in numerous convenient locations. Customers' impressions of First Direct's operation, therefore, reflect how fast the phone is answered (standards require 75 percent of all calls to be answered in 20 seconds or less), the courtesy and professionalism of the employee's voice, and the speed with which the desired transactions can be completed.

Visiting a branch involves different and more time-consuming contacts. Customers can visit a branch only during opening hours and may have to travel some distance to get there. They are exposed to the exterior and interior of the building; may have to wait in line with other customers; and must deal face-to-face with an employee who, in many banks, will be hiding behind a security grill or glass screen. Many people enjoy the social interaction of visiting a retail outlet, especially if they know the staff members who serve them, and don't trust machines. A recent U.S. study found that 73 percent of respondents preferred to bank in a staffed branch, and 64 percent said that they would rather not use technology at all for certain types of transactions (see the box on banking by ATM).

Contact with the Service Organization

An important theme in this chapter is that high-contact encounters between customers and service organizations differ sharply from low-contact ones. The four process-based service categories described in chapter 2 prescribe the minimum level of customer contact needed to obtain service in each instance. However, many service organizations currently provide far higher levels of contact than is theoretically necessary to deliver the service in question. Sometimes these high-contact levels reflect customer preferences for person-to-person service with **customer contact personnel**. However, in many instances they result from a management decision to continue relying on traditional approaches instead of reengineering existing service processes to create innovative, lower-contact approaches.

customer contact personnel: those service employees who interact directly with individual customers either in person or through mail and telecommunications.

NOT EVERYBODY LOVES BANKING BY ATM

Why do some customers prefer to deal with humans rather than machines? Skepticism about technology is not necessarily tied to age or low education. A *Wall Street Journal* reporter asked Marianne Cianciolo, a 38-year-old university public relations professional in Ohio why she felt comfortable making withdrawals from an ATM but wouldn't dare to make a deposit there.[a] "What proof do I have that I deposited that money?" she asked. "They have those little [security] cameras but that's not going to prove how much the deposit was for." Ms. Cianciolo stated that she visited her bank branch at least once a week to cash checks, make deposits, or withdraw funds. "I just like knowing there is a real person who is making note of the transaction," she remarked. "If there's an error, I'm going to catch it right away." Part of the challenge for banking executives is to develop strategies for reducing the perceived risks and disadvantages of electronic service delivery. Another issue is to think of ways to gently discourage branch usage while still continuing to offer this alternative. However, banks that have imposed extra charges for teller services have often received very bad publicity as a result.

[a] Eleena de Lisser, "Customers Thwart Banks' Plans to Cut Branches," *The Wall Street Journal*, 16 May 1997, B1–B5.

Within a given industry, the nature of the task may also serve to determine the level of contact. For instance, in consulting assignments that involve a precisely defined task, relatively little interaction with client personnel may be required. Other assignments, in contrast, may require active discussions between consultants and clients to help define and solve the problems at hand. These two different types of assignments have been referred to as "jobbing" and "sparring," respectively.[2]

Variability is a fact of life in situations in which customers differ widely and service personnel interact with those customers on a one-on-one basis.[3] The longer and more actively customers are involved in the process of service delivery, the greater the likelihood that each customer's experience will be somewhat different from that of other customers (and from previous experiences by the same customer). Not all variations are bad; in fact, many customers seek a tailored approach that recognizes them as individuals with distinctive needs. The challenge is for employees to be flexible, treating each person as an individual rather than as a clone of the last customer.[4]

Many service problems revolve around unsatisfactory incidents between customers and service personnel. In an effort to simplify service delivery, improve productivity, and reduce some of the threats to service quality, some firms are using technology to minimize or even eliminate contact between customers and employees. Thus, face-to-face encounters are giving way to telephone encounters. Also, personal service is being replaced by self-service, often through computers or easy-to-use machines, and Web sites are beginning to replace voice telephone contacts for some types of service transactions.

This chapter builds on our earlier discussion of *processes* in chapter 2 and introduces the notion of a spectrum of customer contact with the service organization that ranges from high to low. We show how the extent of customer contact affects the nature of the service encounter, as well as strategies for achieving *productivity and quality* improvements. As you review the contents of the chapter, including its examples, you should be asking yourself how a strategy of reducing (or increasing) the level of customer contact may affect decisions relating to *product elements*, *place and time*, *people*, and *physical evidence*.

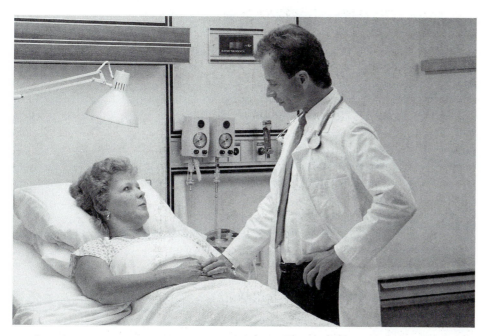

Good medical care involves not only treating the patient's specific health problems but also treating that person as an individual.

Service Encounters: Three Levels of Customer Contact

service encounter: a period of time during which customers interact directly with a service.

A **service encounter** is a period of time during which customers interact directly with a service.[5] In some instances, the entire service experience can be reduced to a single encounter, with ordering, payment, and execution of service delivery on the spot. In other cases, the customer's experience comprises a sequence of encounters, which may be spread out over a period of time, involve a variety of employees, and even take place in different locations (think about flying on a passenger airline). Although some researchers use the term *encounter* simply to describe personal interactions between customers and employees,[6] realistically we also need to think about encounters involving interactions between customers and self-service equipment. As the level of customer contact with the service operation increases, there are likely to be more and longer service encounters. Thus we've grouped services into three **levels of customer contact**, representing the extent of interaction with service personnel, physical service elements, or both (see Figure 3.1). Notice the different locations on the chart of traditional retail banking, telephone banking, and home banking by Web site.

levels of customer contact: the extent to which customers interact directly with elements of the service organization.

high-contact services: services that involve significant interaction among customers, service personnel, and equipment and facilities.

High-contact services tend to be those in which customers visit the service facility in person. Customers are actively involved with the service organization and its personnel throughout service delivery (e.g., hairdressing or medical services). All people-processing services (other than those delivered at home) are high-contact ones. Services from the other three processing categories may also involve high levels of customer contact when, for reasons of tradition, preference, or lack of other alternatives, customers go to the service site and remain there until service delivery is completed. Examples of services that have traditionally been high contact but which technology allows to be low contact today include retail banking, purchase of retail goods, and higher education.

FIGURE 3.1 Levels of Customer Contact with Service Organizations

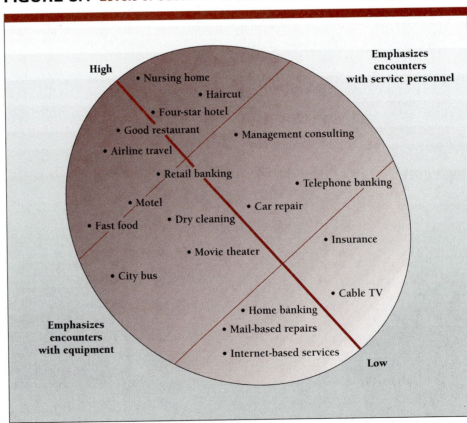

Medium-contact services entail less involvement with service providers. They involve situations in which customers visit the service provider's facilities (or are visited at home or at a third-party location by that provider) but either do not remain throughout service delivery or else have only modest contact with service personnel. The purpose of these contacts is often limited to (1) establishing a relationship and defining a service need (e.g., management consulting or personal financial advising, in which clients make an initial visit to the firm's office but then have relatively limited interactions with the provider during service production), (2) dropping off and picking up a physical possession that is being serviced, or (3) trying to resolve a problem.

Low-contact services involve very little, if any, direct contact between customers and service providers. Instead, contact takes place at arm's length through electronic or physical distribution channels—a fast-growing trend in today's convenience-oriented society. Both mental stimulus processing (e.g., radio and television) and information processing (e.g., insurance) fall naturally into this category. Also included are possession-processing services in which the item requiring service can be shipped to the service site or subjected to remote fixes delivered electronically to the customers' premises (increasingly common for resolving software problems). Finally, many high-contact services are being transformed into low-contact services as customers engage in home shopping, do their banking by telephone, or research and purchase products through the World Wide Web.

SERVICE AS A SYSTEM

The level of contact that a service business intends to have with its customers is a major factor in defining the total service system, which includes three overlapping subsystems: **service operations** (where inputs are processed and the elements of the service product are created), **service delivery** (where final "assembly" of these elements takes place and the product is delivered to the customer), and **service marketing** (which embraces all points of contact with customers, including advertising, billing, and market research). See Figure 3.2.

Parts of this system are visible (or otherwise apparent) to customers; other parts are hidden in what is sometimes referred to as the technical core, and the customer

medium-contact services: services that involve only a limited amount of contact between customers and elements of the service operation.

low-contact services: services that require minimal or no direct contact between customers and the service operation.

service operations: that part of the total service system where inputs are processed and the elements of the service product are created.

service delivery: that part of the total service system where final "assembly" of these elements takes place and the product is delivered to the customer; it includes the visible elements of the service operation.

service marketing: that part of the total service system where the firm has any form of contact with its customers, from advertising to billing; it includes contacts made at the point of delivery.

FIGURE 3.2 **The Service Business as a System**

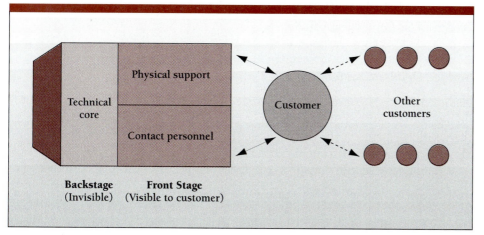

Physical support

Technical core

Contact personnel

Customer

Other customers

Backstage (Invisible)   **Front Stage** (Visible to customer)

Adapted from Eric Langeard, John E. G. Bateson, Christopher H. Lovelock, and Pierre Eiglier, *Services Marketing: New Insights from Consumers and Managers* (Cambridge, MA: Marketing Science Institute, 1981).

backstage (or technical core): those aspects of service operations that are hidden from customers.

front stage: those aspects of service operations and delivery that are visible to customers.

may not even know of their existence.[7] Some writers use the terms *front office* and *back office* in referring to the visible and invisible parts of the operation. Others talk about *front stage* and *backstage*, using the analogy of theater to dramatize the notion that service is a performance.[8] We like this analogy and will be using it throughout the book.

Service Operations System

Like a play in a theater, the visible components of service operations can be divided into those relating to the actors (or service personnel) and those relating to the stage set (or physical facilities, equipment, and other tangibles). What goes on backstage is of little interest to customers. Like any audience, they evaluate the production on those elements they actually experience during service delivery and, of course, on the perceived service outcome. Naturally, if the backstage personnel and systems (e.g., billing, ordering, and accounting) fail to perform their support tasks properly in ways that affect the quality of front-stage activities, customers will notice. For instance, restaurant patrons will be disappointed if they order fish from the menu but are told it is unavailable (in reality, someone forgot to go to the fish market that morning) or find that their food is overcooked (actually caused by improperly set oven controls). Other examples of backstage failures include receiving an incorrect hotel bill because of a keying error, not receiving your grades because of a computer failure in the college registrar's office, or being unable to bury a loved one because of a strike by gravediggers (sadly, such strikes have actually occurred).

The proportion of the overall service operation that is visible to customers varies according to the level of customer contact. Because high-contact services directly involve the physical person of the customer, either customers must enter the service factory (although there may still be backstage activities that they don't see) or service workers and their tools must come to the customers' chosen location. Examples include roadside car repair by automobile clubs or physical fitness trainers who work with clients at their homes or offices. Medium-contact services, in contrast, require a less substantial involvement of the customer in service delivery. Consequently, the visible component of the service operations system is smaller. Low-contact services usually have a strategy of minimizing customer contact with the service provider, so most of the service operations system is confined to a remotely located backstage (sometimes referred to as a technical core); front-stage elements are normally limited to mail and telecommunications contacts. Think for a moment about the telephone company that you use. Do you have any idea where its exchange is located? If you have a credit card, it's likely that your transactions are processed far from where you live.

Service Delivery System

Service delivery is concerned with where, when, and how the service product is delivered to the customer. As seen in Figure 3.2, this sub system not only embraces the visible elements of the service operating system—buildings, equipment, and personnel—but may also entail exposure to other customers.

Traditionally, service providers had direct interactions with their customers. But to achieve goals ranging from cost reduction and productivity improvement to greater customer convenience, many services that don't require the customers to be physically present in the factory now seek to reduce direct contact. Midland Bank's creation of First Direct is a prime example of this trend. As a result, the visible component of the service operations system is shrinking in many industries as electronic technology or redesigned physical flows are used to drive service delivery from higher to lower levels of contact.

Self-service delivery often offers customers greater convenience than face-to-face contact. Machines such as automated fuel pumps, ATMs, or coin-operated food and beverage dispensers can be installed in numerous locations and made accessible 24 hours a day, seven days a week. Cafeteria service allows customers to see menu items before making their selection. Self-guided museum tours allow visitors to enjoy an exhibition at their own pace. But there are potential disadvantages, too. The shift from personal service (sometimes referred to as "high touch") to self-service ("high tech") sometimes disturbs customers. Thus a strategy of replacing employees by machines or other self-service procedures may require an information campaign to educate customers and promote the benefits of the new approach. It also helps to design user-friendly equipment, including free telephone access to an employee who can answer questions and solve problems. Of course, not all self-service is installed in remote locations. Cafeterias and self-guided museum tours are examples of customers taking on tasks that would otherwise have to be assigned to service personnel. Later in this chapter, we discuss the role of the customer as a co-producer of service in collaboration with the service provider.

Using the theatrical analogy, the distinction between high contact and low contact can be likened to the differences between live theater on a stage and a drama created for radio. Customers of low-contact services normally never see the factory where the work is performed; at most, they will talk with a service provider (or problem solver) by telephone. Without buildings and furnishings or even the appearance of employees to provide tangible clues, customers must base judgments about service quality on ease of telephone access, followed by the voice and responsiveness of a telephone-based customer service agent.

When service is delivered through impersonal electronic channels, such as self-service machines, automated telephone calls to a central computer, or the customer's own computer, there is very little traditional "theater" left to the performance. Some firms compensate by giving their machines names, playing recorded music, installing moving color graphics, adding sounds, and creating computer-based interactive capabilities to give the experience a more human feeling (see the box on bank service options, p. 52).

Free phone access to a customer service agent is appreciated by customers if they have a question or a problem when using self-service equipment.

WHAT OPTIONS DO YOU USE FOR DELIVERY OF BANK SERVICES?

Not everyone is comfortable with the trend toward lower-contact services, which is why some firms give their customers a choice. For instance, some retail banks now offer an array of service options. Consider this spectrum of alternatives. Which options do you currently use at your bank? Which would you like to use in the future? And which are currently available?

1. visit the bank in person and conduct transactions with a teller
2. use postal service to send deposits or request new checkbooks
3. use an automated teller machine (ATM)
4. conduct transactions by telephone with a customer service representative
5. use the keys on a telephone to interact with the bank in response to voice commands (or a telephone screen display)
6. conduct home banking through your own computer, using a modem and special software
7. conduct transactions by computer through the World Wide Web

In each instance, what factors explain your preference? Do they relate to the type of transactions you need or a situational element like the weather or time of day? Are you influenced by your feelings of liking (or disliking) human contact in a banking context? Or is there some other explanation?

Note: If you do not have a bank account of your own, please interview someone who does.

Responsibility for designing and managing service delivery systems has traditionally fallen to operations managers. But marketing has to be involved, too, because understanding customers' needs and concerns is important to ensure that the delivery system works well. Moreover, if we're dealing with a service facility where customers may interact with one another—such as a hotel, aircraft, or post office—their behavior has to be managed discreetly so that they will act in ways that are compatible with the firm's strategy, including the comfort and safety of other customers.

Service Marketing System

Other elements, too, may contribute to the customer's overall view of a service business. These include communication efforts by the advertising and sales departments, telephone calls and letters from service personnel, billings from the accounting department, random exposures to service personnel and facilities, news stories and editorials in the mass media, word-of-mouth comments from current or former customers, and even participation in market research studies.

Collectively, the components just cited—plus those in the service delivery subsystem—add up to what we term the service marketing system. In essence, this represents all the different ways in which the customer may encounter or learn about the organization in question. Because services are experiential, each of these elements offers clues about the nature and quality of the service product. Inconsistency among different elements may weaken the organization's credibility in the customers' eyes. Figure 3.3 depicts the service marketing system for a hotel—a high-contact service.

As you know from your own experience, the scope and structure of the service marketing system often vary sharply from one type of organization to another. Figure 3.4 (p. 54) shows how the picture changes when we are dealing with a low-contact service, such as a credit card account. The significance of this approach to

FIGURE 3.3 The Service Marketing System for a Hotel

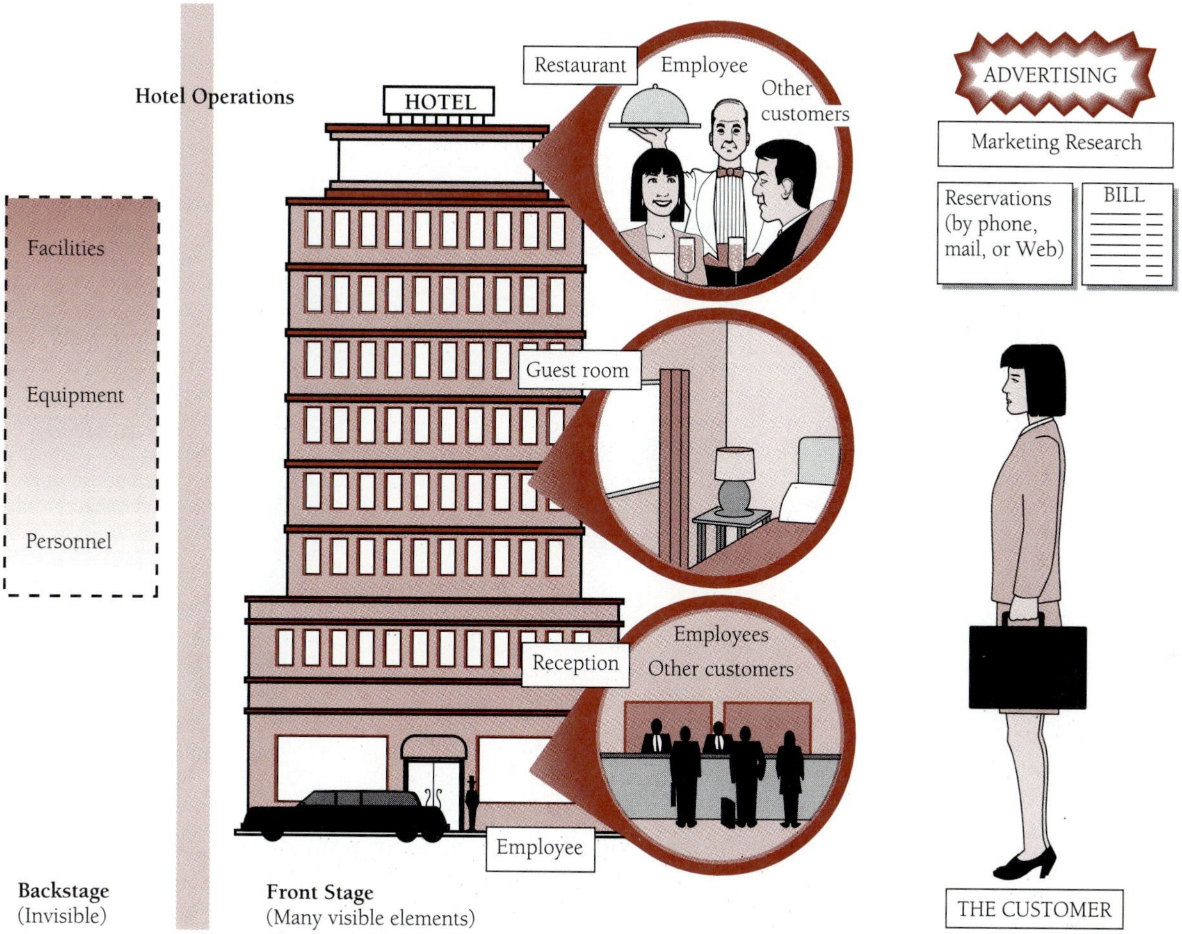

conceptualizing service creation and delivery is that it represents a customer's view, looking at the service business from the outside, as opposed to an internally focused, operations perspective.

Physical Evidence

Because many service performances are inherently intangible, they are often hard to evaluate. As a result, customers often look for tangible clues to the nature of the service. Encounters are sometimes random rather than planned. For instance, what impression would it create on you to see a damaged truck belonging to an express delivery service broken down by the side of the road? Or to observe a poorly groomed flight attendant traveling to (or from) the airport and wearing a uniform that is frayed and dirty? Or to visit a friend in a hospital where the grounds and buildings are beautifully maintained; the interior decor cheerful rather than institutional; and the friendly staff wearing smart, spotlessly clean uniforms?

Because service performances are intangible, physical evidence gives clues to the quality of service and, in some cases, will strongly influence how customers (especially inexperienced ones) evaluate the service. Hence managers need to think carefully about the nature of the physical evidence provided to customers by the service marketing system. Of course, the number of elements that are visible to customers will vary depending on whether service delivery involves high or low customer contact. In low-contact services, additional physical evidence may be communicated

FIGURE 3.4 The Service Marketing System for a Credit Card Account

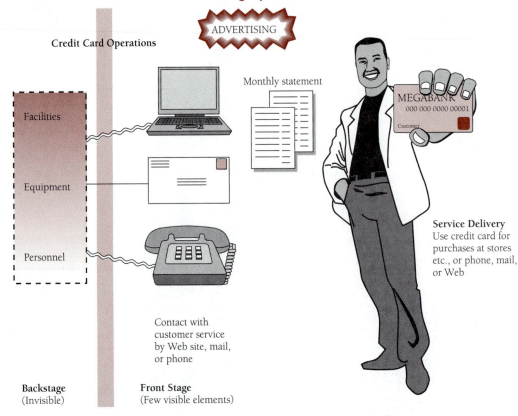

Credit Card Operations

Facilities

Equipment

Personnel

Monthly statement

MEGABANK
000 000 0000 00001
Customer

Service Delivery
Use credit card for
purchases at stores
etc., or phone, mail,
or Web

Contact with
customer service
by Web site, mail,
or phone

Backstage
(Invisible)

Front Stage
(Few visible elements)

through advertising, using video footage on TV or printed illustrations in newspapers, magazines, or brochures. We address this element of the 8Ps in more depth in chapters 9 and 12, but Figure 3.5 is an initial checklist of the main tangible and communication elements to which customers might be exposed.

MANAGING SERVICE ENCOUNTERS

Many services (especially those classified as high contact) involve numerous encounters between customers and service employees, either in person or by phone. Service encounters may also take place between customers and physical facilities or equipment. In low-contact services, customers are having more and more encounters with automated machines that are designed to replace human personnel.

To highlight the risks and opportunities associated with service encounters, Richard Normann borrowed the metaphor **moment of truth** from bullfighting:

moment of truth: a point in service delivery where customers interact with service employees or self-serve equipment and the outcome may affect perceptions of service quality.

> [W]e could say that the perceived quality is realized at the moment of truth, when the service provider and the service customer confront one another in the arena. At that moment they are very much on their own. ... It is the skill, the motivation, and the tools employed by the firm's representative and the expectations and behavior of the client which together will create the service delivery process.[9]

In bullfighting, what is at stake is the life of either the bull or the matador (or possibly both). The moment of truth is the instant at which the latter deftly slays the bull with his sword—hardly a very comfortable analogy for a service organization intent on building long-term relationships with its customers! Normann's point, of course, is that it's the life of the relationship which is at stake. Contrary to bullfighting, the goal of relationship marketing—which is discussed in depth in chap-

FIGURE 3.5 Tangible Elements and Communication Components in the Service Marketing System

1. **Service personnel.** Contacts with customers may be face-to-face, by telecommunications (telephone, fax, telegram, telex, electronic mail) or by mail and express delivery services. These personnel may include
   a. sales representatives
   b. customer service staff
   c. accounting/billing staff
   d. operations staff who do not normally provide direct service to customers (e.g., engineers and janitors)
   e. designated intermediaries whom customers perceive as directly representing the service firm

2. **Service facilities and equipment**
   a. building exteriors, parking areas, landscaping
   b. building interiors and furnishings
   c. vehicles
   d. self-service equipment operated by customers
   e. other equipment

3. **Nonpersonal communications**
   a. form letters
   b. brochures/catalogs/instruction manuals
   c. advertising
   d. signage
   e. news stories/editorials in the mass media

4. **Other people**
   a. fellow customers encountered during service delivery
   b. word-of-mouth comments from friends, acquaintances, or even strangers

ter 6—is to prevent one unfortunate (mis)encounter from destroying what is already, or has the potential to become, a mutually valued, long-term relationship.

Jan Carlzon, the former chief executive of Scandinavian Airlines System, used the moment-of-truth metaphor as a vehicle for transforming SAS from an operations-driven business into a customer-driven airline. Carlzon made the following comments about his airline:

> Last year, each of our 10 million customers came into contact with approximately five SAS employees, and this contact lasted an average of 15 seconds each time. Thus, SAS is "created" 50 million times a year, 15 seconds at a time. These 50 million "moments of truth" are the moments that ultimately determine whether SAS will succeed or fail as a company. They are the moments when we must prove to our customers that SAS is their best alternative.[10]

Managing People in Service Encounters

The last quotation in the previous section immediately makes apparent the link between marketing and human resource management in service organizations. With its own people as part of the product, no service business can afford to divorce its customer contact employees from the firm's marketing strategy. Increasingly, high-contact employees in what have traditionally been service delivery jobs with no sales content are now expected to play a selling role, too. This role shift requires them to be both producers and marketers of a service. As a result, restaurant servers, bank tellers, and even auditors in accounting firms are being asked to promote new services, encourage customers to purchase additional items, or refer them to sales specialists.

Pilots are vital to airline operations, but what is the nature of their service encounters with passengers relative to flight attendants, check-in staff, gate agents, and mechanics?

Making matters even more complex for managers is the fact that primary responsibility for their organization's success often rests with relatively junior personnel in such customer contact positions as bus driver, retail store clerk, telephone-based customer service representative, receptionist in a professional service firm (e.g., architects, lawyers, or management consultants), or car rental agent. These individuals, who are often young and inexperienced and less well educated than their customers, need both technical and interpersonal skills to succeed. Not only must they be able to perform the technical aspects of the job quickly and accurately, but also they must do so while relating well to customers.[11] In chapter 15, we consider how careful recruitment, training, and ongoing mentoring of employees can contribute to improvements in both *productivity* and *quality*.

To cope effectively with all of these challenges, managers should brief employees on what the firm is trying to achieve in the marketplace. However, there are limits to the ability of policy manuals and other control procedures to ensure that employees consistently deliver good service. Service employees also need training, authority, and management support to ensure that their important but often brief encounters with customers result in satisfactory outcomes. Carlzon of SAS made the case for flattening the organization chart and giving customer contact personnel more responsibility. He insists that instead of striving to control employee behavior, managers should be acting as coaches and role models to help them provide better service to customers.[12]

Critical Incidents in Service Encounters

critical incident: a specific encounter between customer and service provider in which the outcome has proved especially satisfying or dissatisfying for one or both parties.

critical incident technique (CIT): a methodology for collecting, categorizing, and analyzing critical incidents that have occurred.

Critical incidents are specific encounters between customers and service employees that are especially satisfying or dissatisfying for one or both parties. The **critical incident technique (CIT)** is a methodology for collecting and categorizing such incidents in service encounters. Conducting such an analysis offers an opportunity to determine what types of incidents during service delivery are likely to be particularly significant in determining whether or not customers are satisfied.

The customer's perspective.   Findings from a CIT study can be very helpful in pinpointing opportunities for future improvements in service delivery *processes*. Determining the most likely "fail points" in service encounters, where there is a risk of significantly upsetting customers, is the first step in taking corrective action. Similarly, CIT findings concerning the nature of incidents that customers seem to find very satisfying may enable managers to train their employees to replicate such positive experiences in the future.

Negative critical incidents that are satisfactorily resolved have great potential for enhancing loyalty because they demonstrate to customers that the organization really cares about them. But the reverse is also true. In a study of 838 critical incidents that led customers to switch to a competitor, unsatisfactory service encounters (cited by 34 percent of respondents) ranked second to core service failures (cited by 44 percent) as a reason for switching. Other key reasons were high, deceptive, or unfair pricing (30 percent); inconvenience from time, location, or delays (21 percent); and poor response to service failures (17 percent). Many respondents described a decision to switch suppliers as the result of interrelated incidents, such as a service failure followed by an unsatisfactory response to resolving the problem.[13] These findings underscore the importance of the dictum "Service is everybody's business," regardless of one's job or departmental affiliation (see the box on critical incidents).

The employee's perspective.   As you reflect on service encounters, you need to recognize that customer-employee contact is a two-way street. Understanding the employee's view of the situation is really important because thoughtless or poorly behaved customers can often cause needless problems for service personnel who are trying hard to serve them well. Continuing dissatisfaction with a succession of negative incidents can even drive good employees to quit their jobs.

Another CIT study examined hundreds of critical incidents from an employee perspective.[14] The results showed that more than 20 percent of all unsatisfactory incidents could be attributed to problem customers, whose bad behavior included drunkenness, verbal and physical abuse, violation of laws or company policies, and

STUDYING CRITICAL INCIDENTS IN THE AIRLINE, HOTEL, AND RESTAURANT BUSINESSES

In a study of critical incidents, a sample of customers was asked,

- think of a time when, as a customer, you had a particularly *satisfying (dissatisfying)* interaction with an employee of an airline, hotel, or restaurant
- when did the incident occur?
- what specific circumstances led up to this situation?
- exactly what did the employee say or do?
- what resulted that made you feel the interaction was *satisfying (dissatisfying)*?

A total of 699 incidents was recorded, split roughly equally between satisfying and dissatisfying incidents. They were then categorized into three groups: (1) employee responses to service failures, (2) employee responses to requests for customized service, and (3) unprompted and unsolicited employee actions.

When employees responded to critical incidents involving a service failure, analysis showed that the outcomes were twice as likely to be dissatisfactory for customers as satisfactory. The reverse was true when customers asked employees to adapt the service in some way to meet a special need or request. In the third grouping, relating to unexpected events and employee behavior, satisfactory and dissatisfactory outcomes were equally matched. (What do you think explains these findings?) Figure 3.6 (pp. 58–59) displays reports on specific incidents, as described in the customers' own words.

FIGURE 3.6 **Customer Reports on Critical Incidents Involving Service Employees**

GROUP 1 SAMPLE INCIDENTS: EMPLOYEE RESPONSE TO SERVICE DELIVERY FAILURES	
Incident	
Satisfactory	Dissatisfactory
A. Response to Unavailable Service	
They lost my room reservation but the manager gave me the V.I.P. suite for the same price.	We had made advance reservations at the hotel. When we arrived we found we had no room—no explanation, no apologies, and no assistance in finding another hotel.
B. Response to Unreasonably Slow Service	
Even though I didn't make any complaint about the hour and a half wait, the waitress kept apologizing and said that the bill was on the house.	The airline employees continually gave us erroneous information; a one-hour delay turned into a six-hour wait.
C. Response to Other Core Service Failures	
My shrimp cocktail was half frozen. The waitress apologized, and didn't charge me for any of my dinner.	One of my suitcases was all dented and looked as though it had been dropped from 30,000 feet. When I tried to make a claim for my damaged luggage, the employee insinuated that I was lying and trying to rip them off.
GROUP 2 SAMPLE INCIDENTS: EMPLOYEE RESPONSE TO CUSTOMER NEEDS AND REQUESTS	
A. Response to "Special Needs" Customers	
The flight attendant helped me calm and care for my airsick child.	My young son, flying alone, was to be assisted by the stewardess from start to finish. At the Albany airport she left him alone in the airport with no one to escort him to his connecting flight.
B. Response to Customer Preferences	
The front desk clerk called around and found me tickets to the Mariners' opening game.	The waitress refused to move me from a window table on a hot day, because there was nothing left in *her* section.
It was snowing outside—car broke down. I checked 10 hotels and there were no rooms. Finally, one understood my situation and offered to rent me a bed and set it up in one of their small banquet rooms.	The airline wouldn't let me bring my scuba gear on board coming back from Hawaii even though I brought it over as carry-on luggage.
C. Response to Admitted Customer Error	
I lost my glasses on the plane; the stewardess found them and they were delivered to my hotel free of charge.	We missed our flight because of car trouble. The service clerk wouldn't help us find a flight on an alternative airline.
D. Response to Potentially Disruptive Others	
The manager kept his eye on an obnoxious guy at the bar, to make sure that he didn't bother us.	The hotel staff wouldn't deal with the noisy people partying in the hall at 3 A.M.
GROUP 3 SAMPLE INCIDENTS: UMPROMPTED AND UNSOLICITED EMPLOYEE ACTIONS	
A. Attention Paid to Customer	
The waiter treated me like royalty. He really showed he cared about me.	The lady at the front desk acted as if we were bothering her. She was watching TV and paying more attention to the TV than the hotel guests.
B. Truly Out-of-the-Ordinary Employee Behavior	
We always travel with our teddy bears. When we got back to our room at the hotel we saw that the maid had arranged our bears very comfortably in a chair. The bears were holding hands.	I needed a few more minutes to decide on a dinner. The waitress said, "If you would read the menu and not the road map, you would know what you want to order."

FIGURE 3.6 *(continued)* **Customer Reports on Critical Incidents Involving Service Employees**

Incident	
Satisfactory	**Dissatisfactory**
C. Employee Behaviors in the Context of Cultural Norms	
The busboy ran after us to return a $50 bill my boyfriend had dropped under the table.	The waiter at this expensive restaurant treated us like dirt because we were only high school kids on a prom date.
D. Gestalt Evaluation	
The whole experience was so pleasant ... everything went smoothly and perfectly.	The flight was a nightmare. A one-hour layover went to three and one half hours. The air conditioning didn't work. The pilots and stewardesses were fighting because of an impending flight attendant strike. The landing was extremely rough. To top it all off, when the plane stopped, the pilots and stewardesses were the first ones off.
E. Performance Under Adverse Circumstances	
The counter agent was obviously under stress, but kept his cool and acted very professionally.	

Adapted from Mary Jo Bitner, Bernard H. Booms, and Mary Stanfield Tetrault, "The Service Encounter: Diagnosing Favorable and Unfavorable Incidents," *Journal of Marketing* 54 (January 1990): 71–84.

failure to cooperate with service personnel. It's simply not true that "the customer is always right." We return to the issue of problem customers and how to deal with them in chapter 6.

THE CUSTOMER AS COPRODUCER

In some service environments, you (and other customers) play a relatively passive role, waiting to be served. As long as you can state your needs clearly and pay promptly when billed, you play a minimal role in the *process* of service delivery (think about leaving clothes at a laundry). In other cases, however, you are expected to be actively involved in the production process—one of the distinctive features of service management noted in chapter 1. This involvement may take two forms. Sometimes, you are given the tools and equipment to serve yourself (as when you take your clothes to a laundromat); at other times, such as in health improvement, you work jointly with health professionals as coproducers of the service from which you wish to benefit. Table 3.1 (p. 60) illustrates the differing levels of participation required of customers across an array of service businesses.

Service Firms as Educators

The more work that customers are expected to do, the greater their need for information about how to perform for best results. The firm should take responsibility for educating inexperienced customers. Lack of knowledge can lead to frustration with the process, cause unsatisfactory results, and even put the customer at risk; consider the unpleasant things that might happen to a customer who smokes a cigarette and spills gas while refueling a car at a self-service pump! Thus, both *promotion* and *education* are important activities in marketing communications strategy for service businesses.

TABLE 3.1 Levels of Customer Participation across Different Services

Low (Customer Presence Required during Service Delivery)	*Moderate* (Customer Inputs Required for Service Creation)	*High* (Customer Coproduces the Service Product)
Products are standardized	Client inputs customize a standard service	Active client participation guides the customized service
Service is provided regardless of any individual purchase	Provision of service requires customer purchase	Service cannot be created apart from the customer's purchase and 62active participation
Payment may be the only required customer input	Customer inputs (information, materials) are necessary for an adequate outcome, but the service firm provides the service	Customer inputs are mandatory and coproduces the outcome
Examples:		
End consumer		
Airline travel	Hair cut	Marriage counseling
Motel stay	Annual physical exam	Personal training
Fast-food restaurant	Full-service restaurant	Weight-reduction program
Business-to-business customer		
Uniform cleaning service	Agency-created advertising campaign	Management consulting
Pest control	Payroll service	Executive management seminar
Interior greenery maintenance service	Independent freight transportation	Install wide area network (WAN)

Adapted from Mary Jo Bitner et al., "Customer Contributions and Roles in Service Delivery," *International Journal of Service Industry Management* 8, no. 3 (1997): 193–205.

The necessary education can be provided in many different ways. Brochures and posted instructions are two widely used approaches. Automated machines often contain detailed operating instructions and diagrams (unfortunately, these are often only intelligible to the engineers who wrote them). Thoughtful banks place a telephone beside their ATMs so that customers can call a real person for help and advice at any time if they are confused about the on-screen instructions. Advertising for new services (or to prospective customers) often contains significant educational content. For instance, the Charles Schwab advertisement reproduced in Figure 3.7 offers basic advice on investing and invites readers to send away for a free resource book. In many businesses, customers look to employees for advice and assistance and are frustrated if they can't obtain it. Service providers, ranging from sales associates and customer service representatives to flight attendants and nurses, must themselves be trained in teaching skills, including one-on-one demonstrations. As a last resort, people may turn to other customers and ask for help.

service preview: a demonstration of how a service works to educate customers about the roles they are expected to perform in service delivery.

Benjamin Schneider and David Bowen suggest giving customers a realistic **service preview** in advance of service delivery to provide a clear picture of the role they will play in service coproduction.[15] For example, a company might show a video to help customers understand their role in the service encounter. This technique is used by some dental surgeons to help patients understand the surgical processes they are about to experience and indicate how they should cooperate to help make things go as smoothly as possible—certainly a sensible goal for all parties involved.

Increasing Productivity and Quality When Customers Are Coproducers

The greater customers' involvement in service production, the greater their potential to influence the processes in which they are engaged. Some researchers argue that firms should view customers as "partial employees," who can influence the

FIGURE 3.7
Charles Schwab Advertising Seeks to Educate Investors

productivity and quality of service processes and outputs.[16] This perspective requires a change in the managerial mind-set, as Schneider and Bowen make clear:

> If you think of customers as partial employees, you begin to think very differently about what you hope customers will bring to the service encounter. Now they must bring not only expectations and needs but also relevant service production competencies that will enable them to fill the role of partial employees. The service management challenge deepens accordingly.[17]

They suggest that customers who are offered an opportunity to participate at an active level are more likely to be satisfied—regardless of whether or not they actually choose the more active role—because it is gratifying to be offered a choice. Managing customers as partial employees requires using the same human resource logic as in managing a firm's regular personnel and should follow these four steps:

1. conduct a "job analysis" of customers' present roles in the business and compare it to the roles that the firm would like them to play
2. determine if customers are aware of how they are expected to perform and have the skills needed
3. motivate customers by ensuring that they will be rewarded for performing well (for instance, satisfaction from better quality and more customized output, enjoyment of participating in the actual process, or a belief that their own productivity speeds the process and keeps costs down)
4. regularly appraise customers' performance. If this is unsatisfactory, try to change their role and the procedures in which they are involved. Alternatively, consider "terminating" these customers (nicely, of course!) and look for new ones.

Effective human resource management starts with recruitment and selection. The same approach should hold true for partial employees. So, if coproduction requires specific skills, firms should target their marketing efforts to recruit new customers who have the competency to perform the necessary tasks.[18] After all, many colleges do the same in their student selection process!

Conclusion

Service businesses can be divided into three overlapping systems. The operations system consists of the personnel, facilities, and equipment required to run the service operation and create the service product; only part of this system, described here as "front stage," is visible to the customer. The delivery system incorporates the visible operations elements and the customers, who in self-service operations take an active role in helping to create the service product, as opposed to being passively waited on. Finally, the marketing system includes not only the delivery system, which is essentially made up of the product and distribution elements of the traditional marketing mix, but also additional components such as billing and payment systems, exposure to advertising and salespeople, and word-of-mouth comments from other people.

In all types of services, understanding and managing service encounters between customers and service personnel is central to creating satisfied customers who are willing to enter into long-term relationships with the service provider. There are wide variations, however, in the nature of such encounters. In high-contact services, for example, customers are exposed to many more tangible clues and experiences than they are in medium-contact and low-contact situations. Critical incidents occur when some aspect of the service encounter is either highly satisfactory or dissatisfactory. In some instances, including self-service, customers participate in the process of creating and delivering services, effectively working as partial employees whose performance will affect the productivity and quality of output. Thus, service managers must be sure to educate and train customers so that they have the skills needed to perform well.

Study Questions and Exercises

1. As a senior bank executive, what actions would you take to encourage more customers to bank by phone, mail, Internet, or ATMs rather than visiting teller in a branch?
2. What are the backstage elements of (a) an insurance company, (b) a car repair facility, (c) a hotel, (d) an airline, (e) a university, (f) a funeral home, (g) a consulting firm, and (h) a television station? Under what circumstances would it be appropriate to allow customers to see some of these backstage elements and how would you do it?
3. What roles are played by front-stage service personnel in low-contact organizations? Are these roles more or less important to customer satisfaction than in high-contact services?
4. Why is it valuable for service operations managers to try to see their business through the eyes of their customers?
5. Use the list in Figure 3.5 to develop a profile of the service marketing system for a variety of services—hospital, airline, consulting engineer, lawyer, college, hotel, dry cleaner, credit union, repair garage, or post office. (You can base your profiles on your own experience or interview other customers.)

6. What is the difference between a moment of truth, a service encounter, and a critical incident?
7. Review Figure 3.6. As a manager, how would you try to prevent future recurrence of each of the 12 dissatisfactory incidents? (Hint: Consider the underlying cause of the problem and possible reasons for the inappropriate response that upset the customer.)
8. Define the term *partial employee* and give examples.
9. Are customers who are playing partial-employee roles more or less likely to be taken advantage of by unscrupulous service providers? Why or why not?

CHAPTER *four*

Service from the Customer's Viewpoint

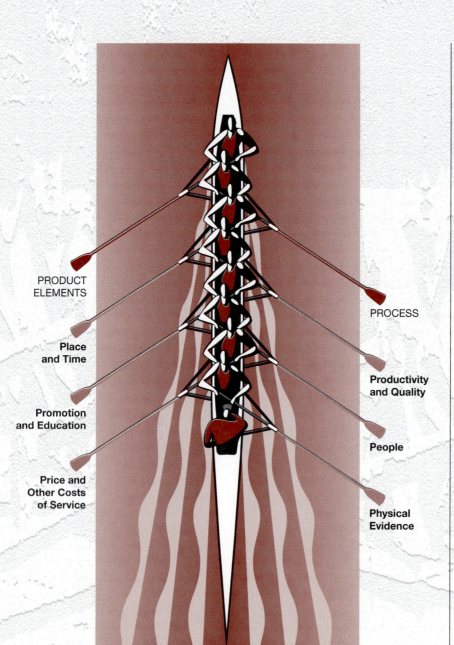

PRODUCT
ELEMENTS

**Place
and Time**

**Promotion
and Education**

**Price and
Other Costs
of Service**

PROCESS

**Productivity
and Quality**

People

**Physical
Evidence**

Learning Objectives

After reading this chapter, you should be able to

- ■ describe the three different types of attributes consumers use to evaluate products and how they relate to service offerings

- ■ discuss why service characteristics like intangibility and quality control problems affect consumer evaluation processes

- ■ explain the purchase process for services

- ■ differentiate between core and supplementary service elements

- ■ construct a simple flowchart, showing a service process from the customer's perspective

Progressive Insurance to the Rescue

Progressive Insurance Corp. prides itself on providing extraordinary customer service—and its accomplishments in this area are impressive.[1] As you read the following examples, think about your own insurance provider and the kind of service you receive. Do you think Progressive is meeting its goal of setting industry standards in providing settlements that are "fast, fair, and hassle-free"?

❏ In late January, a tornado ripped through a Smyrna, Tennessee policyholder's neighborhood. The 24-hour claims unit paged Progressive's on-call claim representative, who contacted the frantic customer. After discovering that the policyholder's garage was on top of his pickup, the claim representative contacted another claim representative who lived in the area. For two hours, this person navigated his way through the storm's debris to find the policyholder's residence. He completed an estimate on what he could see of the truck through the ruins of the garage and advised the policyholder that it was likely the vehicle was a total loss. By the next business day, the claim representative had completed a loss evaluation and presented the customer with a check.

❏ A policyholder had a vandalism claim and scheduled an appointment to have his vehicle inspected at Progressive's St. Cloud, Minnesota, office. Unable to make the appointment, the policyholder telephoned the claim office from his car to cancel. While on the phone, he noticed a Progressive Immediate Response Vehicle (IRV) driving by. The office asked for the IRV vehicle number (displayed on the front fender of each IRV), called the claim representative in the vehicle, and arranged for the policyholder and representative to pull to the side of the road for an inspection. The representative completed the estimate on the spot and sent the very satisfied policyholder on his way.

❏ The crash sight in Tampa, Florida, was chaotic and tense. Two cars were damaged, and although the passengers weren't bleeding, they were shaken up and scared. Lance Edgy, a senior claim representative for Progressive Corp., arrived on the scene just minutes after the collision. He calmed the victims and advised them on medical care, repair shops, police reports, and legal procedures. Edgy invited William McAllister, Progressive's policyholder, into an air-conditioned van equipped with comfortable chairs, a desk, and two cellular phones. Even before the tow trucks cleared away the wreckage, Edgy had offered his client a settlement for the market value of his totaled 1988 Mercury Topaz. McAllister, who did not appear to have been at fault in this accident, stated in amazement: "This is great—someone coming right out here and taking charge. I didn't expect it at all."

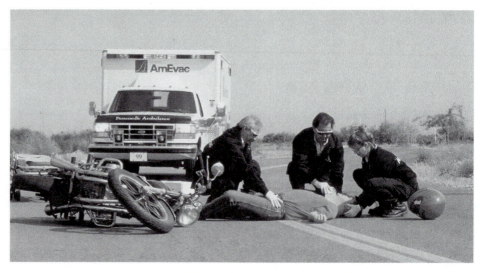

Unexpected accidents create a sudden need for emergency medical service.

HOW CUSTOMERS EVALUATE SERVICE PERFORMANCES

William McAllister, the unfortunate accident victim in the scenario just described, experienced something unusual: He was actually delighted at the service provided by his insurance company. This is not typical of most consumers of insurance services. In fact, customers often feel very hostile toward the insurance industry. As Peter Lewis, CEO of Progressive Corp., notes, "People get screwed seven ways from Sunday in auto insurance. They get dealt with adversarially, and they get dealt with slowly."[2] Unfortunately, many businesses make their customers unhappy. A survey of patients in 120 U.S. hospitals found that over 25 percent felt that they had received cold and impersonal care and were discharged before they felt ready.[3] The 1998 American Customer Satisfaction Index (ACSI) finally showed a slight improvement in overall satisfaction scores after four consecutive years of decline. But although satisfaction with insurance rose slightly, scores for most service categories—including mail and parcel delivery, movies, fast-food restaurants, hospitals, banks, and national broadcast news—were lower than in the previous year.[4] The ACSI is based on telephone interviews of over 50,000 consumers about their current levels of satisfaction, perception of value, expectations, and company or brand loyalty with 200 firms in seven sectors of the economy. Recent results indicate that consumer expectations are rising, but few companies have implemented strategies that can adequately address these changes.

Evaluation of Different Service Types

Some companies may indeed be guilty of bad behavior, as Lewis charges. Or perhaps they have just not paid enough attention to meeting their customers' expectations. However, it's likely that customers' perceptions are also negatively affected by the fact that services—especially those that are more intangible—can be very complex for consumers to evaluate. Unlike goods, their attributes can't be easily determined before, or sometimes even after, a purchase is made. Also, the consequences of making a mistake by choosing the wrong service are often more personally felt, especially when customers are directly involved in service production.

Where goods are concerned, customers often have the ability to redeem an unsatisfactory choice; for example, they can return a defective compact disc (CD) player or take a car in for repairs under warranty. However, these options are not as readily available with services. Possession-processing services are most similar to goods in this respect because the customer's possessions can often be reserviced if the work is not performed adequately the first time. For example, a janitorial service can reclean an office if a customer complains about the quality of the job. In contrast, people-processing services that are performed on people's bodies may be particularly hard to undo. After all, a bad haircut must grow out, and the consequences of a faulty surgical operation or a poorly done tattoo may last forever.

Mental stimulus processing services like education and live entertainment (e.g., theater performances or professional football games) can also be difficult to replace if quality does not meet customers' expectations. For instance, universities don't usually compensate students for poor-quality classroom experiences. Even if a college were willing to let students repeat classes for free with a different instructor, this remedy would still incur significant time and psychological costs (such costs are discussed in depth in chapter 11).

Finally, information-based services can present challenges for customers when service quality is unsatisfactory. Unhappy customers of insurance, banking, or accounting services may be reluctant to switch providers because of the potential time, psychological, and financial costs involved in doing so. If the other people who were involved in the auto accident described at the beginning of this chapter wanted to switch to Progressive for their future insurance needs, they would have to spend time and effort in completing new applications. Drivers who switch to a new insurance company from one that they have used for a long time risk losing the "good customer" discounts—like those from the Automobile Association of America (AAA) and State Farm Insurance—offered as a reward for their loyalty to the firm.

A Continuum of Product Attributes

In chapter 1, we pointed out that one of the basic differences between goods and services is that services are harder for customers to evaluate. We also briefly mentioned three different categories of product characteristics: search, experience, and credence. We expand on the concept of these **product attributes** here because they provide a useful framework for understanding how consumers evaluate different types of market offerings.

All products can be placed on a continuum according to these attributes. As you can see from Figure 4.1 (p. 68), most goods are high in **search attributes**—those characteristics that allow customers to evaluate a product before purchasing it. With features like style, color, texture, taste, sound, and price, prospective consumers can view, try out, taste-test, or test drive the product prior to purchase. This step helps customers understand and evaluate what they will get in exchange for their money and reduces the uncertainty or risk associated with the purchase. Goods such as clothing, furniture, automobiles, electronic equipment, and foods are high in search properties.

Experience attributes can't be evaluated prior to purchase. Customers must "experience" these features to know what they are getting. Vacations, live entertainment, sporting events, and restaurants fall into this category. Even after exposure to colorful brochures and informative videos about the features of a holiday destination or to travel reviews in newspapers and magazines, travelers can't really evaluate (or feel) the dramatic beauty of the Swiss Alps or the magic of scuba diving in Belize until they actually experience it. Nor can customers always rely on the accuracy of information from friends, family, or other personal sources when evaluating these types of products. Friends may have told you about a "great" movie they had just seen, and you may have gone to the theater with high expectations but were disappointed when you "experienced" the film yourself.

product attributes: all features (both tangible and intangible) of a good or service that can be evaluated by customers.

search attributes: product characteristics that consumers can readily evaluate prior to purchase.

experience attributes: product performance features that customers can evaluate only during service delivery.

FIGURE 4.1 How Product Attributes Affect Ease of Evaluation

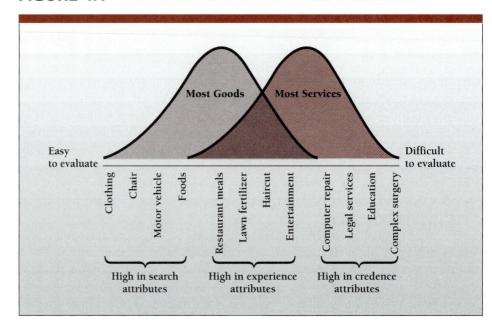

credence attributes: product characteristics that customers may not be able to evaluate even after purchase and consumption.

Credence attributes are characteristics that customers may find impossible to evaluate confidently even after purchase and consumption. For example, few consumers know enough about financial markets to assess whether their financial planner got the best possible returns on their invested funds. Patients can't usually evaluate how well their dentists have performed complex dental procedures, and most college students must simply have faith that their professors are providing a worthwhile educational experience.

Most goods fall to the left of the continuum in Figure 4.1 because they are high in search attributes. Many services can be placed on the right side, reflecting two of the eight basic differences between goods and services discussed in chapter 1: intangibility of service performances and variability of inputs and outputs, leading to quality control problems. These characteristics present special challenges to service managers because services, compared to most goods, are high in experience and credence attributes and relatively low in search attributes.

Intangibility of service performances.   The intangible nature of service performances means that customers can't rely on their senses to evaluate the nature or quality of the basic service benefits. Even when there are many tangible elements (as in a restaurant or hotel), the service package is difficult to demonstrate physically before purchase. Marketers whose products are high in experience characteristics often try to provide more search attributes for their customers. One way to do so is by providing a free trial of the service. Providers of on-line computer services are good examples of this strategy. For example, AOL gives potential users software and a chance to try its services free for a limited number of hours. This reduces customers' concerns about entering into a formal membership relationship without first having an opportunity to experience what the service offers. Of course, AOL is betting that consumers will be dependent on its Internet services after the free trial is over.

Companies also use advertising to help customers visualize service benefits when there are few inherent search attributes. For instance, the only tangible thing owners of a MasterCard get directly from the company is a small plastic card. But that is obviously not the essence of the service provided. Think about the credit card advertisements you have seen recently. They have probably featured exciting products that you could purchase or exotic places to which you could travel by using your card. These ads are designed to help us visualize (and get excited about) the tangible benefits of using our credit cards. Some companies are quite clever in recognizing that their products are intangible and play on this in their advertising campaigns.

Providers of services that are high in credence characteristics have an even greater challenge. Their benefits may be so intangible that customers can't evaluate what they've received even *after* the service has been purchased and consumed, although marketers often try to provide tangible cues to customers. For example, high-contact services may carefully design and maintain their facilities to provide physical evidence of service quality. Professional service providers like doctors, architects, and lawyers often display their degrees and certifications for the same reason—they want customers to "see" the credentials that underlie the services they provide. Financial service providers often choose a physical motif implying protection, strength, or safety.

Since industry standards have changed to allow advertising for most professional services (see chapter 1), many professionals have turned to new marketing arenas to help make their offerings tangible to customers. For example, lawyers use the Yellow Pages, print ads, and television spots to promote their services. Some poorly executed ads have actually had a *negative* impact on people's opinions of lawyers (such as those larger-than-life personal injury attorneys staring down from enormous billboards). But other campaigns are using sophisticated approaches to humanize lawyers and present them as valuable resources for solving clients' problems.

For instance, a Chicago-based firm, Briskman and Briskman, uses typical blue-collar clients in its television ads. These clients talk about problems that led them to seek legal assistance and then describe how the law firm resolved the issues. Another firm, Jacoby and Meyers, uses humor to convince potential clients that the company is "warm and accessible." Its 15-second TV ads and billboards depict situations typically handled by its lawyers—personal injury lawsuits, bankruptcies, divorces, and estates—with a humorous twist and end with the tagline "Jacoby and Meyers: problem solved."[5]

Although we have focused on services that fall in the experience and credence areas of the continuum in Figure 4.1, companies whose products are dominated by search attributes also face an interesting challenge. Marketers of physical goods often choose to play up the *intangible* characteristics of their products to increase their appeal to customers. This strategy of emphasizing intangible service attributes to add value to a tangible good is used in more than just advertising campaigns. It is sometimes an integral part of the product itself. For example, Toyota maintains that when people buy a Lexus, they are not just buying a car—they are also buying a luxury package. Although a high-quality automobile is the core product, the distinguishing features are far more intangible. Lexus uses extraordinary service to create a sense of prestige and luxury for its customers. This culture is present from the showrooms (which are tastefully decorated) to the salespeople (who do not use high-pressure sales tactics) to the service garages (which are brightly lit and spotless). Moreover, every employee's compensation is tied to customer satisfaction ratings. The strategy has paid off for Toyota: Customers ranked Lexus as first overall in dealer service, product reliability and quality for the sixth time in the 1997 Customer Satisfaction Index Study, conducted by J. D. Power & Associates. In spite of the awards, the company maintains that "our pursuit continues. Because while our customers may be satisfied, we never are."[6]

Variability and quality control problems. The continuum of product attributes in Figure 4.1 also has implications for another distinguishing service characteristic—the degree of customer involvement in the production process. Products that are highest in search attributes are most often physical goods that are manufactured in a factory, with no customer involvement, and then purchased and consumed. Quality is much easier to control in this situation because the elements of production can be more closely monitored and failures can be spotted before the product reaches the customer. In fact, some manufacturers like Motorola claim to be able to guarantee product quality at the so-called six-sigma level—that is 99.999 percent. However, quality control for services that fall in the experience and credence ranges is more difficult because production often involves customer involvement.

Customers' evaluations of services may be affected to a great extent by their personal interactions with the physical setting of the business, the employees, and even the other customers. For example, your experience in purchasing a haircut is a combination of the following factors: your impression of the hair salon, how well you can describe what you want to the stylist, the stylist's ability to understand and do what you've requested; and the appearance of the other customers and stylists in the salon. Stylists might add that it is difficult for them to do a good job if customers don't cooperate during service delivery.

For products with lots of credence characteristics, the situation can be very complex. Many of these are pure services, which have few tangible characteristics and rely on the expertise of a professional to provide high quality. In this case, providers must be able to interact with customers effectively to produce a satisfactory product. Problems can occur when this interaction doesn't produce an outcome that meets customers' expectations, even though the service provider may not be at fault.

For example, an architectural firm may design a building that it believes closely matches the features desired by a client. However, the latter may be disappointed when the structure is completed and feel that the architect has delivered a poor product. Although this may be the case, other explanations may include the client's inability to describe his or her needs accurately or to understand from the plans what the architect was proposing. Alternatively, the builder may not have executed the plans accurately or may have cut costs in places that affected the building's appearance and integrity. Computer technology has thus become extremely useful to architects, not only to aid in the technical aspects of building design, but also to create simulations for clients before construction begins. For instance, with the aid of virtual reality devices, clients can simulate the experience of walking around the exterior of a proposed building and then entering it and touring different rooms. The architect can then demonstrate the impact of changes in dimensions, layout, building materials, design, and decor.

Service providers must also work hard to keep the quality of their products consistent over time. This is more difficult when production involves direct interaction with service employees, whose performances are likely to vary from one day to another. But customers don't want variations in quality, as Michael Flatley, the Irish founder, director, and lead dancer of *Lord of the Dance*, knows. As he said in a recent TV interview, "The people who drive hundreds of miles to see this show ... they don't want to know I'm almost 39 ... they don't want to know my legs are sore ... they don't want to know I go home and put my feet in ice. They just want to know that what they're seeing is the best show ever—tonight, not tomorrow night!"[7] Flatley's insistence on providing the best performance possible every time has produced results: His company achieves sold-out performances around the world, and audiences often show their appreciation by giving the dancers a standing ovation.

THE PURCHASE PROCESS FOR SERVICES

Customers buy products to meet specific **needs**, and they evaluate the outcomes of their purchases according to what they originally expected to receive. Having some knowledge of customer needs can help service providers understand *how* and *why* customers react to service delivery. Needs are deeply rooted in people's unconscious minds and concern long-term existence and identity issues. When people feel a need, they are motivated to take some kind of action to fulfill it. Abraham Maslow identified five categories of human needs—physiological, safety, love, esteem, and self-actualization—and proposed that basic needs like food and shelter must be met before others could be fulfilled.[8] Although poverty and deprivation remain pressing issues around the world, physiological needs have ceased to be the sole issue for many people. Greater prosperity means that increasing numbers of individuals are seeking to satisfy social and self-actualization needs. These needs, which are more complex, create a demand for more sophisticated goods and services.

In North America, as in many highly developed nations, many consumers have all the physical goods they want and are now turning to services to fulfill unmet needs. In 1997, Christmas shoppers in the United States spent more money overall than they had a year earlier, but many of them reported that they already had all the material things they needed or wanted to buy and that they would rather give or receive services instead. Overall, they planned to spend 2 percent less on tangible gifts and 45 percent to 55 percent more on entertainment and travel. According to Daniel Bethamy of American Express, consumers want "memorable experiences, not gadgets."[9] This shift in consumer behavior and attitudes provides opportunities for service companies that can effectively understand and meet customers' needs.

needs: subconscious, deeply felt desires that concern long-term existence and identity issues.

Rising disposable incomes are leading many consumers to increase their spending on services like travel and entertainment.

purchase process: the stages a customer goes through in choosing, consuming, and evaluating a service.

When customers decide to buy a service to meet an unfulfilled need, they typically go through a more complex **purchase process** than if they had decided to buy a good. Service characteristics like intangibility and variability make it harder for customers to evaluate alternatives before they buy a service. To make matters worse, they may not be able to determine effectively the quality of their experience during, or even after, they have consumed the service. The purchase process for customers has three separate stages—prepurchase, service encounter, and postpurchase (see Figure 4.2). We describe each of these stages and illustrate the purchase process with the story of how a marketing professor at a university in California decided to have laser surgery on his eyes. Note that each stage involves costs for the customer.

The Prepurchase Stage

prepurchase stage: the first stage in the service purchase process, where customers identify alternatives, weigh benefits and risks, and make a purchase decision.

The decision to buy and use a service is made in the **prepurchase stage**. Individual needs and expectations are very important here because they influence what alternatives a customer will consider. In some instances, the customer may quick-

FIGURE 4.2 The Purchase Process: Customer Activities in Selecting, Using, and Evaluating Service

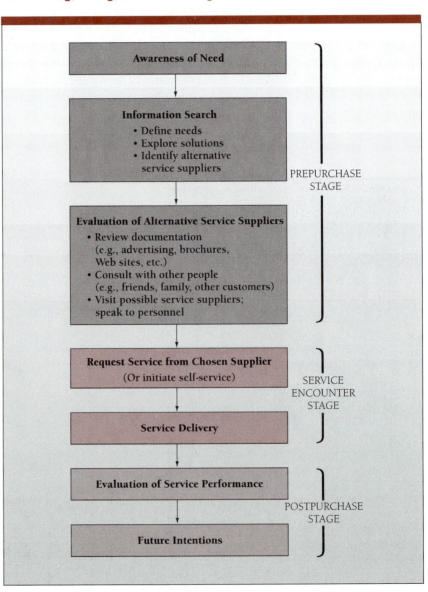

ly select and use a specific service provider, particularly if the purchase is routine and relatively low risk. In other instances, where more is at stake or the customer plans to use a service for the first time, an intensive information search may be conducted (contrast the process of buying a pizza to applying to college). After a customer has conducted an information search, which can range from brief and casual to extended and thorough, he or she may identify several alternative suppliers and then weigh the benefits and risks of each option before making a purchase decision.

This element of perceived risk is especially relevant for services that are high in experience or credence attributes because they are often more difficult to evaluate before purchase and consumption. First-time users are especially likely to have greater uncertainty and to be wary of the perceived risks. Risk perceptions are based on customers' judgments of the likelihood that negative outcomes will occur and on the degree of negativity. Different types of perceived risks are outlined in Table 4.1.

When customers feel uncomfortable with risks, they can use a variety of methods to reduce them during the prepurchase stage. In fact, you have probably tried some of the following risk-reduction strategies yourself before deciding to purchase a service:

- seeking information from respected personal sources (friends and acquaintances)
- relying on the reputation of the firm
- looking for guarantees and warranties
- looking for opportunities to try the service before purchasing
- asking knowledgeable employees about competing services
- examining tangible cues or other physical evidence
- using the World Wide Web to compare service offerings

TABLE 4.1 Perceived Risks in Purchasing and Using Services

Type of Risk	Examples of Customer Concerns
Functional risk (unsatisfactory performance outcomes)	<ul><li>Will this training course give me the skill I need to get a better job?</li><li>Will this credit card be accepted wherever and whenever I want to make a purchase?</li><li>Will the dry cleaner be able to remove the stains from this jacket?</li></ul>
Financial risk (monetary loss, unexpected costs)	<ul><li>Will I lose money if I make the investment recommended by my stockbroker?</li><li>Will I incur lots of unanticipated expenses if I go on this vacation?</li><li>Will repairing my car cost more than the original estimate?</li></ul>
Temporal risk (wasting time, consequences of delays)	<ul><li>Will I have to wait in line before entering the exhibition?</li><li>Will service at this restaurant be so slow that I will be late for my afternoon meeting?</li><li>Will the renovations to our bathroom be completed before our friends come to stay with us?</li></ul>
Physical risk (personal injury or damage to possessions)	<ul><li>Will I get hurt if I go skiing at this resort?</li><li>Will the contents of this package get damaged in the mail?</li><li>Will I fall sick if I travel abroad on vacation?</li></ul>
Psychological risk (personal fears and emotions)	<ul><li>How can I be sure this aircraft won't crash?</li><li>Will the consultant make me feel stupid?</li><li>Will the doctor's diagnosis upset me?</li></ul>
Social risk (how others think and react)	<ul><li>What will my friends think of me if they learn I stayed at this cheap motel?</li><li>Will my relatives approve of the restaurant I have chosen for the family reunion dinner?</li><li>Will my business colleagues disapprove of my selection of an unknown law firm?</li></ul>
Sensory risk (unwanted impacts on any of the five senses)	<ul><li>Will I get a view of the parking lot from my room, rather than the beach?</li><li>Will the bed be uncomfortable?</li><li>Will I be kept awake by noise from the guests in the room next door?</li><li>Will my room smell of stale cigarette smoke?</li><li>Will the coffee at breakfast taste disgusting?</li></ul>

PART I: THE PREPURCHASE STAGE

Dan's Big Decision

Dan Toy has had poor eyesight for most of his life. He inherited bad eyes from one of his parents, and they only got worse when Dan was hit in the face with a baseball bat during a grade school ball game. Dan's vision was first corrected with glasses, then hard contact lenses, and eventually soft contacts. Soft contacts were a reasonable solution for Dan for many years, but they did have drawbacks. Although Dan liked his job as a marketing professor at a university in northern California, his real loves (besides his wife, Lauren, of course) were sports and the outdoors. Contacts were a big improvement over glasses for these athletic pursuits, but they had a tendency to freeze overnight on Dan's climbing trips to places like Mt. Shasta and Mt. Rainier. And he always worried about losing a lens while he was swimming, kayaking, or scuba diving.

Another problem surfaced as Dan got older. It became harder every year to treat his deteriorating vision with soft contact lenses. When his eyes got tired at night, he had to change to glasses to use the computer or read. That really didn't work well either because his eyes had trouble adjusting to the bifocals. So Dan began searching for another solution.

Dan's brother, Scott, a doctor, and his sister-in-law, Sue, a nurse, had both decided to try a new surgical procedure called radial keratotomy (RK) to fix their vision problems. After several operations over a period of 12 months, neither needed to wear glasses or contacts. Both Scott and Sue thought the procedure was miraculous, and they enthusiastically recommended it to Dan. Dan asked his ophthalmologist about RK but found that the treatment could not be used with his degree of near-sightedness. However, his doctor told him about a new procedure that might offer a cure. This new technique, called photorefractive keratectomy (PRK), uses a laser to reshape the cornea of the eye rather than cutting the cornea like the RK surgery.

A few doctors in the United States were beginning to try PRK, and a doctor in Dan's hometown knew something about it. Dan was discouraged to learn that the Federal Drug Administration (FDA) did not yet allow treatment in the United States for eyes as bad as his. (The procedure was approved for −7.0 diopters or lower, and Dan's diopter measurements were −6.25 for the right eye and −10.25 for the left.) However, the doctor recommended several practitioners in Canada that might handle his case. He gave Dan a brochure for the London Place Eye Centre, a clinic in Vancouver, British Columbia (BC), that specializes in Excimer laser eye surgery. Dan checked out the Eye Centre on the Internet and discovered that the lead physician, Don Johnson, had invented the "no touch" technique for performing PRK in 1993. ("No touch" refers to the fact that surgical instruments never touch a patient's eye because corrections are made by using multiple passes with a laser.) Since the laser surgery was introduced, the Eye Centre had performed over 12,000 operations, and Dr. Johnson had also trained a number of American doctors in this technique.

Encouraged by this information, Dan called the clinic. The staff in Vancouver were very helpful and immediately sent Dan a large packet of information about the clinic and the PRK procedure. Because Dan would need to have his preoperation exam done locally, the clinic recommended

Now that we know some of the issues involved in the prepurchase stage, let's consider the story of Dan Toy's decision to have corrective laser surgery on his eyes (see box, Part I).

The Service Encounter Stage

After customers decide to purchase a specific service, they engage in one or more service encounters with the service provider (in some instances, they may even have one or more encounters during the evaluation stage, before making a final choice of provider). These service encounters often begin with a request for service from the chosen provider, perhaps taking the form of an application, a reservation, or a simple order. As we saw in chapter 3, encounters may take the form of personal exchanges between customers and service employees or impersonal interactions with

Dr. Sontag, an opthamologist who had referred other patients to the Eye Centre. Dr. Sontag also had personal experience with PRK; he had undergone laser surgery with Dr. Johnson several years ago, at the age of 57. Dr. Sontag examined Dan's eyes and said he was a candidate for the operation. But he warned Dan that PRK results were typically better for younger patients (Dan was 49) and those with less severe vision problems. There was also some risk that the operation would not produce a significant correction, which might force Dan to rely on glasses because contacts could not usually be worn after the surgery.

Dan questioned Dr. Sontag about his personal reactions to the operation. Dr. Sontag said he was not happy with the results and that he didn't think Dan would be either. Dr. Sontag did not have 20/20 vision and still needed glasses to read. He was also disappointed that his vision wasn't as precise as he expected it to be after the surgery. However, Dr. Sontag did tell Dan to call Bill, a 37-year-old patient who had a positive experience. Dan talked to Bill, who was very enthusiastic about the results of his operation because he was free of glasses for the first time in his life. He said he had some problems with night vision but he had expected that. Bill felt the surgery was one of the best things he had ever done.

These conflicting opinions about the outcome of the PRK surgery created quite a dilemma for Dan, especially because he felt that there were a number of risks associated with this decision. The procedure was quite expensive ($4,000, including all pre- and postoperative exams) and would not be covered by Dan's insurance. Dan would also have to stop wearing contacts four weeks before the operation, which meant suffering through poor vision and Coke-bottle glasses for an entire month. Dan was also concerned about Dr. Sontag's reaction, and the fact that the procedure was not approved by the FDA in the United States also created uncertainty about the decision. Finally, he did not like the possibility that his vision could actually worsen as a result of the operation.

Dan spent several long weeks agonizing over the decision with Lauren, eventually concluding that the potential benefits still outweighed the risks. He decided to go ahead with the operation and set a date that would give him just enough time to meet the four-week "no contact lens" period. He also made reservations at Henley House, a bed and breakfast facility the London Place Eye Centre had recommended. With these arrangements made, Dan took out his contacts for the last time and began the month-long wait for the surgery date.

Costs to Dan during the Prepurchase Stage

- *Time Costs:*   Many hours spent doing research on the Web, talking to family members and others about the surgery, going to doctor's appointments, reading the material sent by the London Place Eye Center, and wondering whether to have the operation.
- *Psychological Costs:*   Anxiety about pain associated with the PRK procedure; worry that his eyesight would not be improved or get worse; embarrassment about having to wear his glasses to work; concern over spending so much money.
- *Monetary Costs:*   A $400 nonrefundable deposit payable when the surgery was scheduled.

equipment, telephones, or computers. In high-contact services, such as restaurants, health care, hotels, and public transportation, customers may be exposed to a variety of service encounters during service delivery.

Customers base decisions about service quality on several factors that affect the outcome of the **service encounter stage**. These factors—which include service environments, service employees, and support services—are discussed briefly here.

Service environments include all of the tangible characteristics of the environment in which service delivery takes place. The facility and equipment, the firm's atmosphere (including cleanliness, odor, or noise), and other customers can all affect what customers expect during a service encounter and their perceptions of service quality. We return to this concept in chapters 9 and 12.

Service employees are the most important factor in most high-contact service encounters, in which they have direct, face-to-face interactions with customers, but

service encounter stage: the second stage in the service purchase process, in which the service delivery takes place through interactions between customers and the service provider.

they can also affect service delivery in low-contact situations. Customers expect service employees to follow specific scripts during the service encounter, and violations of these scripts can cause customer satisfaction to decrease. Employees should be carefully selected, trained, and compensated to handle service encounters effectively. We discuss how to recruit and retain good service employees in chapter 15.

Support services are made up of the materials and equipment plus all of the backstage processes that allow front-stage employees to do their work properly. This element is critical because front-line workers can't do a good job for customers unless they receive high-quality internal service from support personnel. As an old axiom goes, "If you aren't servicing the customer, you are servicing someone who is."[10] We analyze the scripts and steps involved in support processes in more detail in chapter 10.

Let's see (box, Part II) how these factors affected Dan's service encounters as he traveled to Vancouver, BC, to have his eye surgery.

The Postpurchase Stage

postpurchase stage: the final stage in the service purchase process, in which customers evaluate service quality and their satisfaction or dissatisfaction with the service outcome.

During the **postpurchase stage**, customers continue a process they began in the service encounter stage—evaluating service quality and their satisfaction or dissatisfaction with the service experience. The outcome of this process will affect their future intentions, such as whether or not to remain loyal to the service provider and whether to pass on positive or negative recommendations to family members and other associates.

Customers evaluate service quality by comparing what they expected with what they perceive they received. If their expectations are met or exceeded, they believe they have received high-quality service. These satisfied customers are more likely to be repeat purchasers or loyal customers. However, if the service experience does not meet customers' expectations, they will feel that service quality is poor. They may complain, suffer in silence, or switch providers in the future. Service managers must find effective ways to address customers' expectations and perceptions to enhance service satisfaction. We return to this topic in chapter 5, where we take a closer look at customer satisfaction and service quality issues.

It's time to conclude the story of Dan Toy's eye surgery and learn how he evaluated the outcome of his PRK experience (see box, Part III, p. 78).

THE SERVICE OFFERING

service offering: all elements designed into a service experience to provide value to customers.

Because the consumer evaluation and purchase processes are more complex for services, it is especially important that service managers understand how customers view the service offering. One of the best definitions of a **service offering** from a customer perspective comes from FedEx. Its senior managers decided to define service very simply as "all actions and reactions that customers perceive they have purchased." This statement can be applied to any business and clarifies what customers have known all along, namely, that "service" is a bundle made up of the core product plus a cluster of supplementary services.

Core and Supplementary Product Elements

core product: the central benefit provided by a firm to address specific customer needs.

supplementary service elements: additional benefits provided by a firm to add value and differentiation to the core product.

Whatever the business, companies have to think in terms of performing well on all actions and reactions that customers perceive they are purchasing, and they need to be clear about which of these various interactions constitute the **core product** and which represent **supplementary service elements**. The core product provides the central benefit that addresses specific customer needs. It defines the fundamental na-

PART II: THE SERVICE ENCOUNTER STAGE

Dan Goes to Vancouver, BC

Exactly four weeks after Dan made the decision to have eye surgery, he and his wife, Lauren, drove from northern California to Vancouver, BC. Dan was understandably anxious as they approached the Canadian border. Lauren provided what reassurance she could—which wasn't much because she had never been through the process herself. They checked into the Henley House and were pleasantly surprised by its clean, cheerful atmosphere. Although its location and competitive prices also attracted vacationers, over 50 percent of the Henley House guests were eye surgery patients who wanted comfortable lodgings within easy walking distance of the clinic. The friendly proprietors, Anne O'Shaughnessy and Ross Hood, explained the many amenities (e.g., a big-screen television and plenty of videos and large-print books and magazines) that were provided specifically for eye clinic patients. They were very reassuring and told Dan encouraging stories about the positive outcomes other guests had had with their PRK surgery. Dan and Lauren then went to the London Place Eye Centre, where the staff took additional measurements of Dan's eyes and described the procedures that would occur during Dan's surgery the next day. The clinic employees were professional and polite, and the front offices of the facility were brightly lit and full of interesting art and live plants.

Dan and Lauren went for an early morning run on the day of the operation and arrived at the clinic around 10 A.M. They had a brief meeting with Dr. Johnson, who provided explicit information about what to expect during the operation and the days that followed. He said that although the surgery itself was not painful, Dan would probably have significant discomfort for three or four days afterward, including blurred vision, an acute stinging sensation, and a feeling of having sand or eyelashes in his eyes. Dr. Johnson also explained the surgical procedure and warned Dan to expect a small puff of smoke and an odor of something burning as the laser vaporized part of the cornea. He explained that he would correct Dan's left eye for close vision and his right eye for distance. Dan was told that he should not expect 20/20 results with either eye but that his vision should improve dramatically. Dr. Johnson also said that Dan would probably still need glasses for reading.

After the briefing, Dan entered the operating room. He was told to lie perfectly still and not to move—which was particularly unnerving because Dan expected that at any moment the laser might burn off a large piece of his eye. Lauren was astonished to see Dan walk out of the operating room in 20 minutes with both eyes completed. The next few days in Vancouver were somewhat dreamlike for Dan. Although the PRK procedure produced much more intense postoperation discomfort than Dan had expected, his vision improved on a daily basis. Dan and Lauren took another run the day after the operation, and both were surprised by how much detail Dan could see. He even remarked that it was the first time he'd been able to see what Lauren *really* looked like since they were married.

Costs to Dan during the Service Encounter Stage

- *Time Costs:* The 12-hour drive to Vancouver; the four days spent having the surgery, plus pre- and postoperative exams.
- *Psychological Costs:* Anxiety before and during the PRK procedure; worry about the pain and how the healing process was progressing in the days immediately after the surgery.
- *Physical Costs:* The postoperative pain; the fatigue that accompanied recovery.
- *Sensory Costs:* The sound and smell of the laser procedure; very blurred vision for 72 hours.
- *Monetary Costs:* The $4,000 for the surgery ($3,600 plus the $400 deposit)—no insurance coverage or financing was available; gas expenses to Vancouver ($80); restaurant meals for five days (approximately $55 per day); five nights of lodging ($330); postsurgery prescriptions ($100).

PART III: THE POSTPURCHASE STAGE

Dan Evaluates His Experience

Dan's eyes healed so quickly that he drove halfway back from Seattle to northern California a few days after the surgery without using glasses or contacts. In fact, most of the postsurgery changes took place during the first month. He was pleased, as his vision improved week after week. An unexpected side benefit was that he could read newspapers, menus, and computer screens without glasses. Five weeks after the surgery, he had a postoperation examination with Dr. Sontag, who felt that the surgery had been a success. In fact, he stated that Dan had healed so completely that no ophthalmologist would even know he had undergone PRK by examining his eyes.

Almost two years after the operation, Dan still does not need glasses for reading but has noticed some regression in his distance vision. Also, since his operation, new technologies have emerged that allow different prescriptions for eye implants to match changes in vision over time. These methods provide more flexible treatment possibilities and involve less permanent physical changes to the eye. Although Dan has enjoyed his improved vision immensely, he is still not sure that his decision was the best one. Lauren is very impressed by the surgery results, but Dan maintains that he is not yet ready to burst into the song "I can see clearly now ..." until he knows what the long-term outcome of the surgery will be.

Costs to Dan during the Postpurchase Stage

- *Time Costs:* The 12-hour drive from Vancouver; follow-up exams once a month for three months following the surgery.
- *Psychological Costs:* Anxiety about the gradual regression in his vision.
- *Monetary Costs:* Gas expenses from Vancouver ($80).

---

ture of a company's business. Supplemental service elements supply additional benefits to enhance the core product and differentiate it from competitors' offerings.

In most businesses—both service and manufacturing—the core product tends to become a commodity as competition increases and the industry matures. In natural resources, such as oil, minerals, or agricultural produce, the product begins life as a commodity. It's very difficult to protect innovative products from imitation by competitors (brand names and proprietary software are among the few aspects of service design that can be legally protected). Even in manufacturing, where inventions can be patented, it's becoming increasingly difficult to sustain product leadership. Just think about how quickly innovative, high-technology products are cloned and protective patents circumvented.

The maturing of the insurance industry was the driving force behind Progressive Insurance Corp.'s redefinition of its core service. The core product of insurance is risk management—hedging against the possibility of suffering substantial economic loss as a result of injuries or damage to vehicles and other property. All drivers are legally required to obtain a certain minimum level of automobile insurance to protect third parties. The company developed a niche by writing policies for high-risk drivers whom other insurance providers wouldn't touch, charging its customers hefty premiums for its services. As shown in Figure 4.3, supplementary services include giving information and advice, handling applications for coverage, delivering policy documents, and sending out billing statements on a prearranged cycle. When the customer has a loss, additional supplementary services come into play, including documentation of the accident to assign responsibility and identify the nature of the damage incurred; advice to policyholders on how to deal with police, legal, medical, and vehicle repair issues; claims handling; offers of settlement; and payment of claims.

FIGURE 4.3 Core and Supplementary Services: An Example for Car Insurance

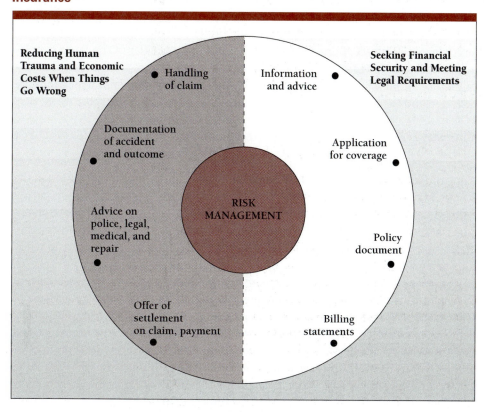

Progressive's profitable environment was threatened when Allstate outsold it in the high-risk market. Moreover, voters in California (which accounted for 25 percent of Progressive's profits) passed a referendum-based law that set strict limits on insurance rates. To remain competitive, Progressive decided to redefine its core business in a way that went well beyond offering its policyholders merely "peace of mind." The company now seeks to "reduce human trauma and economic costs of auto accidents, theft and other perils while building a recognized, trusted, admired, business-generating consumer brand." This strategy proved very profitable, as the company achieved a rapid increase in the number of insurance premiums written in Canada and the United States.

Progressive decided to set new industry standards for auto accident claims in an attempt to please its customers and claimants. It introduced a 24-hour "immediate response" program to respond to claims rapidly and to make settlements "fast, fair and hassle-free."[11] Delivering this level of supplementary service helps the company as well as the customers because adjusters are able to gather accurate information firsthand, which they then feed into Progressive's automated claims management system. The streamlined process reduces costs and builds tremendous goodwill among customers. Progressive's well-designed Web site (www.auto-insurance.com) provides additional supplementary services: information about the company and where to find a local agent; rate comparisons; customer account access; and even some entertainment, including an art gallery, contests, a children's page, and an interactive quiz.

The company also provides outstanding customer service to supplement its core product. According to Progressive's CEO, Peter Lewis, "To the extent that the insurance industry is a commodity, our biggest differentiator is our people. We want the best people at every level of the company, and we pay at the top of the market." Besides choosing its employees carefully and paying them well, the company invests heavily in training. For example, Lance Edgy (the senior claim adjuster who arrived on the scene of the auto accident in the opening story of this chapter) received training not only on insurance regulations but also on negotiations and grief counseling. This training helps him deal sympathetically but effectively with customers when a family member has been killed or badly injured in an accident. The basic supplementary services in Figure 4.3 may be found in other insurance companies; what distinguishes Progressive from many of its competitors is the manner in which they are delivered and the extra benefits of faster, more effective, and more responsive service.

Competing on Supplementary Service Elements

Every business that aspires to market leadership should be working to enhance existing products and to develop new ones. But achieving significant innovation in the core product is nearly always time consuming and expensive, sometimes requiring enormous research investments. In mature product categories, such innovation occurs only infrequently. Think for a moment: What was the most recent successful *major* innovation in airline travel, cars, hotels, or retail financial services? And when did each take place?

Because significant innovation in core products seems to be an infrequent event in many industries, much of the action occurs among supplementary service elements, which offer the best opportunity in mature industries for increasing customers' perceptions of value. This idea is not a new one by any means. Twenty years ago, Ted Levitt observed, "We live in an age in which our thinking about what a product or service is must be quite different from what it was before. It is not so much the basic, generic, central thing we are thinking about that counts, but the whole cluster of satisfactions with which we surround it."[12] Customers expect companies to produce a decent core product—whether it's a manufactured good like a microwave oven or a service like cable television. If they can't, sooner or later they'll go out of business.

Where's the Leverage?[13]

For customers of a mature industry, meaningful differentiation and added value usually come from a whole bundle of supplementary service elements. Performance of the core service is a matter of do or die (Figure 4.4), but there are some differences in the relative role and importance of various supplementary services.

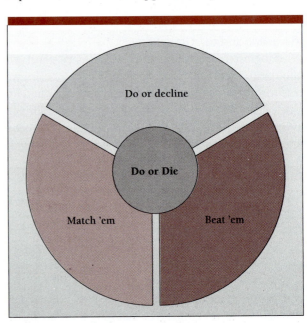

FIGURE 4.4
Service Elements and Competitive Leverage

Do or decline.   At the top of the diagram are the do-or-decline elements. More and more, firms find that providing information (by phone or otherwise), order taking, billing, and problem solving are included in this category. If they can't perform these tasks well—tasks that are generic to almost all service industries—they will appear to be incompetent and uncaring and the stage will be set for a steady decline. Do-or-decline elements for service businesses vary from industry to industry, but companies must provide them at a certain threshold level just to stay in business. For example, before the U.S. banking industry was deregulated, most banks were not very customer-friendly. Banking hours were short, and access to account information was limited to personal interactions with tellers. Monthly statements were virtually impossible to read. After deregulation, however, increased competition forced banks to change their ways. Longer banking hours (including Saturdays), access to ATMs and 24-hour telephone service, and understandable monthly statements became do-or-decline elements as banks struggled to attract customers and remain profitable.

Match 'ems and beat 'ems.   Other supplementary services can be divided into "match 'em" and "beat 'em" elements. Each firm should decide what the basis for its competitive strategy will be. When targeting a specific market segment, on which attributes will superior performance yield a meaningful competitive edge? And where is it enough simply to offer the industry standard of performance on a given service element? To answer this question, you will probably have to find out what customers think of your firm's products and those of competitors on all relevant service attributes.

Another question to ask is how long it will take before a "beat 'em" is copied by the competition and reduced to the stage of a "match 'em"? The best approach is to create supplementary elements that are difficult for competitors to duplicate. For example, Progressive Insurance Corp. has redesigned its entire business around superior customer service. This includes extensive investments in technology (to support its immediate response program), people (for selection, training, and compensation), and facilities (such as the mobile offices that appear at crash sites). Because all of these elements are part of an integrated service management strategy, it would be difficult for competitors to copy them quickly.

Managers must decide where the opportunities lie for adding distinctive extras and when the focus should be on improving basic performance. It may already have occurred to you that whereas many supplementary elements are specific to one industry or service, some are not (e.g., telephone information and order taking, statements and billing, and food and beverage service). We cover the topic of supplementary service elements in more detail in chapter 8, where we examine their role in providing additional value for customers.

MAPPING THE CUSTOMER'S SERVICE EXPERIENCE

To design a service that meets or exceeds the expectations of its customers, service providers must have an idea of what those customers actually experience during their service encounters. One of the most effective ways to do this is to create a description of the steps that customers and employees go through in coproducing a service. These steps can be shown visually by using a tool called a **flowchart**. By depicting all of the service encounters, or occasions when contact takes place between customers and a service provider (see chapter 2), flowcharts can highlight problems and opportunities in the service delivery process. Flowcharts can be used by both high-contact and low-contact services to gain a better understanding of

flowchart: a visual representation of the steps involved in delivering service to customers.

Productivity and Quality: Two Sides of the Same Coin

Product elements

Place and time

Promotion and Education

Price and other costs of service

Process

PRODUCTIVITY AND QUALITY

People

Physical Evidence

Learning Objectives

After reading this chapter, you should be able to

■ define what is meant by both productivity and quality in a service context

■ describe the relationship among customer expectations, service quality, and customer satisfaction

■ explain the gaps model of service quality

■ explain the techniques for identifying the root cause of specific problems

■ discuss productivity and quality measurement techniques

■ identify the components of a service quality information system

A.D. 2032: "Now All Restaurants Are Taco Bells"[1]

Taco Bell seems to have won a place in the hearts of American consumers by providing both value and quality in its 4,600 locations nationwide. The preceding quotation is from the movie *Demolition Man* (set in 2032), but already numerous Internet testimonials indicate that the company may now be an American icon—a coveted position in the ultra-competitive food service market. Moreover, Taco Bell Corp. is now the largest quick-service Mexican-style restaurant chain in the world.

How has a company that was barely a player 15 years ago managed to take such a significant bite out of the fast-food industry's profits? Changes in customers' tastes helped as Mexican cuisine went upscale and gained wider acceptance in the United States. But Taco Bell's expansion is due primarily to its new service strategy—offering the best *value* in fast meals whenever and wherever customers are hungry. Instead of focusing on preparing food (an operations-based approach), the company now defines its business as feeding hungry people (a customer-based approach).

When the company redesigned its competitive strategy in the late 1980s, Taco Bell's management decided that value had two components—quality and price—and that it should provide both to its customers. The first step was to understand how their customers defined quality. Taco Bell surveyed its best customers

in 1987 and 1989 to identify their expectations about fast-food restaurants. The results show that customers wanted FACT: food prepared *fast*, food orders filled *accurately*, food served in a *clean* environment, and food at the right *temperature*. Taco Bell used a statistical tool called conjoint analysis to predict the potential benefits of improving different FACT attributes to various levels, ranging from modest improvements to consistently perfect execution. The results allowed Taco Bell to analyze potential improvements and determine their estimated costs. The company then reengineered its service processes and retrained employees in order to provide its customers with high-quality, low-cost fast food.

Taco Bell plans to continue service "wherever customers are hungry." The company purchased the "fresh-mex" casual dining chain Chevy's in 1993 and is experimenting with several Border Bell restaurants, which offer quick service and a more upscale menu than conventional Taco Bells. It has also increased its presence with nontraditional outlets like mobile carts; kiosks; school lunch programs; and express units in airports, movie theaters, universities, and sports stadiums. If management's vision of having over 200,000 locations by 2003 becomes true, it may be able to claim that in the new millenium almost all restaurants are indeed Taco Bells.

MINDING THE SERVICE *P*s AND Q*s*

As you may have noticed already, productivity and quality are treated jointly in this book as one of the 8Ps of integrated service management. This reflects our belief—and that of others—that they are often two sides of the same coin. In fact, FedEx has even employed an internal slogan, $Q = P$.[2] If the two issues are totally divorced, companies risk introducing productivity efforts that will annoy customers or embarking on quality initiatives that will result in higher costs without increasing revenues. As you can see from Taco Bell's success, the strategic integration of both can provide greater value for customers and service providers. A focus on productivity and quality from the *customers' viewpoint* is critical to a firm's long-term financial success.[3]

Productivity and quality were historically seen as issues for operations managers. Thus, companies focused internally on making process "improvements" that were not necessarily linked to customers' service priorities. However, continuing efforts to understand and improve quality led back to the customer—and to the recognition that quality is customer defined. Relative to work in the manufacturing sector, research in service quality has always been strongly customer driven. In part, of course, this reflects the greater involvement of customers in service delivery systems (especially in people-processing services).

To a large extent, service-based definitions equate quality with customer satisfaction, as defined by the formula

$$\text{Satisfaction} = \frac{\text{Perceived service}}{\text{Expected service}}$$

The theory is quite simple. Service quality is the extent to which a service meets or exceeds customer expectations. If customers perceive the actual delivery of service as better than expected, they'll be happy; if it's below expectations, they'll be mad. And they'll judge quality according to their perceived level of satisfaction with the service. As you recall from chapter 4, customers' expectations play a significant role in all three stages of the purchase process for services. But what do customers expect, and where do their expectations come from?

CUSTOMER EXPECTATIONS

There is no single answer to the question of what customers expect from services, because they have different kinds of expectations about different kinds of services. For example, you would expect a visit to an accountant to talk about your tax returns to be very different from a visit to the veterinarian to get treatment for a sick pet. Customers also have different expectations about different service providers that are offering the same basic core benefits. Whereas they expect no-frills travel on Southwest Airlines, passengers would undoubtedly be very dissatisfied with that same level of service on a Singapore Airlines flight from San Francisco to Hong Kong. Because customer expectations tend to vary from service to service, service providers need to understand the expectations customers have of their specific service offerings.

How Are Expectations Formed?

When customers evaluate the quality of a service, they are judging it against some internal standard that existed before the service experience. This internal standard for judging quality is the basis for customer **expectations**.[4] People's expectations about services are most influenced by their own previous experiences as customers—with a particular service provider, with competing services in the same industry, or

expectations: internal standards that customers use to judge the quality of a service experience.

By promising attentive, personalized service in luxurious surroundings, Shangri-La advertising sets high customer expectations.

with related services in different industries. If they have no relevant personal experience, customers may base their prepurchase expectations on factors like word of mouth or advertising.

Over time, certain norms develop for what customers can expect from various service providers in a given industry. These norms are reinforced by both customer experience and company-controlled factors like advertising, pricing, and the appearance of the service facility and employees. For example, customers don't expect to be greeted by a doorman and a valet at a Super 8 Motel, but they certainly do at a Hilton. Different industries may also have their own norms for quality that affect customer expectations. In the United States, most customers expect extremely reliable service from utilities companies but have accepted less than perfect performance from their TV cable providers. Expectations may even vary among different demographic groups (e.g., between men and women, older and younger consumers, or blue- and white-collar workers). Moreover, expectations also differ from country to country (see the box on rating banking services, p. 90). For instance, although it may be acceptable for a train to arrive several hours late in Greece, rail schedules are so precise in Switzerland that the margin for error is measured in seconds.

Different Levels of Customer Expectations

Customer expectations involve several different elements, including desired service, adequate service, predicted service, and a zone of tolerance that falls between the desired and adequate service levels.[5] We briefly describe each of these elements, which form the model of customer expectations shown in Figure 5.1 (p. 90).

Desired and adequate service levels.   **Desired service** is the type of service customers hope to receive. It is a wished-for level of service—a combination of what customers believe can and should be delivered for their personal needs. Although

desired service: the wished-for level of service quality that a customer believes can and should be delivered.

DO GERMANS AND AMERICANS RATE THEIR BANKING SERVICES DIFFERENTLY?

A recent cross-cultural study tested the conventional wisdom that the United States is a much more customer-centered and service-oriented society than Germany. Researchers from both countries worked together to design a self-administered questionnaire that asked respondents to rate 26 different expectations about excellent service quality and to evaluate their own banks on these factors. Overall, Americans had higher expectations for banking services than did Germans. One of the biggest differences between the two groups was that Americans expected significantly more access to technologically based services like telephone banking. (This difference might be partly explained by the high price of telephone service in Germany, where local calls are as expensive as long distance rates in the United States.)

The U.S. customers ranked trust and friendliness as the two most important attributes of high-quality banking services, whereas Germans wanted competent investment advice and timely service delivery. Still, the two groups did agree on some things. Four of the five top-ranked expectations were the same for both countries, and both groups agreed that bank size, receiving promotional information by mail, and corporate social responsibility were low in importance.

Almost all customers, regardless of nationality, had higher expectations for service quality than their banks actually delivered. And in both countries, women had slightly higher expectations than men. However, the gap between expectations and performance was generally greater for Americans than for Germans. Even though Americans expected and received better banking service than their German counterparts, they reported a higher level of dissatisfaction. In this case, better service performance did not lead to increased perceptions of service quality—perhaps because it created even higher expectations.

Source: Excerpted from Terrence Witkowski and Joachim Kellner, "How Germans and Americans Rate Their Banking Services," *Marketing News*, 7 October 1996, 7. Also Allyson L. Stewart-Allen, "Customer Care: European Marketers Try to Catch Up with Service, Not Servitude, as a Strategic Option," *Marketing News*, 18 November 1996, 17.

adequate service: the minimum level of service that a customer will accept without being dissatisfied.

they would prefer to receive ideal service, customers do not usually have extravagant or unreasonable expectations. They understand that companies can't always deliver the best possible service. For this reason, they also have a lower level of expectations for acceptable service. This lower expectation level, called **adequate service**, is the minimum level of service customers will accept without being

FIGURE 5.1 **Factors That Influence Service Expectations**

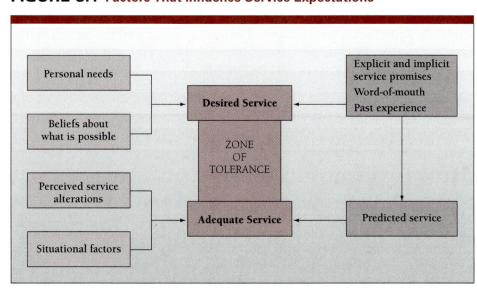

Source: Adapted from Valarie A. Zeithaml, Leonard A. Berry, and A. Parasuraman, "The Nature and Determinants of Customer Expectations of Service," *Journal of the Academy of Marketing Science* 21, no. 1 (1993): 1–12.

dissatisfied. Among the factors that help to set this expectation are the anticipated performance of perceived service alternatives and situational factors related to use of the service on a specific occasion. The levels of both desired and adequate service expectations may reflect both explicit and implicit service promises made by the provider, what the customer has heard through word of mouth, and past experience (if any) with this organization.

Customers have different desired levels of expectations across subcategories of services in an industry. For example, in the restaurant industry, customers expect different things from expensive restaurants than from fast-food establishments. Taco Bell discovered from its customer surveys that customers desired accurate orders prepared quickly and served at the right temperature in a clean environment. Whereas customers of a more upscale restaurant chain might value some of the same basic attributes, they will probably have additional expectations about the atmosphere, the behavior of service employees, and the way the food is presented. The adequate service level is likely to vary for businesses within the same subcategory. Thus, customers may expect a higher level of adequate service from a McDonalds than from, say, a Jack-in-the-Box if they've experienced more consistent service from McDonalds over time.

Predicted service.   **Predicted service** is the level of service customers actually expect to receive from the service provider during a particular service encounter. These estimates of anticipated service performance levels directly affect the customers' level of adequate service. If good service is predicted, the adequate level will be higher than if less optimal service is predicted. For example, if you visit the student health center during the winter, you probably expect to wait a long time to see a doctor because many people are likely to be sick; so a wait of 45 minutes may not fall below your adequate service level. However, on a warm spring afternoon you might be quite impatient if the wait is 20 minutes because you predicted that the health center would not be crowded.

predicted service: the level of service quality a customer believes a firm will actually deliver.

Zone of tolerance.   As we discussed in chapter 1, the inherent nature of services makes consistent service delivery difficult across employees in the same company and even by the same service employee from day to day. The extent to which customers are willing to accept this variation is called the **zone of tolerance**. As you can see from Figure 5.1, adequate service is the minimum level that is acceptable to customers. Service *below* this level will cause frustration and dissatisfaction. Service that rises *above* the desired service level will both please and surprise customers. Another way of looking at the zone of tolerance is to think of it as the range of service within which customers don't pay explicit attention to service performance. When service falls outside the range, customers will definitely react in either a positive or a negative way.

zone of tolerance: the range within which customers are willing to accept variations in service delivery.

The zone of tolerance can increase or decrease for individual customers depending on factors like competition, price, or importance of specific service attributes. These factors most often affect adequate service levels (which move up and down according to situational factors), whereas desired service levels tend to move up very slowly in response to accumulated experiences. For example, an airline passenger's ideal level of service may include being booked on the most direct flight possible to her destination. Now suppose she is traveling on a ticket that has been "purchased" with frequent flyer miles. Her ideal service level probably won't change, but her zone of tolerance for travel time and number of flight changes may increase because she is traveling for "free." Airlines know that passengers in these situations have lower adequate service thresholds and tend to book them accordingly.

UNDERSTANDING SERVICE QUALITY

service quality: customers' long-term, cognitive evaluations of a firm's service delivery.

customer satisfaction: a short-term emotional reaction to a specific service performance.

As you recall from chapter 3, customers compare what they expect to get with what they actually receive during the postpurchase stage of the service purchase process. They decide how satisfied they are with service delivery and outcomes, and they also make a judgment about service quality. Although **service quality** and **customer satisfaction** are related concepts, they are not exactly the same thing. Many researchers believe that customers' perceptions about quality are based on long-term, cognitive evaluations of a firm's service delivery, whereas customer satisfaction is a short-term emotional reaction to a specific service experience.[6]

Customers evaluate their levels of satisfaction or dissatisfaction after each encounter and use this information to update their perceptions of service quality, but attitudes about quality are not necessarily experience dependent. People often base quality judgments about services they have never consumed on word of mouth from acquaintances or on a firm's advertising campaign. However, customers must actually experience a service before they can be satisfied or dissatisfied with the outcome. Figure 5.2 shows the relationship among expectations, customer satisfaction, and service quality.

How Customers Evaluate Service Quality

quality gap: a discrepancy between a service provider's performance and customer expectations.

Before customers purchase a service, they have an expectation about service quality that is based on individual needs, past experiences, word-of-mouth recommendations, and a service provider's advertising. After buying and consuming the service, customers compare its expected quality with what they actually received (see Figure 5.2). Service performances that surprise and delight customers by falling above their desired service levels will be seen as superior in quality. If service delivery falls within their zone of tolerance, they will feel that it is adequate. But if actual quality falls below the adequate service level expected by customers, a discrepancy—or **quality gap**—has occurred between the service provider's performance and customer expectations. Gaps can occur during various parts of a service performance,[7] as shown in Figure 5.3.

FIGURE 5.2 **The Relationship Among Expectations, Customer Satisfaction, and Perceived Service Quality**

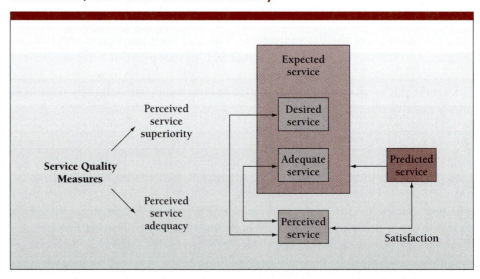

Source: Adapted from Valarie A. Zeithaml, Leonard L. Berry, and A. Parasuraman, "The Nature and Determinants of Customer Expectations of Service," *Journal of the Academy of Marketing Science* 21, no. 1 (1993): 1–12.

FIGURE 5.3 Seven Quality Gaps Leading to Customer Dissatisfaction

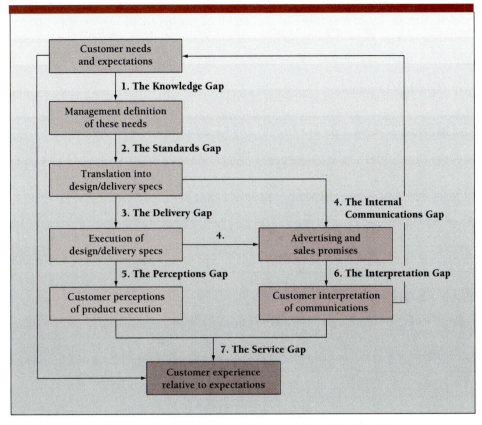

Source: Adapted from Christopher Lovelock, *Product Plus* (New York: McGraw-Hill, 1994), 112.

The service gap is the most critical, because it is the customer's overall assessment of what was expected compared to what was received. The ultimate goal in improving service quality is to narrow this gap as much as possible. To do so, service providers may have to reduce or close the six other gaps in Figure 5.3. The seven potential gaps in service quality are

1. *the knowledge gap*—the difference between what service providers believe customers expect and customers' actual needs and expectations

2. *the standards gap*—the difference between management's perceptions of customer expectations and the quality standards established for service delivery

3. *the delivery gap*—the difference between specified delivery standards and the service provider's actual performance

4. *the internal communications gap*—the difference between what the company's advertising and sales personnel think are the product's features, performance, and service quality level and what the company is actually able to deliver

5. *the perceptions gap*—the difference between what is actually delivered and what customers perceive they have received (because they are unable to accurately evaluate service quality)

6. *the interpretation gap*—the difference between what a service provider's communication efforts actually promise and what a customer thinks was promised by these communications

7. *the service gap*—the difference between what customers expect to receive and their perceptions of the service that is actually delivered

Any of the seven quality gaps can damage relationships with customers. Remember that service quality is a customer's overall attitude about service delivery, which is made up of a number of successful or unsuccessful service experiences. Avoiding service gaps in every service encounter will help a firm improve its reputation for quality service.

Five Quality Dimensions

Service gaps aren't the only ways in which customers judge service quality. They also use five broad dimensions as criteria:[8]

- *Reliability:* Is the company dependable in providing service as promised, over time?
- *Tangibles:* What do the service provider's physical facilities, equipment, personnel, and communication materials look like?
- *Responsiveness:* Are the firm's employees helpful and able to provide prompt service?
- *Assurance:* Are service employees knowledgeable, polite, competent, and trustworthy?
- *Empathy:* Does the service firm provide caring, personalized attention?

Of these five dimensions, reliability has consistently proven to be the most important factor in U.S. customers' judgments of service quality.[9] Reliability is at the heart of service quality because unreliable service is poor service in spite of its other attributes. If the core service is not performed reliably, customers may assume that the company is incompetent and switch to another service provider.

However, reliability poses some significant challenges for service firms. Because customers often enter the service factory and are involved in service production, they experience mistakes directly—often before a firm has an opportunity to correct them. Also, because many services are labor intensive, employees add a large degree of variability to the service production process that is not easily controlled by the service provider. A company's employees are different from one another in their personalities, skills, and attitudes, and the same employee can provide radically different service from one customer to the next, depending on situational factors like customer attitude and task complexity.

Although mistakes occur in every organization, many companies strive to minimize errors to provide greater service reliability for their customers. Leonard Berry describes how the Hard Rock Café Orlando addresses service reliability:

> Performing the service right the first time is a bedrock value at Hard Rock Café Orlando, the immensely successful restaurant chain and merchandise retailer. Hard Rock Café emphasizes "double checking" to minimize errors. The message of double checking is: *Perform the service carefully to avoid mistakes. If a mistake does occur, correct it before it reaches the customer.* Hard Rock Café implements double checking through two "extra" people in the kitchen. One is stationed inside the kitchen and the other at the kitchen counter. The inside person reviews everything that is going on, looking for signs of undercooked or overcooked meals, wilting lettuce, or any below-standard product or performance. The counter person, or "expediter," checks each prepared plate against the order ticket before the food is delivered to the table.[10]

Reliability is an outcome measure because customers judge it after the service experience. The service was either delivered as promised or it wasn't. The other four dimensions—tangibles, responsiveness, assurance, and empathy—are process dimensions because they can be evaluated by customers during service delivery. These dimensions provide companies with the opportunity to delight customers by exceeding their expectations during interactions with employees and the service environment. As we can see in Figure 5.2, exceeding customers' desired levels of expectations leads to positive perceptions of service quality.

Learning from Service Failures

Although every firm should plan for the need to implement effective service recovery (discussed in chapter 7), there's no substitute for doing it right the first time. In fact, there's a real danger in allowing excellent service recovery procedures to substitute for service reliability.[11] When a problem is caused by controllable, internal forces, there is no excuse for allowing it to recur—either from the customer's or the firm's standpoint—because recurring service failures can affect customers' perceptions of service quality and negatively affect service productivity. With prevention in mind, let's look briefly at some simple but powerful tools for monitoring quality and determining the root causes of service failures.

Among the many tools available to quality improvement specialists, the following four are particularly helpful for managers in identifying service failures and designing effective recovery strategies.

Flowcharts.   Flowcharts, introduced in chapter 4, are useful tools for thoroughly examining service delivery processes. Once managers understand these processes, it's easier for them to identify potential failure points, which are weak links in the chain. Knowing what can go wrong, and where, is an important first step in improving productivity and preventing service quality problems.

Control charts.   Control charts offer a simple method for graphing performance over time against specific quality criteria. Because the charts are visual, trends are easily identified. Figure 5.4 shows an airline's performance on the important criterion of on-time departures. The results suggest that this issue should be explored by management because departure performance is erratic and unsatisfactory.

control charts: charts that graph quantitative changes in service performance on a specific variable relative to a predefined standard.

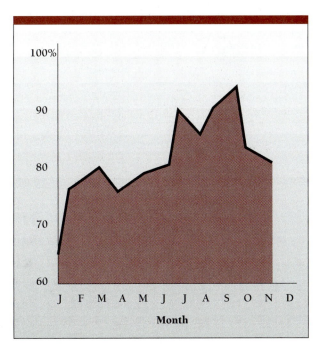

FIGURE 5.4
Control Chart
of Departure Delays
Showing Percentage
of Flights Departing
Within 15 Minutes
of Schedule

fishbone diagram: a chart-based technique that relates specific service problems to different categories of underlying causes (also known as a cause-and-effect chart).

Fishbone diagram.   The **fishbone diagram** (also called a cause-and-effect chart) was first developed by the Japanese quality expert Kaoru Ishikawa for use in manufacturing firms. To produce a fishbone diagram, groups of managers and employees brainstorm factors that might be causing a specific problem. The resulting factors are then categorized into one of five groupings—equipment, people, materials, procedures, and other. It's important to recognize, of course, that failures are often sequential, with one problem leading to another in a different category.

You notice that the fishbone diagram in Figure 5.5 includes eight rather than five groupings.[12] The extra categories are designed to provide additional information for service firms. For example, the People category has been changed to Front-Stage Personnel and Backstage Personnel. This highlights the fact that front-stage service problems are often experienced directly by customers, whereas backstage failures tend to show up more indirectly. "Information" has been split from "Procedures" because many service problems result from information-related failures. For an airline, for instance, inadequate information about flight departures may lead passengers to arrive late at the gate. The expanded fishbone diagram includes a new category—Customers—to acknowledge their increased involvement in service production and delivery.

As discussed before, customers of high-contact services are often heavily involved in front-stage operations. If they don't play their roles correctly, they may reduce service productivity and cause quality problems for themselves and other customers. For instance, an aircraft that seats hundreds of passengers can be delayed

FIGURE 5.5 **Cause-and-Effect Chart for Airline Departure Delays**

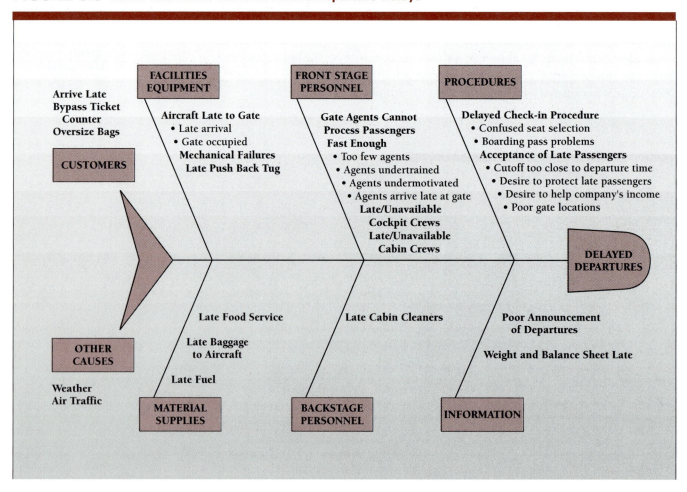

if a single traveler tries to board at the last minute with an oversized bag, which then has to be loaded into the cargo hold. Figure 5.5 displays 27 possible reasons for late departures of a passenger aircraft.

Pareto analysis.   The **Pareto analysis** (which was named after the Italian economist who first developed it) is useful in identifying the principal causes of observed outcomes. This technique often shows that approximately 80 percent of the value of one variable (in this instance, the number of service failures) is accounted for by only 20 percent of the causal variables (i.e., the number of possible causes). This phenomenon is often referred to as the 80/20 rule. In the airline example, 88 percent of the company's late-departing flights were caused by only four (15 percent) of all the possible causes. Thus, it would make sense for managers to focus on these four factors, rather than attempting to tackle all potential causes simultaneously—especially when time and other resources are limited.

Pareto analysis: an analytical procedure to identify what proportion of problem events are caused by each of several different factors.

CUSTOMER SATISFACTION

Customers experience various levels of satisfaction or dissatisfaction after each service experience according to the extent to which their expectations were met or exceeded. Because satisfaction is an emotional state, their postpurchase reactions can involve anger, dissatisfaction, irritation, neutrality, pleasure, or delight.

Satisfaction, Delight, and Loyalty

Obviously, angry or dissatisfied customers are troublesome because they may switch to another company and spread negative word of mouth. But is it sufficient just to satisfy a customer? After all, a firm might reason, products and services are rarely perfect and people are hard to please. Companies that take this approach may be asking for trouble because there is a lot of evidence that merely satisfying customers is not enough.[13] Marginally satisfied or neutral customers can be lured away by competitors. A delighted customer, however, is more likely to remain loyal in spite of attractive competitive offerings. Customer satisfaction plays an especially critical role in highly competitive industries, where there is a tremendous difference between the loyalty of merely satisfied and completely satisfied—or delighted—customers (see Figure 5.6, p. 98). For example, a study of retail banking customers showed that completely satisfied customers were nearly 42 percent more likely to be loyal than merely satisfied customers.

To improve its customer satisfaction levels, a company must first find out how satisfied or dissatisfied its current customers actually are. One common way of measuring satisfaction is to ask customers first to identify what factors are important in satisfying them and then to evaluate the performance of a service provider and its competitors on these factors. Many firms use a five-point scale to measure customer satisfaction, with the following format:

1 = very dissatisfied
2 = somewhat dissatisfied
3 = neutral
4 = somewhat satisfied
5 = very satisfied

The results of these satisfaction surveys can be used to estimate the number of loyal customers a firm has, as well as how many are at risk of defecting.

FIGURE 5.6 How the Competitive Environment Affects the Satisfaction-Loyalty Relationship

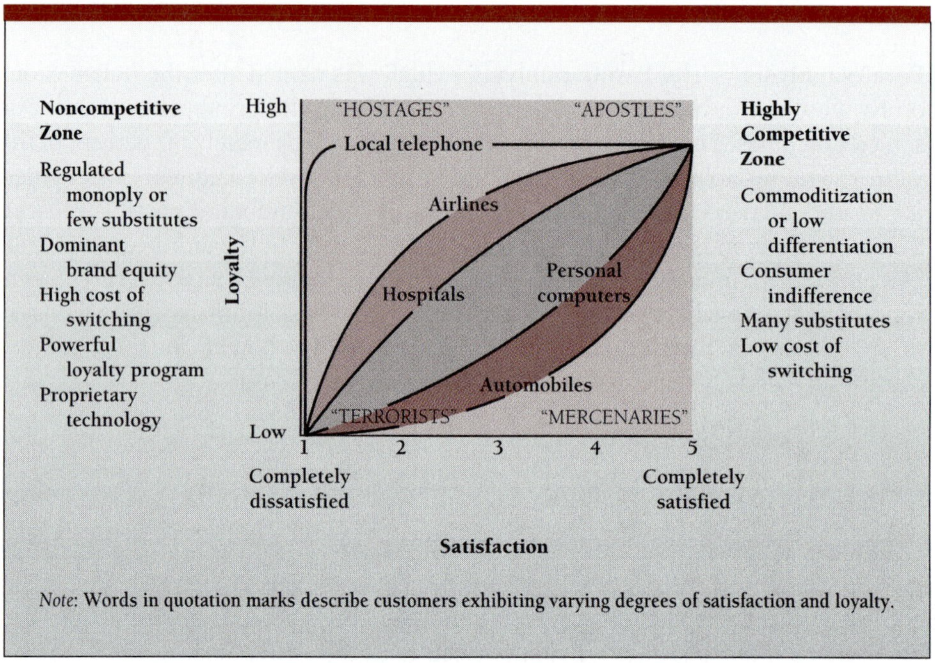

Note: Words in quotation marks describe customers exhibiting varying degrees of satisfaction and loyalty.

Source: Adapted and reprinted by permission of the *Harvard Business Review*. An exhibit from "Why Satisfied Customers Defect," by Thomas O. Jones and W. Earl Sasser, Jr., November–December 1995, 91. Copyright © 1995 by the President and Fellows of Harvard College; all rights reserved.

Figure 5.7 demonstrates that customers with satisfaction ratings of 0 to 3 are very likely to defect, whereas customers who rated their satisfaction as a 4 are somewhat indifferent and can be lured away by a competing service. Only customers with a satisfaction rating of 5 are absolutely loyal. At the extremes of the scale are two customer groups with particular significance to service providers: "terrorists" and "apostles." Terrorists are every company's nightmare. They don't just defect; they make sure that everyone else shares their anger and frustration, too. These customers had a bad experience that was never corrected by the company, and they are dedicated to spreading as much negative word of mouth as possible. In contrast, the apostle is the kind of customer every service provider dreams of. Apostles are customers who are so satisfied with their service experiences, whose expectations have been so far exceeded, that they feel compelled to share their enthusiasm with others. They are extremely loyal, and their obvious delight helps attract other customers. Creating apostles and eliminating terrorists should be a key goal for every service provider.[14]

Using Customer Satisfaction Information

Once a company has gathered satisfaction data from its customers, the next step is to decide on the most appropriate strategies for increasing satisfaction levels. If most of the satisfaction ratings fall in the 2–3 range, there is probably a problem with the firm's delivery of the core service—which is the basic package of benefits that customers expect every business in an industry to be able to provide. These are the do-or-die elements that we talked about in chapter 4, and they often change as customer expectations increase, competitive offerings improve, or new competitors enter the market. The solution for problems here is to make sure that a firm's basic product meets customer-defined industry standards.

FIGURE 5.7 *"Apostles" and "Terrorists" on the Satisfaction-Loyalty Curve*

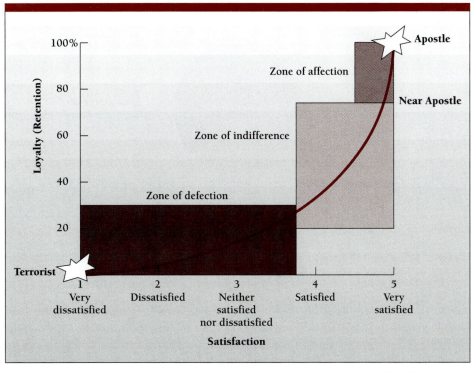

Source: James L. Heshett, W. Earl Sasser, Jr., and Leonard A. Schlesinger, *The Service Profit Chain* (New York: Free Press, 1997), 87.

Neutral or satisfied customers (the 3s and 4s) are probably happy with the core service but would like to have a consistent set of supplementary services that make the basic product more effective or easier to use (see chapter 8). These include both the do-and-decline and match-'em elements described in chapter 4. Companies should also have responsive service recovery processes in place so that when problems do occur, customers don't slide into the dissatisfied category. Service providers with a high proportion of neutral and satisfied customers need to increase their range of supporting services and develop proactive recovery strategies to correct problems that occur during service delivery.

Completely satisfied customers believe that a company thoroughly understands and addresses their own personal preferences, needs, expectations, and problems. Service providers whose customer satisfaction ratings are 5s have obviously listened carefully to their customers and, as a result, have been able to incorporate a significant number of beat-'em elements into their core offering (see chapter 4). Because beat-'em elements can easily turn into match-'em elements if they are copied by competitors, companies must continually listen to customers and find new ways to delight them.

Benefits of Customer Satisfaction

Although every successful marketer wants to provide a service that satisfies customers, this isn't the only goal. Companies can't lose sight of other basic business goals such as achieving a competitive advantage or making a profit. As Figure 5.8 (p. 100) shows, customer satisfaction provides many benefits for a firm, and higher levels of customer satisfaction lead to greater customer loyalty. In the long run, it is more profitable to keep good customers than to constantly attract and develop new customers to replace the ones who leave. Highly satisfied customers spread positive

FIGURE 5.8 Benefits of Customer Satisfaction and Service Quality

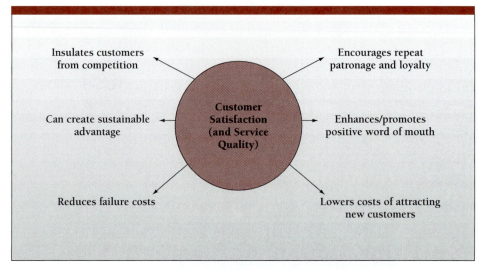

Source: C. H. Lovelock, P. G. Patterson, and R. H. Waller, *Services Marketing: Australia and New Zealand* (Sydney: Prentice Hall, 1998), 119.

word of mouth and in effect become a walking, talking advertisement for a firm, which lowers the cost of attracting new customers. This is particularly important for professional service providers (like dentists, lawyers, engineers, or accountants), because reputation and word of mouth are key information sources for new clients.[15]

High satisfaction is an insurance policy against something going wrong, which it inevitability will because of the variability associated with service production. Long-term customers are more forgiving in these situations because an occasional bad experience will be offset by previous positive ones, and satisfied customers are less susceptible to competitors' offerings. It is no wonder that companies have become obsessed with customer satisfaction, given its direct link to customer retention, market share, and profits.

Return on Quality

return on quality: the financial return obtained from investing in service quality improvements.

Because many strategies to improve customer satisfaction are costly to design and implement, companies need to decide which quality improvement efforts will provide the greatest financial returns. This investment-oriented approach is called **return on quality** (ROQ).[16] A company's research and complaint data may show that some quality defects are much more important to customers than others, and some defects cost more money to fix than others. Moreover, not all quality improvement efforts will necessarily pay for themselves. An ROQ approach can help a firm set priorities based on investing resources to fix those defects that will subsequently yield the best financial returns. The objective should be to undertake a systematic method for rank-ordering quality improvement efforts according to their anticipated financial return.

Building a Quality Information System

Organizations that are known for providing excellent service quality are good at listening to both their customers and their front-line employees. To do this effectively, companies need to create an ongoing service research process that provides managers with useful, timely data. As Leonard Berry says in *On Great Service*, "Companies need to build a service quality information system, not just do a study.

Conducting a service quality study is analogous to taking a snapshot. Deeper insight and an understanding of the pattern of change come from an ongoing series of snapshots taken of various subject matter from many angles."[17]

Berry recommends that ongoing research should be conducted through a portfolio of research techniques that make up a firm's **service quality information system**. Possible approaches include

- transactional surveys
- total market surveys
- mystery shopping
- new, declining, and former customer surveys
- focus group interviews
- employee field reporting

service quality information system: an ongoing service research process that provides timely, useful data to managers about customer satisfaction, expectations, and perceptions of quality.

Transactional surveys.   Transactional surveys are designed to measure customer satisfaction and perceptions about service experiences while they are still fresh in the customer's mind. These surveys are conducted right after a service encounter or within a few days.[18] Many service businesses, including hotels and restaurants, have questionnaires at their service sites for customers to complete. Some companies even provide incentives for customers to complete the surveys. For example, the Olive Garden restaurant sometimes gives customers a discount on their next meal if they complete the customer satisfaction survey that is provided with every bill. Some service providers collect these data electronically. Customers at Einstein's Bagels can use a touch-activated screen that is located at the entrance to record their impressions of service quality.

Total market surveys.   The purpose of total market surveys is to measure customers' overall evaluations of service quality. Because these evaluations are the result of customers' accumulated experience over time (and because this type of data collection is costly), these surveys are administered less frequently than transactional surveys. A wide range of information should be collected, including customers' service expectations and perceptions, the relative importance of the service dimensions discussed earlier, and customers' behavioral intentions about repurchasing and making positive recommendations about a firm's service to others. Companies can also use total market surveys to measure competitors' service quality. However, they will need to sample both customers and noncustomers to get an accurate picture of their competitive position.

Marketers sometimes use a tool called **SERVQUAL**[19] to gather this type of information from customers (see the box on the SERVQUAL scale, p. 102). Customers are asked to complete a series of scales that measure their expectations of a particular company on a wide array of specific service characteristics, including aspects of the five quality dimensions. They then record their perceptions of actual service performance on these same characteristics. When perceived performance ratings are lower than expectations, it is a sign of poor quality; the reverse indicates good quality.

SERVQUAL: a standardized 22-item scale that measures expectations and perceptions about critical quality dimensions.

Mystery shopping.   Mystery shoppers are people who are hired by a company to pose as ordinary customers. During their unannounced visits to service sites, they observe both the physical environment and the interactions between customers and employees. One advantage of this technique is that it provides feedback on the performance of individual service employees. This information can be used to reward exceptional performance, as well as to identify employees who could benefit from additional training or coaching. Companies like Au Bon Pain and Safeway use mystery shopping regularly to improve their customer service.

THE SERVQUAL SCALE

The SERVQUAL scale includes five dimensions: tangibles, reliability, responsiveness, assurance, and empathy. Within each dimension are several items measured on a seven-point scale from *strongly agree* to *strongly disagree*, for a total of 22 items.

SERVQUAL Questions

Note: For actual survey respondents, instructions are also included and each statement is accompanied by a seven-point scale ranging from "strongly agree = 7" to "strongly disagree = 1." Only the end points of the scale are labeled—there are no words above the numbers 2 through 6.

TANGIBLES

- Excellent banks [refer to cable TV companies, hospitals, or the appropriate service business throughout the questionnaire] will have modern-looking equipment.
- The physical facilities at excellent banks will be visually appealing.
- Employees at excellent banks will be neat in appearance.
- Materials associated with the service (like brochures or statements) will be visually appealing in an excellent bank.

RELIABILITY

- When excellent banks promise to do something by a certain time, they will do so.
- When customers have a problem, excellent banks will show a sincere interest in solving it.
- Excellent banks will perform the service right the first time.
- Excellent banks will provide their services at the time they promise to do so.
- Excellent banks will insist on error-free records.

RESPONSIVENESS

- Employees of excellent banks will tell customers exactly when service will be performed.
- Employees of excellent banks will give prompt service to customers.
- Employees of excellent banks will always be willing to help customers.
- Employees of excellent banks will never be too busy to respond to customer requests.

ASSURANCE

- The behavior of employees of excellent banks will instill confidence in customers.
- Customers of excellent banks will feel safe in their transactions.
- Employees of excellent banks will be consistently courteous with customers.
- Employees of excellent banks will have the knowledge to answer customer questions.

EMPATHY

- Excellent banks will give customers individual attention.
- Excellent banks will have operating hours convenient to all their customers.
- Excellent banks will have employees who give customers personal attention.
- The employees of excellent banks will understand the specific needs of their customers.

Adapted from A. Parasuraman, Valarie A. Zeithaml, and Leonard Berry, "SERVQUAL: A Multiple Item Scale for Measuring Consumer Perceptions of Service Quality," *Journal of Retailing* 64 (1988); 12–40.

Service providers should be sensitive to employees' feelings when using this approach, because employees often feel that mystery shoppers are spying on them. Tips for making mystery shopping successful include letting employees know what criteria they are being judged on and evaluating service quality over a series of visits rather than by a single encounter. For example, Au Bon Pain posts its criteria for service quality in each store, along with a list of employees who have received outstanding scores from mystery shoppers.

New, declining, and former customer surveys. Asking former customers why they left can provide helpful—if sobering information—about areas where a firm's service quality is deficient. Surveys that monitor declining patronage can identify why customers are buying fewer services and may predict future customer defections. And new customers can provide information about what attracted them to a specific service provider, including the impact of the firm's reputation and marketing communications. Thus, these surveys are very useful in pointing out the profit effect of service quality.

Surveys of new, declining, or former customers are easiest to do in businesses in which customers use the service on a fairly regular basis and sales transactions are recorded at the individual customer level. For instance, Safeway supermarkets will be able to do this type of research by using their newly introduced "membership" cards to electronically track each customer's purchases over time. Since customer-contact data are collected when customers apply for the card, Safeway can easily contact new, declining, or former customers. The company can also use the membership card to reward loyal customers with special discounts and cash rebates.

Focus group interviews. Focus group interviews involve questioning a group of representative customers about a specific topic or issue. The interviews, which typically last several hours, are done by trained moderators, who keep the participants—typically, six to ten in number—on task. Focus groups are particularly useful ways to get in-depth information about service problems and to identify possible solutions. They can also be used to find out what criteria customers use to evaluate service quality or to get feedback about a new service idea. These data should not be projected onto an entire market segment, however, without additional quantitative research.

Whereas most focus group research involves face-to-face conversations with participants, a few companies have gone high-tech. For example, the cable network Nickelodeon conducts on-line focus groups with 8- to 12-year-old-viewers to gather their reactions to its programming and marketing. The company says the electronic focus groups provide faster, cheaper data than traditional methods but warns that other market research techniques should also be used.[20]

Employee field reporting. Whereas most service quality data are collected from customers, a firm's employees can also be a valuable source of qualitative information. Employee field reporting is a systematic method for finding out what employees learn from their interactions with customers and their direct observations of customer behavior. Data can be collected from employees through written surveys, telephone interviews, or focus groups. Employees can also record critical incidents that occur during service encounters (a technique discussed in chapter 2). For example, employees in a dentist's office can be asked to record patients' reactions to all aspects of the service, including the physical environment, new equipment, or personal interactions.

PRODUCTIVITY ISSUES FOR SERVICE FIRMS

As mentioned at the beginning of this chapter, a key challenge for any service business is to improve service quality for its customers in cost-effective ways. This means that service providers must try to increase productivity in ways that won't have a

Telecommunications allow researchers in one country to watch a live transmission of a focus group being conducted in another part of the world.

inputs: all resources (labor, materials, energy, and capital) required to create service offerings.

outputs: the final outcomes of the service delivery process as perceived and valued by customers.

negative impact on customer satisfaction or perceived quality. But what *is* productivity? Simply defined, productivity measures how efficiently a company can transform **inputs** into **outputs**. Inputs vary according to the nature of the business but may include labor (both physical and intellectual), materials, energy, and capital (land, buildings, equipment, information systems, and financial assets). Service outputs are the final outcomes of the service delivery process as perceived and valued by customers.

Measuring Service Productivity

The intangible nature of service performances often makes it difficult to measure the productivity of service industries. The measurement task is perhaps the most straightforward in possession-processing services because many are quasi-manufacturing organizations, performing routine tasks with easily measurable inputs and outputs. Examples include quick-service garages, which change a car's oil and rotate its tires, or fast-food restaurants, which offer limited and simple menus. But the task is more complicated when the customer's automobile has an engine problem, or when the restaurant in question is famous for its varied and exotic cuisine.

In a people-processing service, such as a hospital, we can look at the number of patients treated in the course of a year and at the hospital's census, or average bed occupancy. But how do we account for the different types of procedures performed—removal of cancerous tumors, treatment of diabetes, or setting of broken bones—and the almost inevitable variability between one patient and another? And how do we evaluate the difference in service outcomes? Some patients get better, some develop complications, and some never recover. There are relatively few standardized procedures in medicine that offer highly predictable outcomes.

Consider information-based services. How should we define the output of a bank or a consulting firm? And how does an architect's output compare to a lawyer's?

Some lawyers like to boast about their billable hours, but what were they actually doing during those hours and how do we measure their output, as opposed to their fees? It's alleged that some lawyers contrive to bill for more than 24 hours of work per day, but is that really an accurate indication of productivity?

Finally, measuring productivity is also a challenge for mental stimulus services like education. Many universities are under pressure to document outputs, and they have been struggling with how to measure the hours professors spend preparing for class, interacting with students, providing service to the university and the community, and contributing to their professional fields. And how do colleges (or their graduates) quantify the value of a college degree? Or the value of a good professor versus a mediocre one?

Thus, variability is a major problem in measuring service productivity, and traditional measures of service output tend to ignore variations in the quality or value of a service. In freight transportation, for instance, a ton-mile of output for freight that is delivered late is treated the same for productivity purposes as a similar shipment delivered on time.[21] Another approach, counting the number of customers served per unit of time, suffers from the same shortcoming. What happens when an increase in the speed with which customers are served is achieved at the expense of perceived quality? Suppose a haircutter serves three customers per hour and finds she can increase her output to four—giving what is technically just as good a haircut—by using a faster but noisier hair dryer, eliminating all conversation, and rushing through the process. Even if the haircut is just as good, her customers may rate the overall service experience less positively because it did not meet their expectations of an adequate level of service on multiple dimensions.

Productivity and Customer Satisfaction[22]

The "productive" hairdresser just described illustrates an important issue for service providers. Although many companies would like to increase both productivity and quality, the two are not always compatible. Managers may have to make trade-offs between quantity and quality, especially when customer satisfaction depends on customized service provided directly by employees. High levels of productivity and customer satisfaction are most profitable—and most possible—for such companies as mail-order firms, clothing stores, and fast-food restaurants, which provide a mixture of goods and services to customers in a fairly standardized way. For example, Taco Bell was very successful in making productivity improvements that added to customer satisfaction and had an extremely positive impact on profitability.

However, for companies whose outputs are more intangible—like airlines, banks, and charter travel agencies—the greatest profits are associated with higher customer satisfaction and relatively lower productivity. Thus, for more customized services, the primary focus should be on increasing customer satisfaction. Firms should make productivity improvements only if they are sure that the changes will not negatively affect customers' perceptions of service quality.

Unfortunately, many attempts to improve service productivity tend to center on efforts to eliminate waste and reduce labor costs. Cutbacks in front-stage staffing mean either that the remaining employees have to work harder and faster or that there are insufficient personnel to serve customers promptly at busy times. Although employees may be able to work faster for a brief period of time, few can maintain a rapid pace for extended periods. They become exhausted, make mistakes, and treat customers in a disinterested way. Workers who are trying to do two or three things at once (e.g., serving a customer face to face while simultaneously answering the telephone and sorting papers) may do a poor job on each task. Excessive

WHEN PRODUCTIVITY IMPROVEMENT CLASHED WITH SERVICE QUALITY AT UPS

Even successful firms like United Parcel Service (UPS) have had customer service decline because of the implementation of internal productivity improvement strategies that were not directly linked to customer priorities. For example, UPS made an assumption that on-time delivery was the most important service feature for its customers. The company did time-and-motion studies to see how delivery processes could be made more efficient and pushed its workers to meet demanding delivery schedules. Much to its surprise, UPS discovered from its customer satisfaction surveys that customers actually wanted more interaction time with its drivers. After performing a return-on-quality analysis, the company designed a program to allow drivers to spend more time with customers by relaxing delivery schedules and hiring more drivers. Drivers received a small bonus for any sales leads they generated. Cost estimates for the first year were $4.2 million, which was quickly offset by over $10 million in additional revenues.

Source: From David L. Kurtz and Kenneth E. Clow, *Services Marketing* (New York: Wiley, 1998), 122.

pressure to improve productivity breeds discontent and frustration among all employees, but it is especially difficult for customer-contact personnel, who are caught between trying to meet customer needs and attempting to achieve management's productivity goals (see the box on service quality at UPS).

Sometimes companies can use technology to streamline service processes in a way that reduces costs and satisfies customers. For example, cost cutting was a very important issue for Taco Bell because its strategy relied on providing customers with high-quality, low-priced fast food. The company's "value menu" pricing meant that profit margins were reduced. Cost cutting was mandatory, but what should be cut? Because improved customer service was an important part of the new strategy, Taco Bell couldn't easily improve productivity by decreasing its labor costs. Instead, it embarked on an approach called "K-minus" (*K* stands for *kitchen*). By using technology to reduce the labor intensity of food preparation, outsourcing some of the most time-intensive chores, and turning restaurant kitchens into strictly food assembly areas, Taco Bell was able to shrink the average kitchen size by 40 percent. Its restaurants moved from 70 percent kitchen and 30 percent dining to 70 percent dining and 30 percent kitchen, freeing both space and employees to serve customers. These dramatic changes significantly reduced operating costs, and customer waiting time decreased more than 70 percent!

We discuss some additional approaches to improving productivity—including involving customers more actively in service production; changing the timing of customer demand; and using intermediaries to handle tasks like reservations, billing, and payment—in greater detail in later chapters.

Conclusion

Service providers can't afford to separate productivity improvement from quality improvement. If the two issues are totally divorced, operations managers may launch productivity efforts that will degrade the service received by customers, and marketing managers may introduce service quality programs that complicate operations, raise costs, and hurt profits. Successful firms base their efforts to improve quality on understanding customers' expectations relative to different quality dimensions and analysis of service quality gaps that can lead to dissatisfaction. When things go wrong, they seek the underlying causes and try to prevent a recurrence. Their efforts to innovate often center on new approaches that will enhance productivity and quality simultaneously.

Firms that succeed in providing high-quality service are good at listening to both their customers and their employees, especially those in direct contact with customers. They build information systems that use a variety of research techniques to measure customer satisfaction and the quality of service delivered. Measuring productivity, however, can be difficult because of the intangible nature of service performances. Unfortunately, many traditional measures of service output ignore variations in the quality of service delivered and its perceived value to customers.

Study Questions and Exercises

1. Define customer expectations and describe where they come from.
2. Discuss the three different levels of expectations. How are they related to a customer's zone of tolerance?
3. Explain the difference between service quality and customer satisfaction.
4. Identify the seven gaps that can occur in service quality. What do you think service marketers can do to prevent each of these gaps?
5. What are the five dimensions customers use in evaluating service quality?
6. Explain the elements of a service quality information system and give examples of each element.
7. How can firms learn from service failures?
8. Define productivity. Why is it hard to measure in services?
9. Why is productivity a more difficult issue for services than for many manufactured goods? Explain the relationship between productivity and quality.

Six

Managing Relationships and Building Customer Loyalty

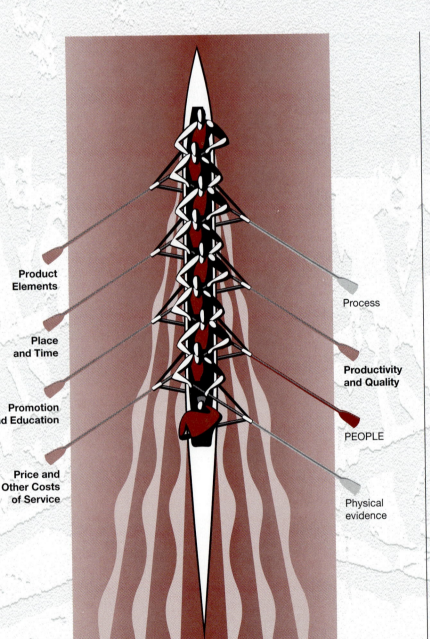

Product Elements

Place and Time

Promotion and Education

Price and Other Costs of Service

Process

Productivity and Quality

PEOPLE

Physical evidence

Learning Objectives

After reading this chapter, you should be able to

- recall the principles of segmentation, particularly as they relate to customer behavior

- understand the bases by which firms can set priorities for targeting specific segments

- understand why capacity-constrained firms need to target multiple market segments

- recognize that not all customers are attractive to a specific organization and consider strategies for dealing with abusive behavior

- calculate the value of a customer who remains loyal and recognize the role that loyalty plays in determining financial success

- develop ideas for creating customer loyalty programs

Creating a Formula for Success in Ski Resorts[1]

Soaring high in the Coast Mountain range of the Canadian province of British Columbia, Whistler and Blackholm ski resorts receive an average of some 30 feet (9 meters) of snow each year and claim to offer the longest ski season and largest skiable terrain in North America. The twin resorts are owned by Vancouver-based Intrawest Corporation, whose other ski properties include Mammoth in California, Copper Mountain in Colorado, Stratton in Vermont, and Mont Tremblant in Quebec.

Whistler and Blackcomb, located 75 miles (120 km) northeast of Vancouver, offer the greatest vertical drop of any ski mountains in North America—no less than 1 mile (1,600 m). Dayskiers from Vancouver and its suburbs have long ceased to be Whistler and Blackholm's only source of business, although the resort still courts their loyalty with big savings on season passes. By creating a major destination resort, Intrawest has been able to appeal to vacationers from across the continent and even overseas.

Whistler's appeal is evident from the fact that it has been named the number one ski resort on the North American continent by three different ski magazines. Intrawest's management believes that it has created a formula for success that can be transferred to other ski resorts.

Their multistep process begins with enhancing the skiing experience on each mountain. To keep skiers loyal, the experience on the slopes must be a good one, requiring a choice of well-maintained terrain that will satisfy all skiers, from beginners to experts, plus sufficient lift capacity to avoid lengthy delays. The second step is to build an attractive and animated resort community so that people will want to stay longer. For many people, après-ski activities are part of the appeal of a skiing vacation. Satisfied skiers not only come back more often but also tell their friends and spend more money. Higher patronage justifies the third step, which is construction of more lodging and additional attractions, drawing yet more people to the resort. Now in the fourth stage, Intrawest is expanding year-round facilities, thus maximizing the use of shops, hotels, convention facilities, and restaurants. By this point, the resort is appealing to nonskiers as well.

The purchase of a condominium or chalet at a resort tends to bring owners back more often throughout the year, even when there is no snow. After all, the mountains are lovely in summer and fall, as well as in winter and early spring, when there is snow on the slopes. The resort operators can also manage properties on behalf of their owners, who derive income from renting to other visitors.

Maintaining the quality of a ski resort requires ongoing investment. Because of inexpensive airfares, skiers can choose between many different resorts for their vacations; and their expectations—which have been rising in recent years—tend to be shaped by the best facilities they have experienced, heard about from their friends, seen on television, or read about in magazines. In 1997, Intrawest spent $16 million to improve facilities at Whistler and Blackholm. Investments included replacing old chair lifts by new express quads to improve reliability, reduce waiting time, and increase lift capacity. A wide range of new trails was opened at Blackholm. Recognizing the growing popularity of snowboarding, the company also purchased a new Pipe Dragon, a unique machine used to shape and groom snowboard half-pipes. Other investments include the purchase of new snow cats for trail grooming and upgrades in snowmaking equipment to ensure good skiing conditions, even on days when Mother Nature is not cooperative. To appeal to summer visitors, investments are also being made in an expanded trail system for the Whistler Mountain Bike Park.

Finally, recognizing the importance of attracting and retaining loyal employees—who form an important element in creating visitor satisfaction—the company plans to construct numerous units of employee housing at the resort.

TARGETING THE RIGHT CUSTOMERS

mass customization: offering a service with some individualized product elements to a large number of customers at a relatively low price.

market segmentation: the process of dividing a market into different groups within which all customers share relevant characteristics that distinguish them from customers in other segments.

segment: a group of current and prospective customers who share common characteristics, needs, purchasing behavior, or consumption patterns.

We hear the term *mass marketing* less and less these days. Instead the talk is of *focus* or *targeting* or **mass customization**. Underlying such terms is the notion of **market segmentation**. More and more firms are trying to decide which types of customers they can serve well and make loyal, rather than trying to be all things to all people. Intrawest targets customers who will not only enjoy the skiing experience that it offers but can also afford this relatively expensive sport. The company is not alone in recognizing the need for ongoing investments. Managers in innovative service firms constantly debate what improvements in product elements—or entirely new services—they need to attract and retain customers in specific segments that are believed to present good opportunities for growth and profits. Market segmentation is a key concept in marketing and is usually a central topic in introductory marketing courses, so if you have not previously taken such a course, please review the key aspects of segmentation in the boxed review that follows.

Whistler Resort would not have grown to its present size if it had continued to rely solely on visitors from nearby Vancouver, which is close enough to allow residents to make an easy day trip to the slopes. Its carefully phased growth is designed to attract vacationers who will spend a week or more. Today, it has even reached the point where it can attract nonskiers in winter and summer alike. Few service businesses can survive by serving just a single **segment**, especially if they have a lot of capacity to fill.

Airbone skier at Whistler.

In this chapter, we emphasize the importance of choosing to serve a mix—or portfolio—of several carefully chosen **target segments** and taking pains to build and maintain their loyalty. We also note that not all segments are worth serving, and it may not be realistic to try to retain them. One researcher makes this point nicely in a discussion of banking:

> A bank's population of customers undoubtedly contains individuals who either cannot be satisfied, given the service levels and pricing the bank is capable of offering, or will never be profitable, given their banking activity (their use of resources relative to the revenue they supply). Any bank would be wise to target and serve only those customers whose needs it can meet better than its competitors in a profitable manner. These are the customers who are most likely to remain with that bank for long periods, who will purchase multiple products and services, who will recommend that bank to their friends and relations, and who may be the source of superior returns to the bank's shareholders.[2]

Even when customers fit the desired profile, a few of them may prove, through their undesirable behavior, to be candidates for prompt termination rather than retention. Although slogans claim that the customer is always right, this is not true in every instance. We address this issue in more depth later in the chapter.

target segment: a segment selected because its needs and other characteristics fit well with a specific firm's goals and capabilities.

Searching for Value, Not Just Numbers

Too many service firms still focus on the *number* of customers they serve—an important issue for operations and human resource planning—without giving sufficient attention to the *value* of each customer. Generally speaking, heavy users, who buy more frequently and in larger volumes, are more profitable than occasional users. Think about the activities that you do on a regular basis. Do you have a favorite restaurant or pizza parlor where you often eat with friends or family? Is there a movie theater that you patronize regularly? Do you ride a bus or train to work or college every weekday? Are you often to be seen at your local laundromat?

If you answered yes to any of these questions, you are probably a lot more interesting to the management of these different organizations than a one-time visitor who is just passing through town. The revenue stream from your purchases—and those of others like you—may amount to quite a considerable sum over the course of the year (go ahead, figure it out). Sometimes your value as a frequent user is openly recognized and appreciated; you sense that the business is tailoring its service features, including schedules and prices, to attract people like you and is doing its best to make you loyal. In other instances, however, you may feel that nobody in the organization knows or cares who you are. You may be a valuable customer, but you certainly don't feel valued.

Matching customers to the firm's capabilities is vital. Managers must think carefully about how customer needs relate to such operational elements as speed and quality, when service is available, the firm's capacity to serve many customers simultaneously, and the physical features and appearance of service facilities. They also need to consider how well their service personnel can meet the expectations of specific types of customers in terms of both personal style and technical competence. Finally, they need to ask themselves, Can my company match or exceed competing services that are directed at the same types of customers?

Relationship Marketing

Traditionally, marketing has overemphasized attraction of new customers. But well-managed organizations work hard to retain their existing customers and increase their levels of spending. A widely circulated statement is that on average it costs a

REVIEW OF PRINCIPLES OF MARKET SEGMENTATION

Market segmentation is central to almost any professionally planned and executed marketing program. The concept of segmentation recognizes that customers and prospects within a market vary across several dimensions and that not every segment constitutes a desirable target for the firm's marketing efforts.

Market Segments

A segment is made up of a group of current and potential customers who share common characteristics, needs, purchasing behavior, or consumption patterns. Effective segmentation should group buyers into segments in ways that result in as much similarity as possible on the relevant characteristics *within* each segment but dissimilarity on those same characteristics *between* each segment. Two broad categories of variables are useful in describing the differences between segments. The first have to do with user characteristics, the second with usage behavior.

User characteristics may vary from one person to another, reflecting demographic characteristics (for instance, age, income, and education), geographic location, and psychographics (the attitudes, values, lifestyles, and opinions of decision makers and users). Another important variable is the specific benefits that individuals and corporate purchasers seek from a particular good or service.

Usage behavior relates to how a product is purchased and used, including when and where the purchase and consumption take place; the quantities consumed (heavy users are always of particular interest to marketers); the frequency and purpose of use; the occasions in which consumption takes place (sometimes referred to as occasion segmentation); and sensitivity to such marketing variables as advertising, pricing, speed and other service features, and availability of alternative delivery systems.

Target Segment

After evaluating different segments in the market, a firm should focus its marketing efforts by targeting one or more segments that fit well with the firm's capabilities and goals. Target segments are often defined on the basis of several variables. For instance, a hotel in a particular city might target prospective guests who shared such user characteristics as (1) traveling on business (demographic segmentation), (2) visiting clients within a defined area around the hotel (geographic segmentation), and (3) willing to pay a certain daily room rate (user response).

Issues for Research

When studying the marketplace, service marketers should be looking for answers to such questions as these:

- In what useful ways can the market for our firm's service be segmented?
- What are the needs of the specific segments that we have identified?
- Which of these segments best fits both our institutional mission and our current operational capabilities?
- What do customers in each segment see as our firm's competitive advantages and disadvantages? Are the latter correctable?
- In the light of this analysis, which specific segment(s) should we target?
- How should we differentiate our marketing efforts from those of the competition to attract and retain the types of customers that we want?
- What is the long-term financial value to us of a loyal customer in each of the segments that we currently serve (and those that we would like to serve)?
- How should our firm build long-term relationships with customers from the target segments? And what strategies are needed to create long-term loyalty?

firm five to six times as much to attract a new customer as it does to implement retention strategies to hold an existing one.[3]

Relationship marketing involves activities aimed at developing long-term, cost-effective links between an organization and its customers for the mutual benefit of both parties. Service firms can use a variety of strategies to maintain and enhance relationships, including such basic ones as treating customers fairly, offering service augmentations, and treating each customer as though he or she were a segment of one—the essence of mass customization.[4] Service extras often play a key role in building and

relationship marketing: activities aimed at developing long-term, cost-effective links between an organization and its customers for the mutual benefit of both parties.

ATTRACTING OLDER PASSENGERS AT SOUTHWEST AIRLINES

Like most airlines, Southwest Airlines's passengers can be divided into two broad groups: business travelers and leisure travelers. Although business travelers fly far more frequently than most leisure travelers, the latter help fill the aircraft outside commuting hours and enable Southwest to offer more frequent service at lower prices. A significant target segment within the broad leisure group is older customers, who are growing in numbers as the population ages and has the time and inclination to travel—and can afford to do so at Southwest's very low fares.

However, many senior citizens are not experienced flyers. In fact, some have never flown before in their lives. To encourage these people to fly, Southwest has created a brochure titled "Travel Tips for Seniors" (see the reproduced cover), which is educational in nature rather than promotional. It begins by pointing out that the airline offers special fares to people aged 65 and older, then continues with bullet-pointed tips on Packing and Travel, Making Reservations, Checking In, and Travel Talk Language. The brochure concludes with a map of the United States, showing the cities that Southwest serves, plus the head office address, the airline's toll-free phone number, and its Web site address.

Through such efforts, the airline seeks to demystify air travel; help older people prepare for a journey by air; and explain each step in what is, for an inexperienced traveler, a relatively complex process. The brochure also explains the terms commonly used in airline travel, many of which (such as *preboard* or *gate agent*) are not often heard outside an airport. In this way, older travelers will know what to expect and—equally important—what is expected of them. Knowledge reduces anxiety, thus eliminating one of the barriers to trying something new. To the extent that readers of the brochure appreciate the advice, try a flight on Southwest, and enjoy it, the airline can expect to create loyal customers and stimulate positive word of mouth.

SOUTHWEST AIRLINES®

TRAVEL TIPS FOR SENIORS

Dreaming of jetting away to explore the history and fun of these United States? Southwest Airlines would like to make getting away as easy and fun as possible for those **age 65 or over** by offering some travel tips to Seniors who are keen on life and life's adventures!

sustaining relationships between vendors and purchasers of industrial goods.[5] Theodore Levitt has this to say about relationship management in professional firms:

> It is not surprising that in professional partnerships, such as law, medicine, architecture, consulting, investment banking, and advertising, individuals are rated and rewarded by the client relationships they control. These relationships, like other assets, can appreciate or depreciate. ... Relationship management requires companywide programs for maintenance, investment, improvement, and even for replacement.[6]

Not all existing customer relationships are worth keeping. Some customers no longer fit the firm's strategy, either because that strategy has changed or because the nature of the customer's behavior and needs has changed. Careful analysis may show that many relationships are no longer profitable for the firm because they cost more to maintain than the revenues they generate. Just as investors need to dispose of poor investments and banks may have to write off bad loans, each service firm needs to regularly evaluate its customer portfolio and consider terminating unsuccessful relationships. Legal and ethical considerations, of course, will determine whether it is proper to take such actions. At a minimum, a firm should focus its advertising and promotional strategy to reach prospects from desired segments and to avoid attracting customers who do not fit the desired profile. Professional firms, such as accounting or legal partnerships, provide a good example of the importance of considering the mix of business. As David Maister emphasizes, marketing is about getting better business, not just more business. Firms should measure and monitor the caliber of their practice, not just its volume.[7]

SEGMENTATION STRATEGIES FOR EFFECTIVE CAPACITY UTILIZATION

Capacity-constrained service businesses need to make the best use of their productive capacity. The problem for these businesses is to find enough customers to use their service at any given time and place. Managers should recognize the risks involved in trying to fill capacity with just any warm body. Instead, they should be asking themselves whether they have attracted the right sorts of customers at the right places, times, and prices. In people-processing services, in which customers

DIFFERENT PRODUCTS FOR DIFFERENT SEASONS AT BOSTON'S SYMPHONY HALL

One of the world's best-known concert halls for classical music is Symphony Hall in Boston, which is widely recognized for its superb acoustics. From September through April, Symphony Hall offers concerts by the world-famous Boston Symphony Orchestra (BSO) under the baton of its long-time conductor Seiji Ozawa. High-priced seats are sold to classical music lovers, who often buy on a subscription basis. The players wear traditional evening dress, with white tie and tails for the men, and the atmosphere is hushed, even reverent, until a piece ends and it's time for applause.

In the late spring and early summer, the BSO season is replaced by the Boston Pops. The Pops has its own conductor, Keith Lockhart; only a minority of the players are also members of the BSO. The attire changes to stylish, modern outfits. Ticket prices are reduced; tables and chairs replace the orchestra-level seats; and concerts of popular music are played to sociable audiences who talk, drink, and eat as the concert proceeds. The overlap between BSO and Pops audiences is probably quite small, and the distinctions between the two series are generally well known to their respective audiences. To fill capacity on days when neither the BSO nor the Pops are playing, Symphony Hall is often rented out for other types of events.

themselves become part of the product, conflicts may arise when people from distinctively different segments come together simultaneously in the same facility. Imagine the dismay among patrons at a bar that prides itself on providing a quiet and romantic environment when a group of rowdy sports fans arrive to celebrate their team's victory in a big game.

Customers as a Product Element

Most businesses face fluctuations in demand over time, with predictable peak and off-peak periods. When customers from a firm's principal target segment are absent, marketers often seek to attract customers from other segments to fill capacity during periods of low demand. In general, there's less risk of customer conflict when different segments patronize a facility at different times. In principle, if the off-peak business is financially profitable, can be handled effectively by the service organization, and is not going to hurt the latter's image, it's worth accepting. Little harm is probably done to an airline's positioning strategy if it uses its aircraft for charter flights when business demand is low. But if a hotel or restaurant gains a reputation for attracting a totally different type of customer in the off-season, it may negate its desired high-season image, particularly if a few high-season customers happen to visit during another season, expecting to find the same types of customers and service levels as before. One solution is to be quite explicit about the different **positioning** strategies. Consider the approach used at Boston's famous Symphony Hall (see the box on Symphony Hall).

When service users share a common facility—such as a hotel, restaurant, retail store, or transport vehicle—other customers become part of the product. As a result, the size and composition of the customer base have important implications for both the image of the service organization and the nature of the service experience. If you are patronizing a high-contact, shared service, you can quickly determine whether it is well or poorly patronized. You can also see what sorts of people are using it—their appearance; age range; apparent income bracket; dress (formal or casual); and whether they have come alone, in couples, or in groups. Also apparent (sometimes obtrusively so) is how these other customers are behaving: Are they quiet or noisy, slow or active in their movements? Do they appear cheerful or glum, considerate toward others or rude?

positioning: a firm's use of marketing tools to create a clear, distinctive, and desirable image in the minds of target consumers, relative to competing products.

Mixing or Separating Different Segments

Because customers contribute strongly to the atmosphere of many high-contact services, a firm should try to attract (and retain) customers from the most appropriate market segments. Managers also need to ensure that prospective customers are aware of what constitutes appropriate dress and behavior. For instance, if you were running a restaurant that thrived on business from casually dressed students, it would probably be unwise to try to attract middle-aged people in business attire. On the one hand, a hotel that has succeeded in building up a clientele of business travelers should consider how they might react to the presence in the lobby or dining room of a large group of tourists on a packaged vacation. On the other hand, some retail establishments, such as coffee houses, thrive on attracting a diverse mix of customers. This diversity becomes part of their culture and works well as long as no one's behavior actively disturbs other people.

A uniform customer base is not always possible or even desirable for many service organizations. Two or more distinct market segments may each contribute importantly to the organization's success, yet they may not mix well. Ideally, potentially conflicting segments should be separated in *place* and *time*. Examples of the former include seating airline passengers in first class, business class, and economy class cabins (based on how much they are willing to pay for enhanced service); placing conventioneers on a different floor of a hotel from other guests; and assigning bank customers with substantial accounts a separate entrance and transaction area—even a special branch office of their own—to offer more privacy. Separation of customers in time can be achieved through sequential rather than joint use of the same service facility by customers from different market segments; in this way, neither group encounters the other.

As you know from your own experience, the way in which other customers behave can affect your own enjoyment of a service. If you like classical music and attend symphony concerts, you expect audience members to keep quiet during the performance, rather than spoiling the music by talking or coughing loudly. In contrast, a silent audience would be pretty deadly during a rock concert or sports event, where active audience participation usually adds to the excitement. There is a fine line, however, between spectator enthusiasm and abusive behavior by hooligan supporters of rival sports teams.

ABUSIVE CUSTOMERS AND HOW TO DEAL WITH THEM

One issue that is of greater concern to service marketers than to goods marketers relates to customers who behave in abusive ways. These customers are a problem for any company, but they have more potential for mischief in service businesses, particularly those in which the customer comes to the service factory. When abusive customers come face-to-face with service personnel and other customers, their behavior can put employees at risk and spoil other customers' service experiences. There's also more potential for theft and vandalism when customers enter the service factory, and customers who act inappropriately ultimately can interfere with a firm's efforts to improve productivity and quality.

Addressing the Challenge of Jaycustomers[8]

Visitors to North America are often puzzled by the term *jaywalker*, that distinctively American word used to describe people who cross streets at unauthorized places or in a dangerous manner. The prefix *jay-* comes from a 19th-century slang term for a stupid person. We could create a whole vocabulary of derogatory terms by adding the prefix *jay-* to existing nouns and verbs. How about **jaycustomer**, for example, to denote someone who "jayuses" a service or "jayconsumes" a product (and then "jaydisposes" of it afterward)? Or "jayemployees" who deliver poor service and abuse customers? Or even "jaymanagers"?

jaycustomer: a customer who acts in a thoughtless or abusive way, causing problems for the firm, its employees, and other customers.

Every service encounters its share of jaycustomers. But opinions on this topic seem to polarize around two opposing views. One is denial: The customer is king and can do no wrong. The other sees the marketplace of customers as positively overpopulated with nasty people (and even nastier corporate purchasers) who simply cannot be trusted to behave in ways that self-respecting suppliers should expect and require. The first view has received wide publicity in enthusiastic management books and in motivational presentations to captive groups of employees, whereas the second view often appears to be more widely held among cynical managers who have been burned at some point in their professional lives. As with so many opposing viewpoints in life, there are important grains of truth in both perspectives. Let's look at different categories of abusive customers and discuss strategies for dealing with each of them.

Six Types of Jaycustomers

Jaycustomers are undesirable. At worst, a firm needs to control or prevent their abusive behavior; at best, it would like to avoid attracting them in the first place. Because defining the problem is the first step in resolving it, we start by considering the different types (or segments) of jaycustomers who prey on suppliers of both goods and services. We identify six broad categories and give them generic names, but many customer-contact personnel have come up with their own special terms of endearment for these charming people. As you reflect on these categories, you may perhaps be stimulated to add a few more of your own.

The thief.   The thief has no intention of paying and intends to steal goods and services (or to pay less than full price by such devices as switching price tickets or contesting certain entries in an itemized bill on baseless grounds). Shoplifting is a major problem in retail stores. What retailers euphemistically call "shrinkage" is estimated to cost them billions in annual revenues. Many services lend themselves to clever schemes for avoiding payment. For those with a technical bent, it is sometimes possible to bypass electricity meters, tap into telephone lines free of charge, or circumvent normal cable TV feeds. Riding free on public transportation, sneaking into movie theaters, or not paying for restaurant meals are also popular pastimes, and we mustn't forget fraudulent forms of payment such as stolen credit cards or checks that are guaranteed to bounce. The challenge for managers is to devise schemes for protecting themselves against thieves while avoiding the temptation to employ Gestapo-like tactics against the bulk of honest customers.

While a graduate student, one of the authors was asked by the regional manager of Greyhound Bus Lines in San Francisco to obtain a book that described how to steal a wide variety of goods and services without getting caught. Wittily—if unwisely—titled *Steal This Book*, the volume included a whole chapter on how to ride long-distance buses free of charge.[9] He found the book invitingly displayed at the Stanford University bookstore. Sure enough, it included a veritable encyclopedia of tips on how to rip off capitalist-pig, Establishment-run enterprises (this was in the 1970s). Greyhound was indeed featured, complete with a host of ideas for riding free and avoiding detection. Feeling a little foolish at ignoring the invitation on the cover, he took the priceless volume to the checkout clerk, wondering if this was the first time that anyone had actually paid for it. Today, its updated contents are probably somewhere on the Internet.

The Greyhound manager had the right idea. Finding out how people steal your product is the first step in taking preventive measures to stop them or corrective measures to catch them and, where appropriate, to prosecute. But managers should try not to alienate their honest customers by degrading the latter's own service experiences. Also, provision must be made for honest but absent-minded customers who forget to pay. Many stores now attach electronic tags to their merchandise, which can be removed only by a cashier. If the customer passes a point near the exit doors with merchandise that still bears a tag, it sets off an alarm, thus offering a clear choice between returning to the register or making a break for it.

The rule breaker.   Just as highways need safety regulations (including "Don't jaywalk"), many service businesses find it necessary to establish rules of behavior for employees and customers. Some of these rules are imposed by government agencies for reasons of health and safety. Air travel is perhaps the best example; there can be few other environments outside of prison where healthy, mentally competent, adult customers are quite so constrained (albeit with good reason). In addition to enforcing government regulations, suppliers often lay down their own set of rules

RIPPING OFF INSURANCE COMPANIES

Elaborate auto insurance scams are on the rise in the United States and are estimated to cost the industry from $15 to $20 billion a year. Inevitably, these losses are recouped from honest customers through higher premiums, adding up to $200 per year to the cost of a typical $1,100 premium for a medium-sized, late-model car.

What sometimes seem like bad-luck fender-benders are often cleverly executed frauds. There are several permutations. In one case, a driver is passed by two other vehicles, one of which then swoops in front of the other, causing it to brake sharply and leading the unsuspecting driver of the newish car into a rear-end collision, for which he or she is forced to take the blame and thus the insurance liability (by this stage, the third car has disappeared). The rear-ended car's occupants—who are not, in fact, injured—soon show up at medical clinics, claiming a need for medical treatment. The lawyers and doctors who assist them are often participating in the scam.

Other variants of the scam involve staged accidents in which two cars are deliberately damaged in a remote location, then driven to the shoulder of a highway, at which point the alleged accident is reported to police. Alternatively, wrecked cars are purchased from auto salvage shops and subjected to additional damage, after which claims are filed.

Courtesy of GAB Robins North America, Inc. and Margeotes, Fertitta + Partners, NY. Illustrator: James F. Kraus.

Insurance companies have belatedly realized that what appears to be an individual accident may instead be one event in a large-scale conspiracy. To catch the perpetrators, companies are using such tactics as videotape surveillance, undercover agents, and matching of policyholders and accident victims through powerful computer databases.

As shown in the accompanying advertisement, insurance carriers and independent claims adjusting companies like GAB Robins North America now use standardized fraud indicators (which, of course, they do not reveal publicly in their advertising) to help their claims adjusters determine whether there is reason to believe that a claim is suspicious and merits an in-depth fraud investigation.

Source: Based on information in Tim Smart, "Accidentally, on Purpose," *Business Week,* 30 June 1997, 72–73.

to facilitate the smooth functioning of the operation, avoid unreasonable demands on employees, prevent misuse of products and facilities, protect themselves legally, and discourage individual customers from behaving in ways that would detract from the quality of the service experience. In addition to formal rules are the unwritten norms of social behavior in any given culture to which customers are expected to adhere without being told. Notices at ski resorts often list rules for safe skiing and warn violators that they may lose their passes. Hence, in the interests of safety, ski patrol members sometimes have to play police officer (see the box on policing the slopes).

There are risks in making lots of rules in any service business. Rules can make an organization appear bureaucratic and overbearing; and they can transform employees, whose orientation should be service to customers, into police officers who see (or are told to see) their most important task as enforcement. A third problem is that there are always going to be some customers who break the rules anyway—either because they haven't bothered to take note of them or just for the fun of it.

How should a firm deal with rule breakers? Much depends on which rules have been broken. In the case of legally enforceable ones—theft, bad debts, guns on aircraft—the courses of action need to be laid down explicitly, as much to protect employees as to punish or discourage wrongdoing. Company rules are a little more ambiguous. Are they really necessary in the first place? If not, get rid of them. Do they deal with health and safety? If so, education and reminders will reduce the need for taking corrective action. The same is true for rules designed to protect the comfort and enjoyment of all customers who are using the same facility. Then there are unwritten social norms such as "Thou shalt not jump the line." Other customers can often be relied on to help service personnel enforce rules that affect everybody else, or even take the initiative in doing so. The fewer the rules, the more explicit the important ones can be.

The belligerent.   You've probably seen the belligerent jaycustomer in a store, at the airport, or in a hotel or restaurant—red in the face and shouting angrily or perhaps icily calm and using insults, threats, and obscenities. Things don't always work as they should: Machines break down, service is clumsy, customers are ignored, flights are delayed, an order is delivered incorrectly, staff are unhelpful, or a promise is broken. Or perhaps the customer is expressing resentment at being told to abide by the rules. Service personnel are often abused, even when they are not to blame. If an employee lacks authority to resolve the problem, that may make the belligerent person still angrier, even to the point of physical attack. Drunkenness and drug abuse add an extra layer of complication. Organizations that care about their employees go to great efforts to develop skills in dealing with these difficult situations. Training exercises that involve role playing help employees develop the self-confidence and assertiveness they need to stand up to upset customers. Employees also need to learn how to defuse anger, calm anxiety, and comfort distress (particularly when there is good reason for the customer to be upset with the organization's performance).

But what is an employee to do when an angry, belligerent customer—what airline personnel call an "irate"—brushes off attempts to defuse the situation? In a

POLICING FOR RECKLESS BEHAVIOR ON THE SLOPES

Ski resorts are getting tough on foolhardy skiers. Skiing is a potentially dangerous sport, not least because of the speeds involved. Inconsiderate skiers pose risks not only to themselves but also to others. Collisions can cause serious injury and even kill. Thus ski patrol members must be safety oriented and sometimes have to take on a policing role. Just as dangerous drivers can lose their licences, so dangerous skiers can lose their lift tickers. At Vail and Beaver Creek in Colorado, ski patrollers recently revoked nearly 400 lift tickets in just a single weekend. At Winter Park near Denver, skiers who lose their passes for dangerous behavior may have to take a 45-minute safety class to get them back.

Okemo Mountain in Vermont positions itself as a family-oriented resort and has come up with a creative way to penalize bad behavior. Ski patrollers may issue a warning to reckless skiers by attaching a bright orange sticker to their lift tickets. If pulled over again for inappropriate behavior, these skiers may be escorted off the mountain and banned for a day or more. "We're not trying to be Gestapos on the slopes," says the resort's marketing director, "just trying to educate people."

Source: Based on Rob Ortega and Emily Nelson, "Skiing Deaths May Fuel Calls for Helmets," *The Wall Street Journal*, 7 January 1998, B1–B16.

public environment, one priority should be to move the irate away from other customers. Sometimes supervisors may have to arbitrate disputes between customers and staff members; at other times, they need to stand behind the employee's actions. If an employee has been physically assaulted by a customer, it may be necessary to summon security officers or the police. Some firms try to conceal such events, fearing bad publicity, but others feel obliged to make a public stand on behalf of their employees.

Telephone rudeness poses a different challenge. Service personnel have been known to hang up on angry customers, but that action doesn't resolve the problem. Bank customers, for instance, tend to get upset when checks are returned because they are overdrawn (they've broken the rules) or a request for a loan is denied. One recommended approach for handling customers who continue to berate a telephone-based employee after the reasons for an action have been carefully explained is to say firmly, "This conversation isn't getting us anywhere. Why don't I call you back in a few minutes when you've had time to digest the information?" In many cases, a breathing space for reflection is exactly what's needed.

The family feuders.   A subcategory of belligerents are those who get into arguments—or worse—with other customers (often members of their own family). Employee intervention may calm the situation or further exacerbate it. Sometimes the trick is to get other customers on your side. Some situations require detailed analysis and a carefully measured response. Others, such as customers who start a food fight in a nice restaurant (yes, such things do happen), require almost instantaneous response. Where necessary, service managers need to be prepared to think on their feet and to act fast.

The vandal.   It's astonishing the level of physical abuse to which service facilities and equipment can be subjected. Soft drinks are poured into a bank's ATMs; graffiti are scrawled on both interior and exterior surfaces; cigarettes are used to burn holes in carpets, tablecloths, and bedcovers; bus seats are slashed and hotel furniture broken; telephone handsets are torn off; customers' cars are vandalized; glass is smashed and fabrics torn—the list is endless. Not all of the damage is done by customers, of course. Much exterior vandalism is done by bored youths, and disgruntled employees have been known to commit sabotage. But much of the problem does originate with wrongly behaved, paying customers. Alcohol and drugs are sometimes the cause, psychological problems may contribute, and plain carelessness plays a role. There are occasions when unhappy customers, feeling mistreated by the service provider, try to get their own back. Finally, there are those charming folks with a constant urge to carve their name on something, so that posterity may remember their visit.

The best cure is prevention. Improved security can discourage some vandals. Good lighting helps, as does open design of public areas. Consultants can suggest pleasing yet vandal-resistant surfaces, protective coverings for equipment, and rugged furnishings. Better education of customers on how to use equipment properly (rather than fighting with it) and warnings about fragile objects can reduce the likelihood of abuse or careless handling. Moreover, there are economic sanctions: security deposits or signed agreements in which customers agree to pay for any damage that they cause.

What should managers do if prevention fails and damage is done? If the perpetrators are caught, they should first clarify whether there are any extenuating circumstances (accidents do happen). Sanctions for deliberate damage can range from a warning to prosecution. As far as the physical damage itself is concerned, fix it fast (within any constraints imposed by legal or insurance considerations). A former general manager of AC Transit in Oakland, California, had the right idea years ago. "If one of our buses is vandalized," he said, "whether it's a broken window, a slashed seat, or graffiti on the ceiling, we take it out of service immediately, so nobody sees it. Otherwise you just give the same idea to five other characters who were too dumb to think of it in the first place!"[10]

The deadbeat. Aside from those who never intended to pay in the first place (our term for them is *thief*), many customers end up as delinquent accounts who fail to pay what is due for the service they have received. But once again, prevention is better than cure. A growing number of service businesses insist on prepayment, most ticket sales being a good example. Direct marketing organizations ask for your credit card number as they take your order. The next best thing is to present the customer with a bill immediately upon completion of service, as most dentists now do. If the bill is to be sent out after the fact, send it fast, while the service is still fresh in the customer's mind.

Not every apparent delinquent is a hopeless deadbeat. Perhaps there's a good reason for the delay; perhaps acceptable payment arrangements can be worked out. A key question is whether such a personalized approach can be cost justified, relative to the results obtained by purchasing the services of a collection agency. There may be other considerations, too. If the client's problems are only temporary, what is the long-term value of maintaining the relationship? Will it create positive goodwill and word of mouth to help the customer work things out? These decisions are judgment calls, but if creating and maintaining long-term relationships is the firm's goal, they bear exploration.

Can Firms Restrict Service to Target Customers Only?

Many marketers would probably like to be able to decline requests for service from prospective customers who do not fit the market position sought by the firm. There are ways to discourage unwanted persons from requesting services—for instance, by insisting on certain standards of dress—but outright refusal to admit someone to a service facility may be viewed as illegal or unethical if that person has the ability to pay and is not behaving in a disorderly manner.

One of marketing's roles is to inform prospective customers in advance about the specific nature of a service, so they know what to expect. This increases the chances of a satisfactory fit between customers and the organization. Sometimes, however, friction develops between customers and staff or between different customers, and employees may have to play police officer and either resolve the problem or ask the offending individuals to leave the premises. In fact, some businesses have employees assigned specifically to this role, like bouncers at a bar. Failure to take action quickly and efficiently may seriously damage the impression that other customers have of the service, thus destroying the chance of obtaining repeat business.

SELECTING THE APPROPRIATE CUSTOMER PORTFOLIO

Artists and writers often prepare a portfolio of their work to show to prospective purchasers or employers. The term portfolio also describes the collection of financial instruments held by an investor or the array of loans advanced by a bank. In financial services, the goal of portfolio analysis is to determine the mix of investments (or loans) that is appropriate to one's needs, resources, and risk preference. In an investment portfolio, the contents should change over time in response to the performance of individual portfolio elements, as well as reflect changes in the customer's situation or preferences.

Creating a Portfolio of Market Segments

We can apply the concept of portfolio to service businesses with an established base of customers. If managers know the annual value of each category of customers (revenues received minus the associated costs of serving them), as well as the proportions represented by each category within the customer base, they can project the ongoing value of all these customers in terms of future revenue streams. There are models for projecting the future value of the **customer portfolio**, based on historical data of customer acquisitions, classes of service purchased, service upgrades and downgrades, and terminations. These historical data can be adapted to reflect pricing and cost changes, promotional efforts, and market-related risks (including the anticipated impact of competitive actions or changes in market dynamics). A simple example of such a model applies to the cable TV industry (see the box on a subscriber portfolio).

customer portfolio: the size and composition of the firm's set of customer relationships.

When service businesses (especially professional firms like accounting or medical practices) are sold, a specific value is often assigned to current clients: The larger the practice and the more profitable each client relationship, the more the business will sell for. A case in point is Comprehensive Accounting Corporation, a franchised bookkeeping service based in Aurora, Illinois. Typically, a privately owned accounting practice can be sold at a price equivalent to 80 percent to 120 percent of its current annual billings. However, when a franchisee sells an ongoing practice,

PREDICTING THE FUTURE MIX OF A CABLE TV COMPANY'S SUBSCRIBER PORTFOLIO

The cable TV industry builds its subscriber base from a variety of segments and is notorious for its churn, reflecting the continuing need to find new customers to replace those who have terminated their service agreements. Marketing efforts also encourage existing subscribers to trade up from basic levels of service by purchasing the more profitable premium channels. However, the growth of satellite broadcasting and the widespread use of VCRs for playing rental videos present competitive threats to cable television, with the result that subscribers often choose to downgrade from one or more premium channels to just basic cable service.

Weinberg and Lovelock created a model to predict the future mix and size of a cable TV company's subscriber base and the resulting revenue stream.[a] The basic ingredients to this model include (1) the current mix—how many customers there are subscribing to each class of service; (2) how much each class of service costs the customer and what it costs the provider; (3) how many new subscribers are attracted to each class each month; (4) what percentage of subscribers in each service class (except the highest) upgrade their service to each of the higher classes; (5) what percentage in each class (except the most basic) downgrade from that class to each of the lower classes; (6) what percentage in each class terminate cable service completely; and (7) the cost to the company of installing new customers, handling a termination, and making changes to existing subscription packages. The result is a formula that can be programmed very easily on a computer to generate changing subscription profiles and operating income.

However, the results are valid only to the extent that current change percentages remain valid. In addition to the potential impact of activities by such competitors as satellite broadcasters, current percentage rates of change may vary in response to the firm's own pricing policies and promotional efforts. To maximize profitability, the cable TV provider may wish to experiment with different marketing and pricing strategies to see which approaches prove most effective in the long run, relative to their costs. If a company operates systems in many different geographic areas (as most now do) marketing researchers can conduct experiments in one or more locations whose results can be generalized to other, similar areas.

[a] Charles B. Weinberg and Christopher H. Lovelock, "Pricing and Profits in Subscription Service Marketing: An Analytical Approach to Customer Valuation," in M. Venkatesan, D. M. Schmalensee, and C. Marshall, *Creativity in Services Marketing* (Chicago: American Marketing Association, 1986).

he or she can expect to get double that amount, reflecting the greater profitability resulting from more efficient back-office systems.[11]

In talking about customer portfolios, it's important to distinguish between existing relationships—all the customers with whom the firm does business—and the mix of customers being served *at any given time*. The former determines valuation, based on current and future earnings potential; the latter is central in decisions on how to optimize use of available capacity over time.

CREATING AND MAINTAINING VALUED RELATIONSHIPS

What is a valued relationship? It's one in which the customer finds value because the benefits received from service delivery significantly exceed the associated costs of obtaining them. For the firm, it's a relationship that is financially profitable over time and in which the benefits of serving customers may extend beyond revenues to include such intangibles as the knowledge and pleasure obtained from working with them. Having a good working relationship between two parties implies that they relate positively to one another, as opposed to just conducting a series of almost anonymous transactions. In a healthy and mutually profitable relationship, both parties have an incentive to ensure that it is extended for many years. The seller, in particular, recognizes that it pays to take an investment perspective, justifying the upfront costs of acquiring new customers and learning about their needs—which may even make the account unprofitable in its first year— by an expectation of future profits.

Relationships versus Transactions

A **transaction** is an event during which an exchange of value takes place between two parties. One transaction—or even a series of transactions—does not necessarily constitute a relationship because relationships require mutual recognition and knowledge between the parties. When each transaction between a customer and a supplier is essentially anonymous, with no long-term record of a customer's purchasing history and little or no mutual recognition between the customer and the firm's employees, no meaningful marketing relationship can be said to exist.

With very few exceptions, consumers buying manufactured goods for household use do so at discrete intervals, paying for each purchase separately and rarely entering into a formal relationship with the original manufacturer, although they may have a relationship with the dealer or retail intermediary. The same is true for many services, ranging from passenger transportation to food service or visits to a movie theater, where each purchase and use is a discrete event. However, in other cases, purchasers receive certain services, or the right to those services, on a continuing basis. The different nature of these situations offers an opportunity for categorizing services as shown in Table 6.1 (p. 124).

First, we can ask, Does the service organization enter into a **membership relationship** with its customers, as with telephone subscriptions, banking, and seeing the family doctor? Or is there no formal relationship? Second, is the service delivered on a continuous basis, as in insurance, broadcasting, and police protection? Or is each transaction recorded and charged separately? The table shows the matrix resulting from this categorization, with examples in each category.

The advantage to the service organization of a membership relationship is that it knows who its current customers are and, usually, what use they make of the services offered. This can be valuable information for segmentation purposes if good

transaction: an event during which an exchange of value takes place between two parties.

membership relationship: a formal relationship between the firm and an identifiable customer that may offer special benefits to both parties.

TABLE 6.1   Relationships with Customers

Nature of Service Delivery	Type of Relationship between the Service Organization and Its Customers	
	"Membership" Relationship	No Formal Relationship
Continuous Delivery of Service	Insurance Cable TV subscription College enrollment Banking	Radio station Police protection Lighthouse Public highway
Discrete Transactions	Long-distance calls from subscriber phone Theater series subscription Travel on commuter ticket Repair under warranty Health treatment for HMO member	Car rental Mail service Toll highway Pay phone Movie theater Public transportation Restaurant

records are kept and the data are readily accessible in a format that lends itself to computerized analysis. Knowing the identities and addresses of current customers enables the organization to make effective use of direct mail, telephone selling, and personal sales calls—all highly targeted methods of marketing communication.

The nature of service relationships also has important implications for pricing. Whenever service is offered on an ongoing basis, there is usually just a single periodic charge that covers all contracted services. Most insurance policies fall in this category, as do tuition and board fees at a residential college. The big advantage of this package approach is its simplicity. Some memberships, however, entail a series of separate and identifiable transactions, with the price being tied explicitly to the number and type of each. Although more complex to administer, such an approach is fairer to customers (whose usage patterns may vary widely) and may discourage wasteful use of what are perceived to be "free" services. In these cases, members may be offered advantages over casual users, for instance, discount rates (telephone subscribers pay less for long-distance calls made from their own phones than from pay phones) or advance notification and priority reservations (theater subscriptions). Some memberships offer certain services (such as rental of equipment or connection to a public utility system) for a base fee and then make incremental charges for each separate transaction above a defined minimum.

When no formal relationship exists between supplier and customer, continuous delivery of the product is normally found only among those free services that economists term *public goods*—for instance, broadcasting, police protection, lighthouse services, and public highways—which are continuously available to all comers and financed from tax revenues.

Membership relationships usually result in customer loyalty to a particular service supplier. (Sometimes, however, there is no choice because the supplier has a monopoly.) As a marketing strategy, many service businesses try to develop formal, ongoing relations with customers to ensure repeat business and/or ongoing financial support. Public radio and television broadcasters, for instance, develop membership clubs for donors and offer monthly program guides in return; performing arts organizations sell subscription series; transit agencies offer monthly passes; airlines create clubs for frequent fliers; hotels develop frequent guest programs, offering priority reservations, upgraded rooms, and other rewards for frequent guests. The marketing task here is to determine how it might be possible to build sales and revenues through such memberships while avoiding a formal membership requirement that would result in freezing out a large volume of desirable casual business.

Discrete transactions—when each usage involves a payment to the service supplier by an essentially anonymous consumer—are typical of services like transportation, restaurants, movie theaters, and shoe repairs. The problem for marketers of these services is that they tend to be less informed about who their customers are and what use each customer makes of the service than their counterparts in membership-type organizations. Managers in businesses that sell discrete transactions have to work a little harder to establish relationships. In small businesses such as hairsalons, frequent customers are (or should be) welcomed as regulars, whose needs and preferences are remembered. Keeping formal records of customers' needs, preferences, and purchasing behavior is useful even in small firms because it helps employees avoid having to ask repetitive questions on each service occasion, allows them to personalize the service given to each customer, and also enables the firm to anticipate future needs. In large companies with substantial customer bases, transactions can still be transformed into relationships by opening accounts, maintaining computerized customer records, and instituting account management programs that may involve a special telephone number to call for assistance or even a designated account representative. Long-term contracts between suppliers and their customers take the nature of relationships to a higher level, transforming them into partnerships and strategic alliances.

The Loyalty Effect

Loyalty is an old-fashioned word that has traditionally been used to describe fidelity and enthusiastic devotion to a country, cause, or individual. More recently, in a business context, it has been used to describe a customer's willingness to continue to patronize a firm over the long term, purchasing and using its goods and services on a repeated and preferably exclusive basis, and voluntarily recommending the firm's products to friends and associates. "Few companies think of customers as annuities," says Frederick Reichheld, author of *The Loyalty Effect* and a major researcher in this field.[12] And yet that is precisely what a loyal customer can mean to a firm: a consistent source of revenues over a period of many years. However, this loyalty cannot be taken for granted. It will continue only as long as the customer feels that he or she is receiving better value (including superior quality relative to price) than could be obtained by switching to another supplier. If the original firm does something to disappoint the customer or if a competitor starts to offer significantly better value, there is a risk that the customer will defect.

Defector was a nasty word during the Cold War. It described disloyal people who sold out their own side and went over to the enemy. Even when they defected towards our side, rather than away from it, they were still suspect. Today, the term **defection** is being used to describe customers who transfer their brand loyalty to another supplier. Reichheld and Sasser popularized the term *zero defections*, which they describe as keeping every customer the company can profitably serve (as already said, there are always some customers a firm is not sorry to lose).[13] Not only does a rising defection rate indicate that something is already wrong with quality (or that competitors offer better value), it may also signal the risk of a coming fall in profits. Large customers don't necessarily disappear overnight; they may signal their mounting disaffection by steadily reducing their purchases. Observant firms record purchase trends carefully and are quick to respond with service recovery strategies (the topic of chapter 7) in the event of complaints or other service failures.

There are many ways to disappoint customers through service quality failures (see chapter 5). A major source of disappointment, especially in high-contact service, is poor performance by employees. Reichheld and other researchers believe that there is an explicit link between customers' satisfaction with service, on the one

loyalty: a customer's voluntary decision to continue patronizing a specific firm over an extended period of time.

defection: a customer's decision to transfer brand loyalty from a current service provider to a competitor.

FIGURE 6.1 The Links in the Service-Profit Chain

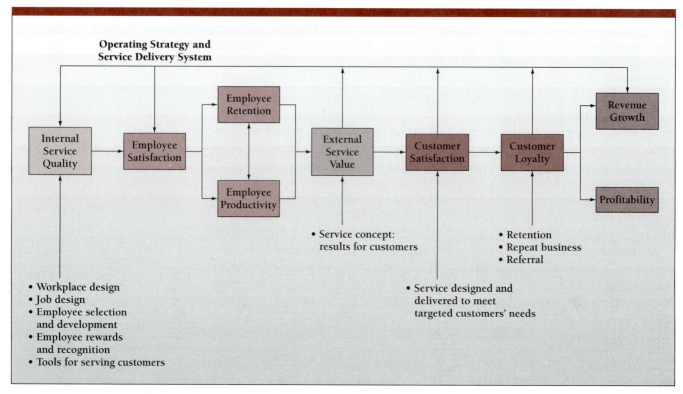

Source: James L. Heskett, Thomas O. Jones, Gary W. Loveman, W. Earl Sasser, Jr., and Leonard A. Schlesinger, "Putting the Service Profit Chain to Work," *Harvard Business Review*, March–April 1994. Copyright © 1994 by the President and Fellows of Harvard College.

hand, and employees' satisfaction with their jobs, on the other. To the extent that service workers are capable, enjoy their jobs, and perceive themselves as well treated by their employer, they will remain loyal to that firm for an extended period of time, rather than constantly switching jobs. Competent and loyal workers tend to be more productive than new ones, to know their customers well, and to be better able to deliver high-quality service. In short, employee loyalty can contribute to customer loyalty through a series of links that Heskett et al. refer to as the "service profit chain."[14] As shown in Figure 6.1, there is a link between human resource strategy and marketing strategy.

Realizing the Full Profit Potential of a Customer Relationship

How much is a loyal customer worth in profit? In 1990, Reichheld and Sasser analyzed the profit per customer in different service businesses, categorized by the number of years that a customer had been with the firm.[15] They found that the longer customers remained with a firm in each of these industries, the more profitable they became to serve. Annual profits per customer, which have been indexed over a five-year period for easier comparison, are summarized in Figure 6.2. The industries studied (average profits from a first-year customer are in parentheses) were credit cards ($30), industrial laundry ($144), industrial distribution ($45), and automobile servicing ($25).

Underlying this profit growth, say the two researchers, are four factors working to the supplier's advantage to create incremental profits. In order of magnitude at the end of seven years, these factors are

FIGURE 6.2 How Much Profit a Customer Generates Over Time

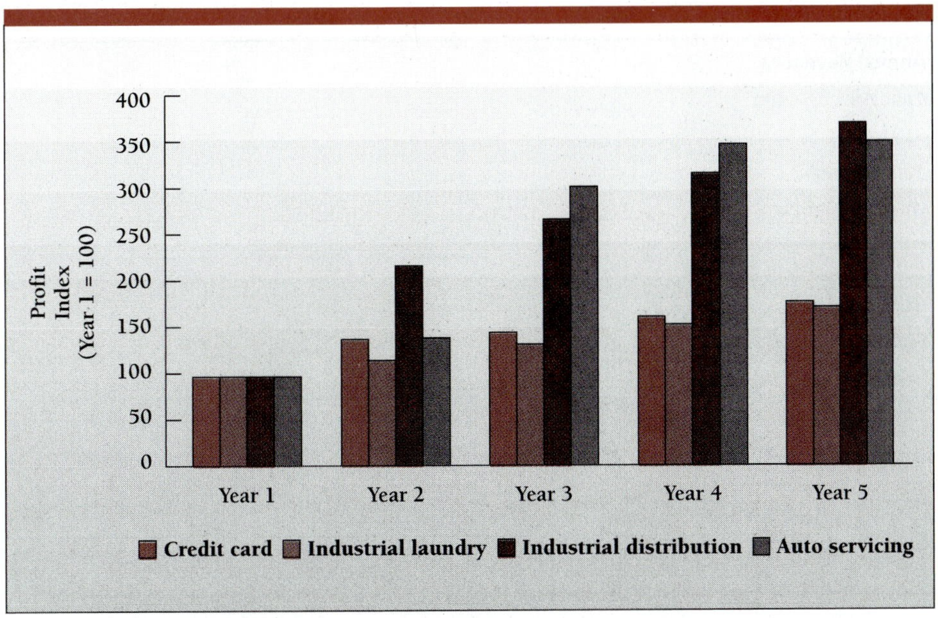

Source: Based on data in Frederick J. Reichheld and W. Earl Sasser, Jr., "Zero Defections: Quality Comes to Services," *Harvard Business Review* 73 (September–October 1995): 59–75.

1. *Profit derived from increased purchases* (or, in a credit card or banking environment, higher account balances). Over time, business customers often grow larger and so need to purchase in greater quantities. Individuals may purchase more as their families grow or as they become more affluent. Both types of customers may decide to consolidate their purchases with a single supplier who provides high-quality service.

2. *Profit from reduced operating costs.* As customers become more experienced, they make fewer demands on the supplier (for instance, less need for information and assistance); they may also make fewer mistakes when involved in operational processes, thus contributing to greater productivity.

3. *Profit from referrals to other customers.* Positive word-of-mouth recommendations act as free advertising, saving the firm from high investments in this area.

4. *Profit from price premium.* New customers often benefit from introductory promotional discounts, whereas long-term customers are more likely to pay regular prices. Moreover, when customers trust a supplier, they may be more willing to pay higher prices at peak periods or for express work.

Reichheld argues that the economic benefits of customer loyalty often explain why one firm is more profitable than a competitor. Furthermore, the upfront costs of attracting these buyers can be amortized over many years. For insights on how to calculate customer value in any given business, see the worksheet in Table 6.2 (p. 128).

For profit-seeking firms, the potential profitability of a customer should be a key driver in marketing strategy. Grant and Schlesinger declare, "Achieving the full profit potential of each customer relationship should be the fundamental goal of every business. ... Even using conservative estimates, the gap between most companies' current and full potential performance is enormous."[16] They suggest analysis of the following three gaps between actual and potential performance:

■ What percentage of its target customers does a firm currently have—market share—and what percentage could it obtain? If there is a large gap between a

TABLE 6.2 **Worksheet for Calculating Long-Term Customer Value**

Acquisition		Ongoing Use	Year 1	Year 2	Year 3	Year *n*
Initial Revenue		**Annual Revenues**				
Application fee[a]	_____	Annual account fee[a]	_____	_____	_____	_____
Initial purchase[a]	_____	Sales	_____	_____	_____	_____
		Service fees[a]	_____	_____	_____	_____
		Value of referrals[b]	_____	_____	_____	_____
Total Revenues	_____		_____	_____	_____	_____
Initial Costs		**Annual Costs**				
Marketing:	_____	Account management	_____	_____	_____	_____
Credit check[a]	_____	Cost of sales	_____	_____	_____	_____
Account set up[a]	_____	Write-offs (e.g., bad debts)	_____	_____	_____	_____
Less Total Costs	_____		_____	_____	_____	_____
Net Profit (Loss)	_____		_____	_____	_____	_____

[a] If applicable.
[b] Anticipated profits from each new customer referred (could be limited to the first year or expressed as the net present value of the estimated future stream of profits through year *n*); this value could be negative if an unhappy customer starts to spread negative word of mouth that leads existing customers to defect.

firm's current share and its potential, it may make sense to develop strategies to attract new customers.

- What is the current purchasing behavior of customers in each target segment? What would be the impact on sales and profits if they exhibited the ideal behavior profile of (1) buying all services offered by the firm, (2) using these to the exclusion of any purchases from competitors, and (3) paying full price? Often, firms need to examine opportunities to cross-sell new services to existing customers. In the meantime, frequent user programs that are designed to reward loyalty can help to cement relationships more tightly. Getting customers to pay higher prices than they have been used to, however, may be more difficult unless competitors are also trying to reduce the availability of discount promotions.

- How long, on the average, do customers remain with the firm? What impact would it have if they remained customers for life? As we showed earlier, the profitability of a customer often increases over time. Management's task is to identify why customers defect and then take corrective action.

Many elements are involved in gaining market share, cross-selling other products and services to existing customers, and creating long-term loyalty. The process starts, as suggested earlier, by identifying and targeting the right customers, and then learning everything possible about their needs, including their preferences for different forms of service delivery. Consistently doing an outstanding job of satisfying these needs should lie at the heart of any service program, as described in chapter 5.

Loyalty Programs

The big challenge for service marketers lies not only in giving prospective customers a reason to do business with their firms but also in offering existing customers incentives to remain loyal and even to increase their purchases. Among the best-known strategies for rewarding frequent users are the frequent flyer programs offered by most passenger airlines (see the box on rewarding frequent flyers).

To record the mileage of passengers enrolled in their frequent flyer programs, the airlines have had to install elaborate tracking systems that capture details of

REINFORCING LOYALTY BY REWARDING FREQUENT FLYERS

The original frequent flyer program was established by American Airlines in 1983. Targeted at business travelers (who fly the most), this promotion enabled passengers to claim travel awards based on the accumulated distance they had traveled on the airline. "Miles" flown became the scoring system that entitled customers to make claims from a menu of free tickets in different classes of service. American was taken by surprise at the enormous popularity of this program. Other major airlines soon felt obliged to follow and implemented similar schemes of their own. Each airline hoped that its own frequent flyer program, branded with a distinctive name such as "AAdvantage" (American) or "Mileage Plus" (United), would induce a traveler to remain loyal, even to the extent of some inconvenience in scheduling. However, many business travelers enrolled in several programs, thereby limiting the effectiveness of these promotions for individual carriers.

To make their programs more appealing, the airlines signed cooperative agreements with regional and international carriers, as well as with "partner" hotels and rental car firms, allowing customers to be credited with mileage accrued through a variety of travel-related activities. What had begun as a one-year promotion by American Airlines was soon transformed into a permanent—and quite expensive—part of the industry's marketing structure.

As time passed, airlines in the United States started to use double and triple mileage bonus awards as a tool for demand management, seeking to encourage travel on less popular routes. A common strategy was to award bonus miles for changing flights at an intermediate hub rather than taking a nonstop flight or for flying during the low season, when many empty seats were available. To avoid giving away too many free seats at peak time, some airlines offered more generous redemption terms during off-peak periods; a few even created blackout periods during key vacation times like Christmas and New Year to avoid cannibalizing seat sales by holders of free tickets.

Competitive strategies often involved bonus miles, too. Bonus wars broke out on certain routes. At the height of its mid-1980s battle with New York Air on the lucrative 230-mile (370-km) New York–Boston shuttle service, the PanAm Shuttle offered passengers 2,000 miles for a one-way trip and 5,000 miles for a round trip completed within a single day. Bonus miles were also awarded for travel in first or business class; and bonuses might also be awarded to encourage passengers to sample new services or to complete market research surveys. In due course, many international airlines felt obliged to introduce their own frequent flyer programs, offering miles (or kilometers) to compete with American carriers and then with one another.

every flight. They have also created systems for recording and maintaining each member's current account status and devised procedures for redeeming miles for free travel (some airlines have outsourced these tasks to independent contractors).

American Airlines was probably the first service firm to realize the value of its frequent customer database for learning more about the travel behavior of its best customers, enabling it to create highly targeted direct mailing lists (such as travelers who fly regularly between a certain pair of cities). The airline was also quick to examine bookings for individual flights to see what percentage of seats was filled by frequent flyers, most of whom were probably traveling on business and therefore less price sensitive than vacationers and pleasure travelers. This information proved to have great value for countering competition from low-cost discount airlines, whose primary target segment was price-conscious pleasure travelers. Rather than reducing all fares on all flights between a pair of cities, American realized that it needed to offer only a limited number of discount fares, primarily on those flights known to be carrying significant numbers of nonbusiness passengers. Even on these flights, the airline would limit the availability of discount fares by requiring an advance purchase or an extended stay in the destination city, so that it would be difficult for business travelers to trade down from full fare to a discount ticket.

A number of other service businesses have sought to copy the airlines with frequent user programs of their own, for example, hotels, car rental firms, telephone

Safeway offers club members discounts on merchandise. At the same time, it automatically collects information on their purchasing behavior.

companies, retailers, and even credit card issuers. Some provide their own rewards. For instance, the Safeway supermarket chain offers a Club Card, which provides savings on its own merchandise and discounts on purchases of services from partner companies. Similarly, car rental firms offer vehicle upgrades, and hotels offer free rooms in vacation resorts. But many firms offer miles credited to a frequent flyer program. In short, air miles have become a promotional currency in the service sector, as illustrated by the WellsMiles program, offered to holders of Wells Fargo Bank credit cards (information about this promotional effort was enclosed in the envelope sent to customers with their monthly billing statements).

Despite the popularity of customer loyalty programs, Dowling and Uncles claim that these programs have proved "surprisingly ineffective" for many firms. They suggest that to succeed in competitive markets, loyalty programs must enhance the overall value of the product or service and motivate loyal buyers to make their next purchase.[17] In some instances, as with the airlines, the benefits are popular with customers, and virtually all players in the industry have felt obliged to offer a loyalty program, if only for defensive reasons. In other cases, the benefits are not perceived as particularly valuable and certainly insufficient to justify a higher price than competitors. This may have been one reason why AT&T, competing against fierce price competition in the telecommunications industry, ended its True Rewards loyalty program in 1998.

The truth is that rewards alone will not enable a firm to retain its most desirable customers. If these customers are not delighted with the quality of service they receive or believe that they can obtain better value from a less expensive service, they may quickly become disloyal. In short, no service business can ever afford to lose sight of the broader goals of providing quality service and good value relative to the price and other costs of service that customers incur.

Conclusion

All marketers need to be concerned about who their customers are, but this concern takes on added dimensions for certain types of services. When customers have a high level of contact with the service organization and with one another, the customer portfolio helps to define the character of the organization because the customers themselves become part of the product. Too diverse a portfolio may result in an ill-defined image, especially if all segments are present at the same time. Abusive customers may spoil the experience for others and hurt profitability in other ways, too. Thus, marketers must be selective in targeting the desired customer segments, and guidelines must be established for customers' behavior while they are using the service.

For services that are constrained by capacity, the marketer's task is not only to balance supply and demand but also to obtain the most desirable types of customers at a particular time. This may require targeting different segments at different times. For profit-seeking businesses, a key issue is which segments will yield the greatest net revenues. Public and nonprofit organizations, although not ignoring financial issues, need to consider which segments will help them best fulfill their nonfinancial objectives. In all instances, accurate market analysis and forecasting assume great importance in guiding marketing strategy.

Finally, marketers need to pay special attention to those customers who offer the firm the greatest value because they purchase its products with the greatest frequency and spend the most on premium services. Programs to reward frequent users—of which the most highly developed are the frequent flyer clubs created by the airlines—not only identify and reward high-value customers but also enable marketers to track their behavior in terms of where and when they use the service, what service classes or types of product they buy, and how much they spend. The greatest success is likely to go to organizations that can give their best customers incentives to remain loyal, rather than spreading their patronage among many other suppliers.

Study Questions and Exercises

1. What criteria should a marketing manager use to decide which of several possible segments should be targeted by the firm?
2. Identify some of the measures that can be used to encourage long-term relationships with customers.
3. What does segmentation have to do with capacity utilization? For what types of services is this a relevant issue?
4. Make a case both for and against the statement that "the customer is always right."
5. Select a people-processing service business; then pick two types of jaycustomer and develop strategies designed (a) to discourage them from using your service in the first place if they have already begun to cause problems, (b) to prevent them from causing distress to other customers and/or to employees, (c) to minimize financial loss to your organization.
6. Explain what is meant by a customer portfolio. How should a firm decide what is the most appropriate mix of customers?
7. What are the arguments for spending money to keep existing customers loyal?
8. Evaluate the strengths and weaknesses of frequent user programs in different types of service industries.

Complaint Handling and Service Recovery

Product
Elements

Place
and time

Promotion
and education

Price and
Other Costs
of Service

Process

PRODUCTIVITY
AND QUALITY

People

Physical
evidence

Learning Objectives

After reading this chapter, you should be able to

■ identify the extent of consumer complaints and the effectiveness of current service recovery practices

■ outline the courses of action open to a dissatisfied consumer

■ explain the factors that affect complaining

■ identify the principles of an effective service recovery system

■ demonstrate the value of a well-planned unconditional guarantee

Why Did the Hotel Guests Pass Up a Free Breakfast?[1]

An alert hostess at a Hampton Inn in California noticed that two guests from an Australian tour group were passing up her hotel's popular complimentary breakfast. On the second morning, she asked if anything was wrong. "To be honest, the food is just not what we're used to at home," they replied, describing a typical Australian breakfast. When they came down the next morning, the hostess greeted them cheerfully. "I think we might be able to give you some breakfast this morning," she smiled, laying out items they had mentioned the previous day. She had made a quick trip to a nearby supermarket and added items from her own kitchen at home. The guests were thrilled. "So this is what 100 percent satisfaction means?" they asked. "*We* get to define satisfaction?" They were so impressed that they arranged to have the other members of their tour group, who were staying at another hotel, move to the Hampton Inn. The two weeks' worth of unexpected revenue from the tour group certainly was a more than adequate return on the extra time and money spent by the hostess to satisfy her guests.

Promus Hotel Corporation offers a unique proposition to guests at its more than 700 Hampton Inns: an *unconditional* guarantee of their satisfaction. Guests define satisfaction on their own terms, and the hotel guarantees the customer-defined satisfaction—without negotiation. These two elements make the Promus guarantee extraordinary and give Hampton Inn a competitive advantage in its lodging segment. Since then, only a few competitors have imitated the Promus "100% Satisfaction Guarantee." More important, mere imitation has not produced the results achieved by Promus because the imitators lack the supporting infrastructure, culture, and above all the *attitude* that makes the guarantee more than a slogan.

Initially, the Hampton Inn guarantee was viewed as a proactive approach to what Ray Schultz, now chairman of Promus Hotel Corp., referred to as "the heartbreak of franchising." Schultz was determined that Hampton Inn would not fall prey to the all-too-familiar deterioration of a lodging chain that traditionally plagues the hotel industry. He recognized how easily quality and service standards could slip as properties aged. Also, he knew how often investments in properties, either hard dollars put into capital improvements or so-called soft dollars put into employee training, for example, were compromised to support short-term earnings.

Furthermore, Schultz recognized the inherent difficulty of maintaining quality standards across a large and diverse multisite franchise system. He knew that the challenge would only intensify, given the company's aggressive growth strategy to increase the number of Hampton Inns from 200 in 1989 to over 700 in 1997. "We cannot compromise the quality of Hampton Inn as we grow because ultimately that would constrain our growth," asserted Schultz. "Deteriorating quality inevitably will result in declining guest satisfaction, lower guest loyalty, and negative word-of-mouth. That's a recipe for further deterioration in revenue and operating cash flow. It is easy to lower service standards. But once lowered, it is very difficult to raise them."

The guarantee has been so successful that Promus has extended it to other chains that it owns, including Embassy Suites and Homewood Suites.

CONSUMER COMPLAINTS

"Thank Heavens for Complainers" was the provocative title of an article about customer complaints, which also featured a successful manager who exclaimed, "The ones I worry about are the ones I never hear from."[2] Customers who complain give a firm the chance to correct problems, restore relationships with the complainer, and improve service quality for all.

Although the first law of service productivity and quality might be "Do it right the first time," we can't ignore the fact that failures continue to occur, sometimes for reasons outside the organization's control. You've probably noticed from your own experience that the various moments of truth in service encounters are especially vulnerable to breakdowns. Such distinctive service characteristics as real-time performance, customer involvement, people as part of the product, and difficulty of evaluation greatly increase the chance of perceived service failures. How well a firm handles complaints and resolves problems may determine whether it retains or loses its customers' patronage.

complaint: a formal expression of dissatisfaction with any aspect of a service experience.

If you're not entirely satisfied with the quality of the services that you use, how do you respond? Do you complain informally to an employee, ask to speak to the manager, file a **complaint** with the head office of the firm, write to some regulatory authority, or telephone a consumer advocacy organization? Or do you just grumble to your friends and family and take your business elsewhere?

If you don't normally tell a company (or outside agency) of your displeasure with unsatisfactory service or faulty goods, you're not alone. Research around the world has exposed the sad fact that most people do not complain, especially if they don't think it will do any good. And even when they do communicate their dissastisfaction, managers may not hear about complaints made to customer-contact personnel.[3]

Customer Responses to Service Failures

service failure: a perception by customers that one or more specific aspects of service delivery have not met their expectations.

What options are open to customers when they experience a **service failure**? Figure 7.1 depicts the courses of action available. This model suggests at least four major courses of action:

- Do nothing.
- Complain in some form to the service firm.
- Take action through a third party (consumer advocacy organization, consumer affairs or regulatory agencies, or civil or criminal courts).
- Switch suppliers and discourage other people from using the service (negative word of mouth).

Following the sequence of possible reactions, we can see a variety of end results, leaving the customer anything from furious to delighted. The risk of defection is high, especially when many competing alternatives are available. One study of customer switching behavior in service industries found that close to 60 percent of all respondents who reported changing suppliers did so because of a perceived failure: 25 percent cited failures in the core service, 19 percent reported an unsatisfactory encounter with an employee, 10 percent reported by an unsatisfactory response to a previous service failure, and 4 percent described unethical behavior by the provider.[4]

Managers need to be aware that the impact of a defection can go far beyond the loss of that person's future revenue. Angry customers often tell many other people about their problems. The Web has made life more difficult for companies that

FIGURE 7.1 Courses of Action Open to a Dissatisfied Customer

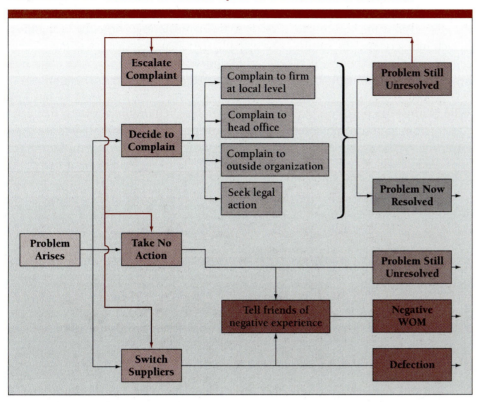

provide poor service, because unhappy customers can now reach thousands of people by posting complaints on bulletin boards or setting up Web sites to publicize their bad experiences with specific organizations.[5]

The TARP Study of Consumer Complaint Handling

The Technical Assistance Research Program Institute (TARP) is a Washington-based research organization that has studied consumer complaint handling in the United States and other countries. In 1986, it published a landmark research study based on its own research and a detailed review of other studies from around the world.[6] Its findings, which were widely publicized, prompted many managers to consider the impact of dissatisfied customers—especially those that never complained but simply defected to a competitor. Let's look at some specific findings.

What percentage of problems are reported?   From its own research and detailed studies, TARP found that for problems with manufactured consumer products, only 25 percent to 30 percent of customers complained. For grocery products or their packaging, the market research firm of A.C. Nielsen found a complaint rate of 30 percent. Even for problems with large ticket durables, TARP determined that the complaint rate was only 40 percent. Similar findings come from other countries. A Norwegian study found that the percentage of dissatisfied consumers who complained ranged from 9 percent for coffee to 68 percent for cars. A German study showed that only a small fraction of customers expressed dissatisfaction, but among this group the complaint rates ranged from 29 percent to 81 percent. A Japanese study found complaint rates of 17 percent among those having a problem with services and 36 percent with goods.

Where do people complain?   Studies show that the majority of complaints are made at the place where the product was bought or the service received. Very few dissatisfied consumers complain directly to the manufacturers or to the head office. In fact, industry-specific studies conducted by TARP suggest that fewer than 5 percent of complaints about large-ticket durable goods or services ever reach corporate headquarters, presumably because retail intermediaries fail to pass them on.

Who is most likely to complain?   In general, research findings suggest that consumers from high-income households are more likely to complain than those from lower-income ones, and younger people are more likely to complain than older ones. People who complain also tend to be more knowledgeable about the products in question and the procedures for complaining. Other factors that increase the likelihood of a complaint include problem severity, importance of the product to the customer, and whether financial loss is involved.

Why don't unhappy customers complain?   According to TARP, dissatisfied customers don't complain for three primary reasons. In order of frequency, customers stated the following:

- They didn't think it was worth the time or effort.
- They decided no one would be concerned about their problem or about resolving it.
- They did not know where to go or what to do.

Unfortunately, this pessimism seems justified because a large percentage of people (40 percent to 60 percent in two studies) reported dissatisfaction with the outcome of their complaints. People also don't complain because of culture or context. A study in Japan found that 21 percent of dissatisfied customers felt awkward or embarrassed about complaining. In some European countries, there is a

Crowded conditions and too much time waiting in line create dissatisfied customers in many service industries, but will they bother to complain?

strong guest–host relationship between service providers and customers (especially in the restaurant industry), and it's considered bad manners to tell customer-contact personnel that you are dissatisfied in any way with the service or the meal. It probably never even occurred to the two Australians in our opening story to complain about the absence of an Australian-style breakfast in an American hotel. Think about some occasions when you were dissatisfied but did not complain. What were the reasons?

Impact on repurchase intentions.   When complaints are satisfactorily resolved, there's a much better chance that the customers involved will remain loyal and continue to repurchase the items in question. Thus, TARP found that intentions to repurchase different types of products ranged from 69 percent to 80 percent among those complainers who were completely satisfied with the outcome of the complaint. This figure dropped to 17 percent to 32 percent (depending on the type of product) for complainers who felt that their complaint had not been settled to their satisfaction.

Variations in Dissatisfaction by Industry

Although significant improvements in complaint-handling practices occurred during the 1980s and early 1990s in some industries, many customers remain dissatisfied with the way in which their problems are resolved. Furthermore, there are discouraging signs that the situation is beginning to deteriorate again. A valuable measure of how well different industries in the United States are performing relative to the needs and expectations of the marketplace is provided by the American Customer Satisfaction Index (ACSI), which measures customers' overall evaluation of the total purchase and consumption experience, both actual and anticipated, and scores them from a maximum of 100 points.[7] The ACSI results show that most manufactured products score higher than most services, highlighting the greater difficulties involved in achieving service quality. The best rated manufacturing company was Mercedes (87 points), and the worst was Compaq Computer (67). The best corporate service performer was FedEx (82), and the worst was McDonald's (60)—only a few points ahead of the Internal Revenue Service at 54.

Figure 7.2 (p. 138) shows industry-wide scores for 1997 in illustrative categories and how they have changed since 1996.[8] Although the overall index turned up slightly, halting a four-year decline, most services were rated worse than the previous year. As these data suggest, many service industries are still a long way from meeting their customers' expectations. Of course, there can be considerable variation in performance between firms within the same industry. For instance, the best-rated airline was Southwest (at 76, unchanged from 1996), and the worst was American (62, a 12.6 percent drop from the previous year).

Consumers in some countries, however, may be getting smarter and more aggessive about seeking satisfactory outcomes for their complaints. Recent findings from a large-scale study of consumer complaints in Australia showed that among the industries studied, a majority of customers who had a serious problem did make the effort to complain.[9] The data in Table 7.1 (p. 138) show considerable disparity from one service industry to another in both the incidence of unsatisfactory service and in customers' likeliness to complain. As you review this table, ask yourself why more Australians were willing to complain about telephone service and other utilities than about restaurants and health services. Other key findings from this study are as follows:

■ Respondents who had experienced at least one problem with products or services within the past 12 months totaled 57 percent.

FIGURE 7.2 American Customer Satisfaction Index Scores for Selected Industries in 1997, Showing Percent Change over 1996

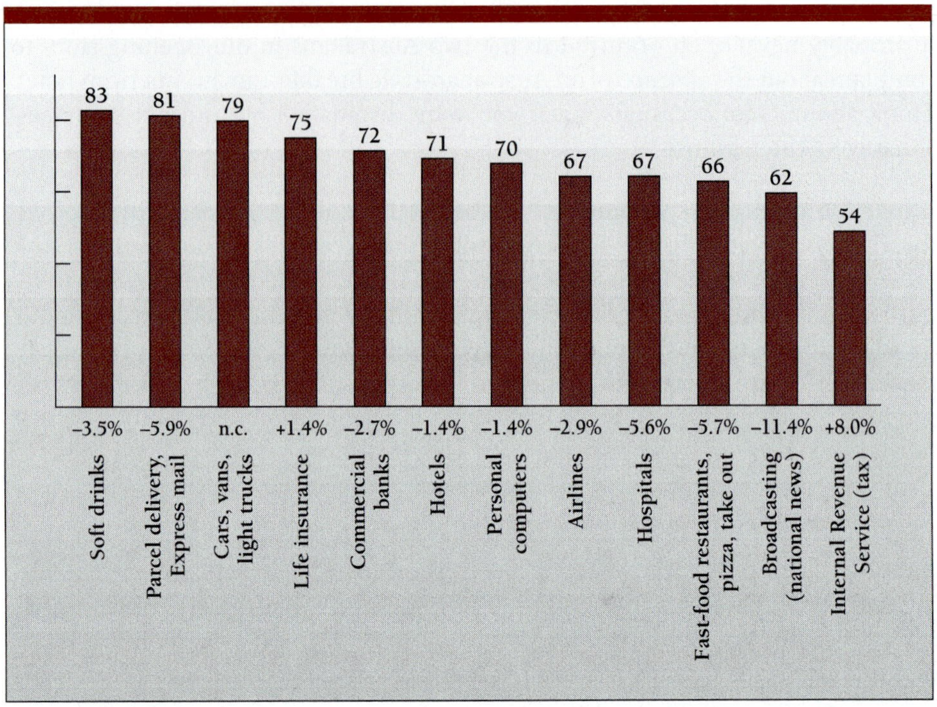

Source: Based on data reported in Ronald B. Lieber and Linda Grant, "Now Are You Satisfied?" *Fortune*, 16 February 1998, 161–166.

- On the average, 73 percent of those respondents who had a serious problem took some action to have it corrected.
- Only 34 percent who took action were satisfied with the way in which the problem was resolved.
- Among those who were not happy with the outcome, 89 percent reported that they would not deal with the same firm again.

TABLE 7.1   Service Problems and Complaining Behavior in Australia

Service Type	Percent of Respondents Experiencing a Problem in Past Year	Percent Taking Action about a Serious Problem
Computers	27	83
Government (e.g., social services)	26	76
Car and motor bike repairs, service	24	75
Small business	21	81
Investment advice	18	80
Housing (purchase and rental)	18	69
Banking	17	75
Public transport	15	52
Telephone	13	93
Restaurants and cafés	13	54
Health (medical, dental, etc.)	12	56
Professional services	11	68
Airlines and coaches	10	79
Accommodation	9	63
Insurance	9	74
Utilities (gas, water, electricity)	9	84
Entertainment and sport	6	59

Source: Society of Consumer Affairs Professionals, SOCAP–TARP *Study of Consumer Complaint Behavior in Australia*, Sydney: SOCAP 1995.

- Complaining households made an average of 3.4 contacts each in an effort to have their most serious problems resolved.
- The further up the management hierarchy customers had to go to get the problem resolved, the more their satisfaction declined.
- On the average, a dissatisfied Australian customer told nine other people, whereas a satisfied customer told only half as many.

Factors Influencing Complaining Behavior

When consumers have an unsatisfactory service encounter, their initial (often unconscious) reaction is to assess what is at stake. On the other hand, studies of consumer complaints have identified two main purposes for complaining. First, consumers will complain to recover some economic loss, seeking either to get a refund or to have the service performed again (e.g., car repairs and dry-cleaning services). They may take legal action if the problem remains unresolved. A second reason for complaining is to rebuild self-esteem. When service employees are rude, aggressive, deliberately intimidating, or apparently uncaring (as when a sales assistant is discussing weekend social activities with colleagues and pointedly ignores waiting customers), the customers' self-esteem, self-worth, or sense of fairness may be negatively affected. They may feel that they should be treated with more respect, and thus become angry or emotional.

On the other hand, there are perceived *costs* in complaining. These may include the monetary cost of a stamp or phone call, the cost in time and effort expended in writing a detailed letter or making a verbal complaint, and the psychological cost of risking an unpleasant personal confrontation with a service provider—especially if this involves someone whom the customer knows and may have to deal with again. Such costs may well deter a dissatisfied customer from complaining. Often, it is simply less stressful to defect to an alternative service supplier, especially when the switching costs are low or nonexistent. If you are unhappy with the service you receive from your travel agent, for example, what is there to prevent you from switching to a different agent next time? However, if you decide to switch doctors or dentists, you may have to ask to have all of your medical records transferred. This requires more effort and might make you feel uncomfortable.

Research findings indicate that customers' intentions to take action about a problem relate directly to its importance. Also, problems associated with service *outcomes* are more likely to cause customers to voice complaints or to switch suppliers than those relating to service *processes*.[10]

Complaining represents a form of social interaction and therefore is likely to be influenced by role perceptions and social norms. One study found that for services in which customers have "low power" (defined as the perceived ability to influence or control the transaction), they are less likely to voice complaints.[11] Professional service providers, such as doctors, dentists, lawyers, and architects, are a good example. Social norms tend to discourage criticism of professional service providers, who are seen as experts in the service being offered. A clear implication is that professionals need to develop comfortable ways for customers to express legitimate complaints.

Complaints as Market Research Data

Responsive service organizations look at complaints as a stream of information that can be used to help monitor productivity and quality and highlight improvements needed to improve service design and execution. Complaints about slow service or bureaucratic procedures, for instance, may provide useful documentation

complaint log: a detailed record of all customer complaints received by a service provider.

of inefficient and unproductive processes. For complaints to be useful as research input, they should be funneled into a central collection point, recorded, categorized, and analyzed. This requires a system for capturing complaints wherever they are made—without hindering timely resolution of each specific problem—and transmitting them to a central location where they can be recorded in a company-wide **complaint log**. This is not a simple matter because there are many different entry points, including

■ the firm's own employees at the front line, who may be in contact with customers face to face or by telecommunications

■ intermediary organizations acting on behalf of the original supplier

■ managers who normally work backstage but who are contacted by a customer who is seeking higher authority

■ suggestion or complaint cards mailed or placed in a special box

■ complaints to third parties—consumer advocate groups, legislative agencies, trade organizations and other customers

The most useful roles for centralized complaint logs are (1) to provide a basis for tracking all complaints to see that they have in fact been resolved, (2) to serve as an early warning of perceived deterioration in one or more aspects of service, and (3) to indicate topics and issues that may require more detailed research. Firms that find ways of centralizing complaint data often discover that this information provides a valuable foundation for additional market research, using sample designs targeted at a broad cross section of customers, including those who—for cultural or other reasons—might be reluctant to initiate a complaint. Personal or telephone interviews also offer much better opportunities than mail or in-store surveys to dig deeper and probe for what lies behind certain responses. A skilled interviewer can solicit valuable information by asking customers such questions as these: Can you tell me why do you feel this way? Who (or what) caused this situation? How did customer-contact employees respond? What action would you like to see the firm take to prevent a recurrence of such a situation?

Tracking complaint trends is key to improving service quality.

Making It Easier for Customers to Complain

How can managers make it easier for unhappy customers to complain about service failures? Many companies have improved their complaint collection procedures by adding special toll-free phone lines, prominently displayed customer comment cards, and video or computer terminals for recording complaints (such as the touch-activated machines that allow customers to record complaints and suggestions just inside the front door at Einstein's Bagel franchises). Some go even further, training their staffs to ask customers if everything is satisfactory and to intervene if a customer is obviously discontented.[12] The hostess at Hampton Inn was clearly very observant: She noticed that the two Australian guests passed up the opportunity for breakfast two mornings in a row and sensed their disappointment.

Of course, just collecting complaints doesn't necessarily help resolve them. In fact, accepting complaints and then ignoring them may make matters worse. Although friendly sympathy from an employee is a lot better than an irritable shrug, the challenge is to have a well-designed service recovery strategy that empowers employees to resolve problems quickly and satisfactorily. At Hampton Inn, the hostess asked the two guests what they would normally eat for breakfast in Australia and then took the initiative during her free time to obtain the preferred items and bring them to the hotel. Recent research suggest that customers' satisfaction with the way in which complaints are handled has a direct impact on the trust they place in that supplier and on their future commitment to the firm.[13]

IMPACT OF SERVICE RECOVERY EFFORTS ON CUSTOMER LOYALTY

Complaint handling, according to TARP, should be seen as a profit center, not a cost center; it has even created a formula to help companies relate the value of retaining a profitable customer to the overall costs of running an effective complaint-handling unit. Plugging industry data into this formula yields some impressive returns on investment: from 50 to 170 percent for banking, 20 to 150 percent for gas utilities, over 100 percent for automotive service, and from 35 percent to an astonishing 400 percent for retailing.[14] Underlying these return rates is a simple fact. When a dissatisfied customer defects, the firm loses more than just the value of the next transaction. It may also lose a long-term stream of profits from that customer and from anyone else who switches suppliers because of negative comments from an unhappy friend. Thus, it pays to invest in **service recovery** efforts designed to protect long-term profits.

service recovery: systematic efforts by a firm after a service failure to correct a problem and retain a customer's goodwill.

Efforts to design service recovery procedures must take into account a firm's specific environment and the types of problems that customers are likely to encounter. Figure 7.3 (p. 142) displays the components of an effective service recovery system.

Service Recovery after Customer Complaints

Service recovery plays a crucial role in achieving or restoring customer satisfaction. Things occur in every organization that negatively affect its relationships with its customers. The true test of a firm's commitment to satisfaction and service quality isn't in the advertising promises or the decor and ambience of its offices, but in the way it responds when things go wrong for the customer. Unfortunately, firms don't always react in ways that match their advertised service promises. Effective service recovery requires thoughtful procedures for resolving problems and handling disgruntled customers. It is critical for firms to have effective recovery strategies

FIGURE 7.3 Components of an Effective Service Recovery System

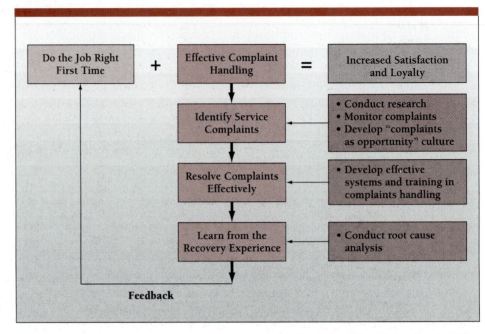

Source: Lovelock, Patterson, and Walker, *Services Marketing—Australia and New Zealand* (Sydney: Prentice Hall, 1998).

because even a single service problem can destroy a customer's confidence in a firm under the following conditions:

- The failure is totally outrageous (for instance, blatant dishonesty on the part of the supplier).
- The problem fits a pattern of failure rather than being an isolated incident.
- The recovery efforts are weak, serving to compound the original problem rather than correct it.[15]

Some complaints are made while service delivery is still taking place; others are made after the fact. In both instances, how the complaint is handled may determine whether the customer remains with the firm or seeks new suppliers in the future. The advantage of getting real-time complaints is that there may still be a chance to correct the situation before service delivery is completed; the disadvantage (from an employee perspective) is that it can destroy motivation, as well as interfere with service delivery. The real difficulty for employees is that they often lack the authority and the tools to resolve customers' problems, especially when it comes to arranging alternatives at the company's expense or authorizing compensation on the spot. When complaints are made after the fact, the options for recovery are more limited. The firm can apologize, repeat the service to achieve the desired solution, or offer some other form of compensation.

Principles of Effective Problem Resolution

Recovering from service failures takes more than just pious expressions of determination to resolve any problems that may occur. It requires commitment, planning, and clear guidelines. Both managers and front-line employees must be prepared to deal with angry customers who are confrontational and sometimes behave in insulting ways toward service personnel who aren't at fault in any way.

GUIDELINES FOR EFFECTIVE PROBLEM RESOLUTION

1. *Act fast.* If the complaint is made during service delivery, time is key in achieving a full recovery. When complaints are made after the fact, many companies have established policies of responding within 24 hours or sooner. Even when full resolution is likely to take longer, fast acknowledgment remains very important.

2. *Admit mistakes but don't be defensive.* Acting defensively may suggest that the organization has something to hide or is reluctant to fully explore the situation.

3. *Show that you understand the problem from each customer's point of view.* Seeing situations through the customers' eyes is the only way to understand what they think has gone wrong and why they are upset. Service personnel should avoid jumping to conclusions with their own interpretations.

4. *Don't argue with customers.* The goal should be to gather facts to reach a mutually acceptable solution, not to win a debate or prove that the customer is an idiot. Arguing gets in the way of listening and seldom diffuses anger.

5. *Acknowledge the customer's feelings.* Acknowledge their feelings either tacitly or explicitly (e.g., "I can understand why you're upset"). This action helps to build rapport, the first step in rebuilding a bruised relationship.

6. *Give customers the benefit of the doubt.* Not all customers are truthful and not all complaints justified. But customers should be treated as though they have a valid complaint until clear evidence to the contrary emerges. If a lot of money is at stake (as in insurance claims or potential lawsuits) careful investigation is warranted; if the amount involved is small, it may not be worth haggling over a refund or other compensation. But it's still a good idea to check records to see if there is a past history of dubious complaints by the same customer.

7. *Clarify the steps needed to solve the problem.* When instant solutions aren't possible, telling customers how the organization plans to proceed shows that corrective action is being taken. It also sets expectations about the time involved (so firms should be careful not to overpromise).

8. *Keep customers informed of progress.* Nobody likes being left in the dark. Uncertainty breeds anxiety and stress. People tend to be more accepting of disruptions if they know what is going on and receive periodic progress reports.

9. *Consider compensation.* When customers do not receive the service outcomes that they paid for or have suffered serious inconvenience and/or loss of time and money because the service failed, either a monetary payment or an offer of equivalent service in kind is appropriate. This type of recovery strategy may also reduce the risk of legal action by an angry customer. Service guarantees often lay out in advance what such compensation will be, and the firm should ensure that all guarantees are met.

10. *Persevere to regain goodwill.* When customers have been disappointed, one of the biggest challenges is to restore their confidence and preserve the relationship for the future. Perseverance may be required to defuse customers' anger and to convince them that actions are being taken to avoid a recurrence of the problem. Truly exceptional recovery efforts can be extremely effective in building loyalty and referrals.

The box on guidelines for effective problem resolution is based on discussions with executives in many different industries. Of course, the service recovery process for a particular firm must take into account its specific environment and the types of problems that its customers are likely to encounter.

Well-managed companies try to act quickly and perform well on each of the 10 guidelines. Research suggests that the slower the resolution of a service problem, the greater the compensation (or "atonement") needed to make customers satisfied with the outcome of the service recovery process.[16] Treating complaints with suspicion is likely to alienate customers. There's a real danger in assuming that all complainers are what we called jaycustomers in chapter 6. The president of TARP notes,

"Our research has found premeditated rip-offs represent 1 to 2 percent of the customer base in most organizations. However, most organizations defend themselves against unscrupulous customers by ... treating the 98 percent of honest customers like crooks to catch the 2 percent who *are* crooks."[17]

SERVICE GUARANTEES

A small but growing number of companies offer customers an unconditional guarantee of satisfaction, promising an easy-to-claim replacement, refund, or credit in the event of dissatisfaction. Christopher Hart argues that these **service guarantees** are powerful tools for both promoting and achieving service quality for the following reasons:

service guarantee: a promise that if service delivery fails to meet predefined standards, the customer is entitled to one or more forms of compensation.

1. Guarantees force firms to focus on what their customers want and expect in each element of the service.

2. Guarantees set clear standards, telling customers and employees alike what the company stands for. Payments to compensate customers for poor service cause managers to take guarantees seriously because they highlight the financial costs of quality failures.

3. Guarantees require the development of systems for generating meaningful customer feedback and acting on it.

4. Guarantees force service organizations to understand why they fail and encourage them to identify and overcome potential failure points.

5. Guarantees build marketing muscle by reducing the risks associated with the purchase and building long-term loyalty.[18]

Many firms have enthusiastically leapt on the service guarantees bandwagon without carefully thinking through what is implied in making and keeping the promises of an unconditional service guarantee. Compare the examples of service guarantees in the box and ask yourself whether you would like to be a customer of either organization.

EXAMPLES OF TWO SERVICE GUARANTEES

1. *Excerpt from the Quality Standard Guarantees from an Office Services Company*

We guarantee 6-hour turnaround on documents of two pages or less ... (does not include client subsequent changes or equipment failures). We guarantee that there will be a receptionist to greet you and your visitors during normal business hours ... (short breaks of less than five minutes are not subject to this guarantee). You will not be obligated to pay rent for any day on which there is not a manager on site to assist you (lunch and reasonable breaks are expected and not subject to this guarantee).

Source: Reproduced in Eileen C. Shapiro, *Fad Surfing in the Boardroom* (Reading, MA: Addison-Wesley, 1995), 180.

2. *Example of L.L. Bean's Guarantee*

Our Guarantee. Our products are guaranteed to give 100% satisfaction in every way. Return anything purchased from us at any time if it proves otherwise. We will replace it, refund your purchase price or credit your credit card, as you wish. We do not want you to have anything from L.L. Bean that is not completely satisfactory.

Source: L.L. Bean mail catalog.

FIGURE 7.4 The Hampton Inn 100% Satisfaction Guarantee

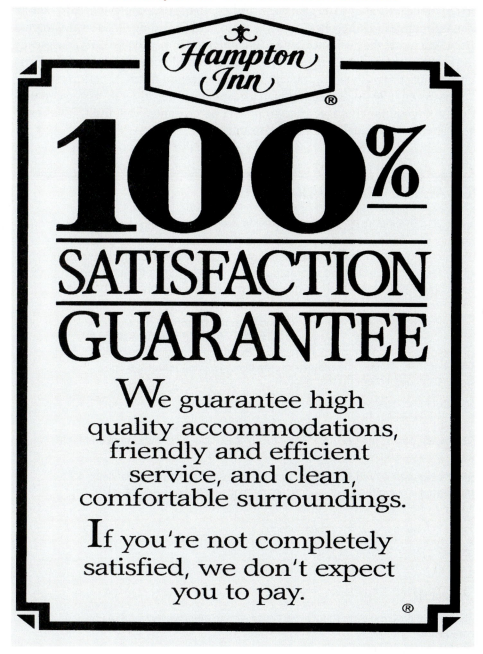

Source: "Hampton Inn 100% Satisfaction Guarantee, Research Justifying the Guarantee" by Promus Companies. Reprinted by permission.

Building Company Strategy around the Service Guarantee at Promus[19]

Promus Hotel Corporation has instituted its "100% Satisfaction Guarantee" (see Figure 7.4) throughout its entire hotel system, including Hampton Inn, Hampton Inn and Suites, Embassy Suites, and Homewood Suites, uniting all of the Promus brands with a single, common commitment to guest satisfaction.

As a business-building program, Promus views the 100% Satisfaction Guarantee as a great success. It has attracted new guests into the system while also serving as a powerful guest-retention program. At least as important, it has become a vital tool for identifying new opportunities for quality improvement and creating the impetus to follow through. The guarantee "turned up the pressure in the hose," as one manager put it, showing where "leaks" existed, and providing the incentive to plug them. As a result, the guarantee has had an important impact on product consistency and service delivery across the Hampton Inn chain. Moreover, studies of the guarantee's impact have shown a dramatic, positive effect on financial performance.

However, fully implementing such a guarantee is no easy task, as some of Promus's competitors who have tried to imitate its guarantee can attest. The boxed story about a "guarantee" is a pointed example.

HOW UNCONDITIONAL IS YOUR GUARANTEE?

Christopher Hart tells this story of an incident at a hotel in a well-known chain during the summer of 1997, while accompanying his two cousins. Jeff and Roxy Hart were nearing the end of an extended vacation weekend. They needed to find an inexpensive place to stay for the night. It was late in the day and their flight left early the following morning. Jeff called Hampton Inn and found nothing available in the area. So he called [name deleted] Inn, which had rooms available and booked one for $62.

We found the hotel [said Chris], noticing a huge banner draped from the bottom of the sign, advertising "Rooms for $55.95, including breakfast." We went inside. After giving the front-desk clerk the basic information, Jeff was told that his room would be $69. "But the reservation agent I just booked the room with quoted me $62. What's the story? And, by the way, what about the $55.95 price advertised on your sign? Can I get a room for that price?"

"Oh," replied the front-desk clerk. "That was a special promotion for the spring. It's over now." [It was late June.]

Jeff replied, "But you're still advertising the price. It's illegal to advertise one price and charge another one."

"Let me get my manager," came the nervous response. Out came the manager. In the middle of the conversation in which Jeff was arguing the same points that he made with the front-desk clerk, Chris interjected, "By the way, I understand you offer a satisfaction guarantee. Right?"

"Not on the $55.95 rooms," came the reply from the manager.

"Well, what rooms is it on?"

"Only the good rooms."

"You mean you have bad rooms?"

"Well, we have some rooms that have not been renovated. Those are the ones we sell for $55.95. But we're sold out of them tonight."

Chris said, "Well, Jeff, you'd better get one of the more expensive rooms because I'm not sure how satisfied you're going to be tomorrow."

The manager quickly added, "Did I mention that the guarantee doesn't apply on weekends?"

"No," barked Jeff, who had worked for 15 years conducting cost-benefit and compliance studies for the U.S. government, "and that's illegal too!"

"Wait just a minute," said the manager, getting a puzzled look like something had just popped into his head. "Let me see something." He then buried his head into the computer, clicking away madly at the keyboard, creating the impression that he was working on our behalf. After an appropriate time, up popped his head, now with a big smile.

"One of the guests who originally reserved a $55.95 room, called and upgraded—but the upgrade wasn't recorded in the computer. I could let you have that room—but I can't guarantee your satisfaction."

"We'll take it," said Roxy, exhausted.

Successful implementation of the 100% Satisfaction Guarantee requires that its underlying philosophy of guest satisfaction be embraced by every employee, from senior management to hourly workers. The challenge is to create a corporate culture based on a proactive commitment to consistently meet guests' expectations of complete satisfaction. However, despite its proven benefits, the guarantee has faced both resistance and skepticism among hotel managers not only at Hampton Inn but also in Embassy Suites and Homewood Suites.

Designing the Guarantee

The first step in designing the guarantee at Hampton Inn was to answer a key question: What would guests want in a guarantee? Research revealed that they were most interested in the quality and cleanliness of their accommodations, friendly and efficient service, and a moderate price. They also wanted a guarantee that was simple and easy to invoke if warranted. In-depth guest interviews yielded an "ideal customer-interaction flow" and a map of 53 "moments of truth" critical to guests' satisfaction with their Hampton Inn stays. These moments of truth translated into concrete and controllable aspects of Hampton Inn's product and service delivery. Throughout the guarantee design process, an important new mindset was reinforced: Listen to the guests, who knew best what satisfied them. Only the guests can make the decision to return to a particular property or positively recommend a Promus property to others.

The vice president of marketing stated, "Designing the guarantee made us understand what made guests satisfied, rather than what *we thought* made them satisfied." It became imperative that everyone from reservation system operators to front-line employees to general managers and personnel at corporate headquarters listen carefully to guests, anticipating their needs to the greatest extent possible, and remedying problems so that guests were satisfied with the solution. Viewing a hotel's function in this customer-centric way had a profound impact on how Promus conducted business.

Concurrent with its guest-based qualitative research, Promus interviewed its most progressive and customer-oriented franchisees and property managers to understand their perceptions of the proposed guarantee. Even among those who fully supported the guarantee concept in principle, pressing concerns remained:

- Will guests try to cheat and rip us off?
- Will our employees give the store away?
- What will be the return on our efforts to increase the satisfaction of our customers?

To prepare for the guarantee, a pilot test was conducted in 30 properties that already had high customer satisfaction. Training was seen as critical. First, general managers were trained in the fundamentals of the guarantee—what it was and how it worked. Then the general managers trained their employees. Managers were taught to take a leadership role by actively demonstrating their support for the guarantee and helping their employees gain the confidence to handle guest concerns and problems. Finally, the guarantee was explained and promoted to guests.

Even in properties that already had a high-satisfaction culture, Promus found that front-line employees were not always *fully empowered* to do whatever was needed to fully satisfy a guest. Furthermore, employees did not always feel they were charged with explicit responsibility for guest satisfaction. They needed to understand that their job responsibilities would now extend beyond the functional roles they were initially hired for (e.g., property maintenance, breakfast staff, or front desk). Managers and employees learned that the guarantee was not about giving money away; it was about making guests satisfied. They learned that satisfying guests by correcting problems had to be a priority. Employees were encouraged to creatively fix problems on the spot and rely on the guarantee as a safety net to catch guests who were still dissatisfied.

After learning the basic guarantee concepts, general managers were asked to form groups of 10 to 12. Their charge was to list the positive and negative aspects of the guarantee on a flipchart. Few groups could come up with more than one or two pages of positive aspects but had little difficulty creating lists of negative ones; one such list ran to 26 pages. Senior corporate managers went through each negative issue, addressing managers' concerns one by one. At all Hampton Inns, Embassy Suites, and Homewood Suites, the concerns remained relatively consistent. Foremost were concerns about management control, as well as concerns about guests abusing the guarantee and cheating (see the box on cheating).

As part of the feedback loop for all Promus brands, the company provides reports to the hotels every quarter, showing the top five reasons for guarantee invocations. Managers are helped to develop clear action plans for eliminating the sources of guarantee payments at their properties. Coupled with an awards program for employees who had undertaken exceptional acts of customer service, guest satisfaction has increased substantially at those properties where the guarantee has been most strongly embraced. Furthermore, once the sources of problems were systematically eliminated, payments became less frequent. When this cycle of success occurred at a property, the staff became guarantee advocates who spread word of their success throughout the chain.

Over time, hotel managers have come to recognize two things: First, the number of guests who invoke the guarantee represents only a small percentage of all guests. Second, the percentage of cheaters in this group amounts to a ridiculously small number. As one manager admitted, "It occurred to me that I was managing my entire operation to accommodate the half of 1 percent of guests who actually invoke the guarantee. And out of that number, maybe only 5 percent were cheating. Viewed this way, I was focused on managing my business to only 0.025% of total revenues."[20]

Experience has shown that guests are not typically looking for a refund; they just want to be satisfied with what they paid for. Because Promus's 100 percent

TRACKING DOWN GUESTS WHO CHEAT

As part of its guarantee tracking system, Promus has developed ways to identify guests who appear to be cheating—using aliases or different satisfaction problems to invoke the guarantee repeatedly. Guests showing high invocation trends receive personalized attention and follow-up from the Promus Guest Assistance Team. Whenever possible, senior managers will telephone these guests to ask about their recent stays. The conversation might go as follows: "Hello, Mr. Jones. I'm the director of guest assistance at Promus Hotel Corporation, and I see that you've had some difficulty with the last four properties you've visited. Since we take our guarantee very seriously, I thought I'd give you a call and find out what the problems were." The typical response is dead silence! Sometimes the silence is followed by questions of how headquarters could possibly know about their problems. These calls have their humorous moments as well. One individual, who had invoked the guarantee 17 times in what appeared to be a trip that took him across the United States and back, was asked, innocuously, "Where do you like to stay when you travel?" "Hampton Inn," came the enthusiastic response. "But," said the Promus executive making the call, "our records show that the last 17 times you have stayed at a Hampton Inn, you have invoked the 100% Satisfaction Guarantee." "That's why I like them!" proclaimed the guest (who turned out to be a long-distance truck driver).

satisfaction guarantee promises that they will be satisfied, it is a powerful vehicle for attracting and retaining guests. A 1996 survey found that

- 54 percent of guests interviewed said they were more likely to consider Promus hotels because of the guarantee
- 77 percent of guests interviewed said they would stay again at the same Promus hotel
- 93 percent of guests interviewed said they would stay at another Promus property
- 59 percent of guests interviewed have already returned

Conclusion

Collecting customer feedback through complaints, suggestions, and compliments is a way of increasing customer satisfaction. It's a terrific opportunity to get into the hearts and minds of customers. In all but the worst instances, complaining customers are indicating that they want to continue their relationship with the service firm. But they are also signaling that all is not well and that they expect the company to make things right.

Service firms need to develop effective strategies for recovering from service failures so that they can maintain goodwill, which is vital for the long-term success of the company. However, service personnel must also learn from their mistakes and try to ensure that problems are eliminated. Even the best recovery strategy isn't as good in the customer's eyes as being treated right the first time. Well-designed, unconditional service guarantees have proved to be a powerful vehicle for identifying and justifying needed improvments, as well for creating a culture in which staff members take proactive steps to ensure that guests will be satisfied.

Study Questions and Exercises

1. Explain the courses of action open to a dissatisfied consumer.
2. Describe the factors that may inhibit a dissatisfied consumer from complaining. How could the service providers in question reduce a complaining customers' discomfort to be sure of receiving important feedback?
3. What are the implications for managers of the TARP study results described in this chapter?
4. Think about the last time you had a less than satisfactory service experience. Did you complain? Why or why not?
5. When was the last time you were delighted with an organization's response to your complaint. Describe in detail what happened. Why do you think you were delighted?
6. Apply the four principles of service recovery at the managerial level to a service organization with which you are familiar. Describe how this organization follows or does not follow these guidelines. What impact do you see this as having on its customers' loyalty?
7. Evaluate the impact on (a) management and (b) customers of the Promus 100% Service Guarantee.

Three

Service Marketing Strategy

CHAPTER
Eight

Service Positioning and Design

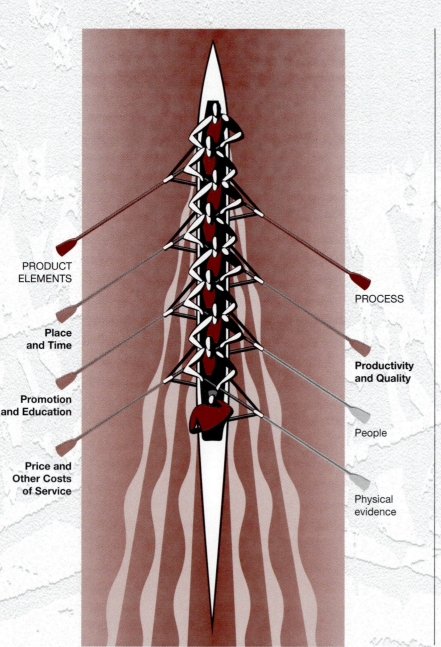

PRODUCT
ELEMENTS

**Place
and Time**

**Promotion
and Education**

**Price and
Other Costs
of Service**

PROCESS

**Productivity
and Quality**

People

Physical
evidence

Learning Objectives

**After reading this chapter,
you should be able to**

■ describe the four basic focus
strategies

■ explain the elements of a
service strategy

■ define the concepts of
competitive positioning and
repositioning

■ use perceptual maps to show a
company's competitive position

■ discuss the six categories of
new services and provide
examples of each

■ design a blueprint that
accurately reflects complexity
and divergence in the delivery
process for a specific service

Desperately Seeking Service Strategies[1]

The basics of a travel agency's business have traditionally been quite straightforward. Customers call for flight, train, hotel, or cruise reservations. The agent finds out what is available, maybe provides a bit of advice, books the transaction, and delivers the tickets. Commissions on airline tickets have long provided about 60 percent of a typical agency's revenues. However, in 1995, most major airlines, led by Delta, announced that they would no longer pay a 10 percent commission on every ticket sold. Regardless of the purchase price, there would be caps of $25 on one way and $50 on round trip domestic tickets.

These commission caps were only the start of trouble for the travel agent industry. Other marketplace changes began to affect the roles that travel agents filled as brokers of information and distributors of other companies' services. Travel agents are like stockbrokers, real estate agents, or consultants—their value is in what they know and what they can find out for customers. But access to information is being reshaped completely by computers and Web-based technologies. Customers can get travel information directly on the Internet at any time and can handle their own bookings, too.

So what should a travel agent do in this challenging new world? Many are trying to survive by cutting costs or adding value by doing the same things better, but a few have created totally new service strategies. Following are profiles of three service revolutionaries; see what you think of their innovative approaches for establishing a secure competitive position.

The Merchandiser

Company: *Travelfest*

Service Strategy: *Revamp the way travel is sold*

Gary Hoover likes to call his travel agency, based in Austin, Texas, the Home Depot of the travel industry.

His goal was to "yank travel out of the retail Stone Age" by designing a travel superstore where customers could shop for tickets and travel-related products in an entertaining and educational environment. Fourteen monitors play travel videos simultaneously in Travelfest stores, and backlit walls show slides from around the world. Customers can browse for travel information in the Europe room, the Africa room, and the Asia room, and children have their own special room to explore. Visa and passport applications are available, and customers can check out the Hotel and Travel Index (a resource used by most travel agents but rarely available to their clients). There are also 10,000 travel-related items for sale, including books, videos, maps, luggage and clothing, water purifiers, and language guides. The store is open from 9 A.M. to 11 P.M. seven days a week, and it accepts mail, Internet, and telephone orders.

The Contractor

Company: *Capital Prestige Travel*

Service Strategy: *Change the service-delivery model*

Derek Messenger, owner of Capital Prestige Travel, spends $1 million a year on statewide travel ads and infomercials about discount cruise sailings. His biggest challenge is having enough trained people to take all the calls his advertising generates. Messenger has solved this problem creatively by using independent contractors who work out of their homes and pay for the privilege of affiliating with a well-known travel agency, which channels calls to them. Each home-based contractor pays $7,800 to Capital Prestige. In return, contractors get a computer, software that connects them to Sabre (a national computerized reservations system), a hookup to Capital Prestige phone lines, and eight days of training. They also get paid 35 percent to 70 percent of the agency's ticket commissions. Capital Prestige takes care of all of the marketing and backup services, such as handling tickets, collecting money, and providing a help line for home agents who run into problems. With its innovative home-agent system, the company has turned fixed costs into variable costs, which saves enough money to generate more business through large-scale promotions and advertising.

The Niche Player

The Company: Aspen Travel

Service Strategy: Specialize in one service-intensive market niche

Aspen Travel started out as a traditional travel agency. Its customer base was largely limited to Jackson Hole, Wyoming, whose isolated mountain location seemed an unlikely spot for building a large corporate clientele. Then a film production company from Los Angeles shot a movie in Jackson Hole, and Aspen did such a good job of handling its travel that the company retained Aspen's services for trips to other locations. Owners Randle Feagin and Andy Spiegel had discovered the perfect niche, and today they do 85 percent of their business with production companies from Los Angeles, New York, and Miami. Word of mouth in the tightly knit film production industry takes care of Aspen's marketing, and faxes, e-mail, and remote ticket printers allow the agency to operate from Jackson Hole. Aspen's specialized knowledge helps it outperform would-be competitors. For example, how many travel agents know how to get an AT&T phone booth to a film site in Belize or transport penguins to the deserts of Moab, Utah, without their collapsing from heatstroke?

SERVICE LEADERSHIP: THE NEED FOR FOCUS

If you ask a group of managers from different service businesses how they compete, many will simply say, "on service." Press them a little further, and they may add "value for money," "convenience," or "our people are the key." Some may even respond to the question "What makes your service different?" by saying "Truthfully, nothing. We're all pretty much the same." But no two services are ever exactly alike. It would be impossible for companies to be identical in the design of their facilities, the employees they attract, the personalities of their leaders, or the cultures they create. As competition intensifies for many businesses in the service sector, creating and communicating *meaningful* differences is becoming increasingly important for **service leadership** and long-term profitability. Competitive strategy can take many different routes, but companies must somehow distinguish themselves from their competitors.[2]

> **service leadership:** achieving and maintaining a company's reputation for innovation and meaningful service differentiation in ways that create competitive advantage in chosen markets.

Four Focus Strategies

It's not usually realistic for a firm to try to appeal to all actual or potential buyers in a market because customers are too numerous; too widely scattered; and too varied in their needs, purchasing behavior, and consumption patterns. Different service firms also vary widely in their abilities to serve different types of customers. So rather than attempting to compete in an entire market, each company needs to focus its efforts on those customers it can serve best. In marketing terms, **focus** means providing a relatively narrow product mix for a particular market segment— a group of buyers who share common characteristics, needs, purchasing behavior, or consumption patterns. This concept is at the heart of virtually all successful service firms, which have identified the strategically important elements in their service operations and have concentrated their resources on them.[3]

> **focus:** the provision of a relatively narrow product mix for a particular market segment.

The extent of a company's focus can be described on two different dimensions— market focus and service focus. **Market focus** is the extent to which a firm serves few or many markets; **service focus** describes the extent to which a firm offers few or many services. These two dimensions define the four basic focus strategies shown in Figure 8.1 and lie at the heart of service leadership.

> **market focus:** the extent to which a firm serves few or many markets.
>
> **service focus:** the extent to which a firm offers few or many services.

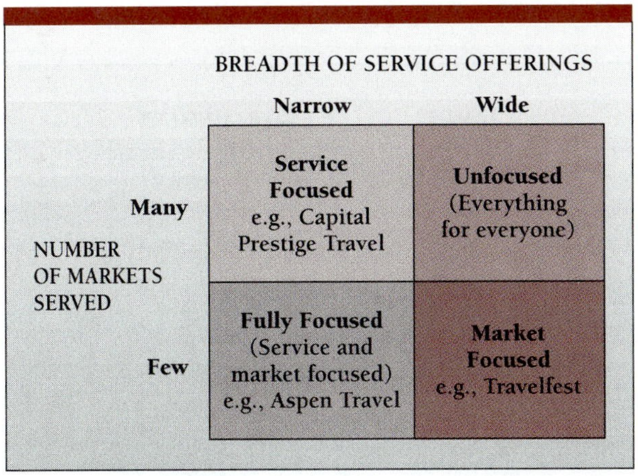

FIGURE 8.1
Basic Focus Strategies for Service Organizations

Source: Adapted from Robert Johnston, "Achieving Focus in Service Organizations," *The Service Industries Journal* 16 (January 1996): 10–20.

A *fully focused* organization provides a very limited range of services (perhaps just a single core product) to a narrow and specific market segment. Among the travel agencies discussed at the beginning of the chapter, Aspen Travel serves the specific needs of the film production industry. A *market-focused* company concentrates on a narrow market segment but has a wide range of services. Each Travelfest store serves a limited geographic market, appealing to families and individuals who are planning vacation trips rather than to business travelers, but offers a broad array of services. *Service-focused* firms offer a narrow range of services to a fairly broad market. Thus, Capital Prestige Travel specializes in the narrow field of discount cruise sailings but reaches customers across a broad geographic market through a telephone-based delivery system. Finally, many service providers fall into the *unfocused* category because they try to serve broad markets and provide a wide range of services.[4]

As you can see from Figure 8.1, focusing requires a company to identify the market segments that it can serve best with the services it offers. Effective market segmentation should group buyers in ways that result in similarity *within* each segment and dissimilarity *between* each segment on relevant characteristics. As discussed in chapter 6, market segments have traditionally been defined by using geographic, demographic, psychographic, or behavioral variables. Because of the dramatic increase in technology-related goods and services, some marketers are now suggesting a new segmentation variable, **technographics**, reflecting customers' willingness and ability to use the latest technology (see Figure 8.2 on p. 156 and the box on classifying technology users on p. 157).

technographics: segmentation of customers based on their willingness and ability to use the latest technology.

CREATING A DISTINCTIVE SERVICE STRATEGY

Once a company has decided which market segment(s) to target, the next task is to establish an overall strategic direction—a service strategy—to achieve and maintain a distinctive competitive position. Leonard Berry emphasizes the importance of these service strategies:

> All great service companies have a clear, compelling service strategy. They have a "reason for being" that energizes the organization and defines the word "service." A service strategy captures what gives the service value to customers. To forge a path to great service, a company's leaders must define correctly that which makes the service compelling. They must set in motion and sustain a vision of service excellence, a set of guideposts that point to the future and show the way.[5]

A company's service strategy can usually be expressed in a few sentences or words that guide and energize its employees. The best service strategies address

FIGURE 8.2 Segmenting Customers Relative to Technology Use

	CAREER	FAMILY	ENTERTAINMENT
OPTIMISTS	**Fast Forwards** These consumers are the biggest spenders, and they're early adopters of new technology for home, office, and personal use.	**New Age Nurturers** Also big spenders but focused on technology for home uses, such as a family PC.	**Mouse Potatoes** They like the on-line world for entertainment and are willing to spend for the latest in technology.
	Techno-strivers Use technology from cell phones and pagers to on-line services primarily to gain a career edge.	**Digital Hopefuls** Families with a limited budget but still interested in new technology; good candidates for the under-$1,000 PC.	**Gadget Grabbers** They also favor on-line entertainment but have less cash to spend on it.
PESSIMISTS	**Hand-shakers** Older consumers—typically managers—who don't touch their computers at work; they leave that to younger assistants.	**Traditionalists** Willing to use technology, but slow to upgrade; not convinced upgrades and other add-ons are worth paying for.	**Media Junkies** Seek entertainment and can't find much of it on-line; prefer TV and other, older media.
	Sidelined Citizens Not interested in technology.		

Data: Forrester Research Inc.

☐ More Affluent   ▨ Less Affluent

Source: Paul C. Judge, "Are Tech Buyers Different?" *Business Week*, 26 January 1998, 65.

basic human needs that don't change much over time. For example, the Hard Rock Café appeals to its target market's need for both food and sensory stimulation (refer to chapter 4 for a review of customer needs). Taco Bell's service strategy is to offer the best-value fast meal whenever and wherever customers are hungry. Although this statement sounds simple enough, it actually symbolizes a major change in the way the company defines itself and its operations (see chapter 5). Figure 8.3 shows the steps involved in identifying an effective service strategy.

A Sustainable Competitive Advantage

The first step in establishing a service strategy is to focus on customers' needs. Important service needs that are not being met by competitors provide opportunities for a company to move into an open position in the marketplace. Two questions should be asked about the needs and expectations of a target market relative to a specific service offering: What attributes are absolutely essential to this group of customers? And what attributes will delight them? The service strategy can then be

CLASSIFYING TECHNOLOGY USERS—FROM MOUSE POTATOES TO MEDIA JUNKIES

As the consumer market for technology soars, companies that sell products from cellular phones to Internet services are discovering that traditional segmentation tactics don't paint an accurate picture of who their customers are and what motivates them to buy. The failure of some highly publicized high-tech products like WebTV and Kodak's PhotoCD have convinced many marketers that a new taxonomy is needed to describe technology customers. They argue that although traditional consumer research may identify who bought a computer, it won't specify that four different people in a household use it—often for entirely different purposes. Market researchers have been scrambling to determine whether the purchase process is different for complex technology products and how people actually use technology in their home and work.

Forrester Research Inc., a technology consulting firm, has designed a study called Technographics to survey 131,000 consumers annually about their motivations, buying habits, and financial ability to buy technology goods and services. Already some big-name companies like Sprint, Visa, Ford, and Bank of America have signed on. "Technology is not just changing the way consumers spend time," says Technographics client Gil Fuchsberg. "It's also changing the way nearly every company is making, selling, and delivering products."

To help companies identify the right target customers, Forrester has defined 10 "technographical" categories, ranging from the tech-crazy "Fast Forwards" to the disinterested "Sidelined Citizens." To get an idea of how this segmentation scheme works, consider the Williams family. Cindy, age 46, is an administrative secretary in Tulsa, Oklahoma. She and her husband, Gary, age 44, have one computer they bought three years ago. They are not connected to the Web and don't use the computer much themselves. Their sons, ages 11 and 12, want an upgraded PC that is better for the computer-based games they love. Because of the Williams's status and income—two traditional segmentation variables—traditional consumer research results would identify them as promising technology buyers.

But Forrester maintains that these results would be misleading and that any high-tech firm that is marketing sophisticated products to the Williams family would be wasting its money. Technographics classifies the Williams as "Traditionalists"—family-oriented buyers who could afford new technological gadgets but are unconvinced of their usefulness. Why would the Williams be traditionalists? The age of their computer (three years old is ancient by tech standards) and the lack of an Internet connection are two big clues. Using this information, high-tech companies might decide to bypass the Williams in spite of their demographic fit because they are unlikely to be avid technology consumers.

Source: Excerpted from Paul C. Judge, "Are Tech Buyers Different?" *Business Week,* 26 January 1998, 64–68.

FIGURE 8.3 Defining a Service Strategy

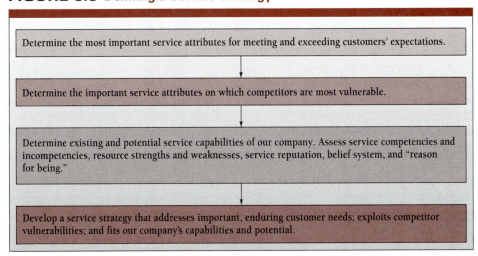

Determine the most important service attributes for meeting and exceeding customers' expectations.

Determine the important service attributes on which competitors are most vulnerable.

Determine existing and potential service capabilities of our company. Assess service competencies and incompetencies, resource strengths and weaknesses, service reputation, belief system, and "reason for being."

Develop a service strategy that addresses important, enduring customer needs; exploits competitor vulnerabilities; and fits our company's capabilities and potential.

Source: Leonard L. Berry, *On Great Service* (New York: Free Press, 1995), 72.

designed to include both the essential attributes and those features that have the potential to exceed customer expectations (see chapter 5).

The remaining three steps in Figure 8.3 help service companies develop a strategy that will provide a **sustainable competitive advantage**—a way of meeting customer needs in a specific market segment better than other competitors (see the box on business travelers). By *sustainable*, we mean a position in the marketplace that can't be taken away or minimized by competitors in the short run. Obtaining and keeping such an advantage is particularly challenging for service companies because many service attributes can be copied easily and quickly.

sustainable competitive advantage: a position in the marketplace that can't be taken away or minimized by competitors for a relatively long period of time.

SERVICE POSITIONING

After a service strategy has been identified, a company must decide how to position its product most effectively. The concept of positioning involves establishing a distinctive place in the minds of customers relative to competing products. Jack Trout[6] distills the essence of positioning into the following four principles:

1. A company must establish a position in the minds of its targeted customers.
2. The position should be singular, providing one simple and consistent message.
3. The position must set a company apart from its competitors.
4. A company cannot be all things to all people—it must focus its efforts.

Domino's Pizza is an example of a company that took these four principles to heart. In an industry whose core product is a commodity, competition is often based on value-added dimensions. Although pizza is the basic product customers purchase from Domino's, they also want service attributes like convenience (home delivery) and speed. For years, Domino's has stressed speed in its advertising with the line "30 minutes or it's on us." As a result, Domino's "owns" the distinctive attribute

---

TRANSPORTING BUSINESS TRAVELERS INTO THE 21ST CENTURY

Amtrak, America's national passenger railroad, provides a good example of a service strategy based on customer needs. Commuter flights established by airlines to offer fast service in the busy Northeast Corridor (which includes Washington, D.C.; New York City; and Boston) have eroded Amtrak's position in the business traveler market. But Amtrak's market research indicates that travelers want both convenience *and* comfort at levels not currently available on most flights. To address these unmet needs, the company plans to introduce a new, high-speed rail service, offering passengers comfortable, reliable, and safe transportation, starting in October 1999. Amtrak's new Canadian-built trains will transport passengers to cities in the Northeast corridor at speeds of up to 150 miles per hour—making its travel times competitive with those of commuter flights when ground travel from airport to city center is included.

Whereas Amtrak will focus on matching the airlines on essential attributes like convenience, reliability, and speed, it also plans to outdo them with features like customer service, spaciousness, and comfort. The company has extended its definition of the "Amtrak travel experience" beyond the core transportation service to include elements that have the potential to delight its customers—including the service provided by on-board staff, the reservations and ticketing processes, and the station environment. The trains' interior decor will also reflect customers' preferences for modern, tasteful design and subdued colors. The seats are spacious and comfortable, and lighting is bright enough to work by but still soft and unobtrusive. Amtrak will also offer a new, upscale "bistro" car and airline-style at-your-seat beverage service to further enhance the quality of its customers' commuter experiences.

Source: Based on Ian P. Murphy, "Amtrak Enlists Customers' Help to Bring Service Up to Speed," *Marketing News*, 27 October 1997, 14; Chad Rubel, "Amtrak Ready to Fly High by Challenging the Airlines," *Marketing News*, 6 May 1996, 1; and information from the Amtrak corporate Web site, http://www.amtrak.com, 11 January 1988.

of speed in the pizza delivery business. That is, when people think of fast, reliable service, Domino's comes to mind. According to Tom Monaghan, the president of Domino's, the secret to the company's success is "A fanatical *focus* on doing *one* thing well."[7]

Positioning and Marketing Strategy

Companies use positioning strategies to distinguish their services from competitors and to design communications that convey their desired position (see chapter 12). There are a number of different positioning strategies to choose from:

1. *Attributes:* Burger King stresses "Have it your way" burgers.
2. *Price and quality:* Supercuts provides good haircuts at a "reasonable" price.
3. *Competitors:* "You better take your Visa card because they don't take American Express."
4. *Usage occasions:* Ski resorts offer downhill and cross-country skiing in the winter, hiking and mountain biking in the summer.
5. *User:* Travelocity's on-line ticketing service is for technologically knowledgeable travelers.
6. *Product class:* It is better to lease a car than to purchase it.

Marketers often use a combination of these positioning approaches. But whatever strategy a company chooses, the primary goal is to emphasize its unique advantages and differentiate it from competitors. Companies that offer similar core benefits may decide to stress different advantages in their marketing efforts. For example, Sprint stresses the price and value of its long-distance services, whereas AT&T emphasizes reliability and expertise. Figure 8.4 (p. 160) summarizes how positioning strategies relate to critical marketing issues like service development and delivery, pricing, and communications.

Service Repositioning

Market positions are rarely permanent. Competitive activity, new technologies, and internal changes may cause a company to reposition itself and its services. **Repositioning** involves changing the position a firm holds in a consumer's mind relative to competing services (see the box on a repositioning success, p. 161). This may be necessary to counter competitive attacks, remain attractive and appealing to current customers, or target new and additional segments. It can involve adding new services or abandoning certain offerings and withdrawing completely from some markets.

repositioning: changing the position a firm holds in a consumer's mind relative to competing services.

Perceptual Maps as Positioning Tools

Many companies use perceptual mapping to help in their positioning strategies. **Perceptual maps**—also called positioning maps—help managers to identify the most critical attributes of competing services from the customer's perspective. They also play an important role in providing a visual picture of a service's unique characteristics, identifying the nature of competitive threats and opportunities and highlighting gaps between customer and management perceptions about competing services (as the Palace Hotel example in the next section illustrates). Any attributes that are important to customers can be placed on the horizontal and vertical axes of a perceptual map.

perceptual map: a graph of how customers perceive competing services.

FIGURE 8.4 Principal Uses of Positioning in Marketing Management

1. Provide a useful diagnostic tool for defining and understanding the relationships between products and markets:
   a. How does the product compare with competitive offerings on specific attributes?
   b. How well does product performance meet consumer needs and expectations on specific performance criteria?
   c. What is the predicted consumption level for a product with a given set of performance characteristics offered at a given price?

2. Identify market opportunities:
   a. *Introduce new products*
      - What segments should be targeted?
      - What attributes should be offered relative to the competition?
   b. *Redesign (reposition) existing products*
      - Should we appeal to the same segments or to new ones?
      - What attributes should be added, dropped, or changed?
      - What attributes should be emphasized in advertising?
   c. *Eliminate products that*
      - do not satisfy consumer needs
      - face excessive competition

3. Make other marketing mix decisions to preempt or respond to competitive moves:
   a. *Distribution strategies*
      - Where should the product be offered (locations and types of outlet)?
      - When should the product be available?
   b. *Pricing strategies*
      - How much should be charged?
      - What billing and payment procedures should be used?
   c. *Communication strategies*
      - What target audience(s) are most easily convinced that the product offers a competitive advantage on attributes that are important to them?
      - What message and attributes should be emphasized and which competitors, if any, should be mentioned as the basis for comparison on those attributes?
      - Which communication channels should be used, personal selling or different advertising media (selected not only for their ability to convey the chosen message to the target audience but also for their ability to reinforce the desired image of the product)?

Some commonly used attributes are

- price
- quality
- type or frequency of use
- service characteristics that offer a unique benefit

A perceptual map is usually limited to two attributes (although three-dimensional models can show three attributes at the same time). When more than three dimensions are needed to describe product performance in a given market, a series of separate charts can be drawn. Computer models that can handle many attributes simultaneously are also available.

A perceptual map is only as good as the quality of the information used in constructing it. Because most markets are dynamic, companies will need to do additional market research and redraw perceptual maps to reflect significant changes in the competitive environment. New market entrants and repositioning of existing competitors may mean that a formerly distinctive position no longer exists. Separate maps may also need to be drawn for different market segments if research shows that there are sharp variations between them. In the case of airlines, for instance, vacationers and business travelers may have different service priorities and are likely to purchase different levels of flight accommodations.

A REPOSITIONING SUCCESS STORY

Charles Schwab & Co., America's largest discount securities broker, was founded in 1975 when fixed commission rates were abolished in the United States. The company's initial service was a very basic one—accurate and timely execution of investment transactions for clients at a lower price than they would pay at a full-service broker.

By 1979–1980, Schwab's customer base and transaction volumes had expanded enough so that the firm could make significant investments in automation. This allowed the company to add services like money market mutual funds and asset management accounts. By adding value through automation, Schwab strategically altered its market position from one based purely on low-price transactions to one that offered value-added service at a low price. By the late 1980s, Schwab's core "transaction with value" business had matured.

The company decided to maintain its core business but also to expand its offerings. In 1992, Schwab launched its OneSource service, which made mutual funds available to customers with no load and no transaction fees. Customers' funds in OneSource were accessible with a single phone call and were tracked on one account statement. This service innovation dramatically reduced customers' costs in two ways: the time spent accessing account information decreased and fees dropped to zero.

In 1995, Schwab introduced its StreetSmart software package, which allowed accountholders to trade through their computers and to obtain on-line access to current investment information. Schwab has since become the dominant provider of on-line brokerage services. Of the 1.5 million active, Web-based brokerage accounts in the United States, 700,000 are held by Schwab. The firm has twice the market share of its closest competitor even though it is one of the most expensive on-line traders. More than half of Schwab's on-line accounts come from its 4.2 million regular discount brokerage accounts. As an enticement to use the Web, regular Schwab customers get a 20 percent discount for cybertrading. Although the discount lowers revenues per trade, increased usage rates and lower operating costs have made on-line trading highly profitable for Schwab. The company continues to strengthen its Internet presence. In 1997, it introduced Schwablink Web, a secure, private on-line site designed exclusively for independent investment managers who do business with Schwab.

Although Schwab's main goal is still to meet the financial needs of its customers, it continues to search for new growth opportunities. The company recently introduced SchwabLife insurance services—discount life insurance, including 5-, 15-, and 20-year policies. Schwab has successfully leveraged its brand name and reputation as a discount brokerage to begin building a franchise in the life insurance industry.

Source: Information on Charles Schwab's strategy through 1987 is drawn from Kent Dorwin, "Repositioning a Leading Stockbroker," *Long Range Planning,* November–December 1988, 13–19. For material from 1988 to 1997, see Matthew Schifrin, "Cyber-Schwab," *Forbes,* 5 May 1997; Adrian J. Slywotzky and David J. Morrison, *The Profit Zone* (New York: Times Books, 1997); and the Schwab Company News Online from 31 July 1997, and 7 October 1997, http://www.schwab.com.

Using Perceptual Maps to Evaluate Positioning Strategies

To demonstrate the value of perceptual mapping, let's look at how the Palace Hotel—a successful four-star property in a city that we call Belleville—used perceptual maps to develop a better understanding of potential threats to its established market position. The Palace was an elegant old hotel located on the edge of Belleville's booming financial district. Its competitors included 8 four-star establishments and the Grand, which had a five-star rating. The Palace had been very profitable for its owners in recent years and boasted an above-average occupancy rate. It was sold out on weekdays most of the year, reflecting its strong appeal to business travelers (who were very attractive because of their willingness to pay higher room rates than vacationers or convention participants). But the general manager and his staff saw problems on the horizon. Permission had recently been granted for four large new hotels in the city, and the Grand had just started a major renovation and expansion project.

To better understand these competitive threats, the hotel's management team worked with a consultant to prepare charts that displayed the Palace's position in the business traveler market both before and after the arrival of new competition. Four attributes were selected: room price, level of physical luxury, level of personal service, and location. Information on competing hotels was not difficult to obtain because the locations were known, the physical structures were relatively easy to visit and evaluate, and the sales staff kept themselves informed about competitors' pricing policies and discounts. A convenient surrogate measure for service level was the ratio of rooms per employee, easily calculated from the published number of rooms and employment data filed with city authorities. Data from travel agents provided additional insights about the quality of personal service at each of the competing hotels.

The Palace's management team created scales for each attribute. Price was simple because the average price charged to business travelers for a standard single room at each hotel was already known. The ratio of rooms per employee formed the basis for a service-level scale, with low ratios indicating high service. This scale was then modified slightly to reflect what was known about the quality of service actually delivered by each major competitor. The level of physical luxury was more subjective. The management team identified the Grand as the most luxurious hotel and decided that the Airport Plaza was the four-star hotel with the least luxurious physical facilities. The other four-star hotels were then rated in relation to these two benchmarks. The location scale was based on each hotel's distance from the stock exchange (which was in the heart of the financial district), because past research had shown that a majority of the Palace's business guests were visiting destinations in this area. The set of 10 hotels lay within a 4-mile (6-km) radius, extending from the stock exchange through the city's principal retail area (where the convention center was also located) to the inner suburbs and the nearby metropolitan airport. Two positioning maps were created to portray the existing competitive situation. The first (Figure 8.5) shows the hotels on the dimensions of price and service level; the second (Figure 8.6) displays them on location and degree of physical luxury.

A quick glance at Figure 8.5 shows a clear correlation between price and service. This is no surprise: Hotels offering higher levels of service can command higher prices. The shaded bar running from upper left to lower right highlights this relationship (which can be expected to continue diagonally downward for three-star and lesser-rated establishments). Further analysis indicates that there appear to be three clusters of hotels within what is already an upscale market category. At the top end, the four-star Regency is close to the five-star Grand; in the middle, the Palace is clustered with four other hotels; and at the lower end, there is another grouping of three hotels. One surprising insight from this map is that the Palace appears to be charging significantly more (on a relative basis) than its service level seems to justify. But since its occupancy rate is very high, guests are evidently willing to pay the present rate.

In Figure 8.6, the Palace is positioned in relation to the competition on location and physical luxury. We would not expect these two variables to be related, and they don't appear to be so. A key insight here is that the Palace occupies a relatively empty portion of the map. It is the only hotel in the financial district, a fact that probably explains its ability to charge more than its service level (or degree of physical luxury) would normally command. There are two clusters of hotels in the vicinity of the shopping district and convention center—a relatively luxurious group of three and a second group of two that offer a moderate level of luxury.

After mapping the current situation, the Palace's management team turned to the future. Their next task was to predict the positions of the four new hotels being constructed in Belleville, as well as the probable repositioning of the Grand (see Figures

FIGURE 8.5 Belleville's Principal Business Hotels: Positioning Map of Service Level versus Price Level

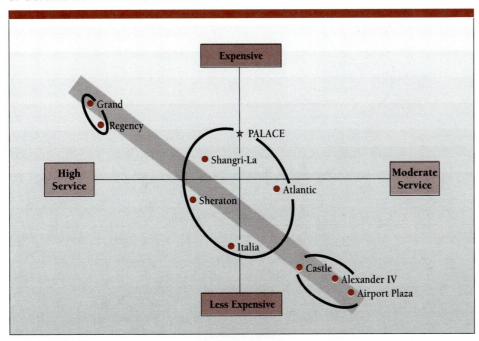

FIGURE 8.6 Belleville's Principal Business Hotels after New Construction: Positioning Map of Location versus Physical Luxury

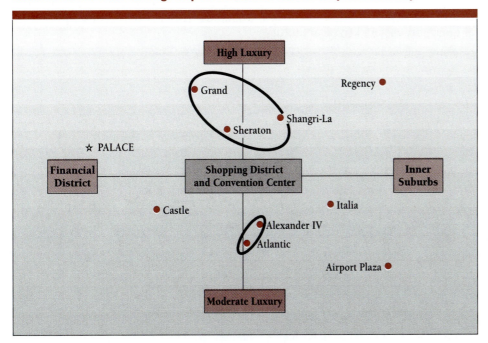

8.7 and 8.8, p. 164). The construction sites were already known. Two would be in the financial district and two in the vicinity of the convention center. Predicting the positions of the four new hotels was not difficult because preliminary details had already been released. The owners of two of the hotels intended to seek five-star status, although this might take a few years to achieve. Three of the newcomers would be affiliated with international chains. Their strategies could be guessed by examining recent hotels opened in other cities by these same chains. Press releases distributed by the Grand had already declared that the "New Grand" would be larger and even more luxurious, and its management planned to add new service features.

FIGURE 8.7 Belleville's Principal Business Hotels, Following New Construction: Positioning Map of Service Level versus Price Level

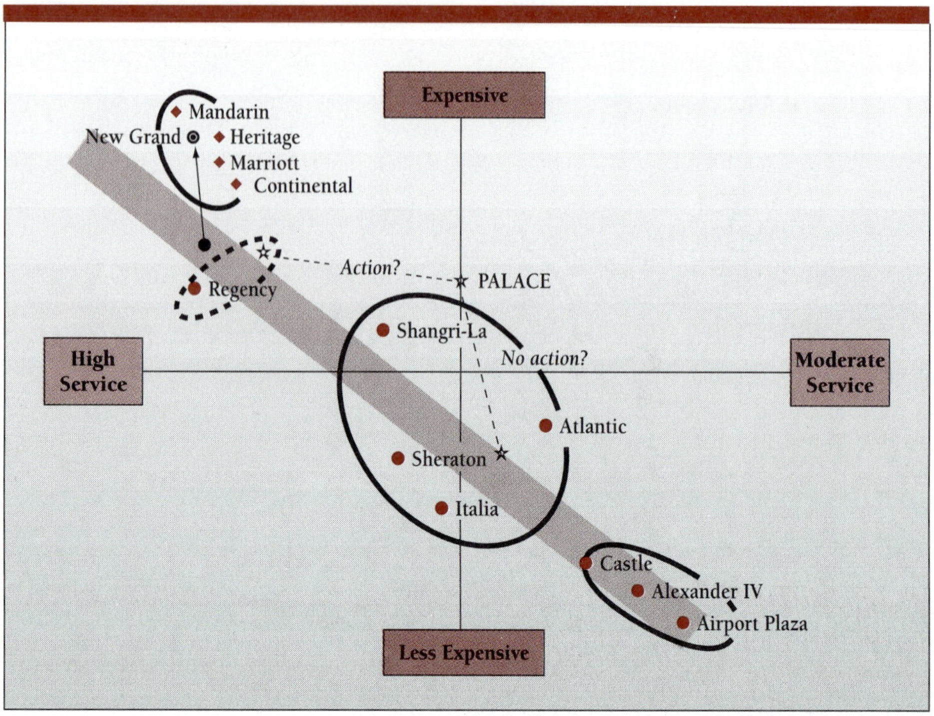

FIGURE 8.8 Belleville's Principal Business Hotels: Positioning Map of Location versus Physical Luxury

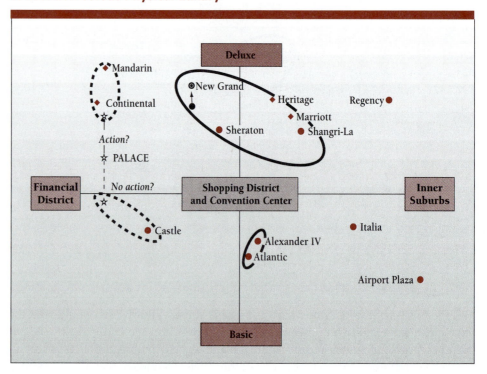

Pricing was easy to project because new hotels use a formula for setting posted room prices (the prices typically charged to individuals on a weekday in high season). This price is linked to the average construction cost per room at the rate of $1 per night for every $1,000 of construction costs. Thus, a 500-room hotel that costs

$100 million to build (including land costs) would have an average room cost of $200,000 and would need to set a price of $200 per room night. Using this formula, Palace managers concluded that the four new hotels would have to charge significantly more than the Grand or the Regency. This would have the effect of establishing what marketers call a price umbrella above existing price levels and would give other competitors the option of raising their prices. To justify the high prices, the new hotels would have to offer customers very high standards of service and luxury. At the same time, the New Grand would need to increase its prices to recover the costs of renovations, new construction, and enhanced service offerings.

Assuming that no changes were made by either the Palace or the other existing hotels, we see that the impact of the new competition clearly posed a significant threat to the Palace. It would lose its unique locational advantage and be one of three hotels in the immediate vicinity of the financial district (see Figure 8.7). The sales staff believed that many of the Palace's existing business customers would be attracted to the Continental and the Mandarin and would be willing to pay higher rates to obtain superior benefits. The other two newcomers were seen as more of a threat to the Shangri-La, Sheraton, and New Grand in the shopping district and convention center cluster. The New Grand and the other entrants would create a high price–high service luxury cluster at the top end of the market, leaving the Regency in what might prove to be a distinctive—and therefore defensible—space of its own.

What action should the Palace take in these circumstances? One option would be to do nothing in terms of service enhancements or physical improvements. But the loss of its unique locational advantage would probably destroy the hotel's ability to charge a price premium, leading to lower prices and profits. Some of the best staff members might be enticed away by the new hotels, leading to a decline in service quality. And without renovations, there would be a gradual decline in physical luxury, too. The net result over time might be to shift the Palace into a new cluster with the Castle, serving guests who wanted to visit destinations in the financial district but were unable (or unwilling) to pay the high prices charged at the Mandarin and Continental. As you can see, doing nothing would have significant strategic implications. If other existing hotels decided to upgrade and the Palace did nothing, it would eventually slide even further down the scales of luxury and service, risking reclassification as a three-star hotel.

An alternative strategy would be to implement renovations, service improvements, and programs to reinforce the loyalty of current guests before the new hotels where completed. The price umbrella these hotels create would allow the Palace to raise its prices to cover the additional costs. The hotel might then move to a new position, where it is clustered with the Regency on the dimensions of price and service. On the dimensions of luxury and location, it would be clustered with the Mandarin and Continental but with slightly lower prices than either competitor.

So what did the Palace actually do? Management selected the second option, concluding that the future profitability of the hotel lay in competing against the Continental (and to a lesser extent against the Mandarin) for the growing number of business travelers visiting Belleville's financial district. The Palace also tried to retain the loyalty of frequent guests by recording their preferences and special needs on the hotel database so that staff could provide more personalized service. Advertising and selling efforts promoted these improvements, and frequent guests were targeted by personal letters from the general manager. Despite the entrance of new and formidable competition, the Palace's occupancy levels and profits have held up very well.

UNDERSTANDING SERVICE PRODUCTS

Creating a competitive advantage presents special challenges for service providers, who often find themselves competing not only with other services but also with goods and customers' self-service options. Figure 8.9 shows four possible delivery alternatives for car travel and word processing, respectively. These alternatives are based on choosing between ownership and rental of the necessary physical goods and self-service or hiring of other personnel to perform the necessary tasks of driving and typing.

Because customers seek to satisfy specific needs, they will often consider reasonable alternatives that offer broadly similar benefits. For example, if your lawn desperately needs mowing, you could buy a lawn mower and do it yourself or you could hire a lawn maintenance service to take care of the chore for you. Such decisions may involve reference to the customers' skills or physical capabilities and their available time, as well as such factors as cost comparisons between purchase and use, storage space for purchased products, and anticipated frequency of need. As you can see, direct competition between goods and services is often inevitable in situations in which they can provide the same basic benefits.

Of course, many services rely on a mixture of both goods and services to satisfy customer needs. Quasi-manufacturing operations like fast-food restaurants sell goods supplemented by value-added service. At each site, customers can view a menu describing the restaurant's products, which are highly tangible and easily distinguishable from those of competitors. The service comes from speedy delivery of freshly prepared food, the ability to order and pick up food from a drive-in location without leaving the car, and the opportunity to eat a meal at a table in a clean environment.

Providers of less tangible services also offer a "menu" of products, representing a bundle of carefully selected elements built around a core benefit. For instance, universities provide many types of undergraduate education, ranging from two-year certification programs to the completion of bachelors' degrees and from full-time residency to evening extension programs. Most also offer graduate studies and non-degree continuing education classes. The supplementary service elements include counseling services, library and computer resources, entertainment opportunities like theater and sports events, and a safe and pleasant campus environment. (We return to the topic of supplementary services in more detail in chapter 9.)

The Power of Service Brands

brand: a name, phrase, design, symbol, or some combination of these that identifies a company's services and differentiates it from competitors.

Because of the difficult competitive challenges to service providers, brands can play an especially important role in defining a company's service offerings. But what *is* a brand? Harry Beckwith argues that for a service, a **brand** is more than a name or a symbol. It is an implicit promise that a service provider will perform up to customer expectations.[8] Brands are very important to service customers because

FIGURE 8.9 Services as Substitutes for Owning and/or Using Goods

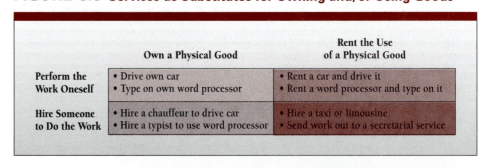

	Own a Physical Good	Rent the Use of a Physical Good
Perform the Work Oneself	• Drive own car • Type on own word processor	• Rent a car and drive it • Rent a word processor and type on it
Hire Someone to Do the Work	• Hire a chauffeur to drive car • Hire a typist to use word processor	• Hire a taxi or limousine • Send work out to a secretarial service

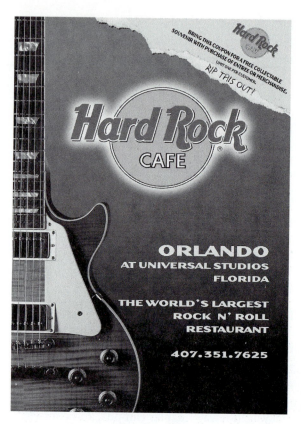

You know what to expect at a
Hard Rock Café.

few services have warranties—in part because they are typically difficult to guarantee. For example, how do you guarantee that a doctor's diagnosis will be accurate? That a professor's class will be educational? That a tax accountant will find every legal deduction? That a theme restaurant will always provide a trendy setting? Because you can't be sure—most of the time—you have to rely on the service provider's brand image. You know what to expect when you patronize a Hard Rock Café. Even nonprofit organizations like Goodwill and the Chicago Symphony Orchestra are using brands to establish positive images in their donors' minds. Both organizations have had a 10 percent increase in donations since they modernized their logos and created a consistent, upbeat image.[9]

To maintain a well-defined brand identity, a firm must reinforce key brand elements in all of its communications—from service encounters to TV advertising. Marketing messages may vary by target audience, but there should be a consistent theme. This includes Web sites, which can be powerful communication links with customers if they are managed effectively. Companies like FedEx, United Parcel Service (UPS), Kinko's, and Sir Speedy use the Internet to provide on-line information and delivery options for their customers. These value-added services help enhance customers' overall brand experiences.

The Branded Customer Experience

Customer satisfaction—the deep kind of satisfaction that builds loyalty—doesn't result from any one thing. A customer's decision to stay or defect is the result of many small encounters with a company. Successful firms recognize this factor and design distinctive service strategies to ensure that ordinary events will be perceived as extraordinary. The Forum Corp., a consulting and training group in Boston, calls this the creation of a "branded customer experience."[10] According to the Forum, the promise of the service brand should be reinforced at every point of contact between a company and its customers. Forum senior vice president Scott Timmins says,

"The question is, what is our brand of customer delight—what are we known for, what do customers expect us to deliver reliably, where's our wow?"

Southwest Airlines has mastered the branded service experience—with a twist. Its brand stands for the opposite of special treatment, but passengers expect that. The airline delights its customers by making and keeping a promise to be fast and cheap, with a little humor on the side. Southwest's positioning strategy is designed to reinforce its image as the "no frills" carrier. This theme is emphasized in its clever advertising campaigns; the sometimes tattered, reusable plastic boarding passes; and the casual appearance and demeanor of its flight attendants.

NEW SERVICE DEVELOPMENT

Competitive intensity and customers' expectations are increasing in nearly all service industries. Thus a company's success lies not only in providing existing services well but also in creating new ones. Six different categories of new products have been identified, ranging from major innovations to simple style changes.[11] We've adapted these classifications for use in a service context.

1. *Major innovations* are new products for markets that have not yet been defined. Examples include FedEx's introduction of express package delivery and Schwab's launch of on-line trading services.

2. *Start-up businesses* are new products for a market already served by products that meet the same generic need. For example, the University of Phoenix competes with other universities by offering undergraduate and graduate degrees in a most untraditional way. It has no regular campus, and courses are taught either in night classes or on-line. Students get most of the benefits of a college degree in half the time—and at a much lower price—than from other universities.[12]

3. *New products* for a currently served market represent an attempt to offer existing customers a product that the firm didn't previously have, although it is available elsewhere. Barnes and Noble's addition of Starbucks Cafés in its retail stores is a new product offering.

4. *Product line extensions* are additions to current product lines or distinctive new ways of delivering existing products. Theme restaurants like the Rainforest Café are good examples of this concept, because they provide food served in a unique setting. Rainforest Cafés are designed to keep customers entertained with aquariums; live parrots; waterfalls; fiberglass monkeys; talking trees that spout environmentally related information; and regularly timed thunderstorms, complete with lightening.[13]

5. *Product improvements* are the most common type of innovation. They involve changes in the features of current products, including improvements to the core service, as well as changes in supplementary services. For instance, Kinko's now offers customers around-the-clock, seven-days-a-week Internet access through special, high-speed modems at most of its locations in the United States and Canada.

6. *Style changes* are the most modest type of innovation, although they are often highly visible. Repainting aircraft in new color schemes, outfitting service employees in new uniforms, or introducing a new bank check design are all examples.

Value-Added Services for Physical Products

Whereas we may tend to think most often of new services for individual consumers, there are many opportunities in the business-to-business sector as well. Corporate purchasers tend to be knowledgeable, demanding, and value conscious.

One concern they have is how to get the best value from their companies' facilities and equipment. Any new physical product may create a need for related possession-processing services, particularly if the product is a high-value, durable item. For industrial equipment, useful services range from transport, installation, refueling, maintenance, and cleaning to consulting advice, upgrading, repair, and ultimate disposal. Historically, such services have generated important revenue streams for many years after the initial sale for products like trucks, factory machinery, locomotives, and computers.

In the case of high-technology equipment, however, revenues from traditional services such as repair and maintenance are shrinking. Ironically, a combination of higher quality and greater reliability often means that machines become technically obsolete before they need major repairs. Moreover, because of more serviceable designs (including plug-in modules), the remaining maintenance work is subject to more competition. Small, independent suppliers may offer to service equipment more cheaply than the original vendor, and many customers have learned how to do their own maintenance. These developments are cutting into traditional sources of after-sales service revenues. In response, high-technology firms have created new value-added professional services such as consultations on how to reengineer business processes or design complex Web sites. Other high-tech services requiring significant professional consultation include specialized education and training, software support, data center design and construction, advice on creating enterprise-wide networks, responsibility for relocating an office and its associated systems, and safe storage of vital records.

Yet another type of high value-added service—which can be applied to any type of manufactured product—is supply chain management. Firms specializing in business logistics will take over the responsibility for transport and warehousing of material inputs, finished goods, and spare parts on a national or even global basis. FedEx, for instance, enters into exclusive, long-term contracts with some clients. Linkages may extend from suppliers' plants to the customer's manufacturing or assembly facilities and from there to wholesalers, retail stores, or end users. The efficiencies obtained through supply chain management are highly dependent on information systems that can track the presence of any item throughout the system.

There are interesting opportunities for services that are linked to goods. Many rental and leasing businesses offer service alternatives to purchasing durable products like cars, furniture, or sports equipment (e.g., mountain bikes or snowboards), and sometimes familiar, nondurable goods are repositioned as services. Many supermarkets now offer attractively packaged take-out (or sometimes home-delivered) meals for customers who are too rushed to cook. The grocery industry hopes that its "home meal replacement" strategy will lure some restaurant customers who like the convenience of not cooking but would rather eat at home.[14]

Some goods and services are integrally linked. Consider optometrists, the professionals popularly known as "eye doctors." They examine patients' eyes and, when necessary, prescribe corrective lenses. Getting new glasses then requires selecting frames and having lenses ground to the right prescription. Many optical stores now perform this task on the site, and some can even deliver a new pair of glasses to a customer within an hour. Years ago, customers might have waited weeks.

Transforming Services into Goods

Some service providers sell goods that are closely related to their core service offerings. For example, many major theme-park operators rely on merchandise sales to supplement profits from rides and other entertainment attractions. Visitors leaving the Indiana Jones Adventure in Disneyland are routed through a store selling Indiana Jones t-shirts and hats, plus various "relics" from the Temple of Doom.

Getting new glasses: Has she purchased a physical good or a service?

Technology can provide interesting new products for capturing service performances through physical goods. The term *frozen services* describes goods that allow customers to self-access inventoried services.[15] For instance, textbooks and the Internet can provide alternative access to the information provided in a classroom lecture. Live entertainment can be recorded and brought back to life on demand through CDs, audiotape, videotape, or film. Expertise in almost any field can be captured on interactive computer software like CD-ROMs or disks or on the Web.

User-friendly technologies, coupled with lower prices and greater affluence, have also created opportunities for goods to replace services in many fields. Telephone-answering machines cut deeply into the business of telephone-answering services. But now, reflecting new technological developments, answering machines themselves face competition from automated voice mail and e-mail. As the wheel of progress turns, customers continue to face changes in how they obtain the product benefits they seek, switching from services to goods and back to services again as new options appear.

The Role of Blueprinting in Service Design

In chapter 4, we introduced flowcharts as a technique for understanding a service experience from the customer's perspective and we'll use flowcharting again in chapter 13 to identify opportunities for companies to delight or disappoint their customers. However, new service design is a complex process that requires a related but more sophisticated approach known as blueprinting. A **blueprint** shows every activity involved in service delivery and production and specifies the linkages among them.[16] Because blueprints show the interrelationships among employees' roles, operational processes, and customer interactions, they can facilitate the process of integrated service management—the integration of marketing, operations, and human resources within a firm to create and sustain a successful service strategy (see chapter 1).

blueprint: a sophisticated form of flowchart, showing each activity involved in service production and delivery and specifying the linkages among them.

Three basic requirements must be met for a service blueprint to be effective:

1. The blueprint must show time and sequencing dimensions in diagrammatic form.
2. It must identify and handle errors, bottlenecks, and other process features.
3. It must precisely define the degree of variation from standards that can occur without affecting customers' evaluations of quality and timeliness.

Blueprints of existing services may suggest new product development opportunities that result from reconfiguring delivery systems, adding or deleting specific elements, or repositioning the service to appeal to other segments. For example, Canadian Pacific Hotels (whose 27 properties include the Toronto York and the Banff Springs Hotel) decided to redesign its hotel services. It had already been successful with conventions, meetings, and group travel but wanted to build greater brand loyalty among business travelers. The company blueprinted the whole guest experience from pulling up at the hotel to getting the car keys from the valet. For each encounter, Canadian Pacific defined an expected service level based on customers' feedback, and it created systems to monitor service performance. It also redesigned some aspects of its service processes to provide guests with more personalized service. The payoff for Canadian Pacific's redesign efforts was a 16 percent increase in its share of business travelers in a single year.

Complexity and Divergence

Service delivery processes can be described along two different dimensions—complexity and divergence.[17] **Complexity** refers to the number of steps required to complete the process, and **divergence** reflects the amount of variability allowed in executing them. Blueprints are a good way to visually document the complexity and divergence in a specific service process.

Service providers can change the levels of complexity and divergence to reposition a specific service offering. We illustrate this concept by blueprinting a florist's service in two different ways. Figure 8.10, on the one hand, presents a low-com-

complexity: the number of steps required to complete a service process.

divergence: the amount of variability allowed in executing the steps in a service process.

FIGURE 8.10 Blueprinting the Services of a Florist That Offers Many Choices

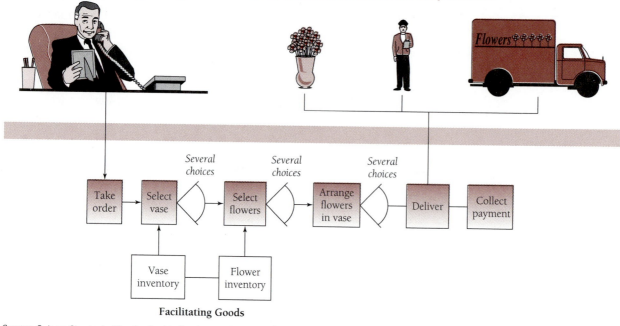

Facilitating Goods

FIGURE 8.11 **Reengineered Florist Blueprint Designed to Offer Eight Alternative Products**

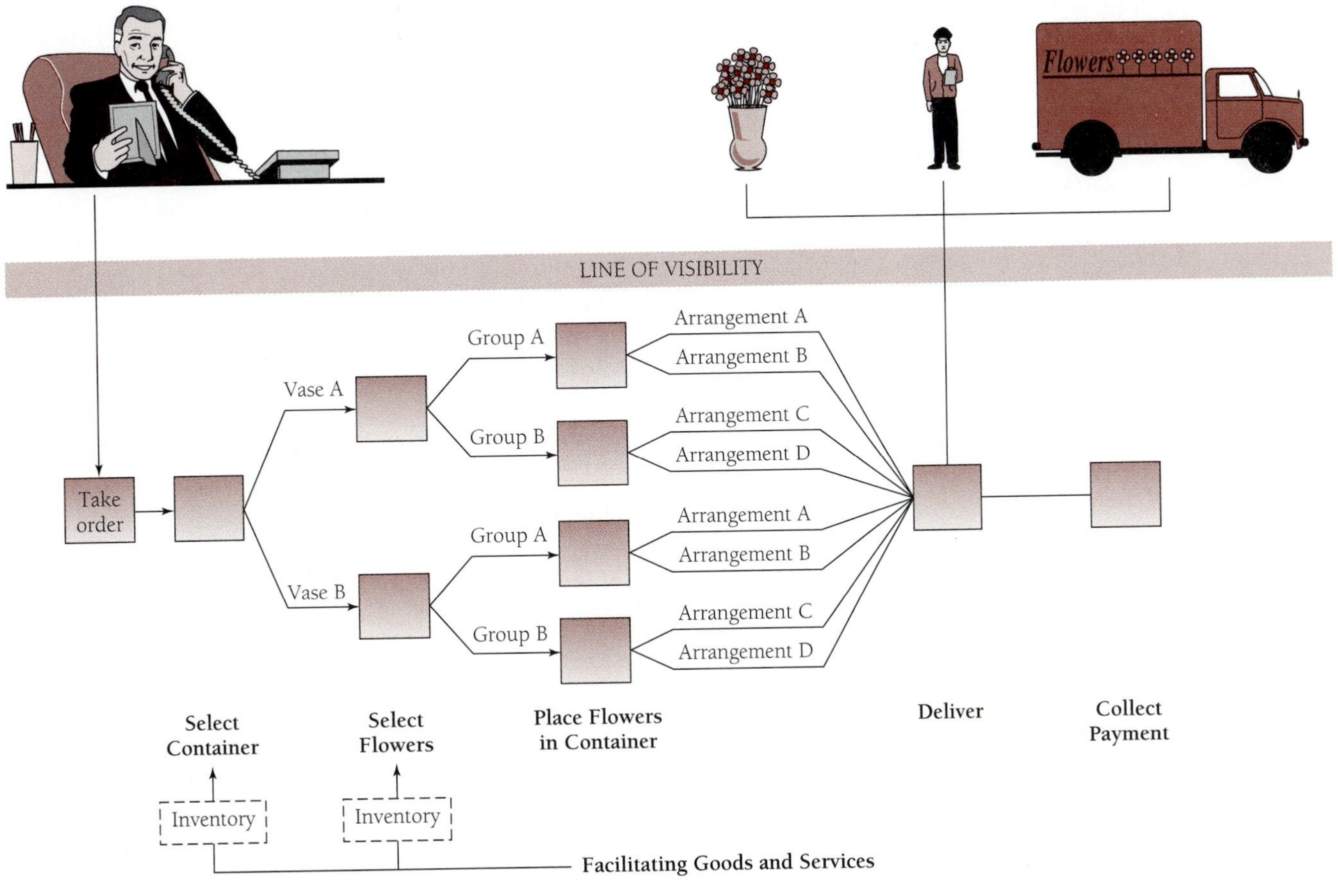

LINE OF VISIBILITY

Take order

Select Container

Select Flowers

Place Flowers in Container

Vase A

Vase B

Group A
Group B

Arrangement A
Arrangement B
Arrangement C
Arrangement D
Arrangement A
Arrangement B
Arrangement C
Arrangement D

Deliver

Collect Payment

Inventory

Inventory

Facilitating Goods and Services

Source: G. Lynn Shostack, "Service Positioning through Structural Change," *Journal of Marketing* 51 (January 1987).

plexity, high-divergence version of the service. This approach implies that the service delivery process will be more customized, with more room for employees' input. The "fans" attached to various steps show where a range of potential actions or events can occur (indicating higher levels of divergence). Figure 8.11, on the other hand, depicts a florist's service that has been reengineered to be less divergent. Although the level of complexity is the same, the choices associated with different steps have been limited. The process is more standardized, and as a result this florist's services can probably be offered to a broader market at lower prices.

Conclusion

All great service companies have a clear, compelling strategy that is designed to create a sustainable competitive advantage. Firms that aspire to become and remain service leaders in their respective industries find meaningful ways to distinguish their offerings from competing alternatives. They achieve this, in part, by focusing on certain market segments or by providing a narrow and carefully selected set of services; some firms do both.

In this chapter, we introduced two tools—perceptual mapping and blueprinting—that companies can use to help define their competitive positions. Perceptual maps present a visual display of how competing firms perform relative to

one another on key service attributes, whereas blueprinting provides a systematic process for examining alternative service designs for both new and existing products. Both techniques can be used to analyze opportunities for developing new services or repositioning existing ones so that companies can establish and maintain a sustainable competitive advantage by effectively addressing the needs and expectations of their target markets.

Study Questions and Exercises

1. Give examples of companies in other industries that are facing the same challenges as the travel agents in the opening section. Describe what service strategies these companies might use to compete effectively.
2. Why should service firms focus their efforts? What options do they have for doing so?
3. Describe what is meant by *positioning*. Choose an industry you are familiar with (like fast-food restaurants or grocery stores) and create a perceptual map, showing the competitive positions of different companies in the industry.
4. Explain why brands might be particularly important for services. Which service brands are you familiar with? What do they tell you about the companies they are associated with?
5. What are the six categories of new services? Provide your own examples for each category.
6. How is a blueprint different from a flowchart? How is it the same?
7. Create a simple service blueprint and explain how it illustrates the service's levels of complexity and divergence.

Nine

Adding Value with Supplementary Product Elements

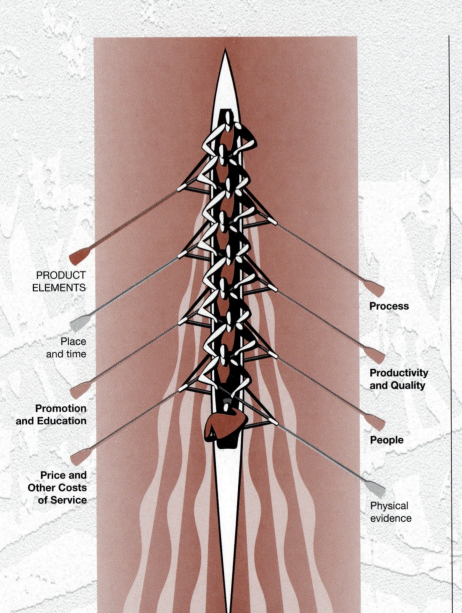

PRODUCT ELEMENTS

Place and time

Promotion and Education

Price and Other Costs of Service

Process

Productivity and Quality

People

Physical evidence

Learning Objectives

After reading this chapter, you should be able to

- discuss several approaches to describing service products

- distinguish between facilitating and enhancing supplementary services

- define the eight petals of the Flower of Service

- show how a company could use each of the petals to enhance its core service

- illustrate how technology offers new opportunities to provide value-added supplementary services

Starbucks Creates a Coffee Cult[1]

Starbucks's founders weren't studying market trends when they opened their first store. They were addressing their personal need for quality coffee. Coffee consumption in America had been declining for the past 10 years and, as a result, the major coffee brands began competing on price by adding cheaper beans to their blends. Canned supermarket coffee often sat on the shelves until it was stale. In desperation, Starbucks's founders decided to open their own store in Seattle in 1971. They named it after Starbuck, the coffee-loving first mate in Herman Melville's classic adventure novel *Moby Dick*, to evoke the romance of the high seas and the seafaring tradition of the early coffee traders. The company's green and black logo comes from a 16th-century Norse woodcut of a two-tailed mermaid and is meant to symbolize the seductive appeal of freshly roasted coffee.

Starbucks didn't introduce espresso and dark-roasted coffee to the United States. Rather, individually owned stores, which had sprung up in a number of cities and college towns, had done so. Although Starbucks initially sold fresh-roasted whole coffee beans, its management soon recognized there was an opportunity to expand into the service sector with upscale, attractive coffee houses where people could consume good coffee and socialize at the same time. The first customers came primarily from a small niche of sophisticated coffee lovers. But as income and education levels rose in America and people traveled more extensively to other countries, the demand for quality coffees—and comfortable coffee houses—began to increase steadily. In Europe, coffee houses traditionally had been associated with intellectual debate, political upheaval, and writers' movements; the

link with this romantic legacy helped Starbucks create a unique place in the U.S. coffee market.

Starbucks has been labeled by some as the coffee equivalent of Pizza Hut—good, consistent, but not too exciting. The secret to its success may indeed lie in educating people about good coffee, then providing a standardized level of customer service and product quality in a pleasing physical setting in every Starbucks outlet worldwide. The company also provides customers with opportunities to satisfy other needs through its promotion of environmental awareness (using recycled products and offering tips on how to recycle coffee grounds), community involvement (cosponsorship of local projects to help children or the homeless), and intellectual pursuits (in-store sales of the best-selling books from the Oprah Winfrey Book Club). Moreover, the stores are a perfect retail setting for coffee-related goods like fresh-roasted beans, coffee makers, and coffee cups, as well as pastries, candies, and other edible treats. They also provide a wealth of attractive brochures with information on such topics as the ingredients and flavors of various specialty beverages and how to make good coffee at home. Starbucks's friendly employees—called "baristas"—are knowledgeable about the 50 types of arabica coffee beans the company sells and are always willing to consult with customers.

By creating a consistently positive branded service experience, Starbucks has become the largest roaster and retailer of specialty coffee in the United States. Its retail stores and airport locations serve over 2 million customers a week, and it is currently expanding into Asia, Latin America, and Europe. Starbucks's coffee is also served in Nordstrom's department stores; Barnes and Noble bookstores; ITT Sheraton Hotels; and on board the aircraft of the Delta Shuttle, Horizons, and United Airlines. Marketing experts rank the Starbucks brand in the exalted company of Levi Strauss and Nike. To protect the brand's value, Starbucks executives carefully monitor quality and turn down as many offers as they accept to put their distinctive logo on new products.

Starbucks has become a pervasive part of American life. As a recent *Fortune* article noted, "It's gotten to the point where you can't escape Starbucks anywhere—even at 30,000 feet. Starbucks is in the freezer; it's in the office cafeteria; it's in Japan." And if Howard Schultz, Starbucks's CEO, has his way, the company will become as much a part of American culture as Levi's famous jeans.

CORE PRODUCTS AND SUPPLEMENTARY SERVICES

Most manufacturing and service businesses offer their customers a package of benefits, involving delivery of not only the core product but also a variety of service-related activities. Increasingly, these services provide the differentiation that separates successful firms from the also-rans. With both services and goods, the core product sooner or later becomes a commodity as competition increases and the industry matures. Although there may still be opportunities to enhance the characteristics of the core product, the search for competitive advantage in a mature industry often emphasizes performance on the supplementary service elements that are bundled with the core. (If a firm can't provide decent core elements, it's eventually going to go out of business.) Starbucks, for example, provides consistently fresh, good-quality coffee and beans (its core offering), but its competitive advantage comes from all of the supplemental benefits it provides for customers in its coffee houses. Our focus in this chapter is on categorizing the supplementary services that surround core products and demonstrating how useful similarities may exist across industries between these various supplementary services.

The Augmented Product

augmented product: the core product (a good or a service), plus all additional elements that add value for the customer.

molecular model: a framework that uses a chemical analogy to describe the structure of service offerings.

Marketing textbook authors have long been writing about the **augmented product**—also referred to as the extended product, or the product package—in an effort to describe the supplementary elements that add value to manufactured goods. Several frameworks can be used to describe augmented products in a services context. Lynn Shostack developed a **molecular model** (Figure 9.1), which uses a chemical analogy to help marketers visualize and manage what she termed a "total market entity."[2] Her model can be applied to either goods or services. At the center is the core benefit, addressing the basic customer need, linked to a series of other service characteristics. She argues that, as in chemical formulations, a change in one element may completely alter the nature of the entity. Surrounding the molecules are a series of bands, representing price, distribution, and market positioning (communication messages).

The molecular model helps identify the tangible and intangible elements involved in service delivery. In an airline, for example, the intangible elements include transportation itself; service frequency; and preflight, in-flight, and postflight service. The aircraft and the food and drinks that are served are all tangible. By highlighting tangible elements, marketers can determine whether their services are tangible dominant or intangible dominant. The more intangible elements there are, the more necessary it is to provide tangible clues about the features and quality of the service.

Two French researchers, Pierre Eiglier and Eric Langeard, proposed a model based on core and peripheral services.[3] The core service is surrounded by a circle that contains a series of peripheral services specific to that particular product. Their

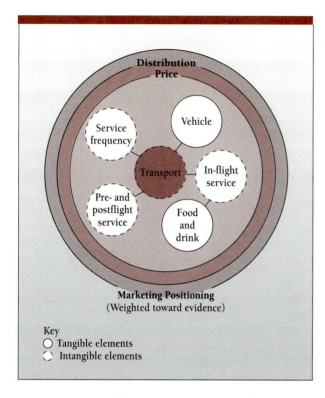

FIGURE 9.1
Shostack's Molecular
Model: Passenger Airline
Service

Source: G. Lynn Shostack, "Breaking
Free from Product Marketing,"
Journal of Marketing, April 1977,
published by the American Marketing
Association. Reprinted with
permission.

approach, like Shostack's, emphasizes the interdependence of the various components. They distinguish between peripheral elements needed to facilitate use of the core service (such as the reception desk at a hotel) and those that enhance the appeal of the core service (such as a bar and telephone service at a hotel).

We use the term *supplementary services* (rather than *peripheral services*) because these elements may add value to the core service and provide a competitive edge. Both models of the augmented product offer useful insights. Shostack wants us to determine which service elements are tangible and which are intangible to help formulate product policy and communication programs. Eiglier and Langeard ask us to think about two issues: first, whether supplementary services are needed to facilitate use of the core service or simply to add extra appeal; and second, whether customers should be charged separately for each service element or whether all elements should be bundled under a single price tag.

CLASSIFYING SUPPLEMENTARY SERVICES[4]

The more we examine different types of services, the more we find that most of them have quite a few supplementary services in common. The first step in identifying existing supplementary services for a product is to develop a flowchart that shows the steps in the service delivery process (see chapter 4, p. 83). In many instances, consumption or use of the core product is sandwiched sequentially between several supplementary services that precede or follow delivery of the core. If you prepare flowcharts for a variety of services, you will soon notice that although core products may differ widely, common supplementary elements—from information to billing and from reservations and order taking to problem resolution—keep recurring.

There are potentially dozens of different supplementary services, but almost all of them can be classified into one of the following eight clusters. We have listed

facilitating supplementary services: supplementary services that facilitate use of the core product or are required for service delivery.

enhancing supplementary services: supplementary services that may add extra value for customers.

Flower of Service: a visual framework for understanding the supplementary service elements that surround and add value to the product core.

them as either **facilitating supplementary services** or **enhancing supplementary services** (similar to the model by Eiglier and Langeard):

FACILITATING SERVICES	ENHANCING SERVICES
■ Information	■ Consultation
■ Order taking	■ Hospitality
■ Billing	■ Safekeeping
■ Payment	■ Exceptions

In Figure 9.2, these eight clusters are displayed as petals that surround the center of a flower—which we call the **Flower of Service**. They are shown clockwise in the sequence in which they are often likely to be encountered by customers, although this sequence may vary widely in practice; for instance, payment may have to be made before service is delivered rather than afterward. In a well-designed and well-managed service organization, the petals and core are fresh and well formed. A badly designed or poorly executed service is like a flower with missing, wilted, or discolored petals. Even if the core is perfect, the overall impression of the flower is unattractive. Think about your own experiences as a customer (or when purchasing on behalf of an organization). When you were dissatisfied with a particular purchase, was it the core that was at fault or was it a problem with one or more of the petals?

Not every core product is surrounded by supplementary elements from all eight clusters. Rather, the nature of the product helps to determine which supplementary services must be offered and which might usefully be added to enhance value and make the organization easy to do business with. In general, people-processing services tend to be accompanied by more supplementary services than do the other three categories; similarly, high-contact services will have more than low-contact services.

A company's market-positioning strategy helps to determine which supplementary services should be included (see chapter 8). A strategy of adding benefits to increase customers' perceptions of quality will probably require more supplementary services (and also a higher level of performance on all such elements) than a strategy of competing on low prices. Firms that offer different levels of service—such as first class, business class, and economy class in airlines—often differentiate them by adding extra supplementary services for each upgrade in service level.

FIGURE 9.2
The Flower of Service: Core Product Surrounded by Clusters of Supplementary Services

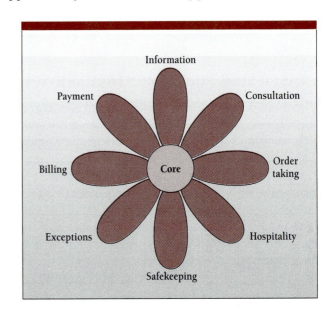

FIGURE 9.3 Examples of Information Elements

- Directions to service site
- Schedules and service hours
- Prices
- Instructions on using core product and supplementary services
- Reminders
- Warnings
- Conditions of sale and service
- Notification of changes
- Documentation
- Confirmation of reservations
- Summaries of account activity
- Receipts and tickets

Information

To obtain full value from any good or service, customers need relevant **information** (Figure 9.3). New customers and prospects are especially hungry for information: They want to know what product will best meet their needs. Other needs may include directions to the site where the product is sold (or details of how to order it), service hours, prices, and usage instructions. Further information, sometimes required by law, could include conditions of sale and use, warnings, reminders, and notification of changes. Finally, customers may want documentation of what has already taken place, such as confirmation of reservations, receipts and tickets, and summaries of account activity.

Companies should be sure that the information they provide is both timely and accurate, because incorrect information can annoy or inconvenience customers. One firm that automated its information services established a fully automated fax request service so that customers could have quicker access to information on upcoming conferences. However, in some cases the faxes were never sent, even after repeated phone calls from annoyed customers. Other customers received multiple pages of unwanted information.[5] In this case, the company put both itself and the advertised conferences in jeopardy by failing to perform an important supplementary service efficiently and effectively.

Traditional ways of providing information to customers include using front-line employees (who are not always as knowledgeable as customers might like), printed notices, brochures, and instruction books. More recent possibilities include videotapes or software-driven tutorials, touch-screen video displays, computer-accessed bulletin boards or Web sites, and menu-driven recorded telephone messages. For example, customers of FedEx and UPS can track the movements of their packages, each of which has been assigned a unique identification number, by accessing the company's Web site.

American Airlines uses several technological options to provide information to its customers in addition to its more traditional channels. In 1996, the airline introduced a convenient and "comprehensive new travel network of products and services" called Personal AAccess to give customers more control and convenience.[6] Personal AAccess provides flight, hotel, and car rental information in addition to frequent flyer mileage balances. Customers can either request free software from American or visit the company's Web site to use the Personal AAccess program.

Another area in which technology is used extensively is in college admissions. Many colleges employ both software and the Web to provide information to potential students. For example, a CD-ROM software package called College Advisor provides

information: a group of supplementary services that facilitates purchase and use by telling customers about service features and performance before, during, and after service delivery.

American Airlines advertises
AAccess.

facts on more than 1,200 colleges and reviews of over 300 top colleges. The Web is full of resources for prospective college students. One of the best sites in North America is College Board Online, which has information about registering and preparing for the Scholastic Aptitude Test™ (SAT), advice on college majors and careers, and an introduction to financing options.[7]

order taking: a group of supplementary services that facilitates purchase by establishing fast, accurate, and responsive procedures for taking applications, placing orders, or making reservations.

Order Taking

Once customers are ready to buy, a key supplementary element comes into play—accepting applications, orders, and reservations (Figure 9.4). The process of **order taking** should be polite, fast, and accurate so that customers do not waste time and

FIGURE 9.4 Examples of Order-Taking Elements

- ■ Applications
  - — Membership in clubs or programs
  - — Subscription services (e.g., utilities)
  - — Prerequisite-based services (e.g., credit and college enrollment)
- ■ Order entry
  - — On-site fulfillment
  - — Mail and telephone orders for subsequent fulfillment
- ■ Reservations and check-in
  - — Seats
  - — Tables
  - — Rooms
  - — Rentals of vehicles or other equipment
  - — Professional appointments
  - — Admissions to restricted facilities (e.g., exhibitions)

endure unnecessary mental or physical effort. These unwanted costs of service can substantially reduce the value of a service to customers by offsetting the benefits they receive (see chapter 11). Only in rare cases are customers willing to wait great lengths of time to place orders for a service. There's a difference, of course, between waiting in line at a ticket window and putting one's name on a list. People will wait overnight for tickets to a popular concert or sports event. Some fans of the Green Bay Packers, a professional football team in the National Football League, have waited up to 32 years for season tickets to the Packers' home games.[8] (Fortunately, they simply put their names on a list and are free to do other things with their time during this lengthy period.)

Technology can be used to make order taking easier and faster for both customers and suppliers. The key lies in minimizing the time and effort required of both parties, while also ensuring completeness and accuracy. For example, many restaurants have incorporated technology into their order-taking systems. Pizza Hut has tested an electronic alternative to the traditional order pad. The server enters orders by number on a handheld device the size of a large calculator, then zaps it toward a small receiver in the ceiling, from where it is downloaded to the kitchen. Taco Bell has been testing a method that enables customers to place their own orders by pressing their selections on a touch-sensitive, countertop menu. Such systems help restaurants by placing the responsibility for an order's accuracy with the customer and providing an instantaneous and accurate record of what has been sold. Some take-out restaurants distribute a fax menu to customers as an alternative to telephone ordering: Fill it out, fax it in, and then drop by to collect your food. A chain of restaurants on the West Coast called World Wrapps even offers its customers the option of e-mailing their orders for the restaurant's "global gourmet meals" to the corporate Web site.

Some service providers establish a formal membership relationship with customers to accomplish order-taking tasks. Banks, insurance companies, and utilities, for instance, require prospective customers to go through an application process designed to gather relevant information and to screen out those who do not meet basic enrollment criteria (like a bad credit record or serious health problems). Universities also require prospective students to apply for admission. Although most students still complete this process in the traditional way, some use high-tech software options like Apply! and Competitor CollegeNET to complete and submit applications electronically. Some universities, like the University of North Carolina at Chapel Hill, even allow applicants to monitor their application status through the Web.[9]

Reservations (including appointments and check-in) represent a special type of order taking that entitles customers to a specified unit of service—for example, an airline seat; a restaurant table; a hotel room; time with a qualified professional; or admission to a facility, such as a sports arena, which has restricted capacity. The scheduling aspect introduces an extra need for accuracy because reserving seats on the wrong flight, say, is likely to be unpopular with customers. Many reservations include confirmation in the form of a ticket that is exchanged for admission, but airlines are moving away from this traditional approach.

Ticketless systems provide enormous cost savings for airlines because there is no travel agent commission (customers book directly) and the administrative effort is drastically reduced (a paper ticket at United is handled 15 times, whereas an electronic ticket requires just one step).[10] But some customers are disenchanted by the paperless process. Although they receive a confirmation number by phone when they make the reservations and need only to show identification at the airport to claim their seats, many travelers feel insecure without tangible proof that they have a seat on a particular flight. Moreover, business travelers complain that needed receipts come days or sometimes weeks after a trip, causing problems for claiming expenses from corporate accounting departments. American Airlines is attempting to address this issue by faxing receipts and itineraries on request at the time a flight is booked.[11]

Billing

billing: a group of supplementary services that facilitates purchase by providing clear, timely, accurate, and relevant documentation of what customers owe, plus information about how to pay.

Billing is common to almost all services (unless the service is provided free of charge). Inaccurate, illegible, or incomplete bills offer a splendid opportunity to disappoint customers who may, up to that point, have been quite satisfied with their experience. Of course, such failures add insult to injury if the customer is already dissatisfied. Billing should also be timely because it will probably result in faster payment, especially if customers are off-site. If customers are at the service facility, they may be very frustrated if they are forced to endure a lengthy wait for their bill.

There are various forms of billing procedures, ranging from verbal statements to a machine-displayed price and from handwritten invoices to elaborate monthly statements of account activity and fees (Figure 9.5). Perhaps the simplest type of billing is self-billing, in which the customer tallies up the amount of an order and either encloses a check or signs a credit card payment authorization. In this type (which ranges from penciled figures on a paper form to sophisticated electronic procedures), billing and payment are combined into a single act. All the seller needs to do is check the customer's arithmetic and credit.

More and more, billing is being computerized. Despite its potential for productivity improvements, computerized billing has its dark side, as when an innocent customer tries futilely to contest an inaccurate bill and is met by an escalating sequence of ever larger bills (compounded interest and penalty charges), accompanied by increasingly threatening, computer-generated letters. America Online infuriated its customers recently with its computerized billing policy (see chapter 11). Other major Internet providers, like Compuserv and Microsoft Network, have been criticized for their complicated billing and cancellation policies.[12]

Bills and account statements are important documents. Customers like them to be clear and informative and itemized in a way that makes plain how the total was computed. Unexplained, arcane symbols that have all the meaning of hieroglyphics on an Egyptian monument (and are decipherable only by the high priests of accounting and data processing) do not create a favorable impression, nor does fuzzy printing or illegible handwriting. The laser printer has proved a boon to firms that want to reorganize billing in more useful ways. With their ability to switch fonts and typefaces, to box and to highlight, these printers can produce statements that are not only more legible but also organize information in more useful ways.

Marketing research has a role to play in billing design. The researcher's job is to ask customers what information they want and how they would like it to be organized. BankBoston learned from research that different customers wanted different types of monthly bank statements. So the bank created two alternative formats that organize information in different ways—a chronological statement and a cate-

FIGURE 9.5
Examples of Billing Elements

- Periodic statements of account activity
- Invoices for individual transactions
- Verbal statements of amount due
- Machine display of amount due
- Self-billing (computed by customer)

gory statement—and offered account holders a choice. Corporate customers value well-presented information, too. American Express (Amex) built its Corporate Card business by offering companies detailed documentation of the spending patterns of individual employees and departments on travel and entertainment. Intelligent thinking about customer's needs led Amex to realize that well-organized information has value to a customer, beyond just the basic requirement of knowing how much to pay at the end of each month.

Busy customers hate to be kept waiting for a bill to be computed in a hotel, restaurant, or rental car lot. Many hotels and rental car firms have now created express checkout options, taking customers' credit card details in advance and documenting charges later by mail. Companies that follow this procedure should be especially certain that their billing is accurate. Because customers use the express checkouts to save time, they are likely to be particularly annoyed if they subsequently have to waste time seeking corrections and refunds. A more reliable express checkout option is now being used by Hertz and several other car rental companies: An agent meets customers as they return their cars, checks the mileage and fuel gauge readings, and then prints a bill on the spot by using a portable and wireless terminal. Many hotels now offer customers the option of previewing their bills before checkout on the TV monitors in their rooms.

Payment

In most cases, a bill requires the customer to take action on **payment** (and such action may be very slow in coming). One exception is bank statements, which detail charges that have already been deducted from the customer's account. Increasingly, customers expect ease and convenience of payment, including credit, when they make purchases in their own countries and while traveling abroad.

There are a variety of options to facilitate paying bills (Figure 9.6). Self-service payment systems, for instance, require customers to insert coins, notes, tokens, or cards in machines. Because equipment breakdowns destroy the whole purpose of

payment: a group of supplementary services that facilitates purchase by offering a choice of easy procedures for making prompt payments.

FIGURE 9.6 Examples of Payment Elements

- **Self-service**
  - Exact change in machine
  - Cash in machine with change returned
  - Insert prepayment card
  - Insert credit, charge, or debit card
  - Insert token
  - Electronic funds transfer
  - Mail a check
- **Direct to Payee or Intermediary**
  - Cash handling and change giving
  - Check handling
  - Credit, charge, or debit card
  - Coupon redemption
  - Tokens, vouchers, etc.
- **Automatic Deduction from Financial Deposits (e.g., Bank Charges)**
- **Control and Verification**
  - Automated systems (e.g., machine-readable tickets operate entry gate)
  - Personal systems (e.g., gate controllers and ticket inspectors)

such a system, good maintenance and rapid-response troubleshooting are essential. Much payment still takes place through hand-to-hand transfers of cash and checks, but credit and debit cards are growing in importance as more and more establishments accept them (see the box on "smart cards"). Tokens, vouchers, coupons, or other prepaid tickets represent further alternatives. Prepaid phone cards have been popular in Europe for some time and are finally becoming more widely used in North America. Emergency phone cards are marketed to parents whose children can use them without money or remembering phone numbers. The card automatically connects them to a prerecorded voice-mail system that gives them explicit dialing directions (e.g., "Press 1 for Mommy at work" or "Press 2 for Grandma").[13]

A key aspect of payment is making sure that people actually pay what is due. Ticket collectors (and electronic gate controllers) at points of entry to a service facility, roving inspectors on buses and trains, and security personnel at retail store exits work to ensure that all users pay the due price. Despite that often-repeated slogan "The customer is always right," a small minority of customers are not always well behaved (recall the pesky jaycustomers from chapter 6)—which creates a need for control systems. However, these tasks have to be well organized so that lines do not back up at exit and entry points. Inspectors and security officers must be trained to combine politeness with firmness in performing their jobs. Honest customers should not feel harassed, but a visible presence often serves as a deterrent.

Consultation

consultation: a group of supplementary services that adds value by providing responses to customers who require advice, counseling, or training to help them obtain maximum benefit from the service experience.

In contrast to information, which suggests a simple response to customers' questions (or printed information that anticipates their needs), **consultation** involves a dialog to probe customers' requirements and then develop a tailored solution (see Figure 9.7). At its simplest, consultation consists of immediate advice from a knowledgeable service person in response to the request "What do you suggest?" (For example, you might ask the person who cuts your hair for advice on different hairstyles and products.) Effective consultation requires an understanding of each customer's current situation before a suitable course of action is suggested. Good customer records can be a great help in this respect, particularly if relevant data can be retrieved easily from a remote terminal. If you are a college student, your advisors probably rely on electronic access to your records to provide consultation about what classes you need to complete your major and graduate.

Counseling is a more subtle approach to consultation because it involves helping customers better understand their situations and encourages them to come up with their own solutions and action programs. This approach can be a particularly valuable supplement to such services as health treatment, when part of the challenge is to get customers to take a long-term view of their personal situation and to adopt more healthful behaviors, which may involve some initial sacrifice. For example, diet centers like Weight Watchers use counseling to help customers change behaviors so that weight loss can be sustained after the initial diet is completed.

There are also more formalized efforts to provide management and technical consulting. "Solution selling," associated with marketing expensive industrial equip-

FIGURE 9.7
Examples of Consultation Elements

- Advice
- Auditing
- Personal counseling
- Tutoring or training in product usage
- Management or technical consultancy

PAYING WITH E-CASH THROUGH RELOADABLE SMART CARDS

The latest technology in card payment systems is what some have called the "electronic wallet," also known as a stored value card. The best-known version is the Mondex card, which contains a microchip that can store money in electronic form. Each time the card is used to make a payment, it is run through a reader that automatically deducts the right amount and credits it to the recipient. Using a small portable reader, individuals can transfer money from one person's card to another. As in refilling a purse with cash after visiting a bank or ATM, the Mondex card can also be reloaded with e-cash from special terminals that can be attached not only to ATMs but also to pay phones and eventually to home computers.

The card was developed by Britain's National Westminster Bank (NatWest) and underwent an extended market test in the town of Swindon, about 80 miles (130 km) west of London. NatWest's partners in the test, which began in June 1995, were Barclay's (another major bank) and British Telecom, which equipped its pay phones with the special equipment needed to read Mondex cards. Numerous retailers were also provided with Mondex readers so that customers could use their cards to make purchases in these stores. All 40,000 NatWest and Barclay's customers in Swindon were offered the chance to participate in the test, and about 10,000 accepted. The test provided detailed information on the nature and extent of card use, together with an indication of the difficulties and opportunities that might accompany broader commercialization of the concept.

Additional tests followed in other countries. In mid-1996, NatWest established a separate company, called Mondex International, and sold off most of its shares to franchisee banks around the world. Mondex use continued in Swindon and by late 1997 had attracted 13,000 users and 700 retail outlets.

In November 1996, Mondex Canada, owned by 10 financial institutions, began the first community-wide test of the card in North America. The community selected was Guelph, Ontario, a middle-class city of 95,000 people, located 40 miles (65 km) west of Toronto. City buses, pay telephones, parking meters, vending machines, and most restaurants and stores were equipped to handle electronic cash. Even farmstands selling sweet corn were participating. The card's carrying case, similar to a small calculator, doubles as a cash tracker, enabling users to check their cash balances and display the previous 10 transactions.

After 10 months, Guelph had 7,500 active Mondex card users, who had collectively loaded C$1 million ($650,000) onto their cards; several major Canadian financial institutions, led by the Royal Bank of Canada, had announced their intention to take Mondex nationwide. The biggest challenge to e-cash, declared the project manager, was the fact that many people still considered cash to be sacred and wouldn't use any form of card. Two other types of smart card, Exact and Visa Cash, have been tested in other Canadian cities.

Using insights from the Canadian experience, New York's two biggest banks began tests in October 1997 in Manhattan's Upper West Side (an area west of Central Park between 60th and 96th Streets). Chase Manhattan offered the Mondex card under the MasterCard banner, but Citibank offered a different technology called Visa Cash card. Despite different technologies, however, both cards can be used in the same retail terminal. They can be refilled from local ATMs and from special kiosks that have been installed in the area. The Mondex MasterCard, which has a powerful microprocessor for off-line operations, can also be refilled with the aid of a gadget called a Personal-ATM. This small device not only allows individuals to make e-cash transactions between themselves but also can be hooked up to a phone line so that users can dial into their banking networks and download cash in the comfort of their homes or offices.

Pundits have long predicted a great future for e-cash, but the technology has been slow to take off. The cards currently being tested may well signal the beginning of significant market penetration for this new payment medium. Canada is well ahead of the United States in the use of debit cards and other electronic payment systems. An important reason is that Canada has only a small number of banks, many of which are extremely large and operate nationally from coast to coast, making coordination and planning much easier. In contrast, despite recent mergers, the United States still has close to 6,000 banks, which tend to be local or regional in coverage. One of the biggest challenges in introducing new service technologies is often the need to coordinate the activities of many different players in the underlying infrastructure.

Source: Derek Austin, "The Future's Brighter," *Banking Technology*, September 1996, 52; "Leaders in North America," *Financial Post*, 26 March 1997, ACT 3; Kalyani Vittala, "Cashless Society Put to Test in Ontario Town, *The New York Times*, 30 September 1997, D2: and Cal Mankowski, "Two New York Banks Launch 'Smart Card' Test," *Reuters Story on Yahoo! News*, 6 October 1997.

ment and services, is a good example: The sales engineer researches the customer's situation and then offers objective advice about what particular package of equipment and systems will yield the best results for the customer. Some consulting services are offered free of charge in the hope of making a sale. However, in other cases the service is "unbundled," and customers are expected to pay for it. Customers' needs for advice can also be met through one-on-one tutorials or group training programs to demonstrate the use of a particular service or piece of equipment.

Hospitality

hospitality: a group of supplementary services that adds value by treating customers like guests and providing amenities that anticipate their needs during interactions with the service provider.

Hospitality is potentially a very pretty petal, reflecting pleasure at meeting new customers and greeting old ones when they return. Well-managed businesses try, at least in small ways, to ensure that their employees treat customers as guests. Courtesy and consideration for customers' needs apply to both face-to-face encounters and telephone interactions (Figure 9.8). Title Nine Sports, a California-based company that sells high-performance women's athletic clothing, has mastered this concept. Customers who are put on hold when they try to reach the company by phone hear this recorded message: "Hey wait! Don't hang up! Our goal is to get you through to a real live person in 20 seconds!" If 20 seconds pass and the customer is still on hold, a new message is played: "Oh brother! We didn't make our goal. If you'd like to be credited for the time you've been waiting, just tell our customer service rep and she'll take care of it." When the customer service representative does answer, he or she apologizes for making the customer wait and offers to send $5 in "Title 9 Bucks," which can be used with any order.

Hospitality finds its full expression in face-to-face encounters. In some cases, hospitality starts (and ends) with an offer of transport to and from the service site, as with courtesy shuttle buses. If customers must wait outdoors before the service can be delivered, a thoughtful service provider will offer weather protection; if indoors, a waiting area with seating and even entertainment (television, newspapers, or magazines) to pass the time. Recruiting employees who are naturally warm, welcoming, and considerate for customer-contact jobs helps to create a hospitable atmosphere.

The Marriott Corporation has made a science of identifying what its hotel guests want in terms of hospitality. In a landmark study, the company's Courtyard by Marriott chain surveyed business travelers about their needs. The results confirmed that they wanted much more than a friendly greeting at the front desk.[14] They valued hassle-free checkout and meal services, plus in-room access to home and work by voice mail, fax, and computer. Marriott provides these items for its business customers in addition to other hospitality services such as quiet lounges, where guests can relax without being distracted by music or TV noise.

The quality of the hospitality services offered by a firm can increase or decrease satisfaction with the core product, especially for people-processing services when

- Greeting
- Food and beverages
- Toilets and washrooms
- Bathroom kits
- Waiting facilities and amenities
  - Lounges, waiting areas, seating
  - Weather protection
  - Magazines, entertainment, newspapers
- Transportation
- Security

FIGURE 9.8
Examples of Hospitality Elements

customers cannot easily leave the service facility (see the box on filling maternity beds, pp. 188–189). For example, both hospitals and airlines provide patients and customers with meals, often accompanied by grumbling about the quantity and quality. Whereas European and Asian airlines have historically provided gourmet food on their flights, carriers based in the United States have only recently started to realize that the way to travelers' hearts—and their pocketbooks—may be through their stomachs. Major airlines like Delta, United, and American want to be perceived as world-class carriers and try to match or beat the competition on service, price, and convenience. They are finding that their meals have taken on greater significance.[15] All three airlines have upgraded their in-flight cuisine to include larger portions and tastier, more exotic meals. Also, when market research showed that most business travelers thought that airline coffee needed major improvement, the airlines listened. United began offering Starbucks coffee on its flights, and Continental now serves Brothers Fog Lifter blend.[16] Despite the importance of these creature comforts to passengers, the airlines still recognize that such amenities do not translate directly into ticket sales. Travelers are more concerned with safety, prices, schedules, and frequent flyer programs. However, when these key elements are perceived as broadly similar across competing airlines, hospitality services can provide a competitive advantage.[17]

Although in-flight hospitality is important, an airline journey doesn't really end until passengers reach their final destination. Air travelers have come to expect departure lounges, but British Airways (BA) came up with the novel idea of an arrivals lounge for its terminals at London's Heathrow and Gatwick airports. Passengers from the Americas, Asia, Africa, and Australia often arrive in London in the early hours of the morning after a long, overnight flight. The airline was already using the slogan "Arrive in better shape" to promote the quality of its in-flight service. A logical extension was to offer holders of first- and business-class tickets or a BA Executive Club gold card (awarded to the airline's most frequent flyers) the opportunity to use a special lounge, where they could take a shower, change, have breakfast, and make phone calls or send faxes before continuing to their final destination, feeling a lot fresher. It's a nice competitive advantage, which BA has promoted actively.

Safekeeping

While visiting a service site, customers often want assistance with their personal possessions. In fact, unless certain **safekeeping** services are provided (like safe and convenient parking), some customers may not come at all. The list of potential onsite safekeeping services is long—provision of coatrooms; baggage transport, handling, and storage; safekeeping of valuables; and even child care and pet care (Figure 9.9, p. 188). Responsible businesses also worry about the safety of their customers. These days, many businesses pay close attention to safety and security issues for customers who are visiting their service facilities. Wells Fargo Bank mails a brochure with its bank statements with information about using its ATM machines safely. It is educating its customers about how to protect both their ATM cards and themselves from theft and personal injury. The bank also makes sure that its machines are in brightly lit, highly visible locations to reduce any risks to its customers or their possessions. Airlines, too, are struggling to protect the safety of both passengers and their physical possessions as overhead bins become more crowded. Falling luggage (in all forms, including briefcases, vodka bottles, and golf umbrellas) and the related injuries are of concern to airlines these days because 4,500 travelers on U.S. carriers are hit by airborne luggage every year.[18]

Another set of safekeeping services relate to physical products that customers buy or rent. These services are particularly applicable to products ordered by mail

safekeeping: a group of supplementary services that adds value by assisting customers with personal possessions that they have brought with them to a service delivery site or purchased there.

HOSPITALS OFFER HOTEL-STYLE PERKS TO FILL MATERNITY BEDS

A calming soak in the Jacuzzi? Some wine with your filet mignon? How about a treat from the dessert tray?

And feel free to breast-feed while you indulge.

With keen competition to fill maternity beds, more hospitals are offering amenities normally found at luxury hotels. Gone are plastic trays, green Jell-O, leathery chicken, and limp vegetables.

At Brigham & Women's Hospital in Boston, new mothers can get afternoon tea and cakes. In Cleveland Clinic, each room has a Jacuzzi. At Santa Monica Hospital in California, restaurants will deliver to rooms.

At Women & Infants Hospital in Providence, R.I., where 8,700 babies were born last year, a Jacuzzi is available, mothers can eat and drink fresh juice at the "nourishment bar," and hungry relatives can sample baked goods from the afternoon dessert tray.

During the last night of a stay, new parents dine in their room on filet mignon or seafood, courtesy of the hospital's "Stork Club."

"It's great to have a real nice meal," said Susan Martin, who held her newborn daughter, Julia, while chablis, steak, and chocolate mousse cake arrived in her room. "It's hard enough when you're going through having a new baby. The extra service helps."

Martin left the hospital with a complimentary baby book, handknit cap for her daughter, and the two wine glasses from the dinner she shared with her husband, Glen.

"We aim to please with food because people aren't sick when they have babies," said Mary Dowd Struck, vice president for patient care at Women & Infants Hospital. "We have it because patients like it."

These are competitive times in the nation's health-care industry, and hospitals see maternity as a prime market.

They've been sprucing up maternity wards since the 1980s. Renovations were made to allow women to go through labor, give birth, and recover in the same room. Facilities were built to include families in the birthing process.

"One of the top reasons somebody comes to a hospital is to give birth," said Alicia Mitchell, spokeswoman for the American Hospital Association. "Hospitals nationwide are looking for ways to make their program or their services distinguished from other hospitals in their area."

- **Caring for Possessions Customers Bring with Them**
  - Child care
  - Pet care
  - Parking facilities for vehicles
  - Valet parking
  - Coat room
  - Baggage handling
  - Storage space
  - Safety deposit and security

- **Caring for Goods Purchased (or Rented) by Customers**
  - Packaging
  - Pickup and return
  - Transportation
  - Delivery
  - Installation
  - Inspection and diagnosis
  - Cleaning
  - Refueling
  - Preventive maintenance
  - Repairs and renovation
  - Upgrade
  - Disposal

FIGURE 9.9
Examples of Safekeeping Elements

Wooing mothers is important for another reason: Marketing studies show women make 75% to 80% of health-care decisions for their families, and often make medical decisions for their elderly parents, said Rhoda Weiss, a national health care marketing consultant in Santa Monica, Calif.

"Hospitals think if a woman delivers a baby there she will have all the hospitalization for her family there," Weiss said.

The majority of U.S. hospitals offer some kind of amenity—food or gifts—as part of their maternity service, and often provide gourmet menus to other patients, Weiss said.

At Santa Monica Hospital, where about 2,500 babies are delivered annually, a VIP suite has a private kitchen, a room for mom and baby, and a room for a nanny, maternity services coordinator Lynn Sullivan said.

All maternity patients may have food delivered from area restaurants, and the hospital distributes beepers to keep new moms and dads connected.

At Cleveland Clinic, where 1,700 babies were delivered last year, each bathroom has a Jacuzzi because research found that about 65% of women choose to control labor pain by soaking in a tub, midwife services director Cindy Cover said.

To keep dads and relatives comfortable, free pizza, chicken, and sandwiches are available.

At Brigham & Women's Hospital where about 8,400 babies were delivered last year, new mothers wait in a heated enclosure while a valet fetches their car. Around 5 a.m. each day, banana bread and muffins are brought for hungry moms awake with their newborns. Lemonade, cookies, and cakes are available for families during afternoon tea, and a chef will prepare meals to order during most of the day.

The 2-year-old maternity facility has showers in each room, and medical equipment is hidden behind wooden panels to add a homey touch, said Lynda Tyer-Viola, assistant nurse manager for obstetrics.

"We went for the designer look—fresh woods, earthy," she said "When you have pictures with your family, it looks like you're in a hotel not a hospital room."

The average cost of a two-day stay and a normal delivery is about $3,500. Adding the amenities is a "minuscule" part of the cost, but can pay big dividends if it helps a hospital secure years of treatment for a family, Weiss said.

Some question the approach, arguing patients value quality care more than comforts.

Source: Rachel Zoll, *Marketing News*, 12 May 1997. Rachel Zoll is a writer for the Associated Press.

or phone. Supplementary services of this nature may include packaging, pickup and delivery, assembly, installation, cleaning, and inspection. Customers who are purchasing durable goods like cars, cameras, and computers may also want to know details about repair and maintenance services, warranties, and maintenance contracts.

Exceptions

Exceptions involve a group of supplementary services that fall outside the routine of normal service delivery (Figure 9.10, p. 190). Astute businesses anticipate exceptions and develop contingency plans and guidelines in advance so that employees will not appear helpless and surprised when customers ask for special assistance. Well-defined procedures make it easier for employees to respond promptly and effectively.

There are several different types of exceptions:

1. *Special requests.* There are many circumstances in which an individual or corporate customer may request some degree of customized treatment that requires a departure from normal operating procedures. In people-processing services, advance requests often relate to personal concerns, including care of children, dietary requirements, medical needs, religious observances, and personal disabilities. Special requests are common among customers who are

exceptions: a group of supplementary services that adds value by responding to special requests, resolving problems, handling complaints and suggestions, and providing compensation for service failures.

Hertz adds value to its car rental services in a variety of ways, including special treatment for customers who are physically challenged.

FIGURE 9.10 Examples of Exceptions Elements

- Special Requests in Advance of Service Delivery
  - Children's needs
  - Dietary requirements
  - Medical or disability needs
  - Religious observance
  - Deviations from standard operating procedures
- Handling Special Communications
  - Complaints
  - Compliments
  - Suggestions
- Problem Solving
  - Warranties and guarantees against product malfunction
  - Resolving difficulties that arise from using the product
  - Resolving difficulties caused by accidents, service failures, and problems with staff or other customers
  - Assisting customers who have suffered an accident or medical emergency
- Restitution
  - Refunds
  - Compensation in kind for unsatisfactory goods and services
  - Free repair of defective goods

spending many hours (or even days) with a people-processing service, especially when they are far from home. The travel and lodging industries are a good example, with customers' medical and dietary needs presenting commonly encountered reasons for special requests.

2. *Problem solving.* Sometimes normal service delivery (or product performance) fails to run smoothly as a result of accidents, delays, equipment failures, or difficulties in using the product.

3. *Handling of complaints, suggestions, and compliments.* This requires well-defined procedures. It should be easy for customers to express dissatisfaction, offer suggestions for improvement, or pass on compliments, and service providers should be able to make an appropriate response quickly.

4. *Restitution.* Customers expect to be compensated for serious performance failures. This may take the form of repairs under warranty, legal settlements, refunds, an offer of free service in the future, or other forms of payment in kind.

Managers need to keep an eye on the level of exception requests. Too many exceptions may indicate that standard procedures need revamping. For instance, if a restaurant constantly receives requests for special vegetarian meals because none are offered, it may be time to revise the menu to include at least one vegetarian dish. On the one hand, a flexible approach to exceptions is generally a good idea because it reflects responsiveness to customers' needs. On the other hand, exceptions should be discouraged if they compromise safety, negatively affect other customers, or place an unrealistic burden on employees.

MANAGERIAL IMPLICATIONS

The eight categories of supplementary services that form the Flower of Service provide many options for enhancing the core product, whether it is a good or a service. Most supplementary services do (or should) represent responses to customers' needs. As mentioned before, some are facilitating services—like information and reservations—that enable customers to use the core product more effectively. Others are extras that enhance the core or even reduce some of its nonfinancial costs (e.g., meals, magazines, and entertainment are hospitality elements that help pass the time on what might otherwise be very boring airline flights). Some of these elements—notably billing and payment—are, in effect, imposed by the service provider. But even if not actively desired by the customer, they still form part of the overall service experience. Any badly handled element can have a negative impact on customers' perceptions of service quality. The information and consultation petals illustrate the emphasis we place on the need for education, as well as promotion, in communicating with service customers (see the box on White Flower Farm, pp. 192–193).

Not every core product will be surrounded by all eight petals. People-processing services tend to be the most demanding in terms of supplementary elements—especially hospitality—because they involve close (and often extended) interactions with customers. When customers do not need to come to the service factory, the need for hospitality may be limited to simple courtesies in letters and telecommunications. Possession-processing services sometimes place heavy demands on safekeeping elements, but there may be no need for this particular petal when providing information-processing services in which customers and suppliers deal entirely at arm's length. Financial services that are provided electronically are an exception, however; companies must ensure that their customers' financial assets are carefully safeguarded in transactions that occur through the phone or on the Web.

THE FLOWER OF SERVICE AT WHITE FLOWER FARM

White Flower Farm, a family-owned nursery in Litchfield, Connecticut, offers a wide selection of plants and bulbs to gardeners throughout Canada and the United States. (To get a visual image of the company, visit its Web site at www.whiteflowerfarm.com.) The core product of White Flower Farm is their plants—a broad selection of extremely healthy, clean, high-quality stock, including some newly available or enhanced varieties not offered by competitors. However, White Flower Farm relies on the following supplementary services to build customer loyalty and maintain its competitive position.

Information

The firm's goal "is to provide you with top quality plants and the information you need to be successful with them." Its catalog, *The Garden Book*, and Web site help customers select plants that will be right for their specific environments. The catalog also contains a pull-out order form, which provides ordering, shipping, and service information. Each order arrives with a "Cultural Instructions" booklet that contains advice on planting and caring for purchases. The website includes an option called The Garden Path, which provides links to other gardening-related Internet locations. Clearly, the company sees itself as an educational organization, as well as a mail-order nursery.

An extract from *The Garden Book*: Echinaceas (purple coneflowers) flower from June to September. "Plants thrive in average soils or hot, dry conditions; shrug off cold; and are equally at home in full sun or partial shade. Blooms last well as cut or dried flowers. ... Butterflies love them also." (Original photo in color.)

Consultation

White Flower Farm prides itself on providing customized advice. *The Garden Book* advises, "Our Customer Service Department is staffed mostly by gardeners, and it's unusual to receive a question that one of them cannot handle. Sometimes we'll need to do a little research and call you back, which we're happy to do. ... If you have a question for which none of [our other] resources provides an answer, we invite you to call our Staff Horticulturist. ... There is no charge for this assistance."

Order Taking

White Flower Farm receives about 150,000 orders each year from some 90,000 different customers. Orders are received primarily by mail, though many come by fax, by telephone, or through

Product Policy Issues

Managers face many decisions concerning what types of supplementary services to offer their customers. These are primarily product policy and positioning issues because companies should make strategic decisions about what supplementary services will help attract and retain customers (see chapter 8). A study of Japanese, American, and European firms serving business-to-business markets found that the Internet. Although 75 percent of the customers live in the northeastern United States, the company caters to people across the continent. Its telephone ordering hours of 9 A.M. to 9 P.M. eastern time reflect that fact. Phone lines are open seven days a week (Saturdays and Sundays are when busy people have time to think about their gardens). Customers can order 24 hours a day through the company's Web site without worrying about time zones or telephone charges. Fax orders may be sent at any time.

Hospitality

The catalog and the Web site encourage customers to visit the nursery (and the colorful pictures in both make it look enormously inviting). Visitors are welcome, in season (April–October), to stroll through the display gardens and the production fields. There is also a retail store that sells plants, seeds, and selected garden equipment.

Safekeeping

Once a customer has placed an order with White Flower Farm, the company believes that its first responsibility is to the plants in question. For this reason, they will not ship a plant until the time is optimal in the customer's climate zone (all zip codes are keyed to these zones). When necessary, plants are maintained in a state of suspended animation in refrigerated sections of the warehouse. Sometimes an order must be broken into two or more shipments so that each plant arrives at its own best planting time. "These split shipments are expensive," concedes the firm's proprietor, Eliot Wadsworth II, "But they're the right thing for the plants." Accompanying instructions urge rapid planting and tell customers how to do it, as well as how to store the plant for a short period if it can't be planted immediately.

Exceptions

If customers have special shipping requests (like delaying or expediting shipments), White Flower Farm will do its best to oblige—as long as the plant will not be harmed in any way. If there is a problem with a shipment, the Customer Service Department will help out. The company encourages complaints and suggestions. All complaints are followed up to determine if there is an ongoing problem. The company guarantees its products with an offer to "cheerfully refund or replace (one time) any item that fails to meet your expectations."

Billing and Payment

The company has combined these two facilitating supplementary services into one. The rationale for requesting advance payment by check, money order, or credit card is that any order involves reserving stock from a limited and perishable inventory. If customers order by mail, they add up the total amount owed and include payment with their orders. This is actually a form of self-service billing. If customers order by phone, the customer service representative tells them how much they owe and asks for a credit card number.

Source: Based on an interview with Eliot Wadsworth II, proprietor of White Flower Farm, plus information from *White Flower Farm: The Garden Book*, Fall 1998, and the firm's Web site, www.whiteflowerfarm.com.

most companies simply added layer on layer of services to their core offerings without knowing what customers really valued.[19] Managers surveyed in the study indicated that they did not understand which services should be offered to customers as a standard package to accompany the core and which could be offered as options for an extra charge. Without this knowledge, developing effective pricing policies can be tricky. There are no simple rules governing pricing decisions for core products and supplementary services. But managers should continually review their own policies and those of competitors to make sure they are in line with both market practice and customer needs. We discuss these and other pricing issues in more detail in chapter 11.

Figures 9.3 to 9.10 can serve as checklists in the continuing search for new ways to augment existing core products and to design new offerings. The lists are not all encompassing because specialized products may require specialized supplementary elements. In general, firms that choose to compete on a low-cost, no-frills basis will require fewer supplementary elements in each category than they would for an expensive, high valued-added product. Different levels of supplementary services around a common core may offer the basis for a product line of differentiated offerings, similar to the various classes of travel offered by airlines for the same flight. Regardless of which supplementary services a firm decides to offer, all of the elements in each petal should receive the care and attention needed to consistently meet defined service standards. Thus, the resulting flower will always have a fresh and appealing appearance, rather than looking wilted or disfigured by neglect.

Conclusion

In mature industries, the core service often becomes a commodity. The search for competitive advantage often centers on the value-creating supplementary services that surround this core. In this chapter, we group supplementary services into eight categories, circling the core like the petals of a flower.

A key insight from the Flower of Service concept is that different types of core products often use similar supplementary elements. As a result, customers may make comparisons across industries: for instance, "If my stockbroker can give me a clear documentation of my account activity, why can't the department store where I shop?" "If my favorite airline can take reservations accurately, why can't the French restaurant up the street?" Such questions suggest that managers should be studying businesses outside their own industries in a search for best-in-class performers on specific supplementary services.

Managers should be aware of the importance of selecting the right mix of supplementary service elements—no more and no less than needed—and creating synergy by ensuring that they are all internally consistent. The critical issue is not how many petals the flower has but ensuring that each petal is perfectly formed and adds luster to the core product in the eyes of target customers.

Study Questions and Exercises

1. In what ways has Starbucks added value to the original agricultural product? What are the specific elements that transform Starbuck's coffee into a service?
2. Review Shostack's molecular model. Apply this model to other service business with which you are familiar, distinguishing carefully between tangible and intangible elements.
3. Distinguish between core, facilitating, and enhancing services.
4. Consider the eight petals of the Flower of Service and use this framework to create flowers for (a) passenger airline service, (b) telephone banking,

(c) visit to a movie theater, (d) watching a movie on television, (e) a management consulting project, and (f) dry cleaning of clothes.

5. Identify the different ways in which information technology can be used to enhance the value of supplementary services (be sure to identify the nature of that value).

6. What do billing and payment have to do with service? List reasons why a company should overhaul its billing and payment system to make it more user-friendly for customers.

7. When it is appropriate for service firms to honor special requests by customers? Are there any ethical considerations that should guide management's decision making in this respect?

8. Identify three services that you use where the core product is essentially a commodity and the differentiation between competing brands is provided by the supplementary services. What additional opportunities do you see for useful differentiation?

Ten

Designing Service Delivery Systems

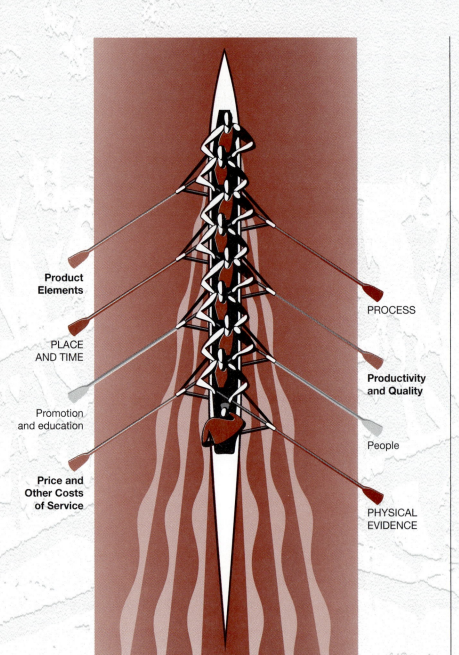

Product Elements

PLACE AND TIME

Promotion and education

Price and Other Costs of Service

PROCESS

Productivity and Quality

People

PHYSICAL EVIDENCE

Learning Objectives

After reading this chapter, you should be able to

■ recognize that successful service delivery systems must address issues of both place and time

■ distinguish between physical and electronic channels of delivery

■ describe the role of intermediaries in service delivery

■ recognize the distinctive challenges to delivery system design posed by high-contact and low-contact service processes

■ explain the role of technology in enhancing the speed, convenience, and productivity of service delivery systems

■ understand the important role of physical evidence in service delivery, including the integration of different elements in a servicescape

Local Copyshop Grows into Global Business Service Provider[1]

In 1970, 22-year-old Paul Orfalea, just out of college, borrowed enough money to open a photocopy shop in Isla Vista, near the campus of the University of California at Santa Barbara. Covering just 100 square feet (less than 10 square meters), the tiny store contained one copy machine and also sold film processing and felt-tip highlighter pens. Orfalea, the son of Lebanese immigrants, called the store Kinko's after the nickname given to him by his college friends because of his curly hair. By 1998, Kinko's was operating a copy and printing chain of 24-hour stores from coast to coast in the United States, plus branches in Canada, Britain, the Netherlands, Australia, and three Asian countries. The company plans to expand to 2,000 locations by the year 2000. Kinko's customers can already print in color in any size, bind their documents as they like, send faxes, and work on in-house computers. The objective is to create a global network to take advantage of digital technologies. Many Kinko's locations have video-conferencing technology, and the company even has its own on-line service, called Kinkonet.

Soon customers will be able to write reports in, say, Chicago and send them by modem to, say, Amsterdam, where they can be printed and bound for a meeting. The traditional approach of creating, printing, and then distributing to another location (often by expensive courier services) will be replaced by a strategy of creating, distributing to another location, and printing there. Of course, this can apply equally well to documents created in suburban New Jersey and then printed and bound in Manhattan (or vice versa).

College students are no longer Kinko's only market segment. The colleges, too, have become customers. For instance, the company prints course packages for colleges, also handling such added-value tasks as obtaining permissions for the use of copyrighted materials. Its major customer base now lies with small businesses, who often need sophisticated services but can't afford to own the equipment nor take time away from other tasks. It is also targeting larger corporations.

Kinko's tries to create a partnership with its customers, offering many advisory services, including how to use color to best advantage and present sales reports more effectively. In 1992, the company launched a national advertising campaign, positioning the firm to its customers as "your branch office." It has also formed partnerships with other suppliers. Federal Express and the U.S. Postal Service sell services at Kinko branches, and Glendale Federal Savings Bank has opened microbranches in Kinko's stores at six California locations. Bankers handle customers' financial transactions as they wait for their print jobs to be completed.

Just as FedEx has changed the world of business logistics, so Kinko's is trying to change the way businesses manage their document production and distribution. With the growing trend for professionals and managers to spend more time in the field and to operate through mobile technology in a "virtual office" far from the corporate base, there is even more need for services available seven days a week, 24 hours a day, in multiple locations. Kinko's most recent slogan is "the new way to office."

EVALUATING ALTERNATIVE DELIVERY CHANNELS

This is both an exciting and challenging time for managers responsible for service delivery. Speed of delivery has become an important factor in competitive strategy.[2] Customers are demanding more convenience and expecting services to be delivered where and when they want them. As Kinko's story shows, new technology means that information-based services (and informational processes related to supplementary services) can be delivered almost anywhere through electronic channels. In many instances, customers no longer need to visit service factories. Physical processes, too, have become much faster. In addition to transforming information-based services from factory delivery to electronic delivery, forward-looking firms are coming up with new formats for face-to-face delivery in new locations, ranging from tiny bank branches in booths at the end of supermarket aisles to massage clinics on airport concourses.

Decisions on Where, When, and How

Delivering a service to customers involves decisions about where, when, and how. Marketing strategy must address the place and the time, paying at least as much attention to speed and scheduling issues as to the more traditional notion of physical location. The service product and its means of distribution and delivery are often closely linked because the nature of the delivery system has a powerful impact on the customers' experience. Although the organization that creates a service concept is much more likely than a manufacturer to control its own delivery systems, there's also a role for intermediaries, including franchisees. For high-contact services, the design of the physical environment and the way in which tasks are performed by customer-contact personnel jointly play a vital role in creating a particular identity for a service firm, shaping the nature of the customer's experience and enhancing both productivity and quality. Low-contact services are expanding in number because of advances in electronic technology. More and more, these low-contact services, often designed specifically with improved productivity in mind, are being delivered by customers themselves through self-service. The challenge is to make self-service a positive experience.

The nature of the service both influences and is shaped by distribution strategy. Many service firms have a variety of options, and the challenge is to select the channel that will best meet the needs of the target segment, as long as price and other costs of service (including time and effort) remain acceptable. Responding to customers' needs for flexibility, some firms offer several alternative choices of **delivery channels**. Options may include serving a customer at a firm's own retail site, delegating service delivery to an intermediary or franchisee, coming to the customer's house or place of business, and (in certain types of services) serving the customer at a distance through physical or electronic channels.

Options for Service Delivery

Decisions on where, when, and how to deliver service have an important impact on the nature of customers' service experiences by determining the types of encounters (if any) with service personnel and the price and other costs incurred. Several factors shape service delivery strategy. A key question is, Does the nature of the service or the firm's positioning strategy require customers to be in direct physical contact with its personnel, equipment, and facilities? (As we saw in chapter 2, this is inevitable for people-processing services but optional for other categories.) If so, do customers have to visit the facilities of the service organization or will it send personnel and equipment to customers' own sites? Alternatively, can transactions between the provider and the customer be completed at arm's length through either telecommunications or modern physical channels of distribution?

delivery channels: the means by which a service firm (sometimes assisted by intermediaries) delivers one or more product elements to its customers.

TABLE 10–1   Method of Service Delivery

Nature of Interaction between Customer and Service Organization	Availability of Service Outlets	
	Single Site	Multiple Sites
Customer goes to service organization	Theater Barbershop	Bus service Fast-food chain
Service organization comes to customer	House painting Mobile car wash	Mail delivery Auto club road service
Customer and service organization transact at arm's length (mail or electronic communications)	Credit card company Local TV station	Broadcast network Telephone company

A second issue concerns the firm's strategy for distribution sites: Should it maintain just a single outlet or offer to serve customers through multiple outlets at different locations? The possible options, combining both the type of contact and the number of sites, can be seen in Table 10.1, which consists of six different cells.

Customers visit the service site.   The convenience of service factory locations and operational schedules may assume great importance when a customer has to be physically present—either throughout service delivery or even just to initiate and terminate the transaction. For example, elaborate **retail gravity models** are sometimes built in deciding where to locate supermarkets relative to prospective customers' homes and workplaces. Traffic counts and pedestrian counts help to establish how many prospective customers a day pass by certain locations. Construction of a freeway or ring road or the introduction of a new bus or rail service may have a significant effect on travel patterns and, in turn, determine which sites are now more desirable and which are less so.

Providers come to the customer.   For some types of services, the supplier visits the customer. This is, of course, essential when the target of the service is some immovable physical item, such as a building that needs to be cleaned, a large machine that needs to be repaired, a house that requires pest-control treatment, or a garden that needs to be landscaped. Because it is more expensive and time consuming for service personnel and their equipment to travel to the customer than vice-versa, the trend has been away from this approach (few doctors make house calls nowadays).

There may still be a profitable niche in serving customers who are willing to pay a premium price for the savings in time and convenience of receiving personal visits from service providers. One young veterinarian has built her business around house calls to sick pets. She has found that customers are glad to pay extra for a service that not only saves them time but also is less stressful for the pet than waiting in a crowded veterinary clinic, full of other animals and their worried owners. Australia is famous for its Royal Flying Doctor Service, in which physicians fly to make house calls at remote farms and stations. Other, more recently established services that are taken to the customer include mobile car washing, office and in-home catering, and made-to-measure tailoring services for business people.

Arm's-length transactions.   In constrast, dealing with a service organization through **arm's-length transactions** may mean that a customer never sees the service facilities and never meets the service personnel face to face. An important consequence is that the number of service encounters tends to be fewer, and those encounters that do take place with service personnel are more likely to be made by telephone or, even more remotely, by mail, fax, or e-mail. The outcome of the service activity remains very important to the customer, but much of the process of service delivery may be hidden. Credit cards and insurance are examples of services

retail gravity model: a mathematical approach to retail site selection that involves calculating the geographic center of gravity for the target population and then locating a facility to optimize customers' ease of access.

arm's-length transactions: interactions between customers and service suppliers in which mail or telecommunications minimize the need to meet face to face.

that can be requested and delivered by mail or telecommunications. Repair services for small pieces of equipment sometimes require customers to ship the product to a maintenance facility, where it will be serviced and then returned by a parcel service (with the option of paying extra for express shipment).

Any information-based product can be delivered almost instantaneously through telecommunication channels to any point in the globe with a suitable reception terminal. As a result, physical logistics services now compete with telecommunications services. When we were writing this book, for instance, we had a choice of mail or courier services for physical shipments of the chapters in either paper or disk form. We could also fax the materials, feeding in the pages one sheet at a time. But by using e-mail, we were able to transmit chapters electronically from one computer to another, with the option of printing them at the receiving end. In fact, we used all three methods, depending on the nature of the page (hand-drawn images were faxed) and the compatibility (or lack thereof) of the authors' and publisher's software.

THE PHYSICAL EVIDENCE OF THE SERVICESCAPE

servicescape: the impressions created on the five senses by the design of the physical environment where service is delivered.

Physical evidence, one of the 8Ps of integrated service management, relates to the tangible objects encountered by customers in the service delivery environment, as well as to tangible metaphors used in such communications as advertising, symbols, and trademarks. The most powerful physical evidence is experienced by customers who come to a service factory and see employees working in a physical environment. The term **servicescape** describes the style and appearance of the physical surroundings where customers and service providers interact.[3] Servicescapes can create positive or negative impressions on each of the five senses, and more and more service firms are paying careful attention to their design. Consider some of the evidence:

- Airlines employ corporate design consultants to help them differentiate the appearance of their aircraft and employees from those of competitors. Although many cabin personnel look interchangeable, others have distinctive uniforms that immediately identify them as employees of, say, Singapore Airlines or British Airways.
- A significant industry has grown up around theme restaurant design, with furnishings, pictures, real or fake antiques, carpeting, lighting, and live or background music all trying to reinforce a desired look and style that may or may not be related to the cuisine.
- The more expensive hotels have become architectural statements. Some occupy classic buildings, lovingly restored at huge expense to a far higher level of luxury than ever known in the past, with antique furnishings and rugs to reinforce their "old world" style. Modern hotels often feature dramatic atriums in which wall-mounted elevators splash down in fountains. Resort hotels invest enormous sums to plant and maintain exotic gardens on their grounds.

As in a theater, scenery, lighting, music and other sounds, special effects, and the appearance of the actors (in this case the employees) and audience members (other customers) all serve to create an atmosphere in which the service performance takes place. In certain types of businesses, servicescapes are enhanced by the judicious use of sounds, smells, and textures of physical surfaces. Where food and drink are served, of course, taste is also highly relevant. For first-time customers in particular, the servicescape plays an important role in helping to frame expectations about both the style and quality of service to be provided. Because services are intangible performances and it's hard to evaluate them in advance (or even after service delivery), customers seek prepurchase clues to quality. Hence, first impressions are important (see the box about a review of a supermarket, pp. 202–203).

Not all servicescapes are expensive and exotic, of course. Firms that are trying to convey the impression of cut-price service do so by locating in inexpensive neightborhoods; occupying buildings with a simple—even warehouse-like—appearance; minimizing wasteful use of space; and dressing their employees in practical, inexpensive uniforms.

Role of Physical Environments

Physical surroundings help to shape appropriate feelings and reactions among customers and employees. Consider how effectively many theme parks use the servicescape concept to enhance their service offerings. The clean streets, colorful costumes, and lively characters all contribute to the sense of fun and excitement that visitors encounter on arrival (and throughout their visit). Alternatively, think about the reception area of a successful professional firm—the offices of a law partnership or a consulting firm—where the decor and furnishings tend to be elegant and designed to impress. Now, look at the two restaurant scenes in the photographs on pages 202 and 203. Imagine you have just walked into each of the two rooms and are looking around. What impression do you think the designer of each room was trying to create? In what ways do the overall room designs, decor, furnishings, and appearance of service personnel help to form that impression? What, specifically, adds to or detracts from the appearance of the servicescape in each instance? Finally, in what ways do the other customers contribute to the newly arrived customer's first impressions?

Physical evidence and the accompanying atmosphere affect buyers' behavior in three ways:

1. as an attention-creating medium to make the servicescape stand out from that of competing establishments and to attract customers from target segments

2. as a message-creating medium, using symbolic cues to communicate with the intended audience about the distinctive nature and quality of the service experience

3. as an effect-creating medium, employing colors, textures, sounds, scents, and spatial design to create or heighten an appetite for certain goods, services, or experiences

Antique stores are a nice example of how carefully crafted design itself can become an important marketing tool. As noted by Philip Kotler,

> Many antique dealers also make use of "organizational chaos" as an atmospheric principle for selling their wares. The buyer enters the store and sees a few nice pieces and a considerable amount of junk. The nice pieces are randomly scattered in different parts of the store. The dealer gives the impression, through his prices and his talk, that he doesn't really know values. The buyer therefore browses quite systematically, hoping to spot an undiscovered Old Master hidden among the dusty canvases of third rate artists. He ends up buying something that he regards as value. Little does he know that the whole atmosphere has been arranged to create a sense of hidden treasures.[4]

Although retailers primarily sell goods, they tend to compete on service. Traditional retail stores face growing competition from nonstore retailers, whose strategy is to make the selection and ordering process for their customers as simple and convenient as possible. Customers select goods from printed catalogs, TV shopping channels, or Web sites and place their orders by mail, phone, or e-mail. They

LET'S GO SHOPPING (MAYBE AT YOUR STORE)

5 CART [RATING]:
- Personnel
- Store Services
- Creativity
- Selection/Inventory
- Overall Store Atmosphere

"Let's Go Shopping" is a regular feature filed by "mystery shoppers" who visit grocery stores across the country to report on how stores measure up in terms of personnel, services, merchandising, selection, and overall store atmosphere.

Loblaws, #029

650 Dupont St. & Christie, Toronto

This chain-operated store's entrance was filled with tantalizing aromas from Movenpick; one of the many kiosks lining the store. The store's most unique asset is its one-stop, "under one roof" shopping experience. The Internet, in-store pharmacy, cleaners, wine store, bank machine etc. prove to be successful additions to the store's business. Everything is done on a larger scale. This is evident in the large aisles and large signage throughout the store and increased SKUs. To enhance the mood of the environment; music, lighting and odors circulate to create customer comfort.

There were 14 cash registers in front of the store, five of which were open. The registers were completely computerized visual systems with scanning. Cashiers provide a choice between paper and plastic bags for those customers who are concerned with recycling. Shopping carts are clean and accessible at the store front with a dollar deposit. There were sufficient cart locations outside the store to attain/dispose of carts.

The pricing on the shelf after a random audit was accurate and highly visible. The overall impression of the shelves was that they were well stocked and faced with a large variety of SKUs. Presidents' Choice, the store's private label products, are aggressively promoted with signage at shelf and throughout the store.

Distinctive servicescapes, from table settings to furniture and room design, create different customer expectations of these two restaurants.

In-Store Marketing:

The promotional weekly flyers, store signs and in-store features were promoted with large signage throughout the store. There was no loyalty card program or coupon clipping here, but there are store coupons available on the shelf. Similar to most stores they did accept manufacturers coupons. The primary displays included a variety of feature/advertised items, which are promoted on well-stocked displays throughout the store. The incremental displays were attractively done and promoted impulse purchases while the aisles are still clear and shoppable. While taking advantage of some good displays to cross promote, there were some obvious missed opportunities. The store has special racking for promoting some products, especially in the seasonal aisle. Overall the impression of in-store promotion was strong.

Staff:

Customer service is definitely not a thing of the past in this store. The staff was extremely customer-focused and seemed to enjoy the work environment. They were well groomed with clean/pressed uniforms. The knowledge of store staff when asked about an item was good. The shopper was directed to the appropriate location but was not taken directly over.

Full of color, the produce section was clean and well maintained. The deli section was also clean and the meat/salads were well stocked. The seafood section filled with the catch of the day looked fresh and inviting. The meat/butcher counter was acceptable. The staff was knowledgeable and helpful in all departments.

General Impressions:

The store's biggest strength is its one-stop shopping benefits. For a taste of international flair one must definitely shop the aisles. The one disappointment of the store was the meat department. The labels indicating specific meats were stained and the overall appearance of the department was unclean.

This store's overall ranking is outstanding. Shopping should be an excellent experience thus endorsing future loyalty to a store.

OVERALL [RATING]: 🛒 🛒 🛒 🛒

Reprinted from *Canadian Grocer*, November 1977, 38.

E-COMMERCE BEGINS TO RESHAPE THE RETAIL LANDSCAPE

Personal computers and the Internet are starting to change the way people shop. From perusing catalogs and shopping by mail or telephone, people are starting to shop in cyberspace for a wide array of both goods and services.

Forrester Research has predicted that on-line sales revenues in the United States will exceed $17 billion by 2001.[a] The firm says that customers are lured into virtual stores by four factors, in the following order of importance: convenience, ease of research (obtaining information and searching for desired items or services), better prices, and broad selection. Enjoying 24-hour service with prompt delivery is particularly appealing to customers whose busy lives leave them short of time.

Traditional retailers are having to respond to stiffer competition from Internet- and telephone-based catalog retailing. One company, softwear and computer retailer Egghead Inc., has decided to get out of physical retailing altogether. It closed its 80 stores across the United States, dismissed

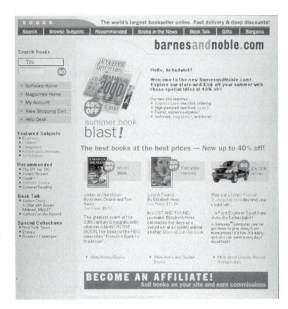

Barnes and Noble has created a user-friendly home page on its Web site.

800 of its 1,000 workers, and shifted its sales entirely to the Internet. Other retailers, such as the giant bookstore chain, Barnes and Noble, have developed a strong Internet presence to complement their full-service bookstores in an effort to counter competition from cybsperspace retailers such as Amazon.com, which claims to be the largest bookseller on Earth, even through it has no stores.

Web sites are becoming increasingly sophisticated but also more user-friendly. They often simulate the services of a well-informed sales assistant in steering customers toward items that are likely to be of interest. Facilitating searches is another useful service on many sites, ranging from looking at what books by a particular author are currently available to finding schedules of flights between two cities on a specific date.

[a]Jose Paulo Vincente, "E-Commerce Shapes U.S. Retail Landscape," *Yahoo News—Reuters*, 5 February 1998.

have to pay for shipping but can choose between regular or express shipment; purchases are delivered directly to their homes or offices. What has been termed *e-commerce* is growing rapidly (see the box on e-commerce).

Store-based retailers are responding to this competitive challenge by trying to make shopping more interesting and enjoyable. Malls have become larger, more colorful, and more elaborate. Within the mall, individual stores try to create their own atmosphere, but tenancy agreements often specify certain design criteria so that each store may fit comfortably into the overall mall servicescape. The presence of food courts and other gathering places encourages social interaction among shoppers. Theatrical touches include live entertainment, special lighting effects, fountains, waterfalls, and eye-catching interior landscaping—ranging from banks of flowers to surprisingly large trees. Individual stores try to add value by offering product demonstrations and such functions as customized advice, gift wrapping, free delivery, installation, and warranty services.

Another illustration of giving more attention to the servicescape can be found in resort hotels. The vacation villages of Club Med, designed to create a totally carefree atmosphere, may have provided the original inspiration for "get-away" vacation environments. The new resorts are not only far more luxurious than Club Med but also draw inspiration from theme park approaches to creating fantasy environments, both inside and outside. Perhaps the most extreme examples come from Las Vegas. Facing competition from numerous casinos in other locations, Las Vegas has been trying to reposition itself, from an adult destination once described in a London newspaper as "the electric Sodom and Gomorrah," to a more wholesome, family resort. The gambling is still there, of course, but many of the huge hotels recently built (or rebuilt) have been transformed into visually striking entertainment centers that feature such attractions as erupting "volcanoes" and mock sea battles.

PLACE AND TIME DECISIONS

How should service managers make decisions on where service is delivered and when it is available? The answer is likely to reflect customers' needs and expectations, competitive activity, and the nature of the service operation. As noted earlier, different distribution strategies may be appropriate for some of the supplementary service elements (the petals of the Flower of Service in chapter 8) than for the core product itself. For instance, as a customer you are probably willing to go to a particular location at a specific time to attend a sporting or entertainment event. But you probably want greater flexibility and convenience when reserving a seat in advance, so you may expect the reservations service to be open for extended hours, to offer booking and credit card payment by phone, and to deliver tickets by mail.

Where Should Services Be Delivered?

Although customer convenience is important, operational requirements set tight constraints for some services. Airports, for instance, are often inconveniently located relative to travelers' homes, offices, or destinations. Because of noise and environmental factors, finding suitable sites for the construction of new airports is a very difficult task. A governor of Massachusetts was once asked what would be an acceptable location for a second airport to serve Boston; he thought for a moment and then responded, "Nebraska!" As a result, airport sites are often far from the city centers to which many passengers wish to travel, and the only way to make them less inconvenient is to install high-speed rail links. A different type of location constraint is imposed by the fact that, by definition, ski resorts have to be in the mountains and beach resorts on the coast. The need for economies of scale is another operational issue that may restrict the choice of locations. Major hospitals consolidate many different health care services—even a medical school—at a single location, requiring a very large facility. Customers requiring complex, inpatient treatment must come to this service factory rather than being treated at home—although an ambulance (or even a helicopter) can be sent to pick them up.

Some service factories, however, can be created on a very small scale, with numerous individual units being located where the customers are. The most obvious locations for consumer services are close to where customers live or work. Modern buildings are often designed to be multipurpose, featuring not only office or production space but also such services as a bank (or at least an ATM), a restaurant, several stores, and even a health club. Some companies even include a children's day-care facility on the site to make life easier for busy working parents.

Interest is growing in placing retail and other services on transportation routes or even in bus, rail, and air terminals. Major oil companies are developing chains of retail stores to complement the fuel pumps at their service stations, thus offering customers the convenience of one-stop shopping for fuel, auto supplies, food,

AIRPORTS TRANSFORMED INTO SHOPPING MALLS

Large airports used to be places where every day thousands of people spent lots of time waiting with little to keep them occupied. Airports were often bound by contract to a single food operator, which translated into expensive drinks and low-quality food at high prices. Other than visiting stores that sold newspapers, magazines, and paperback books, there wasn't much opportunity to shop unless you wanted to spend money on expensive (and often tawdry) souvenirs. The one exception was the duty-free shop at international airports, where opportunities to save money created a brisk trade in alcohol, perfumes, tobacco, and consumer products like cameras.

By the late 1980s, the operators of major international airports in such cities as London and Singapore were starting to see the opportunities for expanded retail operations. After the British Airports Authority was privatized in 1987 (and changed its name to BAA plc), its management began to look for additional revenues to finance the ever-increasing demands for expansion of the seven airports that it managed in the United Kingdom. Property development was one chosen route; another was on-airport retail operations.

Three factors made retailing look very appealing. One was the upscale demographics of airline passengers. A second was that many of them had plenty of time to spare while waiting for their flights. Finally, many terminal interiors had free space that could be put to profitable use. As terminals were expanded, new retail sites could be included as an integral part of the design.

The company recognized that the market for purchases could be divided into several segments, including international, premium brand products at tax-free prices; gifts; and both impulse and necessity products for business and vacation use. So BAA began to broaden the array of stores at its terminals, adding branches of prestige department stores like Harrods, national pharmacy chains like Boots The Chemists, respected franchises like Body Shop, and a variety of brand-name shoe and clothing stores. Food and beverage operations were expanded to offer a broader choice of menus, including well-known chains like McDonald's.

The results have been dramatic: Today, BAA boasts almost 1 million square feet (93,000 square meters) of retail space at its seven British airports (more than 80 percent of which is located at London's Heathrow and Gatwick airports), occupied by over 550 stores. In the past five years, retail revenues from all sources (including parking and catering), have more than doubled, to about $1 billion per year. BAA attributes its success in part to rigorous quality control, including a global money-back guarantee on any item purchased from any airport store, plus a guarantee of "High Street pricing" (prices charged at the airport are the same as in off-airport locations).

and household products. Truck stops on long-distance highways also include laundromats, bathrooms, ATMs, fax machines, and restaurants, in addition to a variety of vehicle maintenance and repair services. In one of the most interesting new retailing developments, airport terminals are being transformed from nondescript areas where passengers and their bags are processed into vibrant shopping malls (see the box on airports transformed into shopping malls).

When Should Service Be Delivered?

In the past, most retail and professional services in industrialized countries followed a traditional and rather restricted schedule that limited service availability to about 40 to 50 hours a week. In large measure, this routine reflected social norms (and even legal requirements or union agreements) about what were appropriate hours for people to work and for enterprises to sell things. The situation caused a lot of inconvenience for working people, who either had to shop during their lunch break (if the stores themselves didn't close for lunch) or on Saturdays (if management chose to remain open a sixth day). But the idea of Sunday shopping was strongly discouraged in most Christian cultures and often prohibited by law, reflecting a long tradition based on religious practice. Among commercial services, only those

Airport retailing is changing dramatically in North America, too. Seeking to capitalize on its expertise in all facets of airport management, BAA has established an American subsidiary. In 1992, it won a 15-year master-developer contract to design, build, lease, and manage the Pittsburgh Airmall, the nation's first custom-built airport retail complex, as part of a new airport terminal. Pittsburgh is US Airways' major hub, and most of its passengers are domestic travelers. Goods and services available at the Airmall range from tasty take-out sandwiches for passengers who don't expect a meal on their flight to $15 massages for tired travelers with aching backs. Sales per passenger at Pittsburgh increased from $2.40 in 1992 to over $7.00 in 1996. Since 1995, BAA has operated Indianapolis International Airport, responsible for all operations and maintenance. A new shopping environment is only one of the improvements underway.

La Guardia Marketplace: Except for the baggage claim sign, you would think you were in a shopping mall rather than an airport.

In New York, La Guardia Airport recently opened La Guardia Marketplace in its newly renovated central terminal. National brand stores and restaurants, from Sbarro to Sunglass Hut, have replaced overpriced, cafeteria-style food vendors and generic drugstores. Tighter security requirements mean that passengers must now check-in earlier for flights, so they have even more time to spend at the airport. A passenger, relaxing in the bright, three-story atrium after making some purchases, contrasts the new facility favorably to the old, which, she says, "was sort of what I had expected in a New York airport: dull, kind of dirty, and not much to do."

To help design, develop, lease, and manage the new retail facility, the airport operator brought in a Boston-based firm, Marketplace Development, which had previously handled projects at O'Hare Airport in Chicago, Philadelphia International, and Boston's South Station rail terminal. Like BAA, the airport's management requires vendors to adhere to a "street pricing" policy.

Source: Based on information supplied by Market Place Development Inc., January 1998; Eileen Kinsella, "Noshing at New York's La Guardia Airport," *The Wall Street Journal*, 21 January 1998, B–10; and BAA plc, February 1998.

devoted to entertainment and relaxation, such as movie theaters, bars, restaurants, and sporting facilities, geared their schedules toward weekends and evening hours, when their customers had leisure time. Even so, they often faced restrictions on hours of operation, especially on Sundays. Today, the situation is changing fast. For some highly responsive service operations, the standard has become **24/7 service**— 24 hours a day, seven days a week, around the world.

24/7 service: service that is available 24 hours a day, seven days a week.

Factors That Encourage Extended Operating Hours

Some services, such as telecommunications and international airlines, are 24-hour operations, every day of the year. Other examples include emergency services, such as from fire and police departments and ambulances, or repairs to vital equipment. Hospitals and first-class hotels provide 24-hour care or room service as a matter of course. Ships and long-distance trains don't stop for the night. Similarly, passenger aircraft operate around the clock, and telephone companies always have operators available on a 24-hour basis.

At least five factors are driving the move toward extended operating hours and seven-day operations. The trend has been most noticeable in the United States and Canada, but it's also spreading elsewhere.

■ *Economic pressure from consumers.* The growing number of two-income families and single wage earners who live alone need time outside normal working hours to shop and use other services because there is nobody else to do it for them. Once one store or firm in any given area extends its hours to meet the needs of these market segments, competitors often feel obliged to follow. Retail chains have often led the way in this respect.

■ *Changes in legislation.* A second factor has been the decline, lamented by some, of support for the traditional religious view that a specific day (Sunday in predominantly Christian cultures) should be legislated as a day of rest for one and all, regardless of religious affiliation. In a multicultural society, of course, which day should be designated as special is a moot point—for observant Jews and Seventh Day Adventists, Saturday is the Sabbath; for Muslims, Friday is the holy day; and agnostics or atheists presumably don't mind. There has been a gradual erosion of such legislation in Western nations in recent years, although it's still firmly in place in some countries and locations. Switzerland, for example, still closes down most retail activities on Sundays—except for bread, which people like to buy freshly baked on Sunday mornings.

■ *Economic incentives to improve asset utilization.* A great deal of capital is often tied up in service facilities. The incremental cost of extending hours is often relatively modest (especially when part-timers can be hired without paying them either overtime or benefits); if extending hours reduces crowding and increases revenues, then it's economically attractive. There are costs involved in shutting down and reopening a facility like a supermarket, yet climate control and some lighting must be left running all night, and security personnel must be paid to guard the premises. Even if the number of extra customers served is minimal, there are both operational and marketing advantages to remaining open 24 hours.

■ *Availability of employees to work during "unsocial" hours.* Changing lifestyles and a desire for part-time employment have combined to create a growing labor pool of people who are willing to work evenings and nights. Some of these workers are students looking for part-time work outside their classroom hours; some are moonlighting, holding a full-time job by day and earning additional income by night; some are parents juggling child-care responsibilities; others simply prefer to work at night and relax or sleep during the day; still others are glad to obtain any paid employment, regardless of hours.

■ *Automated self-service facilities.* Self-service equipment has become increasingly reliable and user-friendly. Many machines now accept card-based payments, in addition to coins and banknotes. Unattended machines may be economically feasible in places that couldn't support a staffed facility. Unless a machine requires frequent servicing or is particularly vulnerable to vandalism, the incremental cost of going from limited hours to 24-hour operation is minimal. In fact, it may be much simpler to leave machines running all the time than to turn them on and off, especially if they are placed in widely scattered locations.

Responding to Customers' Need for Convenience

American and Canadian retailers have led the way in meeting customer needs for greater convenience, but many other countries are now beginning to follow suit. A trend that began in earnest with early-morning to late-evening service in pharmacies and so-called 7-Eleven convenience stores (open 7 A.M. to 11 P.M.) has now extend-

Modern ATMs not only offer 24-hour banking services but also may dispense tickets, stamps, and abbreviated bank statements.

ed to 24-hour service in a variety of retail outlets, from service stations to restaurants to supermarkets. (In continental Europe, which employs the 24-hour system for keeping time, such stores are sometimes referred to as "7-23" stores—for obvious reasons.)

The customer's search for convenience has not been confined to convenient times and places, nor to just purchases of core products. People want easy access to supplementary services, too, especially information, reservations, and problem solving. As one credit card executive observed,

> There are a lot of two-income families. Our customers are busy with their personal lives, and they don't have a lot of time to handle their personal business. They expect us to be available to them when it's convenient for them, not when it's convenient for us; so they expect extended hours. And most of all, they expect one contact to solve their problem.

In many service industries, problem-solving needs were originally met by telephoning a specific store or facility during its regular operating hours. But led by airlines and hotel chains, separate customer service centers have evolved, reached by calling a single number regardless of the caller's location. Some of these centers are operated by the service provider; others are subcontracted to specialist intermediaries (hotel chains, for instance, often delegate the reservations function to independent contractors).

Once a firm departs from locally staffed phones and installs a centralized system, most customers will be calling from distant locations. So, instead of forcing customers to pay the cost of a long-distance call, many firms have installed toll-free numbers. Once one firm offers this convenience, competitors often feel obliged to follow.

Moving to 24/7 Service

Providing extended-hours service is almost mandatory for any organization with a nationwide clientele in countries (or service regions) that cover multiple time zones. Consider a company that serves customers on both the Atlantic and Pacific coasts of North America. Between New York and Los Angeles, for instance, there is a three-hour time difference. If the switchboard closes at 5:00 P.M. eastern time, for instance, customers on the West Coast are denied access to the number after 2:00 P.M. Pacific time (the situation is even worse for those on Alaska-Hawaii time, where it's only 12 noon). The situation is reversed when the supplier is located on the West Coast. Imagine a Canadian supplier in Vancouver, B.C., whose office opens at 8:30 A.M. Pacific time. By then it's already 12:30 P.M. Atlantic time in Halifax, Nova Scotia, and 1:00 P.M. in St. John's, Newfoundland, which has its own time zone. Even having access between 8:30 A.M. and 5:00 P.M. local time is inconvenient for people who want to call a supplier from home before or after work. (If there's a mistake on your bank statement, for instance, you are likely to discover it when you read the mail at home in the evening.)

When a North American business redefines its goal as offering continent-wide service on a daily basis, from first thing in the morning in Newfoundland to mid-evening in Alaska or Hawaii, managers don't need a fancy calculator to figure out that customer service lines will have to be open at least 18 hours a day. At this point, why not go to 24-hour operation and cater to organizations that themselves operate on a 24-hour schedule, as well as to individuals who work odd shifts and get up very early or go to bed very late? It depends on the firm's priorities, the costs involved, and the value that customers place on total accessibility.

Mail-order firms have existed since the 19th century, but it often took weeks from the time the customer selected an item from the catalog and mailed in the order to the time the item arrived. Today, mailing in the order has been replaced by 24-hour telephone response or Web ordering. Catalogs are still sent to prospective customers, but, increasingly, firms are placing their catalogs on an interactive Web site, with animation and sound effects to enhance the presentation. Firms such as Lands' End place a growing threat to conventional retailers because they can offer a wide assortment of styles and sizes, stocked in strategically located warehouses, at competitive prices. Helping to keep costs down is their ability to locate customer service centers in small towns with inexpensive land and wage rates instead of in costly downtown sites or suburban shopping centers.

Servicing Manufactured Products

Most manufactured products create a need for accompanying services, ranging from finance and training to transportation and maintenance. Indeed, the competitiveness of a manufacturer's products in both domestic and global markets is as much a function of the availability and quality of relevant services as the quality of the core product. Increasingly, both manufacturing and service companies rely on computer-based systems to provide the supplementary services that customers need and expect. In turn, servicing these computer systems constitutes a major possession-processing industry.

Powerful computer systems—and the software to run them—have been sold to users all over the world. Although there are many niche players, the market for large computer systems is supplied by a small handful of international firms, dominated by American and Japanese companies. The systems that they sell can be found in such locations as big-city banks and chemical plants near rural towns, even in such exotic locations as remote mining sites in Australia, oil rigs above the Arctic Circle, airports on Pacific islands, hydroelectric projects in the Andes, and ships sailing the seven seas. Although the applications to which they are put vary enormously, computers are only of value when they are up and running (or ready for service). System failures can have disastrous consequences for their users and also for the users' own customers. Supporting the enormous installed base of equipment and software, as well as helping users to plan for future needs, is a big business, attracting suppliers that range from worldwide vendors to local service firms.

Historically, maintaining and repairing computers was a task that had to be performed on the site. Proximity to the customer can give locally based, third-party vendors a competitive edge over original equipment manufacturers (OEMs), who also tend to be more expensive. Varying educational levels among people in the host countries can also make it difficult for global OEMs like Hewlett-Packard to ensure consistent standards of service to their customers around the world—a serious problem when dealing with complex equipment, where speed and accuracy are essential in restoring defective hardware and software to good working order.

If a customer is dependent on a machine or a service 24 hours a day, downtime can be very disruptive. Emergencies don't involve only people; they involve vital equipment and processes, too. If a computer goes down, the consequences can range from personal inconvenience to the shutdown of a major facility; if a transformer blows, electric power may be lost; if a furnace fails in below-freezing conditions, pipes may burst. Sometimes, these types of emergencies are handled by a duty person, reached by a pager or cellular phone, who drives to the site of the problem, makes a physical inspection, and undertakes whatever repairs are necessary. By using modern technology, engineers can sometimes fix problems in high-technology equipment in another location without ever leaving their own offices, and they can even do it from the opposite side of the world (see the box on Hewlett-Packard's worldwide response service, p. 212).

THE PROCESS OF SERVICE DELIVERY

There's more to the design of new service delivery systems, obviously, than just a description of the physical facilities and equipment and a specification of the service personnel required. These are merely ingredients in a recipe. What we need next are "mixing" and "cooking" instructions, so that service staffs know what is expected of them and customers understand their own role in service delivery, including how to interact with personnel and facilities. Clarification in advance of the customer's role is vital in the case of self-service. Finally, as in cooking, we need to specify delivery schedules and the time frames involved for each activity. Increasingly, speed is becoming a vital element in competitive strategy. In many instances, service firms are building their strategies around what are known as fast-cycle operations. It's not only customers who are interested in speedier service; firms can benefit, too, when faster operation leads to improved productivity and lower costs.

Planning and Configuring Service Delivery

Decisions in planning and configuring the service delivery process are summarized in Figure 10.1 (p. 213) and require managers to address the following questions:

- What should be the sequencing of the various steps in the service delivery process? Where (location) and when (scheduling) should these steps take place?
- Should service elements be bundled or unbundled for delivery purposes (for instance, should a service firm take responsibility for all elements or delegate certain supplementary services, such as information and reservations, to an intermediary)?
- What should be the nature of the contact between the service provider and its customers: Should customers come to the provider or the other way around? Or for other types of services (e.g., retailing and banking), should the two

HEWLETT-PACKARD'S GLOBAL SERVICE STRATEGY

In addition to being one of the world's best-known suppliers of computer hardware, the Hewlett-Packard Company (HP) is also at the cutting edge of customer support—not only for its own products but also for customer networks incorporating other vendors' equipment. What is driving HP's global service strategy? The answer is that the company sells its hardware to customers with broadly similar needs around the world. Many of its largest customers are themselves operating on a global basis and have expectations of consistent, high-quality service wherever the equipment may be located. Competition in this industry is fierce, because HP's major competitors—companies like IBM, Compaq, and NEC—are themselves global companies.

In the past, computers had to be serviced locally by an engineer who visited the site in person. This is still true of installations and many mechanical repairs. But today, many problem-solving and repair services can be distributed electronically through telecommunication channels. Through its global Customer Support Business Unit (CBSU), which evolved from an earlier phone-in consulting service based in local sales offices, HP has created enormous economies of scale.

Facing problems of varying quality, failure to capture needed data, and inability to balance workloads across offices, HP developed a centralized North American Response Center in 1984. Subsequently, it extended the concept outside the United States and created CBSU. Employing 16,000 people, CBSU now has extensive global market participation, operating some three dozen response centers around the world, and delivers support services and tools that extend beyond traditional hardware maintenance.

The CBSU maintains a globally standardized set of services that range from site design to systems integration and remote diagnostics. This global standardization includes seamless service at any hour of the day or night from anywhere in the world. In addition to discussing problems with a customer by voice phone, an engineer can run diagnostic tests of faulty hardware or software through telecommunication links, with electronic repairs being transmitted through "remote fixes." Standardization also means capability in several languages. For example, a midnight call might originate in Osaka, Japan, from where it goes to the Tokyo Response Center. A bilingual call coordinator then contacts Mountain View, California, where it is 7 A.M. Pacific time. A Japanese-speaking engineer, based in California, calls the customer back to obtain further information.

To provide this kind of service, HP maintains a global chain of activity locations—its response centers around the world are integrated into a network headed by four major centers: Bracknell (United Kingdom), Atlanta (Georgia) and Mountain View (California) in the United States, and Melbourne (Australia). Each center is staffed during extended daytime hours, seven days a week, by between 12 and 200 engineers. The size of each center is a function of the volume of business in the local region. Problems that can't be resolved in a smaller center may be transferred to one of the major centers; which one actually receives the transfer may depend on the time of day at which the call is made. Because of time-zone differentials, at least one of the major centers is always in full operation at any time.

Unlike some competitors who scatter responsibility for different customer support activities among different divisions and geographies, HP unifies every program under the CBSU banner. It is also, perhaps, the leader in using global account management. In recent years it has developed and implemented an extensive system for coordinating the way in which it manages the accounts of its most important multinational customers.

Source: Updated from information in Christopher Lovelock, *Product Plus* (New York: McGraw-Hill, 1994).

parties deal at arm's length, using mail and telecommunications (ranging from voice telephone to the Web)?

■ What should be the nature of the service process at each step? Should customers be served in batches or individually, or should they serve themselves?

■ What should be the serving protocol: Should the firm operate a reservations system or work on a first-come, first-served basis, with queuing as necessary? Alternatively, should a priority system be established for certain types of customers (such as many firms do for their larger industrial accounts or airlines do for their frequent flyers)?

■ What imagery and atmosphere should the service delivery environment (or servicescape) try to create? For a high-contact service, this involves decisions about (1) facility design and layout; (2) staff uniforms, appearance, and attitudes; (3) the type of furnishings and equipment installed; and (4) the use of music, lighting, and decor.

How Technology Is Revolutionizing Service Delivery

Technological developments during the last 20 years have had a remarkable impact on the way in which services are produced and delivered. Developments in telecommunications and computer technology in particular continue to result in many innovations in service delivery. An important result is that, more than ever before, customers are now able to serve themselves, rather than requiring the assistance of an employee. Four innovations of particular interest are

FIGURE 10.1 Planning Service Delivery Processes

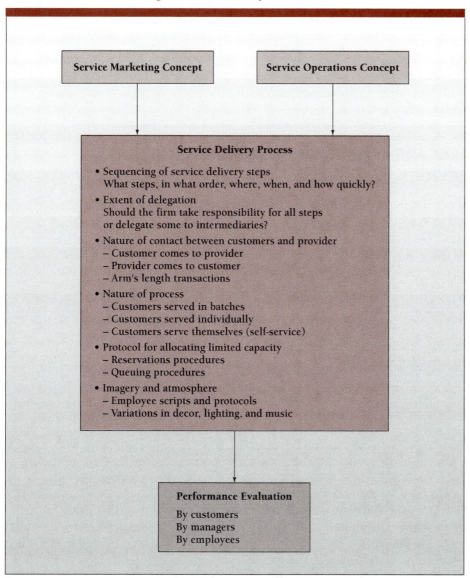

1. development of smart telephones that allow customers to communicate with a service firm's computer by entering commands on the telephone keypad in response to voice commands. Voice recognition technology is also coming into use.

2. creation of freestanding, automated kiosks that enable customers to conduct a variety of simple transactions. Bank ATMs, discussed next, are the best-known example, but many new applications of this technology are coming into use (see the box on electronic kiosks).

3. Development of Web sites that can provide information, take orders, and even serve as a delivery channel for information-based services.

4. development of smart cards with a microchip that can store detailed information about the customer and act as an electronic purse, containing digital money.

One of the most frequently cited service delivery innovations of the past quarter century has been the automated teller machine which has revolutionized the delivery of retail banking services, making them available 24 hours a day, every day of the year, in a wide variety of convenient locations, often far from traditional retail branches. To expand the geographic area in which service can be delivered to their customers, banks have joined regional, national, and even global networks. Thus a bank can also offer service to customers from other banks and collect a fee for doing so. However, a bank's brand identity is weakened when the ATMs used by its customers are branded with the name of other banks or networks. Furthermore, the social bonds between customers and bank staff, which are often responsible for customers' remaining loyal to a particular bank, have now been severed.

The creation of global networks means that once equipped with a valid card and sufficient funds on deposit, customers of a bank in one country can instantly withdraw money in a different currency from another bank's ATM in a country on the

ELECTRONIC KIOSKS DELIVER BOTH COMMERCIAL AND GOVERNMENT SERVICES

Machines similar to bank ATMs are now being used to deliver a broadening array of services. In an effort to make profitable use of hallway space in shopping malls, their owners are starting to install a variety of electronic kiosks. Some are souped-up ATMs that can be programmed to dispense postage stamps or print coupons, bus passes, and even theater tickets, deducting the cost plus a handling fee from the customer's bank account. The ATM manufacturers point out that anything that can be printed on paper and dispensed is a possible service. New derivatives of ATMs can be designed to sell gift certificates, airline tickets, job leads, and long-distance telephone cards.

Government agencies have been using electronic kiosks for several years to dispense information about public services, tourist attractions, and bus routes. Now, in an effort to cut administrative budgets and provide 24-hour service in convenient locations, a number of agencies are using kiosks to automate a variety of transactions. Consumers touch the screen to choose from a menu of services, which can be programmed in multiple languages. They can pay parking tickets, speeding fines, and property taxes; obtain dog licenses and copies of birth certificates; and order license plates for their cars. In Utah, five Quickcourt kiosks assist people in filling out paperwork for no-fault divorces—a process that takes about 45 minutes, requires no lawyer, and costs only $10. Quickcourt also computes child support payments. In San Antonio, Texas, kiosks sell permits to hold garage sales and print out information on property taxes and city job openings. Users can also view pictures of animals available for adoption at the city pound. In New York, users can look up certain kinds of records, such as landlords' histories of building code violations and swipe their credit cards through a slot to pay municipal taxes, license fees, and speeding fines. In New York, a fee of $3.50 is added to credit card transactions.

Source: Based on information in De'Ann Weimer, "Can You Keep 'Em Down on the Mall?" *Business Week*, 15 December 1997, 66, 70; and Carol Jouzaitis, "Step Right Up and Pay Your Taxes and Tickets," *USA Today*, 2 October 1997, p. 4A.

other side of the world. These remarkable machines can now perform most of the functions of a human teller with a high degree of customization. The machines used by banks in Switzerland even know what language the customer prefers to speak. When opening an account, customers select one of four languages (German, French, Italian, or English), and this choice is then encoded onto their ATM cards. These Swiss ATMs greet customers in all four languages, ask them to insert the card, and then immediately switch to their preferred language.[5]

Banks in many countries have started to close branches and shift customers to cheaper, electronic banking channels in an effort to boost productivity and remain competitive in an increasingly competitive marketplace. However, not all customers like to use self-service equipment, and so the migration of customers to new electronic channels may require different strategies for different segments, as well as recognition that some proportion of customers will never voluntarily shift from their preferred high-contact delivery environments. An alternative that appeals to many people, perhaps because it uses a familiar technology, is banking by voice telephone (for a description of First Direct, the world's first, all-telephone bank, operating 24 hours a day, every day of the year, see chapter 3). The mbanx virtual banking enterprise created by Bank of Montreal and its U.S. subsidiary, Chicago-based Harris Bank, offers customers a broad choice of 24-hour delivery channels, including telephone, fax, internet, and ATM. The ultimate in self-service banking will be when one can not only use a smart card as an electronic wallet for a wide array of transactions but also refill it from a special card reader connected to a computer modem.

Promoting and Delivering Services in Cyberspace

The use of the telephone for selling and ordering goods and services has increased rapidly during the past few decades. More recently, entrepreneurs have taken advantage of the Internet to create new services that can be delivered through electronic channels accessed by computers in customers' homes or offices.

The underlying theme is to offer customers more choices: Some people opt for face-to-face contact; others like telephone contact with a human being; still others prefer the greater anonymity and control offered by more impersonal contacts. When purchasing goods, some customers like to visit the store and make a physical examination of the items that interest them. Others watch product demonstrations on television (sometimes called infomercials) and then call a toll-free number to place an order if they have seen something they like. Another group likes to select its purchases from a nicely printed catalog and to order by telephone or mail. Finally, a small but growing number of consumers are choosing to use **cyberspace** as a means of examining and purchasing goods through the World Wide Web. In each instance, although the core product may remain the same, the wide differences in delivery systems mean that the nature of the overall service experience changes sharply as the encounter moves from high contact to low.

cyberspace: a term used to describe the absence of a definable physical location where electronic transactions or communications occur.

Marketplace or Marketspace?

The growth of electronic channels is creating a fundamental change in the nature of marketing, as noted in the banking industry. Customers are moving from face-to-face contacts with suppliers in fixed locations that operate only during fixed hours to remote contacts "anywhere, anytime." More and more services now fall into the category of arm's-length relationships rather than face-to-face interactions.

As Rayport and Sviokla note, "The traditional *marketplace* interaction between physical seller and physical buyer has been eliminated. In fact, everything about this new type of transaction—what we call a *marketspace* transaction—is different from what happens in the marketplace."[6]

marketplace: a physical location where suppliers and customers meet to do business.

The marketplace.   Companies doing business in the **marketplace** need a physical environment in which customers can get together with suppliers to inspect merchandise or conduct service-related business. We cannot get rid of the marketplace for people-processing services because they require customers to enter the physical environment of a service factory. In some instances, customers would not wish to get rid of the marketplace, for it is the physical and social environment that attracts them, as in destination resorts. Shopping malls are being redesigned to create "total experiences," which include not only retail stores but also food services, health clubs, entertainment, exhibitions, and a chance to socialize.

marketspace: a virtual location made possible by telephone and Internet linkages where customers and suppliers conduct business electronically.

The marketspace.   Companies doing business in the **marketspace** may be able to replace contact with physical objects by information about them (as in a paper or electronic catalog). Information-based services, of course, don't even require a physical location. Moreover, the context in which the transaction occurs is also different, with on-screen (or on-telephone) contact replacing physical contact; customers may also have the option to replace service from contact personnel by self-service through intelligent interactive systems.

One of the driving forces behind these moves has been time savings, reflecting a desire by customers for ever faster and more convenient service. Another factor has been interest on the part of some customers in obtaining more information about the goods and services that they buy. Paradoxically, electronic contacts may bring customers "closer" to manufacturers and service suppliers. Managers are beginning to realize that the opportunity to develop increased knowledge of customers may be as important a reason for doing business in the marketspace as seeking cost savings by eliminating physical contact. Conducting dialog with customers about their needs and preferences (information that can be stored for future reference) can lead to delivery of better and more customized service, which may create greater value and therefore command higher prices.

Web sites have become the latest competitive tool for service marketers. Some firms only see them as an alternative to paper brochures; others see them in more creative ways, ranging from order-taking channels to delivery systems in their own right. Delivery through the Internet is possible for any information-based product (physical products, such as clothes from Lands' End, books from Amazon.com, or wine and food from Virtual Vineyards, must necessarily be shipped through physical channels). Among information-based services now delivered through commercial Web sites are software, news, research reports, and even some forms of entertainment. In addition, of course, firms can also deliver information-based services to their customers as e-mail attachments or through corporate **extranets**—a secure, **intranet**-like private network linking a company to its major suppliers and designated customers.

extranet: a secure, private intranet-like network that links a company to its major suppliers and designated customers.

intranet: an internal corporate network, restricted to company personnel, that allows easy access to a series of Web-site-like information bases organized around departments, projects, products, markets, and so forth.

THE ROLE OF INTERMEDIARIES

Many service organisations find it cost effective to delegate certain tasks, most frequently, supplementary service elements. For instance, airlines rely heavily on travel agents to handle customer interactions such as giving out information, taking reservations, accepting payment, and ticketing. Of course, many manufacturers rely on the services of distributors or retailers to stock and sell their products to end users,

FIGURE 10.2 Splitting Responsibilities for Supplementary Service Elements

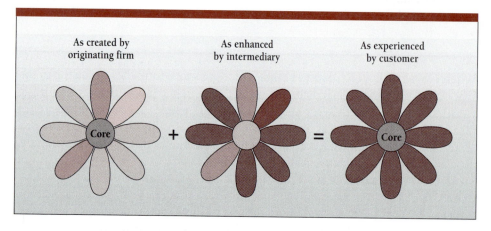

As created by originating firm + As enhanced by intermediary = As experienced by customer

while also taking on the responsibility for such supplementary services as information, advice, order taking, delivery, installation, billing and payment, and certain types of problem solving; in some cases, they may also handle certain kinds of repairs and upgrades. Figure 10.2 uses the Flower of Service framework to illustrate how the firm responsible for a given service concept may work in partnership with one or more intermediaries to deliver a complete service package to its customers.

Even the core product can be outsourced to an intermediary. Trucking companies regularly use independent agents instead of locating company-owned branches in each of the different cities they serve; they may also choose to contract with independent owner-operators, who drive their own trucks, rather than buying trucks and employing full-time drivers. Universities may offer evening or weekend extension courses in local community colleges or other locations, as well as at their main campus, to make access more convenient to prospective students. In such cases, the course is designed centrally but delivered locally. Franchising is also a popular way of delivering many business service concepts through carefully trained and monitored intermediaries, following a standardized format.

A firm's decision of whether or not to subcontract may vary from one part of the world to another. FedEx's operation in the United States is an example of an organization with a totally closed system: The vehicles, aircraft, facilities, and personnel are all its own. But in many countries around the world, FedEx employs local service contractors, referred to as "global service participants," to perform such functions as delivery and pickup.

The Challenge of Maintaining Consistency

A disadvantage of delegating activities is that it entails some loss of control over the delivery system and, thereby, over how customers experience the actual service. Ensuring that an intermediary adopts exactly the same priorities and procedures is difficult but vital to effective quality control. Franchisors usually try to exercise tight control over all aspects of the service performance, not only output specifications but also the appearance of the servicescape, employee performance, and such elements as service schedules.

Even when the work is done well, however, there's still a risk that customers will perceive inconsistencies between the intermediary's approach to the task and the overall positioning sought by the primary service organization. Not every franchise operation can design service sites according to a template. In many cases, the chosen intermediary already has its own delivery site, thus affecting the servicescape

experienced by customers visiting that location. For instance, the use of high schools as satellite campuses for college extension courses may lead prospective users to perceive the product as inferior, regardless of the quality of the facilities and teaching.

Conclusion

Where? When? How? Responses to these three questions form the foundation of service delivery strategy. The customer's service experience is a function of both service performance and delivery characteristics. The where, of course, relates to the places where customers can obtain service delivery. In this chapter, we have presented a categorization scheme for thinking about alternative place-related strategies, including remote delivery from virtual locations.

The when is involved with decisions on scheduling of service delivery. Customers' demands for greater convenience are now leading many firms to extend their hours and days of service. The how concerns channels and procedures for delivering the core and supplementary service elements to customers. Advances in technology are having a major impact on the alternatives available and on their economics.

Study Questions and Exercises

1. Review the evolution of Kinko's. What do you see as the key changes in (a) product strategy and (b) distribution strategy? To what extent have these been customer driven versus technology driven, in each instance?

2. Review the options for service delivery in Table 10.1. What factors constrain a service firm's choice of delivery system? How is technology changing the picture?

3. Compare and contrast the role of servicescapes within two specific industries of your choice. To what extent are these roles strategic in intent (differentiating one firm from its competitors) versus functional (adding value for customers or employees)? Give examples.

4. Visit the Web sites www.Amazon.com and www.BarnesandNoble.com. Compare and contrast their design, structure, and ease of use. As a potential customer, which do you prefer and why? What enhancements would you suggest?

5. Visit the following airline Web sites: www.aa.com, www.british-airways.com, www.singaporeair.com, www.iflyswa.com, and www.ual.com. Visit two or three competing Web sites and compare and contrast their approaches, clarifying your criteria as a prospective customer.

6. Contrast the roles of place strategy and time strategy in influencing customers' service decisions and selections. What market segmentation issues are involved?

7. What marketing and management challenges are raised by the use of intermediaries in a service setting?

8. Identify a service whose delivery strategy fits in each of the categories presented in Table 10.1. What are the implications for management in each case?

9. What is the difference between *marketspace* and *marketplace*? Give examples of service companies that use both of these delivery strategies to reach their target markets.

Price and Other Costs of Service

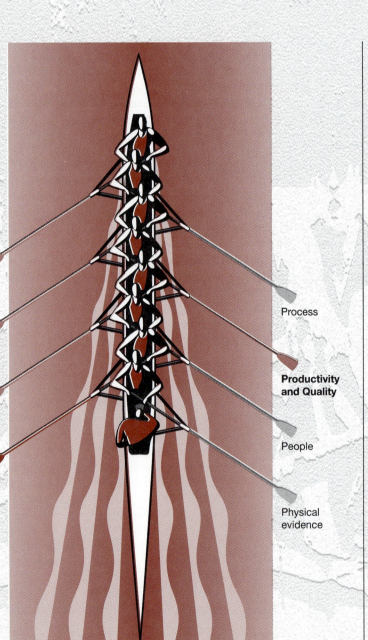

Product
Elements

Place
and Time

Promotion
and Education

PRICE AND
OTHER COSTS
OF SERVICE

Process

Productivity
and Quality

People

Physical
evidence

Learning Objectives

After reading this chapter, you should be able to

■ appreciate the factors that shape pricing strategy

■ define different types of financial costs incurred by companies

■ define the different costs of service incurred by customers

■ understand the concept of net value

■ appreciate ethical concerns in pricing policy

■ formulate pricing strategies and policies for services

America Online: When the Price Isn't Right[1]

For several years, the Internet provider America Online (AOL) enjoyed a loyal—and growing—customer base in spite of its relatively high prices. Originally, it charged a base subscription of $9.95 for 20 hours of access a month, plus $2.95 for each additional hour. This formula kept most subscribers watching the clock, although heavy users racked up monthly bills of $500 or more. But growing competition from Internet providers like Microsoft Network, AT&T, and Netcom forced AOL to consider matching the industry standard of $19.95 for unlimited access.

Surveys of AOL customers showed that they favored the change. So in December 1996, AOL began an intensive media campaign to promote a new flat rate. For $19.95 a month, customers could obtain unlimited Internet access plus AOL's proprietary content, which included games, access to newspaper and magazine sites, and special features like the Motley Fool investment forum.

At first, AOL was delighted with the stampede of new business. Over one-half million people signed up for the service in the first month of the campaign, causing the company's CEO to exclaim, "We will look back on this point in history as the time when the mass market moved to the Internet." Over the next month, the company's customer base grew from 7 million to 8 million members.

By January 1997, however, problems were surfacing as the "mass market" squeezed AOL's service operations to the point where Internet access was virtually impossible. Although AOL had been adding modems for months in anticipation of its pricing changes, the dramatic increase in demand quickly ate up the additional capacity. To make matters worse, existing customers had increased their on-line time substantially because there was no longer any cost for additional hours. By mid-January, AOL was publicly pleading with members to "show some restraint"

during the peak evening period. But skeptical members began staying on line even longer, afraid that it would be difficult to get back on again if they quit.

Customers grew increasingly dissatisfied as Internet access through AOL became virtually impossible. Especially infuriating was the fact that in spite of their inability to use the service, AOL still billed their credit cards automatically each month. And they couldn't cancel easily either—that required logging on through AOL, which was a seemingly impossible feat. Finally, AOL gave into pressure from angry customers and attorneys-general from more than 30 states who threatened to sue if the situation wasn't resolved. It agreed to pay cash refunds for two months' worth of service for members who were having difficulty getting on line. It also agreed to limit its advertising and to allow customers to cancel their subscriptions by fax or regular mail.

Some customers were cynical. They argued that the plan penalized AOL's most substantial users because people could get a refund only if they had been on line for a limited number of hours in December and January. Critics also questioned the value of a free month, as users were still having difficulty in getting on line. However, other members felt that the company was showing good faith in trying to resolve the problem and said they were willing to be patient for another three to four months while AOL increased its service capacity.

Once the dust settled, many industry analysts felt that AOL had emerged the clear winner. Members spent an average of 16 hours on line during the months specified in the settlement, yet only those who had logged fewer than 15 hours were eligible for the refund. Applying for refunds or the month's free service was a cumbersome process, and many people were too busy (or too lazy) to apply. Gambling that it would lose relatively few customers overall, AOL was right. Many members decided that switching to a new provider

wasn't worth the time and effort required to learn a new system and notify everyone of the change in their e-mail address. Thus, AOL still had a nearly 3 million subscriber lead over Compuserv, its nearest competitor and expected to maintain it. "No one else offers the same content and ease of use," remarked one AOL spokesperson. "We've created a community online and our customers respond to that."

However, by early 1998, AOL was in trouble again.

This time, the issue was an allegedly deceptive sales practice in which the company offered 50 free hours of use to attract new subscribers. Lawyers claimed that the promotion was misleading, because it didn't make clear that customers had to use the 50 hours within one month of signing up. Also, by accepting free time, new customers attracted by the promotion were automatically signing up for future AOL use at $19.95 per month.

PAYING FOR SERVICE

Have you ever noticed what a wide variety of terms service organizations use to describe the prices they set? Universities talk about *tuition*, professional firms collect *fees*, and banks add *service charges*. Some bridges and highways impose *tolls*. Transportation operators refer to *fares*, clubs to *subscriptions*, brokers to *commissions*, landlords to *rents*, museums to *admissions charges*, utilities to *tariffs*, and hotels to *room rates*. These diverse terms are a signal that many services take a different approach to pricing than manufacturing firms. Let's look at what makes pricing a particularly challenging task for service managers. The discussion that follows assumes a basic understanding of economic costs incurred by companies—fixed, semivariable, and variable costs—contribution, and break-even analysis (if you haven't previously been exposed to these concepts, you'll find it useful to review the material in the box, p. 222, on understanding costs).

What Makes Service Pricing Different?

In chapter 1, we reviewed some of the key differences between goods and services. Intangible performances are inherently more difficult to price than goods because it's harder to calculate the financial costs involved in serving a customer than it is to identify the labor, materials, machine time, storage, and shipping costs associated with producing a physical good. The variability of both inputs and outputs means that units of service may not cost the same to produce, nor may they be of equal value to customers—especially if the variability extends to greater or lesser quality. To make matters even more complicated, it's not always easy to define a unit of service, thus raising questions about what should be the basis of service pricing (a topic we address later in this chapter).

A very important distinction between goods and services is that many services have a much higher ratio of fixed costs to variable costs than is found in manufacturing firms. Service businesses with high fixed costs include those with an expensive physical facility (hotel, hospital, college, or theater), a fleet of vehicles (airline, bus line, or trucking company), or a network (telecommunications company, Internet provider, or gas pipeline), but their variable costs of serving one extra customer may be minimal. Under these conditions, managers may feel that they have tremendous pricing flexibility and they are tempted to price very low to make an extra sale. However, there can be no profit at the end of the year unless all fixed costs have been recovered. Many service businesses have gone bankrupt by ignoring this fact. In contrast, public and nonprofit organizations can use tax

UNDERSTANDING COSTS, CONTRIBUTION, AND BREAK-EVEN ANALYSIS

Fixed costs—sometimes referred to as overhead—are those economic costs that a supplier would continue to incur (at least in the short run) even if no services were sold. These costs are likely to include rent, depreciation, utilities, taxes, insurance, salaries and wages for managers and long-term employees, security, and interest payments.

Variable costs refer to the economic costs associated with serving one additional customer, such as making a bank transaction, selling a single seat in a train or theater, serving an extra hotel guest for the night in a hotel, or doing one more repair job. With many services, such costs are very low; there is, for instance, very little labor or fuel cost involved in transporting an extra bus passenger. In a theater, the cost of seating an extra patron is probably minimal unless the ticket was sold through an independent agency that takes a fixed percentage of the price as its fee. Selling a hotel room for the night has slightly higher variable costs because the room will need to be cleaned and the linens sent to the laundry after a guest leaves. More significant variable costs are associated with such activities as serving food and beverages or installing a new part when undertaking repairs because they include the provision of often costly physical products in addition to labor. The fact that a business has sold a service at a price that exceeds its variable cost does not mean that the firm is now profitable, for there are still fixed and semivariable costs to be recouped.

Semivariable costs fall between fixed and variable costs. They represent expenses that rise or fall in stepwise fashion as the volume of business increases or decreases. Examples include adding an extra flight to meet increased demand on a specific air route or hiring a part-time employee to work in a restaurant on busy weekends.

Contribution is the difference between the variable cost of selling an extra unit of service and the money received from its buyer. It goes to cover fixed and semivariable costs before creating profits.

Determining and allocating economic costs can be a challenging task in some service operations because of the difficulty of deciding how to assign fixed costs in a multiservice facility, such as a hospital. For instance, certain fixed costs are associated with running a hospital emergency unit (EU), but beyond that, there are fixed costs for running the hospital of which it is a part. How much of the hospital's fixed costs should be allocated to the EU? A hospital director might use one of several approaches to calculate the EU's share of overheads: (1) the percentage of total floor space that it occupies; (2) the percentage of employee hours or payroll that it accounts for; or (3) the percentage of total patient contact hours involved. Each method is likely to yield a totally different fixed-cost allocation. One method might show the emergency unit to be very profitable, another make it seem a break-even operation, and a third suggest that the EU was incurring a big loss.

Break-even analysis. Managers need to know at what sales volume a service will become profitable. This is called the break-even point. *Break-even analysis* involves dividing the total fixed and semivariable costs by the contribution obtained on each unit of service. For instance, if a 100-room hotel needs to cover fixed and semivariable costs of $1 million a year and the average contribution per room night is $50, the hotel will need to sell 20,000 room nights per year out of a total annual capacity of 36,500. If prices are cut by an average of $10 per room night (or variable costs rise by $10), the contribution will drop to $40, and the hotel's break-even volume will rise to 25,000 room nights. The required sales volume needs to be related to *price sensitivity* (will customers be willing to pay this much?), *market size* (is the market large enough to support this level of patronage after taking competition into account?), and *maximum capacity* (the hotel in our example has a capacity of 36,500 room nights per year, assuming that no rooms are taken out of service for maintenance or renovation).

subsidies, donations, and income from endowments to cover all or part of their fixed costs.

The intangibility of service performances and the invisibility of the necessary backstage facilities and labor make it harder for customers to see what they are getting for their money than when they purchase a physical good. Consider the homeowners who call an electrical contractor to repair a defective circuit. Two days later (if they are lucky) an electrician arrives. Carrying a small bag of tools, he disappears into the closet where the circuit board is located, soon finds the problem, replaces a defective circuit breaker, and presto!—everything works. A mere 20 minutes has elapsed. A few days later, the homeowners are horrified to receive a bill for $65, most of it for labor charges. Just think what the couple could have bought for that amount of money—new clothes, several compact disks, a nice dinner. What they fail to think of are all the fixed costs that the owner of the business needs to recoup: the office, telephone, insurance, truck, tools, fuel, and office support staff. The variable costs of the visit are also higher than they appear. To the 20 minutes spent at the house must be added 15 minutes of driving back and forth, plus five minutes to unload (and later reload) needed tools and supplies from the truck on arrival at the customer's house—thus effectively doubling the labor time devoted to this call. Moreover, the firm still has to add a margin to make a profit for the owner. But it is undeniable that customers often feel that they have been exploited.

Another factor that influences service pricing is the time factor because it may affect customers' perceptions of value. Customers may be willing to pay more for a service delivered fast than for one delivered more slowly. Sometimes greater speed increases operating costs, too—reflecting the need to pay overtime wages or use more expensive equipment (a supersonic Concorde costs more to fly per passenger mile than a Boeing 747). In other instances, achieving faster turnaround is simply a matter of giving priority to one customer's business over another's (clothes requiring express dry cleaning take the same amount of time to clean; time is saved by moving them to the head of the line). Also, the use of different distribution channels—electronic banking, say rather than face-to-face banking—not only has different cost implications for the bank but also affects the nature of the service experience for the customer and the total time required to conduct a transaction. Some people like the convenience of fast, impersonal transactions; others dislike technology and prefer to deal with a real teller. So a service transaction that has value for one person may not for another.

Ethical Concerns

Services in general, and credence services in particular, often invite performance and pricing abuses.[2] When customers don't know what they are getting from the service supplier and lack the technical skills to know if a good job has been done, they are vulnerable to paying for work that wasn't necessary or, if it was, was not well performed. There is an implicit assumption among many customers that a high-priced professional—say a lawyer—must be more skilled than one who charges lower fees. Although price can indeed serve as a surrogate for quality, it's sometimes hard to be sure if the extra value is really there.

Pricing schedules for services are often quite complex. Before it went to a flat monthly fee, AOL charged a combination of monthly subscription plus an hourly charge beyond a certain minimum. Complexity makes it easy (and perhaps more tempting) for firms to engage in unethical behavior. The car rental industry, for instance, has attracted some notoriety for advertising bargain rental prices and then telling customers on arrival that other fees, like collision insurance and personal insurance, are mandatory; also, rental agents sometimes fail to clarify certain "small print" contract terms, such as a high mileage charge that is added once the car exceeds a very low threshold of free miles. The situation in some Florida resort towns was so bad at one point that people were saying: "The car is free, but the keys are extra." A common practice when the car is returned is to charge fees for refueling a partially empty tank that are about three times what the driver would pay at the pump. When customers know that they are vulnerable to potential abuse, they

Medical bills contain many different items and can be difficult to understand. The patient may need an explanation.

become suspicious of both the firm and its employees. It's harder for customer service personnel to deliver friendly service under such conditions.

If the firm is honest in the first place, the best approach to such situations is a proactive one, spelling out all fees and expenses clearly in advance so that there are no surprises. A related approach is to develop a simple fee structure so that customers can more easily understand the financial implications of a specific usage situation. Nevertheless, pricing scams continue and sometimes lead to government regulations designed to protect customers.

Understanding the Costs of Service Incurred by Customers

From a customer's standpoint, the monetary price charged by the supplier may be just the first of many costs associated with the purchase and delivery of a service. Let's look at what's involved (as you do so, please consider your own experience in different service contexts).

Purchase price plus other financial costs of service.   Customers often incur financial costs over and above the purchase price. Necessary incidental expenses may include travel to the service site, parking, and purchase of other facilitating goods or services ranging from meals to babysitting. We call the total of all these expenses (including the price of the service itself) the *financial costs of service*. However, there's more to come because the costs of service go beyond just financial outlays (see Figure 11.1).

Nonfinancial costs of service for customers.   In most situations, customers are likely to incur a variety of *nonfinancial costs of service*, representing the time, effort, and discomfort associated with the search, purchase, and use. Customers' involvement in production (which is particularly important in people-processing services and in self-service) means that customers incur such burdens as mental and physical effort and exposure to unwanted sensory experiences as noise, heat, and smells.

FIGURE 11.1 Determining the Total Costs of a Service: More Than Meets the Eye?

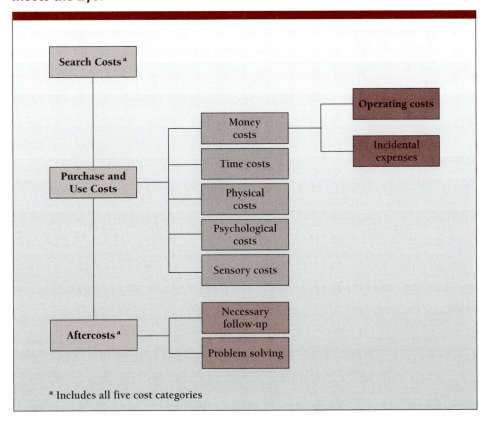

ª Includes all five cost categories

Services that are high on experience and credence attributes may also create psychological costs, such as anxiety. Nonfinancial costs of service can be grouped into four distinct categories.

- **Time costs of service** are inherent in service delivery. There's an opportunity cost to customers for the time they are involved in the service delivery process because they could spend that time in other ways. They could even be working to earn additional income. The customers of AOL saw the time spent trying to get on line as time wasted. (Not for nothing do people jest about the World Wide Wait.)

- **Physical costs of service** (like fatigue, discomfort, and occasionally even injury) may be incurred in obtaining services, especially if customers must come to the service factory and if delivery entails self-service.

- **Psychological costs of service**, like mental effort, feelings of inadequacy, or fear, are sometimes attached to evaluating service alternatives, making a selection, and then using a particular service. The anger and frustration felt by AOL customers when unable to log on compounded the waste of their time.

- **Sensory costs of service** relate to unpleasant sensations affecting any of the five senses. In a service environment, they may include putting up with noise, unpleasant smells, drafts, excessive heat or cold, uncomfortable seating, visually unappealing environments, and even unpleasant tastes.

We sometimes refer to physical, psychological, and sensory costs collectively as effort or hassle.

time costs of service: time spent by customers during all aspects of the service delivery process.

physical costs of service: undesired consequences to a customer's body that occur during the service delivery process.

psychological costs of service: undesired mental or emotional states experienced by customers as a result of the service delivery process.

sensory costs of service: negative sensations experienced through a customer's five senses during the service delivery process.

As shown in Figure 11.1, the total costs of purchasing and using a service also include those associated with search activities. When you were looking for a college, how much money, time, and effort did you spend before deciding where to apply? How much time and effort would you put into comparing alternative haircutters if your current one were to leave? There may be additional costs of service even after the initial service is completed. Thus, a doctor may diagnose a medical problem for a patient and then prescribe a course of physical therapy and drugs that must be continued for several months. Also, service failures may force customers to waste time, money, and effort in trying to resolve the problem.

Understanding Value

When customers purchase a specific service, they are weighing the perceived benefits to be obtained from the service against its perceived costs. Consider your own experience. As a customer, you make judgments about the benefits you expect to receive in return for your anticipated investment of money, time, and effort. Although our focus in this chapter is mainly on the monetary aspects of pricing, you have probably noticed that people often pay a premium to save time, minimize unwanted effort, and obtain greater comfort. In other words, they are willing to pay higher prices (financial costs of service) to reduce the nonfinancial costs of service. However, because not all customers are willing (or able) to pay more, service companies sometimes create several different levels of service. For example, airlines and hotels often have different classes of service, which offer customers the option of paying more in exchange for additional benefits. Some companies create special time-saving advantages for their most loyal customers by establishing frequent user clubs that offer such privileges as special phone numbers for reservations or faster check-in stations.

Research findings suggest that customers' definitions of value may be highly personal and idiosyncratic. Four broad expressions of value emerged from one study: (1) value is low price, (2) value is whatever I want in a product, (3) value is the quality I get for the price I pay, and (4) value is what I get for what I give.[3] In this book, we base our definition of value on this fourth category and use the term **net value**, which is defined as the sum of all the perceived benefits (gross value) minus the sum of all the perceived costs of service. The greater the positive difference between the two, the greater the net value. Economists use the term **consumer surplus** to define the difference between the price customers pay and the amount they would actually have been willing to pay to obtain the desired benefits (or utility) of a specific product.

If the perceived costs of service are greater than the perceived benefits, the service in question will have negative net value. Customers will probably describe the service as poor value and decide not to purchase it. You can think of calculations that customers make in their minds as being similar to weighing materials on an old-fashioned pair of scales, with product benefits in one tray and the costs of obtaining those benefits in the other tray (Figure 11.2). When customers evaluate competing services, they are basically comparing the relative net values. Think about your own decision processes when you go to a restaurant and are trying to select among the different items on the menu.

Increasing Net Value by Reducing Nonfinancial Costs of Service

A marketer can increase the net value of a service by adding benefits to the core product, enhancing supplementary services, or reducing the financial costs associated with the purchase and use of the product. In many instances, service firms also

net value: the sum of all perceived benefits (gross value) minus the sum of all perceived costs.

consumer surplus: the difference between the actual price paid and the customer's perception of the product's monetary worth.

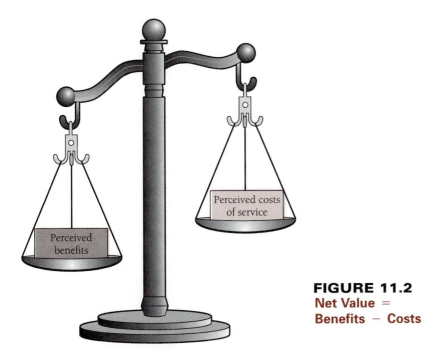

FIGURE 11.2
Net Value =
Benefits − Costs

have the option to improve value by minimizing unwanted nonfinancial costs of service for customers. Possible approaches include

- reducing the time costs of service involved in service purchase, delivery, and consumption
- minimizing unwanted psychological costs of service at each stage
- eliminating unwanted physical costs of service that customers may incur, notably during the search and delivery processes
- decreasing unpleasant sensory costs of service by creating more attractive visual environments; reducing noise; installing more comfortable furniture and equipment; curtailing offensive smells; and ensuring that foods, beverages, or medicines have a pleasant taste

Cutting these types of costs significantly may even allow service firms to increase the monetary price while still offering what is perceived by customers as good value.

Perceptions of net value may vary widely between customers and from one situation to another for the same customer. For example, how customers feel about the net value of a service may be sharply different postuse than preuse, reflecting the experiential qualities of many services. When customers use a service and find that it has cost more and delivered fewer benefits than expected, they are likely to speak angrily of poor value. In extreme cases, when they feel that the supplier misrepresented service features, benefits, costs, or outcomes, they may seek restitution or press legal charges on the grounds of fraud (see the box on unexpected surcharges, p. 228). Good managers try to provide full disclosure of all costs of service for search, purchase, use, and postpurchase activities; in particular, they carefully scrutinize advertising claims and sales presentations to ensure that customers are not misled.

FOUNDATIONS OF PRICING STRATEGY

Now we turn to the issue of how firms should decide on the financial price that they charge for their services. The foundations of a firm's pricing strategy can be described as a tripod, with costs to the provider, competition, and value to the customer as the three legs (Figure 11.3, p. 228).

CUSTOMERS FIND UNEXPECTED SURCHARGES ON NONBANK ATMs

In the past, only banks installed and operated automated teller machines. Today, however, more than 34,000 ATMs in the United States are owned and operated by nonbanking organizations. You find them in all sorts of useful locations—at gas stations, in small stores, and even in clubs. But if you use one, be prepared to pay a premium fee for the transaction.

Banks used to charge their customers an extra dollar when they used a "foreign" ATM (that is, one belonging to another bank) on top of any service charges levied on their own customers, which might be as much as $1.25 per transaction when account balances fell below a certain level. In 1996, banks across the country lobbied the two largest ATM networks—Visa's Plus and Mastercard's Cirrus—to withdraw their ban on any additional surcharges. They argued, successfully, that permitting surcharges would encourage placement of ATMs in useful but out-of-the-way places where volume would be lower.

The big winners from surcharges appear to be several dozen small companies that install inexpensive ATMs that can only dispense cash and connect them to a national network. The surcharges can mount up. In 1996, it's estimated that nonbanks took in $50 million, but by 1997 that figure had jumped to $600 million. The ATM surcharges of all types amounted to $3.7 billion that year.

What upsets many customers is that nonbank ATMs impose a double surcharge: first the $1+ fee for use of a foreign ATM plus an additional charge that may reach as high as $3 for a simple cash withdrawal (and averaged $1.31 in 1997). To make matters worse, nonbank ATMs often fail to disclose the extra surcharge; users first know about it when they find it billed to their bank accounts. As a result of consumer complaints, there is pressure at both the state and federal levels to pass laws banning ATM surcharges.

However, many small business owners appear to like the nonbanks' approach to doing business. When the owner of a minimart was unable to persuade a bank to put an ATM in his store, he leased a machine from a company for about $300 a month. Customers pay an extra $1.50 surcharge for each transaction, of which $0.80 goes to the minimart owner. He claims that because of the machine, his store attracts more customers and sells more merchandise, netting a profit of up to $50 a month after paying the leasing fee.

Source: Dean Foust, Seanna Browder, and Geoffrey Smith, "Mad as Hell at the Cash Machine," *Business Week*, 15 September 1997, 124; Ross Kerber, "High-Fee ATMs, Low Profile Operators," *The Wall Street Journal*, 4 December 1997, B-1.

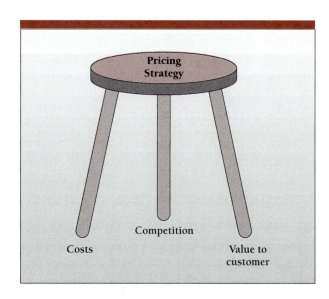

FIGURE 11.3
The Pricing Tripod

The Pricing Tripod

The costs that a firm needs to recover usually imposes a minimum price, a floor, for a specific service offering, and the perceived value of the offering to customers sets a maximum, or ceiling. The price charged by competitors for similar or substitute services typically determines where, within the floor-to-ceiling range, the price should actually be set. Let's look at each leg of the pricing tripod in more detail.

Cost-based pricing.   In cost-based pricing, prices are set relative to financial costs. Companies seeking to make a profit must recover the full costs—variable, semivariable, and fixed—of producing and marketing a service and then add a sufficient margin to yield a satisfactory profit. When variable costs are low, managers may be tempted to establish unrealistically low selling prices that fail to contribute toward fixed and semivariable costs. However, some firms make an exception in the case of **loss leaders**, which are products sold at less than full cost to attract customers who will then be tempted to buy profitable service offerings from the same organization. Managers need to keep track of the actual costs associated with loss leaders so that the amount of promotional subsidy is fully understood.

When industries like electric and telecommunications were tightly regulated, there was little flexibility for charging substantially different prices to different market segments. In fact, these industries often lacked the information needed to calculate the costs of serving different types of user. So managers would determine the total costs incurred during a certain period, divide them by actual unit sales, and thus calculate an average cost per unit of service (defined by such measures as kilowatt-hours or minutes of long-distance calling time). The next step was to add a certain percentage for profit to this average cost and seek permission from the regulatory agency to charge a specific price. As more sophisticated costing analysis began to be used, particularly with the advent of deregulation (or privatization) and increased competition, it became clear that the prices charged to business users had been subsidizing household subscribers, who were, in fact, much more expensive to serve.

Competition-based pricing.   In competition-based pricing, firms marketing services that are relatively undifferentiated from competing offerings keep an eye on what competitors are charging and try to price accordingly. If customers see little or no difference between the services offered in the marketplace, they will be likely to choose the cheapest. In this situation, the firm with the lowest cost per unit of service enjoys an enviable marketing advantage. It has the option of either competing on price at levels that higher-cost competitors cannot afford to match or of charging the going market rate and earning larger profits than competing firms.

In some industries, one firm may act as the price leader, with others taking their cue from this company. You can sometimes see this phenomenon at the local level when several gas stations are situated at opposite corners of an intersection. As soon as one station raises or lowers its prices, each of the others will follow promptly.

During boom times in highly competitive industries such as airlines, hotels, and rental cars, other firms are often happy to go along with the leader, particularly if this supplier does not have the lowest costs, because prices are likely to be set at a level that allows good profits. During a downturn in the economy, however, such industries quickly find themselves with surplus productive capacity—unsold seats, empty rooms, or unrented cars. In an effort to attact more customers, one firm—often not the original leader—may cut prices. However, pricing is the easiest and fastest of the 8Ps to change. Sometimes a price war may result overnight as competitors rush to match the other firm's bargain prices.

---

cost-based pricing: the practice of relating the price to be charged to the costs of producing, delivering, and marketing a product.

loss leaders: products provided at less than cost to attract customers in the hope that they will buy other goods and services at regular prices.

competition-based pricing: the practice of setting prices relative to those charged by competitors.

value-based pricing: the practice of setting prices with reference to what customers are willing to pay for the value they believe they will receive.

Value-based pricing.   No customer will pay more for a service than he or she thinks it's worth. Thus, marketers may need to do some research to determine how customers perceive the value of their services. Value may vary according to the situation. For instance, people may be willing to pay more for repair services during emergencies (such as a car breakdown on an icy winter night).

Price is sometimes used as a means to communicate the quality and value of a service when customers find it hard to evaluate its capabilities in advance. In the absence of tangible clues, customers may associate higher prices with higher levels of performance on important service attributes.[4] Who is the better lawyer: the one who charges $25 an hour or the one who bills $200 an hour? If nothing else, the high fee suggests past success. Later in this chapter we examine the opportunities for value-based pricing strategies with more specificity.

Establishing Monetary Pricing Objectives

Any decision on pricing strategy must be based on a clear understanding of a company's pricing objectives. There are three basic categories of pricing objectives: revenue oriented, capacity oriented, and demand oriented (see Figure 11.4).[5]

Revenue-oriented objectives.   Within certain limits, profit-seeking organizations try to maximize the surplus of income over expenditure. Managers responsible for public and nonprofit service organizations, in contrast, are more likely to be concerned with breaking even or keeping the operating deficit within acceptable bounds; however, they cannot afford to ignore the revenue implications of pricing strategy. In some organizations, one service may be priced to yield a profit that is used to cross-subsidize other services. Such cross-subsidies should be a deliberate choice, not an unplanned outcome of sloppy practice.

Capacity-oriented objectives.   Capacity-constrained organizations seek to match demand and supply to ensure optimal use of their productive capacity at any given time. Hotels, for instance, try to fill their rooms because an empty room is an un-

FIGURE 11.4 Alternative Bases for Pricing

REVENUE ORIENTED

- Profit Seeking
  - Make the largest possible surplus.
  - Achieve a specific target level, but do not seek to maximize profits.
- Cover Costs
  - Cover fully allocated costs (including institutional overhead).
  - Cover costs of providing one particular service or manufacturing one particular product category (after deducting any specific grants and excluding institutional overhead).
  - Cover incremental costs of selling to one extra customer.

CAPACITY ORIENTED

- Vary prices over time to ensure that demand matches available supply at any specific time (thus making the best use of productive capacity).

DEMAND ORIENTED

- Maximize demand (when capacity is not a constraint), subject to achieving a certain minimum level of revenues.
- Recognize differing abilities to pay among the various market segments of interest to the organization and price accordingly.
- Offer methods of payment (including credit) that will enhance the likelihood of purchase.

productive asset. Similarly, professional firms want to keep their staff members occupied; airlines want to fill empty seats; and repair shops try to keep their facilities, machines, and workers busy. When demand exceeds capacity, however, these organizations may try to increase profits and ration demand by raising prices.

Matching hotel demand to the number of rooms available may be achieved by pricing high at peak periods and pricing low in off-peak periods. Repair shops may offer special deals at reduced rates when business is slack. The problem with matching demand to supply through price is that firms may be accused of price gouging when times are good, and some firms are reluctant to engage in price discounting for fear that customers will equate it with a decline in quality.

Demand-oriented objectives. New services, in particular, often have trouble attracting customers. Introductory price discounts may be used to stimulate trial use, sometimes in combination with promotional activities like contests and giveaways. Firms wishing to maximize their appeal among specific types of customers may need to adopt pricing strategies that recognize a differential ability to pay among various market segments, as well as variations in preferences among customers for different levels of service.

Price Elasticity

The concept of elasticity describes how sensitive demand is to changes in price. When **price elasticity** is at unity, sales of a service rise (or fall) by the same percentage that price falls (or rises). When a small change in price has a big impact on sales, demand for that product is said to be price elastic. But when a change in price has little effect on sales, demand is described as price inelastic The concept is illustrated in the simple chart in Figure 11.5, which shows schedules for highly elastic demand (a small change in price results in a big change in the amount demanded) and highly inelastic demand (even big changes in price have little impact on the

price elasticity: the extent to which a change in price leads to a corresponding change in demand in the opposite direction. (Demand is described as price inelastic when changes in price have little or no impact on demand.)

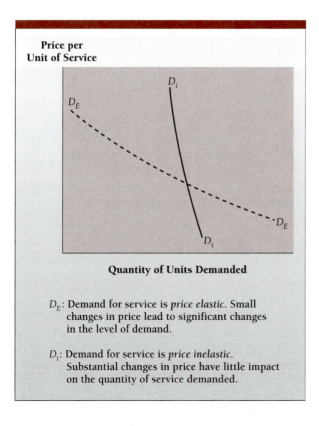

D_E: Demand for service is *price elastic*. Small changes in price lead to significant changes in the level of demand.

D_i: Demand for service is *price inelastic*. Substantial changes in price have little impact on the quantity of service demanded.

FIGURE 11.5
Illustrations of Price Elasticity

amount demanded). In chapter 14, we illustrate and discuss demand curves of varying degrees of elasticity, reflecting the differing behavior of customers in each of several market segments for hotel accommodation.

Most theaters and auditoriums do not have a single, fixed admission price for performances. Instead, the price varies according to (1) the location of the seats, (2) the time of the performance, (3) the projected cost of staging the performance, and (4) the anticipated appeal of the performance. In establishing prices for different blocks of seats (known as scaling the house), it is important to identify what the demand for each price category will be to determine the appropriate number of seats to offer at that price. Poor judgment on this score may result in large numbers of empty seats in some price categories and immediate sellouts (and disappointed customers) in others. Management also needs to know theatergoers' preferences for scheduling of performances—matinees versus evenings, weekends versus weekdays, and possibly even seasonal variations. In each instance, the aim is to manage demand over time to maximize attendance, revenues, or a combination of the two (e.g., maximizing revenues, subject to a minimum attendance goal per performance of 70 percent of all seats sold).

Many service businesses are increasingly concerned with yield management, that is, maximizing the revenue yield that can be derived from available capacity at any given time. Airlines and hotels have become particularly adept at varying their prices for what is essentially the same product in response to the price sensitivity of different market segments at different times of the day, week, or season. But there's a risk that pricing policies may become too complex. Jokes abound about travel agents having nervous breakdowns because they get a different quote every time they call the airline for a fare and because there are so many exclusions, conditions, and special offers. We look at yield management in greater detail in chapter 14.

VALUE STRATEGIES FOR SERVICE PRICING

The key to effective service pricing is to relate the price that customers pay to the value that they receive. Service-pricing strategies are often unsuccessful because they lack any clear association between price and value.[6] Berry and Yadav propose three distinct but related strategies for capturing and communicating the value of a service: uncertainty reduction, relationship enhancing, and low-cost leadership.[7]

Pricing Strategies to Reduce Uncertainty

There are three options in pricing strategies to reduce uncertainty, beginning with a service guarantee that entitles customers to a refund if they are not completely satisfied (see the discussion of Hampton Inn's 100% Satisfaction Guarantee in chapter 7). When well designed and executed, service guarantees remove much of the risk associated with buying an intangible service—especially for services high in experience qualities, in which customers can easily determine after the fact that service was unsatisfactory.

benefit-driven pricing: a strategy of relating prices to the benefits that customers are looking for when using the service.

Benefit-driven pricing involves pricing that aspect of the service that directly benefits customers. This approach forces service marketers to research what aspects of the service the customers do and do not value. For instance, prices for on-line information services are often based on log-on time, but what customers really value is the information that is browsed and retrieved. In fact, poorly organized Web sites often waste customers' time because they make it hard to find what users are looking for. The result is that pricing and value creation are not synchronized. When ESA-IRS, a European on-line provider, implemented a new pricing strategy termed *pricing for information* and based prices on the information actually extracted, the company found that customers were more willing to use a time-consuming feature called

ZOOM, which allowed them to search several complex databases simultaneously with increased precision. They started staying on line longer, and the use of ZOOM tripled as customers began to conduct more detailed searches. From then on, the company changed its marketing focus to selling information rather than selling time.

Flat-rate pricing involves quoting a fixed price in advance of service delivery to avoid any surprises. In essence, the risk is transferred from the customer to the supplier in the event that the service takes longer to deliver or involves more costs than anticipated. Flat-rate pricing can be an effective strategy in industries in which service prices are unpredictable and suppliers are poor at controlling their costs and the speed at which they work. They are also effective in situations in which competitors make low estimates to win business but subsequently claim that they were only giving an estimate, not making a firm pricing commitment.

flat-rate pricing: quoting a fixed, all-in-all price in advance of service delivery.

Relationship Pricing

When developing and maintaining long-term customer relationships is a key objective, pricing strategy can play an important role. Cutting prices to win new business is not the best approach if a firm wants to attract customers who will remain loyal; research indicates that those who are attracted by cut-price offers can easily be enticed away by a better offer from a competitor.[8] Creative pricing strategies focus on giving customers both price and nonprice incentives to consolidate their business with a single supplier.

One relationship-building strategy that has been very successful is MCI's Friends and Family program (since copied by British Telecom), which offers customers discounts on calls they make to specific telephone numbers, *if* the entire group signs up for service with MCI. A key objective is to enlist customers as sales agents: Uncle Bob spots the deal and urges other family members whom he calls regularly to switch to MCI. Subsequently, there is an incentive to cement loyalty: Group members now have a vested interest in discouraging any member from canceling the

Value is important at high prices, too: Holland America Westours highlights its service benefits and reduces uncertainty by specifying that the cruise price is inclusive of airfare, port charges, and taxes, with no tipping required.

MCI service and using another supplier. This strategy is reported to have attracted 10 million new customers to MCI.

A strategy of offering volume discounts for large purchases can often be profitable for both parties because the customer benefits from lower prices and the supplier may enjoy lower variable costs, resulting from economies of scale. Another relationship-building strategy is to offer customers price savings when two or more services are purchased together. The greater the number of different services a customer purchases from a single supplier, the closer the relationship is likely to be: On the one hand, both parties get to know each other better, and on the other hand, it's more inconvenient for the customer to shift its business.

Low-Cost Leadership

Low-priced services reduce the monetary burden for customers and are particularly likely to appeal to both corporate and individual customers who are on a tight financial budget. They may also lead purchasers to buy in larger volumes. One challenge when pricing low is to convince customers that they should not equate price with quality. A second challenge is to ensure that economic costs are kept low enough to enable the firm to make a profit. Some service businesses have built their entire strategy around being the low-cost leader. A classic example of a focused pricing strategy is that of Southwest Airlines (see the Southwest Airlines box).

PUTTING SERVICE-PRICING STRATEGY INTO PRACTICE

Although the main decision in pricing is usually seen as how much to charge, there are actually a lot of other decisions to be made, too. Figure 11.6 summarizes the questions that service marketers need to ask themselves as they prepare to create and implement a well-thought-out pricing strategy. Let's look at each in turn.

SOUTHWEST AIRLINES: LOW-PRICE LEADER WITH A LOW-COST CULTURE

The most consistently profitable airline in North America is Southwest Airlines, which emphasizes relatively short-haul, point-to-point routes within the United States but has no international service. Southwest's strategy is to price low enough to compete with surface travel by car, bus, or train, rather than pricing to compete against other airlines. Whenever it enters a new market, demand increases substantially as people shift from other modes of transportation, start to travel more frequently, or make trips they would not previously have made.

Supporting Southwest's low-price marketing efforts is a low-cost operational strategy and a culture among the airline's dedicated employees of doing everything possible to keep costs low, including working very productively. "Thanks to the Culture at Southwest Airlines," observed a recent annual report, "we do not have to motivate our Employees with programs to reduce costs; rather it is their goal each and every day."

By minimizing the amount of time aircraft spend at the gate, Southwest keeps them in the air more hours per day. The use of only one aircraft type, the Boeing 737, in its 260+ aircraft fleet simplifies the airline's operation and saves further costs. Southwest offers a very basic core service, with few of the supplementary elements found in full-service carriers. But it manages customers' expectations so that travelers are not surprised to find no reserved seats, no meals, and no baggage transfer to other airlines (the absence of each of which contributes to Southwest's record of having the lowest costs per seat-mile of any major American carrier). Despite the absence of such frills, Southwest creates value by saving its customers time and money and by doing a superb job of delivering basic air transportation safely, reliably, and consistently, with friendly employees providing a human touch.

Source: Annual Reports (Dallas: Southwest Airlines, 1996, 1997, 1998), 8.

FIGURE 11.6 Some Pricing Issues

1. How much should be charged for this service?
    a. What costs is the organization attempting to recover? Is the organization trying to achieve a specific profit margin or return on investment by selling this service?
    b. How sensitive are customers to different prices?
    c. What prices are charged by competitors?
    d. What discount(s) should be offered from basic prices?
    e. Are psychological pricing points (e.g., $4.95 versus $5.00) customarily used?

2. What should be the basis of pricing?
    a. Execution of a specific task
    b. Admission to a service facility
    c. Units of time (hour, week, month, year)
    d. Percentage commission on the value of the transaction
    e. Physical resources consumed
    f. Geographic distance covered
    g. Weight or size of object serviced
    h. Should each service element be billed independently?
    i. Should a single price be charged for a bundled package?

3. Who should collect payment?
    a. The organization that provides the service
    b. A specialist intermediary (travel or ticket agent, bank, retailer, etc.)
    c. How should the intermediary be compensated for this work—flat fee or percentage commission?

4. Where should payment be made?
    a. The location at which the service is delivered
    b. A convenient retail outlet or financial intermediary (e.g., bank)
    c. The purchaser's home (by mail or phone)
5. When should payment be made?
    a. Before or after delivery of the service
    b. At which times of day
    c. On which days of the week

6. How should payment be made?
    a. Cash (exact change or not?)
    b. Token (where can these be purchased?)
    c. Stored value card
    d. Check (how to verify?)
    e. Electronic funds transfer
    f. Charge card (credit or debit)
    g. Credit account with service provider
    h. Vouchers
    i. Third-party payment (e.g., insurance company or government agency)?

7. How should prices be communicated to the target market?
    a. Through what communication medium? (advertising, signage, electronic display, sales people, customer service personnel)
    b. What message content (how much emphasis should be placed on price?)

How Much Should Be Charged?

Realistic decisions on pricing are critical for financial solvency. The pricing tripod model (Figure 11.3) provides a useful departure point. Let's just reiterate the three elements involved. The task begins with determining the relevant economic costs and then deciding whether, in a specific situation, the organization should try to recover just variable costs or a share of the fixed and semivariable costs, too, as well as a margin for profit on top. Determining the costs to be recovered at different sales volumes and, as appropriate, the profit margin, sets the relevant floor price.

The second task is to assess market sensitivity to different prices, both the overall value of the service to prospective customers and their ability to pay. This step sets a ceiling price for any given market segment. It's very important to be able to make an accurate prediction of what sales volume might be obtained at different price levels.

Competitive prices provide a third input. The greater the number of broadly similar alternatives that appeal to consumers and the more widely available they are, the greater the pressure on the marketing manager to keep prices at or below those of the competition. The situation is particularly challenging when some competitors choose to compete on the basis of low price, coupled with an operating strategy designed to achieve low costs.

The wider the gap between the floor and ceiling prices, the more room there is for maneuver. If a ceiling price (the maximum that customers are willing to pay) is below the floor price (the lowest price the firm can afford to charge in the light of its costs), the manager has two choices. One is to recognize that the service is noncompetitive, in which case it will have to be discontinued. The other is to modify it in ways that differentiate it from the competition and add value for prospective customers, so that it now becomes competitive at a higher price. Public and nonprofit organizations have a third option, which is to seek third-party funding—such as government subsidies or private donations—to cover some of the costs, thus allowing the service to be sold at a lower price. This approach is commonly used to make such services as health, education, the arts, and urban transportation more easily affordable to a broad cross-section of the population.

Finally, a specific figure must be set for the financial price that customers will be asked to pay. This decision raises the question of whether to price in round numbers or try to create the impression that prices are slightly lower than they really are. On the one hand, if competitors promote such prices as $3.95 and $9.95, a strategy of charging $4.00 or $10.00 may convey a perception of significantly higher prices. On the other hand, rounded prices offer convenience and simplicity—benefits that may be appreciated by both consumers and salespeople because they help to speed up cash transactions, if the price includes relevant taxes.

What Should Be the Basis for Pricing?

Deciding on the basis for pricing requires defining the unit of service consumption. Should it be based on completing a specific service task, such as cleaning a jacket or cutting a customer's hair? Should it be admission to a service performance, like an educational program or a movie, concert, or sports event? Should it be based on time, for example using an hour of a lawyer's time, occupying a hotel room for a night, renting a car for a week, subscribing to a pay-TV service for a month, or paying for a semester's tuition at a university? Should it be tied to value, as when an insurance company scales its premiums to reflect the amount of coverage provided or a real estate agent takes a percentage of the selling price of a house as a commission?

Some service prices are tied to consumption of physical resources, such as food, beverages, electricity, or gas. For example, rather than charging customers for renting a table and chairs, restaurants put a sizable markup on the food and drink consumed. Transportation firms have traditionally charged by distance, with freight companies using a combination of weight or cubic volume and distance to set their rates. Such a policy has the virtue of consistency and reflects calculation of an average cost per mile (or kilometer). However, simplicity may suggest a flat rate, as with postal charges for domestic letters below a certain weight or a zone rate for parcels that lumps geographic distances into broad clusters. Long-distance phone calls reflect a combination of distance and time, but as with transportation, market analysis and competitive practices have largely eliminated strictly distance-based formulas.

In this 1998 ad, Sprint seeks to build long-term loyalty for its telecommunication services by offering free calls on Fridays to small business customers through the year 2000.

Price bundling. As emphasized throughout this book, many services unite a core product with a variety of supplementary services. Food and beverage service on a cruise ship is one example; baggage service on a train or aircraft is another. Should such service packages be priced as a whole (referred to as a bundle), or should each element be separated and priced separately? To the extent that people dislike having to make many small payments, **bundled pricing** may be preferable—and is certainly simpler to administer. But if customers dislike being charged for product elements they don't use, itemized pricing may be preferable.

bundled pricing: the practice of charging a single price for a bundle made up of a core service plus supplementary product elements.

Some firms offer an array of choices. Telephone subscribers, for instance, can select from among several service options, such as a small monthly fee for basic service and extra for each phone call made or a higher flat rate and a certain number of free local, regional, or long-distance calls. At the top of the scale is the option that gives business users unlimited access to long-distance calls over a prescribed area, even internationally. Bundled prices offer a service firm a certain guaranteed revenue from each customer, while giving the latter a clear idea in advance of how much the bill will be. **Unbundled pricing** gives customers flexibility in what they choose to acquire and pay for but may also cause problems. For instance, customers may be annoyed to discover that the ultimate price of what they want, inflated by all the "extras," is substantially higher than the advertised base price that attracted them in the first place.

unbundled pricing: the practice of charging a base price for a core service plus additional fees for optional supplementary elements.

Discounting. A strategy of **discounting** from established prices should be approached cautiously because it dilutes the average price received and reduces the contribution from each sale. There is also a risk that customers who would have been willing to pay more now find themselves enjoying a bargain. Nevertheless, selective price discounting targeted at specific market segments may attract new customers and fill capacity that would otherwise be unused. Volume discounts sometimes cement the loyalty of large corporate customers that might otherwise spread their

discounting: a strategy of reducing the price below the normal level.

purchases among several different suppliers. Another way to use discounting to build loyalty is by offering existing customers a discount off their next purchase.

The challenge for managers is to understand the price elasticities of different segments and to discourage high-paying segments from taking advantage of discounts designed to lure more price-sensitive consumers. Airlines impose restrictions on the availability of discount fares (requiring, for instance, travelers to stay over on Saturday night) to make it difficult for business travelers, whose fares are often being reimbursed by their employers, to travel cheaply. Discount fares, after all, are designed to attract pleasure travelers taking discretionary trips. To compete with car travel, in which several people can travel as cheaply as one, Amtrak offers a 50 percent discount for the second person in a group and free travel for a third.

Who Should Collect Payment?

As seen in chapter 8, the petals of the Flower of Service include information, order taking, billing, and payment. Customers appreciate suppliers who make it easy to obtain price information and place orders, as well as present clear bills and offer convenient payment procedures. Sometimes intermediaries handle these tasks: for example, travel agents, who make hotel and transportation bookings; ticket agents, who sell seats for theaters, concert halls, and sports arenas; and retailers, who act as intermediaries for repair and maintenance work on physical goods. Although the service organization may have to pay a commission, the intermediary is usually able to offer customers greater convenience in terms of where, when, and how payment should be made. Even after paying commissions, the use of intermediaries often offers a net savings in administrative costs to the primary organization.

Where Should Payment Be Made?

Service delivery sites are not always conveniently located. Airports, theaters, and sports arenas, for instance, are often situated some distance from where potential patrons live or work. When consumers purchase a service before using it, there are obvious benefits to using intermediaries that are more conveniently located or paying by mail. A growing number of organizations now accept telephone bookings and sales by credit card; callers simply give their card numbers and have the charge billed directly to their accounts. Early experiments that allowed customers to use their credit cards to pay through the World Wide Web ran into security problems; but as these are resolved through more robust encryption, the Web will doubtless become a popular medium for purchasing an array of goods and services.

When Should Payment Be Made?

The two basic options are to ask customers to pay in advance of use (as with an admission charge, airline ticket, or purchase of postage stamps) or to bill them once service delivery has been completed (as with restaurant bills and repair charges). Occasionally, a service provider may ask for an initial payment in advance of service delivery, the balance being due later. This approach is quite common with expensive repair and maintenance jobs, when the firm—often a small business with limited working capital—must first buy materials.

Asking customers to pay for service in advance of use means that the buyer is paying before the benefits are received. But there may be value to the customer, as well as to the provider. Sometimes it's inconvenient to pay each time a regularly patronized service—such as the post office or public transportation—is used; to save time and effort, customers may prefer the convenience of buying a roll of stamps or a monthly travel pass. Performing arts organizations with limited funds and heavy up-front financing requirements often offer discounted subscription tickets to bring in money in advance. A different form of prepayment, involving the notion of insurance, is found in medical benefits organizations, in which members pay a fixed annual, quarterly, or monthly premium that entitles them to rebates on medical and/or dental work.

How Should Payment Be Made?

As shown in Figure 11.6, there are a variety of ways to pay for service. Cash may appear to be the simplest method, but it raises problems of security, as well as being inconvenient when exact change is required to operate machines. Tokens with a predefined value are sometimes used to simplify the process of paying road and bridge tolls or transit fares. Payment by check for all but the smallest purchases is now fairly widespread and offers customer benefits, although it may require controls to discourage bad checks.

Credit cards are used for many types of purchases and have gained acceptance around the world. Debit cards, first widely used in Europe and Australia, look like credit cards but act more like "plastic checks" because the sum charged is debited directly from the holder's account. Electronic point-of-sale terminals are connected directly to banking networks. As acceptance of credit and debit cards has become more universal, businesses that refuse to accept them may find themselves at a competitive disadvantage. Many companies offer customers the convenience of a credit account (which generates a membership relationship between the customer and the firm).

Other payment procedures include vouchers as supplements to (or instead of) cash, directing the bill to a third party for payment (as often happens in health care). Vouchers are sometimes provided by social service agencies to elderly or low-income people. This policy achieves the same benefits as discounting, without the need to publicize an array of different prices and to require those who collect the money to act as police officers (a role for which they may be unsuited and untrained).

Now coming into broader usage are prepayment systems based on cards that store value on a magnetic strip or in a microchip embedded in the card. Telephone cards are only one example. Service firms that want to accept payment in this form, however, must first install card readers. More sophisticated applications involve partnerships among banks, retailers, and telephone companies. Working together, these partners offer a smart card that serves as an "electronic wallet"; customers can transfer funds to their cards from their bank accounts through the medium of a special telephone attachment. They are also able to transfer funds from one card to another (see the description of the Mondex card on p. 185).

Growing interest in the Internet and World Wide Web as a medium for purchasing a variety of goods and services is leading many firms to work on development of fraud-proof payment systems. One approach involves the creation of prepaid digital cash accounts into which customers would deposit funds that could then be used to pay for purchases ordered over the Internet. A key issue for service marketers in this and other contexts is that for many transactions, the simplicity and speed with which payment can be made may affect the customer's perception of overall service quality.

Communicating Prices to the Target Markets

The final task is to decide how the organization's chosen pricing policies can best be communicated to the target markets. People need to know the price for some product offerings well in advance of purchase; they may also need to know how,

Price advertising by Arby's
restaurant chain.

where, and when the price is payable. This information must be presented in ways that are intelligible and unambiguous so that customers will not be misled and question the ethical standards of the firm. An advertisement by Arby's, a quick-service restaurant chain, clearly specifies the prices of a wide variety of menu items, including combinations, and offers a satisfaction guarantee.

Managers must decide whether or not to include information on pricing in advertising for the service. It may be appropriate to relate the price to the costs of competing products or to alternative ways of spending one's money. Certainly, salespeople and customer service representatives should be able to give prompt, accurate responses to queries about pricing, payment, and credit. Good signs at retail points of sale will save staff members from having to answer basic questions on prices.

Conclusion

The price charged to customers for a service is only one of several costs of service incurred by customers. Others include time, mental and physical effort, and undesirable sensory experiences. Because the net value of a service to customers is the sum of all the benefits minus the sum of all the associated costs, value can be increased by saving customers time, money, or effort (and they may be willing to pay more to achieve such savings). Establishing a pricing strategy for a service business begins with a good understanding of the supplier's underlying financial costs, both fixed and variable. It also requires knowledge of competitive pricing and of the value of the service to target customers.

But pricing strategy goes far beyond just establishing the price itself. Such issues as convenience, security, credit, speed, simplicity, collection procedures, and automation may all play a role in improving customer satisfaction with service organizations. Technology has a significant potential to facilitate creation of a cashless society, but in practice we are still some distance from that point.

1. Is pricing strategy more difficult to implement in some service industries than others? If so, why? Be specific!

2. Review the different costs of service (financial and nonfinancial) explained in this chapter, and show how they apply to the following industries:
   a. airline service
   b. restaurant meals
   c. retail banking
   d. hotels
   e. consulting services
   f. garbage removal
   g. college courses
   h. computer repair in a business setting

3. Why is cost-based pricing (as it relates to financial costs) particularly problematic in service industries?

4. In what ways does competition-based pricing work in favor of many service providers? In what circumstances does it not?

5. How does an understanding of the different costs of service help a firm to create a strategy for improving the value of its service to customers?

6. From a customer perspective, what factors create value in the following services and how do they affect pricing strategy?
   a. a nightclub
   b. a bodyshop that repairs damaged cars
   c. a hairstyling salon
   d. a legal firm specializing in business and taxation law

9. Describe three service marketing situations where there is a price and quality signaling relationship, and why.

10. Identify key ethical considerations in pricing as they relate to specific service industries. Identify ways to ensure that customers are treated ethically in each instance.

Customer Education and Service Promotion

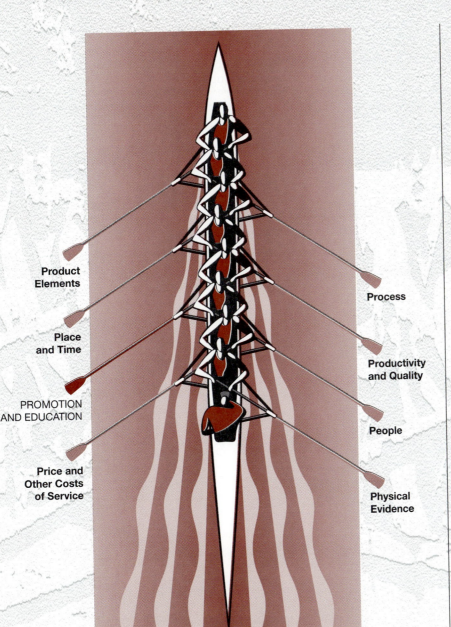

Product Elements

Place and Time

PROMOTION AND EDUCATION

Price and Other Costs of Service

Process

Productivity and Quality

People

Physical Evidence

Learning Objectives

After reading this chapter, you should be able to

- explain the role of marketing communications and how it ties in to other 8P elements

- describe how marketing communications differ between services and goods

- identify the components of the marketing communications mix

- understand how the educational role of service marketing affects communication strategy

- define marketing communication objectives and identify the communication elements necessary.

- recognize the potential value of the Internet (e-mail and Web sites) as a communication channel

Seeing Is Selling: Using Trade Shows to Promote Services[1]

What if you were trying to sell a service that some of your customers can't even imagine? That's the marketing challenge faced by Emily Loughnan, co-owner of Clicksuite, an interactive media company based in Wellington, New Zealand. Clicksuite's core service is producing custom-made interactive media for corporate clients. The company works with a range of media—including CDs, discs, Web sites, interactive videos, and touchscreen kiosks—that allow a viewer to interact with the medium by keying in specific information or choosing options from a menu (e.g., interacting with a bank's ATM to conduct specific transactions).

Because Clicksuite produces leading-edge technology, which many people don't understand, Loughnan spends a lot of her time at trade shows and exhibitions educating potential customers about what her company does. "It's about opening the eyes of the business world to the possibilities of interactive

media," Loughnan says. "Then we can educate them about the company, but they must understand the wider issues first. Trade shows and exhibitions are a pain in the neck, but they help grow the brand and get the name known."

Although trade shows aren't usually the first thing that comes to mind when marketers think about promoting services, they do provide an excellent opportunity for suppliers to educate and impress potential customers. According to consultant Elizabeth Light, they "can be exhausting, expensive and time consuming, but they can also be lots of fun and very profitable." Companies use trade shows to test the waters for a new product or to enhance their image and educate the market about existing brands. Visitors attend exhibitions to learn about the latest goods and services, talk to suppliers, compare competing products, and make purchase decisions.

THE ROLE OF MARKETING COMMUNICATION IN SERVICES

Many people confuse marketing management in general with just advertising, selling, sales promotions, and public relations. This is not surprising because advertising, in particular, is one of the most pervasive—some would say intrusive—elements in modern society. However, these communication activities, although very significant, are what marketers tackle after they have already made decisions about product elements, service delivery systems, and pricing. Communications is not just about promoting new services and urging people to use services with which they

are already familiar. As you can see from the Clicksuite example, spreading the word about a new service is not enough to sell it. Much of Emily Loughnan's communication efforts are devoted to explaining what her product is and educating prospective customers about what Clicksuite can do for them.

Among the tasks assigned to marketing communications are

■ *informing and educating* prospective customers about a firm and the relevant features of the goods and services that it offers

■ *persuading* target customers that a specific service product offers the best solution to their needs, relative to the offerings of competing firms

■ *reminding* customers of the product and motivating them to act

■ *maintaining contact* with existing customers and providing updates and further information on how to obtain the best results from the firm's products

In this chapter, we describe the different elements of the marketing communication mix and their distinctive capabilities, emphasizing the need to think in terms of a total communications program in which different communication elements play different roles in supporting an integrated service strategy. We also highlight how some of the distinctive features of services influence the choice of communication tools and strategies. The chapter ends with coverage of one of the most exciting new developments in marketing—Web sites.

Services versus Goods: Implications for Communication Strategy

Several of the differences between services and goods have important marketing communications implications. Developing a communications strategy for intangible service performances requires different guidelines from those for physical goods.[2] Let's highlight the five most relevant points.

Intangible nature of service performances.   Because advertising can't easily feature the product, it has to focus on the process; the benefits; or such tangible elements as service personnel, other customers, or the servicescape itself. In highly intangible services, it may be necessary to create tangible metaphors that are easy for customers to grasp. Insurance companies often use such an approach: Allstate's ads proclaim that "You're in good hands," Travelers presents an umbrella motif to suggest protection, and Prudential uses the Rock of Gibraltar as a symbol of corporate solidity. Prudential has gone one stage further in the use of this imagery by choosing 1-800-THE-ROCK as its toll-free phone number. Some companies have successfully incorporated animals and animal motifs as physical symbols for their products, for example, the Qantas kangaroo, the U.S. Postal Service eagle, the black horse of Britain's Lloyd's Bank, Merrill Lynch's bull, the lion of Dreyfus investment funds, and the Chinese dragon of Hong Kong's Dragonair.

Customer involvement in production.   Pressures to improve productivity in service organizations often involve technological innovations. In many cases, customers resist new, technologically based systems or avoid self-service alternatives. So innovative firms need to teach their customers how to use new technologies effectively; customers need training to help them perform well, just as employees do. Advertising and publicity can be used to make customers aware of changes in service features and delivery systems that require a different script. Sales promotions can motivate customers by offering them incentives to make the necessary changes in their behavior. Price discounts are one way to encourage self-service on an on-

Here's What "Full Service" Means to Investors at Prudential Securities

Today's market poses challenges to investors everywhere. But at least one million investors have an edge: Prudential Securities. Everyday, we show our clients what "full service" really means.

Each morning, nearly 6,000 Financial Advisors participate in an interactive discussion with Prudential Securities' top analysts.

Our clients have an expert to call on. There are times when you need to speak to someone who can offer you a perspective on your portfolio—not just take orders. At Prudential Securities, you always know where you can turn for advice: your personal Financial Advisor.

"I thought it was important to reach out to my clients right away with what we knew and what we expected next." — Dick Mitchell, Financial Advisor

Our clients can talk to someone who understands their situation. When you need to act quickly, you can't afford to deal with someone who's looking at your account for the very first time. Your Prudential Securities Financial Advisor knows your investment style, your risk tolerance, and how to help keep your portfolio on track.

Our clients receive personalized advice. For important investment decisions, one-size-fits-all recommendations don't fit. Your Prudential Securities Financial Advisor works with you to design personalized solutions based on an understanding of your long-term objectives.

Our clients have an all-star research team in their corner. When you work with a Prudential Securities Financial Advisor, you don't just get overwhelmed with news, you get insight and analysis that can help you make sense of it. Your Financial Advisor connects you to a dedicated team of analysts who, year in and year out, have been honored among the industry's elite by publications such as *The Wall Street Journal.*

Our clients feel more confident trading person-to-person. In a high-tech world, there's a peace of mind you can only get when you work with other people. Trading with a Prudential Securities Financial Advisor helps ensure that your transaction is executed quickly and correctly.

Peter Kann, Prudential Securities' floor broker, at the NYSE.

Call Prudential Securities to speak to a Financial Advisor.
1-800-THE-ROCK
ext.1359 www.prudential.com

 **Prudential** Securities

Prudential tangibilizes its services with photos of its professional staff, an offer of an informative video, and use of its symbol, based on the Rock of Gibraltar.

going basis, particularly for retail delivery systems such as self-service gasoline pumps (where the difference in price per gallon or liter from the full-service option is often substantial). Premiums, sampling, and prize promotions can also be used to encourage customers to adopt new methods (see the box on a FedEx promotion, p. 246). And, of course, well-trained customer-contact personnel can provide one-on-one tutoring to help customers adapt.

Supply and demand management.   Because services can't be inventoried, advertising and sales promotions may help marketers shape demand to match the capacity available at any given time. As we discuss in chapter 14, demand management strategies include reducing usage during peak demand periods and stimulating it during off-peak periods. Pricing is often the first marketing tool to be used for this

FedEx PROMOTES A CHANGE IN CUSTOMER BEHAVIOR

Some years ago, FedEx introduced an automated telephone procedure for customers to request a visit from a courier to pick up a package. Instead of calling the customer service center and speaking to an agent, account holders were invited to call a toll-free number and follow the instructions of a recorded voice to key in their account number, postal code, and the number of packages. To encourage use of this new, more productive order-entry procedure, FedEx offered free coffee mugs plus bags of tea and coffee to each account holder who used the new system four or more times during a three-month period. An underlying element in this promotion came from the recognition that people retain new learning more effectively if they repeat it several times within a short period. (FedEx has since provided a Web site that customers can use for many of the same tasks.)

purpose. An alternative strategy is to offer promotions instead—such as competitions or extra service elements—in an attempt to stimulate demand without using price directly as a weapon. Then, when demand increases, these promotions can be reduced or eliminated.

Reduced role for intermediaries.   Intermediaries, like retailers, often play a significant role in promoting products and educating customers in how to use them. But services are less likely than goods to be sold through channel intermediaries. In fact, service marketers selling directly to customers—such as banks, restaurants, health clubs, and professional firms—may have no need for trade promotions at all. However, some service providers do rely on intermediaries. For instance, firms in the travel and insurance industries, which make extensive use of independent agents and brokers, must compete with other brands sold by these intermediaries not only for physical display space in their retail offices but also for "top-of-mind" recall among the latters' agents. In these environments, service marketers may have to develop special communication campaigns directed at channel intermediaries to win their cooperation.

Importance of contact personnel.   Because of the critical role played by service employees in enhancing customer satisfaction and building loyalty, it's important for service firms to develop employee incentive programs to promote service quality. In some cases, firms also need to motivate and reward effective selling. Possible approaches include cash bonuses, awards, dinners, recognition programs, and eligibility for prize drawings. Advertising should not only encourage customers to buy the service but also target employees as a second audience, motivating them to deliver high-quality service—perhaps by using fellow employees rather than actors—to role-model desired behavior in print and broadcast ads.

Putting Promotion and Education in a Broader Context

Promotional and educational activities in service businesses should be seen in the broader context of managing all of the 8Ps. As an illustration, let's examine an advertisement by CVS. As a retail pharmacy chain that fills doctors' prescriptions for patients, as well as selling a wide array of nonprescription medications, CVS is a possession-processing service. For both legal and ethical reasons, it must take great care to dispense the right drugs in the right amount for the right customer. A failure to customize could have serious medical consequences.

Competing against many other pharmacies that sell the same core products, CVS tries to add value by being easily accessible in both place and time, packaging the drug in an appropriate fashion with the required instructions, and offering personalized

This CVS ad delivers messages about its people, the products that it sells, and the places and times at which its services are available.

advice to customers about their medications. Pharmacists are well-trained professionals whose primary task is to prepare prescription drugs in accordance with tight specifications. However, many customers look to them as people with medical expertise who can offer advice on nonprescription medications as well.

With plenty of space available in a full-page newspaper advertisement, three basic messages are delivered, each with a tie-in to other elements of the 8Ps. The top third of the ad addresses the *people* element. The headline under the CVS brand, "Care that touches everyone... one at a time," promises personalized service. Illustrating this theme are the three photos at the top of the page. At left, a friendly pharmacist is discussing two products with a customer; perhaps she is offering advice on the relative merits of each. At center, a father is confidently giving a small child some medicine (implying that he has received good instructions from CVS). And, at right, another helpful-looking pharmacist is talking on the phone, presumably with a customer calling from home or office.

The central third of the ad invites readers to request information from CVS about prescription medications. Having already promoted personalized, one-to-one education and advice, the ad now tells readers about how to access its recorded telephone information service, which they can use to obtain information about the core *products* of concern to them. On reaching a toll-free number, callers can key in a four-digit code to obtain specific information about each of more than 70 different drugs—many of them widely advertised by their manufacturers—treating 16 different medical conditions. Apart from the convenience of telephone access, some people may actually prefer the anonymity of this approach; after all, how would you like to have a conversation in a store about antianxiety drugs, antide-pressants, or antiulcer medications? Use of this service is potentially a boost to both *productivity and quality* because it's a self-service *process* and the message, being pre-recorded, can be tightly controlled for accuracy and quality of delivery. However, unless people are made aware of this option, they won't use it and there will be no productivity gains.

Finally, the bottom third of the ad promotes the accessibility of the CVS pre-scription service (*place* and *time*). It names those retail sites in the newspaper's cir-culation area (southeastern New England) that are open 24 hours a day and a toll-free number to call to find the nearest store; note the clever number, 1-800-SHOP CVS. Like banks and fast-food restaurants, some CVS pharmacies even offer a drive-through window. There's also an automated telephone service for refilling prescriptions (another productivity tool). The photographs in this ad provide *phys-ical evidence* of the service, notably the pharmacists and the "drive-thru" window. Al-though *price* is never mentioned, the ad implies that customers will pay less in time and effort.

Internal Communications

internal communications: all
forms of communication from
management to employees in a
service organization.

Marketing communications are used to communicate with service employees as well as with external customers. **Internal communications** are especially critical in maintaining and nurturing a corporate culture founded on specific service values (discussed in more detail in chapter 16). Such efforts are vital in large service busi-nesses that operate in widely dispersed sites, sometimes around the world, where employees may be working far from the head office in the home country. Consid-er, for instance, the challenge of maintaining a unified sense of corporate purpose at the overseas offices of Citibank, Swissair, FedEx, Holiday Inn, or McDonalds.

The goals of internal communications include ensuring efficient and satisfac-tory service delivery; achieving productive and harmonious working relationships; and building employee trust, respect, and loyalty. Progress in reaching each goal de-pends, in part, on clear communication between management and employees. Commonly used media vehicles include internal newsletters and magazines; pri-vate corporate TV networks; videotapes; face-to-face briefings; and periodic pro-motional campaigns using displays, prizes, and recognition programs. Sometimes external advertising is targeted at employees, as well as customers. Consider how the pharmacists in the CVS ad are portrayed as friendly, helpful, and knowledge-able. In effect, they are role-modeling the behavior that CVS management would like all its employees (including nonpharmacists) to adopt in their service en-counters with customers.

Ethical Issues in Communication

The tools of communication are very powerful. Few aspects of marketing lend them-selves so easily to misuse (and even abuse) as advertising, selling, and sales pro-motion. Communication messages often include promises about the benefits that customers will receive and the quality of service delivery. When promises are made and then broken, customers are disappointed because their expectations have not been met.[3] Their disappointment and anger will be even greater if they have wast-ed money, time, and effort and have either no benefits to show for it or, worse, have actually suffered a negative impact. Employees, too, may feel frustrated.

Sometimes, unrealistic service promises result from poor internal communica-tions. As we discussed in chapter 5, one of the seven service quality gaps is lack of awareness by advertising personnel of the product's capabilities and limitations. A more sinister reason for misrepresentation is a deliberate attempt to mislead customers. The fact that customers often find it hard to evaluate services makes them more dependent on marketing communication for information and advice. Once a firm gets a reputation for being untrustworthy, it can be hard to shake.

In a world where advertisers are constantly looking for new ways to promote their products, critics argue that some areas of life should be off-limits to advertising. They worry, for instance, about promoting casinos and state lotteries on the grounds that it can attract people to wager more than they can afford, with disastrous consequences for both gamblers and their families. There is also a vigorous ongoing debate about the ethics of advertising to children. Recent controversies have included promotional tie-ins between public schools and fast-food restaurants (see the box on marketing to children).

Setting Communication Objectives

In what specific ways can communication help a service firm to achieve its marketing goals? Figure 12.1 (p. 250) lists an array of common educational and promotional objectives in service settings. Marketers need to be clear about their goals and their priorities. Only then can they formulate specific communications objectives and select the most appropriate messages and communication tools to achieve them. For

QUESTIONS RAISED ABOUT MARKETING TO CHILDREN THROUGH THEIR SCHOOLS

Advertisers are coming under increasing criticism for their efforts to promote products to children within their schools. Corporations first began to focus on schools in the 1980s. Responding to tightly constrained school budgets, they offered mentors, money, equipment, and training programs. Although many corporate gifts really do contribute to improving the quality of education, in other instances the companies are engaging in what one critic has called "strategic philanthropy."

One issue is whether commercial content overwhelms educational value. For instance, at Pembroke Lakes Elementary School in Broward County, Florida, 10-year-olds recently learned how to design a McDonald's restaurant, how it works, and how to apply and interview for a job at McDonald's. These skills were contained in a seven-week class, sponsored by the company and intended to teach children about the world of work. The assistant principal admitted that the school accepted McDonald's offer because the curriculum was developed already and available at no cost.

A second issue is the extent to which corporate brand names should be featured prominently on school property. At Palmer High School in Colorado Springs, Burger King and Sprite advertise on the sides of school buses; Norwest, Cub Foods, and Mountain Dew have posters in school hallways; and the new scoreboard on the football field bears the Pepsi logo. During 1996–1997, the school district took in $145,000, of which 30 percent went to the marketing firm that helped to sell the ads. Each of the 53 schools in the district received a percentage of the balance, amounting to a few thousand dollars for Palmer High.

Yet another issue is whether schools are being exploited when their students contribute to off-site corporate promotional events but receive relatively little in return for their efforts. In May 1997, Red Roof Inns combined a celebration in Phoenix to mark the opening of its 250th budget motel with a promotion to help local high schools raise money for their music programs. The company recruited 250 musicians from seven high-school bands to play at the ceremonies. Because of the school connection, the event (which would hardly have been very newsworthy if limited to just a motel opening) drew overflow crowds and extensive coverage by local media. In exchange, each musician received a hat and a t-shirt displaying the Red Roof logo, and the seven schools received a couple of hundred audiocassettes of their music. If they managed to sell them all, each school could hope to make about $2,800.

Source: Based on information in Pat Wechsler, "This Lesson Is Brought to You By..." *Business Week*, 30 June 1997, 68–69.

FIGURE 12.1 Common Educational and Promotional Objectives in Service Settings

- Create tangible, memorable images of specific companies and their brands.
- Build awareness and interest to stimulate trial of the service.
- Teach customers how to use a service to their own best advantage.
- Communicate special strengths and benefits of a particular brand.
- Stimulate demand in low-demand periods and discourage demand during peak periods (including information on the best times to use the service to avoid crowds).
- Counter competitive claims.
- Reduce uncertainty and the sense of risk by providing useful information and advice.
- Provide reassurance (e.g., by promoting service guarantees).
- Recognize valued customers and employees.
- Reinforce loyalty by encouraging and rewarding frequent usage.
- Reposition a service relative to the competing offerings.

instance, a car rental agency might want to increase repeat purchase rates among business travelers. One strategic element might involve implementing an automatic upgrade program and an express delivery and drop-off system. For this to work, customers need to learn of this initiative and be instructed on how to take advantage of it.

The next step is to consider which elements of the marketing communications mix will best convey the desired messages to chosen market segments. Advertising through such media as television, newspapers, magazines, and posters is usually the most visual element in a campaign, and radio is a commonly used audible medium (often too much so). However, marketers have many other tools at their disposal, including personal selling, public relations, sales promotions, exhibitions, and corporate design. The newest medium available to marketers is the Internet, including e-mail and Web sites.

Key Planning Considerations

Planning a marketing communications campaign must take account of the nature of the service process and the extent to which the product is characterized by *search, experience*, or *credence* qualities (refer to chapter 4). Also important are the nature, characteristics, and behavior of the target market and audience (discussed in chapters 4 and 6). What should be the content, structure, and style of the message? How should it be presented? Which media will be best able to reach the intended audience? Additional considerations include the budget available for execution, time frames (as defined by such factors as seasonality, market opportunities, and known or predicted competitive activities), and methods of measuring and evaluating performance. A useful checklist for marketing communications planning is provided by the 5 Ws model:

> *Who* is our target audience?
>
> *What* do we need to communicate and achieve?
>
> *How* should we communicate this?
>
> *Where* should we communicate this?
>
> *When* do the communications need to take place?

Now let's review the different communication tools available to service marketers.

THE MARKETING COMMUNICATIONS MIX

Service marketers usually have access to many alternative forms of communication, sometimes referred to collectively as the **marketing communications mix**. Communication elements vary in their capabilities according to the types of messages they can convey and the market segments most likely to be exposed to them.

Communication experts draw a broad division between **personal communications** (when a representative of the service firm interacts with customers on an individual basis) and **impersonal communications** (when the service firm sends messages to an audience). In the former, messages are personalized and move in both directions between the two parties. In the latter, messages move in only one direction and are generally targeted at a large market segment of customers and prospects rather than at a single individual. However, as you've probably noticed in your own life as a customer, technology has created a gray area between personal and impersonal communications. It's now very easy for a firm to combine word-processing technology with information from a database to create an impression of personalization. Consider the direct mail you receive. Does it contain a personal salutation or some reference to your specific situation or your past use of a particular product?

As shown in Figure 12.2, the communications mix includes a variety of elements, including personal contact, advertising, publicity and public relations, sales promotion, instructional materials, and corporate design (such as corporate logos, stationery, uniforms, signs, and the color schemes used on company vehicles). In its broadest sense, corporate design may extend to many aspects of the physical evidence provided by the servicescape—the physical environment within which service is delivered.

marketing communications mix: the full set of communication channels (both paid and unpaid) available to marketers.

personal communications: direct communications between marketers and one or more customers that allow two-way dialog (including face-to-face conversations, phone calls, and e-mail).

impersonal communications: one-way communications directed at target audiences who are not in personal contact with the message source (including media advertising and public relations).

FIGURE 12.2 The Marketing Communication Mix for Services

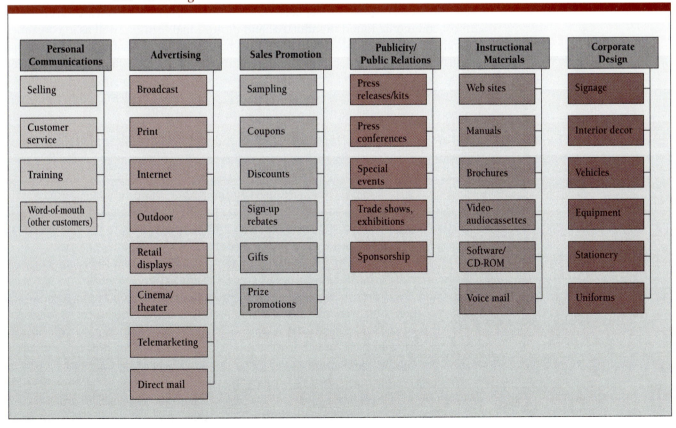

Personal Communications

Communications undertaken on a face-to-face basis (or ear-to-ear during telephone calls) embrace not only selling but also customer service and word of mouth.

personal selling: two-way communications between service employees and customers designed to directly influence the purchase process.

Personal selling refers to interpersonal encounters on a face-to-face (or in telemarketing, voice-to-voice) basis, in which efforts are made to educate customers and promote preference for a particular brand or product. Because face-to-face selling is usually very expensive, it is used most frequently in business-to-business markets, especially when the amounts purchased by each corporate customer are substantial. But there is still widespread use of personal selling in settings where customers encounter service personnel, ranging from department stores to hair salons and car rental agencies. For infrequently purchased services like real estate, insurance, and funeral services, the firm's agents often play a consulting role to help buyers determine their needs and select from suitable alternatives.

The direct nature of personal selling allows a sales representative or account manager to tailor the message to fit each customer's particular needs and concerns; effective teaching often benefits from one-on-one "tutorials." During a sales call, which may take place in person or by phone, communication flows in both directions between the marketer and the customer. By listening carefully, sales representatives can learn more about their customers. In fact, many sales-training programs place heavy emphasis on developing good listening skills. Through one-on-one dialog, needs can be identified, questions answered, and concerns addressed. But not all service personnel who engage in selling are, in fact, trained as salespeople. For instance, professionals in businesses like accounting, engineering, and management consulting are required to attract new clients to their firms, as well as to build lasting relationships with existing ones.

Relationship marketing strategies are often based on account management programs, in which customers are assigned a designated account manager who acts as an intermediary between the customer and the supplier. Account management is most commonly found in industrial and professional firms, as well as in consumer services for which customers are likely to have ongoing needs for information and consultation (two of the supplementary services discussed in chapter 9). Examples of account management for individual consumers can be found in private banking, insurance, stockbroking, medical services, and even in vehicle maintenance and repair for owners of expensive cars like Lexus or Mercedes.

customer service: the provision of supplementary service elements by employees who are not specifically engaged in selling activities.

Customer service.   The primary responsibilities of employees in customer service positions usually involve creating and delivering the service in the customer's presence, as well as providing information, taking reservations and receiving payment, and solving problems. New customers, in particular, often rely on customer service personnel for assistance in learning how to use a service effectively and how to resolve problems. However, it is difficult for these employees to provide good service if they themselves are insufficiently informed, trained, and supported.

When a customer may buy several different products from the same supplier, firms often encourage their customer-contact staff to cross-sell additional services. However, these strategies may fail if not properly planned, and some employees who see their jobs primarily in operational terms resent having to act as salespeople. In the banking industry, for example, a highly competitive marketplace and new technologies have forced banks to add more services in an attempt to increase their profitability. Bank tellers, who have traditionally been operations oriented in providing service, have been asked to promote new services to their customers. Despite training, some employees feel uncomfortable in this role and are not effective as salespeople. For an in-depth illustration of this situation, see the Menton Bank case on pages 373–378.

Word of mouth. The comments and recommendations that customers make about their service experiences can have a powerful influence on other people's decisions. Thus, it's realistic to classify what is often called **word of mouth** as a form of marketing communication, although it's hard for marketers to control this channel. A modest step in this direction is the notice sometimes seen in stores: "If you like our service, tell your friends; if not, please tell us."

Positive word of mouth can act as a powerful and highly credible selling agent. Whose recommendations are you most likely to accept—that of a trusted friend or that of a professional salesperson? Experienced customers can also be useful in assisting new customers and teaching them how to use a service. Conversely, negative word of mouth can be extremely damaging if it serves to "demarket" a company and its service offerings. The most appropriate way to think of unpaid word of mouth is as a form of publicity that marketers seek to cultivate and shape so that it becomes an effective supplement to other communication activities.

word of mouth: positive or negative comments about a service made by one individual (usually a current or former customer) to another.

Advertising

Advertising is often the first point of contact between service marketers and their customers, especially in consumer markets. Paid advertising media include broadcast (television and radio), print (magazines and newspapers), and many types of outdoor media (posters, billboards, electronic message boards, and even buses). There are exciting new opportunities to distribute information through the Internet and World Wide Web. More and more companies are establishing Web sites as an information resource for customers and prospects. Advertising can be supplemented by brochures delivered through intermediaries or by direct marketing through mail, telephone calls (telemarketing), fax, or e-mail.

Some media are more focused than others. Newspapers and television tend to reach mass audiences (although research can identify who reads what sections of a newspaper or watches specific programs). Most papers have regional editions targeted at specific geographic areas, and most network TV channels allow local stations to insert local advertising. Cinemas, a popular advertising medium in some countries, also reach a broad demographic audience but are very localized in terms of the audience. Magazines, in contrast, although often national in scope, are usually focused on relatively well-targeted audiences. Radio tends to be local or regional in coverage, but the audiences reached by each station are often very well segmented.

advertising: any form of nonpersonal communication by a marketer to inform, educate, or persuade members of target audiences.

Direct marketing, which includes both direct mail and telemarketing, allows personalized messages to be sent to highly targeted microsegments, including one-to-one communications. E-mail is growing as a direct advertising medium, although

direct marketing: one-way communications from a company to a list of target customers by mail, telephone, fax, or e-mail.

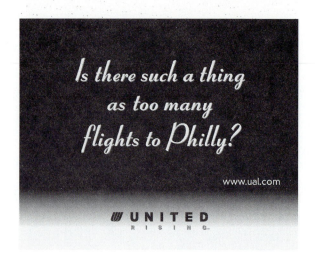

retail displays: presentations in store windows and other locations of merchandise, service experiences, and benefits.

many e-mail address lists are still very unfocused. Unfortunately, many advertisers are simply purchasing address lists for millions of e-mail subscribers and then "spamming" them with unwanted junk mail that often promotes some very dubious services.

Another form of advertising, often linked to sales promotion, is **retail displays** in store windows. Sophisticated Web sites are themselves beginning to replicate retail storefronts with attractive displays in cyberspace, although currently the time required to download the images often gets in the way of effective communication. Later in this chapter, we discuss how service marketers can use the Internet more effectively.

To summarize, advertising is most commonly used to create awareness and stimulate interest in the service offering, to educate customers about service features and applications, to establish or redefine a competitive position, to reduce risk, and to help make the intangible tangible. It plays a vital role in providing factual information about services and educating customers about product features and capabilities. To demonstrate this role, Steve Grove, Gregory Pickett, and David Laband compared newspaper and TV advertising for goods and services.[4] Based on a review of 11,543 TV ads over a 10-month period and 30,940 newspaper display ads over a 12-month period, they found that advertisements for services were significantly more likely than those for goods to contain factual information on the following four dimensions: price, guarantees and warranties, documentation of performance, and availability (where, when, and how to acquire the products). Consumers may rely more on information provided by advertising for services because they lack the ability to use search qualities—and thus their own evaluations, based on tangible product attributes—as effectively as they can for goods.

Publicity and Public Relations

public relations: efforts to stimulate positive interest in a company and its products by sending out news releases, holding press conferences, staging special events, and sponsoring newsworthy activities put on by third parties.

Public relations (PR) involves fostering goodwill toward an organization among individuals and interest groups. It recognizes that all business is about people and relationships with people. Experts in PR know that these relationships must be cultivated and nurtured for a business to be well regarded and patronized.

One of the most basic tasks in public relations is the preparation and distribution of press releases (including photos and sometimes videos) featuring stories about the company, its products, and its employees. Public relations executives also arrange press conferences and distribute press kits when they feel that a story is especially newsworthy. However, unlike paid advertising, there is no guarantee that these stories will appear in the media, and if they do, they may not appear in the positive form desired by the company's PR department (or the outside PR agency retained by the firm). Good relationships with journalists and other media specialists are important in building a receptive climate for news releases. A reputation for openness and honesty is vital when something negative occurs, such as an accident, injuries to customers or employees, or market rejection of a new service.

Among other widely used PR techniques are recognition and reward programs, obtaining testimonials from public figures, community involvement and support, fundraising, and obtaining favorable publicity for the organization through special events and pro bono work. Firms can also win wide exposure through sponsorship of sporting events and other high-profile activities. On a global scale, the selection of Sydney, Australia, to host the summer Olympic Games in 2000 has created numerous opportunities for companies around the world to sponsor different activities and national teams in specific sports.

Sales Promotion

Sales promotions can be described as communications attached to an incentive. They are usually specific to a time period, price, or customer group. Typically, the objective is to accelerate the purchasing decision or to motivate customers to use a specific service sooner, in greater volume with each purchase, or more frequently.[5]

Short-term price promotions can offer service marketers the following advantages that are not available through other marketing tools:[6]

- Because promotional costs vary with volume, price promotions are a good weapon for small companies to use in challenging large competitors.
- Promotions reduce the risk of first-time purchase for customers and thus encourage trial purchases.
- Different segments can be charged different prices for the same service when one group receives a promotional discount and the other doesn't.
- Promotions can add excitement to mundane repetitive purchases and appeal to price-conscious consumers.
- Price promotions are particularly useful for adjusting demand and supply fluctuations.

Sales promotions can take many forms. At least six methods are available to service marketers, including samples, coupons, enrollment rebates, entitlement to future discounts, gift premiums, and prize promotions.[7] Let's look briefly at each in turn.

Sampling gives customers a chance to learn more about a service by trying it free of charge. For instance, a credit card company may offer cardholders a free one-month trial of a credit card protection program, public transit systems might provide free service for a day or two on a newly opened route, or hotels may allow guests free 15-minute previews of first-release movies available on the internal pay-TV system. Sampling, however, is used less frequently for services than for consumer package goods. Service marketers usually prefer to offer price discounts or other promotions rather than give away the service.

Coupons usually take one of three forms: a straight price cut, a discount or fee waiver for one or more patrons accompanying the original purchaser, or a free or discounted augmentation of the basic service (such as free waxing with each car washing). Traditionally, coupons have been printed in newspapers and magazines or sent by direct mail. Some coupons, however, are actually sold in books, which give purchasers the opportunity to use the services of a wide array of restaurants and

sales promotion: a short-term incentive offered to customers and intermediaries to stimulate product purchases.

sampling: a method for allowing customers to use a product on a limited, short-term basis free of charge.

coupons: documented offers for free or discounted product use or purchase.

cafés, laundries, automotive firms, cinemas, and other suppliers. And some coupon systems are now entirely electronic, like the Safeway Members Card described in chapter 6.

short-term discounts: special offers of discounts for purchases during a defined time period.

Short-term discounts are price cuts that are available for only a limited time period, such as any form of "sale" designed to boost business during slow periods. Another example is "charter memberships" in health and fitness clubs, which are sold at decreasing levels of discount before the facility is opened. Such strategies help to build a base of customers quickly and improve initial cash flow.

sign-up rebates: offers to reduce or waive the sign-up fee for joining a membership service.

Sign-up rebates may be offered by membership services that charge a preliminary sign-up fee for applying, enrolling, or making connections to a network, for example, application fees for educational institutions, enrollment fees at many private clubs, and installation fees for connections to pay-TV systems. To attract new enrollments or subscribers, these fees may be waived or else credited toward payment of future charges.

gift premiums: rewards for purchasing a product under defined conditions, typically at a specific time or place.

Gift premiums can add a tangible element to services and provide a distinctive image for sponsoring organizations. For instance, some international airlines provide passengers in first and business classes with a range of free gifts, including toiletries, pens, stationery, and playing cards. Similarly, to encourage customers (who may hold several credit cards) either to increase their credit purchases or to consolidate their charges on a single account, banks and credit card companies may offer prizes to customers who charge more than specified amounts over a given period. Sometimes, however, gifts are offered simply to amuse customers and create a friendly environment. The Conrad Hotel in Hong Kong places a small teddy bear on each guest's bed and a yellow rubber duck in the bathroom; it reports that many guests take these items home.

prize promotions: offers to enter a customer's name in a sweepstakes or other competition that provides an opportunity to win a prize.

Prize promotions introduce an element of chance, like a lottery or sweepstakes. They can be used effectively to add involvement and excitement to the service experience and are generally designed to encourage increased use of the service. Fast-food restaurants, video rental outlets, and service stations sometimes offer lot-

This Supercuts coupon ad offers customers a limited-time price cut.

The Best For The West

Bank of America is the proud sponsor of the PGA TOUR West Coast Swing. This series of eight tournaments raises more than $6 million each year for charities in West Coast communities. This year for the first time, the World Golf Foundation will also benefit. The Foundation's First Tee program is dedicated to bringing golf's character-building values to youth who otherwise would not have had the opportunity.

Bank of America

The First Tee

Bank of America sponsors PGA Tour golf tournaments.

tery-like promotions tied to special events, giving all purchasers tickets with scratch-off award categories. Radio stations may offer listeners the chance to claim instant cash and other prizes if they call within a prescribed time after the announcement is broadcast.

Instructional Materials

Promotion and education often go hand in hand. There is little point in promoting a new service, service feature, or more productive process, if people are unsure of the benefits or don't know how to proceed. Although service personnel are often called on to play teaching roles, they are not always available to help in those locations where customers need them. Traditional approaches use printed materials, ranging from brochures and instruction manuals to step-by-step instructions and diagrams affixed to self-service machines (examine a pay phone, ATM, or ticketing machine the next time you use one). But in recent years, video and audio instructions have also come to the fore. Supermarkets and department stores sometimes feature a touchscreen store directory. Some banks have video terminals in the lobby, where customers can learn about new financial products. Airlines play videos to illustrate aircraft safety procedures and make customers aware of government regulations. The latest instructional media take the form of CD-ROMs and Web sites (which are described in the section on new technologies).

Corporate Design

Many companies have come to appreciate the importance of creating a unified and distinctive visual appearance for all tangible elements that contribute to the corporate image. **Corporate design** strategies are usually created by external consulting

corporate design: the consistent application of distinctive colors, symbols, and lettering to give a firm an easily recognizable identity.

firms and include such features as stationery and promotional literature; retail signs; uniforms; and color schemes for vehicles, equipment, and building interiors. These elements are created by using distinctive colors, symbols, lettering, and layout to provide a unifying and recognizable theme, linking all the firm's operations in the form of branded physical evidence.

Many companies use a trademarked symbol, rather than a name, as their primary logo. Shell Oil, for instance, makes a pun of its name by displaying a yellow scallop shell on a red background, which has the advantage of making its vehicles and service stations instantly recognizable around the world. McDonald's Golden Arches is said to be the most widely recognized corporate symbol in the world. Its early restaurant designs featured an enormous arch, but today local zoning laws may restrict the size and nature of its exterior signs. How easy to recognize are the facilities, vehicles, and personnel of your own bank, favorite fast-food restaurant, taxi service, and local public transit system? Try the quiz in the box on recognizing a service company to see how many internationally used symbols and design elements you are familiar with.

Companies in the highly competitive express delivery industry tend to use their names as the basis for their corporate designs: FedEx uses its name as a symbol, featured in a distinctive red, white, and purple logo, which is applied to buildings, storefronts, vehicles, aircraft, and certain employee uniforms; its arch rival, UPS, is known for its brown uniforms and trucks, bearing the corporate initials in gold. Other carriers, such as Airborne and DHL, also feature their names prominently. One characteristic of a good design is that it must look good in different sizes and not lose too much of its punch when reproduced in black and white.

Servicescape Design

As noted in chapter 8, the term *servicescape* describes the design of any physical location where customers come to place orders and obtain service delivery.[8] It has four dimensions: the interior and exterior of the physical facility, the location, ambient conditions (like temperature or lighting), and interpersonal dimensions (such as the appearance of staff members and how they interact with customers). Each has implications for perceived service quality. Corporate design consultants are often asked to advise on servicescape design, especially the visual presentation of building interiors and exteriors, such as signs, decor, carpeting, and furnishings.

Referring to the dramatic analogy described in chapter 10, we can think of the servicescape concept in terms of the design of the stage on which the service drama is enacted. A good set and costumes can't save a bad play, but they can greatly enhance the audience's enjoyment of a good one. Conversely, a bad stage set can create a poor initial impression that is hard to shake. Consider what conclusions you

---

CAN YOU RECOGNIZE A SERVICE COMPANY FROM THESE CLUES?

1. With which rental car service is the color yellow associated? The color red?
2. Which international airline has a flying kangaroo for its symbol? Which has a maple leaf?
3. Which stockbroker displays a bull?
4. Which oil company paints all its vehicles and service stations in a distinctive bright green with yellow lettering?
5. Name two companies that use a globelike symbol.
6. Which international bank uses a four-pointed star as its symbol?

The answers can be found at the end of the chapter (p. 264).

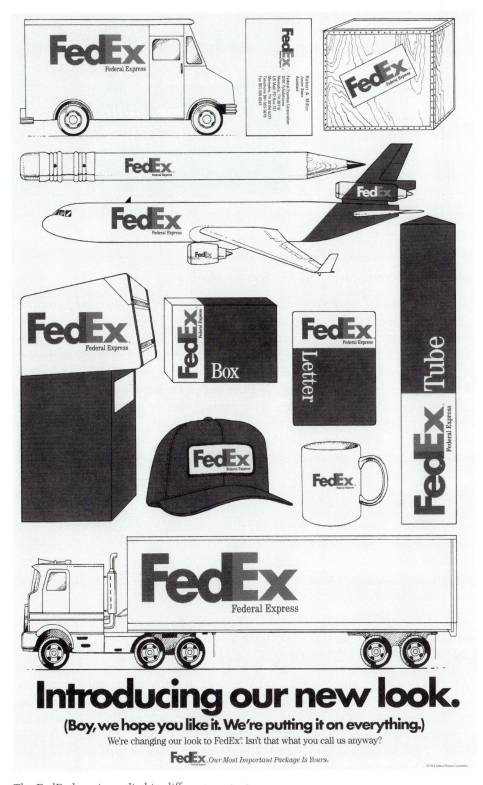

The FedEx logo is applied in different contexts.

might draw about a car rental firm's service if, on arrival, you encounter a smart-looking building with attractive signs, but on entering, you notice in the harsh neon light that the office is small and cramped, the paintwork is peeling and clashing with the faded carpet, the signs are hand-lettered, the desk and furnishings are in contrasting styles, and the agent is wearing a smart uniform shirt tucked into dirty jeans?

"*Captain to Tower...
it's me again.*"
(*15 daily flights to Chicago.*)

www.ual.com

UNITED
R I S I N G.

Does this ad seem familiar? Rather than spending its budget on one large ad, United Airlines is using a series of similar, small format ads in the *Boston Globe* to drive home the message about its frequent flights from Boston.

Integrated Communications for Service Marketing

In a service setting, marketing communications tools are especially important because, wisely used, they can create strong images and a sense of credibility, confidence, and reassurance. Through the use of brand names, recognizable corporate design elements, and well-executed servicescapes, companies can give visibility and personality to their intangible service offerings. Each of the different communication elements described is a potentially powerful tool that can be used to create and promote a distinctive corporate, brand, or product identity; communicate with current and prospective customers; and sell specific products. Marketing communications, in one form or another, are essential to a company's success. Without them, prospects may never learn of a service firm's existence or what it has to offer.

A key task for service marketers is to select the most appropriate mix of communication elements to convey the desired messages efficiently and effectively to the target audience. Different communication elements may be used in ways that mutually reinforce one another. Sequencing these elements is often important because one element may pave the way for others. For example, advertising may encourage prospects to request further information by mail, or it may pull them into a retail site or trade show where they may then be exposed to displays or interact directly with a salesperson (see the box on trade shows and exibitions).

IMPACT OF NEW TECHNOLOGIES ON MARKETING COMMUNICATION

As mentioned earlier, the Internet and World Wide Web are becoming increasingly important marketing communications tools. Owners of personal computers are spending more and more time on line and less time watching television or reading printed material. By late 1997, Internet users in the United States were spending about 13 to 14 hours on line a week—double the amount of time just a year previously.[9] Although the number of North American Internet subscribers currently exceeds that of users living elsewhere in the world by a ratio of four to one, subscriptions in other countries are increasing rapidly.

None of this is lost on marketers, who are rushing to establish a presence on the Web. Advertising expenditures on the Internet are growing rapidly; in 1998 they accounted for about one percent of all U.S. media advertising.[10] A key dimension of Web advertising is its ability to measure performance. On the Internet, a marketer can track the number of people who "click through" a specific ad in one location to obtain more information from the advertiser's own Web page and identify what is purchased.[11]

PARTICIPATING IN TRADE SHOWS AND EXHIBITIONS

Trade shows and exhibitions combine a variety of communication elements. For instance, an exhibitor's booth creates a small servicescape in itself (some displays at large exhibitions are very dramatic), and there are brochures to take away, videos to watch, and sales personnel to meet face to face. Often, there are special promotions to attract prospective customers and reward old ones. The public relations department will try to maximize the company's exposure in news coverage of the show and related events. There are three basic categories of shows—exhibitions, trade shows, and conference trade exhibitions—each targeting a different type of market.

Exhibitions (or *expos*) are usually open to the public and an entry fee is charged. These shows allow companies to promote their products and services to a huge number of potential customers. For example, an exhibition held the day before the 1996 Boston Marathon drew hundreds of exhibitors and over 100,000 visitors from around the world. Because of its size and the variety of goods and services that were exhibited, it was almost as big an event as the race itself.

Trade shows focus on business-to-business selling. They are not usually open to the public, and there is no entry fee. Not as many people pass by each booth as in an exhibition, but those who do are more likely to be potential customers. In many industries, trade shows are a great opportunity for service providers to find out about the latest products in their areas. For example, cosmetic surgeons in Europe, New Zealand, and the United States recently attended trade shows to learn about advances in technology and equipment that will allow them to perform highly effective, nonsurgical treatments with mysterious names like "botox," "vein sclerotherapy," and "collagen replacement therapy."

Conference trade exhibitions give exhibitors a small but very focused audience because conferences usually attract people who are interested in specific disciplines and topics. In the higher education industry, for example, publishers like Prentice Hall (who published this text) set up elaborate exhibits at conferences attended by university professors. The booths contain copies of the latest textbooks, software, and videos for classroom use, and company representatives are available to answer questions and demonstrate the products. Professors can browse through the books or view the videos to see which ones best suit their teaching style and students.

Exhibitions and trade shows can be very profitable promotional tools. For example, 50 percent of the sales leads generated at trade shows can be closed with just one sales call, and a sales representative who usually reaches four or five prospective clients per day can average five qualified leads per *hour* at a show, or 35 in just one seven-hour day. This assumes, of course, that marketers have targeted the right audience and have designed informative, attractive booths.

Source: Elizabeth Light, "Tradeshows and Expos—Putting Your Business on Show," *Her Business*, March–April 1998, 14–18; and Susan Greco, "Trade Shows versus Face-to-Face Selling," *Inc.*, May 1992, 142.

Advertisers are using their Internet sites for a variety of communications tasks, such as promoting consumer awareness and interest, providing information and consultation, stimulating product trials and sales, and facilitating personal communications with customers. Many companies have found that the interactive nature of the Internet increases customers' involvement dramatically because it is actually a form of self-service marketing, one in which customers are in complete control of the time and extent of contact with the Web sites they visit. This can also be useful for self-paced learning, when the site content of interest is educational in nature.

Designing an Internet Communications Strategy

The ability to communicate and establish a rapport with individual customers is one of the Web's greatest strengths. For this reason, the Internet is fast becoming almost as common in business-to-business marketing as business cards and fax machines. Marketing through the Web allows companies to supplement conventional communications channels at a very reasonable cost.[12] But like any of the elements of the marketing communications mix, Internet advertising should be part of an integrated, well-designed communications strategy. The 5 Ws model of communications planning, presented earlier in the chapter, provides useful guidelines for marketing on the Web.[13] Let's briefly look at each element of the model in the context of Internet marketing.

Who. Marketers need to consider what target markets they want to reach and whether these markets have access to the Web. In early 1998, some 20 percent of the American population was using the Internet on a regular basis (by the time you read this, the figure will almost certainly be higher). The key question for a marketing manager is whether the demographics of these Internet users match those of the firm's target market segment. If so, it should definitely consider maintaining a Web site. For example, some lawyers who are specializing in intellectual property law target clients who are computer programmers and corporate clients that sell software and Internet-related services. These lawyers want to attract potential clients through their Web sites, and they follow up with interviews in trendy cyber cafés while sipping cappuccino and discussing the latest Web technologies.[14]

Although most marketers depend on their customers to access Web sites from home or work, a few enterprising firms bring the Internet to customers. Kinko's, the California-based chain of copy centers, wants to be "the first and largest retail provider of Internet services in the country" by providing traveling executives and small business owners with 24-hour access to computers and the Web. Another company, AtcomInfo Inc., is going after traveling executives by locating high-technology kiosks in airports' frequent flyer lounges and in hotels' business centers.[15]

What. A Web site should contain information that a company's target market will find useful and interesting. It should also stimulate product purchases and encourage repeat visits. Whereas Internet users rank content as the most important factor in their decision to return to a Web site (they are actually annoyed by sites and companies that waste their time with "frivolous content"), they also want the experience to be "enjoyable" (either because they found the information they wanted or because the site was unique or entertaining).[16] Companies that do business internationally should be especially careful to investigate the legal, logistical, and cultural implications of their Web sites to avoid damaging their image among global customers. They need to remember that once they establish an Internet presence, their site is available worldwide to anyone with Web access.[17]

When. A Web site is a very dynamic medium. Visitors expect it to be updated regularly or they soon lose interest in returning. Unlike pamphlets and brochures, which may be redesigned only once a year, a Web presence must be maintained and upgraded constantly . As Internet technology evolves, Web sites are becoming increasingly sophisticated. Many companies regularly add new content, attractive graphics, and interactive capabilities or animation to make their sites attractive to both first-time and repeat visitors.[18] Web sites should probably be updated once every four months, even if it just means changing the appearance of the site cosmetically by using a different layout or new illustrations. Remember that it's very easy for customers to compare competitors' offerings on the Internet—that information is literally at their fingertips. For example, customers who are shopping for books on-line can browse the Web sites of competing book retailers like Barnes and Noble,

Borders, and Amazon.com in a matter of minutes before making a decision about where to "shop."[19]

Where.   Firms need to actively promote their Web sites to existing and potential customers. Web addresses should be kept simple. They should be displayed everywhere the company name appears, including business cards, brochures, advertisements, trade show entries, catalogs, Yellow Pages, and promotional items. Some firms use a direct mail approach by sending out postcards with their Web addresses, along with an incentive for customers to visit the site. Web addresses are becoming common features of our daily lives. Just think of how many times a day you see them—on television, in newspapers and magazines, and even on the menu of your favorite take-out restaurant.

Why.   Companies must provide reasons for people to visit—and revisit—their Web sites. They might use their sites to provide valuable information that isn't available anywhere else, such as a description of a new technological breakthrough that could save customers time and money or a comparison of different options for corrective eye surgery. Palo Alto Software offers its Web site visitors the opportunity to download free business and market-planning samples, small-business advice, product information and support, and a decision analysis case study.[20]

Transportation firms offer interactive sites that enable travelers to evaluate alternative routes and schedules for specific dates, download printed information, and make reservations. Some sites offer discounts on lodging and airfare if reservations are made over the Internet. Many banks now have interactive sites that allow customers to pay bills electronically, apply for loans, and check their account balances. A Web-based business called Home Debut, which allows house shoppers to look for a new residence on line, also provides information about specific neighborhoods and links to school districts, day care, restaurants, and health care providers.[21] The Whistler and Blackholm Ski Resorts in British Columbia uses a Web site to promote advance on-line purchases of lift tickets at a discount. The site provides instructions on how the on-line ticket window works and where to pick up the tickets, plus responses to frequently asked questions.

Conclusion

Many different communication elements are available to service marketers as they seek to create a distinctive position in the market for both their firm and its products and to reach prospective customers. The options include paid advertising, personal selling and customer service, sales promotions, public relations, and corporate design and the evidence offered by the servicescape of the service delivery site. Informational materials, from brochures to Web sites, often play an important role in teaching customers how to make good choices and obtain the best use from the services they have purchased.

Some of the distinctive characteristics of services suggest that a different approach is needed for marketing communications strategy than that used to market goods. Advertising, for instance, may provide much-needed tangible clues to service quality and performance without raising expectations unrealistically. Internal, as well as external, public relations management is critical in ensuring sound and enduring relationships, credibility, and goodwill. Public relations activities and the proactive generation of publicity and positive word of mouth should be regarded as a valuable long-term investment, necessary in building a service firm's reputation and place within a community.

ANSWERS TO SYMBOL QUIZ ON PAGE 258

1. Hertz (yellow), Avis (red).
2. Qantas (kangaroo), Air Canada (maple leaf). Some other Canadian airlines also display a maple leaf.
3. Merrill Lynch (bull).
4. British Petroleum (BP). In New York and New Jersey, Hess has similar colors.
5. AT&T, Cable & Wireless. (UPS now paints a globe on all its trucks to emphasize its worldwide delivery capabilities; Continental Airlines shows part of a globe).
6. Citibank (also its parent, Citicorp).

Study Questions and Exercises

1. What role do personal selling, advertising, and public relations play in (a) attracting new customers to a service business and (b) retaining existing customers?
2. Contrast the relative effectiveness of brochures and Web sites for promoting (a) a ski resort, (b) a hotel, (c) the services of a consulting firm, and (d) a full-service stockbroker.
3. In what ways do the physical aspects of a servicescape "communicate"?
4. This book links promotion and education. In what situations should service marketers think of themselves primarily as teachers rather than promoters?
5. Review the box on marketing to children through their schools (p. 249). Do you believe the three examples cited are unethical (or at least undesirable) practices? Why or why not?
6. Consider each of the following scenarios and determine which elements of the marketing communications mix you would employ and for what purposes:
   a. a newly established hair salon in a suburban shopping center
   b. an established restaurant facing declining patronage because of the arrival of new competitors
   c. a large, single-office accounting firm doing business in a major city and serving primarily business clients.
7. For which categories of services are customers at greatest risk when a firm makes advertising claims that it knows to be fraudulent? What types of customers are most likely to be hurt?
8. Locate a Web site for a service provider. What do you think the firm's communications objectives for the site are, and are they being achieved? Would you change anything about the site?
9. How do the following distinguishing characteristics of services (described in chapter 1) affect the role of marketing communications?
   a. intangible nature of service performances
   b. management of supply and demand
   c. reduced role for intermediaries
   d. importance of contact personnel
   e. customer involvement in production

four

Integrating Marketing with Operations and Human Resource Management

Tools for Service Marketers

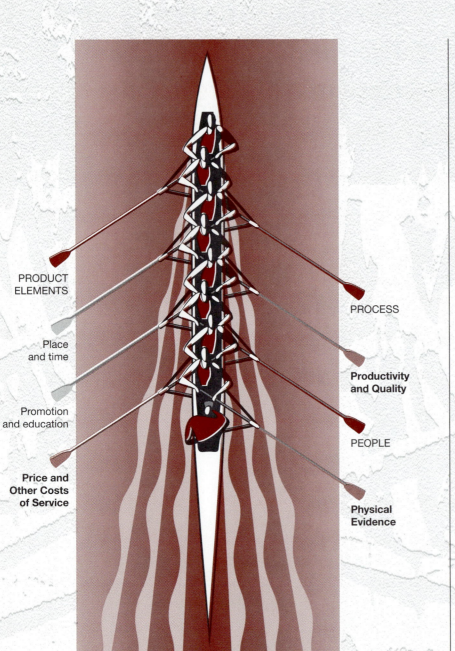

PRODUCT
ELEMENTS

Place
and time

Promotion
and education

**Price and
Other Costs
of Service**

PROCESS

**Productivity
and Quality**

PEOPLE

**Physical
Evidence**

Learning Objectives

**After reading this chapter,
you should be able to**

- describe in what ways services
  are like theater performances

- explain how role and script
  theories relate to service
  delivery

- develop a flowchart showing
  how front-stage actions are
  supported by backstage
  activities

- discuss the value of
  flowcharting in managing
  capacity and reengineering
  service processes

- outline how trade-off analysis
  can be used to develop an
  optimal mix of attributes for a
  new service

 *Crossing the English Channel . . . by Train*

The British were not amused in 1802 when one of Napoleon's generals suggested digging a tunnel under the English Channel to link Britain and France. They saw it as a military threat and imagined foreign troops using it to invade their country. But once raised, the idea never went away again.

In 1987, work finally began on twin rail tunnels and a third, smaller service tunnel between them. The Chunnel as it soon became known, runs over 23 miles (38 km) below the seabed from near the English town of Dover to the French town of Calais. It took seven years to complete, required the removal of 17 million tons of earth, and cost more than $13 billion by the time it was opened by Britain's Queen Elizabeth II and France's President François Mitterand in May 1994.

Until that date, all passengers and freight wishing to cross the English Channel had two options: air or ferry. For passengers, air travel is fast but expensive. It takes slightly more than an hour to fly to Paris from one of London's major airports, but travel time from city center to city center is closer to three hours, with the risk of traffic delays. Before the Chunnel, the other option on the London–Paris route was to travel by a combination of train, ferry, and then train again—usually a trip of six to eight hours. Cars, buses, and trucks could drive to one of several ports on the south coast of England and load their vehicles onto car ferries for a sea crossing, which takes from 50 minutes to four hours, depending on the route and the type of vessel (conventional ferries compete against faster hovercraft and water-jet catamarans). Rough seas, which are not uncommon, may lead to delays or even cancellations.

With the advent of the Chunnel, three new travel options became available. Eurostar provides passenger rail service from London to Paris or from London to Brussels, Belgium (some trains serve intermediate points, too), and Le Shuttle carries cars, buses, and trucks on railcars between Folkestone (near Dover) and Calais. International rail freight is also available.

Rather than allowing the new London–Paris passenger service to be operated by British Rail and the SNCF (the existing national railways), a new company was created and named Eurostar. New trains of a striking appearance, designed to cruise at up to 186 miles per hour (300 km/h), were derived from the successful French TGV (train à grande vitesse). These trains cut the travel time between central London and central Paris to three hours. (Completion of a new, high-speed track between London and the Chunnel will eventually reduce the time to two and one-half hours.) New station facilities were constructed.

But a host of decisions awaited Eurostar management: Who were the target market segments? What amenities should be offered at the stations and on board the trains? What types of service personnel were needed? How should the service be promoted? What would be the best way to win passengers from the competition? And how should the services be priced?

The most important decision positioned Eurostar against the airlines, rather than against existing trains and ferries. The argument was simple: From city center to city center, Eurostar was as fast as air travel. Other decisions followed quickly. Prices for the two classes of travel, first and standard, would be set with reference to business and economy air fares (there's no first-class air service between London and Paris). Each stage of the journey, from reservations to arrival at the destination, was carefully examined. Reservations and ticketing must be state of the art. Passenger facilities at the dramatic new Waterloo International Station in London would be equal to or better than those in a major air terminal (renovating the existing Gare du Nord in Paris would present more of a problem). Train exteriors and interiors would have a stylish appearance. The passenger cars would be furnished to offer greater comfort and more amenities than a competing airliner, as well as being quieter, smoother, and more spacious. In a two-class seating format, an 18-car Eurostar train would be capable of carrying 792 passengers (double the capacity of a Boeing 747).

Personal service by Eurostar employees, at the terminals and in the trains, would equal or exceed that given by airline personnel, requiring careful selection and training. Customer service personnel would have to be multilingual (at a minimum, English and French would be required, as well as Dutch on trains serving Brussels). Their uniforms would be stylish and make them immediately recognizable as Eurostar employees.

Marketers at Eurostar also addressed the needs of different market segments, starting with business travelers. As in business-class air travel, first-class Eurostar passengers receive complimentary meals, drinks, and newspapers at their seats (those in standard class can purchase food from a roving refreshment cart or visit one of two buffet cars). Unlike air travel,

passengers have a choice of smoking or nonsmoking cars, and there are no restrictions on the use of laptop computers or mobile phones. Public pay phones are provided, too. There is also a special Premium First service whose amenities include special lounges in the terminals, a fast check-in lane before departure, a wider choice of meals and wines on board, and complimentary taxi service on arrival. Passengers arriving in London can opt for free LimoBike service, which provides chauffeur-driven motorbikes to beat the traffic.

To promote and reward loyalty, Eurostar has created a Frequent Traveller program that rewards passengers with free rail and air travel, car rentals, and hotel stays. Eurostar's most frequent users can use the executive lounges at the terminal stations.

As required by law, special attention has been given to the special needs of disabled travelers, including the design of both the stations and train interiors, as well as staff training. Services for small children and their parents include baby-changing facilities—both on board the trains and in the terminals—and bottle warming. A recently introduced Eurostar service takes travelers directly to the rail station at the entrance to Paris Disneyland. On board the special trains, children will find Disney entertainment and free activity packs, as well as encounter Disney characters waiting at the station to greet them on arrival.

DESIGNING FOR SUCCESS

Meeting—and exceeding—customers' expectations takes more than just luck and an interesting service concept. It requires a systematic approach to all of the elements that make up the service experience. Customer satisfaction and delight can be designed *into* a service or designed *out* of it, depending on how effectively a company orchestrates the delivery processes for both its core and supplementary service offerings.

Eurostar is a good example of successfully designing a new service to meet customers' needs in the face of long-entrenched competitors. Engineers created a rail transportation system—track, power, and vehicles—that is extraordinarily fast, reliable, and safe. The train operator, Eurostar, then systematically identified all points of customer contact and used feedback from market research to design delivery processes and a servicescape that would meet their expectations. Among the many different professional skills employed in creating the Eurostar experience have been those of architects, fashion designers, seating experts, interior designers, and artists. The company also recognizes that its customer-contact personnel play key roles in creating a satisfying service experience for travelers. Selective recruitment, careful training, and ongoing supervision and support help to ensure superior performance. There is a sense of occasion about traveling Eurostar that is largely missing from air travel today.

As the Eurostar example shows, good service delivery has elements of both art and science. We cover both of these aspects in this chapter as we explore some of the methods service providers use to enhance the effectiveness of their service delivery processes.

Service as an Art Form

All the world's a stage and all the men and women merely players. They have their exits and their entrances and each man in his time plays many parts.

As You Like It
WILLIAM SHAKESPEARE

As pointed out in earlier chapters, the theater is a good metaphor for services because service delivery consists of a series of processes that customers experience as a *performance*.[1] It is a particularly useful approach for high-contact service providers (like physicians, educators, restaurants, and hotels) and for businesses that serve many people simultaneously rather than providing individualized service (like professional sports, hospitals, and entertainment). Figure 13.1 shows the relative importance of theatrical dimensions for different types of service businesses. As you can see, watch repair has very few front-stage theatrical components compared to services like airlines and spectator sports.

Service facilities contain the *stage* on which the drama unfolds. Sometimes the setting changes from one act to another (e.g., when Eurostar's rail passengers move from the station to the boarding platform to the interior of the train). The stage may have minimal props or elaborate scenery, as in the award-winning appearance of Waterloo International Station (which cost $130 million to complete). Some service dramas are tightly scripted and highly structured, whereas others are improvisational in nature.

Some services are more ritualized than others. In highly structured environments, such as dental offices, "blocking" may define how the actors (in this case, receptionists, dental hygienists, technicians, and dentists) should move relative to the stage (the dentist's office), items of scenery (furniture and equipment), and other actors.

Not all service providers require customers to attend performances at the company's "theater." Often, the customer's own facilities provide the stage where actors perform with their props. For example, outside accountants are often hired to provide specialized services at a client's site. (Although this may be convenient for customers, it isn't always wonderful for the visiting accountants, who may even find themselves working in rat-infested basements checking inventories of frozen foods for hours in a cold storage locker.)[2] Telecommunication linkages offer an alternative performance environment, allowing customers to be involved in the drama

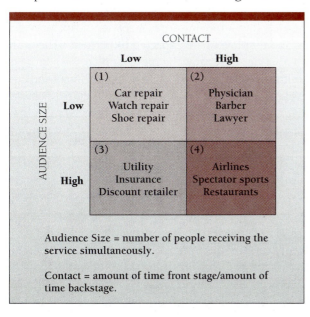

FIGURE 13.1
Relative Importance of Theatrical Dimensions

Source: Stephen J. Grove and Raymond P. Fisk, "The Dramaturgy of Service Exchange: An Analytical Framework for Services Marketing," in *Emerging Perspectives of Services Marketing*, L. L. Berry, I. L. Shostack, and G. D. Upah, eds. (Chicago: American Marketing Association, 1983), 45–49. Reprinted with permission.

from a remote location—a delivery option long desired by those traveling accountants, who would much prefer to do their clients' work in the comfort of their own offices through modems and computers.

Front-stage personnel are members of a cast, playing roles as *actors* in a drama and supported by a backstage production team. Sometimes they are expected to wear special costumes when on stage like the protective clothing, traditionally white, worn by dental professionals; Eurostar's stylish blue and yellow uniforms; or the more utilitarian brown ones worn by UPS drivers. Many front-stage employees must conform to both a dress code and grooming standards (e.g., Disney's rule that men at its parks can't wear mustaches or beards). Depending on the nature of their work, employees may be required to learn and repeat specific lines, ranging from announcements in several languages to a singsong sales spiel (just think of the last telemarketer who called you) to the parting salutation of "Have a nice day!" And just as in the theater, companies often use scripting to define actors' behavior, as well as their lines. Eye contact, smiles, and handshakes may be required in addition to a spoken greeting. Other rules of conduct may include bans on smoking, eating and drinking, or gum chewing while on duty.

Role and Script Theories

Role and script theories offer some interesting insights for service providers. If we view service delivery as a theatrical experience, both employees and customers act out their parts in the performance according to predetermined roles. Steve Grove and Ray Fisk define a **role** as "a set of behavior patterns learned through experience and communication, to be performed by an individual in a certain social interaction in order to attain maximum effectiveness in goal accomplishment."[3] Roles have also been defined as combinations of social cues, or expectations of society, that guide behavior in a specific setting or context.[4] In service encounters, employees and customers each have roles to play. The satisfaction of both parties depends on **role congruence**, or the extent to which each person acts out his or her prescribed role during a service encounter. Employees must perform their roles to customers' expectations or risk dissatisfying or losing customers all together, and customers also must play by the rules, or they will fall into one of the six jaycustomer categories described in chapter 6.

Scripts, sequences of behavior that both employees and customers are expected to follow during service delivery, are learned through experience, education, and communication with others.[5] Much like a movie script, a service script provides detailed actions that customers and employees are expected to perform. The more experience a customer has with a service company, the more familiar the script becomes. Any deviations from this known script may frustrate both customers and employees and can lead to high levels of dissatisfaction. If a company decides to change a service script (e.g., by using technology to turn a high-contact service into a low-contact one), service personnel and customers should be educated about the new script and the benefits it provides.

Some scripts are highly routinized and allow service employees to move through their duties quickly and efficiently (such as flight attendants' scripts for economy class). This approach helps to overcome two of the inherent challenges to service firms—how to reduce variability and ensure uniform quality. The risk is that frequent repetition may lead to mindless service delivery that ignores customers' needs.

Not all services involve tightly scripted performances. For providers of highly customized services—like doctors, educators, hairstylists, and consultants—the service script is flexible and may vary by situation and by customer. When customers are new to a service, they may not know what to expect and be fearful of

role: a combination of social cues that guides behavior in a specific setting or context.

role congruence: the extent to which both customers and employees act out their prescribed roles during a service encounter.

scripts: learned sequences of behaviors obtained through personal experience or communications with others.

A uniformed hotel employee leads a guest through the check-in script; her warmth humanizes the experience for him.

behaving incorrectly. Organizations should be ready to educate new customers about their roles in service delivery because inappropriate behaviors can disrupt service delivery and make customers feel embarrassed and uncomfortable. As service delivery procedures evolve in response to new technology or other factors, revised scripts may need to be developed.

Defining customer and employee scripts is a good way to start the flowcharting process. These scripts provide a full description of the service encounter and can help identify potential or existing problems in a specific service process. Table 13.1 (p. 272) shows a script for teeth cleaning and a simple dental examination, involving three players—the patient, the receptionist, and the dental hygienist. Each has a specific role to play. In this instance, the script is driven primarily by the need to execute a technical task both proficiently and safely (note the mask and gloves). The core service task of examining and cleaning teeth can be accomplished satisfactorily only if the patient cooperates in an experience that is at best uncomfortable and at worst painful. Several script elements refer to information flows. Confirming, as well as honoring, appointments avoids delays for customers and ensures effective use of dental professionals' time. Obtaining patient histories and documenting analysis and treatment are vital for maintaining complete dental records and also for accurate billing. Payment on receipt of treatment improves cash flow and avoids the problem of bad debts. Adding greetings, thanks, and goodbyes helps to humanize the experience.

The examination of existing scripts may suggest ways to modify the nature of customer and employee roles with a view to improving service delivery, increase productivity, and enhance the nature of the customer's experience.

To Delight or Disappoint?

At each step of the service drama, a firm has many opportunities to act improperly and lose its customers. But as we learned in chapter 4, smart managers understand their customers' expectations They are aware of what customers are looking for, not only in end benefits but also in the service delivery process itself. Perhaps

TABLE 13.1   Script for Teeth Cleaning and Simple Dental Examination

Patient	Receptionist	Dental Hygienist
1. Phone for appointment	2. Confirm needs and set date	
3. Arrive at dental office	4. Greet patient; verify purpose; direct to waiting room; notify hygienist of arrival	5. Review notes on patient
6. Sit in waiting room		7. Greet patient and lead way to treatment room
8. Enter room; sit in dental chair		9. Verify medical and dental history; ask about any issues since previous visit
		10. Place protective covers over patient's clothes
		11. Lower dental chair; put on own protective face mask, gloves, and glasses
		12. Inspect patient's teeth (option to ask questions)
		13. Place suction device in patient's mouth
		14. Use high-speed equipment and hand tools to clean teeth in sequence
		15. Remove suction device; complete cleaning process
		16. Raise chair to sitting position; ask patient to rinse
17. Rinse mouth		18. Remove and dispose of mask and gloves; remove glasses
		19. Complete notes on treatment; return patient file to receptionist
		20. Remove covers from patient
		21. Give patient free toothbrush; offer advice on personal dental care for future
22. Rise from chair		23. Thank patient and say goodbye
24. Leave treatment room	25. Greet patient; confirm treatment received; present bill	
26. Pay bill	27. Give receipt; agree on date for next appointment; document agreed-on date	
28. Take appointment card	29. Thank patient and say goodbye	
30. Leave dental office		

OTSU (opportunity to screw up): performance during a service encounter that disappoints customers by falling below their minimal level of expectations.

ISSO (ideal service scenario): performance during a service encounter that matches or exceeds customer expectations on all dimensions.

you've heard of the ancient and not-so-honorable art of **OTSU** or the splendid art of **ISSO**?[6] The former term was coined by David Maister, formerly a Harvard professor. It stands for the **o**pportunity **t**o **s**crew **u**p. At every step in the service delivery, there are many different opportunities to make mistakes. Some service firms seem to know them all and to delight in practicing them on their defenseless customers. In sharp contrast to the evil OTSU is the ideal way a service ought to perform at each step if the customer is to be truly satisfied. We call this the **i**deal **s**ervice **s**cenario, or ISSO for short. OTSUs also relate to servicescapes (see box).

Identifying OTSUs and ISSOs is critical in delivering a service that is guaranteed to please audiences. As noted in chapter 4, customers entertain both desired and adequate service levels. On the one hand, ISSOs are opportunities for service companies to meet—and, it is hoped to exceed—the desired service levels of their customers. On the other hand, even a single serious OTSU can cause a drop below the adequate level of service, resulting in a very dissatisfied customer.

This is where flowcharting comes back into our picture (or play). We introduced it in chapter 4 when we looked at the basic steps involved in a customer's interactions with Progressive Insurance Corp. In the following section, you'll see how flowcharting can be used as a tool to minimize OTSUs and maximize ISSOs as the service drama takes place.

THE RESTAURANT EXPERIENCE: A PLAY IN THREE ACTS

Our example, which we call *The Restaurant Experience*, is a play in three acts—each divided into several scenes, or steps, in the service process. Our goal is to help you envision good service by thinking carefully about the customer's situation at each

COSMETIC SURGEONS FLUNK SERVICESCAPES 101

It appears that plastic surgeons could use some OTSU training along with their other courses in medical school. That's the diagnosis of two experts, Kate Altork and Douglas Dedo, who did a study of patients' reactions to doctors' offices. They found that many patients will cancel surgery, change doctors, or refuse to consider future elective surgery if they feel uneasy in the doctor's office. The study results suggest that patients don't usually "doctor-jump" because they don't like the doctor but because they don't like the context of the service experience. The list of common patient dislikes includes graphic posters of moles and skin cancers decorating office walls, uncomfortable plastic identification bracelets, claustrophobic examining rooms with no windows or current reading material, bathrooms that aren't clearly marked, and not enough wastebaskets and water coolers in the waiting room.

What do patients want? Most requests are surprisingly simple and involve creature comforts like tissues, water coolers, telephones, plants, and bowls of candy in the waiting room and live flower arrangements in the lobby. Patients also want windows in the examining rooms and gowns that wrap around the entire body. They would like to sit on a real chair when they talk to a doctor instead of perching on a stool or examining table. Finally, preoperative patients prefer to be separated from postoperative patients because they are disturbed by sitting next to someone in the waiting room, say, whose head is enclosed in bandages.

Dr. Altork's study results suggest that cosmetic surgery patients would rather visit an office that looks more like a health spa than a hospital ward. By thinking like service marketers, savvy surgeons could use this information to create patient-friendly environments that will complement rather than counteract their technical expertise.

Source: Lisa Bannon, "Plastic Surgeons Are Told to Pay More Attention to Appearances," *The Wall Street Journal*, 15 March 1997, B1.

step in the front-stage process, as well as considering what your own definition of good service might be at that point (you have undoubtedly starred in the customer's role yourself many times). We also examine some of the horrible things that might go wrong—both front stage and backstage.

Act I: Appointment with Destiny

The play opens with the first act, "Appointment with Destiny" (see Figure 13.2, pp. 274–275). In this particular drama, the act has six scenes, beginning with the selection of the restaurant and concluding with being seated at a table. These six steps make up the customers' initial experience of the restaurant performance. They all take place front-stage, but much is also taking place backstage. Each element of the front-stage action is supported by a series of backstage activities: assignment of staff, delivery and preparation of food, maintenance of facilities and equipment, and storage and transfer of data (depicted here by the broad arrows, which link requests for tables to the seating capacity and reservations database).

Screwing up creatively. Let's follow our customers through each step, keeping in mind the accompanying OTSUs (we consider the ISSOs later). In the first scene our customers select Chez Jean, a French restaurant, and then proceed to Scene 2 to make a reservation. But much can go wrong with these simple steps. The potential for OTSUs is everywhere. Put yourself for a moment in the position of a restaurant manager who is looking for ways to bungle the reservations process. Here are some helpful hints:

■ Don't list your phone number in restaurant guides, the telephone directory, or your ads. In this way, nobody but your family and close friends will know how to reach you.

FIGURE 13.2 **The Restaurant Experience: Act I, Appointment with Destiny**

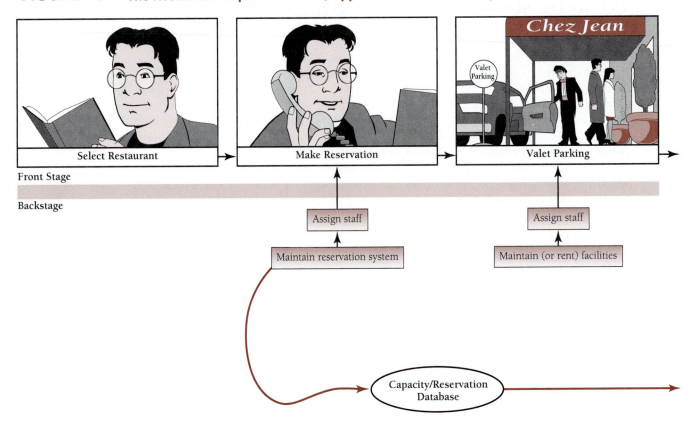

- Let the phone ring 10 to 15 times before answering; you want to be sure that you deal only with the most committed customers, rather than wasting time answering dumb questions from people who are just shopping around.

- Better yet, leave the phone off the hook. It gets rid of that distracting ringing noise in the background and gives the impression that the restaurant must be immensely successful.

- If you feel that someone must occasionally answer the phone, assign the task to an employee who doesn't speak the same language as your customers. Then, neither party will understand the other.

- Alternatively, put the reservations phone in the kitchen, next to the potato-peeling machine or the dishwasher. The background noise may make meaningful communication impossible, but customers always enjoy a challenge.

- To show prospective customers who's boss, pick employees with a naturally rude and offhand manner to take reservations. Give them no training and don't monitor their performance (you wouldn't want to spoil their act).

- Don't bother to have a reservations book or computer anywhere near the phone. Then, employees taking calls will have to guess when tables might be free and will be forced to keep the reservations in their heads until they have a moment to record them. It's good memory training.

These OTSUs are funny when you talk about them. John Cleese made millions laugh with his portrayal of an inept hotel manager in the British television series "Fawlty Towers," and Chevy Chase has entertained American movie audiences for years by playing a customer tortured by inept, rude, or downright cruel service employees. However, customers don't always see the funny side when the joke is on

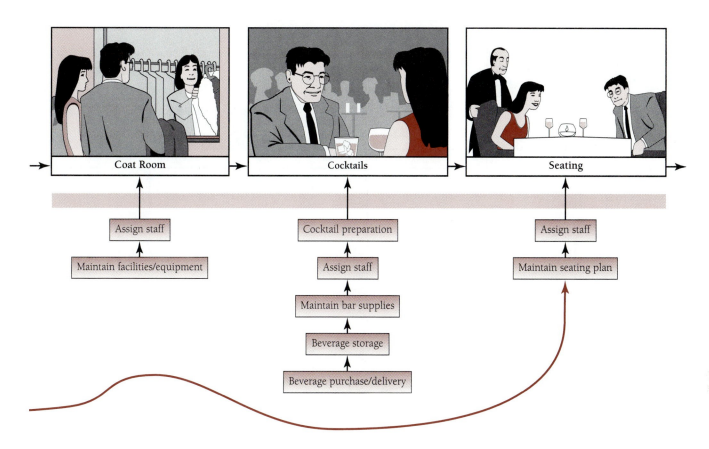

them. It's only by identifying all the possible OTSUs associated with a particular task that service managers can put together a delivery system that is explicitly designed to avoid all possible mistakes.

Identifying ISSOs.   By identifying ideal service scenarios (ISSOs), service providers can design each step in a system to satisfy and even delight its customers. Here are some possible ISSOs for Act I, Scene 2. First, there would be a highlighted listing in the phone directory so that customers could quickly find the number. The telephone line would be staffed during normal business hours, as well as during the specific hours when meals were being served. The phone would be picked up within three rings by a pleasant-voiced person who would answer with the name of the restaurant and his or her own name. That person would be able to check the desired reservation date and time and provide a response within 15 seconds. At no point in the process would customers be put on hold.

If the preferred time was not free, the reservation taker would volunteer other times available on the same date. He or she would also be able to respond knowledgeably and cheerfully to any questions customers might have about the restaurant—how to get there, the nature of the menu, prices, table availability, presence of a nonsmoking section, and whether the restaurant is suitable for children. When taking the reservation, the employee would get the customer's name right and confirm the agreed-on time and size of the party. Finally, he or she would thank the customer for the reservation and conclude by saying, "We look forward to your visit."

More OTSUs as Act I unfolds.   If our customers get past the reservations hurdle, they arrive outside the restaurant, where, as an extra service to its patrons, the management provides valet parking. Assignment of the right staff here is very im-

FIGURE 13.3 The Restaurant Experience: Act II, "Banquet of the Gods"

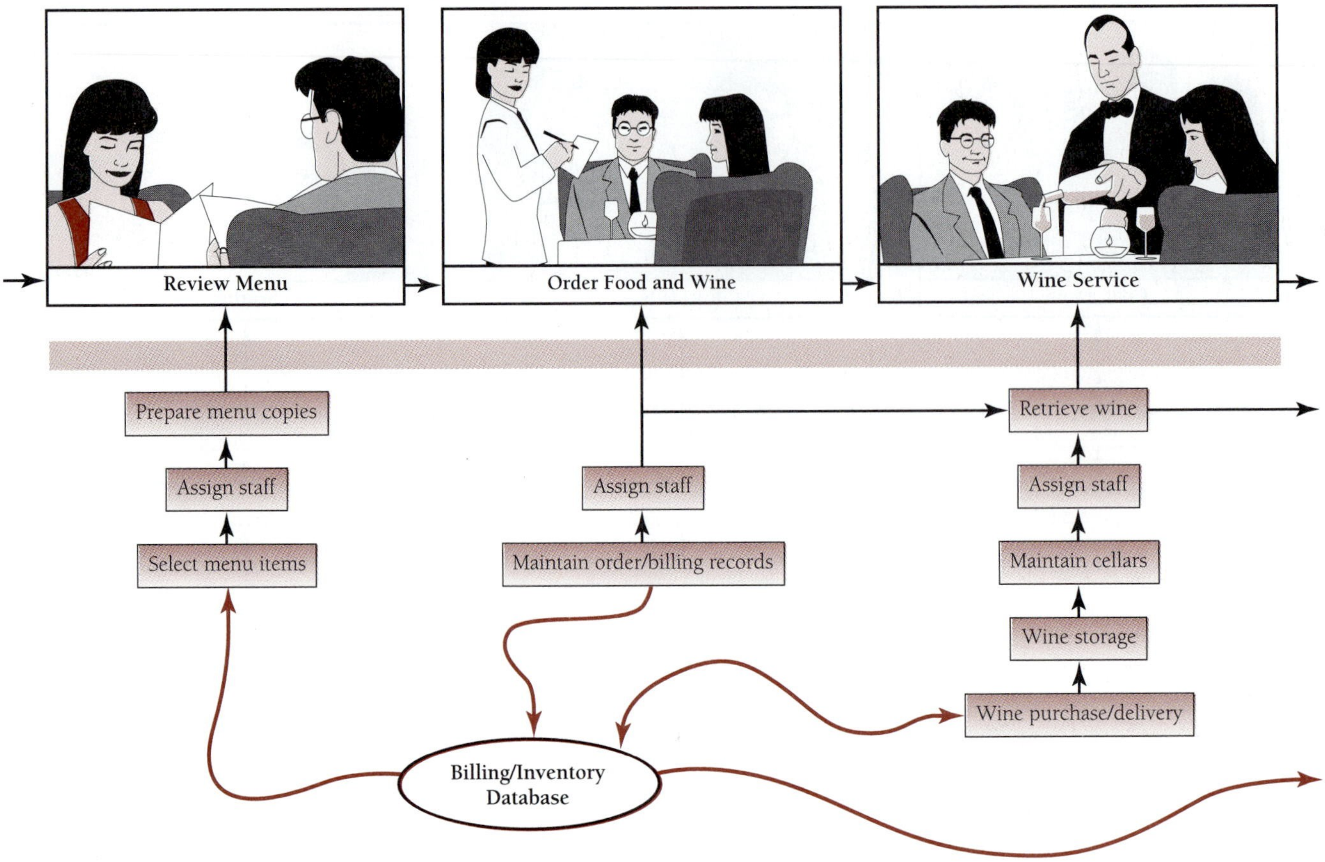

portant to customers who take pride in their cars. How would you feel, as you arrive in your late-model Mercedes or Jaguar (or even your lovingly cared-for family Ford), if you are greeted by some 17-year-old boys in leather vests and cutoff jeans? One has long greasy hair, and the other has shaved most of his hair off and has a nose ring and a tattoo proclaiming that he is "Born to Race." Do you give them the keys to your car? Or do you just decide to leave, there and then? Now imagine yourself as the customer in each of the three remaining scenes depicted in Act I of our play: dropping off coats at the coatroom, ordering cocktails in the lounge, and being seated at your table. What are the potential ISSOs and OTSUs for each of these scenes?

The opening scenes of a service drama are particularly important because customers' first impressions can affect their evaluations of quality during the later stages of service delivery. That is, customers' perceptions of their service experiences tend to be cumulative.[7] On the one hand, if a few things go wrong and the customers haven't walked out yet, they'll be looking for other things that aren't quite right. On the other hand, if the first steps go really well, the customers' zones of tolerance may increase so that they are more willing to overlook minor mistakes later. For example, customer research done by Marriott Hotels indicates that four of the five top factors contributing to customer loyalty come into play during the first 10 minutes of service delivery.[8]

Act II: Banquet of the Gods

In Act II, our customers finally experience the core service they came for. If all goes well, they will have a good meal, nicely served in a pleasant atmosphere, with perhaps a fine wine to enhance the effects. If the restaurant fails to satisfy customers'

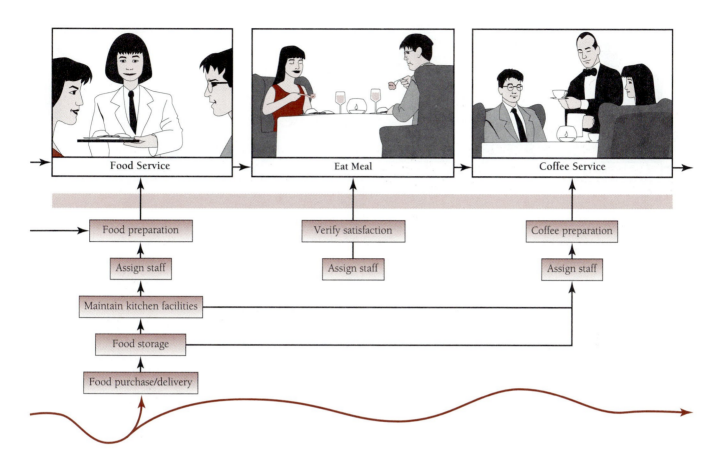

expectations during Act II, it's clearly going to be in serious trouble. For simplicity, we've included just six scenes in Figure 13.3 rather than showing the meal course by course. In practice, if you were actually running a full-service restaurant, you would need to go into greater detail in identifying all of the steps involved in service delivery.

The curtain rises as our two customers review their menus. Opportunities for ISSOs and OTSUs immediately arise. Is the menu information complete? Is it intelligible? If the menu is in French, can the staff provide translations into English or other languages? Will explanations and advice be given in a friendly and noncondescending manner for guests who have questions about specific menu items or are unsure about which wine to order? After our guests decide on their meals, they place their order with the server, who must then pass it on to personnel in the kitchen, bar, and billing desk. Mistakes in transmitting information are a rich source of OTSUs in many organizations. Bad handwriting or unclear verbal requests can lead to delivery of the wrong items altogether—or of the right items incorrectly prepared.

In subsequent scenes of Act II, our customers at Chez Jean will be evaluating not only the quality of food and drink but also how promptly it is served (not too promptly, for that would suggest frozen foods cooked by microwave) and how graciously. A technically correct performance by the server can still be spoiled by such human failures as a disinterested, cold, or ingratiating manner. As before, a great deal of activity is taking place behind the scenes—much of it far removed from direct customer contact, and some of it necessarily occurring long before the customers' arrival.

A common OTSU in Scene 2 is the unavailability of a menu item. Tracing this problem back to its source may reveal that somebody in purchasing forgot to order a certain type of food in sufficient quantity for the anticipated demand. Alterna-

FIGURE 13.4 The Restaurant Experience: Act III, "Return to Reality"

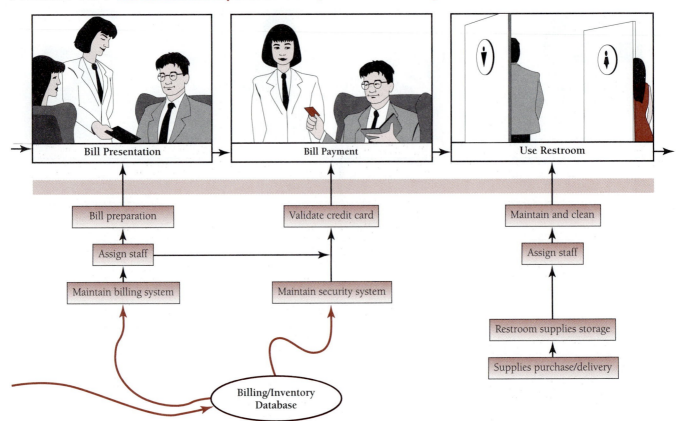

tively, the necessary food may have spoiled because it wasn't stored right, or maybe the cooks accidentally burned it because the oven controls were inaccurate due to the lack of proper maintenance.

In chapter 5 we looked at root cause analysis (or fishboning), which is a specific quality control technique for tracing problems to their source. This is a good tool for identifying the existence and causes of OTSUs. It starts with a team of managers and staff brainstorming all possible reasons why a particular type of failure might occur; then they group them into various categories and document actual practices to determine which of these possible causes are most frequently the source of the problem in question.

Act III: Return to Reality

Let's go on to Act III, "Return to Reality," which continues to be a busy time both front stage and backstage as the drama moves to its close (Figure 13.4). The core service has now been delivered, and we'll assume that our customers are happily digesting it. Act III should be short. The action in each of the remaining scenes should move smoothly, quickly, and pleasantly. There should be no shocking surprises at the end. But a number of the supplementary service elements discussed in chapter 9 must still be delivered to complete the experience. Ideally, the scenario should look like this:

■ an accurate, intelligible bill is presented promptly as soon as the customer requests it

■ payment is handled politely and expeditiously, and all major credit cards are acceptable

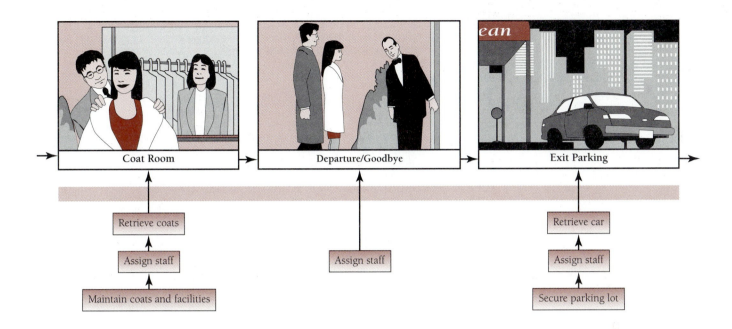

- the restrooms are clean and properly supplied
- the right coats are promptly retrieved from the coatroom
- a staff member opens the door, thanks the guests for their patronage, bids them goodnight, and expresses the hope that they will come again
- the customer's car is brought promptly to the door in the same condition as it was left

But how often is this ideal achieved in Act III? How often do OTSUs intervene to ruin the customers' experience and spoil their good humor? Do you remember how many times the experience of a nice meal in Act II was completely spoiled for you by one or more OTSUs in Act III? One of the most commonly cited OTSUs is the inability to get the bill when customers have finished their meal and are ready to leave. This seemingly minor mistake can taint the rest of the dining experience even if everything else has gone well. Making customers wait unnecessarily is akin to stealing their time.

Some restaurants have created ISSOs by offering customers who are in a hurry ways of getting through the restaurant experience pleasantly and quickly. For example, The Olive Garden restaurant chain introduced its Pronto! program in 1996 to encourage lunch customers to tell their server "Pronto!" if they wanted fast service. Bennigan's puts a stop watch at every table with a guarantee to have lunch and a bill on a customer's table within 15 minutes or the meal is free. European and Canadian diners in a hurry can patronize Movenpick Marché. In this classy chain of cafeterias, service means food that is fast but artfully prepared and presented.[9] These restaurants have designed both their front-stage and their backstage processes to provide quick service that still meets customers' expectations for quality see Table 13.2.

TABLE 13.2   In-and-Out Food Service

Restaurant Hospitality, a trade magazine for the restaurant industry, offers the following 10 ways of serving customers quickly without making them feel as if they've been pushed out the door.[a] As you'll see, some of these tactics involve front-stage processes, whereas others take place backstage—but it is the interaction between front stage and backstage that creates the desired service delivery.

1. Distinguish between patrons in a hurry and those who are not.
2. Design specials that are quick.
3. Guide hurried customers to the quick specials.
4. Place the quickest, highest-margin menu items either first or last on the menu.
5. Offer dishes that can be prepared ahead.
6. Warn customers when they order slow delivery items.
7. Consider short-line buffets, roving carts, and more sandwiches.
8. Offer "wrap"-style sandwiches, which are a quickly prepared, filling meal.
9. Use equipment built for speed, like combination ovens.
10. Eliminate preparation steps that require cooks to stop cooking.

[a] Paul B. Hertneky, "Built for Speed," *Restaurant Hospitality*, January 1997, 58.

The Grand Finale

It's clear that even in the simplified form presented here, the service delivery process is very complex. As you've seen, the core service in Act II is surrounded on either side by supplementary product elements in Acts I and III. Our restaurant example was deliberately chosen to illustrate a high-contact, people-processing service with which all readers were likely to be familiar. But many possession-processing services (like repair or maintenance) and information-processing services (like insurance or accounting) involve much less contact with customers as much of the service operation takes place backstage. In these situations, an OTSU committed front stage is likely to represent a higher proportion of the customer's service encounters with a company and therefore may be viewed even more seriously. The worst OTSUs are those that directly affect external customers as they wait for service front stage. But other OTSUs, even when their impact is confined backstage, may still hinder employees' productivity, leading to increased costs and lower morale.

SERVICE AS A SCIENCE

Our restaurant example emphasizes the importance of preventing failures at each point in an existing process and making sure that each step is designed to meet customers' expectations. But polishing existing processes until they shine, both front stage and backstage, is not the only way to improve service outcomes. Managers may need to completely rethink the underlying delivery processes. Flowcharts can provide valuable insights by indicating how to reengineer business processes, improve capacity planning, and better define employees' roles. These efforts will help companies integrate their marketing, operations, and human resources efforts—and thus move closer to achieving the goal of integrated service management.

Reengineering Business Processes

The design of business processes has important implications for the nature of the customer's experience as well as the cost, speed, and productivity with which the desired outcome is achieved. Improving productivity in services often requires speeding up the overall process (or cycle time), because the cost of creating a service is usually related to how long it takes to deliver each step in the process, plus any dead time between each step.

When they are relaxing or being entertained, customers don't mind *spending* time. But when they are busy, they hate *wasting* time (see chapter 11). Even when

Modern communications technology can help speed up backstage processes.

customers aren't directly involved in the process, the elapsed time between ordering and receiving a service may be seen as costly (e.g., waiting for the repair of a broken machine, installation of a new computer system, receipt of legal advice, or delivery of a consulting report).

Reengineering involves analyzing and redesigning business processes to achieve faster and better performance. To reduce the overall time for a process, analysts must identify each step, measure how long it takes, look for opportunities to speed it up (or even eliminate it altogether), and cut out dead time. Running tasks in parallel rather than in sequence is a well-established approach to speeding up processes (a simple household example would be to cook the vegetables for a meal while the main dish was in the oven rather than waiting to cook them after the main dish was removed). Service companies can use blueprinting—a technique described in chapter 8—to diagram these aspects of service operations in a systematic way.

reengineering: the analysis and redesign of business processes to create dramatic performance improvements in such areas as cost, quality, speed, and customers' service experiences.

Examination of business processes may also lead to the creation of alternative delivery forms that are so radically different that they constitute entirely new service concepts. Options may include eliminating certain supplementary services, addition of new ones, transforming personal service into self-service, and rethinking the location where service delivery takes place. Figure 13.5 illustrates this principle with simple flowcharts of four ways to deliver meal service from the full-service restaurant shown in Figures 13.2–13.4. Compare what occurs front stage at a fast-food restaurant, a drive-in restaurant, home delivery, and home catering. From the customer's perspective, what has been added and deleted from the scenario at Chez Jean? And in each instance, what needs to change backstage?

Capacity Planning

A **bottleneck** in the service delivery process creates an irritating situation for customers. There they are, moving nicely through the cafeteria line, when they run into a five-minute wait at the cashier's station. Why does this dead time occur? Perhaps the two cashiers on duty can't process customers as quickly as the meal servers

bottleneck: a point of congestion in a service delivery process.

FIGURE 13.5 Flowcharts for Meal Delivery Scenarios

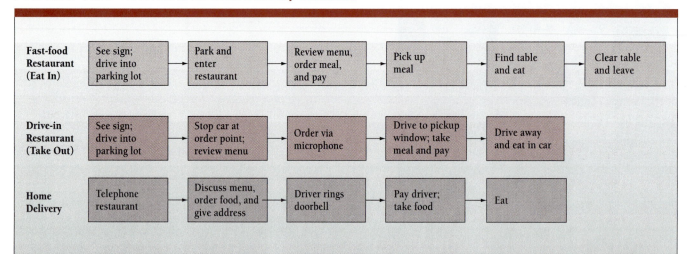

and self-service stations further up the line. The solution may be to add a third cashier at busy times or find faster ways to process each transaction (such as better training for cashiers, installing cash registers that operate more rapidly, or rounding up all prices to make giving change faster). For example, a grocery chain in the western United States, called Lucky's, addresses this issue with the "Rule of 3." When each of all currently open checkout stations have more than three customers waiting in line, the manager and assistant manager are responsible for opening up additional stations so that the store can speed the checkout process. We return to capacity management in greater detail in chapter 14. A related issue is the management of waiting lines, which is addressed in chapter 15. Managing capacity and waiting lines are major challenges for people-processing services like cafeterias and airlines, but companies also face these issues when processing inanimate objects or information and mental stimulus services.

Flowcharts can help address capacity-related issues in all types of services. By calculating the average processing time at each step, relative to the available capacity, service providers can identify potential bottlenecks and explore possible solutions. However, the word *average* implies some variability. If a clump of customers arrives, each requiring an above-average in-process time, temporary delays will still occur. There are now some excellent software packages for this type of analysis. One, Process Charter, creates flowcharts that can be used for both time and cost analyses for service processes. It also runs simulations for different service scenarios so that managers can see the trade-offs between waiting times and costs. The software even has a way to build in the estimated time a customer is willing to wait before becoming dissatisfied with the service delivery.

Understanding Employee Roles

Many of the benefits of flowcharts come from the research and analysis involved in creating them, especially if employees themselves are directly involved in the task. Participation in making flowcharts for specific processes helps employees gain a clearer understanding of their roles and responsibilities and makes them feel part of a team that is responsible for implementing a shared service vision. Flowcharts also encourage managers and employees to understand the service delivery process as it's experienced by customers.

An additional benefit of flowcharts is to help backstage personnel see how their work relates to their front-stage colleagues. The former provide a series of internal services, represented by each of the vertically stacked boxes in Figures 13.2 to 13.4, that support front-stage activities. If they do their jobs poorly, they may create problems for their coworkers with customer-contact responsibilities. As you can see, OTSUs and ISSOs also apply to "internal customers," or employees and suppliers who provide service for others working within the organization. It's not always possible to give either external or internal customers exactly the service they would like, but flowcharts can be a valuable tool in deciding how to manage expectations and in facilitating discussion about how to improve service processes.

CREATING NEW SERVICE DRAMAS

In this chapter, we've discussed how to improve existing service operations by thinking of them as dramas whose evolution can be charted. But as you'll recall from chapter 8, flowcharts tools are also very useful for designing new services. Flowcharts are to service design what architectural sketches and detailed blueprints are to the design of buildings and equipment. Different configurations of the service can be examined from the perspective of cycle time, costs, labor requirements, need for specialized equipment, and facilities design. Flowcharts can also help evaluate how well alternative approaches are likely to satisfy customers—not only in creating desired outcomes, but also in terms of financial and time costs and the demands placed on customers during the service delivery process. In fact, such analysis may reveal opportunities to offer alternative versions of the process to meet the needs of different customer segments (see the discussion of blueprints in chapter 8).

Using Research to Design New Services

When a company is designing a new service from the beginning, how can it decide what features and prices will create the best value for target customers? It's hard to know without asking the customers—thus the need for research. Let's examine how the Marriott Corporation used market research to help with new service development in the hotel industry.

When Marriott was designing a new chain of hotels for business travelers (which eventually became known as Courtyard by Marriott), it hired marketing research experts to help establish an optimal design concept.[10] Because there are limits to how much service and how many amenities can be offered at any given price, Marriott needed to know how customers would make trade-offs to arrive at the most satisfactory compromise in value for money. The intent of the research was to get respondents to indicate which service features they valued most. Marriott's goal was to determine if a niche existed between full-service hotels and inexpensive motels, especially where demand was not high enough to justify a large, full-service hotel. If such a niche existed, executives wanted to develop a product to fill that gap.

A sample of 601 consumers from four metropolitan areas participated in the study. Researchers used a sophisticated technique known as conjoint analysis, which asks survey respondents to rank between different groupings of attributes. The objective is to determine which mix of attributes at specific prices offers the highest degree of utility. The 50 attributes in the Marriott study were divided into the following seven factors (or sets of attributes), each containing a variety of different features based on detailed studies of competing offerings:

1. *External factors*—building shape, landscaping, pool type and location, hotel size
2. *Room features*—room size and decor, climate control, location and type of bathroom, entertainment systems, other amenities
3. *Food-related services*—type and location of restaurants, menus, room service, vending machines, guest shop, in-room kitchen
4. *Lounge facilities*—location, atmosphere, type of guests
5. *Services*—reservations, registration, checkout, airport limosine, bell desk, message center, secretarial services, car rental, laundry, valet
6. *Leisure facilities*—sauna, whirlpool, exercise room, racquetball and tennis courts, game room, children's playground
7. *Security*—guards, smoke detectors, 24-hour video camera

For each of these seven factors, respondents were presented with a series of stimulus cards displaying different levels of performance for each attribute. For instance, the "Rooms" stimulus card displayed nine attributes, each of which had three to five different levels. Thus, *amenities* ranged from "small bar of soap" to "large soap, shampoo packet, shoeshine mitt" to "large soap, bath gel, shower cap, sewing kit, shampoo, special soap" to the highest level, "large soap, bath gel, shower cap, sewing kit, special soap, toothpaste" and so on.

In the second phase of the analysis, respondents were shown a number of alternative hotel profiles, each featuring different levels of performance on the various attributes contained in the seven factors. They were asked to indicate on a five-point scale how likely they would be to stay at a hotel with these features, given a specific room price per night (see Figure 13.6).

Transforming Research Findings into Reality

The research yielded detailed guidelines for the selection of almost 200 features and service elements, representing those attributes that provided the highest utility for the customers in the target segments at prices they were willing to pay. An important aspect of the study was that it focused on not only what travelers wanted but also identified what they liked but weren't prepared to pay for (there's a difference, after all, between wanting something and being willing to pay for it). Using these inputs, the design team was able to meet the specified price while retaining the features most desired by the target market.

Marriott was sufficiently encouraged by the findings to build three Courtyard by Marriott prototype hotels. After testing the concept under real-world conditions and making some refinements, the company subsequently developed a large chain whose advertising slogan became "Courtyard by Marriott—the hotel designed by business travelers." The new hotel concept filled a gap in the market with a product that represented the best balance between the price customers were prepared to pay and the physical and service features they most desired. The success of this project has led Marriott to develop additional customer-driven products—Fairfield Inn and Marriott Suites—by using the same research methodology.

FIGURE 13.6 Sample Description of a Hotel Offering

Room Price per Night is $44.85

Building Size; Bar/Lounge

Large (600 rooms), 12-story hotel with

- Quiet bar/lounge
- Enclosed central corridors and elevators
- All rooms with very large windows

Landscaping/Court

Building forms a spacious outdoor courtyard

- View from rooms of moderately landscaped courtyard

    Many trees and shrubs

    Swimming pool plus fountain

    Terraced areas for sunning, sitting, and eating

Food

Small, moderately priced lounge and restaurant for hotel guests/friends

- Limited breakfast with juices, fruit, Danish, cereal, bacon, and eggs
- Lunch—soup and sandwiches only
- Evening meal—salad, soup, sandwiches, six hot entrees including steak

Hotel/Motel Room Quality

Quality of room furnishings, carpet, etc. similar to

- Hyatt Regencies
- Westin "Plaza" Hotels

Room Size and Function

Room 1 foot longer than typical hotel/motel room

- Space for comfortable sofa-bed and and two chairs
- Large desk
- Coffee table
- Coffee maker and small refrigerator

Service Standards

Full service including

- Rapid check-in/check-out systems
- Reliable message service
- Valet (laundry pick up/deliver)
- Bellman
- Someone (concierge) arranges reservations and tickets, generally at no cost
- Cleanliness, upkeep, management similar to

    Hyatts

    Marriotts

Leisure

- Combination indoor-outdoor pool
- Enclosed whirlpool (Jacuzzi)
- Well-equipped playroom/playground for kids

Security

- Night guard on duty 7 P.M. to 7 A.M.
- Fire/water sprinklers throughout hotel

"X" the **One** box below that best describes how likely you are to stay in this hotel/motel at this price:

Would stay there almost all the time	Would stay there on a regular basis	Would stay there now and then	Would rarely stay there	Would not stay there
☐	☐	☐	☐	☐

This full profile description of a hotel offering is one of the 50 cards developed by a fractional factorial design of the seven facets each at the five levels (developed by the Marriott's development team). Each respondent received five cards following a blocking design.

Source: Jerry Wind et al., "Courtyard by Marriott: Designing a Hotel Facility with Customer-Based Marketing Models," *Interfaces*, January/February 1989, 25–47.

Conclusion

Service delivery involves a series of processes that customers experience as a performance. The theater is a good analogy for service delivery, complete with actors, stage sets, scripts, and costumes. Backstage activities (which the customer doesn't see) exist only to create and support good performances onstage. These front-stage activities involve customers in service delivery and may require them to interact with facilities, equipment, employees, and even other customers.

At each step in the service drama, the firm has many opportunities to make mistakes and offend its customers. But there are many chances to please them as well. Scripts, flowcharts and conjoint analysis are useful tools for managers in identifying possible problems (OTSUs) and opportunities (ISSOs) as the service drama unfolds.

Study Questions and Exercise

1. Which types of service businesses does the theater metaphor fit best? Why?
2. Discuss the concept of employee and customer roles.
3. Develop two different customer scripts: one for a standardized service and one for a customized service. Compare the two scripts and describe any significant differences.
4. What are OTSUs and ISSOs? Why are these concepts important to a service provider?
5. Think about your university's course registration process. Can you identify any OTSUs? Any ISSOs?
6. Describe some of the ways in which service managers can use flowcharts to improve service delivery.
7. For each of the flowcharts of front-stage processes in Figure 13.5, complete the necessary backstage processes and information flows.
8. What research would you conduct to design:
   a. a new health club, targeted at people aged 18 to 25
   b. a repair service for high-tech equipment in home offices
   c. an internet-based travel agency

Balancing Demand and Capacity

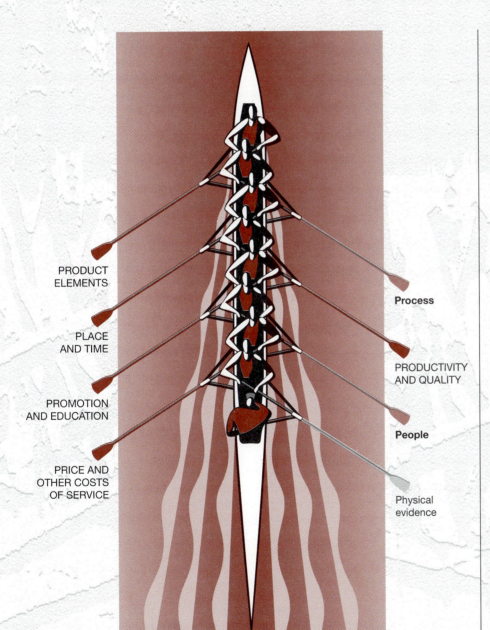

PRODUCT
ELEMENTS

PLACE
AND TIME

PROMOTION
AND EDUCATION

PRICE AND
OTHER COSTS
OF SERVICE

Process

PRODUCTIVITY
AND QUALITY

People

Physical
evidence

Learning Objectives

After reading this chapter, you should be able to

- understand the elements that make up productive capacity for a service organization

- explain how to use capacity management techniques to meet variations in demand

- understand the concept of demand cycles

- recognize different patterns of demand and their underlying causes

- formulate demand management strategies appropriate to specific situations

Cape Cod: A Seasonal Tourist Destination

Cape Cod is a remarkable peninsula of narrow land, jutting out into the Atlantic off the Massachusetts coast like a long arm, bent at the elbow. Native Americans have lived there for thousands of years. The Pilgrims landed at that spot in 1619 but continued across Cape Cod Bay to found Plymouth; however, not long afterward, more immigrants from England settled on the Cape itself. Fishing, whaling, agriculture, and salt works were among the principal industries in the 19th century. By the mid-20th century, all but fishing—itself in decline—had virtually disappeared and tourism was beginning to assume some significance. Events in the early 1960s put the Cape firmly in the public eye. John F. Kennedy became president of the United States and was regularly photographed at his family's vacation home in Hyannisport; while in office he signed legislation creating the Cape Cod National Seashore, preserving large areas of the Outer Cape as a national park. Also, the song, "Old Cape Cod," commissioned by tourism promoters and sung by popular vocalist Patti Page, unexpectedly climbed to the top of the charts and was heard around the world. With its beaches and salt marshes, sand dunes and fishing harbors, picturesque towns and lobster dinners, the Cape rapidly became a resort destination, drawing millions of visitors each year from New England, the mid-Atlantic states, eastern Canada, and beyond—in season, that is.

In summer, the Cape is a busy place. Colorful umbrellas sprout like giant flowers along the miles of sandy beaches. The parking lots are full. There are lines outside most restaurants, and managers complain about the difficulty of hiring and retaining sufficient serving staff. Stores and movie theaters are busy (especially when it rains), the Mid-Cape Highway is clogged, and hotels sport "no vacancy" signs. Fishing

trips have to be booked well in advance. Vacation cottages are rented, it's hard to get a car reservation on the ferries to the islands of Nantucket or Martha's Vineyard, and the visitor centers at the National Seashore are crowded with tourists.

Return for a weekend in midwinter, however, and what do you find? A few walkers brave the chill winds on the otherwise empty beaches. You can park in almost any legal space you wish. Many restaurants have closed (their owners are wintering in Florida), and only the most popular of the remaining establishments even bother to suggest reservations. The stores have laid off seasonal workers and, in some cases, cut the hours of remaining employees. As a result, there is seasonal unemployment.

It's rare in winter to be unable to see the movie of your choice at your preferred time. The main problem on the Mid-Cape Highway is being stopped for speeding. If a motel has a "no vacancy" sign, that means it's closed for the season; others offer bargain rates. Recreational fishing? You must be crazy—there may even be ice on Cape Cod Bay! Owners of vacation cottages have drained their water systems and boarded up the windows. You can probably drive your vehicle straight onto one of the car ferries to the islands (although the sailing schedules are more limited), and the rangers at the visitor centers are happy to talk with the few visitors who drop by during the limited opening hours.

Faced with such a sharply peaked season, economic development agencies are working to extend the Cape's tourism beyond the peak months of July and August and to build demand during the spring and fall months. Among their targets are tourists from Europe, who appreciate the old-world charm of the Cape and tend to spend more money than visitors from Boston or New York.

THE UPS AND DOWNS OF DEMAND

Fluctuating demand for service, as that experienced by retailers, movie theaters, motels, restaurants, ferries, and other establishments on Cape Cod, is not just found in vacation resorts. It's a problem that besets a huge cross-section of businesses, serving both individual and corporate customers. These demand fluctuations, which may range in length from seasonal to hourly, play havoc with the efficient use of productive assets.

Effective Use of Productive Capacity

Unlike manufacturing, service operations create a perishable **inventory** that cannot be stockpiled for sale at a later date. This is a problem for any capacity-constrained service that has wide swings in demand. The problem is found most commonly among services that process people or physical possessions, such as transportation, lodging, food service, repair and maintenance, entertainment, and health care. It also affects labor-intensive, information-processing services that have cyclical shifts in demand, for example, accounting and tax preparation.

Effective use of productive capacity is one of the secrets of success in such businesses. However, the goal shouldn't be to utilize staff, labor, equipment, and facilities as much as possible but rather to use them as productively as possible. This chapter is very much concerned with issues of *productivity* and *quality*, which is introduced in chapter 1 and discussed in more depth in chapter 5. Successful service managers recognize that managing demand and managing capacity are essential not only to productive use of the firm's assets but also to give customers the high-quality service experiences they seek.

From Excess Demand to Excess Capacity

The problem is a familiar one: "It's either feast or famine for us!" sighs the manager. "In peak periods, we're disappointing prospective customers by turning them away. And in low periods, our facilities are idle, our staff is standing around looking bored, and we're losing money." At any given moment, a fixed-capacity service may face one of four conditions (see Figure 14.1):

■ **Excess demand**—the level of demand exceeds the maximum available capacity, with the result that some customers are denied service and business is lost.

■ Demand exceeds optimum capacity—no one is actually turned away, but conditions are crowded and all customers are likely to perceive a deterioration in the quality of service.

inventory: for *manufacturing*, physical output stockpiled after production for sale at a later date; for *services*, future output not yet reserved in advance, such as the number of hotel rooms still available for sale on a given day.

excess demand: demand for a service at a given time exceeds the firm's ability to meet customers' needs.

FIGURE 14.1 Implications of Variations in Demand Relative to Capacity

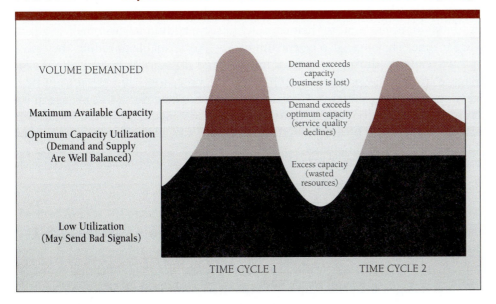

■ Demand and supply are well balanced—at the level of optimum capacity—staff and facilities are busy without being overworked, and customers receive good service without delays.

■ **Excess capacity**—demand is below optimum capacity and productive resources are underutilized, resulting in low productivity. In some instances, customers may find the experience disappointing or have doubts about the viability of the service.

excess capacity: a firm's capacity to create service output is not fully utilized.

We've drawn a distinction between **maximum capacity** and **optimum capacity**. When demand exceeds the maximum available capacity, some potential customers may be turned away and their business lost forever. But when demand is operating between optimum and maximum capacity, there's a risk that all customers being served at that time may receive inferior service and thus become dissatisfied.

maximum capacity: the upper limit to a firm's ability to meet customer demand at a particular time.

optimum capacity: the point beyond which a firm's efforts to serve additional customers will lead to a perceived deterioration in service quality.

Sometimes optimum and maximum capacities are one and the same. At a live theater or sports performance, a full house is grand because it stimulates the players and creates a sense of excitement and audience participation. The net result is a more satisfying experience for all. But with most other services, customers may feel that they get better service if the facility is not operating at full capacity. The quality of restaurant service, for instance, often deteriorates when every table is occupied because the staff is rushed and there's a greater likelihood of errors or delays. If you're traveling alone in an aircraft with high-density seating, you tend to feel more comfortable if the seat next to you is empty. When repair and maintenance shops are fully scheduled, delays may result if there is no slack in the system to allow for unexpected problems in completing particular jobs.

There are two basic solutions to the problem of fluctuating demand. One is to adjust the level of capacity to meet variations in demand. This approach, which entails cooperation between operations and human resource management, requires an understanding of what constitutes productive capacity and how it may be increased or decreased on an incremental basis. The second approach is to manage the level of demand, using marketing strategies to smooth out the peaks and fill in the valleys to generate a more consistent flow of requests for service. Some firms use both approaches.

MEASURING AND MANAGING CAPACITY

Many service organizations operate processes that are capacity constrained; that is, there's an upper limit to their capacity to serve additional customers at a particular time. They may also be constrained by being unable to reduce their productive capacity during periods of low demand. In general, organizations that engage in physical processes, such as people processing and possession processing, are more likely to face capacity constraints than those that engage in information-based processes. A radio station, for instance, may be constrained in its geographic reach by the strength of its signal, but within that radius any number of listeners can tune in to a broadcast.

Defining Productive Capacity

productive capacity: the extent of the facilities, equipment, labor, infrastructure, and other assets available to a firm to create output for its customers.

What do we mean by **productive capacity**? The term refers to the resources or assets that a firm can employ to create goods and services. In a service context, productive capacity can take at least five potential forms.

1. *Physical facilities designed to contain customers* and used for delivering people-processing or mental-stimulus processing services. They include clinics,

hotels, passenger aircraft, buses, restaurants, swimming pools, movie theaters, concert halls, and college classrooms. In these cases the primary capacity constraint is likely to be defined by such furnishings as beds, rooms, seats, tables, or desks. In some cases, local regulations may set an upper limit to the number of people allowed in the interest of health or fire safety.

2. *Physical facilities designed for storing or processing goods* that either belong to customers or are being offered to them for sale. They include supermarket shelves, pipelines, warehouses, parking lots, freight containers, and railroad freight wagons.

3. *Physical equipment used to process people, possessions, or information* may embrace a huge range of items and be very situation specific. Machinery, telephones, hair dryers, computers, diagnostic equipment, airport security detectors, toll gates, cooking ovens, bank ATMs, repair tools, and cash registers are among the many items whose absence in sufficient numbers for a given level of demand can bring service to a crawl or a complete stop.

4. *Labor*, a key element of productive capacity in all high-contact services and many low-contact ones, may be used for both physical and mental work. Staffing levels for customer-contact personnel, from restaurants to hospitals to customer service hotlines, need to be sufficient to meet anticipated demand; otherwise customers are kept waiting or service is rushed. Professional services are especially dependent on highly skilled staffs to create high value-added, information-based output. Abraham Lincoln captured it well when he remarked, "A lawyer's time and expertise are his stock in trade."

5. Many organizations are dependent on access to sufficient capacity in the public or private *infrastructure* to be able to deliver quality service to their own customers. Capacity problems of this nature may include busy telephone circuits, electrical power failures (or brown-outs caused by reduced voltage), congested airways that lead to air traffic restrictions on flights, and traffic jams on major highways.

Measuring Capacity

Measures of capacity utilization include the number of hours (or percentage of total available time) that facilities, labor, and equipment are productively employed in revenue operation, as well as the percentage of available space (e.g., seats, cubic freight capacity, and telecommunications bandwidth) that is actually utilized in revenue operations. Human beings tend to be far more variable than equipment in their ability to sustain consistent levels of output over time. One tired, unmotivated, or poorly trained employee who is staffing a single station in an assembly-line service operation like a cafeteria restaurant or a motor vehicle license bureau can slow the entire service to a crawl.

In a well-planned, well-managed service operation, the capacity of the facility, supporting equipment, and service personnel will be in balance. Similarly, sequential operations will be designed to minimize the likelihood of bottlenecks at any point in the process. In practice, however, it's difficult to achieve this ideal all the time.

Stretching and Shrinking the Level of Capacity

Some capacity is elastic in its ability to absorb extra demand. A subway car, for instance, may offer 40 seats and allow standing room for another 60 passengers with adequate handrail and floor space for all. Yet at rush hours, when there have been delays on the line, perhaps 200 standees can be accommodated under sardinelike conditions. Service personnel may be able to work at high levels of efficiency for short periods of time but would quickly tire and begin providing inferior service if they had to work that fast all day long.

Even where capacity appears fixed, as when it's based on the number of seats, there may still be opportunities to accept extra business at busy times. Some airlines, for instance, increase the capacity of their aircraft by slightly reducing leg room throughout the cabin and cramming in another couple of rows. Similarly a restaurant may add extra tables and chairs. Upper limits to such practices are often set by safety standards or by the capacity of supporting services, such as the kitchen.

Another strategy for stretching capacity within a given time frame is to utilize the facilities for longer periods—for example, restaurants that open at 5 P.M. for "early-bird" dinners and offer late suppers until midnight, universities that offer evening classes and summer programs, and airlines that extend their schedules from, say, 14 to 20 hours a day. Alternatively, the average amount of time that customers (or their possessions) spend in process may be reduced. Sometimes this is achieved by minimizing slack time, as when the bill is presented promptly to a group of diners who are relaxing at the table after a meal. At other times, it may be achieved by cutting back the level of service—offering, say, a simpler menu at busy times of day.

Chasing Demand

chase demand: adjusting the level of capacity to meet the level of demand at any given time.

Another set of options involves tailoring the overall level of capacity to match variations in demand, a strategy known as **chase demand**. Managers can take several actions to adjust capacity as needed:[1]

- *Schedule downtime during periods of low demand.* To ensure that 100 percent of capacity is available during peak periods, repair and renovations should be conducted when demand is expected to be low. Employee holidays should also be taken during such periods.

- *Use part-time employees.* Many organizations hire extra workers during their busiest periods for example, postal workers and retail shop assistants at Christmas, extra staff for tax preparation firms at the end of the financial year, and additional hotel employees during holiday periods and major conventions.

- *Rent or share extra facilities and equipment.* To limit investment in fixed assets, a service business may be able to rent extra space or machines at peak times. Firms with complementary demand patterns may enter into formal sharing agreements.

- *Cross-train employees.* Even when the service delivery system appears to be operating at full capacity, certain physical elements—and their attendant employees—may be underutilized. If employees can be cross-trained to perform a variety of tasks, they can be shifted to bottleneck points as needed, thereby increasing total system capacity. In supermarkets, for instance, the manager may call on stockers to operate cash registers when checkout queues start to get too long. Likewise, during slow periods, the cashiers may be asked to help stock shelves.

Creating Flexible Capacity

Sometimes, the problem lies not in the overall capacity but in the mix that's available to serve the needs of different market segments. For instance, on a given flight, an airline may have too few seats in economy even though there are empty places in business class; or a hotel may find itself short of suites one day when standard rooms are still available. One solution lies in designing physical facilities to be flexible. Some hotels build rooms with connecting doors. With the door between two rooms locked, the hotel can sell two bedrooms; with the door unlocked and one of the bedrooms converted into a sitting room, the hotel can now offer a suite.

Facing stiff competition from Airbus Industrie, the Boeing Company received what were described, tongue-in-cheek, as "outrageous demands" from prospective customers when it was designing its new 777 airliner. The airlines wanted an aircraft in which galleys and lavatories could be relocated (plumbing and all) almost anywhere in the cabin within a matter of hours. Boeing gulped but solved this challenging problem. Airlines can rearrange the passenger cabin of the "Triple Seven" quickly, reconfiguring it with varying numbers of seats allocated among one, two, or three classes.

One nice example of highly flexible capacity comes from an ecotourism operator in the south island of New Zealand. During the spring, summer, and early autumn months, the firm provides guided walks and treks, and during the snow season it offers cross-country skiing lessons and trips. Bookings all year round are processed through a contracted telephone-answering service, guides and instructors are employed on a part-time basis as required; the firm has negotiated agreements to use national park huts and cabins, and it has an exclusive arrangement with a local sports goods store whereby equipment can be hired or purchased by clients at preferential rates. As needed, charter bus service for groups can be arranged. Yet despite this capacity to provide a range of services, the owners' capital investment in the business is remarkably low.

UNDERSTANDING THE PATTERNS AND DETERMINANTS OF DEMAND[2]

Now let's look at the other side of the equation. To control variations in demand for a particular service, managers need to determine what factors govern the **demand cycle**. Research should begin by finding answers to a series of important questions about the patterns of demand and their underlying causes (see the box on patterns and causes of demand, p. 294).

demand cycle: a period of time during which the level of demand for a service will move up and down in a somewhat predictable fashion before repeating itself.

As you think about some of the seemingly random causes, consider how rain and cold affect the use of indoor and outdoor recreational or entertainment services. Then reflect on how heart attacks and births affect the demand for hospital services. Imagine what it is like to be a police officer, firefighter, or ambulance driver—you never know exactly where your next call will come from nor what the nature of the emergency will be. Finally, consider the impact of natural disasters, such as earthquakes, tornadoes, and hurricanes, not only on emergency services but also for disaster recovery specialists and insurance firms.

Multiple Influences on Demand

Most periodic cycles that affect demand for a particular service vary in length from one day to twelve months. Often, multiple cycles operate simultaneously. For example, demand levels for public transport may vary by time of day (highest during commuting hours), day of week (less travel to work on weekends but more leisure travel), and season of year (more travel by tourists in summer). The demand for service during the peak period on a Monday in summer may be different from that during the peak period on a Saturday in winter, reflecting day-of-week and seasonal variations jointly.

QUESTIONS ABOUT THE PATTERNS OF DEMAND AND THEIR UNDERLYING CAUSES

1. **Do demand levels follow a predictable cycle?** If so, is the duration of the demand cycle

   - one *day* (varies by hour)?
   - one *week* (varies by day)?
   - one *month* (varies by day or by week)?
   - one *year* (varies by month or by season or reflects annual public holidays)?
   - some other period?

2. **What are the underlying causes of these cyclical variations?**

   - employment schedules
   - billing and tax payment and refund cycles
   - wage and salary payment dates
   - school hours and vacations
   - seasonal changes in climate
   - occurrence of public or religious holidays
   - natural cycles, such as coastal tides

3. **Do demand levels seem to change randomly?** If so, could the underlying causes be

   - day-to-day changes in the weather?
   - health events whose occurrence cannot be pinpointed exactly?
   - accidents, fires, and certain criminal activities?
   - natural disasters, from earthquakes to storms to mud slides and volcanic eruptions?

4. **Can demand for a particular service over time be disaggregated by market segment** to reflect such components as

   - use patterns by a particular type of customer or for a particular purpose?
   - variations in the net profitability of each completed transaction?

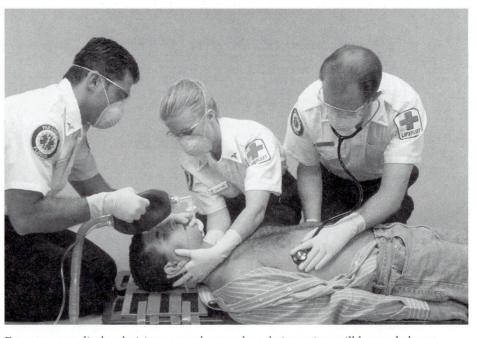

Emergency medical technicians never know when their services will be needed next.

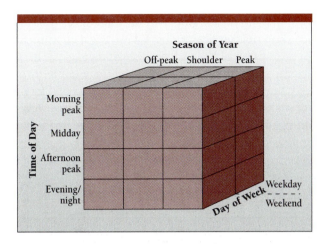

FIGURE 14.2
Identifying Variations in Demand by Time Period

Figure 14.2 shows how the combination of four time-of-day periods (morning peak, midday, afternoon peak, and evening or night), two day-of-week periods (weekday and weekend), and three seasonal periods (peak, shoulder, and off-peak) can be combined to create 24 different demand periods. In theory, each of these might have its own distinct demand level (at a given price) and customer profiles (with resulting differences in needs and expectations). But in practice, analysis might show close similarities between many of the periods. Such a finding would make it possible to collapse the framework into a total of perhaps three to six cells, each requiring a distinct marketing treatment to optimize the use of available capacity and obtain the most desirable customer mix.

Analyzing Demand

No strategy for smoothing demand is likely to succeed unless it's based on an understanding of why customers from a specific market segment choose to use the service when they do. It's difficult for hotels to convince business travelers to remain on Saturday nights because few executives do business over the weekend. Instead, hotel managers may do better to promote weekend use of their facilities for conferences or pleasure travel. Attempts to get commuters to shift their travel to off-peak periods will probably fail because this travel is determined by employment hours. Instead, efforts should be directed at employers to persuade them to adopt flextime, or staggered working hours. These firms recognize that no amount of price discounting is likely to develop business out of season. However, resort areas like Cape Cod may have good opportunities to build business during the "shoulder seasons" of spring and fall (which some consider the most attractive times to visit the Cape) by promoting different attractions—such as hiking, birdwatching, visiting museums, and looking for bargains in antique stores—and altering the mix and focus of services to target a different type of clientele.

Keeping good records of each transaction helps enormously in analyzing demand patterns in the past. Computer-based services, such as telecommunications, can track customers' consumption patterns by date and time of day automatically. Where relevant, it's also useful to record weather conditions and other special factors (a strike, an accident, a big convention in town, a price change, launch of a competing service, etc.) that might have influenced demand.

Random fluctuations are usually caused by factors beyond management's control, but analysis will sometimes reveal that a predictable demand cycle for one segment is concealed within a broader, seemingly random pattern. This fact illustrates the importance of breaking down demand on a segment-by-segment basis. For instance, a repair and maintenance shop that services industrial electrical equipment may already know that a certain proportion of its work consists of regularly scheduled contracts to perform preventive maintenance. The balance may come from walk-in business and emergency repairs. Although it might seem hard to predict or control the timing and volume of such work, further analysis could show that walk-in business was more prevalent on some days of the week than others and that emergency repairs frequently followed thunderstorms (which tend to be seasonal in nature and can often be forecast a day or two in advance). Not all demand is desirable. In fact, some requests for service are inappropriate and make it difficult for the organization to respond to the legitimate needs of its target customers (see the box on discouraging demand).

DISCOURAGING DEMAND FOR NONEMERGENCY CALLS

Have you ever wondered what it's like to be a dispatcher for an emergency service such as 911 in the United States or 999 in Britain? What is considered to be an emergency differs widely among different people.

Imagine yourself in the huge communications room at police headquarters in New York City. A gray-haired sergeant is talking patiently by phone to a woman who has dialed 911 because her cat has run up a tree and she's afraid it's stuck there. "Ma'am, have you ever seen a cat skeleton in a tree?" the sergeant asks her. "All those cats get down somehow, don't they?" After the woman has hung up, the sergeant turns to a visitor and shrugs. "These kinds of calls keep pouring in," he says. "What can you do?" The trouble is, when people call the emergency number with complaints about noisy parties next door, pleas to rescue cats, or requests to turn off leaking fire hydrants, they may be slowing response times to fires, heart attacks, or violent crimes.

At one point, the situation in New York City was so bad that officials were forced to develop a marketing campaign to discourage people from making inappropriate requests for emergency assistance through the 911 number. The problem was that what might seem to be an emergency to the caller—a beloved cat stuck in a tree or a noisy party that was preventing a tired person from getting needed sleep—was not a life- (or property-) threatening situation of the type that the city's emergency services were poised to resolve. Therefore, a communications campaign, using a variety of media, was developed to urge people not to call 911 unless they were reporting a dangerous emergency. For help in resolving other problems, they were asked to call their local police station or other city agencies. The following advertisement appeared on New York buses and subways.

SAVE 911 for the real thing
CALL YOUR PRECINCT OR CITY AGENCY
WHEN IT'S NOT A <u>DANGEROUS</u> EMERGENCY
(noisy party, open hydrant, abandoned car, etc.)
911 NEW YORK CITY'S DANGEROUS EMERGENCY NUMBER

Discouraging **undesirable demand** through marketing campaigns or screening procedures, of course, will not eliminate random fluctuations in the remaining demand. But it may help to keep peak demand levels within the service capacity of the organization.

undesirable demand: requests for service that conflict with the organization's mission, priorities, or capabilities.

STRATEGIES FOR MANAGING DEMAND

Many services, such as health care or repair and maintenance, involve multiple actions delivered sequentially. What this means is that a service organization's capacity to satisfy demand is constrained by one or more of its physical facilities, equipment, and personnel and by the number and sequence of services provided. Consequently, financial success in capacity-constrained businesses is, in large measure, a function of management's ability to use productive capacity—staff, labor, equipment, and facilities—as efficiently and as profitably as possible.

Services involving tangible actions to customers or their possessions are likely to be subject to capacity constraints than are information-based services. In the latter, however, similar capacity problems may occur when customers are obliged to go to a service site for delivery, as in live entertainment or traditional retail banking.

In a well-designed, well-managed service operation, the capacity of the facility, supporting equipment, and service personnel will be in balance. Similarly, sequential operations will be designed to minimize the risk of bottlenecks at any point in the process. This ideal, however, may prove difficult to achieve. Not only does the level of demand vary over time, often randomly, but also the time and effort required to process each person or thing may vary widely at any point in the process. In general, processing times for people are more variable than for objects or things, reflecting varying levels of preparedness ("I've lost my credit card"), argumentative versus cooperative personalities ("If you won't give me a table with a view, I'll have to ask for your supervisor"), and so forth. But service tasks are not necessarily homogeneous. In both professional services and repair work, diagnosis and treatment times vary according to the nature of the customers' problems.

Dividing Up Demand by Market Segment

Can marketing efforts smooth out random fluctuations in demand? The answer is generally no because these fluctuations usually are caused by factors beyond the organization's control. But detailed market analysis sometimes may reveal that a predictable demand cycle for one segment is concealed within a broader, seemingly random pattern. For example, a retail store might experience wide swings in daily patronage, but a core group of customers visits every weekday to buy staple items like newspapers and candy.

The ease with which total demand can be broken down into smaller components depends on the nature of the records kept by management. If each customer transaction is recorded separately and backed up by detailed notes (as in a medical or dental visit or an accountant's audit), the task of understanding demand is greatly simplified. In subscription and charge account services, when each customer's identity is known and itemized monthly bills are sent, managers can gain some immediate insights into usage patterns. Some services, such as telephone and electrical, even have the ability to track subscriber consumption patterns by time of day. Although these data may not always yield specific information on the purpose for which the service is being used, it is often possible to make informed judgments about the volume of sales generated by different user groups.

Managing Demand under Different Conditions

There are five basic approaches to managing demand. The first, which has the virtue of simplicity but little else, involves *taking no action and leaving demand to find its own levels*. Eventually customers learn from experience or word of mouth when they can expect to stand in line to use the service and when it will be available without delay. The trouble is, they may also learn to find a competitor who is more responsive. More interventionist approaches involve influencing the level of demand at any given time by taking active steps to *reduce demand in peak periods* and to *increase demand when there is excess capacity*.

Two more approaches both involve *inventory of demand until capacity becomes available*. A firm can accomplish this either by introducing a booking or *reservations system*, which promises access to capacity at specified times, or by *creating formalized queuing systems* (or by a combination of the two).

Table 14.1 links these five approaches to the two problems of excess demand and excess capacity and provides a brief strategic commentary on each. Many service businesses face both situations at different points in the cycle of demand and should consider the interventionist strategies described.

TABLE 14.1   Alternative Demand Management Strategies for Different Capacity Situations

Approach Used to Manage Demand	Capacity Situation Relative to Demand	
	Insufficient Capacity (Excess Demand)	Excess Capacity (Insufficient Demand)
Take no action	Unorganized queuing results (may irritate customers and discourage future use)	Capacity is wasted (customers may have a disappointing experience for services like theater)
Reduce demand	Higher prices will increase profits; communication can encourage usage in other time slots (can this effort be focused on less profitable and desirable segments?)	Take no action (but see above)
Increase demand	Take no action, unless opportunities exist to stimulate (and give priority to) more profitable segments	Lower prices selectively (try to avoid cannibalizing existing business; ensure all relevant costs are covered); use communications and variation in products and distribution (but recognize extra costs, if any, and make sure appropriate trade-offs are made between profitability and usage levels)
Inventory demand by reservation system	Consider priority system for most desirable segments; make other customers shift to outside peak period or to future peak	Clarify that space is available and that no reservations are needed
Inventory demand by formalized queuing	Consider override for most desirable segments; try to keep waiting customers occupied and comfortable; try to predict wait period accurately	Not applicable

Using Marketing Strategies to Shape Demand Patterns

Four of the 8Ps have a part in stimulating demand during periods of excess capacity and in decreasing it (demarketing) during periods of insufficient capacity. Price is often the first variable to be proposed for bringing demand and supply into balance, but changes in product, distribution strategy, and communication efforts can also play an important role. Although each element is discussed separately, effective demand management often requires changes in two or more elements jointly.

Price and other costs.   One of the most direct ways of reducing excess demand at peak periods is to charge customers more money to use the service during those periods. Other costs, too, may have a similar effect. For instance, if customers learn that they are likely to face increased costs in time and effort during peak periods, those who dislike spending time in crowded and unpleasant conditions may decide to try later. Similarly, the lure of cheaper prices and an expectation of no waiting may encourage at least some people to change the timing of their behavior, whether it entails shopping, travel, or visiting a museum.

Some firms use pricing strategy in sophisticated ways in order to balance supply and demand. For the monetary price of a service to be effective as a demand management tool, managers must have some sense of the shape and slope of a product's demand curve—that is, how the quantity of service demanded responds to increases or decreases in the price per unit at a particular time (Figure 14.3 shows a sample demand curve). It's important to determine whether the demand curve for a specific service varies sharply from one time period to another (will the same person be willing to pay more for a weekend stay in a hotel on Cape Cod in summer than in winter? The answer is probably yes). If so, significantly different pricing schemes may be needed to fill capacity in each time period. To complicate matters further, there may be separate demand curves for different segments within each time period (business travelers are usually less price sensitive than vacationers).

One of the most difficult tasks for service marketers is to determine the nature of all these different demand curves. Research, trial and error, and analysis of parallel situations in other locations or in comparable services are all ways of learning

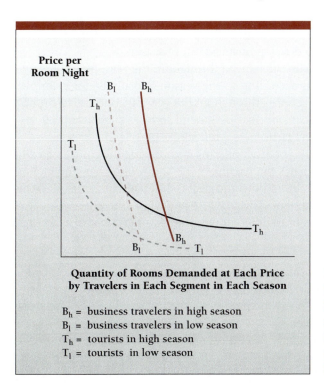

**Quantity of Rooms Demanded at Each Price
by Travelers in Each Segment in Each Season**

B_h = business travelers in high season
B_l = business travelers in low season
T_h = tourists in high season
T_l = tourists in low season

FIGURE 14.3

**Differing Demand Curves
for Business Travelers
and Tourists in High and
Low Seasons
(Hypothetical Hotel
Example)**

to understand the situation. Many service businesses explicitly recognize the existence of different demand curves by establishing distinct classes of service, each priced at levels appropriate to the demand curve of a particular segment. In essence, each segment receives a variation of the basic product, with value being added to the core service through supplementary services to appeal to higher-paying segments. For instance, first-class service on airlines offers travelers larger seats, free drinks, and better food; in computer and printing firms, product enhancement takes the form of faster turnaround and more specialized services; and in hotels, a distinction is made between rooms of different sizes and amenities and with different views.

In each case, the objective is to maximize the revenues received from each segment. When capacity is constrained, however, the goal in a profit-seeking business should be to ensure that as much capacity as possible is utilized by the most profitable segments available at any given time. Airlines, for instance, hold a certain number of seats for business passengers, who pay full fare, and place restrictive conditions on excursion fares for tourists (such as requiring advance purchase and a Saturday night stay) to prevent business travelers from taking advantage of cheap fares designed to attract tourists, who can help fill the aircraft. Pricing strategies of this nature are known as *yield management* and are discussed in the following chapter.

Product elements.   Although pricing is often a commonly advocated method of balancing supply and demand, it is not quite as universally feasible for services as for goods. A rather obvious example is provided by the respective problems of a ski manufacturer and a ski slope operator during the summer. The former can either produce for inventory or try to sell skis in the summer at a discount. If the skis are sufficiently discounted, some customers will buy before the ski season to save money. However, in the absence of skiing opportunities, no skiers would buy lift tickets on a midsummer day at any price. So, to encourage summer use of the lifts, the operator has to change the service product offering (see the box on ski slopes in the summer).

There is similar thinking in a variety of other seasonal businesses. Tax preparation firms offer bookkeeping and consulting services to small businesses in slack months, educational institutions offer weekend and summer programs for adults and senior citizens, and small pleasure boats offer cruises in the summer and a dockside venue for private functions in the winter. These firms recognize that no amount of price discounting is likely to develop business out of season.

Many service offerings remain unchanged throughout the year, but others undergo significant modifications according to the season. Hospitals, for example, usually offer the same array of services throughout the year. In contrast, resort hotels sharply alter the mix and focus of their peripheral services such as dining, entertainment, and sports to reflect customers' preferences in different seasons.

There can be variations in the product offering even during the course of a 24-hour period. Some restaurants mark the passing of the hours with changing menus and levels of service, variations in lighting and decor, different bar hours, and the presence or absence of entertainment. The goal is to appeal to different needs within the same group of customers or to different customer segments or both, according to the time of day.

Modification of the place and time of delivery.   Rather than trying to modify demand for a service that continues to be offered at the same time in the same place, some firms respond to market needs by modifying the time and place of delivery. Three basic options are available.

The first is a strategy of *no change:* Regardless of the level of demand, the service continues to be offered in the same location at the same times. A second strategy *varies*

SUMMER ON THE SKI SLOPES

Ski resorts used to shut down once the snow melted and the slopes became unskiable. The chair lifts stopped operating, the restaurants closed, and the lodges were locked and shuttered until winter approached. In time, however, some ski operators recognized that a mountain offers summer pleasures, too, and kept lodging and restaurants open for hikers and picknickers. Some even built Alpine slides—curving tracks in which wheeled toboggans could run from the summit to the base—and thus created demand for tickets on the ski lifts. With the construction of condominiums for sale, demand increased for warm-weather activities as the owners flocked to the mountains in summer and early fall.

The arrival of the mountain-biking craze in the 1980s created opportunities for equipment rentals as well as chairlift rides. Killington Resort in Vermont has long encouraged summer visitors to ride to the summit, see the view, and eat at the mountaintop restaurant, but now it also rents mountain bikes and related equipment like helmets. In or near the base lodge, where, in winter, skiers would find rack after rack of skis for rent, the summer visitor can now choose from rows of mountain bikes. Bikers transport their vehicles up to the summit on specially equipped lifts, and then ride them down designated trails. Serious hikers reverse the process—climbing to the summit on trails that avoid descending bikes, getting refreshments at the restaurant, and then taking the chair lift back down to the base. Once in a while, a biker will actually choose to ride up the mountain, but such gluttons for punishment are few and far between.

Most large ski resorts look for a variety of additional ways to attract guests to their hotels and rental homes during the summer. Mont Tremblant, Quebec, for instance, is located beside an attractive lake. In addition to swimming and other water sports on the lake, the resort offers such activities as a championship golf course, tennis, roller blading, and a children's day camp—and hikers and mountain bikers come to ride the lifts up the mountain.

Riding the chair lift up Mont Tremblant to hike and bike rather than ski.

the service schedule to reflect changes in customer preference by day of week, by season, and so forth. Theaters and cinema complexes often offer matinées at weekends, when people have more leisure time throughout the day; during the summer, cafés and restaurants may stay open later because of daylight saving time and the general inclination of people to enjoy the longer, balmier evenings outdoors; and shops may extend their hours before Christmas or during school holidays.

A third strategy involves *offering the service to customers at a new location.* One approach is to operate mobile units that take the service to customers rather than requiring them to visit fixed service locations. Traveling libraries, mobile car wash services, in-office tailoring services, home-delivered meals and catering services, and vans equipped with primary care medical facilities are examples. A cleaning and repair firm that wishes to generate business during low demand periods might offer free pickup and delivery of portable items that need servicing. Service firms whose productive assets are mobile may choose to follow the market when that, too, is mobile. For instance, some car rental firms establish seasonal branch offices in resort communities. In these new locations, they often change the schedule of service hours (as well as certain product features) to conform to local needs and preferences.

Promotion and education.   Even if the other variables of the marketing mix remain unchanged, communication efforts alone may be able to help smooth demand. Signs, advertising, publicity, and sales messages can be used to educate customers about the timing of peak periods and encourage them to use the service at off-peak times, when there will be fewer delays. Examples include post office requests to "Mail early for Christmas," public transport messages urging noncommuters—such as shoppers or tourists—to avoid the crush during rush hours; and communications from sales representatives for industrial maintenance firms that advise customers when preventive maintenance work can be done quickly. In addition, management can ask service personnel (or intermediaries like travel agents) to encourage customers with discretionary schedules to favor off-peak periods.

Changes in pricing, product characteristics, and distribution must be communicated clearly. If a firm wants to obtain a specific response to variations in marketing mix elements, it must, of course, inform customers fully about their options. As discussed in chapter 12, short-term promotions, combining both pricing and communication elements, as well as other incentives, may give customers attractive incentives to shift the timing of service use.

Conclusion

Several of the 8Ps of integrated service management underlie the discussion in this chapter. The first is *productivity and quality*. Because many capacity-constrained service organizations have heavy fixed costs, even modest improvements in capacity utilization can have a significant effect on the bottom line. Managers can transform fixed costs into variable costs through such strategies as using rented facilities or part-time labor. Creating a more flexible approach to productive capacity allows a firm to adopt a strategy of chase demand, thereby improving productivity. However, managers need to be careful not to lower service quality by trying to squeeze in too many customers.

Decisions on *place* and *time* are closely associated with balancing demand and capacity. Demand is often a function of where the service is located and when it is offered. As in the Cape Cod example, the appeal of many destinations varies with the seasons. Marketing strategies involving *product elements, price and other costs*, and *promotion and education* are often useful in managing the level of demand for a service at a particular place and time.

In the following chapter, we address strategies for regulating demand by queuing and reservations systems, as well as the role of reservations in yield management strategies.

Study Questions and Exercises

1. Review each of the services described in the opening description of Cape Cod. Are there any that might attract increased business in winter? Is so, what strategy would you recommend to build winter time demand? (Be realistic!)
2. Why is capacity management particularly significant in a service setting?

3. What is meant by *chasing demand*?
4. What does *inventory* mean for service firms and why is it perishable?
5. Give examples of several service firms (other than those described in this chapter) that use *flexible capacity* strategies to balance supply and demand.
6. Select a service organization of your choice and identify its particular patterns of demand with reference to Figure 14.1.
    a. What is the nature of this service organization's approach to capacity and demand management?
    b. What changes would you recommend in relation to its management of capacity and demand and why?
7. Name some specific companies in your community (or region) that change their pricing to encourage patronage during what would otherwise be periods of low demand.
8. What marketing and management challenges are raised by the use of intermediaries in a service setting?

CHAPTER Fifteen

Managing Waiting Lines and Reservations

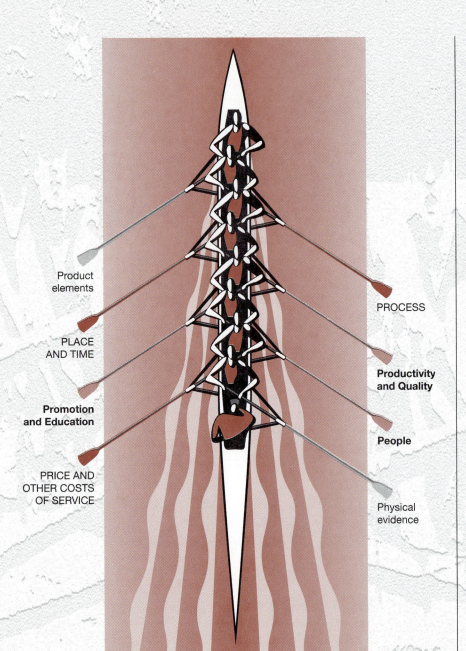

Product elements

PLACE AND TIME

Promotion and Education

PRICE AND OTHER COSTS OF SERVICE

PROCESS

Productivity and Quality

People

Physical evidence

Learning Objectives

After reading this chapter, you should be able to

■ understand how well-designed environments can reduce the perceived burden of waiting for service

■ recognize the several different designs of queues

■ calculate expected waiting times under defined conditions

■ know the basics of designing an effective reservation system

■ understand the principles of yield management and the use of segmented reservations to improve profitability

Cutting the Wait at First National Bank of Chicago[1]

How should a big retail bank respond to increased competition from new financial service providers? The First National Bank of Chicago decided that enhancing service to its customers would be an important element in its strategy. One opportunity for improvement was to reduce the amount of time that customers spent waiting in line for service in the bank's retail branches—a frequent source of complaints. Recognizing that no single action could resolve the problem satisfactorily, the bank adopted a three-pronged approach.

First, technological improvements were made to the service operation, starting with the introduction of an electronic queuing system, which not only routed customers to the next available teller but also gave supervisors on-line information to help match staffing to customer demand. Also, computer enhancements provided tellers with more information about their customers, enabling them to handle more requests without leaving their stations. New cash machines for tellers saved them from selecting bills and counting them twice (yielding a time savings of 30 seconds for each cash withdrawal transaction).

Second, changes were made in human resource strategies. The bank adopted a new job description for teller managers that made them responsible for customer queuing times and for expediting transactions. It created an officer-of-the-day program, under which a designated officer, equipped with a beeper, was assigned to help staff with complicated transactions that might otherwise slow them down. A new job category of peak-time teller was introduced, paying premium wages for 12 to 18 hours of work a week. Existing full-time tellers were given cash incentives and recognition to reward improved productivity on predicted high-volume days. Moreover, management reorganized meal arrangements. On busy days, lunch breaks were reduced to half-hour periods and the staff received catered meals; also, the bank cafeteria was opened earlier to serve peak-time tellers.

A third set of changes centered on customer-oriented improvements to the delivery system. Quick-drop desks were established on busy days to handle deposits and simple requests, and newly created express teller stations were reserved for deposits and check cashing. Lobby hours were expanded from 38 to 56 hours a week, including Sundays. A customer brochure, "How to Lose Wait," alerted customers to busy periods and suggested ways of avoiding delays.

Subsequently, internal measures and customer surveys showed that the improvements had not only reduced wait times but also increased customer perceptions that First Chicago was "the best" bank in the region for minimal waits. The bank also found that adoption of extended hours had deflected some of the noon rush to before-work and after-work periods.

WAITING TO GET PROCESSED

You asked for a table for two last Saturday at a restaurant but were told that there would be a 40-minute wait; no washing machines were available when you went to the laundromat last night; your travel agent told you the flight you wanted to take on vacation was fully booked; and the line to get into the latest hit movie stretches around the block. Groan! A friend's car is having problems, but the local garage told her that mechanics can't deal with it until next Tuesday. At least that is better than the plumber, who cannot get to your apartment to fix that annoying drip for another 10 days. Calling another airline to check on schedules, you were put on hold and had to listen to a combination of canned music and ads for Florida vacations for nine minutes. That delay came on top of the six minutes you waited in line in the bookstore at lunchtime to pay for books and the extra 25 minutes you waited this afternoon at your doctor's office beyond the appointment time you set up three weeks ago. Life is such a hassle! You begin to understand road rage.

All these disappointments result from too many people wanting the same service at the same time. One of the challenges of services is that, being performances, they cannot normally be stored for later use. A teller at the First National Bank of Chicago cannot prepackage a check-cashing transaction for the following day; it must be done in real time. In an ideal world, nobody would ever have to wait to conduct a transaction at First Chicago (or at any other service organization). But firms cannot afford to provide extensive extra capacity that would be unutilized most of the time. As shown in the previous chapter, there are a variety of procedures for bringing demand and supply into balance. But what is a manager to do when the possibilities for shaping demand and adjusting capacity have been exhausted and yet supply and demand are still out of balance? Not taking any action and leaving customers to sort things out is no recipe for service quality or customer satisfaction. Rather than allowing matters to degenerate into a random free-for-all, customer-oriented firms must try to develop strategies for ensuring order, predictability, and fairness.

In those businesses in which demand regularly exceeds supply, managers can often take steps to inventory demand. This task can be achieved in one of two ways: (1) by asking customers to wait in line (queuing), usually on a first-come, first-served basis, or (2) by offering them the opportunity to reserve or book space in advance.

STEALING THE CUSTOMER'S TIME

It's estimated that Americans spend 37 billion hours a year (an average of almost 150 hours per person) waiting in lines, "during which time they fret, fidget, and scowl," according to the *Washington Post*.[2] Similar or worse situations seem to prevail around the world. Richard Larson suggests that when everything is added up, the average person may spend as much as one-half hour per day waiting in line, which would translate to 20 months of waiting in an 80-year lifetime.[3]

Nobody likes to be kept waiting. It's boring, time wasting, and sometimes physically uncomfortable, especially if there is nowhere to sit or you are outside. In short, it has a negative impact on service quality. Yet waiting for a service process is an almost universal phenomenon: Virtually every organization faces the problem of waiting lines somewhere in its operation. People are kept waiting on the phone, they line up with their supermarket carts to check out their grocery purchases, and they wait for their bills after a restaurant meal. They sit in their cars, waiting for traffic lights to change, to enter drive-in car washes, and to pay at toll booths.

Physical and inanimate objects wait for processing, too: Letters pile up on an executive's desk; shoes sit on racks waiting to be repaired at the shoe repair store; checks wait to be cleared at a bank; an incoming phone call waits to be switched

to a customer service representative. In each instance, a customer may be waiting for the outcome of the work—an answer to a letter, a pair of shoes, a credited check, or a useful conversation (instead of being kept on hold, listening to a recorded message that keeps repeating, "Your call is important to us").

The Nature of Queues

A waiting line—known to operations researchers (and also the British) as a **queue**—occurs whenever the number of arrivals at a facility exceeds the capacity of the system to process them. In a very real sense, queues are basically a symptom of unresolved capacity management problems, sometimes reflecting a deliberate policy of cost containment and productivity improvement without regard for the quality of customers' service experiences.

queue: a line of people, vehicles, other physical objects, or intangible items waiting their turn to be served or to proceed.

The analysis and modeling of queues is a well-established branch of operations management. Queuing theory has been traced to 1917, when a Danish telephone engineer was charged with determining how large the switching unit in a telephone system had to be to keep the number of busy signals within reason.[4] Not all queues take the form of a physical line in a single location. When customers deal with a service supplier at arm's length, as in information-processing services, they call from home, office, or college, using telecommunication channels like voice telephone or the Internet. Typically, calls are answered in the order received, often requiring customers to wait their turn in a virtual line. Some physical queues are geographically dispersed. Travelers wait at many different locations for the taxis they have ordered by phone to arrive and pick them up.

The advent of sophisticated Web sites now makes it possible for people to do things for themselves, such as obtaining information or making reservations, that formerly required calling on the telephone or visiting a service facility in person. Companies often promote the time savings that can be obtained. Although accessing the Web can be slow sometimes, at least the wait is conducted while the customer is comfortably seated and able to attend to other matters.

Increasing capacity by adding more tellers was only one of several actions taken to reduce waiting times at First National Bank of Chicago. But adding extra servers is not always the optimal solution in situations in which customer satisfaction must be balanced against cost considerations. Like First Chicago, managers should consider a variety of alternatives, such as

- rethinking the design of the queuing system
- redesigning processes to shorten the time of each transaction
- managing customers' behavior and their perceptions of the wait
- installing a reservations system

Elements of a Queuing System[5]

We can divide queuing systems into seven elements, as shown in Figure 15.1 (p. 308). Let's take a look at each, recognizing that strategies for managing waiting lines can exercise more control over some elements than others.

Customer population.   When planning queuing systems, operations managers need to know who their customers are and something about their needs and expectations. There is, obviously, a big difference between a badly injured patient arriving at a hospital emergency unit and a sports fan arriving at a stadium ticket office. Although neither are inanimate physical objects at a repair shop that, in theory, could be left to wait for several weeks, the hospital needs to be more geared for

United Airlines advises customers to make reservations and select seats on their own computers to avoid waiting in line at the airport.

FIGURE 15.1 Elements of a Queuing System

1. The *customer population* from which demands for service originate (sometimes known to operations researchers as the calling population)
2. The *arrival process*—times and volumes of requests for service
3. *Balking*—decision by an arriving customer not to join the queue
4. *Queue configuration*—design of the system in terms of the number, location, and arrangement of lines
5. *Reneging*—decision by a customer already in the queue to leave rather than wait any longer
6. *Customer selection policies*—formal or ad hoc policies of whom to serve next (also known as queue discipline)
7. The *service process*—physical design of the service delivery system, roles assigned to customers and service personnel, and the flexibility to vary system capacity

speed than the stadium. Based on customer research, the population can often be divided into several distinct market segments, each with differing needs and priorities.

Arrival process.   The rate at which customers arrive over time—relative to the capacity of the serving process—and the extent to which they arrive individually or in clusters will determine whether or not a queue starts to form. We need to draw a distinction between the *average* arrival rate (e.g., 60 customers per hour = one customer every minute) and the *distribution* of the arrivals during any given time period. In some instances, arrival times are largely random (e.g., individuals entering a store in a shopping mall); in other instances, some degree of clustering can be predicted, such as arrivals of students in a cafeteria within a few minutes of the end of classes. Managers who anticipate surges of activity at specific times can plan their staff allocations around them, for example, opening an additional checkout line.

Balking.   If you're like most people, you tend to be put off by a long line at a service facility and may often decide to come back later (or go somewhere else). Sometimes balking is a mistake, as the line may actually be moving faster than you think. Managers can disguise the length of lines by having them wind around corners, as often occurs at theme parks. Alternatively, they may indicate the expected waiting time from specific locations in the queuing area by installing information signs.

balking: a decision by a customer not to join a queue because the wait appears to be too long.

Queue configuration.   There are many different types of queues. The following are common ones, which you may have experienced yourself in people-processing services (see also Figure 15.2, p. 310, for diagrams of each type):

queue configuration: the way in which waiting lines are organized.

- *Single line, single stage.* Customers wait to conduct a single service transaction, for example, waiting for a bus or at a single ticket window.
- *Single line, sequential stages.* Customers proceed through several serving operations, as in a cafeteria line. In these systems, bottlenecks will occur at any stage where the process takes longer to execute than at previous stages. Many cafeterias have lines at the cash register because the cashier takes longer to calculate how much you owe and to make change than the servers take to slap food on your plate.
- *Parallel lines to multiple servers (single or sequential stages).* This system offers more than one serving station, allowing customers to select one of several lines in which to wait. Fast-food restaurants usually have several serving lines in operation at busy times of day, each offering the full menu. A parallel system can have either a single stage or multiple stages. The disadvantage of this design is that lines may not move at equal speed. How many times have you chosen what seemed to be the shortest line only to watch in frustration as the lines on either side of you moved much faster because someone in your line had a complicated transaction?
- *Designated lines.* Different lines can be assigned to specific categories of customer, for example, express lines (say, six items or less) and regular lines at supermarket checkouts and different check-in lines for first-class, business-class, and economy-class airline passengers.
- *Single line to multiple servers ("snake").* Customers wait in a single line, often winding sinuously back and forth between rope barriers (hence the name). As each person reaches the head of the queue, he or she is directed to the next available serving position. This approach is encountered frequently in bank lobbies, post offices, and airport check-ins. Its big advantages are

FIGURE 15.2 Alternative Queuing Configurations

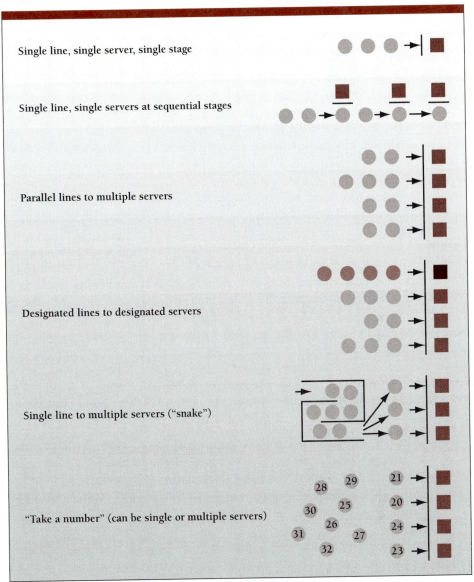

fairness and reduced anxiety. The presence of ropes or other barriers makes it difficult for inconsiderate people to break into line. At the margin, it may also discourage people from leaving the line.

■ *Take a number.* In this variation of the single line, arriving customers take a number and are then called in sequence, thus saving the need to stand in a queue. This procedure allows them to sit down and relax (if seating is available) or to guess how long the wait will be and do something else in the meantime (but risk losing their place). Users of this approach include large travel agents or specialized departments in supermarkets, such as the butcher or baker.

Hybrid approaches to queue configuration also exist. For instance, a cafeteria with a single serving line might offer two cash registers at the final stage. Similarly, patients at a small medical clinic might visit a single receptionist for registration; proceed sequentially through multiple channels for testing, diagnosis, and treatment; and conclude by returning to a single line for payment at the receptionist's desk.

Reneging. You know the situation (perhaps all too well). The line is not that long, but it's moving at a snail's pace. The man at the front of the queue has been there for at least five minutes and his problem seems nowhere near solution. There are two other people ahead of you, and you have an uneasy feeling that their transactions are not going to be brief either. You look at your watch for the third time and realize that you only have a few minutes left before your next appointment. Frustrated, you leave the line. In the language of queue management, you have reneged. One of the things planners need to determine is how long a wait has to be before customers are likely to start reneging. The consequences may include irritated customers who will return later, as well as lost business.

Customer selection policies. Most waiting lines work on the principle of first come, first served. Customers tend to expect this—it's only fair, after all. In many cultures (but not all), people get very resentful if they see later arrivals being served ahead of them for no good reason. There are, however, some valid exceptions. Medical services will give priority to emergency cases, and airline personnel will allow passengers whose flights are due to leave soon to check in ahead of passengers taking later flights.

Service process. Poorly designed service processes can lead to waits that are longer and more burdensome than necessary. All of the elements of the service system discussed in chapter 3 come into play here. The root cause for waits is sometimes found in one or more delays behind the scenes, so that customer-contact employees are themselves kept waiting for a necessary action to occur somewhere else in the system. Flowcharts, employee interviews, and analysis of past service failures can help to pinpoint where such problems might occur. The physical design of the front-stage service delivery system (refer to chapters 3 and 9) plays a key role in effective queue management. Important design issues include

1. how customers are served—batch processes serve customers in groups, whereas flow processes serve them individually
2. whether customers will be served by personnel, by equipment (self-service), or by a combination of the two
3. how fast service transactions can be executed (thus determining capacity)
4. whether service comes to the customers or whether they must come to the service site and move from one step to another
5. the quality of the serving and waiting experience, including personal comfort and such design issues as the impression created by the servicescape (see chapter 9)

Matching Queuing Systems to Market Segments

The basic rule in most (but not all) queuing systems is first come, first served. Market segmentation is sometimes used to design queuing strategies that set different priorities for different types of customers. Allocation to separate queuing areas may be based on

- *urgency of the job*—at many hospital emergency units, a triage nurse is assigned to greet incoming patients and decide which ones require priority medical treatment and which can safely be asked to register and wait their turn
- *duration of service transaction*—banks, supermarkets, and other retail services often institute express lanes for shorter, less complicated tasks
- *payment of a premium price*—airlines usually offer separate check-in lines for first-class and economy-class passengers, with a higher ratio of personnel to

reneging: a decision by a customer to leave a queue before reaching its end because the wait is proving to be longer or more burdensome than originally anticipated.

She was lucky and got straight through the checkout line without having to wait.

passengers in the first-class line, resulting in reduced waits for those who have paid more for their tickets

■ *importance of the customer*—a special area may be reserved for members of frequent user clubs; airlines often provide lounges, offering newspapers and free refreshments, where frequent flyers can wait for their flights in greater comfort.

MINIMIZING THE PERCEIVED LENGTH OF THE WAIT

Operations managers should know better than to treat people who are waiting for service like inanimate objects (although that doesn't stop some organizations from doing so!). As we saw in chapter 11, customers view the time and effort spent on consuming services as a cost. People don't like wasting their time on unproductive activities, any more than they like wasting money. They also prefer to avoid unwanted mental or physical effort, including anxiety or discomfort. The unwanted costs of waiting reduces the value of a service and may be equated with poor quality.

Research shows that people often think they have waited longer for a service than they actually have. Studies of public transportation, for instance, have shown that travelers perceive time spent waiting for a bus or train as passing from one and a half to seven times more slowly than the time actually spent traveling in the vehicle.[6]

The Psychology of Waiting Time

The noted philosopher William James, observed, "Boredom results from being attentive to the passage of time itself." Based on this observation, David Maister formulated eight principles about waiting time.[7] Adding two additional principles gives us a total of 10, summarized in Figure 15.3. Let's examine each proposition in turn and review some appropriate actions.

Unoccupied time feels longer than occupied time.   When you're sitting around with nothing to do, time seems to crawl. The challenge for service organizations is to give customers something to do or to distract them while they are waiting. Doc-

FIGURE 15.3 **Ten Propositions on the Psychology of Waiting Lines**

1. Unoccupied time feels longer than occupied time
2. Preprocess waiting and postprocess waiting feels longer than in-process waiting
3. Anxiety makes waiting seem longer
4. Uncertain waiting is longer than known, finite waiting
5. Unexplained waiting is longer than explained waiting
6. Unfair waiting is longer than equitable waiting
7. The more valuable the service, the longer people will wait
8. Solo waiting feels longer than group waiting
9. Physically uncomfortable waiting feels longer than comfortable waiting
10. Waiting seems longer to new or occasional users than to frequent users

tors and dentists stock their waiting rooms with piles of magazines (all too often, many months old and irrelevant to patients' interests) for people to read. Car repair facilities may have a television for customers to watch. One tire dealer goes further, providing free popcorn, soft drinks, coffee, and ice cream. Theme parks supply roving bands of entertainers to amuse customers waiting for the most popular attractions.

Preprocess and postprocess waiting feels longer than in-process waiting. There's a difference between waiting to buy a ticket to enter a theme park and waiting to ride on a roller coaster once you're inside. There's also a difference between waiting for coffee to arrive near the end of a restaurant meal and waiting for the server to bring you the check once you're ready to leave. Rental car firms sometimes start the process early by assigning an agent to obtain information on customers' needs while they wait in line; in that way, service delivery—namely, assigning a specific car—can begin as soon as each person reaches the head of the line. These firms also try to minimize customer waiting when the car is returned, employing agents with wireless, hand-held terminals to meet customers in the parking area, enter fuel and mileage, and then compute and print bills on the spot.

preprocess waiting: waiting before service delivery begins.

postprocess waiting: waiting after service delivery has been completed.

in-process waiting: waiting during service delivery.

Customers must wait in line even at fast-food restaurants, but they can pass the time studying the menu.

Anxiety makes waiting seem longer. Can you remember waiting to meet someone and worrying about whether the time or the location was correct? While waiting in unfamiliar locations, especially outside and after dark, people often worry about their personal safety.

Uncertain waiting is longer than known, finite waiting. Although any wait may be frustrating, we can usually adjust mentally to a wait of known length. It's the unknown that keeps us on edge. Imagine waiting for a delayed flight and not being told how long the delay is going to be. You don't know whether you have time to walk around the terminal or whether to stay at the gate in case the flight is called.

Unexplained waiting is longer than explained waiting. Have you ever been in a subway or elevator that has stopped for no apparent reason? Not only is there uncertainty about the length of the wait, there is also added worry about what is going to happen. Has there been an accident on the line? Will you have to leave the train in the tunnel? Is the elevator broken? Will you be stuck for hours in close proximity with strangers?

Unfair waiting is longer than equitable waiting. Expectations about what is fair or unfair sometimes vary from one culture or country to another. In countries like the United States, Canada, or Britain, for example, people expect everybody to wait one's turn in line and are likely to get irritated if they see others jumping ahead or being given priority for no apparent good reason.

The more valuable the service, the longer people will wait. People will queue overnight under uncomfortable conditions to get good seats at a major concert or sports event that is expected to sell out.

Solo waiting feels longer than group waiting. Waiting with one or more people you know is reassuring. Conversation with friends can help to pass the time; not everyone is comfortable talking to a stranger.

Physically uncomfortable waiting feels longer than comfortable waiting.[8] "My feet are killing me!" is one of the most frequently heard comments when people are forced to stand in line for a long time. And whether seated or unseated, a wait seems more burdensome if the temperature is too hot or too cold, if it's drafty or windy, and if there is no protection from rain or snow.

Unfamiliar waiting seems longer than familiar waiting.[9] Frequent users of a service know what to expect and are less likely to worry while waiting. New or occasional users of a service, in contrast, are often nervous, wondering not only about the probable length of the wait but also about what happens next. They may also be concerned about such issues as personal safety.

The implications of these findings? When increasing capacity is simply not feasible, you should try to be creative and look for ways to make waiting more palatable for your customers. An experiment at a large bank in Boston found that installing an electronic news display in the lobby didn't reduce the perceived waiting time for teller service but did lead to greater customer satisfaction.[10] Heated shelters equipped with seats make it pleasanter to wait for a bus or train in cold weather. Restaurants solve the waiting problem by inviting dinner guests to have a drink in the bar until their table is ready (that approach makes money for the house, as well as keeping the customer occupied). In similar fashion, guests waiting in line for a show at a casino may find themselves queuing in a corridor lined with slot ma-

chines. The doorman at a Marriott Hotel has taken it upon himself to bring a combination barometer-thermometer to work each day, hanging it on a pillar at the hotel entrance, where guests can spend a moment or two examining it while they wait for a taxi or for their car to be delivered from valet parking.[11] Theme park operators cleverly design their waiting areas to make the wait look shorter than it really is, find ways to give customers in line the impression of constant progress, and make time seem to pass more quickly by keeping customers amused or diverted while they wait.

Giving Customers Information on Waiting

Does it help to tell people how long they are likely to have to wait for service? Common sense would suggest that this is useful information because it allows customers to decide whether they can afford to wait now or come back later. It also enables them to plan the use of their time while waiting. An experimental study in Canada looked at how students responded to waiting while conducting transactions by computer—a situation similar to waiting on the telephone in that there are no visual clues to the probable waiting time.[12] The study examined dissatisfaction with waits of 5, 10, or 15 minutes under three conditions: (1) The subjects were told nothing, (2) they were told how long the wait was likely to be, or (3) they were told what place they had in line. The results suggested that for 5-minute waits, it was not necessary to provide information to improve satisfaction. For waits of 10 or 15 minutes, offering information appeared to improve customers' evaluations of service. However, for longer waits, it may be more positive to let people know how their place in line is changing than to let them know how much time remains before they will be served. One conclusion we might draw is that people prefer to see (or sense) that the line is moving than to watch the clock.

CALCULATING WAITING TIMES

Queue management involves extensive data gathering. Questions of interest include the rate at which customers (or things requiring service) arrive per unit of time and how long it takes to serve each one. The box on check-in service at Logan Airport (p. 316) describes the procedures used by a consulting firm to collect information about the behavior of passengers at that point.

A typical operations strategy is to plan on the basis of average "throughput" to get the best use of employees and equipment. As long as customers (or things) continue to arrive at this same average rate, there will be no delays. However, fluctuations in arrivals (sometimes random, sometimes predictable) will lead to delays if the line backs up following a clump of arrivals. Planners also need to know how easily customers will just walk away when they spot a lengthy line (balking) and how long they will wait for service before leaving (reneging).

Predicting the Behavior of Simple Queuing Systems

Underlying the practice of queue management are mathematical models that enable planners or consultants to calculate a variety of statistics about queue behavior and thus make informed decisions about changes or improvements to existing queuing systems. For basic queuing situations, the formulas are quite simple and yield interesting insights (see the box, p. 317). More complex environments may require powerful simulation models that are beyond the scope of this book. Given certain information about a particular queuing situation, you can use these formulas to calculate such statistics as (1) average queuing length, (2) average waiting times

IMPROVING CHECK-IN SERVICE AT LOGAN AIRPORT

To streamline its check-in service at Boston's Logan International Airport, a major airline turned to Massachusetts Institute of Technology Professor Richard Larson, who heads a consulting firm called QED. Technicians from QED installed pressure-sensitive rubber mats on the floor in front of the ticket counters. Pressure from each customer's foot on approaching or leaving the counter recorded the exact time on an electronic device embedded in the mats. From these data, Larson was able to profile the waiting situation at the airline's counters, including average waiting times, how long each transaction took, how many customers waited longer than a given length of time (and at what hours on what days), and even how many left a long line. Analysis of these data, collected over a long time period, yielded information that helped the airline to plan its staffing levels to match more closely the demand levels projected at different times.

Source: Malcolm Galdwell, "The Bottom Line for Lots of Time Spent in America," *Washington Post*, February 1993.

for customers, (3) average total time for customers in the service system, (4) impact of increasing the number of service channels, and (5) impact of reducing the average serving time. The math is easy but requires reference to a statistical table, which we have reproduced as an appendix at the end of this chapter.

RESERVATIONS

Ask someone what services come to mind when you talk about reservations, and they will probably cite airlines, hotels, restaurants, car rentals, and theater seats. Suggest synonyms like *bookings* or *appointments*, and they may add haircuts, visits to such professionals as doctors and consultants, vacation rentals, and service calls to fix anything from a broken refrigerator to a neurotic computer.

reservation: a confirmed and recorded commitment to provide a customer with designated service at a specified time and place.

A **reservation** is supposed to guarantee that an agreed service will be available at the place and time the customer wants it. Systems vary from a simple appointment book for a doctor's office, using handwritten entries, to a central, computerized data bank for an airline's worldwide operations. When goods require servicing, their owners may not wish to be parted from them for long. Households with only one car, for example, or factories with a vital piece of equipment often cannot afford to be without such items for more than a day or two. Thus a reservations system may be necessary for service businesses in such fields as repair and maintenance. By requiring reservations for routine maintenance, management can ensure that some time will be available for emergency jobs, which because they carry a premium price, generate a much higher margin.

Designing a Reservations System

Reservation systems are commonly used by many people-processing services, including restaurants, hotels, airlines, hairdressing salons, doctors, and dentists. These systems enable demand to be controlled and smoothed out in a more manageable way. By capturing data, reservation systems also help organizations to prepare financial projections.

Taking bookings also serves to presell a service, to inform customers, and to educate them about what to expect. Customers who hold reservations should be able to count on avoiding a queue because they have been guaranteed service at a specific time. A well-organized reservations system allows the organization to deflect demand for service from a first-choice time to earlier or later times, from one class of service to another (upgrades and downgrades), and even from first-choice locations to alternatives.

CALCULATING STATISTICS FOR SIMPLE QUEUES

With the information provided, used in conjunction with the appendix table at the end of this chapter, you will be able to make simple calculations about queue waiting times and how many people are likely to be waiting in a given queue under specified conditions.

The formulas are very simple; don't be discouraged by the use of Greek letters for the notation.

Terminology

Certain terms and notation are used in queue analysis:

M = *number of serving channels*

λ (lambda) = *arrival rate* (here, average number of customers arriving per hour)

μ (mu) = *service rate* (the capacity of a channel to provide service, expressed here as number of customers per channel per hour)

ρ (rho) = λ/μ = *flow intensity* (average percent utilization of serving channel's capacity)

$U = \lambda/M\mu$ = *capacity utilization of the overall facility* (expressed as percent of the capacity of all channels combined)

L_q = *expected length of line* (here, average number of people waiting)

$W_q = L_q/\lambda$ = *expected waiting time* (before a new arrival is served)

You should note that unless the average number of customers served (μ) exceeds the average number of arrivals (λ), it will never be possible to serve all the customers desiring service.

Example

Let's consider a simple example. A theater ticket office has one agent (M) who, on average, can serve 25 customers per hour (μ). This implies an average serving time of ($1 \div 25$) = 0.04 hours = 2.4 minutes per customer. Let's assume that customers arrive at an average rate of 20 per hour (λ) in the busy period, which means that the flow intensity is $\rho = 20/25 = 0.80$. We can now use the table in the appendix to calculate the

- expected length of the line (L_q): looking down the column for one serving line (M) to $\rho = 0.80$, we can see that the line length will average **3.2 persons**
- expected waiting time before service (W_q): ($3.2 \div 20$) $\times$ 60 = **9.6 minutes**
- expected total time in system ($W_q + 60/\mu$): 9.6 mins. + 2.4 mins. = **12.0 minutes**
- average capacity utilization ($U = \lambda/M\mu$): 20 $\div$ (1 $\times$ 25) = **80%** (in other words, 20 percent of the time, the agent will be idle)

Let's suppose that customers are complaining about this wait, and management wants to speed up service. The choices are to add a second agent, maintaining a single line of customers, so $M = 2$, or to purchase new equipment that halves the time required to issue a ticket and receive payment. Here are the comparative results:

1. Using the table in the appendix, when $M = 2$ and $\rho = 0.80$:
   - the expected line length (L_q) is only 0.15 persons
   - the expected wait (W_q): (0.15 $\div$ 20) $\times$ 60 = 0.45 minutes
   - the expected time in the system ($W_q + 60/\mu$): 0.45 + 2.4 = 2.85 minutes total
   - the flow intensity (U): 20 $\div$ (2 $\times$ 25) = 40% (the two agents will each be idle 60 percent of the time)

2. However, if instead we halve the serving time, from 2.4 to 1.2 minutes, then μ = (60 $\div$ 1.2) = 50 customers per hour per channel, and ρ = (20 $\div$ 50) = 0.40. Using the data in the appendix for $M = 1$ and $\rho = 0.40$, the following results occur:
   - the expected line length is 0.27 persons
   - the expected wait is (0.27 $\div$ 20) $\times$ 60 = 0.81 minutes
   - the expected time in the system is 0.81 + 1.2 = 2.01 minutes total
   - the flow intensity is 20 $\div$ (1 $\times$ 50) = 40%

Both approaches cut the time sharply from the original 12 minutes, but halving the servicing time yields slightly better time savings than doubling the number of channels. In this instance, the decision on which approach to adopt would probably depend on the relevant costs involved—the capital cost of adding a second channel, plus the wages and benefits paid to a second employee, versus the capital costs of investing in new technology and training (assuming no increase in wages). In both instances, an agent is now idle 60 percent of the time.

However, problems arise when customers fail to arrive or when service firms overbook. Marketing strategies for dealing with these operational problems include

- requiring a deposit
- cancelling nonpaid bookings after a certain time
- providing compensation to victims of overbooking

The challenge in designing reservation systems is to make them fast and user-friendly for both staff and customers. Many firms now allow customers to make their own reservations on a Web site—a trend that seems certain to grow. Whether customers talk to a reservations agent or make their own bookings, they want quick answers to queries about service availability at a preferred time. They also appreciate further information about the type of service they are reserving. For instance, can a hotel assign a specific room on request? Or at least, can it assign a room with a view of the lake rather than one with a view of the parking lot and the nearby power station?

Information Needs

Service managers require substantial information to help them develop effective demand management strategies and then monitor subsequent marketplace performance. Information needs include

- historical data on the level and composition of demand over time, including responses to changes in price or other marketing variables
- forecasts of the level of demand for each major segment under specified conditions
- segment-by-segment data to help management evaluate the impact of periodic cycles and random demand fluctuations
- sound cost data to enable the organization to distinguish between fixed and variable costs and to determine the relative profitability of incremental unit sales to different segments and at different prices

The eternal optimist: "I'd like to make a reservation for Friday evening."

- in multisite organizations, identification of meaningful variations in the levels and composition of demand on a site-by-site basis
- customer attitudes toward queuing under varying conditions
- customer opinions on whether the quality of service delivered varies with different levels of capacity utilization

Where might all this information come from? Although some new studies may be required, much of the needed data is probably already being collected within the organization—although not necessarily by marketers. A stream of information comes into most service businesses, especially from distilling the multitude of individual transactions conducted. Sales receipts alone often contain much useful data. Most service businesses collect detailed information for operational and accounting purposes. Although some do not record details of individual transactions, a majority are able to associate specific customers with specific transactions. Unfortunately, the marketing value of these data is often overlooked, and they are not always stored in ways that permit easy retrieval and analysis for marketing purposes. Nevertheless, collection and storage of customer transaction data can often be reformatted to provide marketers with some of the information they require, including how existing segments have responded to past changes in marketing variables.

Other information may have to be collected through special studies, such as customer surveys or reviews of analogous situations. It may also be necessary to collect information on competitive performance because changes in the capacity or strategy of competitors may require corrective action.

YIELD MANAGEMENT

Service organizations often use percentage of capacity sold as a measure of operational efficiency. Transport services talk of the load factor achieved, hotels of their occupancy rate, and hospitals of their census. Similarly, professional firms can calculate what proportion of a partner's or an employee's time is classified as billable hours, and repair shops can look at utilization of both equipment and labor. By themselves, however, these percentage figures tell us little of the relative profitability of the business attracted because high utilization rates may be obtained at the expense of heavy discounting or even outright giveaways.

More and more, service firms are looking at their **yield**—that is, the average revenue received per unit of capacity. The aim is to maximize this yield to improve profitability, and the strategies are collectively known as **yield management**. They are widely used in such capacity-constrained industries as passenger airlines, hotels, and car rentals. Formalized yield management programs, based on mathematical modeling, are of greatest value for service firms that find it expensive to modify their capacity but incur relatively low costs when they sell another unit of available capacity.[13] Other characteristics encouraging use of these programs are fluctuating demand levels, the ability to segment markets by the extent of price sensitivity, and the sale of services well in advance of use.

yield: the average revenue received per unit of capacity offered for sale.

yield management: strategies, typically based upon mathematical modeling, that are designed to maximize the revenue from the sale of capacity.

Segmentation Issues in Reservations Strategy

Yield analysis forces managers to recognize the **opportunity cost** of accepting business from one customer or market segment when another might subsequently yield a higher rate. Consider the following problems in different types of capacity-constrained service organizations:

opportunity cost: the potential value of the income or other benefits foregone as a result of deciding on one course of action instead of pursuing other opportunities.

■ Should a hotel accept an advance booking from a tour group for 200 room nights at $80 each when they may be sold later at short notice to business travelers at the full posted rate of $140?

■ Should a railroad with 30 empty freight cars at its disposal accept an immediate request for a shipment worth $900 per car or hold the cars idle for a few more days in the hope of getting a priority shipment that would be twice as valuable?

■ How many seats on a particular flight should an airline sell in advance to tour groups and passengers traveling at special excursion rates?

■ Should an industrial repair and maintenance shop reserve a certain proportion of productive capacity each day for emergency repair jobs that offer a high contribution margin and the potential to build long-term customer loyalty, or should it only make sure that there are sufficient jobs, mostly involving routine maintenance, to keep its employees fully occupied?

■ Should a print shop process all jobs on a first-come, first-served basis, with a guaranteed delivery time for each job, or should it charge a premium rate for rush work and tell customers with standard jobs to expect some variability in completion dates?

Such decisions deserve to be handled with a little more sophistication than the "bird in the hand is worth two in the bush" mindset. So managers need a way of figuring out the chances of getting more profitable business if they wait. Good information, based on detailed record keeping of past usage and supported by current market intelligence and good marketing sense, is the key.

A Scientific Approach to Capacity Allocation

The decision to accept or reject business should represent a realistic estimate of the probability of obtaining higher-rated business, together with a recognition of the importance of maintaining established (and desirable) customer relationships. Managers who make such decisions on the basis of guesswork and "gut feel" are little better than gamblers who bet on rolls of the dice.

There has to be a clear plan, based on analysis of past performance and current market data, that indicates how much capacity should be allocated on specific dates to different types of customers at certain prices. Based on this plan, "selective sell" targets can be assigned to advertising and sales personnel, reflecting the allocation of available capacity among different market segments on specific future dates. The last thing a firm wants its sales force to do is to encourage price-sensitive market segments to buy capacity on dates when sales projections predict that there will be strong demand from customers willing to pay full price. Unfortunately, in some industries, the lowest-rated business often books the furthest ahead: Tour groups, which pay much lower room rates than individual travelers, may ask airlines and hotels to block space more than a year in advance.

Figure 15.4 illustrates capacity allocation in a hotel, where demand from different types of customers varies not only by the day of the week but also by the season. These allocation decisions by segment, captured in reservation databases that are accessible worldwide, tell reservations personnel when to stop accepting reservations at certain prices, even though many rooms may still be unbooked.

Charts similar to those in Figure 15.4 can be constructed for most capacity-constrained businesses. In some instances, capacity is measured in seats for a given performance, in seat miles, or in room nights; in others, it may be measured in machine time, labor time, billable professional hours, vehicle miles, or storage volume—whichever is the scarce resource. Unless it's easy to divert business from one

FIGURE 15.4 Setting Capacity Allocation Sales Targets over Time

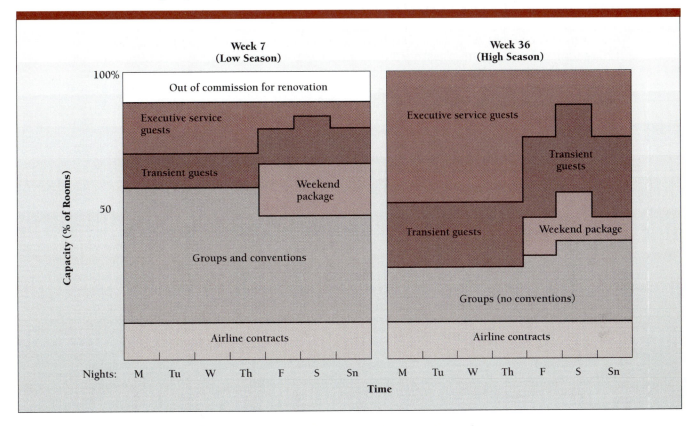

facility to a similar alternative, allocation planning decisions will have to be made at the level of geographic operating units. Thus each hotel or repair and maintenance center may need its own plan. In contrast, transport vehicles represent mobile capacity that can be allocated to different geographic areas.

In large organizations, like major airlines or hotel chains, the market is very dynamic because the situation is changing all the time. For instance, the demand for both business and pleasure travel reflects current or anticipated economic conditions. Although many business travelers are not price sensitive, some companies insist that employees shop for the best travel bargains they can find within the constraints of their travel needs. Pleasure travelers, however, are usually very price sensitive; a special promotion, involving discounted fares and room rates, may encourage people to undertake a trip that they would not otherwise have made.

Viewed from the perspective of the individual hotel or airline, competitive activity can play havoc with patronage forecasts. Imagine that you are a hotel owner, and a new hotel opens across the street with a special discount offer. How will it affect you? Or consider the impact if an existing competitor is destroyed by fire. The airline business is notoriously changeable. Fares can be slashed overnight. A competitor may introduce a new nonstop service or cut back its existing schedule on another route. Travel agents and knowledgeable customers watch these movements carefully and may be quick to cancel one reservation (even if it involves paying a penalty) to take advantage of a better price or a more convenient schedule elsewhere.

Advances in software and computing power have made it possible for firms to use very sophisticated mathematical models for yield management analysis (see the box on Flight 2015, p. 322). These models integrate massive historical databases on ridership with real-time information on current bookings to help analysts pinpoint how many customers would want to travel at a particular price on a given flight.

PRICING SEATS ON FLIGHT 2015

American Airlines Flight 2015 is a popular flight from Chicago to Phoenix, departing at 5:30 P.M. The 125 seats in coach (economy class) are divided into seven fare categories, referred to by yield management specialists as buckets, with round-trip ticket prices ranging from $238 for a bargain excursion fare (with various restrictions and a cancellation penalty) to an unrestricted fare of $1,404. Seats are also available at a higher price in the small first-class section. Scott McCartney tells how ongoing analysis changes the allocation of seats between each of the seven buckets in economy class:

> In the weeks before each Chicago–Phoenix flight, American's yield management computers constantly adjust the number of seats in each bucket, taking into account tickets sold, historical ridership patterns, and connecting passengers likely to use the route as one leg of a longer trip.

> If advance bookings are slim, American adds seats to low-fare buckets. If business customers buy unrestricted fares earlier than expected, the yield management computer takes seats out of the discount buckets and preserves them for last-minute bookings that the database predicts will still show up.

> With 69 of 125 coach seats already sold four weeks before one recent departure of Flight 2015, American's computer began to limit the number of seats in lower-priced buckets. A week later, it totally shut off sales for the bottom three buckets, priced $300 or less. To a Chicago customer looking for a cheap seat, the flight was "sold out."

> One day before departure, with 130 passengers booked for the 125-seat flight, American still offered five seats at full fare because its computer database indicated 10 passengers were likely not to show up or take other flights. Flight 2015 departed full and no one was bumped.

Source: Scott McCartney, "Ticket Shock: Business Fares Increase Even as Leisure Travel Keeps Getting Cheaper," *The Wall Street Journal*, 3 November 1997, A1, A10.

There's evidence that yield management programs can improve revenues significantly—many airlines report increases of 5 percent or more after starting such programs. But a word of warning is in order: Yield management shouldn't necessarily mean short-term yield maximization at all costs. Strategies can easily become rigid, full of rules and regulations designed to prevent less price-sensitive segments from taking advantage of lower-priced offers and stiff penalties for canceled reservations. Even worse is a policy of cynical overbooking without thought for the consequences to disappointed customers, who thought they had firm reservations. To maintain goodwill and build relationships, managers have to take the long-term perspective. Therefore, yield management programs should build in strategies for retaining valued customer relationships, even to the extent of not charging the maximum feasible amount on a given transaction (perceptions of price gouging do not build trust). There should also be thoughtfully planned contingencies for victims of overbooking, with recovery programs designed to maintain goodwill even under conditions of inherent disappointment.

Conclusion

The time-bound nature of services is a critical management issue today, especially with customers becoming more time sensitive and more conscious of their personal time constraints and availability. People-processing services are particularly likely to impose the burden of unwanted waiting on their customers because customers cannot avoid coming to the "factory" for service. Reservations can shape the timing of arrivals, but sometimes queuing is inevitable. Managers who can save customers time (or at least make time pass more pleasantly) may be able to create a competitive advantage for their organizations. However, opportunities to improve the quality of the service experience must be balanced against productivity concerns. Yield management techniques can help firms in certain capacity-constrained industries to develop sophisticated pricing strategies designed to improve profitability by selling to different segments at different prices.

Study Questions and Exercises

1. Why should service marketers be concerned about the amount of time that customers spend in (a) preprocess waits and (b) in-process waits?

2. Give examples, based on your own experience, of reservations systems that worked really well or really badly.

3. How might the principles of yield management be applied to rental car companies?

4. Review the 10 propositions on the psychology of waiting lines. Which are the most relevant in (a) a supermarket; (b) a city bus stop on a cold, dark evening; (c) check-in at the airport; (d) a doctor's office, where patients are seated; (e) a ticket line for a football game that is expected to be sold out?

5. What are the seven elements of a queuing system? Which are under the control of the customer and which of the service provider?

6. For an organization serving a large number of customers, what do you see as the advantages and disadvantages of the different types of queues?

7. Using the formulas on page 317 and the appendix, calculate answers to the following problems:

   a. At Frank's office cafeteria, customers select their meals from different food stations and then go to the cashier to pay. Frank knows that Maureen, the cashier, can check out a customer every 30 seconds, on average. With an arrival rate of 80 customers an hour during the 11 A.M. to 2 P.M. lunch period, what is the average length of the line that Frank can expect to see at the checkout station? How many minutes will he have to wait?

   b. Maureen goes on maternity leave and is replaced by Willy, whom Frank times at one customer every 42 seconds. On average, how much longer will the line now be and how long will Frank have to wait?

   c. In response to complaints about delays at the checkout line, management assigns JoAnn to operate a second cash register during Maureen's absence. JoAnn can process the average customer in 36 seconds, and following retraining, Willy manages to improve his performance to the same level. How long, on average, will each line now be and how many minutes can Frank expect to wait (in either line)?

   d. Willy is sick one day, so JoAnn must work alone. Now, how long, on average, is the line? The wait?

8. What segmentation principles and variables are inherent in the yield management example from American Airlines?

Appendix

Poisson Distribution Table

Calculating the Expected Number of People Waiting in Line for Various Values of *M* and ρ

Flow Intensity (ρ)	Number of Service Channels (*M*)			
	1	2	3	4
0.10	0.0111			
0.15	0.0264	0.0008		
0.20	0.0500	0.0020		
0.25	0.0833	0.0039		
0.30	0.1285	0.0069		
0.35	0.1884	0.0110		
0.40	0.2666	0.0166		
0.45	0.3681	0.0239	0.0019	
0.50	0.5000	0.0333	0.0030	
0.55	0.6722	0.0149	0.0043	
0.60	0.9000	0.0593	0.0061	
0.65	1.2071	0.0767	0.0084	
0.70	1.6333	0.0976	0.0112	
0.75	2.2500	0.1227	0.0147	
0.80	3.2000	0.1523	0.0189	
0.85	4.8166	0.1873	0.0239	0.0031
0.90	8.1000	0.2285	0.0300	0.0041
0.95	18.0500	0.2767	0.0371	0.0053
1.0		0.3333	0.0454	0.0067

CHAPTER

Sixteen

Service Employees: From Recruitment to Retention

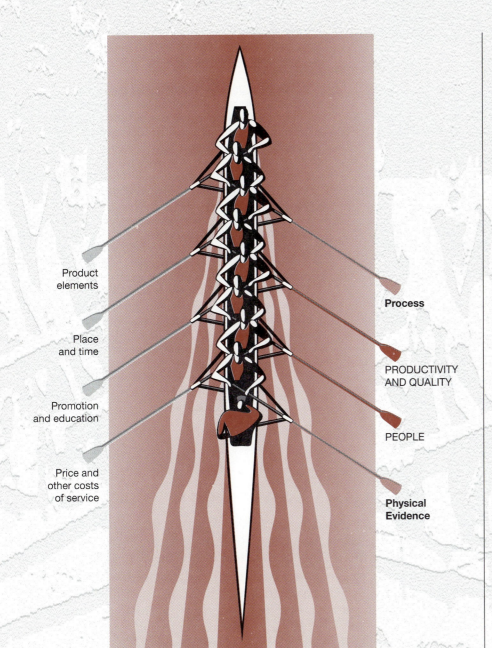

Product elements

Place and time

Promotion and education

Price and other costs of service

Process

PRODUCTIVITY AND QUALITY

PEOPLE

Physical Evidence

Learning Objectives

After reading this chapter, you should be able to

■ appreciate that expenditures on human resources are an investment that will pay dividends, rather than as a cost to be minimized

■ understand the strategic importance of recruitment, selection, training, motivation, and retention of employees

■ define what is meant by the control and involvement models of management

■ understand the benefits and implications of employee empowerment

■ recognize how the culture of a company affects the service received by customers

Southwest Airlines: A Company of People

In early 1998, Southwest Airlines was rated the best company to work for in America.[1] What's its secret? This extract from the company's annual report for 1996 provides some insights:[2]

Southwest Airlines believes our number one asset is our People; therefore, we devote a significant amount of time and effort hiring, training, and retaining our Employees. At Southwest, we are not interested in hiring clones. We target individuals from diverse backgrounds who will support and enhance our Culture. Regardless of the job, we hire People with attitudes that are outrageously positive. Our Employees enjoy working together as a team and take pleasure in team results, rather than emphasizing individual accomplishments.

Southwest Employees are not afraid to "color outside the lines." We encourage our Employees to be creative and have fun on the job. As a result, our Employees tend to go out of their way to ensure our Customers have an enjoyable and memorable flight. Although our Employees take our Customers very seriously, they do not take themselves seriously. They are warm, caring, compassionate, and always willing to go the extra mile to deliver Positively Outrageous Service to our Customers as well as the communities we serve.

Finding a person who fits that bill is not an easy task! In fact, we accepted approximately 124,000 external job applications in 1995 and interviewed 38,000 individuals for 5,473 positions.

Once Southwest hires someone to join our Family, we focus on nurturing and developing that Employee. We provide exceptional training programs which are specifically designed to help our Employees excel and succeed in an extremely competitive and dynamic environment.

Without sufficient retention of our incredibly talented Employees, our recruiting, hiring, and training efforts would be in vain. What is our secret? Although we offer competitive compensation packages, including, among other things, competitive wages and generous profitsharing, it is the psychic satisfaction of pride, excitement, fun, and collective fulfillment that is the key to our Culture and retaining the best Employees in America.

It is Southwest's philosophy that Employees with a sense of ownership in the Company will focus more on longterm versus shortterm goals. Empowerment to each and every Employee not only provides high spirit but avoids complacency and prevents a hierarchy or bureaucracy from slowing down creativity and innovation. In other words, the Southwest Spirit and Culture enhance job satisfaction which translates into thousands and thousands of dedicated Employees.

In every respect, our Employees are the best. And even though our competition may try to imitate Southwest, they cannot duplicate the most important element of our success—the Southwest Spirit inherent in each and every one of our 20,000 Employees.

HUMAN RESOURCES: AN ASSET WORTH MANAGING

Many organizations have used the phrase "People are our most important asset," but all too few companies act as though their top management really believes it. Southwest Airlines is one of the exceptions. At first sight, a highly unionized, low-cost, short-haul airline, trying to make a profit in a fiercely competitive industry, seems an unlikely place to find extraordinary management commitment—at all levels of the organization—to putting people first. Yet the results speak for themselves. For more than 20 years, Southwest has been the most consistently profitable airline in the United States. For the past five years, it has topped the U.S. Department of

Our flight operations team would like to note that our 25th anniversary arrived right on time.

THIS COMES AS NO SURPRISE TO THESE SEVEN ORIGINAL EMPLOYEES. THEY'VE SPENT THE PAST 25 YEARS CREATING A LEGACY OF ON-TIME ARRIVALS. SO AFTER ALL THEIR HARD WORK, THE LAST THING THEY'RE GOING TO BE LATE TO IS AN ANNIVERSARY PARTY.

[Left to right: Charlie Marcel, Flight Crew Training Instructor; Bob Pratt, Captain; Dan Johnson, Dispatcher; Willie Wilson, Manager-Flight Crew Operations Administration; Sam Cohn, Captain; Gene VanOverschelde, Captain; Scott Johnson, Dispatcher.]

Southwest Airlines devoted its twenty-fifth anniversary to honoring employees who had been with the company since its founding. Pictured is the flight operations team.

Transportation rankings of airlines with the fewest customer complaints, best on-time performance, and best baggage handling. It has grown relentlessly, even as competitors have failed.

As Southwest makes clear, key elements in **human resource management** (HRM) include recruitment, selection, training, and retention of employees. Successful service firms like Southwest are characterized by a distinctive culture of service, leadership, and role modeling by members of top management and the active involvement of human resource managers in strategic decisions. Employees are seen as a resource to be nurtured rather than as a cost to be minimized. They are empowered to make decisions on their own rather than continually asking their supervisors for permission.

Hal Rosenbluth, owner of a chain of successful travel agencies, argues in his book, *The Customer Comes Second*, that a company's first focus should be on its employees: "Only when people know what it feels like to be first in someone else's eyes," he writes, "can they sincerely share that feeling with others."[3] In a service organization, other employees have to serve **internal customers** as they work backstage to support the efforts of front-stage colleagues who are serving customers directly.

human resource management (HRM): the function responsible for coordinating tasks related to job design and employee recruitment, selection, training, and motivation; it also includes planning and administering other employee-related activities.

internal customers: employees who are recipients of services from an internal supplier (another employee or department) as a necessary input to performing their own jobs.

HIGH-CONTACT SERVICE ENCOUNTERS

Most people can recount some horror story of a dreadful experience they have had with a service business—and usually they love to talk about it. If pressed, many of these same people can also recount a really good service experience. Service personnel usually feature prominently in such dramas—either in roles as uncaring, incompetent, mean-spirited villains or as heroes who went out of their way to provide aid, anticipating customers' needs or resolving problems in a helpful and empathetic manner. Think about your own recent service experiences. In what ways have you been treated particularly well or badly by service personnel?

Role of Front-Stage Personnel

In high-contact service encounters, we tend to remember the role played by front-stage personnel better than any other aspect of the operation. In many respects, these employees *are* the service. A single employee may play many roles: part of the product and part of the delivery system, advisor and teacher, marketer, and even—if the customers get unruly—police officer (like a bouncer in a bar). Service people may also play a vital role in lower-contact jobs, in which customers interact with the firm by telephone and an agent's voice is the only form of human contact.

Customer-contact personnel must attend to both operational and marketing goals. On the one hand, they help to "manufacture" the service output. On the other hand, they may also be responsible for marketing it (e.g., "We've got some nice desserts to follow your main course" or "We could clean your machine at the same time that we repair the motor" or "Now would be a good time to open a separate account to save for your children's education"). In the eyes of their customers, service personnel may also be seen as physical evidence of the service experience. In short, the service person may perform a triple role as operations specialist, marketer, and part of the service product itself. This multiplicity of roles—known as boundary spanning—may lead to role conflict among employees, especially when they feel as physically and psychologically close to customers as they do to managers and other employees.[4] Table 16.1 highlights some of the conflicts between operations and marketing goals that may trap employees in the middle. Organizations whose services involve extensive service encounters tend to be harder to manage than those without them. Because of the human element, consistent service delivery becomes harder to achieve, thereby complicating the task of those responsible for productivity and quality improvement.

Several special characteristics may be important in recruiting and training high-contact employees: interpersonal skills, personal appearance and grooming, knowledge of the product and the operation, selling capabilities, and skills in coproduction (i.e., working jointly with customers to create the desired service). Additional characteristics, particularly valuable in selling situations, include monitoring nonverbal clues (such as the customer's body language) and adjusting one's behavior in the context of social situations. Both technical and interpersonal skills are necessary but neither alone is sufficient for optimal job performance.[5]

Emotional Labor

emotional labor: the act by an employee of expressing socially appropriate (but sometimes false) emotions toward customers during service transactions.

Service encounters entail more than just correct technical execution of a task. They also involve such human elements as personal demeanor, courtesy, and empathy. This brings us to the notion of **emotional labor** (or emotional work), defined as the act of expressing socially appropriate (but sometimes false) emotions during service transactions.[6] For instance, some jobs require service workers to act in a friendly fashion toward customers; others to appear compassionate, sincere, or even self-effacing. Trying to conform to customers' expectations on such dimensions can prove to be a psychological burden for some service workers when they see themselves having to act out emotions they do not feel (see the box on displaying emotions, p. 330).

Customer-contact employees comply with so-called display rules through acting and the expression of spontaneous and genuine emotion.[7] Display rules generally reflect the norms imposed both by society—which may vary from one culture

TABLE 16.1   Operations and Marketing Perspectives on Operational Issues

Operational Issues	Typical Operations Goals	Common Marketing Concerns
Productivity improvement	Reduce unit cost of production	Strategies may cause decline in service quality
Make-versus-buy decisions (outsourcing)	Trade off control against comparative advantage and cost savings	"Make" decisions may result in lower quality and lack of market coverage; "buy" decisions may transfer control to unresponsive suppliers and hurt the firm's image
Facilities location	Reduce costs; provide convenient access for suppliers and employees	Customers may find location unattractive and inaccessible
Standardization	Keep costs low and quality consistent; simplify operations tasks; recruit low-cost employees	Consumers may seek variety, prefer customization to match segmented needs
Batch versus unit processing	Seek economies of scale, consistency, efficient use of capacity	Customers may be forced to wait, feel "one of a crowd," be turned off by other customers
Facilities layout and design	Control costs; improve efficiency by ensuring proximity of operationally related tasks; enhance safety and security	Customers may be confused, shunted around unnecessarily, find facility unattractive and inconvenient
Job design	Minimize error, waste and fraud; make efficient use of technology; simplify tasks for standardization	Operationally oriented employees with narrow roles may be unresponsive to customer needs
Learning curves	Apply experience to reduce time and costs per unit of output	Faster service is not necessarily better service; cost saving may not be passed on as lower prices
Management of capacity	Keep costs down by avoiding wasteful underutilization of resources	Service may be unavailable when needed; quality may be compromised during high-demand periods
Quality control	Ensure that service execution conforms to predefined standards	Operational definitions of quality may not reflect customer needs, preferences
Management of queues	Optimize use of available capacity by planning for average throughput; maintain customer order, discipline	Customers may be bored and frustrated during wait, see firm as unresponsive

Source: Copyright © 1989 by Christopher H. Lovelock. Reprinted from "Managing Interactions Between Operations and Marketing and Their Impact on Customers," chapter 15 in Bowen et al. (eds.), *Service Management Effectiveness* (San Francisco: Jossey Bass, 1990), p. 362.

to another—and by specific occupations and organizations. For instance, customers' expectations for nurses are different from those for bill collectors. Expectations may also reflect the nature of a particular encounter (what emotions would you expect a waiter to display if you discovered a cockroach in your water glass?). Acting requires employees to simulate emotions that they do not actually feel, accomplished

DISPLAYING EMOTIONS

Think for a moment of the following different service jobs and ask yourself what type of emotions you expect individuals working in each position to display to customers in the course of doing their job: emergency room nurse, bill collector, flight attendant, dentist, computer repair technician, supermarket checker, kindergarten teacher, prosecuting attorney, employee in a flower shop, police officer on highway patrol, server in a family restaurant, server in an expensive French restaurant, stockbroker, and undertaker.

by careful presentation of verbal and nonverbal cues, such as facial expression, gestures, and voice tone. Within limits, such acting skills can be taught, and some people are natural actors. Under certain conditions, service providers may spontaneously experience the expected emotion without any need for acting, as when a firefighter feels sympathy for an injured child taken from a burning building.

Human resource (HR) managers need to know that performing emotional labor, day after day, can be stressful for employees as they strive to display toward customers feelings that may be false. From a marketing standpoint, however, failure to display the emotions that customers expect can be damaging and may lead to complaints that "employees don't seem to care." The challenge for HR managers is to determine what customers expect, recruit the most suitable employees, and train them well. When service personnel have been exposed to traumatic events, such as injuries or deaths of customers or coworkers, professional counseling may be needed to allow the workers to express their feelings to others. Special training on how to handle these emotions is often offered to workers in such fields as policing, firefighting, and emergency medical care because of the frequency with which they are likely to be exposed to traumatic situations in the normal course of their jobs.

JOB DESIGN AND RECRUITMENT

The goal of job design is to study the requirements of the operation, the nature of customers' desires, the needs and capabilities of employees, and the characteristics of operational equipment to develop job descriptions that strike the best balance between these sometimes conflicting demands. Some of the most demanding jobs in service businesses are so-called boundary-spanning positions, in which employees are expected to be fast and efficient at executing operational tasks, as well as courteous and helpful in dealing with customers. Many service encounters are potentially a three-cornered fight among the needs of partially conflicting parties: the customer, the server, and the service firm. If the job is not designed carefully or the wrong people are picked to fill it, there's a real risk that employees may become stressed and unproductive.

Empowerment of Employees[8]

How important is the much-advocated practice of empowering employees to use their own discretion to serve customers better? Job designs should reflect the fact that service personnel may encounter customers' requests for assistance in remote sites at any hour of the day and night. Under the right conditions, providing employees with greater discretion (and training them to use their judgment) may enable them to provide superior service without referring to rule books or higher authority. From a humanistic standpoint, the notion of encouraging employees to exercise initiative and discretion is an appealing one. **Empowerment** looks to the

empowerment: authorizing the employee to find solutions to service problems and to make appropriate decisions about responses to customers' concerns without having to ask for a supervisor's approval.

performer of the task to find solutions to service problems and to make appropriate decisions about customizing service delivery. It depends for its success on what is sometimes called **enablement**—giving workers the tools and resources they need to take on these new responsibilities.

Advocates claim that the empowerment approach is more likely to yield motivated employees and satisfied customers than the production-line alternative, in which management designs a relatively standardized system and expects workers to execute tasks within narrow guidelines. But is the choice between these two approaches really so obvious? The truth is, different situations may require different solutions. The payoffs from greater empowerment must be set against increased costs for selection and training, higher labor costs, slower service as customer-contact personnel devote more time to individual customers, and less consistency in service delivery.

Control versus involvement. The production-line approach to managing people is based on the well-established **control model of management** and organization design, with its clearly defined roles, top-down control systems, hierarchical organizational structure, and assumption that management knows best. Empowerment, in contrast, is based on the **involvement** (or commitment) **model of management**, which assumes that most employees can make good decisions—and produce good ideas for operating the business—if they are properly socialized, trained, and informed. It also assumes that employees can be internally motivated to perform effectively and that they are capable of self-control and self-direction. Although broad use of the term *empowerment* is relatively new, the underlying philosophy of employee involvement is not.

In the control model, four key features are concentrated at the top of the organization; in the involvement model, in contrast, these features are pushed down through the organization:

1. information about organizational performance (e.g., operating results and measures of competitive performance)
2. rewards based on organizational performance (e.g., profit sharing and stock ownership)
3. knowledge that enables employees to understand and contribute to organizational performance (e.g., problem-solving skills)
4. power to make decisions that influence work procedures and organizational direction (e.g., through quality circles and self-managing teams)

Levels of employee involvement. The empowerment and production-line approaches are at opposite ends of a spectrum that reflects increasing levels of employee involvement as additional knowledge, information, power, and rewards are pushed down to the front line. Empowerment can take place at several levels:

- *Suggestion involvement* empowers employees to make recommendations through formalized programs, but their day-to-day work activities do not really change. McDonald's, often portrayed as an archetype of the production-line approach, listens closely to its front line; innovations ranging from Egg McMuffin to methods of wrapping burgers without leaving a thumbprint on the bun were invented by employees.

- *Job involvement* represents a dramatic opening up of job content; that is, jobs are redesigned to allow employees to use a wider array of skills. In complex service organizations such as airlines and hospitals, where individual employees cannot offer all facets of a service, job involvement is often

enablement: giving employees the skills, tools, and resources they need to use their own discretion confidently and effectively.

control model of management: an approach based on clearly defined roles, top-down control systems, a hierarchical organizational structure, and assumption that management knows best.

involvement model of management: an approach based on the assumption that employees are capable of self-direction and—if properly trained, motivated, and informed—can make good decisions about service operations and delivery.

accomplished through teams. To cope with the added demands accompanying this form of empowerment, employees require training and supervisors need to be reoriented from directing the group to facilitating its performance in supportive ways.

■ *High involvement* gives even the lowest-level employees a sense of involvement in the total organization's performance. Information is shared. Employees develop skills in teamwork, problem solving, and business operations, and they participate in work-unit management decisions. There is profit sharing and employee ownership of stock.

As shown in Table 16.2, a strategy of empowerment is most likely to be appropriate when certain factors are present within the organization and its environment. It's important to emphasize that not all employees are necessarily eager to be empowered. Many employees do not seek personal growth in their jobs and would prefer to work according to specific directions rather than having to use their own initiative.

Recruiting the Right People for the Job

There's no such thing as the perfect, universal employee. First, some service jobs require prior qualifications, as opposed to giving employees the necessary training after they are hired. A nurse can apply for a job as a hotel receptionist, but the reverse is not true unless the applicant has nursing qualifications. Second, different positions—even within the same firm—are best filled by people with different styles and personalities. It helps to have an outgoing personality in many front-stage jobs that involve constantly meeting new customers; a shy, retiring person might be more comfortable working backstage and always dealing with the same people. Someone who loves to be physically active might do better as a restaurant server or courier than in a more sedentary job as a reservation agent or bank teller. Finally, as Robert Levering and Milton Moskowitz, authors of *The 100 Best Companies to Work for in America*, stress, "No company is perfect for everyone. This may be especially true in good places to work since these firms tend to have real character...their own culture. Companies with distinctive personalities tend to attract—and repel—certain types of individuals."[9]

Recruiting criteria should reflect the human dimensions of the job, as well as the technical requirements. This brings us back to the notion of emotional labor and service as theater. The Walt Disney Company, which is in the entertainment business, actually uses the term *casting* and assesses prospective employees in terms of their potential for onstage or backstage work. Onstage workers, known as *cast members*, are assigned to those roles for which their appearance, personalities, and skills provide the best match.

TABLE 16.2   Factors Favoring a Strategy of Employee Empowerment

- Business strategy is based on competitive differentiation and on offering personalized, customized service
- The approach to customers is based on extended relationships rather than on short-term transactions
- The organization uses technologies that are complex and nonroutine in nature
- The business environment is unpredictable and surprises are to be expected
- Existing managers are comfortable with letting employees work independently for the benefit of both the organization and its customers
- Employees have a strong need to grow and deepen their skills in the work environment, are interested in working with others, and have good interpersonal and group process skills

Source: Based on David E. Bowen and Edward E. Lawler III, "The Empowerment of Service Workers: What, Why, How, and When," *Sloan Management Review*, Spring 1992, 32–39.

Who Must Be Hired versus What Can Be Taught

As part of its turnaround efforts in the early 1980s, British Airways started paying more attention to its passengers' concerns and opinions. When research findings showed that travelers wanted warmer, friendlier service from flight attendants, the airline first tried to develop these characteristics through training. But human resource managers soon concluded that although good manners and the need to smile could be taught, warmth itself could not. So the airline changed its recruitment criteria to favor candidates with naturally warm personalities. It also changed its recruitment advertising to capture the challenges of the work instead of emphasizing the glamour of travel. For instance, one such ad showed a drawing of a small child, sitting in an airline seat and clutching a teddy bear. The headline read, "His mum told him not to talk to strangers. So what's he having for lunch?"

What makes outstanding service performers special? Often it's things that *cannot* be taught, qualities that are intrinsic to the people, qualities they would bring with them to any employer. As one study of high performers observed, "Energy . . . cannot be taught, it has to be hired. The same is true for charm, for detail orientation, for work ethic, for neatness. Some of these things can be enhanced with on-the-job training . . . or incentives. . . . But by and large, such qualities are instilled early on."[10] The logical conclusion is that service businesses that are dependent on the human qualities of their front-stage service personnel should devote great care to attracting and hiring the right candidates.

Other skills, too, may manifest themselves at a relatively early age. Andersen Consulting recently ran a series of full-page recruitment advertisements in magazines like *Business Week*. They featured faded color photographs—designed to look 15 to 20 years old—of children enjoying themselves in different play situations, which the ad then linked to the talents that the target audience might have developed as young adults.

Southwest Airlines, America's leading short-haul airline, believes that the selection process starts not with the candidate but with the individuals responsible for

Recruitment advertising by Andersen Consulting.

recruiting. In a sense, it is they who must ensure that new hiring decisions reflect and reinforce the company's distinctive culture. Everyone hired to work in the airline's People Department—Southwest doesn't use the terms *human resources* or *personnel*—comes from a marketing or customer-contact background. This marketing orientation is displayed in internal research on job descriptions and selection criteria, whereby each department is asked, "What are you looking for?" rather than told, "This is what we think you need." Southwest invites supervisors and peers (with whom future candidates will be working) to participate in the in-depth interviewing and selection process. More unusually, it invites its own frequent flyers to participate in the initial interviews for flight attendants and to tell candidates what they, the passengers, value. The People Department admits to being amazed at the enthusiasm with which these busy customers have greeted this invitation and at their willingness to devote time to this task.

Challenges and Opportunities in Recruiting Workers for Technology-Based Jobs

It used to be thought that only manufacturing jobs could be exported. Today, however, technology allows both backstage and front-stage service jobs to be located around the world. American insurance companies, for instance, have recruited workers in Ireland to process claims. Paperwork is flown in daily from the United States, and digitized information is transmitted back to mainframe computers on the other side of the Atlantic (because of the five-hour time difference, the Irish are using these mainframes when they would normally be underutilized). Barbados, Jamaica, Singapore, India, and the Philippines are emerging as other potential English-speaking locations for telecommunicated services, not only for backstage work but also for such front-stage supplementary services as airline reservations and technical help lines (see the box on solving a skills shortage). Customers may be unaware of where the service person they are talking to is located. Their interest lies in dealing with people who have the personal and technical skills—plus the enabling technological support—to provide high-quality service.

Expert systems can be used to leverage employees' skills to perform work that previously required higher qualifications, more extensive training, or simply years of experience. Some systems are designed to train novices by gradually enabling them to perform at higher levels. Many expert systems capture and make available to all the scarce expertise of outstanding performers. American Express uses a well-

TECHNOLOGY SOLVES A SKILLS SHORTAGE

In the early 1990s, Singapore Airlines (SIA) was having trouble recruiting and retaining check-in agents for its home base at Changi Airport. It was getting harder to recruit people with the necessary skills at the wages SIA was willing to offer. Also, once they were on the job, many agents found it rather unchallenging. The predictable result: relatively high turnover and constant repetition of the expensive recruitment and training process. As part of a major program to update its departure control systems, SIA computer specialists created new software for check-in procedures, featuring screen formats with pull-down windows, menu-driven commands, and other innovations on the video terminal displays—all designed to speed and simplify usage. The net result is that SIA has been able to lower the educational criteria for the check-in position. The job is now open to people who previously would not have qualified and who view the work and the wages as fairly attractive. Because the new system is so much easier to use, only one week's training is needed—a significant savings for SIA. Employee satisfaction with this job is up, and turnover is down. Finally, agents are able to process passengers faster, making the former more productive and the latter happier.

known expert system called Authorizer's Assistant (originally called Laura's Brain, after a star authorizer), which contains the expertise of its best credit authorizers. It has improved the quality and speed of credit decisions dramatically and contributed enormously to corporate profitability.[11] An **expert system** contains three elements: a knowledge base about a particular subject; an inference engine that mimics a human expert's reasoning in order to draw conclusions from facts and figures, solve problems, and answer questions; and a user interface that gathers information from—and gives it to—the person using the system. Like human experts, such systems can give customized advice and may accept and handle incomplete and uncertain data.

expert system: an interactive computer program that mimics a human expert's reasoning to draw conclusions from data, solve problems, and give customized advice.

Rapid developments in information technology are permitting service businesses to make radical improvements in business processes and even completely reengineer their operations.[12] These developments sometimes result in wrenching changes for existing employees. Moreover, firms have redefined jobs, created new employee profiles for recruiting purposes, and hired employees with a different set of qualifications.

A growing number of customer-contact employees work by telephone, never meeting customers face to face. As with other types of service work, these jobs can be very rewarding or they can place employees in an electronic equivalent of the old-fashioned sweatshop. As discussed in the box on BT, recruiting people with the right skills and personalities, training them well, and giving them a decent working environment are some of the keys to success in this area.

SERVICE JOBS AS RELATIONSHIPS

Marketing theory argues that successful relationships are built on mutually satisfying exchanges from which both customers and suppliers gain value. This same notion of value can be applied to any employee who has a choice of whether or not

RECRUITING EMPLOYEES WHO WORK BY PHONE AT BT

BT (formerly British Telecom) is not only a major supplier of telecommunication services but also an active user of its own medium, the telephone, for managing relationships with its business accounts. In common with a growing number of firms that do business by phone, it is very dependent for its success on recruiting and retaining employees who are good at telephone-based transactions with customers whom they never see. Executives responsible for BT's telephone account management (TAM) operation, serving small businesses, are highly selective in their recruitment efforts. They look for bright, self-confident people who can be trained to listen to customers' needs and use structured, probing questions to build a database of information on each of the 1,000 accounts for which an account manager is responsible.

BT begins its recruitment process with a telephone interview, to see if candidates have the poise, maturity, and good speaking voice to project themselves well and inspire trust in a telephone-based job. (Curiously, most recruiters of telephone-based employees leave this all-important telephone test until much later in the process.) Those who pass this screen proceed to written tests and personal interviews.

Successful candidates receive intensive training. BT has built special training schools to create a consistent approach to customer care. Would-be account managers receive 13 weeks of training over a 12-month period, interspersed with live front-line experience at their home bases. They must develop in-depth knowledge of all the services and customer-premises equipment that BT sells, as well as the skills needed to build relationships with customers and to understand their business needs. Modern telecommunications technology is bewildering, for so much is changing so rapidly. Customers need a trusted advisor to act as consultant and problem solver. It is this role that BT's TAM program has succeeded in filling. For all the impressive supporting technology, the program would fail without good people at the other end of the phone.

to work for a particular organization (and the best employees usually do have opportunities to move on, if dissatisfied). The net value of a job is the extent to which its benefits exceed its associated costs. The most obvious benefits are pay, health insurance, and pension funding. However, most jobs also generate other benefits. Some offer learning or experience-building opportunities; some positions provide deep satisfaction because they are inherently interesting or give a sense of accomplishment; still others provide companionship, a valued chance to meet other people, dignity and self-worth, opportunities to travel, and the chance to make a social contribution.

But working in any job has its costs, too, beginning with the time spent on the job and traveling to and from work. Most jobs also entail some monetary costs, ranging from special clothes to commuting to child care. Stress can be a psychological and physical cost in a demanding job. Unpleasant working conditions may involve exposure to noise, smells, and temperature extremes. And, of course, some jobs require intense physical or mental effort. Decisions to change the nature of the service operation frequently affect employees, too. The perceived value of their jobs may go up or down as a result. But not everybody has the same priorities and concerns; there is segmentation among employees, as well as among customers. Part of the human resources challenge is to match round pegs to round holes of the right diameter.

Front-stage service jobs add another dimension: frequent customer contact—sometimes, but not always, involving extended relationships with the same customers. Depending on the employee's personality, these encounters may be seen in the abstract as a benefit to enjoy or a cost to be borne. In reality, good training, good support, and satisfied customers should increase the pleasure (or diminish the pain), and the reverse should also be true.

In job design, it is not enough just to ensure that the firm gets its money's worth out of its employees. Managers must also consider the design of the working environment and whether employees have the tools and facilities they need to deliver excellent service. Knowledgeable human resource managers know that if a job is changed through redesign, it will become more (or less) attractive to certain types of employees—and they can usually predict which ones. To an increasing degree, health and safety legislation requires changes in the workplace to eliminate physical and even psychological hazards, but only management can create a positive working climate, and that takes a long time. Reducing the negative aspects of the job and improving its positive ones may make it easier for firms to hire and retain the best available employees, without having to pay premium salaries and conventional benefits. Employees who enjoy their work are more likely to give good service to customers than unhappy ones.

Employee Retention and Customer Retention

Researchers have found strong correlations between employees' attitudes and perceptions of service quality among customers of the same organization.[13] One retail banking study showed that when employees reported a strong service orientation in the branch where they worked, customers reported that they received higher-quality service. A follow-up study determined that customers' intentions to switch to a competitor could be predicted, based on employee perceptions of the quality of service delivered. It also found that employee turnover probabilities were predictable, based on customers' perceptions of service quality. Simply put, when customers reported high-quality service, employees were less likely to leave. A reasonable inference is that it is not very rewarding to work in an environment in which service is poor and customers are dissatisfied. A study of a truck rental business found that higher levels of employee satisfaction were related to both lower turnover and lower worker's compensation claims.[14]

When jobs are low-paid, boring, and repetitive, with minimal training, service is likely to be poor and turnover high. Poor service generates high customer turnover, too, making the working environment even less rewarding. As a result, the firm spends all its resources trying to recruit both new customers and new employees. Loyal employees, in contrast, know the job and, in many cases, the customers, too. To the extent that long-term employees are customer oriented, knowledgeable, and motivated, better service and higher customer retention should result. Researchers have been able to document the economic value of both customer retention (see chapter 7) and employee retention[15] (see the box on loyal customers at State Farm Insurance). Many companies diminish their economic potential through human resource strategies that ensure high turnover of personnel—both their own employees and independent agents working with customers on the firm's behalf.

Cycles of Failure, Mediocrity, and Success

All too often, bad working environments translate into dreadful service, with employees treating customers the way their managers treat them. Businesses with high employee turnover are frequently stuck in what has been termed the cycle of failure. Others, which offer job security but little scope for personal initiative, may suffer from an equally undesirable cycle of mediocrity. However, there is potential for both vicious and virtuous cycles in service employment, the latter being termed the cycle of success.[17]

The cycle of failure.   In many service industries, the search for productivity is all-encompassing. One solution takes the form of simplifying work routines and hiring workers as cheaply as possible to perform repetitive work tasks that require little or no training. The cycle of failure captures the implications of such a strategy, with its two concentric but interactive cycles—one involving failures with employees; the second, with customers (Figure 16.1, p. 338).

The *employee cycle of failure* begins with a narrow design of jobs to accommodate low skill levels, emphasis on rules rather than service, and use of technology to control quality. A strategy of low wages is accompanied by minimal effort in selection or training. Consequences include bored employees who lack the ability to respond to customers' problems, become dissatisfied, and develop a poor service attitude. Outcomes for the firm are low service quality and high employee turnover.

LOYAL AGENTS EQUAL LOYAL CUSTOMERS AT STATE FARM

One factor underlying the ongoing success of State Farm Insurance in the United States is the interactive effect of both customer and agent retention. According to industry studies, State Farm's customer retention rate exceeds 90 percent, consistently the best performance of all national insurers that sell through agents. At the same time, more than 80 percent of newly appointed agents remain associated exclusively with State Farm through their fourth year, whereas the rate is only 20 percent to 40 percent for other companies in the industry. The average State Farm agent has 18 years of tenure compared to between six and nine years for competitors, making State Farm agents more experienced. This underlying synergy at State Farm comes from the fact that agents who are committed to building a long-term relationship with the company are more likely to build lasting relationships with customers, too. In turn, it's easier for agents to work with (and sell to) loyal customers whose needs, lifestyles, and attitudes to risk they know well. The net result is that the agents' productivity is 50 percent higher than industry norms.

FIGURE 16.1 The Cycle of Failure

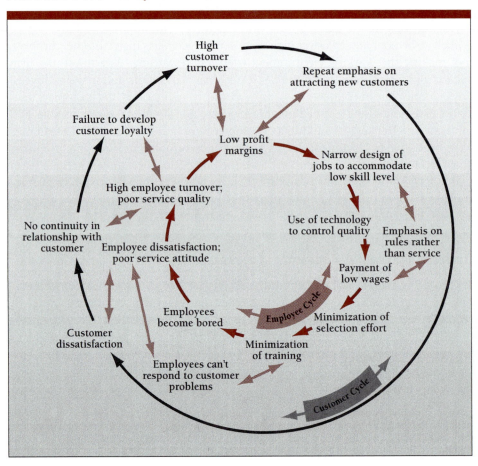

Source: Schlesinger and Heskett

Because of weak profit margins, the cycle repeats itself with the hiring of more low-paid employees to work in this unrewarding atmosphere.

The *customer cycle of failure* begins with repeated emphasis on attracting new customers, who become dissatisfied with employee performance and the lack of continuity implicit in continually changing faces. These customers fail to develop any loyalty to the supplier and turn over as rapidly as the staff, thus requiring an ongoing search for new customers to maintain sales volume. The departure of discontented customers is especially worrying in light of what we now know about the greater profitability of a loyal customer base. For conscientious managers, it should be deeply disturbing to contemplate the social implications of an enormous pool of nomadic service employees moving from one low-paying employer to the next and experiencing a stream of personal failures, in part because of the unwillingness of employers to invest in efforts to break the cycle.

Managers have offered a veritable litany of excuses and justifications for perpetuating this cycle:

■ "You just can't get good people nowadays."

■ "People just don't want to work today."

■ "To get good people would cost too much and you can't pass on these cost increases to customers."

- "It's not worth training our front-line people when they leave you so quickly."

- "High turnover is simply an inevitable part of our business. You've got to learn to live with it."[17]

Too many managers make short-sighted assumptions about the financial implications of low-pay and high-turnover human resource strategies. Part of the problem is failure to measure all relevant costs. Often omitted are three key variables: the cost of constant recruiting, hiring, and training (which is as much a time cost for managers as a financial cost); the cost of lower productivity of inexperienced new workers; and the cost of constantly attracting new customers (requiring extensive advertising and promotional discounts). Also ignored are two revenue variables: future revenue streams that might have continued for years but are lost when unhappy customers take their business elsewhere and potential income from prospective customers who are discouraged by negative word of mouth from even trying the service. Finally, there are less easily quantifiable costs, such as disruptions to service while a job remains unfilled and the loss of the departing employee's knowledge of the business (and its customers).

The cycle of mediocrity.   Another vicious employment cycle, the cycle of mediocrity (Figure 16.2), is most likely to be found in large, bureaucratic organizations—often typified by state monopolies, industrial cartels, or regulated oligopolies—where

FIGURE 16.2 The Cycle of Mediocrity

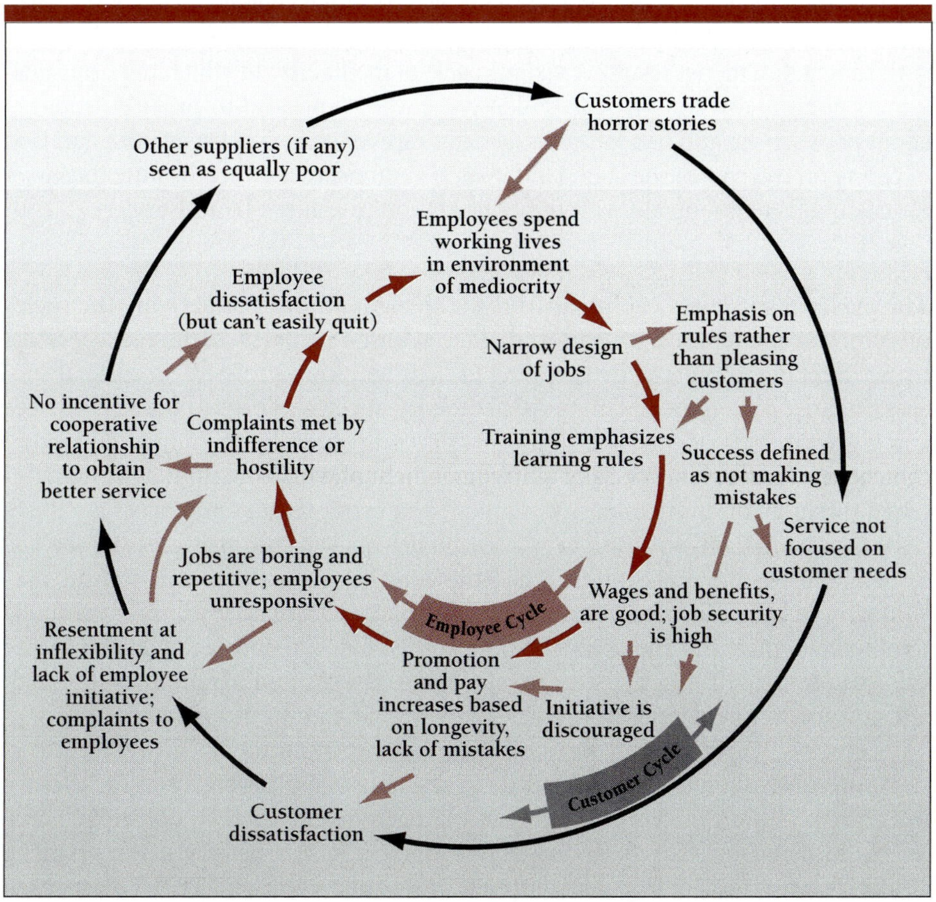

Source: Lovelock

there is little incentive to improve performance and where fear of entrenched unions may discourage management from adopting more innovative labor practices.

In these environments, service delivery standards tend to be prescribed by rigid rule books, oriented toward standardized service, operational efficiencies, and prevention of both employee fraud and favoritism toward specific customers. Employees often expect to spend their entire working lives with the organization. Job responsibilities tend to be narrowly and unimaginatively defined, tightly categorized by grade and scope of responsibilities, and further rigidified by union work rules. Salary increases and promotions are based on longevity, with successful performance in a job being measured by the absence of mistakes rather than by high productivity or outstanding customer service. Training, such as it is, focuses on learning the rules and the technical aspects of the job, not on improving human interactions with customers and coworkers. Because there are minimal allowances for flexibility or employee initiative, jobs tend to be boring and repetitive. However, in contrast to cycle-of-failure jobs, most positions provide adequate pay and often good benefits, combined with high security—thus making employees reluctant to leave. This lack of mobility is compounded by an absence of marketable skills that would be valued by organizations in other fields.

Customers find such organizations frustrating to deal with because of bureaucratic hassles, lack of service flexibility, and unwillingness of employees to make an effort to serve them better on such grounds as "That's not my job." What happens when there is nowhere else for customers to go, either because the service provider holds a monopoly or because all other available players are perceived as being as bad or worse? We shouldn't be surprised if dissatisfied customers display hostility toward service employees, who, feeling trapped in their jobs and powerless to improve the situation, protect themselves through such mechanisms as withdrawal into indifference, playing overtly by the rule book, or countering rudeness with rudeness. The net result? A vicious cycle of mediocrity in which unhappy customers continually complain to sullen employees (and also to other customers) about poor service and bad attitudes, generating ever greater defensiveness and lack of caring on the part of the staff. Under such circumstances, there is little incentive for customers to cooperate with the organization to achieve better service.

The cycle of success. Some firms reject the assumptions underlying the cycles of failure or mediocrity. Instead, they take a long-term view of financial performance, seeking to prosper by investing in their employees to create a cycle of success (Figure 16.3). As with failure or mediocrity, success applies to both employees and customers. Broadened job designs are accompanied by training and empowerment practices that allow front-stage personnel to control quality. With more focused recruitment, more intensive training, and better wages, employees are likely to be happier in their work and to provide higher-quality, customer-pleasing service.

Regular customers also appreciate the continuity in service relationships resulting from lower turnover, and so are more likely to remain loyal. Profit margins tend to be higher, and the organization is free to focus its marketing efforts on reinforcing loyalty through customer retention strategies, which are usually much less costly to implement than strategies for attracting new customers.

The deregulation of many service industries and privatization of government corporations have often been instrumental in rescuing organizations from the cycle of mediocrity. In both the United States and Canada, formerly monopolistic regional telephone companies have been forced to adopt a more competitive stance. In many countries, once mediocre public corporations—such as BT and British Airways—have undergone radical culture changes in the wake of privatization and exposure

FIGURE 16.3 The Cycle of Success

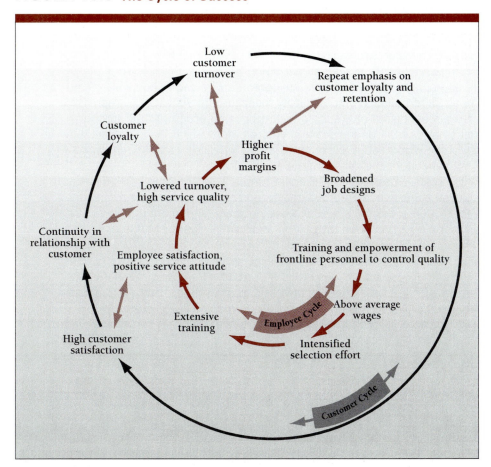

Source: Schlesinger and Heskett

Children, as well as adults, like to return to service outlets where friendly staff members treat them well.

to a more competitive environment. A slimming down of the ranks (usually resulting in retention of the more dynamic and service-oriented employees), redefinition of performance criteria, intensive training, and major reorganizations have created service firms that are much better able to offer customers good service (see the box on Beth Israel Hospital, pp. 342–343).

REWORKING THE SOCIOLOGY OF THE WORKPLACE AT BETH ISRAEL HOSPITAL

Boston's Beth Israel Hospital (BI) is a major teaching hospital, affiliated with Harvard Medical School, that also serves the local community. At BI, managers are trying to rework the sociology of the workplace in ways that are appropriate to the complex environment of a caring hospital—rather than to introduce somebody else's formulation of total quality management. As Laura Avakian, BI's vice-president for human resources, points out, such a task cannot be accomplished through a quick fix. "You can't just tell employees: 'Congratulations, you're empowered!'" she declares. In fact, changing the sociology of the workplace is a slow process, which takes years of constant effort. Moreover, it must reflect the culture and values of the institution itself.

In 1986, BI began creating a plan, PREPARE-21 ("Prepare for the 21st Century"), which seeks to expand and deepen employee participation, improve quality, and cut costs. As a nonprofit institution, the hospital can't offer stock ownership, but employees do share 50 percent of all cost savings, referred to as "gains." The plan has been in full operation since October 1989, with the expectation that it will continue to evolve over many years.

PREPARE-21 includes formalized training, of course. However, much of management's task involves creating the right environment for employees. This, in turn, requires good measurement and communication systems. Says Dr. Mitchell T. Rabkin, the hospital's president, "Deming [the quality pioneer] understood the importance of measuring in order to empower employees to know what was going on, thus allowing an employee to recognize before the boss that something was coming unstuck."

The Role of Unions

If HRM innovations are to achieve their full potential, employee cooperation is often essential. The power of organized labor is widely cited as an excuse for not adopting new approaches in both service and manufacturing businesses. "We'd never get it past the unions," managers say, wringing their hands and muttering darkly about restrictive work practices. Unions are often portrayed as the bad guys in the media, especially when high-profile strikes inconvenience millions. Examples of particularly disruptive industrial disputes range from British, French, and Japanese railway workers to employees of certain U.S. airlines, and from Irish bank personnel to Canadian postal workers. On the other hand, polls showed that customers and the general public were overwhelmingly sympathetic to union concerns of unfair treatment of part-time employees when the Teamsters Union struck United Parcel Service in 1997.

American managers have a reputation for being especially antagonistic toward unions. Jeffrey Pfeffer observes wryly that "the subject of unions and collective bargaining is...one that causes otherwise sensible people to lose their objectivity."[18] He urges a pragmatic approach to this issue, emphasizing that "the effects of unions depend very much on what *management* does." In reviewing numerous studies of the impact of unions (across many U.S. industries), he notes that unions do raise wage levels—especially for low-wage workers—as well as reducing turnover, improving working conditions, and leading to better resolution of grievances. They can also have a positive impact on productivity, but only in those companies where both management's and labor's leadership skills are strong. These improvements in productivity, he suggests, may reflect the greater selectivity in recruitment that is possible when jobs pay better and thus attract more candidates, together with the lower turnover often found in unionized firms and the resulting presence of a more experienced work force. Clearly we are talking about cycles of success here, not cycles of mediocrity.

The hospital has also focused on developing good internal communication systems, including an informal weekly newsletter written by Dr. Rabkin. He remarks, "Knowledge is empowering. When customers and visitors ask, the employees know what is going on and why. They feel they *are* the hospital, rather than answering, 'They don't tell me nothing!' If you don't tell them, if they don't know, then distorted rumors start circulating. Worse yet, they feel excluded and not a true part of the hospital. Employees, in general, are well motivated and want to do well. Furthermore, no one knows the job better than individual employees themselves. Therefore, if you create an environment in which they feel comfortable enough, knowledgeable enough, about the business to feel that they *own* the business in a sense, they will contribute—providing, of course, that their capacity to contribute is enhanced by a responsive upper structure of the organization."

Rabkin and Avakian are strong believers in the importance of enlightened managers who can coach employees in their use of quality tools and who can engage them in active problem solving. All BI supervisors participate in an intense 40-hour leadership development track. One problem that top management has sought to address is that of uneven committment to PREPARE-21, particularly by physicians. However, these individuals are becoming more involved as they realize that the hospital's management is not assailing the quality of their care. Rabkin and Avakian note, "Physicians will buy in when we talk about improving quality of care through improving the quality of the *systems* by which they deliver care."

Although it may take time and effort to persuade existing employees to change their orientation and working habits, there's less of a problem with newcomers. In recruiting new employees, the hospital uses value-based interviewing, so that job applicants may be screened for participation and teamwork skills, as well as for credentials.

The United States is a useful site for comparative research on the impact of unions because firms in the same industry vary widely in the extent of unionization. Among the firms featured in *The 100 Best Companies to Work for in America* are 27 that are strongly unionized, including such successful service firms as Alagasco (natural gas distribution) and Southwest Airlines.[19] Perhaps the most striking contrasts are to be found in the airlines. Among the better regarded U.S. carriers, American Airlines is unionized but Delta is not. Management-union confrontations contributed significantly to the collapse and disappearance of unpopular Eastern Airlines. But compare this situation with that of Southwest Airlines, which is almost 90 percent unionized yet boasts the lowest costs per mile, highest profits, best on-time performance, best baggage handling, and highest customer satisfaction of any U.S. airline (as measured by the fewest complaints to the U.S. Department of Transportation). The airline's unusually good labor-management relations are widely seen as a direct result of its chairman's hands-on efforts. The one area on which management will not negotiate is work rules. It's also worth noting that 30 percent of Southwest employees own 10 percent of the company's stock.

The inescapable conclusion is that the presence of unions in a service company is not an automatic barrier to high performance and innovation, unless there is a long history of mistrust, acrimonious relationships, and confrontation. However, management cannot rule by fiat: Consultation and negotiation with union representatives are essential if employees are to accept new ideas (conditions that are equally valid in non-unionized firms, too).

HUMAN RESOURCE MANAGEMENT IN A MULTICULTURAL CONTEXT

The trend toward a global economy means that more and more service firms are operating across national frontiers. Other important trends are increased tourism and business travel, plus substantial immigration of people from different cultural back-

EURO DISNEY AND THE CHALLENGES OF MULTICULTURALISM

Few service ventures of recent years have attracted as much media comment and coverage as the Walt Disney Co.'s latest venture, Disneyland Paris. Although most of the reported financial losses stem from real estate problems and low occupancy in the hotels, the cultural difficulties of creating and running an American-style theme park in the heart of Europe have been widely publicized. Because Disneyland Paris replicates three successful Disney theme parks, top management's objective has been to ensure that the park adapts itself to European conditions without losing the American feel that has always been seen as one of its main draws. For officials of the European company, Euro Disney, the new park just outside of Paris has proved even more of a challenge than Disney's first foreign theme park, Tokyo Disneyland, which opened in Japan in 1983. Unlike the California, Florida, or Tokyo parks, no one nationality dominates the Paris park. Thus, handling languages and cultures has required careful planning, not least in terms of employee recruitment, training, and motivation.

Knowledge of two or more languages has been an important criterion in hiring "cast members" (front-line employees). Months before opening day, recruitment centers were set up in Paris, London, Amsterdam, and Frankfurt. During the park's first season (1992), approximately two-thirds of those hired were French nationals; the balance included another 75 nationalities, principally British, Dutch, German, and Irish. Some knowledge of French is required of all employees; about 75 percent spoke this language fluently, another 75 percent spoke English, roughly 25 percent spoke Spanish, and 25 percent spoke German.

The reservations center caters to people of many tongues, with special phone lines for each of 12 different languages. The main information center in the park, City Hall, is staffed by cast members speaking a broad cross-section of languages. Special procedures have been instituted at the park's medical center to handle medical emergencies involving speakers of less commonly encountered languages. With over 70 nationalities represented among its employees, there is a high probability that a cast member can be found somewhere on site to interpret in such a situation. The company has noted the language capabilities of every employee, can access them by computer (who

grounds into developed economies such as those of the United States, Canada, Australia, New Zealand, and many European countries. The net result is pressure on service organizations to serve a more diverse array of customers—with different cultural expectations and speaking a variety of languages—and to recruit a more diverse work force.

Striking a balance between diversity and conformity to common standards is not a simple task as societal norms vary across cultures. When McDonald's opened a fast-food restaurant in Moscow, management trained staff members to smile at customers. However, this particular norm did not exist in Russia, and some patrons concluded that staff members were making fun of them. Another example of cultural conflicts comes from the troubled early history of Euro Disney (see the box on the challenges of multiculturalism).

Part of the HRM challenge as it relates to culture is to determine which performance standards are central and which should be treated more flexibly. For instance, some public service agencies in Britain (and elsewhere) that require employees to wear uniforms have been willing to allow Sikh employees to wear a matching turban with badge, but others have generated conflict by insisting on traditional uniform caps. Multiculturalism may also require new HRM procedures. Thus, the decision to be more responsive to customers (and even employees) whose first language is not English may require changes in recruiting criteria, the use of role-playing exercises, and language training.[20]

do we have on duty who speaks Turkish?), and can page them immediately by beeper or walkie-talkie.

However, Euro Disney has encountered many cultural problems in training and motivation. The company's 1990 Annual Report announced that "a leading priority was to indoctrinate all employees in the Disney service philosophy, in addition to training them in operational policies and procedures." The apparent goal was to transform all employees, 60 percent of whom were French, into clean-cut, user-friendly, American-style service providers. Since the founding of Disneyland in 1958, Disney has been known for its strict professional guidelines. "The Look Book," for example, dictated that female employees should wear only clear nail polish; very little, if any, makeup; and, until recent years, only flesh-colored stockings. Men could not have beards or mustaches and had to keep their hair short and tapered. Guests should be greeted within 60 seconds of entering a facility and helped as needed.

According to media reports, a key challenge has been to train French employees to adopt Disney standards. The park's manager of training and development for Disney University was quoted as saying, "The French are not known for their hospitality. But Disney is." During the first four months of operations, more than 1,000 employees left the park. According to management, half quit, and the rest were asked to leave. Subsequently, the women's grooming guidelines were modified because "what is considered a classic beauty in Europe is not considered a classic beauty in America." Female cast members can now wear pink or red nail polish, red lipstick and different colored stockings as long as they "complement [the] outfit and are in dark, subdued colors."

Another Disney trademark is to smile a lot. Yet as one observer commented, "If the French are asked to smile, they will answer, 'I'll smile if I want to. Convince me.'" The training had to be adapted to suit the European work force. Although Disney stressed total customer satisfaction, in the eyes of some employees the company had imposed controls that had made that goal impossible to deliver.

Source: Adapted from Christopher Lovelock and Ivor Morgan, "Euro Disney: An American in Paris" in Christopher Lovelock, *Services Marketing* 3d ed. (Upper Saddle River, NJ: Prentice Hall, 1996), pp. 127–140.

Conclusion

It's probably harder to duplicate high-performance human assets than any other corporate resource. To the extent that employees understand and support the goals of an organization, have the skills needed to succeed in performing their jobs, work well together in teams, recognize the importance of ensuring customer satisfaction, and have the authority and self-confidence to use their own initiative in problem solving, the marketing and operational functions should actually be easier to manage.

Study Questions and Exercises

1. List five ways in which investment in hiring and selection, training, and ongoing motivation of employees will pay dividends in customer satisfaction for such organizations as (a) an airline, (b) a hospital, and (c) a restaurant.
2. Define what is meant by the control and involvement models of management.
3. What is emotional labor? Explain the ways in which it may cause stress for employees in specific jobs. Illustrate with suitable examples.
4. Identify the factors favoring a strategy of employee empowerment.
5. What is the distinction between empowerment and enablement? Can you have one without the other?

6. Highlight specific ways in which technology—particularly information technology—is changing the nature of service jobs. Provide examples of situations in which its use is likely to (a) enhance and (b) detract from employee job satisfaction.

7. What can a marketing perspective bring to the practice of human resource management?

8. What important ethical issues do you see facing human resource managers in high-contact service organizations?

Cases

VICK'S PIZZA CORPORATION

Victor Firenze, chief executive of Vick's Pizza Corporation, looked somber as he addressed senior executives of the national restaurant chain that bore his nickname. "We're facing yet another lawsuit for injuries because of alleged dangerous driving by one of our delivery drivers," he announced at the company's head office in Illinois. "It comes on top of some very bad publicity about accidents involving our drivers in recent years."

Background

Speed had always been a key strategic thrust for Vick's Pizza, which used the slogan "It's quick at Vick's." Not only was pizza prepared rapidly at the company's restaurants, but home deliveries arrived fast, too. The company's promise to deliver a pizza within 30 minutes of a phone order or to cut $3 off the price had boosted it from a single pizzeria 20 years earlier to the status of a national chain, with thousands of outlets and more than $3 billion in sales. But now a growing number of critics were saying that, in Vick's case at least, speed was a killer.

Vick's executives argued that the system did not promote fast or reckless driving. "The speed takes place in the store—not on the road," declared a spokesperson. "We can custom-make a pizza within 10 to 12 minutes. Our average delivery area is only 1 to 2 miles, so there's enough time to deliver."

The Safety Problem

The company's own records indicated that during the previous year, accidents involving Vick's drivers had cost 20 lives, 18 of them during pizza runs. But it had declined to specify how many of the victims were employees. Randell Meins, Vick's vice president of corporate communications, stated in a TV interview that the company had always encouraged drivers to take care, had never penalized late drivers, was urging franchise owners and store managers to promote safe driving, and would soon implement a new safety course for all Vick's drivers.

Meins cited the owner of several franchises in Ohio, who had declared, "We never ask a driver to break the speed limit. We never want them to do anything unsafe on the road. And we always tell them to fasten their seat belts." While acknowledging that "even one death is too many," Meins noted that with 230 million pizzas delivered last year, this works out to only one death per 11.5 million pies. "We're not minimizing the deaths by any means," Meins said. "But that's what the mathematics show."

Martina Gomes, director of a nonprofit safety research and advocacy group, expressed outrage over Vick's statistic. "Great!" she said. "Now we know the value of the life of a 17-year-old—11.5 million pizzas." Gomes offered her own statistical analysis. Vick's, she said, employed some 75,000 part-time drivers. Assuming that this amounted to the equivalent of 20,000 full-time drivers—four for each of the 5,000 Vick's outlets—she claimed that 20 deaths in one year meant that the company's drivers faced a death rate between three and six times higher than that in the construction industry and twice as high as that of miners. "The point is this," said Gomes. "Would parents let their kids drive for Vick's if they knew they were three times more likely to die doing that job than if they were working in construction?"

Scott and Linda Hurding's 17-year-old son had been the latest Vick's driver to die, the only Vick's employee so far during the current year. Hustling to deliver pizzas in a semi-rural area near Dallas, Texas, Mike Hurding often covered 100 miles a night. His parents and classmates said he was proud that he almost always made the delivery within the 30-minute limit and was determined never to get the "King of the Lates" badge, allegedly given every week by his franchisor to the driver most often late on deliveries.

Mike died when the company-owned pickup he was driving in a delivery run skidded off a wet road and hit a utility pole in an effort to avoid another car that was braking to make a left-hand turn. A police reconstruction of the accident concluded that Mike had been driving 45 mph on a road with a 30 mph speed limit and was not wearing a seat belt. The other driver was not charged. Vick's subsequently offered the Hurding family about $5,000 in worker's compensation to cover funeral costs. Gomes estimated that the 20 deaths during the previous year had cost Vick's some $90,000 in death benefits. Like many other critics of the company, she argued that Vick's was unconcerned because the cost was so low. Accordingly, she had written to Victor Firenze, asking Vick's to pay $500,000 to each accident victim, abandon the 30-minute rule, and hire only drivers aged 18 or older.

Linda Hurding, Mike's mother, told a TV reporter that Vick's guarantee to deliver each pizza within 30 minutes or knock $3 off the price was just "a license to speed." Blaming this policy for their son's death, the Hurding parents and a group of family friends had started a petition drive, asking for federal restrictions on the policy. Within a month of beginning their drive, the petitioners had delivered the first batch of more than 1,500 signatures to the offices of their U.S. senator. "We're angry and we're fighting," the Hurdings said. Meanwhile, a state agency in Texas was looking into the case to determine whether Vick's policy violated the Occupational Safety and Health Act under its jurisdiction.

Vick's faced criticism and legal action on other fronts as well. In Eugene, Oregon, the widow of a motorcyclist allegedly struck and killed by a Vick's driver nine months earlier had sued the company for damages. In Atlanta, attorney Anders Mundel had just filed suit on behalf of Wilson and Jennifer Groncki, who suffered neck, back, and arm injuries when their car was broadsided by a driver who had run a stop sign as she left a Vick's store with four pizzas for delivery. The Gronckis alleged that the store manager had rushed to the scene of the wreck and yelled, "Let's get this pizza on the road!" In addition to unspecified monetary damages, the suit sought to force Vick's to abandon the 30-minute rule, which the attorney called "a grossly negligent corporate policy."

Mundel was also helping other lawyers around the country to press cases against the company and had organized an information network, including a Web site, to coordinate the filing of cases in different jurisdictions. "Even if Vick's franchisees, managers, and executives do not actively encourage reckless driving," he argued, "the 30-minute rule acts as an inherent encouragement, putting great pressure on the drivers."

As part of her research, safety advocate Gomes had interviewed a number of current and former Vick's employees, several of whom preferred to remain anonymous for fear of reprisals from the managers where they worked. Gomes claimed that her research showed that "the vast majority" of the company's drivers were under 18. Nelson Chen, a 20-year-old college student and former part-time Vick's employee who had worked in several Vick's outlets in southern California over a three-year period, told Gomes that he and other drivers "speeded all the time. I would even run stop signs—anything to make those deliveries." Sue, a 19-year-old driver in Kansas, said managers "get uptight when pizzas are running late and start yelling at everyone to hurry up, hurry up!" A consultant familiar with the industry agreed: "There's a lot of pressure to speed. It's not written in the manuals, but it's there. If a driver goes out with four deliveries and ends up with only a minute to make that last one but figures he's two minutes away, he's going to speed; he's going to cut corners."

Responding to the Problem

Two weeks after Mike Hurding's death, Vick's sent a letter to its corporate-owned stores and its franchisees stating that it was company policy to hire drivers 18 or older. This directive, however, was not binding on the franchisees, who operated some 65 percent of all Vick's restaurants.

The newly filed Atlanta lawsuit, together with continuing criticism of the company, had been widely reported in the media. Vick Firenze and his colleagues were worried. Historically, the company had enjoyed a positive public image and a reputation as a generous donor to local community activities. "We definitely have a perception problem," said Randell Heins. "We're taking a lot of heat right now. But the last thing we need to do is to panic," warned the senior vice president of marketing. "The 30-minute guarantee is very, very important to our customers. Sales could be hard hit if we drop it."

■ Questions for Discussion

1. Make a flowchart of Vick's service delivery system from receipt of the order to delivery of the pizza to the customer. Why are pizzas sometimes delivered late?
2. How important is the 30-minute guarantee?
3. How serious is the present situation for Vick's Pizza Corporation? How well has it handled the situation so far?
4. If you were a senior manager of Vick's Pizza Corporation, what do you think the company should do now? Why?

ARROW MANAGEMENT

"We provide value to our customers in two ways," stated Gary Chamberlain, owner and founder of Arrow Management. "First, we do jobs they could do themselves but don't want to. Second, we help them save money on their equipment and facilities maintenance." After a slow start in Portland, Oregon, in the early 1990s, Chamberlain had found a profitable niche for his company in Menlo Park, California.

Chamberlain's father was a contractor who introduced Gary to the engineering business at an early age. He was a project manager for his father's construction company and then worked in both engineering consulting and mechanical engineering firms. This experience gave him the ability to communicate well with different players in the contracting and maintenance industries. In both appearance and behavior, Chamberlain created an energetic and efficient impression. His athletic activities (he was a national triathlon champion in 1990 and had become an avid mountain biker) kept him physically fit and trim. Chamberlain had no college degree but felt his hands-on training gave him the skills he needed to design and implement his service concept successfully.

Arrow Management did business with 6 to 10 companies a year. Its clients included universities, large biotechnical and pharmaceutical firms, manufacturing plants, and office buildings that had large physical facilities. Chamberlain had two employees (including himself) but had had as many as seven in the past. He preferred to keep his company small because he felt quality was thus easier to control.

Arrow Management's Services

Chamberlain had developed an effective method for collecting and providing accurate information to businesses about mechanical or electrical equipment at their facilities that requires routine maintenance. He and his employees traveled to clients' sites to locate and inspect their equipment—primarily heating and air-conditioning units or specialized climate control devices—and record data. Arrow Management provided accurate, timely documentation that was presented in a professional, attractive, and user-friendly report. These reports were generated at Arrow's office through computerized mapping techniques and were then delivered to the clients.

Because the task of equipment maintenance was usually outsourced to building contractors at $80 to $90 an hour, clients saved money if they didn't have to pay the contractors to spend time locating the equipment before servicing it. The data could also be used to ensure that contractors who were bidding on maintenance jobs didn't overprice their services. Several of Arrow Management's clients would not award maintenance contracts until Chamberlain had analyzed the bids for accuracy.

Prices were calculated and billed on a per-project basis. Chamberlain estimated the costs and labor involved and added a small contingency for unexpected overruns (in case the project took longer to complete or was more expensive than he expected). He had discovered several years earlier that he could make more money by collecting fewer pieces of data and that service quality from the client's perspective actually increased. Based on this information, he streamlined his service delivery processes so he could concentrate on doing a few things well. Reducing the number of services Arrow Management offered had allowed Chamberlain to standardize procedures and improve his profit margins significantly.

Winning and Keeping Customers

Much of the company's income was generated from repeat business. For example, Stanford University in Palo Alto, California, used Arrow Management on a regular basis. Chamberlain stated that he had become the "voice of Stanford" for the Athletic Department in quality control for equipment maintenance. Contractors who were hired to maintain the department's equipment did not get paid until he certified that their work had been completed satisfactorily.

Current clients referred many of Arrow Management's new customers. Chamberlain had tried direct mailings to attract additional business but had not been satisfied with the results. He estimated that 800 mailed flyers might generate one or two new clients. Recently he had been experimenting with magnets that displayed the company logo and phone number. These seemed to be more effective because people tended to keep them longer and were more likely to have the information in front of them when a need arose.

Chamberlain encouraged people who were considering his service to check with existing customers and to inspect his work. He sometimes made a preliminary report, using a Polaroid camera to document the location and condition of a company's equipment for potential customers. Chamberlain also attempted to minimize perceived risks by suggesting that potential clients could hire Arrow Management for a small project or the most undesirable jobs so they could judge the quality of its work themselves.

"Anybody can do the technical work," said Chamberlain, "but it's the relationships that make it fun or worthwhile." He believed that relationship management was the key to quality service. It helped him understand what clients needed and expected and also enabled him to complete jobs more efficiently. He used his outgoing manner and aggressive charm to get employees inside his clients' organizations to provide the information he needed in a timely manner so he could complete his own work faster. Chamberlain was aware of small ways in which he could make key employees' lives better so that they would be willing to help him in the future. (An example was the time he fixed a broken heating system in a manager's office for free so that she wouldn't continue to freeze every winter.) Chamberlain was also able to deal very effectively with building contractors who bid on maintenance jobs for his clients. He understood their side of the business and could speak in their terms. Because he was not intimidated by the contractors, he was able to represent his clients' interests well.

What Keeps the Boss Up at Night?

"Nothing related to work," Chamberlain said with a grin. He believed he had found a niche that was fairly resistant to competition. Chamberlain referred to himself as the "Kelly Boy" of maintenance management (a reference to the international temporary employment agency whose female workers were once popularly referred to as Kelly Girls). Although his clients could do the work themselves, they preferred to hire him because they were typically short-staffed and had difficulty in meeting the necessary maintenance completion dates without additional help. Chamberlain felt that he could outbid larger companies for jobs. He stated that many consulting firms were not interested in doing what Arrow Management does because "it's grunt work and you have to be willing to get dirty."

Chamberlain had no formal business plan and no definite goals for the future. He was satisfied with keeping his company and client base small. "If you're a worrier, being self-employed could eat you alive," he remarked. "You need to have a passion for what you're doing, and customers sense this when selecting a vendor. If I didn't have to work for a living, I'd probably choose my current career as a way to keep occupied anyway."

■ Questions for Discussion

1. What is the nature of the service that Arrow Management is offering? What processes are involved?
2. How has Arrow Management addressed each of the 8Ps in its overall marketing strategy?
3. What special risks or challenges does Chamberlain face as owner and primary employee of his company? What unique opportunities does he have?
4. Why is relationship management important to the outcome of Chamberlain's work? Is relationship management different for business services than for consumer services?
5. Do you agree with Chamberlain's assessment of his competitive position? Why or why not?

HAMPTON INN: THE 100% SATISFACTION GUARANTEE

Hampton Inn, a subsidiary of Promus Hotel Corporation, was the first company in the lodging industry to offer its customers an unconditional service guarantee.

> HAMPTON INN: 100% SATISFACTION GUARANTEE
> We guarantee high quality accommodations, friendly and
> efficient service, and clean, comfortable surroundings.
> If you're not completely satisfied, we don't expect you to pay.

Guests were encouraged to act as quality-assurance inspectors by identifying deficiencies and reporting them to hotel employees. Reporting systems were set up to identify cases in which the guarantee was invoked and to monitor the problems that triggered them.

Following the introduction of the guarantee on a pilot basis at 30 inns in 1989, guests were asked whether the guarantee had influenced their decision to stay at that Hampton Inn. They were also asked if the guarantee would influence their decision to return to that Hampton Inn or to another Hampton Inn in the future. Finally, guests were asked what they thought of the guarantee, whether they believed it was truly unconditional, and what changes if any they had noticed in the employees' behavior. The most commonly heard comments were these:

- "It helps ensure I'll get the service I deserve."
- "No one else offers this."
- "They stand behind what they say."
- "I'll get my money's worth."
- "It makes their employees try harder."

Later research documented the financial benefits of the guarantee, showing that the revenues from greater patronage greatly exceeded the costs of administering the program. In subsequent years, the guarantee was extended to other hotels operated by Promus, including Hampton Inn & Suites, Embassy Suites, and Homewood Suites. The chairman and other executives emphasized the guarantee's power to align the organization's processes, systems, and policies to create positive, lasting change.

Soon, a few competing chains started to offer their own guarantees, although Promus executives felt that these competitive programs were often poorly designed and administered.

Among many managers, the 100% satisfaction guarantee fostered a proactive attitude toward problem prevention. They saw that it was financially more advantageous for managers and employees to prevent problems from occurring in the first place than to spend money through the reactive response of giving refunds to dissatisfied guests. For example, a manager discovered late one evening that his hotel would lose its water supply overnight. Rather than conjure up myriad excuses to offer to his guests, he thought about how to minimize their dissatisfaction with this potentially disastrous situation. Knowing that his guests would want coffee, he arranged for a caterer to deliver several urns of coffee before breakfast and checkout. He also went to the local WalMart store and purchased over 100 one-gallon jugs, which were filled with water and then placed outside guests' doors so that they could wash and brush their teeth. In the morning, the manager personally called all guests at their appropriate wake-up times, taking responsibility for the problem and apologizing for any inconvenience. His proactive strategy paid off—there were zero guarantee invocations that day.

Continuing Doubts among Hotel Owners and Managers

Despite mounting evidence of the guarantee's financial and operational benefits for the chain, many owners and managers of Promus properties continued to harbor doubts. They overlooked the guarantee's value as a retention strategy, whose documented return on investment clearly outperformed investment in more traditional marketing and advertising efforts designed to attract new guests. Hotel managers typically had misgivings about "giving the store away" or being taken advantage of by guests. Furthermore, they viewed guarantee refunds as an expense that should be minimized rather than an investment in building a loyal base of guests, who as long as they continued to be satisfied with their stays at Promus properties, amounted to annuities: steady streams of future revenue.

The general manager of one hotel later recalled his initial reaction to the guarantee:

> I didn't agree with it. They were expecting me to give up
> control of my property and my guests' satisfaction. I didn't
> want to give my employees full discretion to give away

money; I wanted them to check everything through me so
that I would have the last say with every guest. Many of us
viewed the guarantee solely as an expense item on our profit
and loss statements. Given how dedicated I was to managing
my bottom line, I viewed the guarantee as an expense line
item that I wanted to control and manage. After all, that's the
way I had been doing business for years.

At a meeting to promote the benefits of the guarantee, some general managers said
they felt more comfortable *negotiating* with customers for what each side felt was a fair
remedy—a partial refund, $10 off the guest's bill, or a free room the next night. Responding to these views, Promus's chairman countered,

But that isn't what guests are paying for! The guests pay for a
night's stay. If they aren't satisfied, then they don't pay, pure
and simple. Anything further is a compromise of what we
stand for—the absolute satisfaction of our customers. This
isn't a program to give away money. This is a program to
enhance the quality of our hotel system.

Over time, hotel owners and managers came to recognize the value of the guarantee as a framework for making capital investment decisions. Any documentation of a
trend of guarantee invocations in a specific area (e.g., numerous complaints about threadbare carpeting) made clear the need for investment and lowered the priority on a more
discretionary item, such as the latest telephone technology. The guarantee also freed
managers from having to resolve every guest problem themselves. Employees were empowered to resolve customer issues and ensure each guest's total satisfaction, leaving the
managers time to dedicate their attention to more strategic issues that might otherwise
have been neglected.

The Problem of Uncontrollables

One ongoing barrier to managers' acceptance of the guarantee concept involved the
issue of "uncontrollables," which they felt they could do nothing about. During the
chain-wide implementation of the guarantee at Hampton Inn, one general manager,
surprised and pleased to receive a personal call from a vice president at the head office,
voiced his concern regarding the numerous guarantee invocations at his property. Many
of his guests' visits, he said, were marred by noise from other guests in public areas or
other rooms. "It's just one of those uncontrollables," he ventured. "I've had this problem for years, and I lose a number of people every year to the noise. I consider it a natural part of doing business." He explained that his property was adjacent to a youth
athletic-tournament facility. "I often have several teams staying here. The kids do get
rowdy running upstairs and downstairs, visiting one another, and running down the
halls. We try to keep them quiet, but first, they are kids and, second, we need to keep
the large volume of business they generate."

Discussing the situation objectively, he and the vice president found a solution. The
manager would dedicate the bottom floor of one wing to the sports teams, effectively
isolating the noise and saving other guests from being disturbed. But what if the hotel
were almost full and a last-minute guest had to be assigned a room in that wing? The solution was to be proactive: Front-desk employees would explain to such guests that it
might be noisy and if that was likely to be a problem, they might be more comfortable
staying at another hotel. When this procedure was implemented, most guests decided to
stay at the Hampton Inn in question rather than returning to their cars and trying to
find other accommodations.

Subsequently, a few people occasionally invoked the guarantee at that property, even after warnings about noise; most guests, however, were satisfied with their stay, and in fact appreciated the staff's candor. Often, the noise turned out to be less than the receptionist had suggested, so that guests were pleased with their decision to stay.

The Problem of Full-Service Functions

One area in which managers and owners still felt overly vulnerable concerned the implied obligation to refund the entire cost of a full-service function (e.g., a meeting or wedding banquet) when the guarantee was invoked for any reason. For instance, should customer dissatisfaction with the setup of a meeting room require a refund of the entire fee? Should the entire wedding banquet fee be refunded because coffee was delivered late? Senior Promus executives debated how best to address these concerns within the spirit of the 100% satisfaction guarantee.

■ Questions for Discussion

1. Evaluate the philosophy behind introduction of the 100% satisfaction guarantee. Is this the best way to improve service quality?
2. What are the implications of the guarantee for (a) guests, (b) managers, and (c) Promus?
3. Because certain events are "uncontrollable," wouldn't it be more realistic to exclude them from the guarantee?
4. As a member of the Promus senior management team, how would you address hotel managers' concerns about applying guarantees to full-service functions?

☞✓ FOUR CUSTOMERS IN SEARCH OF SOLUTIONS

Among the many customers of Bell Telephone in Toronto, Ontario, are four individuals living on Willow Street in a middle-class suburb of the city. Each of them has a telephone-related problem and decides to call the company about it.

Winston Chen

Winston Chen grumbles constantly about the amount of his home telephone bill (which is, in fact, in the top 2 percent of all household phone bills in Ontario). There are many calls to countries in Southeast Asia on weekday evenings, almost daily calls to Kingston (a smaller city not far from Toronto) around midday, and calls to Vancouver, BC, most weekends. One day, Chen receives a telephone bill that is even larger than usual. On reviewing the bill, he is convinced that he has been overcharged, so he calls Bell's customer service department to complain and request an adjustment.

Marie Portillo

Marie Portillo has missed several important calls recently because the caller received a busy signal. She phones the telephone company to determine possible solutions to this problem. Portillo's telephone bill is at the median level for a household subscriber. Most of the calls from her house are local, but there are occasional international calls to Mexico or to countries in South America. She does not subscribe to any value-added services.

Eleanor Vanderbilt

During the past several weeks, Eleanor Vanderbilt has been distressed to receive a series of obscene telephone calls. It sounds like the same person each time. She calls the telephone company to see if it can stop this harassment. Her phone bill is in the bottom 10 percent of all household subscriber bills and almost all calls are local.

Richard Robbins

For more than a week, the phone line at Richard Robbins's house has been making strange humming and crackling noises, making it difficult to hear what the other person is saying. After two of his friends comment on these distracting noises, Robbins calls Bell and reports the problem. His guess is that it is being caused by the answering machine, which is getting old and sometimes loses messages. Robbins's phone bill is at the 75th percentile for a household subscriber. Most of the calls are made to locations within Canada, usually during evenings and weekends, although there are a few calls to the United States, too.

■ Questions for Discussion

1. Based strictly on the information in the case, how many possibilities do you see to segment the telecommunications market?
2. As a customer service representative at the telephone company, how would you address each of the problems and complaints reported?
3. Do you see any marketing opportunities for Bell in any of these complaints?

SULLIVAN'S AUTO WORLD

Viewed from Wilson Avenue, the dealership presented a festive sight. Strings of triangular pennants in red, white, and blue fluttered gaily in the late afternoon breeze. Rows of new model cars gleamed and winked in the sunlight. Geraniums graced the flower beds outside the showroom entrance. A huge rotating sign at the corner of Wilson Avenue and Victoria Street sported the Ford logo and identified the business as Sullivan's Auto World. Banners below urged, "Let's Make a Deal!'

Inside the handsome, high-ceilinged showroom, three of the new model Fords were on display—a dark green 4 × 4 sport utility vehicle, a red convertible, and a white Taurus. Each car was polished to a high sheen. Two groups of customers were chatting with salespeople, and a middle-aged man sat in the driver's seat of the convertible, studying the controls.

Upstairs in the comfortably furnished general manager's office, Carol Sullivan-Diaz finished running another spreadsheet analysis on her laptop computer. She felt tired and depressed. Her father, Walter Sullivan, had died four weeks earlier at the age of 56 of a sudden heart attack. As executor of his estate, the bank had asked her to temporarily assume the position of general manager of the dealership. The only visible change that she had made to her father's office was the installation of a fax machine and laser printer, but she had been very busy analyzing the current position of the business.

Sullivan-Diaz did not like the look of the numbers on the printout. Auto World's financial situation had been deteriorating for 18 months, and it had been running in the red for the first half of the current year. New-car sales had declined, reflecting a turndown in the regional economy. Margins had been squeezed by promotions and other efforts to move new cars off the lot. Industry forecasts of future sales were discouraging, and so were her own financial projections for Auto World's sales department. Service revenues, which were below average for a dealership of this size, had also declined, although the service department still made a small surplus.

Had she had made a mistake last week, Carol wondered, in turning down Bill Froelich's offer to buy the business? It was true that the price offered had been substantially below the offer from Froelich that her father had rejected two years earlier, but the business had been more profitable then.

The Sullivan Family

Walter Sullivan had purchased a small Ford dealership in 1977, renaming it Sullivan Auto, and it had become one of the best known in the metropolitan area. Six years earlier, he had borrowed heavily to purchase the current site at a major highway intersection, in an area of a suburb with many new housing developments. There had been a dealership on the site, but the buildings were 30 years old. Sullivan had retained the service and repair bays, but he had torn down the showroom in front of them and replaced it by an attractive modern facility. On moving to the new location, which was substantially larger than the old one, he had renamed his business Sullivan's Auto World.

Everybody had seemed to know Walt Sullivan. He had been a consummate showman and entrepreneur, appearing in his own radio and TV commercials, and was active in community affairs. His approach to car sales had emphasized promotions, discounts, and deals to maintain volume. He was never happier than when making a sale.

Carol Sullivan-Diaz, aged 28, was the eldest of Walter and Carmen Sullivan's three daughters. After obtaining a bachelor's degree in economics, she had earned an MBA and had then embarked on a career in health care management. She was married to Dr. Roberto Diaz, a surgeon at St. Luke's Hospital. Her 20-year-old twin sisters, Gail and Joanne, were students at the local university and lived with their mother.

In her own student days, Sullivan-Diaz had worked part time in her father's business on secretarial and bookkeeping tasks and also as a service writer in the service department, so she was quite familiar with the operations of the dealership. At business school, she had decided on a career in health care management. After graduation, she had worked as an executive assistant to the president of St. Luke's, a large teaching hospital. Two years later, she joined Metropolitan Health Plan as assistant director of marketing, a position she had now held for almost three years. Her responsibilities included attracting new members, handling complaints, doing market research, and instituting member retention programs.

Carol's employer had given her a six-week leave of absence to put her father's affairs in order. She doubted that she could extend that leave much beyond the two weeks still remaining. Neither she nor other family members were interested in making a career of running the dealership. However, she was prepared to take time out from her health care career to work on a turnaround if that seemed a viable proposition. She had been successful in her present job and believed it would not be difficult to find another health management position in the future.

The Dealership

Like other car dealerships, Sullivan's Auto World operated both sales and service departments, often referred to in the trade as front end and back end, respectively. However, Auto World did not have a body shop for repairing damaged bodywork. Both new and used vehicles were sold because a high proportion of new purchases involved trading in the purchaser's existing vehicle. Auto World would also buy well-maintained used cars at auction for resale. Purchasers who decided that they could not afford a new car would often buy a "preowned" vehicle instead, whereas shoppers who came in for a used car could sometimes be persuaded to buy a new one.

The front end of the dealership employed a sales manager, seven salespeople, an office manager, and a secretary. One salesperson had given notice and would be leaving at the end of the following week. The service department, when fully staffed, comprised a service manager, a parts supervisor, nine mechanics, and two service writers. The Sullivan twins often worked part time as service writers, filling in at busy periods, when one of the other writers was sick or on vacation or when—as currently—there was an unfilled vacancy. The job entailed scheduling appointments for repairs and maintenance, writing up each work order, calling customers with repair estimates, and assisting customers when they returned to pick up the cars and pay for the completed work.

Sullivan-Diaz knew from her own experience as a service writer that it could be a stressful job. Few people liked to be without their car, even for a day. When a car broke down or was having problems, the owner was often nervous about how long it would take to get it fixed and, if the warranty had expired, how much the labor and parts would cost. Customers were quite unforgiving when a problem was not fixed completely on the first attempt and they had to return their vehicles for further work.

Major mechanical failures were not usually difficult to repair, although the replacement costs for parts might be expensive. It was often the "little" things like water leaks and wiring problems that were the hardest to diagnose and correct, and it might be necessary for the customer to return two or three times before a problem was resolved. In these situations, parts and materials costs were relatively low, but labor costs mounted up quickly, being charged out at $45 an hour. Customers could often be quite abusive, yelling at service writers over the phone or arguing with service writers, mechanics, and the service manager in person.

Turnover in the service writer job was high, which was why Carol—and more recently her sisters—had often been pressed into service by their father to "hold the fort," as he described it. More than once, she had seen an exasperated service writer respond sharply to a complaining customer or hang up on one who was being abusive over the telephone. Gail and Joanne were currently taking turns to cover the vacant position, but there were times when both of them had classes and the dealership had only one service writer on duty.

By national standards, Sullivan's Auto World was a medium-sized dealership, selling around 1,100 cars a year, equally divided between new and used vehicles. In the most recent year, its revenues totaled $26.6 million from new and used car sales and $2.9 million from service and parts—down from $30.5 million and $3.6 million, respectively, in the previous year. Although the unit value of car sales was high, the margins were quite low. The reverse was true for service. Industry guidelines suggested that the contribution margin (known as the departmental selling gross) from car sales should be about 5.5 percent of sales revenues and from service, around 25 percent of revenues. In a typical dealership, 60 percent of the selling gross came from sales and 40 percent from service. The selling gross was then applied to fixed expenses, such as administrative salaries, rent or mortgage payments, and utilities.

For the most recent 12 months at Auto World, Sullivan-Diaz had determined that the selling gross figures were 4.6 percent and 24 percent, respectively, both of them lower than in the previous year and insufficient to cover the dealership's fixed expenses. Her father had made no mention of financial difficulties, and she had been shocked to learn from the bank after his death that Auto World had been two months behind in mortgage payments on the property. Further analysis also showed that accounts payable had also risen sharply in the previous six months. Fortunately, the dealership held a large insurance policy on Sullivan's life, and the proceeds from this had been more than sufficient to bring mortgage payments up to date, pay all overdue accounts, and leave some funds for future contingencies.

The opportunities for expanding new-car sales did not appear promising, given the state of the economy. However, recent promotional incentives had reduced the inventory to manageable levels. From discussions with Larry Winters, Auto World's sales manager, Sullivan-Diaz had concluded that costs could be reduced by not replacing the departing salesperson, maintaining inventory at somewhat lower levels, and trying to make more efficient use of advertising and promotion. Although Winters did not have Walter's exuberant personality, he had been Auto World's leading salesperson before being promoted and had shown strong managerial capabilities in his current position.

As she reviewed the figures for the service department, Sullivan-Diaz wondered what potential might exist for improving its sales volume and selling gross. Her father had never been very interested in the parts and service business, seeing it simply as a necessary adjunct of the dealership. "Customers always seem to be miserable back there," he had once remarked to her. "But here in the front end, everybody's happy when someone buys a new car." The service facility was not easily visible from the main highway, being hidden behind the showroom. The building was old and greasy, although the equipment was modern and well maintained.

Customers were required to bring in cars for servicing before 8:30 A.M. After parking their cars, customers entered the service building by a side door and waited their turn to see the service writers, who occupied a cramped room with peeling paint and an interior window overlooking the service bays. Customers stood while work orders for their cars were written up by hand on large sheets. Ringing telephones frequently interrupted the process. Filing cabinets containing customer records and other documents lined the far wall of the room.

If the work was routine, such as an oil change or tune-up, customers were given an estimate immediately. For more complex jobs, they would be called with an estimate later in the morning, once the car had been examined. Customers were required to pick up their cars by 6:00 P.M. on the day the work was completed. On several occasions, Carol had urged her father to computerize the service work order process, but he had never acted on her suggestions.

The service manager, Rick Obert, who was in his late 40s, had held the position since Auto World opened at its current location. The Sullivan family considered him to be technically skilled, and he managed the mechanics effectively. However, his manner with customers could be gruff and argumentative.

Customer Survey Results

Other data that Sullivan-Diaz had studied carefully were the results of the customer satisfaction surveys that were mailed to the dealership monthly by a research firm retained by the Ford Motor Company. Purchasers of all new Ford cars were sent a questionnaire by mail within 30 days and asked to use a five-point scale to rate their satisfaction with the dealership sales department, vehicle preparation, and characteristics of the vehicle itself. The questionnaire asked how likely the purchaser would be to recommend the dealership, the salesperson, and the manufacturer to someone else. Other questions asked if the customers had been introduced to the dealer's service department and been given explanations about what to do if their cars needed service. Finally, there were some classification questions relating to customer demographics.

A second survey was sent to new-car purchasers nine months later. This questionnaire began by asking about satisfaction with the vehicle and then asked customers if they had taken their vehicles to the selling dealer for service of any kind. If so, respondents were then asked to rate the service department on 14 different attributes—ranging from the attitudes of service personnel to the quality of the work performed—and then to rate their overall satisfaction with service from the dealer. Customers were also asked where they would go in the future for maintenance service, minor mechanical and electrical repairs, major repairs in those same categories, and body work. The options listed for service were selling dealer, another Ford dealer, "some other place," or "do-it-yourself." Finally, there were questions about overall satisfaction with the sales department and the dealership in general, as well as the likelihood of purchasing another Ford Motor Company product and buying it from the same dealership.

Dealers received monthly reports summarizing customers' ratings of their dealership for the most recent month and for several previous months. To provide a comparison with other Ford dealerships, the reports also included regional and national rating averages. After analysis, completed questionnaires were returned to the dealership; because these included each customer's name, a dealer could see which customers were satisfied and which were not.

In the 30-day survey of new purchasers, Auto World achieved better-than-average ratings on most dimensions. One finding that puzzled Carol was that almost 90 percent of respondents answered yes when asked if someone from Auto World had explained what to do if they needed service, but less than a third said that they had been introduced to someone in the service department. She resolved to ask Larry Winters about this discrepancy.

The nine-month survey findings disturbed her. Although vehicle ratings were in line with national averages, the overall level of satisfaction with service at Auto World was consistently low, placing it in the bottom 25 percent of all Ford dealerships. The worst ratings for service concerned promptness of writing up orders, convenience of scheduling the work, convenience of service hours, and appearance of the service department. On length of time to complete the work, availability of needed parts, and quality of work done ("Was it fixed right?"), Auto World's rating was close to the average. For interpersonal variables such as attitude of service department personnel, politeness, understanding of customer problems, and explanation of work performed, its ratings were relatively poor.

When Sullivan-Diaz reviewed the individual questionnaires, she found that there was a wide degree of variation between customers' responses on these interpersonal variables, ranging all the way across a five-point scale from "completely satisfied" to "very dissatisfied." Curious, she had gone to the service files and examined the records for several dozen customers who had recently completed the nine-month surveys. At least part of the ratings could be explained by which service writers the customer had dealt with. Those who had been served two or more times by her sisters, for instance, gave much better ratings than those who had dealt primarily with Jim Fiskell, the service writer who had recently quit.

Perhaps the most worrying responses were those relating to customers' likely use of Auto World's service department in the future. More than half indicated that they would use another Ford dealer or "some other place" for maintenance service (such as oil change, lubrication, or tune-up) or for minor mechanical and electrical repairs. About 30 percent would use another source for major repairs. The rating for overall satisfaction with the selling dealer after nine months was below average, and the customer's likelihood of purchasing from the same dealership again was a full point below that of buying another Ford product.

An Unwelcome Disturbance

Sullivan-Diaz pushed aside the spreadsheets she had printed out and shut down her laptop. It was time to go home for dinner. She saw the options for the dealership as basically twofold: either prepare the business for an early sale at what would amount to a distress price, or take a year or two to try to turn it around financially. In the latter case, if the turnaround succeeded, the business could subsequently be sold at a higher price than it presently commanded, or the family could install a general manager to run the dealership for them.

Bill Froelich, owner of another, nearby dealership, had offered to buy Auto World for a price that represented a fair valuation of the net assets, according to Auto World's accountants, plus $150,000 in goodwill. However, the rule of thumb when the auto industry was enjoying good times was that goodwill should be valued at $1,000 per vehicle sold each year.

As Carol left her office, she saw the sales manager coming up the stairs leading from the showroom floor. "Larry," she said, "I've got a question for you."

"Fire away!" replied the sales manager.

"I've been looking at the customer satisfaction surveys. Why aren't our sales reps introducing new customers to the folks in the service department? It's supposedly part of our sales protocol, but it only seems to be happening about one-third of the time!"

Larry Winters shuffled his feet. "Well, Carol, basically I leave it to their discretion. We tell them about service, of course, but some of the guys on the floor feel a bit uncomfortable taking folks over to the service bays after they've been in here. It's quite a contrast, if you know what I mean."

Suddenly, the sound of shouting arose from the floor below. A man of about 40, wearing a windbreaker and jeans, was standing in the doorway, yelling at one of the salespeople. The two managers could catch snatches of what he was saying, in between various obscenities: "… three visits … still not fixed right … service stinks … who's in charge here?" Everybody else in the showroom had stopped what they were doing and had turned to look at the newcomer.

Winters looked at his young employer and rolled his eyes. "If there was something your dad couldn't stand, it was guys like that, yelling and screaming in the showroom and asking for the boss. Walt would go hide out in his office! Don't worry, Tom'll take care of that fellow and get him out of here. What a jerk!"

"No," said Sullivan-Diaz, "I'll deal with him! One thing I learned when I worked at St. Luke's was that you don't let people yell about their problems in front of everybody else. You take them off somewhere, calm them down, and find out what's bugging them." She stepped quickly down the stairs, wondering to herself, "What else have I learned in health care that I can apply to this business?"

■ Questions for Discussion

1. How does marketing cars differ from marketing services for those same vehicles?
2. Compare and contrast the sales and service departments at Auto World.
3. Make a flowchart of the servicing of a car that comes in for repair or maintenance.
4. How should Carol Sullivan-Diaz handle the angry customer in the showroom?
5. What useful parallels do you see between running an automobile sales and service dealership and managing health care services?
6. What advice would you give to Carol about
   a. improving service quality
   b. marketing the service department and the dealership
   c. selling Auto World now versus attempting a turnaround?

DR. BECKETT'S DENTAL OFFICE

"I just hope the quality differences are visible to our patients," mused Dr. Barbro Beckett as she surveyed the office that housed her well-established dental practice. She had recently moved to her current location from an office she felt was too cramped to allow her staff to work efficiently—a factor that was becoming increasingly important as the costs of providing dental care continued to rise. Although Beckett realized that productivity gains were necessary, she did not want to compromise the quality of service her patients received.

Management Comes to Dentistry

The classes Beckett took in dental school taught her a lot about the technical side of dentistry but nothing about the business side. She received no formal training in the mechanics of running a business or understanding customers' needs. In fact, professional guidelines discouraged marketing or advertising of any kind. That was not a major problem when Beckett started her practice 22 years ago. In the 1960s and 1970s, profit margins were good. But by the 1990s the dental care industry had changed dramatically. Costs rose as a result of labor laws, malpractice insurance, and the constant need to invest in new equipment and staff training as new technologies were introduced. By 1998, Beckett's overhead was between 70 and 80 percent of revenues before accounting for wages or office rental.

As overhead was rising, there was a movement in the United States to reduce health care costs to insurance companies, employers, and patients by offering managed health care through large health maintenance organizations (HMOs). The HMOs set the prices for various services by putting an upper limit on the amount that their doctors and dentists could charge for various procedures. The advantage to patients was that their health insurance covered virtually all costs. But the price limitations meant that HMO doctors and dentists would not be able to offer certain services that might provide better care but were too expensive. Beckett had decided not to become an HMO provider because the reimbursement rate was only 80 to 85 percent of her usual charge. She felt that she could not provide high-quality care to patients at these rates.

These changes presented some significant challenges to Beckett, who wanted to offer the highest level of dental care rather than being a low-cost provider. With the help of a consultant, she decided that her top priority was differentiating the practice on the basis of quality. She and her staff developed an internal mission statement that reflected this goal. The mission statement (which is prominently displayed in the back office) reads, "It is our goal to provide superior dentistry in an efficient, profitable manner within the confines of a caring, quality environment."

Because higher-quality care was more costly, Beckett's patients sometimes had to pay fees for costs that were not covered by their insurance policies. If the quality differences weren't substantial, these patients might decide to switch to an HMO dentist or another lower-cost provider.

Redesigning the Service Delivery System

The move to a new office gave Beckett a unique opportunity to rethink almost every aspect of her service. She wanted the work environment to reflect her own personality and values, as well as providing a pleasant place for her staff to work.

Facilities and Equipment

Beckett first looked into the office spaces that were available in the Northern California town where she practiced. She didn't find anything she liked, so she hired an architect from San Francisco to design a contemporary office building with lots of light and space. This increased the building costs by $100,000, but Beckett felt that it would be a critical factor in differentiating her service.

Beckett's new office is Scandanavian in design (reflecting her Swedish heritage and attention to detail). The waiting room and reception area are filled with modern furniture in muted shades of brown, grey, green, and purple. Live plants and flowers are abundant, and the walls are covered with art. Classical music plays softly in the background. Patients can enjoy a cup of coffee or tea and browse through the large selection of current magazines while they wait for their appointments.

The treatment areas are both functional and appealing. There is a small conference room with toys for children and a VCR that is used to show patients educational films about different dental procedures. Literature is available to explain what patients need to do to maximize their treatment outcomes.

The chairs in the examining rooms are covered in leather and are very comfortable. Each room has a large window that allows patients to watch birds eating at the feeders that are filled each day. There are also attractive mobiles hanging from the ceiling to distract patients from the unfamiliar sounds and sensations they are experiencing. Headphones are available with a wide selection of music.

The entire back-office staff members (including Beckett) wear matching uniforms in cheerful shades of pink, purple, and blue that match the office décor. All the technical equipment looks very modern and is spotlessly clean. State-of-the-art computerized machinery is used for some procedures. Beckett's dental degrees are prominently displayed in her office, along with certificates from various programs that she and her staff have attended to update their technical skills.

Service Personnel

There are eight employees in the dental practice, including Beckett (who is the only dentist). The seven staff members are separated by job function into front-office and back-office workers. Front-office duties (covered by two employees) include receptionist and secretarial tasks and financial and budgeting work. The back office is divided into hygienists and chair-side assistants.

The three chair-side assistants help the hygienists and Beckett with treatment procedures. They have specialized training for their jobs but do not need a college degree. The two hygienists handle routine exams and teeth cleaning plus some treatment procedures. In many offices, hygienists assume a superior attitude because of their education (a bachelor's degree and specialized training are required) and experience. According to Beckett, this attitude can destroy any possibility of teamwork among the office staff. She feels very fortunate that her hygienists view themselves as part of a larger team whose members are working together to provide quality care to patients.

Beckett values her friendships with the staff members, and she also understands that they are a vital part of the service delivery. "Ninety percent of patients' perceptions of quality comes from their interactions with the front desk and the other employees—not from the staff's technical skills," she states. When the dentist began to redesign her practice, she discussed her goals with the staff and involved them in the decision-making process. The changes meant new expectations and routines for most employees, and some were not willing to adapt. There was some staff turnover (mostly voluntary) as the new office procedures were implemented. The current group works very well as a team.

Beckett and her staff meet briefly each morning to discuss the day's schedule and patients. They also have longer meetings every other week to discuss more strategic issues and resolve any problems that have developed. During these meetings, employees make suggestions about how to improve patient care. Some of the most successful staff suggestions include thank-you cards to patients who refer other patients; follow-up calls to patients after major procedures; a "goodie box" for patients, including toothbrush, toothpaste, mouthwash, and floss; buckwheat pillows and blankets for comfort during long procedures; coffee and tea in the waiting area; and a photo album in the waiting area with pictures of staff members and their families.

The expectations for staff performance (in both technical competence and patient interactions) are very high, but Beckett gives her employees many opportunities to update their skills by attending classes and workshops. She also rewards their hard work by giving monthly bonuses if business is good. Because she shares the financial data with her staff, they can see the difference in revenues if the schedule is slow or patients are dissatisfied. This provides an extra incentive to improve the service delivery. The entire office also goes on trips together once a year (paid for by Beckett), and spouses are welcome (but must cover their own expenses). Past destinations for these excursions have included Hawaii and Washington, D.C.

Procedures and Patients

With the help of a consultant, all the office systems (including billing, ordering, lab work, and patient treatment) have been redesigned. One of the main goals was to standardize some of the routine procedures so that errors were reduced and all patients would receive the same level of care. There are specific times allotted for each procedure, and the staff works very hard to see that these are met. Office policy dictates that patients should be kept waiting no longer than 20 minutes without being given the option to reschedule, and employees often call patients in advance if they know there will be a delay. They also attempt to fill in cancellations to make sure that office capacity is maximized. Staff members will substitute for each other when necessary or help with tasks that are not specifically in their job descriptions to make things run more smoothly.

Beckett's practice includes about 2,000 active patients (and many more who come infrequently). They are mostly white-collar workers with professional jobs (university employees, health care workers, and managers or owners of local establishments). She does no advertising—all of her new business comes from positive word of mouth by current patients.

The dentist believes that the referrals are a real advantage because new patients don't come in cold, they have already been told about her service by friends or family, so she doesn't have to sell herself. All new patients must have an initial exam so that Beckett can perform a needs assessment and educate them about her service. She believes that this is the first indication to patients that her practice is different from others they might have experienced. Patients may then have to wait another three or four months for a routine cleaning and exam because the office is so busy, but they don't seem to mind.

The Biggest Challenge

"Redesigning the business was the easy part," Beckett sighs. "Demonstrating the high level of quality to patients is the hard job." She says it is especially difficult because most people dislike going to the dentist or feel that it's an inconvenience and come in with a negative attitude. Beckett tries to reinforce the idea that high-quality dental care depends on a positive long-term relationship between patients and the dental team. This philosophy is reflected in the patient mission statement hanging in the waiting area: "We are a caring, professional dental team serving motivated, quality-oriented patients interested in keeping healthy smiles for a lifetime. Our goal is to offer a progressive and educational environment. Your concerns are our focus."

Although Beckett enjoys her work, she says it can be difficult to maintain a positive attitude. The job requires precision and attention to detail, and the procedures are often painful to patients. She feels as if she is often "walking on eggshells" because she knows patients are anxious and uncomfortable, which makes them more critical of her service delivery. It is not uncommon for patients to say negative things to Beckett before treatments even begin (as "I really hate going to the dentist—it's not you, but I just don't want to be here."). When this occurs, she reminds herself that she is providing high-quality service whether patients appreciate it or not. "The people will usually have to have the dental work done anyway," Beckett says. "So I just do the best job I can and make them as comfortable as possible." Even though patients seldom express appreciation for her services, she hopes that she has made a positive difference in their health or appearance that will benefit them in the long run.

■ Questions for Discussion

1. Which of the 8Ps are addressed in this case? Give examples of each.
2. Why do people dislike going to the dentist? Do you feel that Beckett has addressed this problem effectively?
3. How do Beckett and her staff educate patients about the service they are receiving? What else could they do?
4. What supplementary services are offered? How do they enhance service delivery?
5. Contrast your own dental care experiences with those offered by Beckett's practice. What differences do you see? Based on your review of this case, what advice would you give (a) to your current or former dentist and (b) to Beckett?

■✓ ROYAL WINNIPEG BALLET

The Royal Winnipeg Ballet (RWB) demonstrates the crunch facing the arts today: you need money to perform the magic. As Peter Carter wrote in the *Financial Post*, "It was as if the place had been hexed by the evil witch in a fairy tale. The performances stayed stellar and the artistic reputation remained intact, but debt and personnel problems hung around like twin vultures."

In September 1993, the RWB staff and committee members gathered for a retreat at a hostel 30 miles north of Winnipeg. The company was at a crossroad. Both the artistic director and executive director were new to the company. They were replacing individuals who had not always been popular with the company. These two new individuals had to establish a close, trustful working relationship in order to allow the company to function at all, let alone to grow. The organization faced a deficit of $800,000 at a time when government agencies were cutting back on funding programs to the arts. Though the deficit was the most visible issue, the RWB also faced other problems.

Like many art groups, the RWB had two "heads," reporting to the board of directors. The artistic director—always a former dancer—was responsible for all aspects of programming: choosing ballets to be performed, casting, music, production (scenery, stage, lights) as well as the dance itself; indeed, the artistic director sometimes "took rehearsal," overseeing preparation of a performance. Thus the artistic director was intimately involved with all the dancers and all elements of the dance itself.

On the same level, also reporting to the board, was the executive director. As the title indicated, this individual was responsible for managing all aspects of the business, such as fund-raising, public relations, accounting, insurance, and human resource management.

The parallel responsibilities—artistic and business—generated conflict between the staffs. The most visible symbol was created by the financial crisis. The dancers had faced a three-month layoff during the summer. Their union contracts tied pay to specific performances; however, in the past, they had sufficient notice of layoffs to arrange for their salaries to be spread over long periods of time. This time, the decision was made by the organization's board, with input from the associate artistic director and the controller. The business staffs continued to work with 52-week contracts, leading to some resentment between artistic and business staffs.

In the following years, no progress had been made to reduce the deficit. Still, there have been changes. In 1994, Mark Godden, the company's resident choreographer, resigned to move to Montreal, where his wife was offered a job with Les Grands Ballets Canadiens. In 1995, two soloists and one principal resigned to join other companies, and artistic director William Whitener resigned following artistic differences. Shortly afterward, general manager Jeffrey Bentley returned to the United States for personal reasons. By 1996, the RWB had chosen André Lewis (former associate artistic director) to be artistic director. Robert Sochasky, the controller, was appointed acting general manager.

Revenue

As with most arts groups, revenue for the RWB does not come primarily from ticket sales. The RWB depends on income from ballet school tuition, profits from souvenir sales, individual donations, and corporate sponsorship. The RWB obtains funding from the municipal, provincial, and federal governments.

The RWB has been overwhelmingly successful: the average per-capita donation in Winnipeg is $1.71, compared to $1.12 in San Francisco, and $0.86 in Toronto. However, the other cities are much larger. San Francisco raises $8 million, or 42 percent of its operating budget, whereas Toronto raises $2.3 million, or 20 percent of its operating budget. The higher per-capita rates in Winnipeg actually increase difficulties of fund-raising during government cutbacks. RWB fund-raising seems to face a saturated marketplace. Many potential donors have already made contributions. Because Winnipeg is relatively small, many small businesses receive appeals not only from the RWB but also from every arts group in the city.

Fund-Raising

Fund-raising involves corporate donations, individual donations, and special events. The RWB sponsors one or more special events a year. In 1994, the RWB's fundraiser was called Points of Steel, focused on a party held at a hangar at the airport. The theme: motorcycles and bikers. Susan Glass, president of the board of the RWB, created the idea when she realized the ballet fans and bikers had similar demographics: people in mid- to upper-income brackets who use discretionary income to make the purchase.

Like many arts groups, the RWB offers special benefits to those who buy season tickets, donate money, or both. Season-ticket holders ("subscribers") had privileges for exchanging tickets if they could not attend, replacing lost tickets, and attending extra performances at a discount. They also received advance information about performances. Donors were known as "Friends," categorized by amount: "corps" members donated less than $100, "soloist" under $500, and so on. Each group carried some perks: passes to dress rehearsals, subscription to a dance magazine, invitations to receptions.

Those donating $750 or more each year were placed in a special category—the "high-end donors." These donors become members of President's Council. These "perks" include access to a VIP room where members can check their coats and stop by for free drinks during intermission. Council members also get invited to special events with dancers, including world-famous ballerina Evelyn Hart. On opening night, Council members and these guests are invited to dinner with a guest speaker from the Company. Many Council members feel these events offer unique low-key networking opportunities as well as venues for entertaining corporate clients—an alternative to football or hockey games.

Despite the attractiveness of these benefits, only 45 donors belonged to the President's Council by March 1995. At that time, the development committee encouraged RWB's Director of Development, Jane Corbett, to enlist the aid of some marketing professors to conduct focus groups with potential donors. Most President's Council members were over age 50. The RWB hoped to attract younger professionals, aged 30 to 45, so that the group could grow.

Potential Donors

The focus groups immediately identified differences between younger and older patrons. Those under 40 talked frankly about a "stuffy" image, although younger males saw the ballet as "a great place to take a date."

While some older subscribers liked the classics, younger subscribers emphasized the need for more variety. Young professionals expressed concern about getting to an 8 P.M. performance directly from work, with little time for dinner. The performances usually ended around 11 P.M., too late for post-performance dining. Both males and females were uncomfortable retrieving their cars from parking lots late at night.

When asked about their donations, younger professionals felt their first priority involved donations to United Way or medical research. "The ballet is a lifestyle, not a charity," someone said. Older subscribers accepted donations as a way of life, even an obligation.

With regard to benefits associated with Friends categories, reaction was mixed. Some were disturbed by the association of donation levels privileges, especially opportunities to meet dancers. Others suggested that the benefits were not particularly appealing. To a young professional who barely had time to attend performances, rehearsal passes offer little benefit. They would prefer sweatshirts, transportation to a safe parking area, or packages that included reasonably priced dinners.

Perhaps the biggest surprise to the RWB staff was the strong negative reaction to the name of the high-end donor group: President's Council. "Who's the president?" they sneered. Others denounced the idea as "elitist." Brochures listed names of prominent community business and political leaders who belonged to President's Council. Potential donors did not respond positively. They felt intimidated: "I have nothing in common with those people."

Recruiting Potential Donors

The Community Leaders Subcommittee was charged with recruiting new members to the President's Council. They wanted to maintain the senior members, but also to be more attractive to newcomers. In March 1996 the development manager resigned to take a position in private industry. This position was primarily responsible for recruiting high-end and corporate donors.

■ **Questions for Discussion**

1. What research would you recommend for the RWB?
2. What marketing suggestions would you offer to reach high-end donors?
3. What motivates donations to the RWB?
4. What are the qualifications for a development manager?

✎ MR. MAHALEEL GOES TO LONDON

It was a Friday in mid-February, and Kadir Mahaleel, a wealthy businessman from the Southeast Asian nation of Tailesia, was visiting London on a trip that combined business and pleasure. Mahaleel was the founder of Eximsa, a major export company in Tailesia. Business brought him to London every two to three months. These trips gave him the opportunity to visit his daughter, Leona, the eldest of his four children, who lived in London. Several of his 10 grandchildren were attending college in Britain, and he was especially proud of his grandson Anson, who was a student at the Royal Academy of Music. In fact, he had scheduled this trip to coincide with a violin recital by Anson at 2 P.M. on this particular Friday.

The primary purpose of Mahaleel's visit was to resolve a delicate matter regarding his company. He had decided that the time had come to retire and wished to make arrangements for the company's future. His son Victor was involved in the business and ran Eximsa's trading office in Europe. However, Victor was in poor health and unable to take over the firm. Mahaleel believed that a group of loyal employees was interested in buying his company if the necessary credit could be arranged.

Before leaving Tailesia, Mahaleel had discussed the possibility of a buyout with Li Sieuw Meng, his trusted financial adviser, who recommended that he talk to several banks in London because of the potential complexity of the business deal: "The London banks are experienced in buyouts. Also, you need a bank that can handle the credit for the interested buyers in New York and London, as well as Asia. Once the buyout takes place, you'll have significant cash to invest. This would be a good time to review your estate plans as well."

Referring Mahaleel to two competing institutions, The Trust Company and Global Private Bank, Li added, "I've met an account officer from Global who called on me several times. Here's his business card; his name is Miguel Kim. I've never done any business with him, but he did seem quite competent. Unfortunately, I don't know anyone at The Trust Company, but here's their address in London."

After checking into his hotel in London the following Wednesday, Mahaleel telephoned Kim's office. Because Kim was out, Mahaleel spoke to the account officer's secretary, described himself briefly, and arranged to stop by Global's Lombard Street office around midmorning on Friday.

On Thursday, Mahaleel visited The Trust Company. The two people he met were extremely pleasant and had spent some time in Tailesia. They seemed very knowledgeable about managing estates and gave him some good recommendations about handling his complex family affairs. However, they were clearly less experienced in handling business credit, his most urgent need. Without a substantial loan, his employees would not be able to buy the business from him.

The next morning, Mahaleel had breakfast with Leona. As they parted, she said, "I'll meet you at 1:30 P. M. in the lobby of the Savoy Hotel, and we'll go to the recital together. We mustn't be late if we want to get front-row seats."

On his way to Global Private Bank, Mahaleel stopped at Mappin & Webb's jewelry store to buy his wife a present for their anniversary. His shopping was pleasant and leisurely; he purchased a beautiful emerald necklace that he knew his wife would like. When he emerged from the jewelry store, the weather had turned much colder and he was caught in an unexpected snow flurry. He had difficulty finding a taxi and his arthritis started acting up, making walking to the Global office out of the question. At last he caught a taxi and arrived at the Lombard Street location of Global Bancorp about noon. After going into the street-level branch of Global Retail Bank, he was redirected by a security guard to the Private Bank offices on the second floor.

It was 12:15 when he arrived at the nicely appointed reception area of the Private Bank. There he was met by Miguel Kim's secretary, who told him, "Mr. Kim was disappointed that he couldn't be here to greet you, but he had a lunch appointment with one of his clients that was scheduled over a month ago. He expects to return about 1:30. In the meantime, he has asked another senior account officer, Sophia Costa, to assist you."

Sophia Costa, 41, was a vice president of the bank and had worked for Global Bancorp for 14 years (two years longer than Miguel Kim). She had visited Tailesia once but had not met Mahaleel's financial adviser nor any member of the Mahaleel family. An experienced relationship manager, Costa was knowledgeable about offshore investment management and fiduciary services. Kim had looked into her office at 11:45 A.M. and asked her if she would cover for him in case a prospective client, a Mr. Mahaleel, whom he had expected to see earlier, should happen to arrive. He told Costa that Mahaleel was a successful Tailesian businessman planning for his retirement but that he had never met the prospect personally; then he rushed off to lunch.

■ Questions for Discussion

1. Prepare a flowchart of Mahaleel's service encounters.
2. Putting yourself in Mahaleel's shoes, how do you feel (both physically and mentally) after speaking with the receptionist at Global? What are your priorities right now?
3. As Sophia Costa, what action would you take in your first five minutes with Mahaleel?
4. What would constitute a good outcome of the meeting for both the client and the bank? How should Costa try to bring about such an outcome?

■ RED LOBSTER

"It felt like a knife going through me!" declared Mary Campbell, 53, after she was fired from her waitressing job at a restaurant in the Red Lobster chain. But instead of suing for what she considered unfair dismissal after 19 years of service, Campbell called for a peer review, seeking to recover her job and three weeks of lost wages.

Three weeks after the firing, a panel of employees from different Red Lobster restaurants was reviewing the evidence and trying to determine whether the server had, in fact, been unjustly fired for allegedly stealing a guest comment card completed by a couple of customers whom she had served.

Peer Review at Darden Industries

Red Lobster was owned by Darden Industries, which also owned another large restaurant chain known as the Olive Garden and had a total of 110,000 employees. The company had adopted peer review of disputed employee firings and disciplinary actions in 1994. Key objectives were to limit workers' lawsuits and ease workplace tensions. Advocates of this approach, which had also been adopted at several other companies, believed that it was very effective in channeling in constructive ways the pain and anger

This case was prepared by Christopher Lovelock. It is based on a story by Margaret A. Jacobs, "Red Lobster Tale: Peers Decide Fired Waitress's Fate," *The Wall Street Journal*, 20 January 1998. Personal names have been changed.

that employees felt after being fired or disciplined by their managers. By reducing the incidence of lawsuits, a company could also save on legal expenses.

A Darden spokesperson stated that the peer review program had been "tremendously successful" in keeping valuable employees from unfair dismissal. Each year, about 100 disputes ended up in peer review, with only 10 resulting in lawsuits. Red Lobster managers and many employees also credited peer review with reducing racial tensions. Campbell, who said she had received dozens of calls of support, chose peer review over a lawsuit not only because it was much cheaper but also because "I liked the idea of being judged by people who know how things work in a little restaurant."

The Evidence

The review panel included a general manager, an assistant manager, a server, a hostess, and a bartender, who had all volunteered to review the circumstances of Campbell's firing. Each panelist had received peer review training and was receiving regular wages plus travel expenses. The instructions to panelists were simply to do what they felt was fair.

Mary Campbell had been fired by Jean Larimer, the general manager of the Red Lobster in Marston, where the former worked as a restaurant server. The reason given for the firing was that Campbell had asked the restaurant's hostess, Eve Taunton, for the key to the guest comment box and had stolen a card from it. The card had been completed by a couple of guests whom Campbell had served and who seemed dissatisfied with their experience at the restaurant. Subsequently, the guests learned that their comment card, which complained that their prime rib of beef was too rare and their waitress was "uncooperative," had been removed from the box.

Jean Larimer's Testimony

Larimer, who supervised 100 full- and part-time employees, testified that she had dismissed Campbell after one of the two customers complained angrily to her and her supervisor. "She [the guest] felt violated because her card was taken from the box and her complaint about the food had been ignored." Larimer drew the panel's attention to the company rule book, pointing out that Campbell had violated the policy that forbade removal of company property.

Mary Campbell's Testimony

Campbell testified that the female customer had requested that her prime rib be cooked "well done" and subsequently complained that it was fatty and undercooked. The waitress politely suggested that "prime rib always has fat on it" but arranged to have the meat cooked some more. However, the woman still seemed unhappy with the food. After pouring steak sauce over the meat, she then pushed away her plate without eating it all. When the customer remained displeased, Cambell offered a free dessert. But the guests left after paying the bill, filling out the guest comment card, and dropping it in the box. Admitting that she was consumed by curiosity, Campbell asked Eve Taunton, the restaurant's hostess, for the key to the box. After removing and reading the card, she pocketed it. Her intent, she declared, was to show the card to Larimer, who had been concerned earlier that the prime rib served at the restaurant was overcooked, not undercooked. However, she forgot about the card and later, accidentally, threw it out.

Eve Taunton's Testimony

At the time of the firing, Taunton was a 17-year-old student, working at Red Lobster for the summer. "I didn't think it was a big deal to give her [Campbell] the key," she said. "A lot of people would come up to me to get it."

The Panel Deliberates

Having heard the testimony, the members of the review panel had to decide whether Ms. Larimer had been justified in firing Ms. Campbell. The panelists' initial reactions were split by rank, with the hourly workers supporting Campbell and the managers supporting Larimer. But then the debate began in earnest in an effort to reach consensus.

■ Questions for Discussion

1. Evaluate the concept of peer review. What are its strengths and weaknesses? What type of environment is required to make it work well?
2. Review the evidence. Do you believe the testimony presented?
3. What decision would you make and why?

TURBULENT SKIES FOR CONSTELLATION AIRLINES

Rhett Javonski, CEO of Constellation Airlines, was meeting with senior executives of the airline to decide what posture it should take in new talks with striking flight attendants on wages and work rules. The International Flight Attendants Union (IFAU) had agreed to resume negotiations the following day, March 26, in New York City.

On March 7, 6,500 flight attendants had struck the airline after management had imposed new work rules, boosting work by 12 hours a month, reducing wages by 22 percent, and establishing a two-tier wage scale. Management estimated that these changes would save Constellation some $120 million per year. Javonski, who had been appointed CEO six months earlier, insisted that the proposed changes were essential to return the airline to profitability after an extended period of losses.

Negotiations with the union had broken down on February 5 after management had rejected the union's offer of wage and benefit cuts amounting to $35 million a year. Both parties were then released from federal mediation for a 30-day cooling-off period, at the end of which the attendants went on strike and the airline replaced them with 3,000 newly trained attendants who were working longer hours at lower wages. Union members picketed airports served by Constellation and distributed press releases claiming that with such inexperienced flight attendants it was now unsafe to fly this airline.

Constellation Airlines

Constellation was among the largest airlines in the United States, with both a domestic and international route network. In the intensively competitive market of the late 1980s and early 1990s, Constellation had sought to increase market share by maintaining competitive fares and schedules, even when this meant that many flights were unprofitable. However, after a $200 million loss in 1991, the board of directors dismissed the airline's CEO and senior vice president–marketing, replacing the former by Avery Stobaugh, previously the airline's vice president of finance. Stobaugh, an accountant by profession, began by getting rid of inefficient, unprofitable operations and sold off many of the older aircraft (such as Boeing 727s and DC-10s) in Constellation's aging fleet. Schedules were reduced, routes that were too competitive and profit draining were curtailed, and more than 3,000 jobs were eliminated.

By 1995, however, Constellation was finding itself in increasing difficulties again. The previous year, it had lost $141 million on revenues of $4.3 billion. Growing success overseas—an operating profit of $130 million—contrasted with increasing domestic losses. Severe capital constraints made it difficult for Constellation to order the new equipment, such as the Airbus 320 and Boeing 777, needed for more efficient operations. Attempts to cut labor costs had met with limited success. In 1994, pilots and noncontract personnel accepted a 17-month pay freeze, but machinists and flight attendants rejected a similar freeze and won new contracts that provided for a 30 percent wage increase over three years with no productivity givebacks (in the form of more flexible work rules).

Part of Constellation's problem in labor negotiations was that the airline was a subsidiary of Constellation Services Corporation, a large holding company that also owned an international hotel chain, a large trucking operation, and other subsidiaries. "There's always the perception that the parent will bail out a subsidiary," remarked one observer. This crutch was removed when the parent firm spun off the airline as an independent company in February 1995.

A New Chief Executive

During the fiscal year ending September 1997, traffic increased by 13.3 percent to 32 billion passenger miles, and the average load factor rose to 65.2 percent. However, the airline lost $193 million that year; during the fourth quarter alone, losses totaled $123 million. Stobaugh announced that he was taking early retirement, and the board replaced him by Javonski, who had previously been president of an all-freight airline and was known as a tough, no-nonsense executive with a strong track record in cost cutting and profitability improvement.

Javonski moved quickly to reduce expenses, dismissing hundreds of office workers and reaching agreements with pilots and machinists for pay cuts of about 15 percent. He then turned his attention to the flight attendants, whose contract was up for renegotiation.

Constellation Flight Attendants

The airline had some 6,500 flight attendants. According to the company, the average flight attendant received wages and benefits worth $44,000 a year. Because the airline had done little hiring in recent years, it employed a higher proportion of senior flight attendants than its competitors. The great majority of flight attendants were college educated. Some had been recruited directly from college; others had worked previously as teachers, nurses, social workers, or in office positions. Others had worked for the airline in reservations, on ticket counters, or as gate agents and saw a cabin position as a step up in pay and prestige.

Candidates were attracted to the job by the pay and benefits (which increased with seniority), the opportunity to travel, free or reduced-fare flights for family members, and a working schedule that was limited to about 14 to 15 days per month. During their time off, many attendants worked at second jobs—some had small businesses of their own—or pursued their education. However, although salaries and benefits improved with seniority, the opportunities for further career progression were minimal. There were possibilities to work on the ground in supervisory or training positions, but the pay was no higher (and sometimes lower) than the earnings of a senior attendant. Also the hours were longer.

The Federal Aviation Authority (FAA) limited the number of hours that attendants could fly each month, as well as setting minimum requirements for days off from flying assignments. The flight attendants' union had negotiated work rules that improved on FAA requirements, so that a Constellation attendant would normally fly about 75 hours a month. However, this excluded time spent waiting at airports and on call, as well as overnight stays in distant cities. On the average, an attendant could expect to spend about 250 hours a month away from home.

Junior attendants served in the "ready reserves," on call for five hours at a time and ready to arrive at the airport within 50 minutes to fly wherever they were needed. Attendants resented the uncertainty and idle time. However, with seniority came priority in bidding on schedules for the following month.

Attendants worked in randomly selected teams of five to seven persons, which were changed monthly. Through this bidding system, attendants could ask to fly on their preferred schedules. Because of the priority system, senior attendants had a better chance of avoiding weekend and holiday travel; flying on routes that were perceived as more glamorous; and picking schedules that would avoid the need to stay overnight in distant cities and allow them more time with their families, on second jobs, or in additional education.

Recruitment and training of flight attendants was strongly influenced by FAA requirements. The Constellation training program had historically lasted about five weeks. Most of this period was spent in classroom instruction, with more than half the time being devoted to FAA-prescribed sections on safety procedures and medical first aid, including cardiopulmonary resuscitation (CPR). The course also covered passenger handling and on-board services, as well as personal grooming and familiarization with the company. There were approximately three dozen written tests.

Education in safety procedures included timed emergency exercises, resembling an obstacle course and designed to simulate real-world disasters. Trainees found themselves working in darkness, fire and smoke, and even underwater as they sought to help others and themselves escape from a simulated accident. Between 5 percent and 10 percent of trainees failed to complete the program satisfactorily. Training continued after graduation, with attendants being required to attend short refresher and update courses in safety each year.

In spite of the emphasis on safety training, an attendant's day-to-day work focused on providing service to the passengers. She or he would greet passengers as they boarded, help them to find seating assignments or stow carry-on baggage, and give special assistance to young children traveling alone or to infirm and disabled passengers. Safety procedures were emphasized before take-off, but once the flight was airborne the focus of the job switched to food and beverage service or "glorified waitressing," as many of them described it.

The nature of the attendant's job was tightly prescribed and included strict dress codes and grooming requirements. Yet a flight attendant's work was not closely monitored in the air. One attendant on each flight was given the coordinating role of flight service manager, who then assigned specific duties to each attendant based on passenger seating. However, the flight service manager did not evaluate her or his fellow attendants. Written complaints and commendations from crew members and passengers were placed in an attendant's employment file; too many negative complaints about poor service could lead to disciplinary action. Failures to observe safety requirements could be punished by fines or termination.

Many attendants expressed regret that there wasn't more time to give personal attention to passengers, as they recognized that the quality of personal service they provided was a significant factor in passenger satisfaction. Although Constellation had a good reputation for service on its international flights, many observers felt that the company's food and cabin service on domestic flights could be improved.

The Strike

Having reached agreement for new contracts with pilots and machinists amounting to a 15 percent cut in pay, Javonski proposed even more significant cuts for the airline's flight attendants. A spokesperson for the airline stated, "We are essentially seeking a 22 percent pay reduction and work rule changes that would amount to being available for duty less than two more hours per week. These cuts would save Constellation some $120 million annually."

The attendants countered with an offer to reduce wages and benefits by 15 percent, a move that they said would save Constellation $35 million a year. They stated that a 22 percent cut, which would save the company some $45 million annually, was excessive, as were the work rule changes, which they claimed would be worth $42 to $75 million.

With neither side able to reach an agreement, the two parties entered a 30-day cooling-off period, which Javonski used to train 1,500 Constellation reservation agents and other employees as flight attendants. He also recruited 1,500 new employees for attendants' jobs and began training them, too. However, the airline gave no guarantee of permanent employment as flight attendants to any of these individuals. Under the proposed new work rules and a continuation of current schedules, Constellation would need only 3,500 attendants at the lowest point of the winter season and 5,000 during the summer high season.

On March 3, four days before the union would be free to strike, Javonski claimed that a strike that was successful in shutting down the airline for a considerable period might force him to break up Constellation and sell off routes, aircraft, gates, and maintenance facilities to other carriers.

The day before the strike, the two parties were still talking and still trading charges. The airline claimed that the average flight attendant's pay was $35,000—double the starting price at many airlines. The union said the $35,000 figure was inflated. Constellation offered to reduce its pay cut demand to 17 percent but refused to budge on work rule changes. The union rejected the offer. It was reported in the news that personal antipathy between Javonski and the union president, Valarie Gilmore, had not facilitated negotiations.

The Strike Begins

The International Flight Attendants Union struck Constellation at 12:01 A.M. on May 7. The airline's newly hired flight attendants crossed picket lines to the jeers of picketing IFAU members. The pilots crossed the picket lines "regretfully," stating that their contract contained a no-strike agreement, and 85 percent of the company's machinists crossed picket lines, too. Industry observers were not surprised, pointing out that airline unions rarely displayed solidarity in a labor dispute that affected only one of them.

On the first day of the strike, Constellation claimed that it had operated 52 percent of its schedule and said that it planned to restore all flights "within the next several days." Substantial fare cuts were offered through the end of the year to lure passengers. Union representatives disputed Constellation's schedule claims and stated that the newly hired flight attendants were not properly trained in safety procedures.

Three days into the strike, Constellation announced that it was continuing to restore flights and that the figure was now up to 54 percent of the total flight schedule. That day, the airline took the International Association of Machinists to court to force them to stop honoring flight attendant picket lines.

On March 11, Constellation announced that it would meet the union with a federal mediator in Philadelphia the following day. However, these talks broke off after four hours, with no new meetings scheduled. That same day, striking machinists obeyed a court order to return to work, and the airline announced that 62 percent of its flights were now operating.

The Strike Continues

During the next 12 days, Constellation continued to rebuild its schedules, and the strike continued to receive broad media coverage. The TV news coverage showed sign-carrying picketers shivering outside terminals at northern airports. Strikers spoke of their commitment to Constellation and claimed that Javonski was just a financial manipulator, bent on making money by breaking up the airline.

The newspapers reported that although Constellation passengers arriving at airports were mostly ignoring picket lines, a well-known movie actor had switched to another airline when she learned that she had been booked on a Constellation flight. It was also reported that the airline was losing over $1 million a day.

Passengers confirmed union claims that on-board service was poor and that flight attendants were slow and inexperienced. Said one traveler after a transcontinental flight, "It was just amateur hour on board! They took forever to serve the drinks and then forgot to come back and collect money from those who had had alcoholic drinks. The meal service was a shambles." Many travelers also complained of delayed flights.

Both the union leadership and the rank and file continued to allege that flying on Constellation was unsafe, because the new attendants lacked both experience and adequate training. Management refuted the charge, stating that the FAA's stringent criteria had been fully met. Noting that "several hundred" IFAU members had defied their union and returned to work, Constellation argued that the rank and file were not behind the strike and demanded that the leadership take a strike vote. Union leaders, however, scoffed at the claim and stated that the membership was "overwhelmingly" behind the strike.

The union's claim of safety problems received a significant boost a few days later when smoke filled the cabin of a Constellation airliner that was descending for landing at San Francisco International Airport. Although the aircraft landed safely and there were no injuries, the shaken passengers told reporters that the flight attendants had panicked and that the situation in the cabin had been chaotic. The incident received wide publicity, and the authorities announced that there would be an investigation. Financial analysts noted that the value of the airline's stock had fallen by 15 percent since the beginning of the strike.

On March 25, Constellation and the union announced that they would resume negotiations the next day in New York.

■ Questions for Discussion

1. How important is the role of flight attendants from the standpoint of (a) airline operations and (b) customer satisfaction?
2. From the employees' standpoint, what do you see as the benefits and disadvantages of working as a flight attendant today? Is it a desirable job as (a) a junior employee, (b) a senior employee?
3. Evaluate the current strike situation. How strong a position does (a) the airline and (b) the flight attendants union have at the present time? How is that position likely to change in the coming weeks?
4. When the company and union resume negotiations, what bargaining position do you recommend for (a) the flight attendants union and (b) the airline?

■✔ MENTON BANK

"I'm concerned about Karen," said Margaret Costanzo to David Reeves. Costanzo was a vice president of Menton Bank and manager of the Victory Square branch, the third largest in Menton's 292-branch network. Reeves, the branch's customer service director, was responsible for coordinating the work of the customer service representatives (CSRs, formerly known as tellers) and the customer assistance representatives (CARs, formerly known as new accounts assistants).

Costanzo and Reeves were discussing Karen Mitchell, a 24-year-old CSR who had applied for the soon-to-be-vacant position of head CSR. Mitchell had been with the bank for three and a half years. She had applied for the position of what had then been called head teller a year earlier, but the job had gone to a candidate with more seniority. Now that individual was leaving—his wife had been transferred to a new job in another city—and the position was once again open. Two other candidates had also applied.

Both Costanzo and Reeves were agreed that according to all the criteria used in the past, Mitchell would have been the obvious choice. She was both fast and accurate in her work, presented a smart and professional appearance, and was well liked by customers and her fellow CSRs. However, the nature of the teller's job had been significantly revised nine months earlier to add a stronger marketing component. They were now required to stimulate customer interest in the broadening array of financial services offered by the bank. "The problem with Karen," as Reeves put it, "is that she simply refuses to sell."

The New Focus on Customer Service

Facing aggressive competition for retail business from other financial institutions, Menton Bank had taken a number of steps in recent years to strengthen its position. In particular, it had invested heavily in technology, installing the latest generation of automated teller machines (ATMs) and 24-hour automated telephone banking. Customers could also call a central customer service office to speak with a bank representative about service questions or problems with their accounts, as well as to request new account applications or new checkbooks, which would be sent by mail. Recently, Menton had introduced home banking through the Internet. Complementing these new channels were a variety of new retail financial products. Finally, the appearance of the branches was being improved, and a recently implemented pilot program was testing the impact of a radical redesign of the branch interior on the quality of customer service. As more customers switched to electronic banking, the bank planned to close a number of its smaller branches.

In the most recent six months, Menton had seen a significant increase in the number of new accounts opened, as compared to the same period of the previous year. Also, quarterly survey data showed that the bank was steadily increasing its share of new deposits in the region.

Customer Service Issues

Bank officers had found that existing "platform" staff—known as new accounts assistants—were ill equipped to sell many of the new products now offered because they lacked product knowledge and skills in selling. As Costanzo recalled,

> The problem was that they were so used to sitting at their desks waiting for a customer to approach them with a specific request, such as a mortgage or car loan, that it was hard to get them to take a more positive approach that involved actively probing for customer needs. Their whole job seemed to revolve around filling out forms.

Internal research showed that the mix of activities performed by tellers was starting to change. More customers were using the ATMs and automated telephone banking for a broad array of transactions, including cash withdrawals and deposits (from the ATMs), transfers of funds between accounts, and a review of account balances. As home banking caught on, this trend was expected to accelerate. But Costanzo noted that customers who were older or less well educated still seemed to prefer "being served by a real person, rather than a machine."

Three sites were included in the pilot test of "new look" branches, featuring a redesigned interior. One was the Victory Square branch, located in a busy commercial and retail area, about 1 mile from the central business district and less than 10-minutes' walk from the campus of a major university. The other test branches were in two different metropolitan areas and were located in a shopping mall and next to a big hospital, respectively.

Each of these three branches had previously been remodeled to include at least five ATMs (Victory Square had seven), which could be closed off from the rest of the branch so that they would remain accessible to customers 24 hours a day. Further remodeling was then undertaken to locate a customer service desk near the entrance; close to each desk were two electronic information terminals, featuring color touch screens that customers could activate to obtain information on a variety of banking services. The teller stations were redesigned to provide two levels of service: an express station for simple deposits and cashing of approved checks, and regular stations for the full array of services provided by tellers. The number of stations open at a given time was varied to reflect the volume of anticipated business, and staffing arrangements were changed to ensure that more tellers were on hand to serve customers during the busiest periods.

Human Resources

With the new environment came new staff training programs and new job titles. Front-line staff at all Menton branches received new job descriptions and job titles: customer assistance representatives (for the platform staff), customer service representatives (for the tellers), and customer service director (instead of assistant branch manager). The head teller position was renamed head CSR. The training program for each group began with staff from the three test branches and was being extended to all. It included information about both new and existing retail products (CARs received more extensive training in this area than did CSRs). The CARs also attended a 15-hour course, offered in three separate sessions, on basic selling skills. This program covered key steps in the sales process, including building a relationship, exploring customers' needs, determining a solution, and overcoming objections.

The sales training program for CSRs, in contrast, consisted of just two 2-hour sessions designed to develop skills in recognizing and probing customers' needs, presenting product features and benefits, overcoming objections, and referring customers to CARs. All front-office staff were taught how to improve their communication skills and professional image: Clothing, personal grooming and interactions with customers were all discussed. Said the trainer, "Remember, people's money is too important to entrust to someone who doesn't look and act the part!"

The CARs were instructed to rise from their seats and shake hands with customers. Both CARs and CSRs were given exercises designed to improve their listening skills and their powers of observation. All employees who were working where they could be seen by customers were ordered to refrain from drinking soda and chewing gum on the job.

Although Menton Bank's management anticipated that most of the increased emphasis on selling would fall to the CSRs, they also foresaw a limited selling role for the CSRs, who would be expected to mention various products and facilities offered by the bank as they served customers at the teller windows. For instance, if a customer happened to say something about an upcoming vacation, the CSR was supposed to mention traveler's checks; if a customer complained about bounced checks, the CSR should recommend speaking to a CAR about opening a personal line of credit that would provide automatic overdraft protection; and if a customer mentioned investments, the CSR was expected to refer him or her to a CAR who could provide information on money market accounts, certificates of deposit, or Menton's discount brokerage service. All CSRs were supplied with their own business cards. When making a referral, they were expected to write the customer's name and the product of interest on the back of a card, give it to the customer, and send that individual to the customer assistance desks.

To motivate CSRs to sell specific financial products, the bank decided to change the process under which employees at the three test branches were evaluated. All CSRs had traditionally been evaluated twice yearly on a variety of criteria, including accuracy, speed, quality of interactions with customers, punctuality, job attitudes, cooperation with other employees, and professional image. The evaluation process assigned a number of points to each criterion, with accuracy and speed being the most heavily weighted. In addition to appraisals by the customer service director and the branch manager, with input from the head CSR, Menton had recently instituted a program of anonymous visits by what was popularly known as the "mystery client." Each CSR was visited at least once a quarter by a professional evaluator, posing as a customer. This individual's appraisal of the CSR's appearance, performance, and attitude was included in the overall evaluation. The number of points scored by each CSR had a direct impact on merit pay raises and on selection for promotion to the head CSR position or to platform jobs.

To encourage improved product knowledge and consultative selling by CSRs, the evaluation process was revised to include points assigned for each individual's success in sales referrals. Under the new evaluation scheme, the maximum number of points assigned for effectiveness in making sales—directly or through referrals to CARs—amounted to 30 percent of the potential total score. Although CSR-initiated sales had risen significantly in the most recent half year, Reeves sensed that morale had dropped among this group, in contrast to the CARs, whose enthusiasm and commitment had risen significantly. He had also noticed an increase in CSR errors. One CSR had quit, complaining about too much pressure.

Karen Mitchell

Under the old scoring system, Karen Mitchell had been the highest scoring teller/CSR for four consecutive half-year periods. But after 12 months under the new system, her ranking had dropped to fourth out of the seven full-time tellers. The top-ranking CSR, Mary Bell, had been with Menton Bank for 16 years but had declined repeated invitations to apply for a head teller position, saying that she was happy where she was, earning at the top of the CSR scale, and did not want "the extra worry and responsibility." Mitchell ranked first on all but one of the operationally related criteria (interactions with customers, where she ranked second) but sixth on selling effectiveness (Exhibit 1).

Costanzo and Reeves had spoken to Mitchell about her performance and expressed disappointment. Mitchell had informed them, respectfully but firmly, that she saw the most important aspect of her job as giving customers fast, accurate, and courteous service:

> I did try this selling thing but it just seemed to annoy people. Some said they were in a hurry and couldn't talk now; others looked at me as if I were slightly crazy to bring up the subject of a different bank service than the one they were currently transacting. And then, when you got the odd person who seemed interested, you could hear the other customers in the line grumbling about the slow service.
>
> Really, the last straw was when I noticed on the computer screen that this woman had several thousand in her savings account so I suggested to her, just as the trainer had told us, that she could earn more interest if she opened a money market account. Well, she told me it was none of my business what she did with her money, and stomped off. Don't get me wrong, I love being able to help customers, and if they ask for my advice, I'll gladly tell them about what the bank has to offer.

Selecting a New Head CSR

Two weeks after this meeting, it was announced that the head CSR was leaving. The job entailed some supervision of the work of the other CSRs (including allocation of work assignments and scheduling part-time CSRs at busy periods or during employees' vacations), consultation on—and, where possible, resolution of—any problems occurring at the teller stations, and handling of large cash deposits and withdrawals by local retailers. When not engaged on such tasks, the head CSR was expected to operate a regular teller window.

The pay scale for a head CSR ranged from $8.00 to $13.50 per hour, depending on qualifications, seniority, and branch size; CSRs earned $6.20 to $10.30 per hour, and CARs earned $7.10 to $12.00. Full-time employees (who were not unionized) worked a 40-hour week, including some evenings until 6 P.M. and certain Saturday mornings. Costanzo indicated that the pay scales were typical for banks in the region, although the average CSR at Menton was better qualified than those at smaller banks and therefore higher on the scale. Mitchell was currently earning $9.10 per hour, reflecting her education, which included a diploma in business administration, three-and-a-half years' experience, and significant past merit increases. If promoted to head CSR, she would qualify for an initial rate of $11.00 an hour. When applications for the positions closed, Mitchell was one of three candidates. The other two candidates were Jean Warshawski, 42, another CSR at the Victory Square branch; and Curtis Richter, 24, the head CSR at one of Menton Bank's small suburban branches, who was seeking more responsibility.

Warshawski was married, with two sons in school. She had started working as a part-time teller at Victory Square some three years previously, switching to full-time work a year later in order, as she said, to put away some money for her boys' college education. Warshawski was a cheerful woman with a jolly laugh. She had a wonderful memory for people's names, and Reeves had often seen her greeting customers on the street or in a restaurant during her lunch hour. Reviewing her evaluations over the previous three years, Reeves noted that she had initially performed poorly on accuracy, and at one point, when she was still a part-timer, had been put on probation because of frequent inaccuracies in the balance in her cash drawer at the end of the day. Although Reeves considered her much improved on this score, he still saw room for improvement. The customer service director had also had occasion to reprimand her for tardiness during the past year. Warshawski attributed this to health problems with her elder son, who, she said, was now responding to treatment.

Both Reeves and Costanzo had observed Warshawski at work and agreed that her interactions with customers were exceptionally good, although she tended to be overly chatty and was not as fast as Mitchell. She seemed to have a natural ability to size up customers and to decide which ones were good prospects for a quick sales pitch on a specific financial product. Although slightly untidy in her personal appearance, she was very well organized in her work and was quick to help her fellow CSRs, especially new ones. She was currently earning $8.20 per hour as a CSR and would qualify for a rate of $10.40 as head CSR. In the most recent six months, Warshawski was ranked ahead of Mitchell as a result of being very successful in consultative selling (Exhibit 1, p. 378).

Richter, the third candidate, was not working in one of the three test branches, so had not been exposed to the consultative selling program and its corresponding evaluation scheme. However, he had received excellent evaluations for his work in Menton's small Longmeadow branch, where he had been employed for three years. A move to Victory Square would increase his earnings from $9.40 to $10.40 per hour. Reeves and Costanzo had interviewed Richter and considered him intelligent and personable. He had joined the bank after dropping out of college midway through his third year but had recently started taking evening courses to complete his degree. The Longmeadow branch was located in an older part of town, where commercial and retail activity were rather stagnant. This branch (which was rumored to be under consideration for closure) had not yet been renovated and had no ATMs, although there was an ATM accessible to Menton customers one block away. Richter supervised three CSRs and reported directly to the branch manager, who spoke very highly of him. Because there were no CARs in this branch, Richter and another experienced CSR took turns in handling new accounts and loan or mortgage applications.

Costanzo and Reeves were troubled by the decision that faced them. Before the bank's shift in focus, Mitchell would have been the natural choice for the head CSR job, which in turn could be a stepping stone to further promotions, including customer assistance representative, customer service director, and eventually manager of a small branch or a management position in the head office. Mitchell had told her superiors that she was interested in making a career in banking and that she was eager to take on further responsibilities.

Compounding the problem was the fact that the three branches that were testing the improved branch design and new customer service program had just completed a full year. Costanzo knew that sales and profits were up significantly at all three branches, relative to the bank's performance as a whole. She anticipated that top management would want to extend the program systemwide after making any modifications that seemed desirable.

EXHIBIT 1   Menton Bank: Summary of Performance Evaluation Scores for Customer Service Representatives at Victory Square Branch for Latest Two Half-Year Periods

CSR Name[c]	Length of Full-Time Bank Service	Operational Criteria[a] (max.: 70 points)		Selling Effectiveness[b] (max.: 30 points)		Total Score	
		1st Half	2nd Half	1st Half	2nd Half	1st Half	2nd Half
Mary Bell	16 years, 10 months	65	64	16	20	81	84
Scott Dubois	2 years, 3 months	63	61	15	19	78	80
Bruce Greenfield	12 months	48	42	20	26	68	68
Karen Mitchell	3 years, 7 months	67	67	13	12	80	79
Sharon Rubin	1 year, 4 months	53	55	8	9	61	64
Swee Hoon Chen	7 months	—	50	—	22	—	72
Jean Warshawski	2 years, 1 month	57	55	21	28	79	83

[a] Totals were based on sum of ratings points against various criteria, including accuracy, work production, attendance and punctuality, personal appearance, organization of work, initiative, cooperation with others, problem-solving ability, and quality of interaction with customers.

[b] Points were awarded for both direct sales by CSR (e.g., traveler's checks) and referral selling by CSR to CAR (e.g., debit card, certificates of deposit, and personal line of credit).

[c] These were full-time CSRs only (part-time CSRs were evaluated separately).

■ Questions for Discussion

1. Identify the steps taken by Menton Bank to develop a stronger customer orientation.
2. Compare and contrast the jobs of CAR and CSR. How important is each to (a) bank operations and (b) customer satisfaction?
3. Evaluate the strengths and weaknesses of Karen Mitchell and other candidates for head CSR.
4. What action do you recommend for filling the position of head CSR?

MUSEUM OF FINE ARTS, BOSTON

It was a sunny July day at Boston's Museum of Fine Arts (MFA). Patricia B. Jacoby, deputy director for marketing and development, was lunching with colleagues in the museum's outdoor restaurant and reflecting on the progress made in building up marketing capabilities during the past three years. Sipping her iced tea, she reminded her colleagues of the challenges facing the MFA at the start of a new fiscal year.

> It's not enough to say that we now have a marketing orientation at the MFA. We must live this orientation through our behavior, as part of our everyday operations. We have to maintain the momentum in our dealings with all the museum's stakeholders—members, current and prospective visitors, the local community, staff, trustees and overseers, volunteers and, of course, the media.

Background

By the late 1990s, Boston's Museum of Fine Arts could boast a permanent collection that ranked it among the best in the United States. *Connoisseur's World* magazine described it as second in quality and scope only to the holdings of New York's Metropolitan Museum of Art. Many art experts saw the MFA as having world-class collections in such fields as

This case was prepared by Christopher H. Lovelock. Copyright © 1998 by the J. Paul Getty Trust.

French Impressionist paintings; American paintings and decorative arts; Egyptian, classical Greek, and Asian arts; and European silver. However, its modern and contemporary art holdings were generally held to be less significant.

Founded in 1870, the museum was located one mile west of Boston's fashionable Back Bay area and two miles from downtown. There was good access by bus and rapid transit and paid parking was available. Adjacent was the School of the Museum of Fine Arts. The MFA's public facilities included two restaurants, a self-service cafeteria, a large retail store, auditoriums for lectures and other presentations, and two recently renovated outdoor garden courts. Behind the scenes were storage areas, workshops, library facilities, and offices.

Unlike many major American museums, the MFA received no ongoing support from city, state, or federal funds. Government grants were limited to special projects. The basic admissions fee was $10; students and senior citizens paid $8, while accompanied children aged 17 and under entered free. Wednesday evenings were free to all, but donations were welcomed. An admission surcharge was sometimes imposed for major exhibitions. But museum members, who paid an annual fee, could enter without charge at any time.

In mid-1997, the museum employed 700 staff members, divided into three broad areas: curatorial and collections; development and marketing; and operations. The three deputy directors in charge of these areas reported to Malcolm Rogers, the museum's director. In turn, Rogers was responsible to the board of trustees. The MFA also benefited from the services of a large volunteer staff.

The MFA's curators, whom some likened to university faculty (although none had tenure), worked within departments organized around specific art fields and had both programmatic and project responsibilities. Their programmatic tasks involved knowing, managing, and shaping the museum's collections, a role that involved working closely with scholars, collectors, and colleagues and also participating in outside professional activities. Project responsibilities included developing exhibitions, selecting the works of art to display, and deciding how to present them. Curators also presented and interpreted the museum's permanent collection, wrote publications, and conducted lectures and gallery talks.

For the fiscal year ending 30 June, 1997, the MFA's operating revenues were $85.2 million (including $12.8 million from the Museum School). After deducting operating expenses, the MFA had ended the year with an estimated surplus of $0.7 million, which would be applied to rebuilding reserves. Exhibit 1 provides a 20-year summary of MFA financial results; Exhibit 2 (p. 380) shows 20-year attendance numbers.

EXHIBIT 1 Museum of Fine Arts: Annual Operating Surpluses (or Deficits), Fiscal Years Ending June 30, 1977–1997

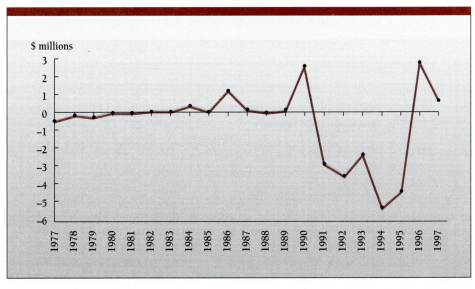

EXHIBIT 2 Museum of Fine Arts: Annual Attendance for Fiscal Years Ending June 30, 1978–1997

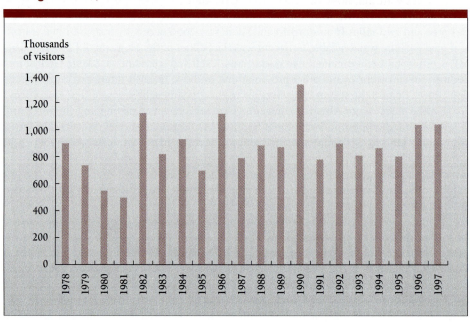

Recent History

During the past quarter-century, the MFA had experienced mixed fortunes. In the late 1960s and early 1970s, it was viewed by some observers as elitist and poorly managed. People accused the MFA of hoarding its remarkable collections, much of them in storage, rather than inviting visitors to come inside and enjoy them. In 1976, Jan Fontein, curator of the Asiatic Department, was named director of the museum and an experienced manager appointed as deputy director in charge of the institution's business affairs. At its close in 1987, Fontein's 11-year tenure was described as "a huge success" by *The Boston Globe*, which noted:

> The sleepy, dusty mausoleum of the 1960s today is like a thriving city center, bursting with special exhibitions, lectures, and concerts. The shop and restaurants are packed and the line of cars waiting to get in stretches around the block.

The MFA's financial situation improved sharply under Fontein, with the operating results moving into surplus. Reflecting improved marketing and development efforts (aided by a booming economy), donations rose significantly, membership almost tripled over 10 years to 41,049 in 1985–86, and retail and catalog sales leaped from $0.9 million to $11.4 million over the same period. Several "blockbuster" exhibitions fueled the growth in admissions, including *Pompeii: AD 79* (1978), *The Search for Alexander* (1981–82), and *Renoir* (1985–86). Admissions fees rose from $1.75 in 1976 to $4.00 in 1983. The most visible change at the MFA was the new West Wing, which included the Gund Gallery, designed to house large exhibitions.

Reflecting the tighter financial controls and budgetary discipline imposed by the associate director's office, costs were held in check—despite inflation and the greater demands of an enlarged physical plant. The associate director (who left in 1989) also emphasized the need for strategic planning and a stronger marketing orientation.

Fontein was succeeded as director by Alan Shestack, a distinguished art scholar. Shestack served six years as director of the MFA, resigning in September 1993 to become deputy director of the National Gallery of Art in Washington. One highlight of his tenure was the exhibition *Monet in the 90s*, which attracted 537,502 visitors to become the best attended exhibition ever staged at the MFA.

On other fronts, however, these were difficult years. An extended recession hurt fund raising and left the museum with continued heavy indebtedness. Although the Monet show contributed to an operating surplus of $2.4 million in 1989–90, the MFA's financial situation deteriorated sharply thereafter. The previous associate director had left and his successor focused actively on cost cutting, including staff layoffs. An important symbol of the museum's straitened circumstances was the decision in 1991 to close the original grand entrance on Huntington Avenue, thus yielding annual savings of some $100,000. However, critics noted that the MFA was literally closing its face to the local community and leaving only one remaining entrance for visitors on a side street. In a further cost savings, opening hours for visitors were cut back and expenditures on development and public information were sharply curtailed. Yet the annual operating deficit continued to rise, exceeding $5 million in 1993–94 (Exhibit 1).

The museum's financial difficulties were compounded by poor budgeting. The MFA had failed to develop a base budget that identified the base number of visitors it could expect, and to prepare incremental budgets for specific projects and exhibitions.

A New Director Arrives

In June 1994, the board appointed Malcolm Rogers, 45, an Oxford educated British art historian who was then deputy director of the National Portrait Gallery in London. Among his many talents was proven skill as a fund raiser. State support for the arts in the United Kingdom had declined sharply, requiring British museums to cut costs but raise funds from corporate and private donors; Rogers had done this with great success. The National Portrait Gallery was also known for its successful merchandising operation, which had brought in substantial revenues and taken the gallery's name around the world.

Arriving in Boston, Rogers found a dispirited institution. Reflecting financial difficulties and recent staff cutbacks, morale was low. Corporate memberships had slumped and attendance had declined since the heady year of the Monet show. The new director lost no time in making his presence felt. One of his first acts was to throw a breakfast for the entire staff. Addressing the crowd, he introduced what would become a central theme:

> We are one museum, not a collection of departments. The
> museum consists of security guards, curators, technicians,
> benefactors, volunteers, public relations personnel. We all
> have our individual professional expertise. And by working
> cooperatively with colleagues, we all have areas that can be
> improved.

Rogers' "one museum" theme, repeated at frequent intervals, sent the message that the director's agenda took precedence over that of the traditionally independent curators in terms of setting priorities for acquisitions and exhibitions. The curator of contemporary art subsequently resigned. While recognized for his good humor and friendly, outgoing manner, the new director also showed that he could be blunt and decisive. To address the deficit, he took a tough line with expenditures and began a program to cut staff size by 20%.

Developing a Stronger Marketing Orientation

The director's cutbacks did not extend to services for museum visitors. Instead, he set about creating a more welcoming environment. Said Rogers:

> I'm firmly committed to the idea that museums are here to
> serve the community, and that's going to be one of the
> keynotes of my work here in Boston—to encourage the MFA
> to turn out toward its public and to satisfy as broad a
> constituency as possible.

Early in his tenure, Rogers reopened the Huntington Avenue entrance, making a major publicity event out of the occasion. He reversed the trend of curtailing admission hours. Daily schedules were gradually extended and seven-day operations instituted. On three evenings a week, the museum remained open until almost 10 P.M., with the staff working to make Friday nights at the museum a popular venue for a younger crowd. To mark the 125th anniversary, Rogers initiated a policy of "Community Days," opening the museum free of charge on three Sundays each year. The Education Department offered free programs throughout the day on these occasions.

In each subsequent year, Rogers undertook other, high-profile activities to improve the museum's facilities and image. He raised funds to restore a derelict interior courtyard and installed new exterior lighting for better display of the MFA's imposing facade at night to passersby on busy Huntington Avenue. A second garden courtyard was opened, while the restaurant was extended and a new roof-top terrace added. Making the MFA an evening destination of choice, especially for people living in or close to the city, was another of Rogers' objectives. The broader variety of exhibitions (to encourage multiple visits per year), the upgrading of the restaurants, and the improvement in the museum's overall atmosphere were all designed to help achieve this goal. Rogers enjoyed a much higher public profile than his predecessors. Said Pat Jacoby: "Malcolm personifies marketing: He's accessible, he's an advocate of PR, he cares about the visitors, and he believes that the MFA can set the standard for other museums."

As director, Rogers selected a mix of exhibitions that combined high scholarly content with popular appeal. He believed that museums of the MFA's size and stature needed to mount accessible and popular shows on a regular basis. Rogers' view, shared by the senior staff, was that one show in five should be of a blockbuster nature, which meant hosting such an exhibition at least once every two years. In early 1997, the director personally championed the popular but controversial exhibition, *Herb Ritts: Works*, featuring the black-and-white photographs of the Los Angeles–based artist.

On the other hand, Rogers also recognized the importance of displaying art from the MFA's permanent collection to best advantage, including small revolving shows in a designated gallery. The new curator of European paintings had recently rehung all 15 European galleries in innovative ways designed to stimulate the audience and engage them more actively. The project included new, user-friendly descriptions of the paintings, with captions printed in a larger font and using everyday language rather than heavy academic prose. Commenting on blockbuster shows, the curator noted, "The big shows do bring people to the permanent collection. But the big show is a monster that museums have created. Linking a museum's health to its spectacular exhibitions is a problem."

The Marketing Organization

Overall responsibility for marketing-related activities at the MFA was in the hands of Patricia B. Jacoby, who held the recently created position of deputy director for marketing and development. Jacoby, whose background was in development and external relations, had joined the museum in 1991. She created a team to work on marketing issues throughout the museum: herself, Paul Bessire, associate director of marketing, Dawn Griffin, director of public relations, and Bill Wondriska, senior marketing consultant. Wondriska described the team's work as follows:

> Marketing is more than a narrow set of ideas, expressions, and applications. In its broadest sense, it's everything that carries the signature of the institution, how it presents itself both externally, to its guests, and internally, to its staff. We have to ensure that the external strategy is supported by those who work here. We have a multitude of experiences to communicate, but we're trying to speak with a single voice.

Griffin aimed to create the sense that "there's always something going on here. With the variety of programming that we offer, we can appeal to adults and children: 'There's something for *you!*'" Underlying all this was the element of quality, so that people might expect something worth coming to see.

Jacoby and her colleagues were concerned to ensure that the MFA should make itself a welcoming place that visitors found accessible. She had established a department of visitor services, hiring the former chief concierge at the Four Seasons Hotel in Beverly Hills to create a commitment to customer service among the guards, the information booth attendants, the ticket sellers, and everyone who worked with the customers. In another new departure, the MFA commissioned development of a Web site (www.mfa.org), which provided information about the museum and its exhibitions.

In fall 1996, a trustee marketing committee was formed, with membership drawn from all areas of the museum. Objectives included (1) becoming familiar with museum priorities that related to accessibility, new audiences, and the visitor experience; (2) developing a thorough understanding of marketing goals, objectives, strategies, and evaluations; (3) offering advice concerning the marketing program; (4) reviewing the marketing plan and budget and conveying recommendations to the budget and finance committee; and (5) becoming informed advocates for the marketing program and MFA itself. The chair of the committee, Stephen A. Greyser, a marketing professor at the Harvard Business School, believed that museums and other arts organizations should be "mission driven, but market sensitive—blending a strong and clear sense of mission with professional marketing strategy, plans, and programs." He saw effective marketing as a way to help "animate the whole organization" as well as outside target audiences, anticipating that the MFA could reach out to new audiences while also attracting more frequent visits from existing attendees.

At one meeting, a committee member urged the group to focus on making MFA exhibitions "fun and exciting experiences," whereupon a curator expressed discomfort with the word "fun," although she conceded that some exhibitions might be more entertaining than others.

At the MFA, as at other major museums, curators were sometimes uncomfortable with marketing activities. As the deputy director for curatorial affairs explained, promotional activities often overemphasized the most popular and familiar objects at the expense of the most artistically significant, thus giving an unbalanced impression of the collection or exhibition:

> In a very real sense, the need to stimulate attendance
> undercuts the educational message (of course, getting people
> in the door provides the opportunity to deliver that message).
> Many curators have a hard time understanding why, at some
> elemental level, the general public don't perceive the magic in
> the works of art that they do. The reality that the general
> visitor brings far less to the interaction with a work of art
> than a highly trained curator often results in the perception
> that marketing "dumbs down" the object, the project, and the
> institution. At worst, willfulness on each side undercuts the
> other, and nasty comments all around are the result. By
> contrast, in the best possible case, communication and
> involvement from both sides about goals and means of
> achieving them, and the explicit acknowledgment of criteria
> used to come to a solution, ought to create understanding and
> a positive working relationship.

The Museum Audience

To understand better the MFA's existing audience, a detailed visitor study was commissioned in 1995. This study involved conducting 100 interviews per month for a total of 12 months. Randomly selected adult visitors were targeted as they exited the museum. Neither school groups nor tour groups (which collectively accounted for one eighth of all museum visitors) were included in these surveys. Goals included obtaining baseline

EXHIBIT 3 **Museum of Fine Arts: Highlights of Findings from 1996 and 1987 Visitor Studies**

Demographics

- Visitors to the Museum are still predominantly female, White, affluent and older; Asian visitors are still the single largest group among minority visitors.
- Sixty percent of visitors continue to be drawn from within Massachusetts; New England states, New York, California, and international remain the largest tourist draws.

Members

- Members are more affluent than the average visitor.
- In terms of benefits, members overwhelmingly continue to value unlimited free admission, discount at the Museum Shop, and subscription to *Preview* magazine.

Time & Money Spent

- Although the median number of visits "in the past 12 months" has gone down from 3.8 to 2 visits, visitors today spend the same amount of time (2.5 hours on average) at the Museum as they did in 1987.
- A high a percent of visitors still spend money on things other than admission. Spending levels remain highest at the cafe/restaurant and at the Museum Shop.

MFA Collection

- No one part of the Museum dominates as visitors continue to express an interest in a wide range of the Museum's collection. Their reasons for visiting are as varied as the Museum's collection.

Improvements

- Most visitors, then as now, feel positive about the MFA. However, many are still dissatisfied with signage and the difficulties in finding their way around. Visitors continue to want more benches/seating areas in the exhibit halls and around the Museum.
- Unprompted complaints about parking have increased since 1987.

information on demographics, reasons for first and repeat visits, what visitors saw and did at the MFA, and how they experienced the museum. The intention was to use these data to help develop a strategy for increasing attendance. Highlights of the findings, and a comparison with a previous study in 1987, appear in Exhibit 3.

To attract financial support and encourage more frequent visits, the MFA had developed an extensive membership program, with different categories offering an increasing scale of benefits. For instance, a $50 individual membership allowed free admission, whereas a sustaining membership of $900 included invitations to selected opening receptions, reciprocal membership benefits at 21 major art museums around the United States, special programs with curatorial staff, and acknowledgment by name in the annual report. Larger donors received additional privileges. Membership revenues had risen at a much faster rate than the number of members in recent years. In 1996–97, members accounted for 231,000 of the 1.1 million visits recorded at the museum.

Enterprise Activities

In addition to operating revenues from admission fees, memberships, and unrestricted endowment income, the MFA obtained substantial revenues from merchandising and other services collectively known as "Enterprise" activities. In 1996–97, merchandise sales through the museum shop and other channels amounted to $39.5 million. After deducting cost of goods sold and other costs associated with merchandise operations, the MFA realized a net contribution of $ 1.9 million. Similarly, food service yielded a contribution of $0.8 million on sales of $ 5.3 million. Parking fees yielded revenues of $1.6 million, but not all related costs, such as security, were broken out separately.

Responsibility for all these activities rested with John Stanley, deputy director of operations. Discussing merchandising, Stanley declared:

> We see merchandising as central to the mission of the museum for both philosophical and legal reasons. If we sell items that are unrelated to our collection, we will be liable for unrelated business income tax and will lose our not-for-profit postal rate for mailing items purchased from our catalog.

Merchandise sales included jewelry, children's toys, decorative arts (such as posters, pictures, book ends, and vases), books, and paper products like calendars and note cards. More than half of all sales were catalog orders, handled through the MFA's distribution center outside the city. The main museum store, soon to be expanded, accounted for about 20 percent of sales. A small exhibition shop outside the Gund Gallery catered to visitors attending special exhibitions. There were five satellite stores within the Greater Boston area: Two in central Boston did particularly well because they were located in popular tourist areas. Three other stores (one under construction) were located in suburban shopping malls. Planning for merchandise keyed to upcoming exhibitions required a long lead time, because commissioning new items might require as much as two years' advance notification to suppliers.

Development and Sponsorship

A capital campaign had been launched in 1992. The goal of $110 million was designed to boost annual operating support and the museum's endowment, not to finance new construction projects or to fund new acquisitions. Support had been broad, and the campaign was expected to meet or even exceed its target by the closing date of June 1998. Jacoby noted that revenues from the enlarged endowment would eliminate the structural deficit once the campaign was completed.

Rogers was a firm believer in securing corporate sponsorship for exhibitions and other activities. Jacoby observed:

> Malcolm is willing to try new things. He's willing to put a corporate logo on the museum banner, if need be, to underwrite an exhibition. Bell Atlantic is underwriting the Picasso show this fall with a million dollars, while Fleet Bank is underwriting the new Monet show the following year with $1.2 million. As hackneyed as the word "partnership" has become, I think he really understands the concept. He's willing to meet a sponsor half-way, to try to understand their needs as well as the museum's needs and to make things work, rather than saying, "Oh no, we're too pure to display a corporate logo!"

The MFA had received both funding and marketing assistance for its exhibitions from corporate sponsors. In 1996, a large bank had supported an exhibition of works by Winslow Homer, a popular 19th century American artist. The bank not only donated a large sum to help mount the exhibition, but also offered its customers a credit card featuring a Homer image and promoted Homer within its branches, in mailed statement inserts, and on its ATMs. The exhibition had been very successful, attracting some 270,000 visitors. But critics, including some curators, felt that such actions smacked too much of commercialism. One member of the marketing team commented, "That's always going to happen when you push the envelope."

The Herb Ritts Exhibition

Few major shows at the MFA had generated as much controversy as *Herb Ritts: Works*. It was championed by Malcolm Rogers, who hoped that it would appeal to a wide audience, from newcomers to frequent visitors to the museum. Ritts, 44, had made his name as a photographer of both fashion and celebrities. His images were widely featured in publications such as *Vogue* and *Vanity Fair*. Additionally, he had shaped corporate advertising campaigns for many well-known fashion houses and cosmetics firms. Recently, he had begun directing commercials and music videos.

The exhibition—which would also be shown in Vienna, Ft. Lauderdale, Paris, and Australia—featured some 230 of Ritts's photographs, all in black and white and ranging in size from intimate portraits to ten-foot murals. It was the first time that a show had been sponsored by a major fashion house, Donna Karan of New York. The exhibits included shots of celebrities such as Madonna and other Hollywood stars, images of people, animals, and landscapes from Africa, layouts from the fashion world, and studies of the human form, including some controversial male and female nudes. The MFA budgeted $450,000 to promote the show, advertising it in a wide array of both general and specialist media, ranging from newspapers and magazines to theater programs and public transit vehicles. For the first time, the MFA advertised in national media, encompassing both fashion publications and upscale general audience magazines.

Reviews by the critics were generally unenthusiastic. The *Boston Sunday Herald* review was headlined "Putting on the Glitz." *The Boston Globe* described the show as "fun, all style and little substance, slick and seductive. ... It's a quick read—art for the attention span of the '90s." Addressing Malcolm Rogers's hope that Ritts would lure new young audiences to the museum, the *Globe's* critic declared, "That might work. ... But will this show turn young viewers on to *other* art?" One Boston gallery owner remarked: "I don't think that quality should ever be sacrificed in the name of new audiences." Nevertheless, when the show closed on February 9, 1997, it had achieved a total attendance of 253,694, making it the sixth most popular exhibition in MFA history. The press coverage, including national TV, was the broadest ever achieved by the museum.

Looking to the Future

The next major exhibition scheduled to be held at the MFA was *Picasso: The Early Years, 1892–1906.* Organized by the MFA and the National Gallery of Art in Washington, it was scheduled to run in Boston from early September to the beginning of January, 1998. Surveying the beginnings of the artist's career, the show would include images from Picasso's so-called "Blue" and "Rose" periods. More than 100 paintings, drawings, and sculptures had been selected for display from major collections around the world. The exhibition was sponsored by a substantial grant from Bell Atlantic, a major regional telecommunications company.

Pat Jacoby recognized that promoting this exhibition was only one of many challenges she faced in seeking to ensure the museum's continued success in serving its many audiences. As she reflected on the future role and responsibilities of marketing at the Museum of Fine Arts, she remembered a recent presentation by Malcolm Rogers, in which he had declared:

> Marketing is central to the life of a great museum that's trying to get its message out. It's part of our educational outreach, our social outreach. Unfortunately, certain people don't like the word "marketing." What I see out there—and also to a certain extent inside the museum—is a very conservative culture that cannot accept that institutions previously considered "elite" should actually be trying to attract a broader public and also listening to what the public is saying. But it's all to do with fulfilling your mission.
>
> Clearly part of a museum's mission is guardianship of precious objects, but unless we're communicating those objects to people effectively and our visitors are enjoying them—and the ambiance of the setting in which they are displayed and interpreted—then we're only operating at 50% effectiveness or less. Having said this, I want to stress that the mission comes first and that marketing is absolutely the

servant of our mission. I believe that museums stand for a commitment to certain eternal values that they bring to an ever-broadening public. We're not just in the business of finding out what people want and then giving it to them.

■ Questions for Discussion

1. Define the core product and supplementary services of a large museum like the MFA.
2. Prepare a flowchart of a tourist visiting Boston who calls from the hotel to get information about the MFA and then goes to visit it.
3. What differentiates the MFA from a for-profit institution like a department store, a theme park, or a movie theater? How does this distinction affect management priorities and decisions?
4. Evaluate the efforts made by the museum management to make the MFA more marketing oriented. What should be done to get better understanding of marketing and its objectives from curators?
5. Evaluate the role of Malcolm Rogers. Is he a good leader? Has he been an effective service marketer?

Endnotes

CHAPTER 1

1. Gross domestic product (GDP) and gross national product (GNP) are both widely used measures of a nation's economic activity. They differ simply in their treatment of international transactions. For the United States, there is little difference between the two measures because only a tiny percentage of Americans work abroad and the foreign earnings of U.S. firms are broadly equal to the U.S. earnings of foreign firms. However, differences between GDP and GNP are substantial in countries where many nationals work abroad (e.g., Pakistan) or where foreign investment in the country greatly exceeds investment abroad by domestic firms (e.g., Canada). Note that different countries may collect and report statistics in different ways.
2. James C. Cooper and Kathleen Madigan, "Fragile Markets Are Tying the Fed's Hands," *Business Week*, 4 November 1997, 33.
3. World Bank, *El Mundo del Trabajo en una Economia Integrada*, Washington, D.C.: World Bank, 1995.
4. Javier Reynoso, "Service Competition in Latin America: Managerial and Research Implications Towards the 21st Century," in *Pursuing Service Excellence: Practices and Insights*, ed. E. E. Scheuing, S. W. Brown, B. Edvardsson, and R. Johnston (New York: International Service Quality Association, 1998), pp. 55–60.
5. Regis McKenna, *Real Time* (Boston: Harvard Business School Press, 1997).
6. See, for instance, the discussion of outsourcing information-based services in James Brian Quinn, *Intelligent Enterprise* (New York: Free Press, 1992), ch. 3, 71–97.
7. Timothy K. Smith, "Why Air Travel Doesn't Work," *Fortune*, 3 April 1995, 42–56; Bill Saporito, "Going Nowhere Fast," *Fortune*, 3 April 1995, 58–59.
8. See, for instance, Valarie A. Zeithaml, A. Parasuraman, and Leonard L. Berry, *Delivering Quality Service* (New York: Free Press, 1990), and Barbara R. Lewis and Gard O. S. Gabrielsen, "Intra-organisational Aspects of Service Quality Management," *The Service Industries Journal*, April 1998, pp. 64–89.
9. See Christopher H. Lovelock and Charles B. Weinberg, *Public and Nonprofit Marketing*, 2d ed. (Redwood City, CA: Scientific Press/Boyd and Davis, 1989); and Philip Kotler and Alan Andreasen, *Strategic Marketing for Nonprofit Organizations*, 5th ed. (Upper Saddle River, NJ: Prentice Hall, 1996).
10. Leonard L. Berry, "Services Marketing Is Different," *Business*, May–June, 1980.
11. W. Earl Sasser, R. Paul Olsen, and D. Daryl Wyckoff, *Management of Service Operations: Text, Cases, and Readings* (Boston: Allyn & Bacon, 1978).
12. G. Lynn Shostack, "Breaking Free from Product Marketing," *Journal of Marketing*, April 1977.
13. Bonnie Farber Canziani, "Leveraging Customer Competency in Service Firms," *International Journal of Service Industry Management*, 8, no. 1 (1997): 5–25.
14. Gary Knisely, "Greater Marketing Emphasis by Holiday Inns Breaks Mold," *Advertising Age*, 15 January 1979.
15. Curtis P. McLaughlin, "Why Variation Reduction Is Not Everything: A New Paradigm for Service Operations," *International Journal of Service Industry Management*, 7, no. 3 (1996): 17–31.

16. This section is based on Valarie A. Zeithaml, "How Consumer Evaluation Processes Differ between Goods and Services," in J. A. Donnelly and W. R. George, *Marketing of Services* (Chicago: American Marketing Association, 1981), 186–190.

17. The 4Ps classification of marketing decision variables was created by E. Jerome McCarthy, *Basic Marketing: A Managerial Approach* (Homewood, IL: Irwin, 1960).

18. Since the late 1970s, many theorists have tried to go beyond the 4Ps to capture the complexity of services marketing in memorable fashion, emphasizing singly or in combination such factors as processes, personnel, and peripheral clues. Our 8Ps model of service management has been derived and expanded from a framework that encompassed seven elements—the original 4Ps plus participants, physical evidence, and process—proposed by Bernard H. Booms and Mary J. Bitner, "Marketing Strategies and Organization Structures for Service Firms," in J. H. Donnelly and W. R. George, *Marketing of Services* (Chicago: American Marketing Association, 1981), 47–51. Subsequently, Booms created a cartoon diagram showing seven little "pea people," two of them carrying oars, lifting a peapod-shaped boat. This gave us the idea for the metaphor of a racing eight, comprising eight rowers (the eighth being labeled productivity and quality), plus a coxswain to control the boat's speed and direction.

19. For a review of the literature on this topic, see Michael D. Hartline and O. C. Ferrell, "The Management of Customer Contact Service Employees," *Journal of Marketing*, 60, no. 4 (October 1996): 52–70.

20. K. Douglas Hoffman and John E. G. Bateson, "Ethical Issues in Services Marketing," *Essentials of Services Marketing* (New York: Dryden Press, 1997), 100–120.

21. Siegmund Warburg, cited by Derek Higgs, London, September 1997.

CHAPTER 2

1. Melvin T. Copeland, "The Relation of Consumers' Buying Habits to Marketing Methods," *Harvard Business Review*, 1 (April 1923): 282–289.

2. These classifications are derived from Christopher H. Lovelock, "Classifying Services to Gain Strategic Marketing Insights," *Journal of Marketing* 47 (Summer 1983): 9–20.

3. For more detailed illustrations of the impact of information technology on services, see Frances Cairncross, *The Death of Distance* (Boston: Harvard Business School Press, 1997), and Larry Downes and Chunka Mui, *Unleashing the Killer App* (Boston: Harvard Business School Press, 1998).

CHAPTER 3

1. Based on material in Delphine Parmenter, Jean-Claude Larréché, and Christopher Lovelock, "First Direct: Branchless Banking" (Fontainebleau, France: INSEAD, 1997); Saul Hansell, "500,000 Clients, No Branches," *New York Times*, 3 September 1995, 3–1; and Christopher Lovelock, *Product Plus: How Product + Service = Competitive Advantage* (New York: McGraw-Hill, 1994).

2. Jean Gadrey and Faïz Gallouj, "The Provider-Customer Interface in Business and Professional Services," *The Service Industries Journal* 18 (April 1998), 1–15.

3. Curtis P. McLaughlin, "Why Variation Reduction Is Not Everything: A New Paradigm for Service Operations," *International Journal of Service Industry Management* 7, no. 3 (1996): 17–39.

4. Lance A. Bettencourt and Kevin Gwinner, "Customization of the Service Experience: The Role of the Frontline Employee," *International Journal of Service Industry Management* 7, no. 2 (1996): 2–21.

5. Lynn Shostack, "Planning the Service Encounter," in J. A. Czepiel, M. R. Solomon, and C. F. Surprenant (eds.), *The Service Encounter* (Lexington, MA: Lexington Books, 1985), 243–254.

6. Carole F. Surprenant and Michael R. Solomon, "Predictability and Personalization in the Service Encounter," *Journal of Marketing* 51 (Winter 1987): 73–80.

7. Richard B. Chase, "Where Does the Customer Fit in a Service Organisation?" *Harvard Business Review*, November–December 1978.

8. Stephen J. Grove, Raymond P. Fisk, and Mary Jo Bitner, "Dramatizing the Service Experience: A Managerial Approach," in T. A. Schwartz, D. E. Bowen, and S. W. Brown, *Advances in Services Marketing and Management* (Greenwich, CT: JAI Press, 1992), Vol. I, 91–122.

9. Normann first used the term *moments of truth* in a Swedish study in 1978; subsequently it appeared in English in Richard Normann, *Service Management: Strategy and Leadership in Service Businesses*, 2d ed. (Chichester, UK: Wiley, 1991), 16–17.

10. Jan Carlzon, *Moments of Truth* (Cambridge, MA: Ballinger, 1987), 3.

11. Mary Jo Bitner, Bernard H. Booms, and Mary Stanfield Tetreault, "The Service Encounter: Diagnosing Favorable and Unfavorable Incidents," *Journal of Marketing* 54 (January 1990): 71–84.

12. Carlzon, *Moments of Truth*, 59–74.

13. Susan M. Keaveney, "Customer Switching Behavior in Service Industries: An Exploratory Study," *Journal of Marketing* 59 (April 1995): 71–82.

14. Mary Jo Bitner, Bernard Booms, and Lois A. Mohr, "Critical Service Encounters: The Employee's View," *Journal of Marketing* 58 (October 1994): 95–106.

15. Benjamin Schneider and David E. Bowen, *Winning the Service Game* (Boston: Harvard Business School Press, 1995), 92.

16. David E. Bowen, "Managing Customers as Human Resources in Service Organizations," *Human Resources Management* 25, no. 3 (1986): 371–383.

17. Schneider and Bowen, *Winning*, 85.

18. Bonnie Farber Canziani, "Leveraging Customer Competency in Service Firms," *International Journal of Service Industry Management* 8, no. 1 (1997): 5–25.

CHAPTER 4

1. Excerpted from the 1st Quarter News Release, Progressive Insurance Corp. Web site, www.auto-insurance.com, January 1998; the 3rd Quarter News Release, Progressive Insurance Corp. Web site, www.auto-insurance.com, January 1998; and Ronald Henkoff, "Service Is Everybody's Business," *Fortune*, 27 June 1994, 48.

2. Henkoff, "Service Is Everybody's Business," 50.

3. Lucette Lagnado, "Patients Give Hospitals Poor Scorecards," *The Wall Street Journal*, 28 January 1997, B1.

4. Ronald Lieber, "Now Are You Satisfied? The 1998 American Customer Satisfaction Index," *Fortune*, 16 February 1998, 161–166.

5. Ian P. Murphy, "Humanizing the Lawyer," *Marketing News*, 17 February 1997, B1.

6. From the Lexus Web site, www.lexus.com, January 1998.

7. Quoted from a TV interview with Michael Flatley on "Dateline NBC," 13 October 1997.

8. Abraham H. Maslow, *Motivation and Personality* (New York: Harper and Bro., 1954).

9. Stephanie Anderson Forest, Katie Kerwin, and Susan Jackson, "Presents That Won't Fit under the Christmas Tree," *Business Week*, 1 December 1997, 42.

10. Bill Fromm and Len Schlesinger, *The Real Heroes of Business* (New York: Currency Doubleday, 1993), 241.

11. From the Progressive Insurance Corp. Web site, www.auto-insurance.com, January 1998; and Henkoff, "Service Is Everybody's Business," 48–60.

12. Theodore Levitt, "What's Your Product and What's Your Business?" in *Marketing for Business Growth* (New York: McGraw-Hill, 1973), 7.

13. From Christopher Lovelock, *Product Plus* (New York: McGraw-Hill, 1994), 29–31.

CHAPTER 5

1. From *Interesting Facts about Taco Bell*, the company's promotional literature, which is available through the Taco Bell Guest Service Center (1-800-Taco-Bell) or through the Taco Bell Web site on the Internet <www.tacobell.com>; "RB Top 100," *Restaurant Business*, 20 November 1990; Ronald Henkoff, "Service Is Everybody's Business," *Fortune*, 27 June 1994, 48–60; and Leonard A. Schlesinger and Roger Hallowell, "Taco Bell Corp." (Boston: Harvard Business School Publishing Division, 1991).

2. Christopher H. Lovelock, "Federal Express: Quality Improvement Program, Lausanne: IMD case, 1990" (distributed by European Case Clearing House).

3. James Brian Quinn, *Intelligent Enterprise* (New York: Free Press, 1992), 325.

4. See Benjamin Schneider and David E. Bowen, *Winning the Service Game* (Boston: Harvard Business School Press, 1995); and Valarie A. Zeithaml, Leonard L. Berry, and A. Parasuraman, "The Nature and Determinants of Customer Expectations of Services," *Journal of the Academy of Marketing Science* 21 (1993).

5. Valarie A. Zeithaml, Leonard L. Berry, and A. Parasuraman, "The Behavioral Consequences of Service Quality," *Journal of Marketing* 60 (1996): 35.

6. See Roland T. Rust, Anthony J. Zahorik, and Timothy L. Keiningham, *Service Marketing* (New York: HarperCollins, 1996), 229; J. Joseph Cronin and Steven A. Taylor, "Measuring Service Quality: A Reexamination and Extension," *Journal of Marketing* 56 (1992): 55–68; and Richard L. Oliver, "A Conceptual Model of Service Quality and Service Satisfaction: Compatible Goals, Different Concepts," in *Advances in Services Marketing and Management: Research and Practice*, Teresa A. Swartz, David E. Bowen, and Stephen W. Brown, eds. (Greenwich, CT: JAI Press, 1993), Vol. 2.

7. From Valarie A. Zeithaml, Leonard L. Berry, and A. Parasuraman, "Communication and Control Processes in the Delivery of Service Processes," *Journal of Marketing* 52 (1988): 36–58; Christopher Lovelock, *Product Plus* (New York: McGraw-Hill, 1994), 112–113; and K. Douglas Hoffman and John E. G. Bateson, *Essentials of Services Marketing* (Fort Worth, TX: Dryden Press, 1997), 300–301.

8. Valarie A. Zeithaml, A. Parasuraman, and Leonard L. Berry, *Delivering Quality Service: Balancing Customer Perceptions and Expectations* (New York: Free Press, 1990).

9. A. Parasuraman, Valarie A. Zeithaml, and Leonard L. Berry, "SERVQUAL: A Multiple-Item Scale for Measuring Consumer Perceptions of Service Quality," *Journal of Retailing* 64 (1988): 12–40.

10. Leonard L. Berry, *On Great Service* (New York: Free Press, 1995), 84.

11. Steven W. Brown, Deborah L. Cowles, and Tracy L. Tuten, "Service Recovery: Its Value and Limitations as a Retail Strategy," *International Journal of Service Industry Management* 7, no. 5 (1996): 32–47.

12. Lovelock, *Product Plus*, 217–218.

13. See, for example, Thomas O. Jones and W. Earl Sasser, "Why Satisfied Customers Defect," *Harvard Business Review*, November–December 1995, 88–99; and Zeithaml, Berry, and Parasuraman, "Behavioral Consequences of Service Quality."

14. Jones and Sasser, "Why Satisfied Customers Defect," 96.

15. Philip L. Dawes, Grahame R. Dowling, and Paul G. Patterson, "Criteria Used to Select Management Consultants," *Industrial Marketing Management* 21 (1992): 187–193.

16. Roland T. Rust, Anthony J. Zahorik, and Timothy L. Keiningham, "Return on Quality (ROQ): Making Service Quality Financially Accountable," *Journal of Marketing* 59 (1995): 58–70.

17. Berry, *On Great Service*, 33.

18. Emil Becker, "Service Quality Requires Strategy and Tactics," *Marketing News*, 29 January 1996, 4.

19. Parasuraman, Zeithaml, and Berry, "SERVQUAL."

20. Tibbett Speer, "Nickelodeon Puts Kids Online," *American Demographics*, January 1994, 16–17.

21. James L. Heskett, *Managing in the Service Economy* (New York: Free Press, 1986).

22. This section is based on material from Eugene W. Anderson, Claes Fornell, and Roland T. Rust, "Customer Satisfaction, Productivity, and Profitability: Differences Between Goods and Services," *Marketing Science* 16 (1997): 131; Eugene W. Anderson, Claes Fornell, and Donald R. Lehmann, "Customer Satisfaction, Market Share and Profitability," *Journal of Marketing* 56 (1994): 53–66; and Lenard Huff, Claes Fornell, and Eugene W. Anderson, "Quality and Productivity: Contradictory and Complimentary," *Quality Management Journal* 4 (1996): 22–39.

CHAPTER 6

1. Based on information in *Intrawest Annual Report 1997* and *Whistler Resort: 1997–98 Winter Ski Season* (Vancouver: Intrawest Corp., 1998).

2. Roger Hallowell, "The Relationships of Customer Satisfaction, Customer Loyalty, and Profitability: An Empirical Study," *International Journal of Service Industry Management* 7, no. 4 (1996): 27–42.

3. According to Paul S. Bender, *Design and Operation of Customer Service Systems* (New York: AMACOM, 1976), a lost customer reduces profits by $118, whereas it costs $20 to keep a customer satisfied.

4. Leonard L. Berry and A. Parasuraman, *Marketing Services: Competing through Quality* (New York: Free Press, 1991), especially chapter 8, 132–150.

5. Barbara Bund Jackson, "Build Relationships That Last," *Harvard Business Review* November–December 1985, 120–128.

6. Theodore Levitt, *The Marketing Imagination*, new expanded ed. (New York: Free Press, 1986), 121.

7. David H. Maister, *True Professionalism* (New York: The Free Press, 1997).

8. This section is adapted from Christopher Lovelock, *Product Plus* (New York: McGraw-Hill, 1994), chap. 15.

9. Abbie Hoffman, *Steal This Book* (San Francisco: Grove Press, 1972).

10. Quoted in Lovelock, *Product Plus*, p. 236.

11. Christopher H. Lovelock and Penny Pittman Merliss, "Comprehensive Accounting Corporation," Harvard Business School Case 9-585-123. Reprinted in C. H. Lovelock and Charles B. Weinberg, *Marketing Challenges: Cases and Exercises*, 2nd ed. (New York: McGraw-Hill, 1989).

12. Frederick F. Reichheld, *The Loyalty Effect* (Boston: Harvard Business School Press, 1996).

13. Frederick F. Reichheld and W. Earl Sasser, Jr., "Zero Defections: Quality Comes to Services," *Harvard Business Review*, October 1990.

14. James L. Heskett, W. Earl Sasser, Jr., and Leonard A. Schlesinger, *The Service Profit Chain* (New York: Free Press, 1997).

15. Reichheld and Sasser, "Zero Defections."

16. Alan W. H. Grant and Leonard H. Schlesinger, "Realize Your Customer's Full Profit Potential," *Harvard Business Review* 73 (September–October, 1995): 59–75.

17. Gerald R. Dowling and Mark Uncles, "Do Customer Loyalty Programs Really Work?" *Sloan Management Review*, Summer 1997, 71–81.

CHAPTER 7

1. Based on information in Christopher W. Hart with Elizabeth Long, *Extraordinary Guarantees* (New York: AMACOM, 1997).

2. Oren Harari, "Thank Heavens for Complainers," *Management Review*, March 1997, 25–29.
3. Technical Assistance Research Programs Institute (TARP), *Consumer Complaint Handling in America: An Update Study,* Part II (Washington, D.C.: TARP and U.S. Office of Consumer Affairs, April 1986).
4. Susan M. Keveaney, "Customer Switching Behavior in Service Industries: An Exploratory Study," *Journal of Marketing* 59 (April 1995): 71–82.
5. Bernd Stauss, "Global Word of Mouth," *Marketing Management*, Fall 1997, 28–30.
6. TARP, *Consumer Complaint Handling.*
7. Claes Fornell et al., "The American Customer Satisfaction Index: Nature, Purpose, and Findings," *Journal of Marketing* 60 (October 1996): 7–18.
8. Ronald B. Lieber and Linda Grant, "Now Are You Satisfied?" *Fortune*, 16 February 1998, 161–166.
9. Society of Consumer Affairs Professionals (SOCAP), *Study of Consumer Complaint Behaviour in Australia* (Sydney: SOCAP, 1995).
10. Terrence Levesque and Gordon H. G. McDougall, "Customer Dissatisfaction: The Relationship between Types of Problems and Customer Response," *Canadian Journal of Administrative Sciences* 13, no. 3 (1996): 264–276.
11. Cathy Goodwin and B. J. Verhage, "Role Perceptions of Services: A Cross-Cultural Comparison with Behavioral Implications," *Journal of Economic Psychology* 10 (1990): 543–558.
12. Christopher W. L. Hart, James L. Heskett, and W. Earl Sasser Jr., "The Profitable Art of Service Recovery," *Harvard Business Review*, July–August, 1990, 148–156.
13. Stephen S. Tax, Stephen W. Brown, and Murali Chandrashekaran, "Customer Evaluations of Service Complaint Exercises: Implications for Relationship Marketing," *Journal of Marketing* 62 (April 1998): 60–76.
14. TARP, *Consumer Complaint Handling.*
15. Leonard L. Berry, *On Great Service: A Framework for Action* (New York: Free Press, 1995), 94.
16. Christo Boshoff, "An Experimental Study of Service Recovery Options," *International Journal of Service Industry Management* 8, no. 2 (1997): 110–130.
17. John Goodman, quoted in "Improving Service Doesn't Always Require Big Investment," *The Service Edge*, July–August 1990, 3.
18. Christopher W. L. Hart, "The Power of Unconditional Service Guarantees," *Harvard Business Review*, July–August 1990: 54–62.
19. The information on Promus Hotel Corporation is based on Christopher W. Hart with Elizabeth Long, *Extraordinary Guarantees.*
20. Christopher W. Hart with Elizabeth Long, *Extraordinary Guarantees.*

CHAPTER 8

1. From J. Case and J. Useem, "Six Characters in Search of a Strategy," *Inc. Magazine*, March 1996, 46–55.
2. George S. Day, *Market Driven Strategy* (New York: Free Press, 1990), 164.
3. See R. H. Hayes and S. C. Wheelwright, *Restoring Our Competitive Edge* (New York: Wiley, 1984); J. L. Heskett, *Managing in the Service Economy* (Boston: Harvard Business School Press, 1986); and J. L. Heskett, W. E. Sasser, and C. W. L. Hart, *Service Breakthroughs: Changing the Rules of the Game* (New York: Free Press, 1990).
4. Robert Johnston, "Achieving Focus in Service Organizations," *The Service Industries Journal* 16 (January 1996), 10–20.
5. Leonard L. Berry, *On Great Service* (New York: Free Press, 1995), 62–63.
6. Jack Trout, *The New Positioning: The Latest on the World's #1 Business Strategy* (New York: McGraw-Hill, 1997). See also Al Ries and Jack Trout, *Positioning: The Battle for Your Mind*, revised ed. (New York: Warner Books, 1993).
7. Harry Beckwith, *Selling the Invisible* (New York: Warner Books, 1997), 103.
8. Beckwith, *Selling the Invisible.*
9. Laura Koss Feder, "Branding Culture: Nonprofits Turn to Marketing to Improve Image and Bring in the Bucks," *Marketing News*, 1 January 1998, 1.
10. Thomas A. Stewart, "A Satisfied Customer Isn't Enough," *Fortune*, 21 July 1997, 112–113.
11. Donald F. Heaney, "Degrees of Product Innovation," *Journal of Business Strategy*, Spring 1983, 3–14.
12. See James Traub, "Drive-Thru U.," *The New Yorker*, 20 and 27 October 1997; and Joshua Macht, "Virtual You," *Inc. Magazine*, January 1998, 84–87.
13. Chad Rubel, "New Menu for Restaurants: Talking Trees and Blackjack," *Marketing News*, 29 July 1996, 1.
14. Cyndee Miller, "It's Not Take-out; It's Now 'Home Meal Replacement,'" *Marketing News*, 9 June 1997, 2.

15. Richard Normann, a Paris-based consultant, used this term in a speech at the conference Management del Terzario, organized by Centro di Formazione, Milan, Italy, December 1994.

16. G. Lynn Shostack, "Designing Services That Deliver," *Harvard Business Review*, January–February 1984, 133–139.

17. G. Lynn Shostack, "Service Positioning through Structural Change," *Journal of Marketing* 51, (January 1987).

CHAPTER 9

1. From Howard Schultz and Dori Jones Yang, *Pour Your Heart into It* (New York: Hyperion, 1997); Jennifer Reese, "Starbucks: Inside the Coffee Cult," *Fortune*, 9 December 1996, 190; and David Bank, "Starbucks Faces Growing Competition: Its Own Stores," *The Wall Street Journal*, 21 January 1997, B1.

2. G. Lynn Shostack, "Breaking Free from Product Marketing," *Journal of Marketing*, April 1977.

3. Pierre Eiglier and Eric Langeard, "Services as Systems: Marketing Implications," in P. Eiglier, E. Langeard, C. H. Lovelock, J. E. G. Bateson, and R. F. Young, *Marketing Consumer Services: New Insights* (Cambridge, MA: Marketing Science Institute, 1977), 83–103. An earlier version of this article was published in French in *Révue Française de Gestion*, March–April 1977, 72–84.

4. The Flower of Service concept was first introduced in Christopher H. Lovelock, "Cultivating the Flower of Service: New Ways of Looking at Core and Supplementary Services," in P. Eiglier and E. Langeard (eds.), *Marketing, Operations, and Human Resources: Insights into Services* (Aix-en-Provence: IAE, Université d'Aix-Marseille III, 1992), 296–316.

5. Stephan A. Butscher, "Automating Services Can Cause More Problems Than It Solves," *Marketing News*, 24 November 1997, 4.

6. The Future of Travel Is in Your Hands, *American Airlines AAdvantage Newsletter*, June/July 1996, 1.

7. Amy Dunkin, "Tackling Admissions with a PC," *Business Week*, 11 November 1996, 132–134.

8. Roger Thurow, "The Longest Wait: Packer Fans Buy Seats after 32 Years," *The Wall Street Journal*, 12 September 1997, B1.

9. Dunkin, "Tackling Admissions with a PC."

10. Calmetta Coleman, "Fliers Call Electronic Ticketing a Drag," *The Wall Street Journal*, 17 January 1997, B1.

11. Ibid.

12. Jared Sandberg, "On-line Services Make It Hard for Users to Quit," *The Wall Street Journal*, 20 January 1997, B1.

13. Kelly Shermach, "Youth Market for Phone Cards Mainly Overlooked," *Marketing News*, 14 April 1997, 8.

14. Gail Gaboda, "For Business Travelers, There's No Place Like Home," *Marketing News*, 15 September 1997, 19.

15. Karen Schwartz and Ian P. Murphy, "Airline Food Is No Joke," *Marketing News*, 13 October 1997, 1.

16. Lisa Miller and Nancy Keates, "The Bitter Search for the Perfect Brew," *The Wall Street Journal*, 12 September 1997, B12.

17. Schwartz and Murphy, "Airline Food Is No Joke."

18. Nancy Keates, "Rising Concern: Falling Luggage inside Airplanes," *The Wall Street Journal*, 10 November 1997, B1.

19. James C. Anderson and James A. Narus, "Capturing the Value of Supplementary Services," *Harvard Business Review*, January–February 1995, 75–83.

CHAPTER 10

1. Ann Marsh, "Kinko's Grows Up—Almost," *Forbes*, 1 December 1997, 270–272; and www.kinkos.com, January 1998.

2. See, for example, Regis McKenna, "Real-Time Marketing," *Harvard Business Review*, July–August 1995, 87–98; Jeffrey F. Rayport and John J. Sviokla, "Exploiting the Virtual Value Chain," *Harvard Business Review*, November–December 1995; and Regis McKenna, *Real Time* (Boston: Harvard Business School Press, 1997).

3. Mary Jo Bitner, "Servicescapes: The Impact of Physical Surroundings on Customers and Employees," *Journal of Marketing* 56 (April 1992): 57–71.

4. Philip Kotler, "Atmospherics as a Marketing Tool," *Journal of Retailing* 49, no. 4 (1973): 48–64.

5. Jose Paulo Vincente, "E-Commerce Shapes U.S. Retail Landscapes," *Yahoo News—Reuters*, 5 February 1998.

6. Jeffrey F. Rayport and John J. Sviokla, "Managing in the Marketspace," *Harvard Business Review*, November–December 1994, 141–150.

CHAPTER 11

1. From Amy Barrett, Paul Eng, and Kathy Rebello, "For $19.95 a Month, Unlimited Headaches for AOL," *Business Week,* 27 January 1997, 35; Jared Sandberg and Rebecca Quick, "Heaviest AOL Users Left Out in the Cold in Settlement Pact," *The Wall Street Journal,* 31 January 1997, B3; David S. Jackson, "AOL Buys Some Time," *Time,* 10 February 1997; Susan Gregory Thomas, "AOL's Busy Signal," *US News & World Report,* 10 February 1997, 68; and "Fifty Hours Free—Sort Of," *Business Week,* 19 January 1997, 4.

2. Leonard L. Berry and Manjit S. Yadav, "Capture and Communicate Value in the Pricing of Services," *Sloan Management Review* 37 (Summer 1996): 41–51.

3. Valarie A. Zeithaml, "Consumer Perceptions of Price, Quality, and Value: A Means-End Model and Synthesis of Evidence," *Journal of Marketing,* 52 (July 1988): 2–21.

4. For a review of the literature in this area and findings from a research study, see Injazz J. Chen, Atul Gupta, and Walter Rom, "A Study of Price and Quality in Service Operations," *International Journal of Service Industry Management* 5, no. 2 (1994): 23–33.

5. Christopher H. Lovelock and Charles B. Weinberg, *Public and Nonprofit Marketing* (Redwood City, CA: Scientific Press, 1989), 256.

6. Hermann Simon, "Pricing Opportunities and How to Exploit Them," *Sloan Management Review* 33 (Winter 1992): 71–84.

7. Berry and Yadav, "Capture and Communicate Value."

8. Frederick F. Reichheld, *The Loyalty Effect* (Boston: Harvard Business School Press, 1996), 82–84.

CHAPTER 12

1. Elizabeth Light, "Tradeshows and Expos—Putting Your Business on Show," *Her Business,* March–April 1998, 14–18; and Susan Greco, "Trade Shows versus Face-to-Face Selling," *Inc.,* May 1992, 142.

2. William R. George and Leonard L. Berry, "Guidelines for the Advertising of Services," *Business Horizons,* July–August 1981.

3. Louis Fabien, "Making Promises: The Power of Engagement," *Journal of Services Marketing* 11, no. 3 (1997): 206–214.

4. Stephen J. Grove, Gregory M. Pickett, and David N. Laband, "An Empirical Examination of Factual Information Content among Service Advertisements," *The Service Industries Journal* 15 (April 1995): 216–233.

5. Ken Peattie and Sue Peattie, "Sales Promotion—A Missed Opportunity for Service Marketers," *International Journal of Service Industry Management* 5, no. 1 (1995): 6–21.

6. Paul W. Farris and John A. Quelch, "In Defense of Price Promotion," *Sloan Management Review,* Fall 1987, 63–69.

7. Christopher H. Lovelock and John A. Quelch, "Consumer Promotions in Services Marketing," *Business Horizons,* May–June 1983.

8. Mary Jo Bitner, "Servicescapes: The Impact of Physical Surroundings on Customers and Employees," *Journal of Marketing* 56 (April 1992): 57–71.

9. From an on-line article by Leslie Adler entitled "Internet Becomes Increasingly Important Ad Medium," *Yahoo! Reuters News,* 20 October 1997.

10. Patrick Barwise and John Deighton, "Digital Media: Cutting through the Hype," *Financial Times,* 9 November 1998 [Mastering Marketing supplement], 2–4.

11. J. William Gurley, "How the Web Will Warp Advertising," *Fortune,* 9 November 1998, 199–120.

12. Kenneth Leung, "Keep This in Mind about Internet Marketing," *Marketing News,* 23 June 1997, 7.

13. J. D. Mosley-Matchett, "Include the Internet in Marketing Mix," *Marketing News,* 24 November 1997, 6.

14. Margaret A. Jacobs, "Young Lawyers Surf for Clients in New Media," *The Wall Street Journal,* 11 April 1997, B1.

15. Cyndee Miller, "New Services for Consumers without Home Page at Home," *Marketing News,* 22 April 1996, 1.

16. Marshall Rice, "What Makes Users Revisit a Web Site?" *Marketing News,* 17 March 1997, 12.

17. J. D. Mosley-Machett, "Remember: It's the *World* Wide Web," *Marketing News,* 20 January 1997, 16.

18. Sharon McDonnell, "For Older Sites, Time for Makeover," *New York Times Cybertimes,* 12 January 1997.

19. Patrick M. Reilly, "Booksellers Prepare to Do Battle in Cyberspace," *The Wall Street Journal,* 28 January 1997.

20. Kelly Shermach, "Marketers Assess Internet Efforts," *Marketing News,* 23 October 1995, 40.

21. "It's Called Shopping for Homes from Home," *Marketing News,* 14 April 1997, 12.

CHAPTER 13

1. Stephen J. Grove and Raymond P. Fisk, "The Dramaturgy of Services Exchange: An Analytical Framework for Services Marketing," in *Emerging Perspectives on Services Marketing*, L. L. Berry, G. L. Shostack, and G. D. Upah, eds. (Chicago: American Marketing Association, 1983), 45–49.

2. Elizabeth MacDonald, "Oh, the Horrors of Being a Visiting Accountant," *The Wall Street Journal*, 10 March, 1997, B1.

3. Grove and Fisk, "Dramaturgy of Services Exchange."

4. Michael R. Solomon, Carol Suprenant, John A. Czepiel, and Evelyn G. Gutman, "A Role Theory Perspective on Dyadic Interactions: The Service Encounter," *Journal of Marketing* (Winter 1985): 99–111.

5. See ibid.; P. Abelson, "Script Processing in Attitude Formation and Decision-Making," in *Cognitive and Social Behavior*, J. S. Carrol and J. W. Payne, eds. (Hillsdale, NJ: Erlbaum, 1976), 33–45; and Ronald H. Humphrey and Blake E. Ashforth, "Cognitive Scripts and Prototypes in Service Encounters," in *Advances in Service Marketing and Management* (Greenwich, CT: JAI Press, 1994), 175–199.

6. Christopher H. Lovelock, *Product Plus* (New York: McGraw-Hill, 1994), 160–176.

7. See for example, Eric J. Arnould and Linda L. Price, "River Magic: Extraordinary Experience and the Extended Service Encounter," *Journal of Consumer Research*, 20 (June 1993): 24–25; "Collaring the Cheshire Cat: Studying Customers' Services Experience through Metaphors," *The Service Industries Journal* 16 (October 1996): 421–442; and Nick Johns and Phil Tyas, "Customer Perceptions of Service Operations: Gestalt, Incident or Mythology?" *The Service Industries Journal* 17 (July 1997): 474–488.

8. "How Marriott Makes a Great First Impression," *The Service Edge* 6 (May 1993): 5.

9. Paul B. Hertneky, "Built for Speed," *Restaurant Hospitality*, January 1997, 54–62.

10. Jerry Wind, Paul E. Green, Douglas Shifflet, and Marsha Scarbrough, "Courtyard by Marriott: Designing a Hotel Facility with Consumer-based Marketing Models," *Interfaces*, January–February 1989, 25–47.

CHAPTER 14

1. Based on material in James A. Fitzsimmons and M. J. Fitzsimmons, *Service Management for Competitive Advantage* (New York: McGraw-Hill, 1994), and W. Earl Sasser, Jr., "Match Supply and Demand in Service Industries," *Harvard Business Review*, November–December 1976.

2. This section is adapted from Christopher H. Lovelock, "Strategies for Managing Capacity-constrained Service Organisations," *Service Industries Journal*, November 1984.

CHAPTER 15

1. Based on an example in Leonard L. Berry and Linda R. Cooper, "Competing with Time Saving Service," *Business* 40, no. 2 (1990): 3–7.

2. Malcolm Galdwell, "The Bottom Line for Lots of Time Spent in America," *Washington Post*, February 1993.

3. Dave Wielenga, "Not So Fine Lines," *Los Angeles Times*, 28 November 1997, E1.

4. Richard Saltus, "Lines, Lines, Lines, Lines … the Experts Are Trying to Ease the Wait," *Boston Globe*, 5 October 1992, 39, 42.

5. This section is based in part on James A. Fitzsimmons and Mona J. Fitzsimmons, *Service Management for Competitive Advantage* (New York: McGraw-Hill, 1994), 264–290; and David H. Maister, "Note on the Management of Queues" 9-680-053, Harvard Business School Case Services, 1979, rev. February 1984.

6. Jay R. Chernow, "Measuring the Values of Travel Time Savings," *Journal of Consumer Research* 7 (March 1981): 360–371. [This entire issue was devoted to the consumption of time.]

7. David H. Maister, "The Psychology of Waiting Lines," in J. A. Czepiel, M. R. Solomon, and C. F. Surprenant, *The Service Encounter* (Lexington, MA: Lexington Books/D.C. Heath, 1986), 113–123.

8. M. M. Davis and J. Heineke, "Understanding the Roles of the Customer and the Operation for Better Queue Management," *International Journal of Operations & Production Management* 14, no. 5, 1994: 21–34.

9. Peter Jones and Emma Peppiatt, "Managing Perceptions of Waiting Times in Service Queues," *International Journal of Service Industry Management* 7, no. 5, 1996: 47–61.

10. Karen L. Katz, Blaire M. Larson, and Richard C. Larson, "Prescription for the Waiting-in-Line Blues: Entertain, Enlighten, and Engage," *Sloan Management Review*, Winter 1991, 44–53.

11. Bill Fromm and Len Schlesinger, *The Real Heroes of Business and Not a CEO among Them* (New York: Currency Doubleday, 1994), 7.

12. Michael K. Hui and David K. Tse, "What to Tell Customers in Waits of Different Lengths: An Integrative Model of Service Evaluation," *Journal of Marketing* 80, no. 2 (April 1996): 81–90.

13. Sheryl E. Kimes, "Yield Management: A Tool for Capacity-constrained Service Firms," *Journal of Operations Management* 8, no. 4 (October 1989): 348–363.

CHAPTER 16

1. Robert Levering and Milton Moskowitz, "The 100 Best Companies to Work for in America" *Fortune*, 12 January 1998, 84–95.

2. Southwest Airlines Co. *1995 Annual Report* (Dallas, TX, 1996), 14.

3. Hal E. Rosenbluth, *The Customer Comes Second* (New York: William Morrow, 1992), 25.

4. David E. Bowen and Benjamin Schneider, "Boundary-spanning Role Employees and the Service Encounter: Some Guidelines for Management and Research," in J. A. Czepiel, M. R. Solomon, and C. F. Surprenant, *The Service Encounter* (Lexington, MA: Lexington Books, 1985), 127–148.

5. David A. Tansik, "Managing Human Resource Issues for High Contact Service Personnel," in D. E. Bowen, R. B. Chase, and T. G. Cummings, *Service Management Effectiveness* (San Francisco: Jossey-Bass, 1990), 152–76.

6. Arlie R. Hochschild, *The Managed Heart: Commercialization of Human Feeling* (Berkeley: University of California Press, 1983).

7. Blake E. Ashforth and Ronald W. Humphrey, "Emotional Labor in Service Roles: The Influence of Identity," *Academy of Management Review* 18, no. 1 (1993): 88–115.

8. This section is closely based on David E. Bowen and Edward E. Lawler III, "The Empowerment of Service Workers: What, Why, How and When," *Sloan Management Review*, Spring 1992, 32–39.

9. Robert Levering and Milton Moskowitz, *The 100 Best Companies to Work for in America* (New York: Currency/Doubleday, 1993).

10. Bill Fromm and Len Schlesinger, *The Real Heroes of Business* (New York: Currency/Doubleday, 1994), 315–316.

11. Rajendra Sisodia, "Expert Marketing with Expert Systems," *Marketing Management*, Spring 1992, 32–47.

12. Thomas H. Davenport, *Process Innovation: Reengineering Work through Information Technology* (Boston: Harvard Business School Press, 1993).

13. Benjamin Schneider and David E. Bowen, *Winning the Service Game* (Boston: Harvard Business School Press, 1995).

14. Benjamin Schneider, "HRM—A Service Perspective: Towards a Customer-focused HRM?" *International Journal of Service Industry Management* 5, no. 1 (1994), 64–76.

15. James L. Heskett, W. Earl Sasser, and Leonard A. Schlesinger, *The Service Profit Chain* (New York: The Free Press, 1997). Frederick F. Reichheld, *The Loyalty Effect* (Boston: Harvard Business School Press, 1996), Chap. 4 and 5.

16. The terms *cycle of failure* and *cycle of success* were coined by Leonard L. Schlesinger and James L. Heskett, "Breaking the Cycle of Failure in Services," *Sloan Management Review*, Spring 1991, 17–28. The term *cycle of mediocrity* comes from Christopher H. Lovelock, "Managing Services: The Human Factor," in W. J. Glynn and J. G. Barnes (eds.), *Understanding Services Management* (Chichester, UK: John Wiley & Sons, 1995), 228.

17. Schlesinger and Heskett, "Breaking the Cycle of Failure."

18. Jeffrey Pfeffer, *Competitive Advantage Through People* (Boston: Harvard Business School Press, 1994), 160–163.

19. Levering and Moskowitz, *The 100 Best Companies*.

20. Christopher Lovelock, *Product Plus: How Product + Service = Competitive Advantage* (New York: McGraw-Hill, 1994), chap. 19.

Glossary

adequate service: the minimum level of service that a customer will accept without being dissatisfied. (p. 90)

advertising: any form of nonpersonal communication by a marketer to inform, educate, or persuade members of target audiences. (p. 253)

arm's-length transactions: interactions between customers and service suppliers in which mail or telecommunications minimize the need to meet face to face. (p. 199)

augmented product: the core product (a good or a service), plus all additional elements that add value for the customer. (p. 176)

backstage (or technical core):   those aspects of service operations that are hidden from customers. (p. 49)

backstage activities: all aspects of the service operation that aren't typically visible to customers during the normal course of service delivery. (p. 82)

balking: a decision by a customer not to join a queue because the wait appears to be too long. (p. 309)

benefit: an advantage or gain that customers obtain from performance of a service or use of a physical good. (p. 5)

benefit-driven pricing: a strategy of relating prices to the benefits that customers are looking for when using the service. (p. 232)

billing: a group of supplementary services that facilitates purchase by providing clear, timely, accurate, and relevant documentation of what customers owe, plus information about how to pay. (p. 182)

blueprint: a sophisticated form of flowchart, showing each activity involved in service production and delivery and specifying the linkages among them. (p. 170)

bottleneck: a point of congestion in a service delivery process. (p. 281)

brand: a name, phrase, design, symbol, or some combination of these that identifies a company's services and differentiates it from competitors. (p. 166)

bundled pricing: the practice of charging a single price for a bundle made up of a core service plus supplementary product elements. (p. 237)

business ethics: the principles of moral conduct that should guide behavior in the business world. (p. 22)

chase demand: adjusting the level of capacity to meet the level of demand at any given time. (p. 292)

competition-based pricing: the practice of setting prices relative to those charged by competitors. (p. 229)

complaint: a formal expression of dissatisfaction with any aspect of a service experience. (p. 134)

complaint log: a detailed record of all customer complaints received by a service provider. (p. 140)

complexity: the number of steps required to complete a service process. (p. 171)

consultation: a group of supplementary services that adds value by providing responses to customers who require advice, counseling, or training to help them obtain maximum benefit from the service experience. (p. 184)

consumer surplus: the difference between the actual price paid and the customer's perception of the product's monetary worth. (p. 226)

control charts: charts that graph quantitative changes in service performance on a specific variable relative to a predefined standard. (p. 95)

control model of management: an approach based on clearly defined roles, top-down control systems, hierarchical organizational structure, and assumption that management knows best. (p. 331)

core product: the central benefit provided by a firm to address specific customer needs. (p. 76)

corporate design: the consistent application of distinctive colors, symbols, and lettering to give a firm an easily recognizable identity. (p. 257)

cost-based pricing: the practice of relating the price to be charged to the costs of producing, delivering, and marketing a product. (p. 229)

coupons: documented offers for free or discounted product use or purchase. (p. 255)

credence attributes: product characteristics that customers may not be able to evaluate even after purchase and consumption. (p. 68)

critical incident: a specific encounter between customer and service provider in which the outcome has proved especially satisfying or dissatisfying for one or both parties. (p. 56)

critical incident technique (CIT):   a methodology for collecting, categorizing, and analyzing critical incidents that have occurred. (p. 56)

customer-contact personnel: those service employees who interact directly with individual customers either in person or through mail and telecommunications. (p. 46)

customer portfolio: the size and composition of the firm's set of customer relationships. (p. 122)

customer satisfaction: a short-term emotional reaction to a specific service performance. (p. 92)

customer service: the provision of supplementary service elements by employees who are not specifically engaged in selling activities. (p. 252)

customization: tailoring service characteristics to meet each customer's specific needs and preferences. (p. 28)

cyberspace: a term used to describe the absence of a definable physical location where electronic transactions or communications occur. (p. 215)

defection: a customer's decision to transfer brand loyalty from a current service provider to a competitor. (p. 125)

delivery channels: the means by which a service firm (sometimes assisted by intermediaries) delivers one or more product elements to its customers. (p. 198)

demand cycle: a period of time during which the level of demand for a service will move up and down in a somewhat predictable fashion before repeating itself. (p. 293)

desired service: the wished-for level of service quality that a customer believes can and should be delivered. (p. 89)

direct marketing: one-way communications from a company to a list of target customers by mail, telephone, fax, or e-mail. (p. 253)

discounting: a strategy of reducing the price below the normal level. (p. 237)

divergence: the amout of variability allowed in executing the steps in a service process. (p. 171)

emotional labor: the act by an employee of expressing socially appropriate (but sometimes false) emotions toward customers during service transactions. (p. 328)

empowerment: authorizing the employee to find solutions to service problems and to make appropriate decisions about responses to customers' concerns, without having to ask for a supervisor's approval. (p. 330)

enablement: giving employees the skills, tools, and resources they need to use their own discretion confidently and effectively. (p. 331)

enhancing supplementary services: supplementary services that may add extra value for customers. (p. 178)

exceptions: a group of supplementary services that adds value by responding to special requests, resolving problems, handling complaints and suggestions, and providing compensation for service failures. (p. 189)

excess capacity: a firm's capacity to create service output is not fully utilized. (p. 290)

excess demand: demand for a service at a given time exceeds the firm's ability to meet customers' needs. (p. 289)

exchange: the act of giving or taking one thing of value in return for something else of value. (p. 21)

expectations: internal standards that customers use to judge the quality of a service experience. (p. 88)

experience attributes: product performance features that customers can evaluate only during service delivery. (p. 67)

expert system: an interactive computer program that mimics a human expert's reasoning to draw conclusions from data, solve problems, and give customized advice. (p. 335)

extranet: a secure, private intranet-like network that links a company to its major suppliers and designated customers. (p. 216)

facilitating supplementary services: supplementary services that facilitate use of the core product or are required for service delivery. (p. 178)

fishbone diagram: a chart-based technique that relates specific service problems to different categories of underlying causes (also known as a cause-and-effect chart). (p. 96)

flat-rate pricing: quoting a fixed, all-in-one price in advance of service delivery. (p. 233)

flowchart: a visual representation of the steps involved in delivering service to customers. (p. 81)

Flower of Service: a visual framework for understanding the supplementary service elements that surround and add value to the product core. (p. 178)

focus: the provision of a relatively narrow product mix for a particular market segment. (p. 154)

franchising: the licensing of independent entrepreneurs to produce and sell a branded service according to tightly specified procedures. (p. 10)

front stage: those aspects of service operations and delivery that are visible to customers. (p. 49)

front-stage activities: all aspects of the service operation that are directly experienced by the customer. (p. 82)

gift premiums: rewards for purchasing a product under defined conditions, typically at a specific time or place. (p. 256)

goods: physical objects or devices that provide benefits for customers through ownership or use. (p. 14)

high-contact services: services that involve significant interaction among customers, service personnel, equipment, and facilities. (p. 48)

hospitality: a group of supplementary services that adds value by treating customers like guests and providing amenities that anticipate their needs during interactions with the service provider. (p. 186)

human resource management (HRM): the function responsible for coordinating tasks related to job design and employee recruitment, selection, training, and motivation; it also includes planning and administering other employee-related activities. (p. 327)

impersonal communications: one-way communications directed at target audiences who are not in personal contact with the message source (including media advertising and public relations). (p. 251)

information: a group of supplementary services that facilitates purchase and use by telling customers about service features and performance before, during, and after service delivery. (p. 179)

information-based services: all services in which the principal value comes from the transmission of data to customers (includes both mental stimulus processing and information processing). (p. 40)

information processing: intangible actions directed at customers' assets. (p. 32)

in-process waiting: waiting during service delivery. (p. 313)

inputs: all resources (labor, materials, energy, and capital) required to create service offerings. (p. 104)

intangibility: a distinctive characteristic of services that makes it impossible to touch or hold on to them in the same manner as physical goods. (p. 28)

intangible: something that is experienced and cannot be touched or preserved. (p. 15)

integrated service management: the coordinated planning and execution of those marketing, operations, and human resources activities that are essential to a service firm's success. (p. 18)

internal communications: all forms of communication from management to employees in a service organization. (p. 248)

internal customers: employees who are recipients of services from an internal supplier (another employee or department) as a necessary input in performing their own jobs. (p. 327)

internal services: service elements in any type of business that facilitate creation of, or add value to, its final output. (p. 7)

intranet: an internal corporate network, restricted to company personnel, that allows easy access to a series of Web-site-like information bases organized around departments, projects, products, markets, and so forth. (p. 216)

inventory: for *manufacturing*, physical output stockpiled after production for sale at a later date; for *services*, future output not yet reserved in advance, such as the number of hotel rooms still available for sale on a given day. (p. 289)

involvement model of management: an approach based on the assumption that employees are capable of self-direction and—if properly trained, motivated, and informed—can make good decisions about service operations and delivery. (p. 331)

ISSO (ideal service scenario): performance during a service encounter that matches or exceeds customer expectations on all dimensions. (p. 272)

jaycustomer: a customer who acts in a thoughtless or abusive way, causing problems for the firm, its employees, and other customers. (p. 116)

levels of customer contact: the extent to which customers interact directly with elements of the service organization. (p. 48)

loss leaders: products provided at less than cost to attract customers in the hope that they will buy other goods and services at regular prices. (p. 229)

low-contact services: services that require minimal or no direct contact between customers and the service operation. (p. 49)

loyalty: a customer's voluntary decision to continue patronizing a specific firm over an extended period of time. (p. 125)

market focus: the extent to which a firm serves few or many markets. (p.154)

marketing communications mix: the full set of communication channels (both paid and unpaid) available to marketers. (p. 251)

marketplace: a physical location where suppliers and customers meet to do business. (p. 216)

market segmentation: the process of dividing a market into different groups within which all customers share relevant characteristics that distinguish them from customers in other segments. (p. 110)

marketspace: a virtual location made possible by telephone and Internet linkages where customers and suppliers conduct business electronically. (p. 216)

mass customization: offering a service with some individualized product elements to a large number of customers at a relatively low price. (p. 110)

maximum capacity: the upper limit to a firm's ability to meet customer demand at a particular time. (p. 290)

medium-contact services: services that involve only a limited amount of contact between customers and elements of the service operation. (p. 49)

membership relationship: a formal relationship between the firm and an identifiable customer that may offer special benefits to both parties. (p. 123)

mental stimulus processing: intangible actions directed at people's minds. (p. 32)

molecular model: a framework that uses a chemical analogy to describe the structure of service offerings. (p. 176)

moment of truth: a point in service delivery where customers interact with service employees or self-serve equipment and the outcome may affect perceptions of service quality. (p. 54)

needs: subconscious, deeply felt desires that concern long-term existence and identity issues. (p. 71)

net value: the sum of all perceived benefits (gross value) minus the sum of all perceived costs. (p. 226)

opportunity cost: the potential value of the income or other benefits foregone as a result of deciding on one course of action instead of pursuing other opportunities. (p. 319)

optimum capacity: the point beyond which a firm's efforts to serve additional customers will lead to a perceived deterioration in service quality. (p. 290)

order taking: a group of supplementary services that facilitates purchase by establishing fast, accurate, and responsive procedures for taking applications, placing orders, or making reservations. (p. 180)

OTSU (opportunity to screw up): performance during a service encounter that disappoints customers by falling below their minimal level of expectations. (p. 272)

outputs: the final outcomes of the service delivery process as perceived and valued by customers. (p. 104)

Pareto analysis: an analytical procedure to identify what proportion of problem events are caused by each of several different factors. (p. 97)

payment: a group of supplementary services that facilitates purchase by offering a choice of easy procedures for making prompt payments. (p. 183)

people: personnel (and sometimes other customers) who are involved in service production. (p. 19)

people processing: services that involve tangible actions to people's bodies. (p. 32)

perceptual map: a graph of how customers perceive competing services. (p. 159)

personal communications: direct communications between marketers and one or more customers that allow two-way dialog (including face-to-face conversations, phone calls, and e-mail). (p. 251)

personal selling: two-way communications between service employees and customers designed to directly influence the purchase process. (p. 252)

physical costs of service: undesired consequences to a customer's body that occur during the service delivery process. (p. 225)

physical evidence: visual or other tangible clues that provide evidence of service quality. (p. 20)

place and time: management decisions about when, where, and how to deliver services to customers. (p. 18)

positioning: a firm's use of marketing tools to create a clear, distinctive, and desirable product image in the minds of target consumers relative to competing products. (p. 114)

possession processing: tangible actions to goods and other physical possessions belonging to customers. (p. 32)

postprocess waiting: waiting after service delivery has been completed. (p. 313)

postpurchase stage: the final stage in the service purchase process, in which customers evaluate service quality and their satisfaction or dissatisfaction with the service outcome. (p. 76)

predicted service: the level of service quality a customer believes a firm will actually deliver. (p. 91)

preprocess waiting: waiting before service delivery begins. (p. 313)

prepurchase stage: the first stage in the service purchase process, where customers identify alternatives, weigh benefits and risks, and make a purchase decision. (p. 72)

price and other costs of service: expenditures of money, time, and effort that customers incur in purchasing and consuming services. (p. 20)

price elasticity: the extent to which a change in price leads to a corresponding change in demand in the opposite direction. (Demand is described as price inelastic when changes in price have little or no impact on demand). (p. 231)

privatization: transforming government-owned organizations into investor-owned companies. (p. 9)

prize promotions: offers to enter a customer's name in a sweepstakes or other competition that provides an opportunity to win a prize. (p. 256)

process: a particular method of operations or series of actions, typically involving steps that need to occur in a defined sequence. (p. 18)

product: the core output (either a service or a manufactured good) produced by a firm. (p. 14)

product attributes: all features (both tangible and intangible) of a good or service that can be evaluated by customers. (p. 67)

product elements: all components of the service performance that create value for customers. (p. 18)

productive capacity: the extent of the facilities, equipment, labor, infrastructure, and other assets available to a firm to create output for its customers. (p. 290)

productivity: how efficiently service inputs are transformed into outputs that add value for customers. (p. 18)

promotion and education: all communication activities and incentives designed to build customers preference for a specific service or service provider. (p. 19)

psychological costs of service: undesired mental or emotional states experienced by customers as a result of the service delivery process. (p. 225)

public relations: efforts to stimulate positive interest in a company and its products by sending out news releases, holding press conferences, staging special events, and sponsoring newsworthy activities put on by third parties. (p. 254)

purchase process: the stages a customer goes through in choosing, consuming, and evaluating a service. (p. 72)

quality: the degree to which a service satisfies customers by meeting their needs, wants, and expectations. (p. 18)

quality gap: a discrepancy between a service provider's performance and customer expectations. (p. 92)

queue: a line of people, vehicles, other physical objects, or intangible items waiting their turn to be served or to proceed. (p. 307)

queue configuration: the way in which waiting lines are organized. (p. 310)

reengineering: the analysis and redesign of business processes to create dramatic performance improvements in such areas as cost, quality, speed, and customers' service experiences. (p. 281)

relationship marketing: activities aimed at developing long-term, cost-effective links between an organization and its customers for the mutual benefit of both parties. (p. 113)

reneging: a decision by a customer to leave a queue before reaching its end because the wait is proving to be longer or more burdensome than originally anticipated. (p. 311)

repositioning: changing the position a firm holds in a consumer's mind relative to competing services. (p. 159)

reservation: a confirmed and recorded commitment to provide a customer with designated service at a specified time and place. (p. 316)

retail displays: presentations in store windows and other locations of merchandise, service experiences, and benefits. (p. 254)

retail gravity model: a mathematical approach to retail site selection that involves calculating the geographic center of gravity for the target population and then locating a facility to optimize customers' ease of access. (p. 199)

return on quality: the financial return obtained from investing in service quality improvements. (p. 100)

role: a combination of social cues that guides behavior in a specific setting or context. (p. 270)

role congruence: the extent to which both customers and employees act out their prescribed roles during a service encounter. (p. 270)

safekeeping: a group of supplementary services that adds value by assisting customers with personal possessions that they have brought with them to a service delivery site or purchased there. (p. 187)

sales promotion: a short-term incentive offered to customers and intermediaries to stimulate product purchase. (p. 255)

sampling: a method for allowing customers to use a product on a limited, short-term basis free of charge. (p. 255)

scripts: learned sequences of behaviors obtained through personal experience or communications with others. (p. 270)

search attributes: product characteristics that consumers can readily evaluate prior to purchase. (p. 67)

segment: a group of current and prospective customers who share common characteristics, needs, purchasing behavior, or consumption patterns. (p. 110)

sensory costs of service: negative sensations experienced through a customer's five senses during the service delivery process. (p. 225)

service: an act or performance that creates benefits for customers by bringing about a desired change in—or on behalf of—the recipient. (p. 5)

service delivery: that part of the total service system where final "assembly" of these elements takes place and the product is delivered to the customer; it includes the visible elements of the service operation. (p. 49)

service encounter: a period of time during which customers interact directly with a service. (p. 48)

service encounter stage: the second stage in the service purchase process, in which the service delivery takes place through interactions between customers and the service provider. (p. 75)

service factory: the physical site where service operations take place. (p. 32)

service failure: a perception by customers that one or more specific aspects of service delivery have not met their expectations. (p. 134)

service focus: the extent to which a firm offers few or many services. (p. 154)

service guarantee: a promise that if service delivery fails to meet predefined standards, the customer is entitled to one or more forms of compensation. (p. 144)

service leadership: achieving and maintaining a company's reputation for innovation and meaningful service differentiation in ways that create competitive advantage in chosen market. (p. 154)

service marketing: that part of the total service system where the firm has any form of contact with its customers, from advertising to billing; it includes contacts made at the point of delivery. (p. 49)

service offering: all elements designed into a service experience to provide value to customers. (p. 76)

service operations: that part of the total service system where inputs are processed and the elements of the service product are created. (p. 49)

service preview: a demonstration of how a service works to educate customers about the roles they are expected to perform in service delivery. (p. 60)

service quality: customers' long-term, cognitive evaluations of a firm's service delivery. (p. 92)

service quality information system: an ongoing service research process that provides timely, useful data to managers about customer satisfaction, expectations, and perceptions of quality. (p. 101)

service recovery: systematic efforts by a firm after a service failure to correct a problem and retain a customer's goodwill. (p. 141)

servicescape: the impressions created on the five senses by the design of the physical environment where service is delivered. (p. 200)

service sector: the portion of a nation's economy represented by services of all kinds, including those offered by public and nonprofit organizations. (p. 5)

SERVQUAL: a standardized 22-item scale that measures expectations and perceptions about critical quality dimensions. (p. 101)

short-term discounts: special offers of discounts for purchases during a defined time period. (p. 256)

sign-up rebates: offers to reduce or waive the sign-up fee for joining a membership service. (p. 256)

standardization: reducing variation in service operations and delivery. (p. 28)

supplementary service elements: additional benefits provided by a firm to add value and differentiation to the core product. (p. 76)

sustainable competitive advantage: a position in the marketplace that can't be taken away or minimized by competitors for a relatively long period of time. (p. 158)

tangible: capable of being touched, held, or preserved in physical form over time. (p. 28)

target segment: a segment selected because its needs and other characteristics fit well with a specific firm's goals and capabilities. (p. 111)

technographics: segmentation of customers based on their willingness and ability to use the latest technology. (p. 155)

technology: the application of a scientifically designed system for using procedures, materials, equipment, and facilities to achieve practical purposes. (p. 42)

time costs of service: time spent by customers during all aspects of the service delivery process. (p. 225)

transaction: an event during which an exchange of value takes place between two parties. (p. 123)

24/7 service: service that is available 24 hours a day, seven days a week. (p. 207)

unbundled pricing: the practice of charging a base price for a core service plus additional fees for optional supplementary elements. (p. 237)

undesirable demand: requests for service that conflict with the organization's mission, priorities, or capabilities. (p. 297)

value: the worth of a specific action or object relative to an individual's needs at a particular time. (p. 21)

value-based pricing: the practice of setting prices with reference to what customers are willing to pay for the value they believe they will receive. (p. 230)

values: underlying beliefs held by people about the way life should be lived and business conducted, including what constitutes appropriate behavior for both individuals and organizations. (p. 22)

variability: a lack of consistency in inputs and outputs during the service production process. (p. 16)

word of mouth: positive or negative comments about a service made by one individual (usually a current or former customer) to another. (p. 253)

yield: the average revenue received per unit of capacity offered for sale. (p. 319)

yield management: strategies, typically based upon mathematical modeling, that are designed to maximize the revenue from the sale of capacity. (p. 319)

zone of tolerance: the range within which customers are willing to accept variations in service delivery. (p. 91)

Credits

Chapter 1
p. 3: © 1994–1998 Net Contents Inc. dba Virtual Vineyards. **p. 10:** S. Meltzer/PhotoDisc, Inc. **p. 12:** British Airways and M&C Saatchi. **p. 22:** Churchill & Klehr/Simon & Schuster/PH College.

Chapter 2
p. 27: C. Borland/PhotoDisc, Inc. **p. 29:** PhotoDisc, Inc. **p. 30:** Motorola, Inc. **p. 33:** Federal Express Corporation. **p. 35:** Feld Entertainment. **p. 37:** US Airways Inc. **p. 41:** The Corcoran Group.

Chapter 3
p. 47: PhotoDisc, Inc. **p. 51:** PhotoDisc, Inc. **p. 56:** J. Luke/PhotoDisc, Inc. **p. 61:** Charles Schwab & Company, Inc.

Chapter 4
p. 66: Michal Heron/Simon & Schuster/PH College. **p. 71:** Seaworld.

Chapter 5
p. 89: Far Eastern Plaza Hotel. **p. 104:** Focus Visions Network, Inc.

Chapter 6
p. 110: Courtesy of Intrawest Corporation. Photo by Randy Links. **p. 113:** Courtesy of Southwest Airlines Co. **p. 118:** GAB Robins North America, Inc. **p. 130:** Safeway Inc.

Chapter 7
p. 136: Grand Union Supermarket. **p. 140:** PhotoDisc, Inc. **p. 145:** Promus Hotel Corporation.

Chapter 8
p. 167: Hard Rock Café Entertainment, Inc. **p. 170:** Cole Vision Corp.

Chapter 9
p. 180: American Airlines. **p. 190:** © 1997 Hertz System, Inc. Hertz is a registered service mark and trademark of Hertz System, Inc. **p. 192:** © 1998 White Flower Farm–Litchfield, CT.

Chapter 10
p. 202: New York Convention & Visitors Bureau. **p. 203:** Loews Hotel. **p. 204:** barnesandnoble.com. **p. 207:** Photograph courtesy of Market Place Development. **p. 209:** PhotoDisc, Inc.

Chapter 11
p. 224: Michal Heron/Simon & Schuster/PH College. **p. 233:** Holland America Line. **p. 237:** Sprint Communications Group. **p. 240:** © Arby's, Inc. March 1998. All rights reserved.

Chapter 12
p. 245: Reprinted with the permission of the Prudential Insurance Company of America. All rights reserved. **p. 247:** CVS Corporation. **pp. 253, 254, 260:** Fallon McElligott. **p. 256:** © 1998 Supercuts. **p. 257:** PGA TOUR, Inc. **p. 259:** Federal Express Corporation.

Chapter 13
p. 271: Radisson Hotels International, Inc. **p. 281:** Property of AT&T Archives, reprinted with permission of AT&T.

Chapter 14
p. 294: Michal Heron/Simon & Schuster/PH College. **p. 301:** Courtesy of Intrawest Corporation. Photo by Randy Links.

Chapter 15
p. 308: Fallon McElligott. **p. 312:** PhotoDisc, Inc. **p. 313:** LAIMA E. DRUSKIS PHOTOGRAPHY/Simon & Schuster/PH College. **p. 318:** PhotoDisc, Inc.

Chapter 16
p. 327: Courtesy of Southwest Airlines Co. "Southwest Airlines: 25 Years of LUV," 1996 Annual Report (Dallas, TX, 1997). **p. 341:** NCR Retail Systems.

Index

Boldface pages locate chapter opening "cases," "i" locates illustrations, "t" locates tables.